The Practice of
Public Relations

5th EDITION

The Practice of Public Relations

Fraser P. Seitel
Senior Vice President
Director of Public Affairs
The Chase Manhattan Bank

MACMILLAN PUBLISHING COMPANY
New York

MAXWELL MACMILLAN CANADA
Toronto

MAXWELL MACMILLAN INTERNATIONAL
New York   Oxford   Singapore   Sydney

To my dad, who I miss

Editors: David Boelio, Fred Easter
Production Supervisor: J. Edward Neve
Production Manager: Nick Sklitsis
Text Designer: Patricia Smythe
Cover Designer: Eileen Burke
Cover illustration: photograph: Bill Longcore

This book was set in 10/12 New Aster by The Clarinda Company,
printed and bound by R. R. Donnelley & Sons.
The cover was printed by Lehigh Press.

Copyright © 1992 by Macmillan Publishing Company, a division of Macmillan, Inc.

Printed in the United States of America

Macmillan Publishing Company
866 Third Avenue, New York, New York 10022

Macmillan Publishing Company is
part of the Maxwell Communication
Group of Companies.

Maxwell Macmillan Canada, Inc.
1200 Eglinton Avenue, East
Suite 200
Don Mills, Ontario, M3C 3N1

Library of Congress Cataloging-in-Publication Data

Seitel, Fraser P.
   The practice of public relations / Fraser P. Seitel.
      p.   cm.
   Includes index.
   ISBN 0-02-408830-7
   1. Public relations—United States.   I. Title.
HM263.S42   1992
659.2—dc20
                                                                                        91-8696
                                                                                             CIP

Printing: 2 3 4 5 6 7 8   Year: 2 3 4 5 6 7 8 9

Foreword

The profession of public relations has never had more dignity than it possesses today. Once confused with the word *publicity,* it is now seen as a process that is a vital function of management. The public relations practitioner once operated at the lowest management levels. Today, it is a wise company that includes the public relations professional in the inner circle of top management.

Each year, I see new opportunities opening for students who have had solid training in the principles, practice, and ethics of public relations. Each year, I see increasing respect for the profession.

Virtually every business today operates within the view of the public eye. The well-being of stockholders, employers, and customers is tied to policies formulated, tested, and disseminated by public relations professionals.

Fraser P. Seitel brings to the study of public relations the practice of public relations at the highest levels. As senior vice president and director of public affairs at Chase Manhattan Bank, he is a decision maker in his own company and a first-hand observer of the results of public relations practice in major corporations with which the banking business is associated.

Like many of the students who will be reading this text, Mr. Seitel had his undergraduate education in communications. He holds two master's degrees—one an MBA. His experience as a classroom teacher encouraged him to balance the theoretical principles in the book with up-to-date cases, a number of which have not yet run their course and are still to be found on today's front pages. In this fifth edition, for example, Mr. Seitel examines in depth the strategies of Exxon, Perrier, and Domino's—among many others—in image and product crises that threatened severe damage to the corporations.

The Practice of Public Relations has been a popular text through four editions. It is the best of both possible worlds when the author of a text like this is not only a fine public relations practitioner, but a top corporate executive as well.

In my opinion, the principles, insights, and cases in *The Practice of Public Relations* will benefit communications students, business administration students, and a wide range of executives in both corporate and nonprofit organizations.

Ralph L. Lowenstein, Dean
College of Journalism and Communications
University of Florida

As senior vice-president and director of public affairs for The Chase Manhattan Bank, Fraser P. Seitel manages a staff of 40 professionals in the traditional areas of public relations work: community affairs, consumer relations, employee communications, financial communications, media relations, philanthropic activities, speech and article writing, and whatever else his management sees fit to hand him.

A Chase Manhattan veteran for two decades and a former Hill & Knowlton account executive, Mr. Seitel has supplemented his professional public relations career with steady teaching assignments at Fairleigh Dickinson University, Pace University, New York's Professional Development Institute, Chicago's Ragan Report Workshops, and Colorado's Estes Park Institute. After studying and examining many texts in public relations, he concluded that none of them "was exactly right." Therefore, in 1980, he wrote the first edition of *The Practice of Public Relations* "to give students a feel for how stimulating this field really is."

In more than a decade of use at hundreds of colleges and universities, Mr. Seitel's book has introduced thousands of students to the excitement, challenge, and uniqueness of the practice of public relations.

Preface

Public Relations is the field of the '90s. It's pertinent. It's dynamic. It's at the center of the action.

In virtually every crisis with which our society is faced—from George Bush in the Persian Gulf to Exxon in Alaska's Gulf of Valdez to Perrier in the face of product contamination—the practice of public relations stands at center stage.

It would be a real shame, therefore, to introduce someone to such a fascinating field with a boring book. And while the fifth edition of *The Practice of Public Relations* may be a lot of things—boring it ain't!

The focus of this book is on the practical nature of public relations work: communicating, writing, and solving problems. The knowledge provided here is meant to be used.

This book is designed to ensure that students fully understand how public relations theory relates to public relations practice. The field's philosophical underpinnings are supported by numerous practical examples and some of the most familiar and frustrating cases in recent history.

Part One deals with the theoretical side of public relations practice, including the importance of management and planning, ethics, and research in public relations work. Part Two deals with the practical communications applications of the field; Part Three with the myriad publics with which the field deals; and Part Four with emerging trends, including crisis management and the law.

The more than 40 case studies confront the reader with the most complex public relations conundrums of recent days—Exxon, Perrier, Tylenol, General Motors' "Roger and Me," Coors Beer's "Mouse in the Can," Hill & Knowlton's defense of the antiabortion stand of the Catholic church, and more.

Beyond this, a handful of unique elements sets this book apart:

◆ A full-color section explores the vast arsenal of promotional weaponry available to public relations professionals—from comic books and brochures to sports stars and spokesmodels.

◆ "Between the Lines" features complement the text with provocative examples of what's right and what's wrong about public relations practice.

◆ Chapter Summaries and Discussion Starter questions highlight the key messages delivered in each chapter.

◆ Updated Suggested Readings and "Top-of-the-Shelf" book reviews supplement the text with the field's most current literature.

◆ "Tips from the Top" interviews with the field's best-known professionals—from the White House press secretary to the chief of the world's largest public relations firm to a public relations patriarch—add unique insights.

All-in-all then, *The Practice of Public Relations* rounds into its fifth edition and second decade as a timely, readable, and relevant book. At least that's the view of this author.

Acknowledgments

You might think that updating a textbook for the fifth time is no sweat. Boy are you wrong!

For one thing, the practice of public relations keeps changing. For another, my new publisher, Macmillan, and its ever-watchful editor-in-chief, David Boelio, and Production Supervisor Par Excellence, J. Edward Neve, demanded that this fifth edition be better than the previous four. So, no matter how much I tried to avoid it, I had to work to improve this book.

Fortunately, the usual cast of benevolent souls assisted me through these labors.

♦ First and foremost, this edition marks the publishing debut of Bradley Pick. Mr. Pick, a public relations student and professional of uncommon ability, not only updated all Suggested Readings and provided all "Top-of-the-Shelf" reviews, but also authored the description of computer-oriented public relations supports in Chapter 23. Mr. Pick's contribution to this edition is substantial. He is a very good man.

♦ I am indebted as well to the willing, well-known experts in the field who provided "Tips-from-the-Top" interviews: Marlin Fitzwater, Roger Ailes, Carol Sanger, Bob Dillenschneider, Peter Gummer, and others. I appreciate their participation very much.

♦ Yolanda Rhymer once again served splendidly as Queen of Secretarial Support. I also am grateful for the valuable administrative aid of Laura Johnson, Michelle Coletta, Sophia DeGraffenreidt, Sharon Reis, and Marvelous Mac Randall.

♦ Keith McDavid, an extraordinary designer and most decent English gentleman, once again designed the full-color section, which adds materially to the visual presentation of this book.

♦ I also thank the public relations teachers whose insightful suggestions aided this Fifth Edition:

Llyle J. Barker	Ohio State University
William G. Briggs	San Jose State University
Larissa Grunig	University of Maryland
Joseph T. Nolan	University of North Florida
Maria P. Russell	Syracuse University
Melvin L. Sharpe	Ball State University

♦ The constructive critiques of the books other editions by colleagues at leading universities helped make this fifth edition an all-around better book: E. Brody, Memphis State University; John S. Detweiler, University of Florida; Jim Eiseman, University of Louisville; Sandy Grossbart, University of Nebraska; Marjorie Nadler, Miami University; Sharon Smith, Middle Tennessee State University; Robert Wilson, Franklin University: Paul Brennan, Nassau Community College; Carol L. Hills, Boston University; George Laposky, Miami-Dade Community College; Mack Palmer, University of Oklahoma; Judy VanSlyke Turk, Louisiana State University; Roger B. Wadsworth, Miami-Dade Community College; James E. Grunig, University of Maryland; Robert T. Reilly, University of Nebraska at Omaha; Kenneth Rowe, Arizona State University; Dennis L. Wilcox, San Jose State University; Albert Walker, Northern Illinois University; Stanley E. Smith, Arizona State University; Dr. Jan Quarles, University of Georgia; Pamela J. Creedon, Ohio State University; Joel P. Bowman, Western Michigan University; Thomas H. Bivins, University of Oregon; Joseph T. Nolan, University of North Florida; Frankie A. Hammond, University of Florida; Bruce Joffe, George Mason University; and Marjorie Nadler, Miami University.

♦ Last but not least, I appreciate most sincerely the support and patience of A. Wright Elliott, executive vice-president of communications at Chase Manhattan, and the Seitel family three—Rosemary, Raina, and David.

Thank you one and all. Onward and upward.

Fraser P. Seitel

Contents

8   Fundamentals of Public Relations Writing   191

9   Writing for the Eye   221

10   Writing for the Ear   247

11   Public Relations Marketing   273

Appendices   607

FINANCIAL TIMES

Career Choice

PUBLIC RELATIONS

Growing up to be more specialist

Public relations has taken a long time to shake off its image of an industry staffed by smooth-talking young men and gushing young women dispensing gin-and-tonic and half truths. But it is growing up—Perrier water and professionalism are the new bywords.

Greater specialisation has increased the effectiveness —and acceptance—of public relations as an integral part of corporate and marketing management.

Corporate PR now covers such different specialist fields as investor relations, employee communications, government affairs, community relations, environmental policy, and crisis management.

In most large consultancies, consumer marketing is being divided into sectors, with separate teams handling food and nutrition, travel and leisure, health care and medications.

The industry is expanding fast, and becoming increasingly international in outlook.

These changes over the past few years, have led to a rapid growth in its demand for graduates; and a similar heightening of interest on campus in public relations careers.

The number recruited direct from universities by the top PR companies is still relatively small, however, and the competition is hot.

Charles Barker this year had 250 applications for four jobs; Valin Pollen, 350 contenders for three openings.

Even the larger PR companies usually visit only a few universities, and do not circulate all with their vacancies; but they will consider applications from any of them.

The class of degree is perhaps more important than the subject; though a corporate and financial specialist, such as Valin Pollen, tends to favour graduates with qualifications in economics or business studies, or with a clearly demonstrable interest in that field.

"We are looking for people with the kind of intellect that can deal with a multiplicity of projects quickly, wittily, and simultaneously," says David Roberts, VP's executive director responsible for training and resources.

But that has to be allied, of course, with an ability to communicate and relate to people at all levels, and with an aptitude for teamwork. Public relations is no place for the shy and the tongue-tied; or for the idealistic and sensitive. Weathering the demands of some clients and the querulous scepticism of journalists requires a fairly thick skin.

Most companies are looking for graduates involved in a lot of extracurricular activity—writing for the university newspaper or magazine, taking part in the debating or drama society. Valin Pollen takes a close interest in the sort of holiday jobs that its applicants have done.

It takes a flair for communication and self-projection; a demonstration of confidence, originality and imagination in the first contact with a consultancy—either in the letter of application or the initial written exercises that are sometimes set— even to reach the interview stage. Then the going really gets tough.

After the interviews, the short-listed are put through a gruelling series of tests. Charles Barker begins with group discussions and exercises in writing press releases, progresses through initiative tests, and ends with crisis management games.

Those who come through find themselves with a job, worth £10-11,000 a year—and a rigorous fast-track training programme. At Valin Pollen, a three-week induction course "jet propels the entrant from the cloistered atmosphere of university into the realities of the commercial world."

After that introduction to the services the agency provides, and its commercial relationship with clients, the trainee is attached to an account team, learning how it develops advertising and media plans, and how it uses the design and production departments.

As soon as possible, the trainee is given increasing responsibility for specific clients, becoming involved in project planning and presentations, and emerges after a year or so as a fully—fledged account executive.

From then on, ability dictates how fast the promotion ladder is climbed; but graduates can expect to double or even treble their starting salaries within five years; and the larger companies provide continuing training to improve performance and skills.

Philip Rawstorne

(Page 54)

What Is Public Relations?

The power and pervasiveness of the practice of public relations in the last decade of the twentieth century is, as Bart Simpson would say, "Radical, dude!"

Consider the following.

♦ In mid-summer 1990, Iraqi President Saddam Hussein, "the Bully of Baghdad," the man President George Bush compared to Adolf Hitler, suddenly appeared on television sets around the world in civilian suit and shiny tie, sitting amid two dozen frightened foreign hostages, lecturing, smiling, joking, and stroking the hair of terrified tots. The poignant home video—obviously broadcast to shore up the public image of the man who ruthlessly invaded neighboring Kuwait—was horrifying.

♦ Meanwhile Saddam's arch-enemy, President Bush, took great pains to transmit his own public image as a man on vacation in good old Kennebunkport, Maine, golfing, fishing, playing, and not letting the Baghdad Butcher get under his presidential skin.

♦ As Spring 1991 arrived and the Iraqi military was vanquished by a relentless allied force, citizens of the world embraced a new cadre of "media darlings," led by Chairman of the Joint Chiefs of Staff Colin Powell, Pentagon operations chief and senior media briefer Lieutenant General Thomas Kelly, and the decade's first bona fide hero of heroes, allied forces commander General "Stormin'" Norman Schwarzkopf.

People everywhere in the 1990s it seemed—especially world leaders—were greatly concerned about their "public relations image."

And why shouldn't they be?

Public relations has become enormously important in a world linked by technological marvels like communications satellites, fax machines, personal computers, and cellular phones—where an outbreak of face-to-face communication and relationship building can sweep down the mightiest walls of oppression from Poland and Hungary to East Germany and Czechoslovakia, from South Africa to the Soviet Union.

♦ In politics, public relations has never been more critical. Former President Ronald Reagan, "the great communicator," was admired most for his ability to lead the nation through language and rhetoric and symbolism. His Soviet counterpart, Mikhail Gorbachev, was every bit Reagan's communications equal. In fact, Gorbachev's crowning achievements of *glasnost* and *perestroika* were, first, a public relations program to enhance the USSR in the eyes of the world and, second, the opening up of what had been the world's most shuttered society.

♦ In business, public relations has transcended words and symbols and marketing enhancement and become a coveted counseling resource of management. Companies as varied as Johnson & Johnson, Perrier, and Procter & Gamble all have turned to public relations guidance when faced with corporate tragedy. Little wonder that in a study of the chief executive officers of 200 organizations in the United States, Canada, and the United Kingdom, the value of communication in general and the practice of public relations in particular was valued highly.[1]

♦ In the United States alone, public relations is a multi-billion-dollar business practiced by 159,000 professionals, according to the U.S. Bureau of Labor Statistics.

♦ Almost 200 colleges and universities offer a public relations sequence or degree program. Many more offer public relations courses. In the vast majority of college journalism programs, public relations sequences rank first or second in enrollment.

♦ By the end of the century, public relations is predicted to experience phenomenal growth, accounting for as many as one million jobs and thereby more than tripling the number of such jobs over the next decade.[2]

By every measure the numbers are growing, as are the role and influence of public relations in our society. The U.S. government has 9,000 communications workers employed by the United States Information Agency alone. Another 1,000 communications specialists work in the Department of Defense. The fifty largest public relations agencies do upwards of $10 billion in fee income annually.[3] Indicative of salary trends for communications executives, one public relations man in 1988 left his $640,000-per-year job at Mobil Oil to make even more money on his own.[4]

Yes, indeed, public relations is hot, hot, hot.

The field's strength stems from its roots: "a democratic society where people have freedom to debate and to make decisions—in the community, the marketplace, the home, the workplace, and the voting booth. Private and public organizations depend on good relations with groups and individuals whose opinions, decisions, and actions affect their vitality and survival."[5]

So pervasive has the influence of public relations become in our society that some even fear it as a pernicious force; they worry about "the power of public relations to exercise a kind of thought control over the American public."[6]

All of this is quite remarkable when you consider that only a decade ago public relations was still a maligned and misunderstood art form, more renowned for the three-martini lunch than for just about anything else.

How times have changed. The practice of public relations has acquired new-found respect. Indeed, in an era of unrelenting questioning by the media and the public, an organization must not only be sensitive to but also highly considerate of its many publics.

A primary vehicle through which an organization shows its public sensitivity and consideration is its public relations professionals. Accordingly, the practice of public relations has shed its old misconceptions, acquired new responsibilities, and inherited an increasing amount of power, prestige, and pay.

On the other hand, along with its new stature, the practice of public relations is faced with unprecedented pressure.

◆ The very name *public relations* is being challenged by such euphemisms as *public affairs, corporate communications, public information,* and a variety of others.

◆ As public relations positions take on greater credibility, the competition to attain them becomes more intense. Today the profession finds itself vulnerable to encroachment by people without a public relations background, such as lawyers, marketers, and general managers of every stripe.

◆ Educational institutions, which have recognized the need to practice public relations intensively, have nonetheless been slow to recognize the need to teach it. This omission is particularly true in university business schools.

◆ Even though organizations throughout society desperately need professionals with general interests and broad-reaching ideas in sensitive public relations jobs, there is a continuing trend toward specialization in the field.

◆ The field is plagued by the disturbing shallowness of a society that seems hooked on easy answers and quick fixes, on wonder drugs and magic bullets to solve problems. Few people have time for complexity. And public relations, properly practiced, recognizes the interplay of complex factors—of people and movements interacting, of sequences of events—all of which determine what the results will be. In other words, few people understand what public relations is all about.[7]

The public relations profession is buffeted by countervailing pressures. It has earned the respect of management, yet must still fight for its identity

---

BETWEEN   THE   LINES

Image War in the Middle East

While most Americans in the fall of 1990 were focusing on whether war would break out as a result of Iraq's invasion of Kuwait and threats against Saudi Arabia, a more subdued battle of images was being waged in the United States.

Just as President Bush took pains to play a round of golf at his vacation home and Iraqi President Hussein hammed it up with young hostages and answered newsman Dan Rather's questions, so too did the Middle Eastern nations themselves line up for serious public relations warfare.

Saudi Arabia hired a long-time advisor to former President Ronald Reagan to produce a 28-page booklet called "King Fahd of Saudi Arabia, The Man, His Work, and His Country." The elaborately designed booklet was distributed to members of Congress, their staffs, and journalists, two weeks after Iraq's invasion of Kuwait.

Meanwhile, supporters of the exiled government in Kuwait hired America's largest public relations firm, Hill & Knowlton, to tell Kuwait's story. The president of Citizens for Free Kuwait said Hill & Knowlton was hired to help with the networks, congressmen, and the ordinary American voter, "to explain to the Midwest what Kuwait is."

Of the three battling nations, only Iraq demurred from public relations support. Huffed the press officer at the Iraqi Embassy in Washington, "The concept of PR doesn't appeal to us. If you need something to be said, you can say it yourself." He derided the Saudi and Kuwaiti public relations efforts, calling them "begging" and adding "they spoil the image of the Arab in the Western world."[8]

The Iraqi press aide neglected to add, however, that only a month before the invasion he, himself, had appeared on American television in a most unMoslem setting: "The Oprah Winfrey Show."

---

with the general public. It has earned acceptance in most organizations, yet must fight for its rightful role in society. It is blessed with unlimited opportunities in the years ahead, yet its very survival is threatened by encroachment from outsiders.

Few other professions are subject to as continuous a current of controversy as is the practice of public relations. In any event, it is irrefutable that public relations today, in a comparatively short time and despite a number of handicaps, has evolved from a fringe function to a basic element of society. It has indeed entered its Golden Age.

Overview of Public Relations

Public relations affects almost everyone who has contact with other human beings. All of us, in one way or another, practice public relations daily. For an organization, every phone call, every letter, every face-to-face encounter is a public relations event.

To be sure, public relations is not yet a profession like law, accounting, and medicine, in which practitioners are trained, licensed, and supervised. Nothing prevents someone with little or no formal training from hanging out a shingle as a public relations specialist. Such frauds embarrass professionals in the field and, thankfully, are becoming harder and harder to find.

Over the last decade, public relations has steadily built its reputation, increased its prominence, and earned respect across a wide span of society. As today's institutions strive to understand more clearly the forces of change, adapt their activities to new pressures and aspirations, and listen and communicate more effectively, public relations becomes more important. Institutions rely on their practitioners to help win public support and trust, without which they will be rendered powerless.

As the field increases in prominence, it grows in professional stature. The International Association of Business Communicators, a broad-based group that started with an internal communications focus, has 11,500 members. The Public Relations Society of America, with a national membership of almost 15,000, has accredited about one-third of its members through a standardized examination. The society has also investigated legal licensing—similar to that of the accounting and legal professions—for public relations practitioners.

The society's main objective is to increase the field's professionalism. It has a code of standards (see Appendix A), which dwells heavily on a practitioner's ethical responsibilities. The society also provides additional opportunities in specialized areas of practice: association, corporation, counseling, educational institutions, educators, financial institutions, government, health, investor relations, and utilities. These sections have their own publications, seminars, and programs.

Thousands of practitioners are former newspaper and broadcast reporters, magazine writers, journalism school graduates, advertising agency alumni, and lawyers. Increasingly, practitioners are graduates of college public relations courses.

In an attempt to understand what public relations is and what it can and cannot accomplish, here are a few approaches toward a definition.

Approaches to a Definition

First, professional public relations is not

◆ The $10 million basketball center glad-handing of local businessmen at the cigar company's annual luncheon

◆ The sultry screen actress seductively caressing the after-shave lotion to the clicks of photographers' shutters

◆ The fast-talking hustler eagerly touting his contacts to a prospective client

◆ A former church secretary compromised by a defrocked evangelist (Jessica Hahn), the jilted wife of a boastful billionaire (Ivana Trump), or a major league team owner booted from baseball for actions detrimental to the game (George Steinbrenner).

Yet all of these and worse have, from time to time, been mistaken as part of the practice of public relations. As *PR Reporter*, one of the industry's leading publications, put it (only slightly tongue-in-cheek), "Exconvicts, child molesters, political fixers, call girls and their procurers, gambling casino bouncers, and a variety of glad-handing front men have been described as 'public relations counselors.' "

Although all organizations have, by their existence, some kind of public relations, not all enjoy *good* public relations. That's what this book is all about—professional public relations, the kind you must work at.

Whereas marketing and sales have as their primary objective selling an organization's products, public relations attempts to sell the organization itself. Central to its concern is the public interest.

Advertising also generally aims to sell products through paid means. Good public relations, on the other hand, cannot be bought; it must be earned. The credibility derived from sound public relations work may far exceed that gained through paid advertising.

Product publicity, although one aspect of public relations, is more closely aligned with advertising. In general, the elements of the marketing mix—advertising, product promotion, sales, publicity, and the like—may be but a small part of public relations. As Syracuse University professor William Ehling has said, "Organizations in general and business enterprises in particular face a large class of problems which cannot be solved by the thinking, policies, and procedures of marketing." Ehling points out that the "maximum contribution of public relations" is at the CEO's "elbow" and not as part of the marketing mix.[9]

The earliest college teachers of public relations exhorted students to

> learn new ways of using knowledge you already have—a different viewpoint, as if you moved to one side and looked at everything from unfamiliar angles. Project yourself into the minds of people you are trying to reach, and see things the way they do. Use everything you've learned elsewhere—English, economics, sociology, science, history—you name it.[10]

Two decades later, it is still widely thought that a broad background is essential to manage public issues effectively. Although specific definitions of public relations may differ, most who practice it agree that good public relations requires a firm base of theoretical knowledge, a strong sense of ethical judgment, solid communication skills, and, most of all, an uncompromising attitude of professionalism.

Searching for a Single Definition

What, then, is public relations? A lot of people seem to have a pretty good idea, but few seem to agree. American historian Robert Heilbroner describes the field as "a brotherhood of some 100,000, whose common bond is its profession and whose common woe is that no two of them can ever quite agree on what that profession is."[11]

Basically, Heilbroner is right, although there have been a great many efforts over the years to come up with a suitable public relations definition. Perhaps the first recorded definition was found in the Bible: "To do good, and communicate, forget not."[12]

In 1923, Edward Bernays described the function of his fledgling public relations counseling business as one of providing "information given to the public, persuasion directed at the public to modify attitudes and actions, and efforts to integrate attitudes and actions of an institution with its publics and of publics with those of that institution."[13]

In 1939, in an article entitled "The Public Be Not Damned," *Fortune* magazine said, "Public relations is the label used to describe, at one and the same time, techniques and objectives" and "the conduct of individual businesses, as organizations of people banded together in an effort to make a living for themselves and a profit for investors."[14]

In 1944, the *Dictionary of Sociology* defined the field as "the body of theory and technique utilized in adjusting the relationships of a subject with its publics. These theories and techniques represent applications of sociology, social psychology, economics, and political science, as well as of the special skills of journalists, artists, organizational experts, advertising men, etc., to the specific problems involved in this field of activity."[15]

Today, although a generally accepted definition of *public relations* still eludes practitioners, substantial headway toward a clearer understanding of the field is being made. One of the most ambitious searches for a universal definition was commissioned in 1975 by the Foundation for Public Relations Research and Education. Sixty-five public relations leaders participated in the study, which analyzed 472 different definitions and offered the following 88-word sentence:

> Public relations is a distinctive management function which helps establish and maintain mutual lines of communications, understanding, acceptance, and cooperation between an organization and its publics; involves the management of problems or issues; helps management to keep informed on and responsive to public opinion; defines and emphasizes the responsibility of management to serve the public interest; helps management keep abreast of and effectively utilize change, serving as an early warning system to help anticipate trends; and uses research and sound and ethical communication techniques as its principal tools.[16]

Another definition emerged from an assembly of public relations associations in 1978.

> Public relations practice is the art and social science of analyzing trends, predicting their consequences, counseling organization leaders, and implementing planned programs of action which will serve both the organization's and the public's interest.[17]

In 1980, the Task Force on the Stature and Role of Public Relations, chartered by the Public Relations Society of America, offered two definitions that project a perspective of the field at the highest policy-making level and encompass all its functions and specialities.

◆ Public relations helps an organization and its publics adapt mutually to each other.
◆ Public relations is an organization's efforts to win the cooperation of groups of people.[18]

Defining by Functions

Communications professor John Marston suggested that *public relations* be defined in terms of four specific functions: (1) research, (2) action, (3) communication, and (4) evaluation.[19] Applying the R-A-C-E approach involves researching attitudes on a particular issue, identifying action programs of the organization that speak to that issue, communicating those programs to gain understanding and acceptance, and evaluating the effect of the communication efforts on the public.

This formula is similar to one of the most repeated definitions of *public relations,* developed by *Public Relations News,* a leading newsletter for practitioners.

> Public relations is the management function which evaluates public attitudes, identifies the policies and procedures of an individual or an organization with

the public interest, and plans and executes a program of action to earn public understanding and acceptance.[20]

The key word in this definition is *management*. Top public relations professionals think of themselves as "managers" in the truest sense of the word. One public relations consultant defines the field as "the profession which seeks to manage the interdependencies of a client individual or organization and the constituents—other individuals and organizations—which make up its environment."[21] Still another scholar in the field, cognizant of the new "sense of empowerment" sweeping not only the world's former dictatorships but also the rank and file of American industry, says, "Public relations now means *personal relations*—or at least personalized relationships."[22]

Underlying these definitions is an unstated word—*performance*. Without proper performance, good public relations is impossible. Stated another way, performance must precede publicity. Or, in the less grandiose terminology of public relations professor Mack Palmer, "First lay the egg, then cackle."

Modern Shorthand Definitions

Other attempts to define the field have been less esoteric but no less germane. For the British Institute of Public Relations, "public relations is a deliberate, planned, and sustained effort to establish and maintain mutual understanding between an organization and its publics." For *Fortune* magazine, "public relations is good performance today publicly appreciated because it is adequately communicated."

To one counselor, public relations is communicating truth—good works well told. To others it's

◆ Persuasive communication designed to influence specific publics
◆ The winning of public acceptance by acceptable performance
◆ Doing good and getting credit for it
◆ Performance plus Recognition

And then there's Murray, the cabdriver, who opined on the way to LaGuardia airport in late 1988 that "public relations is propaganda and common sense properly disseminated." Not bad, Murray.

A Harmonizing Process

Perhaps the best way to approach a definition of public relations is to consider it, as educator Melvin Sharpe has done, as a process that "harmonizes" long-term relationships among individuals and organizations in society.[23]

Professor Sharpe applies five principles to this process:

1. Honest communication for credibility
2. Openness and consistency of actions for confidence
3. Fairness of actions for reciprocity and goodwill
4. Continuous two-way communication to prevent alienation and build relationships
5. Environmental research and evaluation to determine the actions or adjustments needed for social harmony

This approach recognizes three realities of today's increasingly democratic, globally interdependent social system: (1) the economic and social stability of an organization depends greatly on public opinion, (2) all people have the right to information that will affect their lives, and (3) unless communication achieves continuous, accurate feedback, the organization won't accurately be able to assess how it is viewed by its publics and to adjust its actions appropriately.

Stated another way, in the words of scholar DeWitt Reddick, "Public relations is the *lubricant* which makes the segments of an order work together with minimum friction and misunderstanding." The goal of effective public relations, then, is to harmonize internal and external relationships so that an organization can enjoy not only public goodwill, but also stability and longevity.

Interpreting Management to the Public

Public relations practitioners are basically interpreters. On the one hand, they must interpret the philosophies, policies, programs, and practices of their management to the public; on the other hand, they must translate the attitudes of the public to their management.

To accomplish these tasks accurately and truthfully, practitioners must gain attention, understanding, acceptance, and, ultimately, action from target publics. But first they have to know what management is thinking.

Good public relations can't be practiced in a vacuum. No matter what the size of the organization, a public relations department is only as good as its access to management. For example, it's useless for a senator's press secretary to explain the reasoning of an important decision without first finding out what the senator had in mind. So, too, an organization's public relations staff is impotent without firsthand knowledge of the reasons for management's decisions and the rationale for organizational policy.

The public relations department in a profit-making or nonprofit enterprise can counsel management. It can advise management. It can even exhort management to action. But management must call the shots on organizational policy. Practitioners must fully understand the whys and wherefores of policy and communicate the ideas accurately and candidly to the public. Anything less can lead to major problems.

Interpreting the Public to Management

The flip side of the coin is interpreting the public to management. Simply stated, this task means finding out what the public really thinks about the firm and letting management know. Regrettably, corporate history is filled with examples of public relations departments failing to anticipate the true sentiments of the public.

General Motors paid little attention to an unknown consumer activist named Ralph Nader, who spread the message that GM's Corvair was unsafe at any speed. When Nader's assault began to be believed, the automaker assigned private detectives to trail him. In short order, General Motors was forced to acknowledge its act of paranoia, and the Corvair was eventually sacked, at great loss to the company.

In the mid-1970s, as both the price of gasoline and oil company profits rose rapidly, Mobil infuriated a suspicious public by purchasing Marcor, parent of the Montgomery Ward department store chain, instead of spending its earnings on new oil exploration and development.

Government leaders, too, sometimes incorrectly interpret the public's sentiments. Late in his presidency, Jimmy Carter tried to enlist public support for his flagging economic program with a nationally televised address that discussed America's "malaise" and the need to get the nation moving again. Carter's speech backfired, it was generally agreed, because many Americans resented the notion that they and their country were languishing. The Carter malaise speech was later used to great advantage by Ronald Reagan in his successful bid for the presidency in 1980.

In the early 1990s, America was just beginning to recover from an unprecedented wave of greed and duplicity, perpetrated by some of the richest and most well-known financiers in the nation. Ivan Boesky, who donated millions to charity and polished his image with a book on financial advice, received a reduced jail term, only after fingering associates in insider-trading schemes. One Boesky associate, Michael Milken, hailed by corporate leaders throughout the nation as the "king of junk bonds," was also fined and sentenced to prison in the winter of 1990 for his role in illegal transactions. Milken, with the help of high-priced public relations counsel, attempted to alter his public image by buying tickets to ballgames for underprivileged children and making known his sizable charitable contributions. And then there was the stirring saga of Donald Trump, a boastful and self-aggrandizing New York promoter, who saw his marriage crumble along with his far-flung real estate and gambling empire in the recession of late 1990. The public seemed to take a perverse delight in watching "the Donald's" troubles increase.

These examples indicate that organizations are often insensitive to the public's concerns. As Joseph T. Nolan, veteran public relations teacher and practitioner, has put it:

> Nobody has a larger stake in our economic system—or a larger say in our society—than U.S. business. Whether that system and that society continue to work to the satisfaction of business will depend, ultimately, on how successfully individual businesses demonstrate that they can work for the good of everybody.[24]

The Publics of Public Relations

The term *public relations* is really a misnomer. *Publics relations*, or *relations with the publics*, would be more to the point. Practitioners must communicate with many different publics—not just the general public—each having its own special needs and requiring different types of communications. Often, the lines that divide these publics are thin, and the potential overlap is significant. Therefore, priorities, according to organizational needs, must always be reconciled (Figure 1–1).

Technological change, in particular, has brought greater interdependence to people and organizations, and there is growing concern in organizations today about managing extensive webs of interrelationships. Indeed, managers have become interrelationship conscious.

Internally, managers must deal directly with various levels of subordinates, as well as with cross-relationships that arise when subordinates interact with one another. Externally, managers must deal with a system that includes government regulatory agencies, labor unions, subcontractors, consumer groups, and many other independent—but often related—organizations. The public relations challenge in all of this is to manage effectively the communications between managers and the various publics with whom they interrelate.

Definitions differ on precisely what constitutes a public. One time-honored definition suggests that a public arises when a group of people (1) face a similar indeterminate situation; (2) recognize what is indeterminate and problematic in that situation; and (3) organize to do something about the problem.[25]

Publics can also be classified into several overlapping categories:

1. **Internal and external** Internal publics are inside the organization: supervisors, clerks, managers, stockholders, and the board of directors. External publics are those not directly connected with the organization: the press, government, educators, customers, the community, and suppliers.

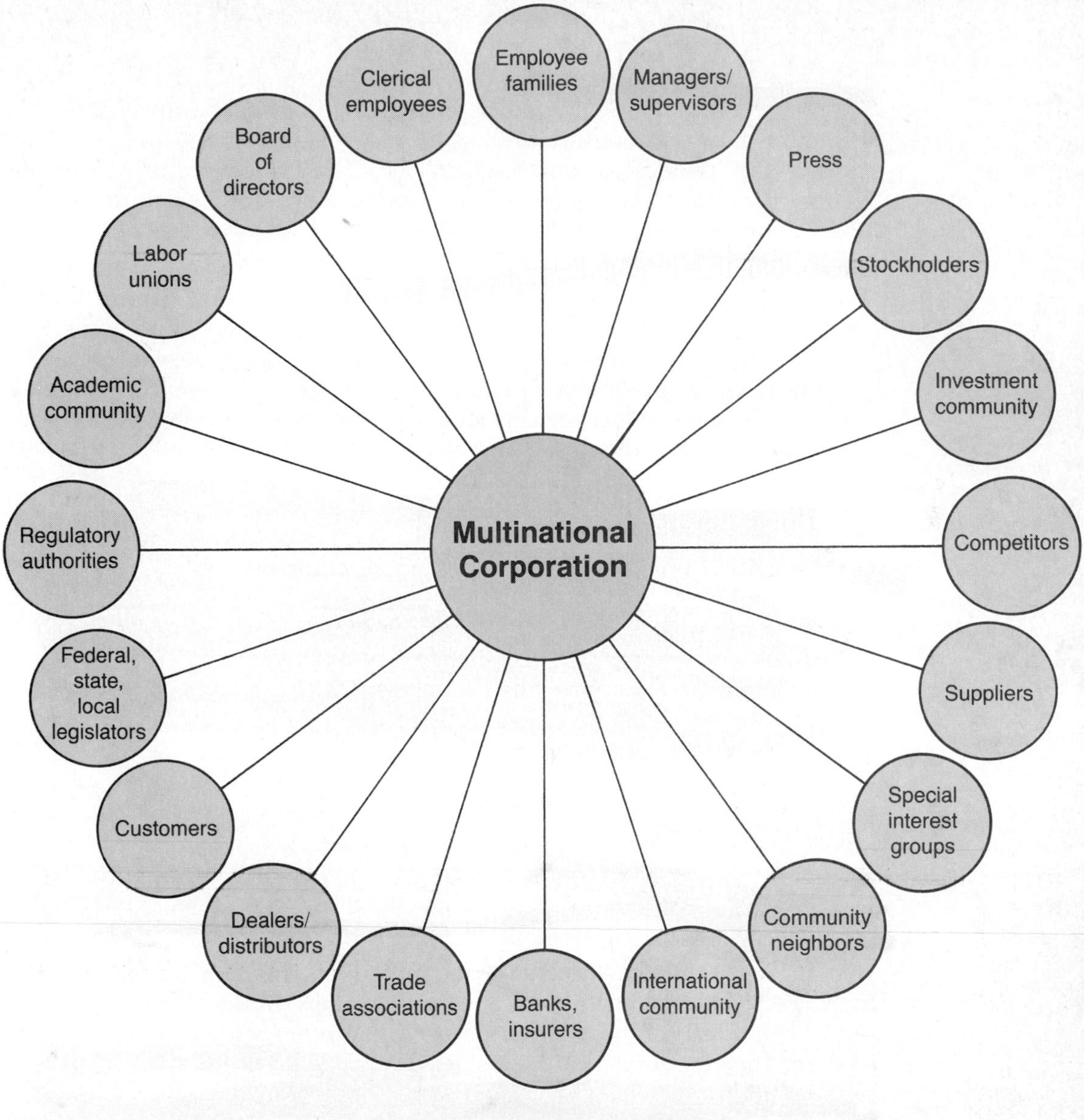

FIGURE 1—1 Twenty key publics of a typical multinational corporation. *(Art by Lou Braun)*

2. **Primary, secondary, and marginal** Primary publics can most help—or hinder—the organization's efforts. Secondary publics are less important, and marginal publics are the least important of all. For example, members of the Federal Reserve Board of Governors, who regulate banks, would be the primary public for a bank awaiting a

regulatory ruling, whereas legislators and the general public would be secondary.

3. **Traditional and future** Employees and current customers are traditional publics; students and potential customers are future ones. No organization can afford to become complacent in dealing with its changing publics. Today, a firm's publics range from women to minorities to senior citizens to homosexuals. Each might be important to the future success of the organization.

4. **Proponents, opponents, and uncommitted** An institution must deal differently with those who support it and those who oppose it. For supporters, communications that reinforce beliefs may be in order. But changing the opinions of skeptics calls for strong, persuasive communications. Often, particularly in politics, the uncommitted public is crucial. Many a campaign has been decided because the swing vote was won over by one of the candidates.

The typical organization is faced with a myriad of critical publics with whom it must communicate on a frequent and direct basis. It must be sensitive to the self-interests, desires, and concerns of each public. It must understand that self-interest groups today are themselves more complex. Therefore, the harmonizing actions necessary to win and maintain support among such groups should be arrived at in terms of public relations consequences.[26] And while management must always speak with one voice, its communications inflection, delivery, and emphasis should be sensitive to all its constituent publics.

The Essence of Public Relations

Ethics, truth, credibility—these values are what good public relations is all about. Cover-up, distortion, and subterfuge are the antitheses of good public relations.

Much more than customers for their products, managers today desperately need constituents for their beliefs and values. In the 1990s, the role of public relations will be much more to guide management in framing its ideas and making its commitments. The counsel that management will need must come from advisors who understand public attitudes, public moods, public needs, and public aspirations.

Winning this elusive goodwill takes time and effort. Credibility can't be won overnight, nor can it be bought. If management policies aren't in the public's best interest, no amount of public relations can obscure that reality. Public relations is not effective as a temporary, defensive measure to compensate for management misjudgment. (See the Exxon Case Study at the end of this chapter.) If management errs seriously, the best—and only—public relations advice must be to get the story out immediately.

If public relations has come of age as a serious and substantive profession, does that mean the end of the slick-talking image merchant? Hardly. People will always be interested in finding an angle or sneaking one by in the flimflammiest traditions of P. T. Barnum. But clearly the profession is growing more sophisticated.

One public relations professional who probably summed up the opinion of many colleagues about exactly what it is he does for a living was Peter F. Jeff, a Michigan practitioner who wrote to a local editor:

> A public relations professional is a bridge builder, not a drum beater— building long-term relationships between a company or organization and its publics based on two-way communication (i.e., listening and speaking). A public relations professional serves as an interpreter, helping the company adapt and adjust to the political, social, and economic climate . . . and assisting the public in more fully understanding the company.[27]

Summary

In today's information society, the presence of public relations has never been more pervasive. Nor has its power been more potent, as the demands increase to communicate effectively. No matter what it's called, the practice of public relations is here to stay. As public relations counselor Philip Lesly has put it, "Whether the references are favorable, unfavorable or neutral, the significant fact is that the field has been growing rapidly in public awareness."[28]

No less an authority than Abraham Lincoln once said, "Public sentiment is everything . . . with public sentiment nothing can fail. Without it, nothing can succeed. He who molds public sentiment goes deeper than he who executes statutes or pronounces decisions. He makes statutes or decisions possible or impossible to execute."

Stated another way, no matter how you define it, the practice of public relations has become an essential element in the conduct of relationships in the 1990s.

DISCUSSION STARTERS

1. Why has the practice of public relations become so pervasive in the 1990s?
2. Why are others—lawyers, accountants, general managers, etc.—interested in penetrating the practice of public relations?
3. Why is the practice of public relations generally misunderstood by the public?
4. Why isn't there one all-encompassing definition of the field?
5. Explain the approach toward defining public relations by the nature of its functions.
6. Explain the approach toward defining public relations as a "harmonizing" process.
7. Why is a public relations professional fundamentally an "interpreter"?
8. What are the four overlapping categories of publics?

9. What is the essence of proper public relations practice?
10. Has public relations truly rid itself of charlatan practitioners? Will it ever?

NOTES

1. James G. Grunig, "IABC Study Shows CEO Value PR," *IABC Communication World* (August 1990): 5.
2. John V. Pavlik, *Public Relations: What Research Tells Us* (Newbury Park, CA: Sage Publications, 1987), 85.
3. Jack O'Dwyer, *O'Dwyer's Directory of Public Relations Firms* 1990 (New York: J. R. O'Dwyer Co., 1990): 7.
4. Paula Span, "Chronicles of the PR Warrior," *Washington Post*, 28 April 1988, C1.
5. "The Design for Undergraduate Public Relations Education," a study co-sponsored by the public relations division of the Association for Education and Journalism and Mass Communication, the Public Relations Society of America, and the educators' section of PRSA, 1987, 1.
6. Jeff Blyskal and Marie Blyskal, *PR: How the Public Relations Industry Writes the News* (New York: William Morrow, 1985), 61.
7. Philip Lesly, "Public Relations Numbers Are up But Stature Down," *Public Relations Review* (Winter 1988): 3.
8. Jason DeParle, "Gulf Crisis Starts a Costly Fight for Good Press," *The New York Times*, 3 September 1990, 31.
9. William Ehling, "How to Get Maximum Benefit from Public Relations by Positioning It Properly in the Organization," *PR Reports Tips & Tactics*, No. 10 (August 13, 1990): 1.
10. Berton J. Ballard, lecture at San Jose State University, San Jose, CA, 1948. Cited in Pearce Davies, "Twenty-Five Years Old and Still Growing," *Public Relations Journal* (October 1977): 22–23.
11. Cited in Scott M. Cutlip and Allen H. Center, *Effective Public Relations*, 6th ed. (Englewood Cliffs, NJ: Prentice-Hall, 1985), 5.
12. Heb. 13:16.
13. Edward L. Bernays, *Crystallizing Public Opinion* (New York: Liveright, 1961), LV.
14. "The Public Be Not Damned," *Fortune* (March 1, 1939): 83.
15. Pratt Henry Fairchild, ed., *Dictionary of Sociology* (New York: Philosophical Library, 1944).
16. Rex F. Harlow, "Building a Public Relations Definition," *Public Relations Review* 2, no. 4 (Winter 1976): 36.
17. First World Assembly of Public Relations Associations, Mexico City, Mexico, 1978.
18. Philip Lesly, "Report and Recommendations: Task Force on Stature and Role of Public Relations," *Public Relations Journal* (March 1981): 32.
19. John E. Marston, *The Nature of Public Relations* (New York: McGraw-Hill, 1963), 161.
20. Denny Griswold, *Public Relations News*, International Public Relations Weekly for Executives, 127 East 80th Street, New York, NY 10021.
21. Robert L. Simpson, "Six Rules for Selling PR," Simpson and Associates, 200 West 9th St., Wilmington, DE 19801, 1989.
22. "In New Decade of Personalized Relationships and Communication, Changes in

Techniques, Strategies, and Practitioners' Attitudes Are Predictable," *PR Reporter*, No. 1 (January 1, 1990): 1.

23. This definition was developed by Dr. Melvin L. Sharpe, professor and coordinator of the Public Relations Sequence, Department of Journalism, Ball State University, Muncie, IN 47306.
24. Joseph T. Nolan, "Protect Your Public Image with Performance," *Harvard Business Review* (March-April 1975): 142.
25. John Dewey, *The Public and Its Problems* (Chicago: Swallow Press, 1927).
26. Sharpe, loc. cit.
27. Peter F. Jeff, "Dissent! Public Relations," *Grand Rapids Press*, 2 March 1990.
28. "Never Mind How Field Defines Itself: Power Brokers, Public Think 'PR' Pandemic," *Public Relations Reporter* (January 4, 1988): 6.

TOP OF THE SHELF

Cutlip, Scott M., Allen H. Center, and Glen M. Broom. *Effective Public Relations,* 6th ed. Englewood Cliffs, NJ: Prentice-Hall, 1985.

From its opening-chapter description of the profession to its final section on public relations and higher education, *Effective Public Relations* offers a comprehensive and detailed look at the field.

This book's strength is its breadth. Part One provides solid instruction in public relations fundamentals, explaining the nature of the profession, its role as a management function, and the skills required to be a successful practitioner. Students also learn the basics of traditional public relations activities from employee relations to community relations to media relations. Particularly helpful are guidelines for developing and executing a communications plan. Part Two shows public relations at work on behalf of business, trade associations, voluntary agencies, government, and schools.

Effective Public Relations, with 670 pages and 23 chapters, is written by three veteran public relations professors. Its ample coverage alone makes it a most worthwhile public relations resource.

Albrecht, Karl. *At America's Service.* Homewood, IL: Dow Jones-Irwin, 1988.

Awad, Joseph. *The Power of Public Relations.* New York: Praeger, 1985.

Baskin, Otis W., and Craig E. Aronoff. *Public Relations: The Profession and the Practice,* 2nd ed. Dubuque, IA: Wm. C. Brown Publishers, 1988.

Baxter, Bill L. "Education for Corporate Public Relations," *Public Relations Review* (Spring 1985): 38–41. This article, based on a survey by the Public Relations Society of America, indicates that public relations courses stress journalism and general writing skills.

Brody, E. W. *The Business of Public Relations.* New York: Praeger, 1987.

SUGGESTED
READINGS

Brough, B. *Publicity and Public Relations Guide for Business.* Sunnyvale, CA: Oasis Press, 1986.

Cantor, Bill (Chester Burger, ed.). *Experts in Action: Inside Public Relations,* 2nd ed. White Plains, NY: Longman, 1989.

Center, Allen H., and Frank E. Walsh. *Public Relations Practices: Case Studies,* 2nd ed. Englewood Cliffs, NJ: Prentice-Hall, 1985.

Center, Allen H., and Patrick Jackson. *Public Relations Practices: Managerial Case Studies and Problems,* 4th ed. Englewood Cliffs, NJ: Prentice-Hall, 1990.

Dilenschneider, Robert L., and Dan J. Forrestal. *Dartnell Public Relations Handbook,* 3rd ed. Chicago, IL: Dartnell Publishing Co., 1987.

Dunn, S. W. *Public Relations: A Contemporary Approach.* Homewood, IL: Dow Jones-Irwin, 1986.

Haberman, David, and Harry Dolphin. *Public Relations: The Necessary Art.* Iowa City: Iowa State University Press, 1988.

Lesly, Philip. *Bonanzas and Fool's Gold Treasures and Dross from the Nuggetizing of Our Lives.* Chicago: Lesly Co., 1987.

Newsom, Doug, and Alan Scott. *This Is PR: The Realities of Public Relations,* 4th ed. Belmont, CA: Wadsworth, 1989.

Olasky, Marvin N. "Roots of Modern Public Relations: The Bernays Doctrine," *Public Relations Quarterly* (March 1985): 25–27. The author suggests that the beginning of modern public relations was the so-called Bernays doctrine that posited the notion that communication, done skillfully, could effectively "engineer public consent" to bring about social goals.

Randall, Craig. "Hype Springs Eternal," *United Inflight Magazine* (November 1985): 48–51, 130–148.

Reilly, Robert T. *Public Relations in Action,* 2nd ed. Englewood Cliffs, NJ: Prentice-Hall, 1987.

Simon, Raymond. *Public Relations Management: Casebook,* 3rd ed. Columbus, OH: Publishing Horizons, 1986.

Stevens, Art. *The Persuasion Explosion.* Washington, DC: Acropolis Books, 1985.

Sullivan, Michael. *Management Audit for Public Relations Firms.* Doylestown, PA: Sullivan Associates (P. O. Box 229), 1987.

Wood, Robert J. *Confessions of a PR Man.* Scarborough, Ontario: The New American Library of Canada, Ltd., 1989.

CASE STUDY   Exxon Corporation's Bad Good Friday

At 8:30 A.M. on March 24, 1989—Good Friday, no less—Lawrence G. Rawl, chairman and chief executive of the Exxon Corporation, one of the world's largest companies, was in his kitchen sipping coffee when the phone rang.

"What happened? Did it lose an engine? Break a rudder?" Rawl asked the caller.

"What happened" was that an Exxon tanker had run aground and was dumping gummy crude oil into the frigid waters of Prince William Sound, just outside the harbor of Valdez, Alaska.

What was about to happen to Mr. Rawl and his company—and to the environment—was arguably the worst environmental disaster in the history of the United States.

The facts, painfully portrayed in media across the country, were these: The *Exxon Valdez*, a 978-foot tanker, piloted by a captain who was later revealed to be "legally drunk," ran aground on a reef 25 miles southwest of the port of Valdez. The resulting rupture caused a spill of 250,000 barrels, the largest spill ever in North America, affecting 1,300 square miles of water, damaging some 600 miles of coastline, and murdering as many as 4,000 cute little Alaskan sea otters.

The disaster also cemented the name, "Exxon," in the all-time Public Relations Hall of Shame.

Exxon's dilemma broke down roughly into five general categories.

1. To Go or Not to Go

The first problem that confronted Exxon and its top management after news of the Good Friday spill was whether Chairman Rawl should personally fly to Prince William Sound to demonstrate the company's concern. This was what Union Carbide chairman Warren Anderson did when his company suffered a devastating industrial explosion in Bhopal, India. It was also what Ashland Oil chairman John R. Hall did when his company suffered an oil spill earlier in 1989.

If Rawl went to Alaska, the reasoning went, he might have been able to reassure the public that the people who run Exxon acknowledged their misdeed and would make amends. What better show of concern than the chairman flying to the local scene of the tragedy?

On the other hand, a consensus of executives around Rawl argued that he should remain in New York. "What are you going to do?" they asked. "We've already said we've done it, we're going to pay for it, and that we're responsible for it." Rawl's more effective role, said these advisors, was right there at Exxon headquarters in Manhattan.

In the end, the latter view triumphed. Rawl didn't go to Alaska. He left the cleanup in "capable hands" and sent a succession of lower-ranking executives to Alaska to deal with the spill. As he summarized in an interview one year after the Prince William Sound nightmare, "We had concluded that there was simply too much for me to coordinate from New York. It wouldn't have made any difference if I showed up and made a speech in the town forum. I wasn't going to spend the summer there; I had other things to do."

Rawl's failure to fly immediately to Valdez struck some as shortsighted. Summarized one media consultant, "The chairman should have been up there walking in the oil and picking up dead birds."

2. Where to Establish Media Central

The second dilemma that confronted Exxon was where to establish its media center.

This decision started correctly enough with Exxon senior managers concluding that the impact of the spill was so great that news organizations should be kept informed on a real-time basis. Exxon, correctly, wanted to take charge of the news flow and give the public, through the news media, a credible, concerned, and wholly committed corporate response.

It decided the best place to do this would be in Valdez, Alaska, itself. "Just about every news organization worth its salt had representatives in Valdez," said Exxon's publicity chief. "But in retrospect, we should have sent live broadcasts of news conferences to several points around the country."

The problem was that Valdez was a remote Alaskan town with limited communications operations. This complicated the ability of Exxon to disseminate information quickly. As *Oil & Gas Journal* summarized later, "Exxon did not update its media relations people elsewhere in the world. It told reporters it was Valdez or nothing."

Additionally, there was a four-hour time difference between Valdez and New York. Consequently, "Exxon statements were erratic and contradictory," said the publisher of another oil bulletin. The phone lines to Valdez quickly became jammed, and even Rawl couldn't find a knowledgeable official to brief him. That left news organizations, responsible for keeping the public informed, cut off from Exxon information during the early part of the crisis. Because news conferences took place at horrible viewing hours for television networks and too late for many morning newspapers, predictable accusations of "Exxon cover-up" resulted. Summarized one Exxon official about the decision to put the center in Valdez, "It didn't work."

3. *Rapidity of Response*

A cardinal rule in any crisis is "keep ahead of the information flow." Try not to let events get ahead of you. Keep in front of the information curve. Here Exxon had serious problems.

First, it took Chairman Rawl a full week to make any public comment on the spill. When he did, it was to blame others: the U.S. Coast Guard and Alaskan officials were "holding up" his company's efforts to clean up the spill. But Rawl's words were too little, too late. The impression persisted that, in light of the delay to admit responsibility, Exxon was not responding vigorously enough.

A full ten days after the crisis, Exxon placed an advertisement in 166 newspapers. To some readers, the ad seemed self-serving

and failed to address the many pointed questions raised about Exxon's conduct.

"It seems the company was a bit too relaxed in its capabilities," offered the president of the Public Relations Society of America. Meanwhile, one group that wasn't "relaxed" was the Alaska State Legislature, which enacted a tax increase on oil from the North Slope fields within weeks of the Exxon spill. Congressional committees in Washington moved just as quickly to increase liability limits and potential compensation for oil-spill damage and to increase the money available through the industry-financed Offshore Oil Pollution Compensation Fund.

When Exxon hesitated, its opponents seized the initiative. Summarized another public relations executive, "They lost the battle in the first 48 hours."

4. *How High the Profile*

Exxon's response in the face of this most challenging crisis in its history was, to put it mildly, "muted."

From an operations and logistics view, Exxon did a good job. The company immediately set up animal rescue projects, launched a major cleanup effort, and agreed to pick up a substantial percentage of the cost. But it made the mistake of downplaying the crisis in public.

Exxon's public statements sometimes contradicted information from other sources. At one point, an Exxon spokesman said that damage from the oil spill would be "minimal." Others watching the industry said the damage was likely to be "substantial."

Chairman Rawl, an otherwise blunt and outspoken chief, seemed defensive and argumentative in his public comments. In one particularly disastrous personal appearance on the *CBS Morning News*, Rawl glared at interviewer Kathleen Sullivan and snapped,

"I can't give you details of our Cleanup Plan. It's thick and complicated. And I haven't had a chance to read it yet. The CEO of a major company doesn't have time to read every plan."

Exxon's attempts at calming the public also were criticized. Its ad drew fire for not "expressing enough concern." It hired an outside firm to do a series of video news releases to show how the company was cleaning up the spill. At an estimated cost of more than $3 million, a 13-minute tape was shown at the corporation's annual meeting. The video, called, "Progress in Alaska," attracted intense criticism from those attending the conference, as well as from the press. The film implied, argued *Boston Globe* reporter Robert Lenzner, that "The brutal scenes of damage to Alaskan waters seen nightly on television news programs were false." *USA Today* called the tape, "Exxon's worst move of the day." When the consultant who devised the video wrote an op-ed article in *The New York Times* defending Exxon's approach in Alaska, the Alaskan representative to the National Wildlife Federation responded with a blistering letter to the editor, noting that the consultant omitted in his article that the spill resulted in the deaths of more than 15,000 sea birds and numerous otters and eagles.

Exxon then added an environmental expert to its board of directors, but only after pension funds, which control a large chunk of its stock, demanded such a response.

5. Dealing with the Aftermath

Finally, Exxon was forced to deal with all the implications of what its tanker had wrought in Valdez.

The company became embroiled in controversy when Exxon USA sent a $30,000 contribution to the Alaska Public Radio Network, which covered the crisis on a daily basis. The network, sniffing "conflict of interest," flatly turned down Exxon's attempted largesse. Subsequently, a special appropriations bill was introduced in the Alaskan legislature to forward an identical amount to Alaska Public Radio.

The accident and the company's reaction to it also had consequences for the oil industry. Plans to expand drilling into the Alaskan National Wildlife Refuge were shelved by Congress, and members called for new laws increasing federal involvement in oil spills.

The company's employees, too, felt confused, embarrassed, and betrayed. Summarizing the prevailing mood at the company, one Exxon worker said, "Whenever I travel now I feel like I have a target painted on my chest."

The lessons of the Exxon Valdez Good Friday oil spill would not soon be forgotten by corporate managers. The episode, predicted some, "will become a textbook example of what not to do when an unexpected crisis thrusts a company into the limelight." Said another, Exxon's response "is fast becoming the stuff of PR legend."

FIGURE 1—2

Reprinted by permission of UFS, Inc.

AN OPEN LETTER TO THE PUBLIC

On March 24, in the early morning hours, a disastrous accident happened in the waters of Prince William Sound, Alaska. By now you all know that our tanker, the Exxon Valdez, hit a submerged reef and lost 240,000 barrels of oil into the waters of the Sound.

We believe that Exxon has moved swiftly and competently to minimize the effect this oil will have on the environment, fish and other wildlife. Further, I hope that you know we have already committed several hundred people to work on the cleanup. We also will meet our obligations to all those who have suffered damage from the spill.

Finally, and most importantly, I want to tell you how sorry I am that this accident took place. We at Exxon are especially sympathetic to the residents of Valdez and the people of the State of Alaska. We cannot, of course, undo what has been done. But I can assure you that since March 24, the accident has been receiving our full attention and will continue to do so.

L. G. Rawl
Chairman

FIGURE 1–3

QUESTIONS

1. What would you have recommended Chairman Rawl do upon learning of the Prince William Sound oil spill?
2. How would you have handled the media in this case?
3. What would have been your "timing" in terms of public relations responses in this case?
4. What would be your overall public relations strategy—i.e., aggressive, low-key, etc.—if you were Exxon's public relations director?
5. Do you think this case will ever qualify as a "textbook example" of what not to do in a crisis?

For further information about the *Exxon Valdez* case, see Richard Behar, "Exxon Strikes Back," *Time* (26 March, 1990): 62–63; Claudia H. Deutsch, "The Giant with a Black Eye," *The New York Times*, 2 April 1989, B1–4; E. Bruce Harrison, with Tom Prugh, "Assessing the Damage," *Public Relations Journal* (October 1989): 40–45; John Holusha, "Exxon's Public-Relations Problem," *The New York Times*, 21 April 1989, D1–4; Peter Nulty, "Exxon's Problem: Not What You Think," *Fortune* (April 23, 1990): 202–204; James Lukaszewski, "How Vulnerable Are You? The Lessons from Valdez," *Public Relations Quarterly* (Fall 1989): 5–6; Phillip M. Perry, "Exxon Falters in PR Effort Following Alaskan Oil Spill," *O'Dwyer's PR Services Report*, (July 1989) 1,: 16–22; Allanna Sullivan, "Rawl Wishes He'd Visited Valdez Sooner," *The Wall Street Journal*, 30 June 1989, B7; and Paul Wiseman, "Firm Finds Valdez Oil Fowls Image," *USA Today*, (26 April 1990): B1.

Tips from the Top

MARLIN FITZWATER

In November 1988, Marlin Fitzwater became the first White House Press Secretary ever to be appointed by two presidents, Presidents Reagan and Bush. Fitzwater guided press relations through the Iran-contra affair and reassured the nation as America undertook at least four major military actions. He provided the government explanations when U.S. forces attacked Iranian oil platforms in the Persian Gulf, when American warships escorted Kuwaiti tankers, when the first paratroopers went into Panama, and when the largest deployment since World War II occurred in the Persian Gulf and Saudi Arabia. With a reputation for professionalism and fairness, Fitzwater has conducted hundreds of press briefings and represented the practice of public relations with distinction in a decade of service in the White House.

What is the primary mission of the president's press secretary?
The press secretary speaks for the president and the administration in terms of explaining decisions and issues to the American people.

What is the greatest challenge to the president's press secretary?
The greatest challenge is to accurately and in a timely manner reflect the president's views on the issues before the government.

The press secretary must measure his value in terms of how honestly and accurately he portrays the position and the ideas of the president.

How close was your access to President Reagan?
Access was not an issue. President Reagan was in constant and close communication with all of his senior staff, certainly including the press secretary.

How would you compare your role in the Bush White House to the Reagan White House?
The role is the same in terms of daily press briefings, the continuous search for information, and the brokering of relations between the White House press corps and the government. The difference is in the personalities and media strategies of the presidents.

President Reagan was an expert in delivering speeches, prepared addresses, and formal press conferences. President Bush is a master of the informal press conference and personal press relations. President Bush gave over 122 press conferences in two years, compared to only 47 in President Reagan's eight years. These strategies were designed to utilize the strengths of both presidents.

President Reagan was called "the great communicator," but President Bush has enjoyed the highest public approval rating of any president in the last several decades and obviously has been successful in his communications as well.

What is President Bush's view of public relations?

President Bush believes it's important to inform the American people about his policies and programs. He prefers the basic communication skills, such as press conferences and interviews, rather than gimmicks or advertising techniques. His speeches are not peppered with props or visual aids. His language is simple. His message is straightforward.

What's been your most challenging assignment thus far as Press Secretary?

Announcing the invasion of Panama at 1:00 in the morning on December 17, 1989. It was crucial to offer an explanation throughout the night to the American people that would inspire confidence in our ability to achieve a victory, while at the same time demonstrating our efforts to minimize casualties.

On a sustained basis, the most challenging assignment was providing daily explanations of our policy in the Persian Gulf. It required a daily analysis and understanding of our situation in the conflict over a period of several months. The daily press briefing was an essential element in building public support for the United States' growing involvement in the implementation of the U.N. resolutions against Iraq.

What's your view on whether a press secretary should create quotes for the president?

The press secretary should reflect the president's thinking and disseminate the president's quotes. He should not create them.

What is the caliber and attitude of the journalists with whom you dealt at the White House?

The White House press corps represents the highest quality journalists in America. They are inquisitive, smart, relentless, and insightful.

How objective are they?

The White House press corps reports with considerable objectivity. However, some of them have definite points of view. But these points of view are normally an important aspect of their reporting and are sanctioned, if not encouraged, by their organizations.

What advice would you give to public relations practitioners of the future?

Don't forget the basics. We are in the midst of a technology explosion in terms of information dissemination, but the basic principles of information collection are the same. Don't lose sight of honesty, accuracy, and sensitivity as you utilize the new technology.

The Evolution of
Public Relations

The practice of public relations has been shaped by several underlying and pervasive societal trends, as it has enhanced its role and stature. Four trends, in particular, are directly related to the evolution of public relations: (1) the growth of big institutions; (2) the increasing incidence of change, conflict, and confrontation in society; (3) the heightened awareness and sophistication of people everywhere, as a result of technological innovations in communications; and (4) the increased importance of public opinion as democracy washes over the world in the 1990s. See p. 39

♦ The bigness of today's society has played a significant role in the development of public relations. The days of the mom-and-pop grocery store, the tiny community college, and the small local bank are rapidly disappearing. In their places have emerged supermarket chains and 24-hour-a-day 7-Elevens, statewide community college systems with populous branches in several cities, and the beginnings of multibank, multistate banking networks. As institutions have grown larger, as the U.S. population has burgeoned to nearly 251 million, and as people have had to deal increasingly with bureaucracy, so too have institutions themselves refined their methods of communicating with their publics. Specifically, the public relations profession has evolved to interpret these large institutions to the publics they serve.

♦ The increasing incidence of change, conflict, and confrontation in society is yet another reason for the evolution of public relations. Women's rights and affirmative action, consumerism and environmental awareness, labor-management disputes, and the unhappiness of the general public with large institutions have all contributed materially to the need for more and better communications and the existence of more and better communicators.

Then, too, the rapidity of societal change has added to the necessity for professional public relations. Today, nothing stands still for long. The credibility of organizations is challenged constantly, and their role in society can change instantly. Our expectations of an organization's responsibilities are ever-changing. And the emerging technologies of the computer age—robotics, genetic engineering, telecommunications, and the rest—continually put added pressure on an organization to adapt not only its communicated messages but its methods of communicating as well.

♦ A third factor in the development of public relations has been the heightened awareness of people everywhere. First came the invention of the printing press. Later it was the pervasiveness of mass communications: the print media, radio, and television. Then it was the development of cable, satellite, videotape, video discs, video typewriters, portable cameras, word processors, fax machines, and all the other communications technologies that have helped fragment audiences and deliver Marshall McLuhan's "global village."

In a world where the image of a lone protestor blocking a line of tanks in Beijing's Tiananmen Square can be flashed around the world to be

FIGURE 2–1 The communications revolution sweeping the world was no more vividly illustrated than in 1989, when Chinese students, including this brave protestor, stood up for freedom in the face of military might. People for the American Way, a lobbying group, recalled this protest when, in 1990, U.S. Senator Jesse Helms threatened to censor government arts funding. *(Courtesy of People for the American Way)*

seen on the evening news; when an earthquake in San Francisco can be witnessed in "real-time" by people in their living rooms in Bangor, Maine; when a dictator in the Persian Gulf can be interviewed live by a reporter in Washington, there can be no doubt that the "communications revolution" has arrived.

◆ Finally, the outbreak of democracy in Latin America, Eastern Europe, and even the Soviet Union and South Africa has heightened the power of public opinion in the world. Just as increasing numbers of Americans had their voices heard through the civil rights movements, various consumer movements, the women's rights movement, and political movements through the ages, so too have oppressed peoples around the world risen up and spoken out. Accordingly, the practice of public relations, as a facilitator in understanding more clearly and managing more effectively in the midst of such democratic revolution, has increased in prominence.

Ancient Beginnings

Although we think of public relations as a twentieth-century phenomenon, its roots are ancient. Leaders in virtually every great society throughout history understood the importance of influencing public opinion through persuasion. For example, the Babylonians of 1800 B.C. hammered out their messages on stone tablets so that farmers could learn the latest techniques of harvesting, sowing, and irrigating.[1] The more food the farmers grew, the better the citizenry ate and the wealthier the country became—a good example of planned persuasion to reach a specific public for a particular purpose; in other words, public relations.

Later on, the Greeks put a high premium on communication skills. The best speakers, in fact, were generally elected to leadership positions. Occasionally, aspiring Greek politicians enlisted the aid of Sophists (individuals renowned for both their reasoning and their rhetoric) to help fight verbal battles. Sophists would gather in the amphitheaters of the day and extol the virtues of particular political candidates. Often, their arguments convinced the voters to elect those candidates. Thus, the Sophists set the stage for today's lobbyists, who attempt to influence legislation through effective communication techniques.

The Romans, particularly Julius Caesar, were also masters of persuasive techniques. When faced with an upcoming battle, Caesar would rally public support through assorted publications and staged events. Similarly, during World War I, a special U.S. public information committee, the Creel Committee, was formed to channel the patriotic sentiments of Americans in support of the U.S. role in the war. Stealing a page from Caesar, the committee's massive verbal and written communications effort was successful in marshaling national pride behind the war effort. According to a young member of the Creel Committee, Edward L. Bernays (later considered by many to be the father of public relations), "This was the first time in our history that information was used as a weapon of war."[2]

Even the Catholic Church had a hand in the beginnings of public relations. In the 1600s, under the leadership of Pope Gregory XV, the Church established a college of propaganda to "help propagate the faith." In those days, the term *propaganda* did not have a negative connotation; the Church simply wanted to inform the public about the advantages of Catholicism.

Early American Experience

The American public relations experience dates back to our founding as a republic. Influencing public opinion, managing communications, and persuading individuals at the highest levels were at the core of the American Revolution. The colonists tried to persuade King George III that they should be accorded the same rights as Englishmen. "Taxation without representation is tyranny!" became their public relations slogan to galvanize fellow countrymen.

When King George refused to accede to the colonists' demands, they combined the weaponry of sword and pen. Samuel Adams, for one, organized committees of correspondence as a kind of revolutionary Associated Press to disseminate speedily anti-British information throughout the Colonies. He also staged events to build up revolutionary fervor, like the Boston Tea Party, where colonists, masquerading as Indians, boarded British ships in Boston Harbor and pitched chests of imported tea overboard—as impressive a media event as has ever been recorded, *sans* television.

Thomas Paine, another early practitioner of public relations, wrote periodic pamphlets that urged the colonists to band together. In one issue of *Common Sense,* Paine wrote poetically, "These are the times that try men's souls. The summer soldier and the sunshine patriot will, in this crisis, shrink from the service of their country." The people listened, were persuaded, and took action—testifying to the power of early American communicators.

Later American Experience

The creation of the most important document in our nation's history, the Constitution, also owed much to public relations. Federalists, who supported the Constitution, fought tooth and nail with Anti-Federalists, who opposed it. Their battle was waged in newspaper articles, pamphlets, and other forms of persuasion, in an attempt to influence public opinion. To advocate ratification of the Constitution, political leaders like Alexander Hamilton, James Madison, and John Jay banded together, under the pseudonym Publius, to author letters in leading newspapers. Today, those letters are bound in a document called *The Federalist Papers* and are still used in the interpretation of the Constitution.

After ratification, the Constitutional debate continued, particularly over the document's apparent failure to protect individual liberties against government encroachment. Hailed as the Father of the Constitution, Madison framed the Bill of Rights in 1791, which ultimately became the first ten amendments to the Constitution. Fittingly, the first of those amendments safeguarded, among other things, the practice of public relations: "Congress shall make no law respecting an establishment of religion, or prohibiting the free exercise thereof; or abridging the freedom of speech, or of the press, or the rights of the people peaceably to assemble, and to petition the government for a redress of grievances." In other words, people were given the right to speak up for what they believed in and the freedom to try to influence the opinions of others. Thus was the practice of public relations ratified.[3]

Into the 1800s

The practice of public relations continued to percolate in the nineteenth century. Among the more prominent—yet negative—antecedents of modern public relations that took hold in the 1800s was press agentry. Two of the better-known—some would say notorious—practitioners of this art were Amos Kendall and Phineas T. Barnum.

In 1829, President Andrew Jackson selected Kendall, a writer and editor living in Kentucky, to serve in his administration. Within weeks Kendall became a member of Old Hickory's "kitchen cabinet" and eventually became one of Jackson's most influential assistants.

Kendall performed just about every White House public relations task. He wrote speeches, state papers, and messages and turned out press releases. He even conducted basic opinion polls. Although Kendall is generally credited with being the first authentic presidential press secretary, his functions and role went far beyond that.

Among Kendall's most successful ventures in Jackson's behalf was the development of the administration's own newspaper, the *Globe.* Although it was not uncommon for the governing administration to publish its own national house organ, Kendall's deft editorial touch refined the process to increase its effectiveness. Kendall would pen a Jackson news release, distribute it for publication to a local newspaper, and then reprint the press clipping in the *Globe*, to underscore Jackson's nationwide popularity. Indeed, that popularity continued unabated throughout Jackson's years in

---

BETWEEN THE LINES

Buffalo "Bull" Was More Like It

To the people of LeClaire, Iowa, who honored him one hundred years later with a 1989 commemorative plaque mounted on the museum bearing his name, Buffalo Bill Cody was a hero who hunted bison to feed the troops in the frontier West of the late 1800s.

But to Iowa historians, Mr. Cody was a blatant self-promoter in the best traditions of P. T. Barnum.

"We're learning that Buffalo Bill was a very average person who, by his own promotion, transformed himself into an international figure of mythic proportions," said Malcolm Rohrbough, a University of Iowa historian. Indeed, according to Mr. Rohrbough, Mr. Cody symbolized the tragic slaughter of 10 million hapless buffaloes—nearly driving the species to extinction. In other words, Buffalo Bill epitomized the very worst environmental traditions of the nation.

Maybe.

But to the people of LeClaire and to thousands of school children, Buffalo Bill stands for everything that is good and brave and noble about America.

Ah, the power of publicity.*

*Robert Johnson, "Mr. Cody's Public Relations Aide Couldn't Be Reached for Comment," *The Wall Street Journal*, 22 February 1989; B2.

---

office, with much of the credit going to the president's public relations advisor.*

Most public relations professionals would rather not talk about Phineas T. Barnum as an industry pioneer. Barnum was a huckster—pure and simple. His end was to make money, and his means included publicity. He remained undaunted even when the facts sometimes got in the way of his promotional ideas. "The public be fooled" might well have been his motto.

---

*Kendall was most decidedly not cut from the same swath as today's neat, trim, buttoned-down press secretaries. On the contrary, Jackson's man was described as "a puny, sickly looking man with a weak voice, a wheezing cough, narrow and stooping shoulders, a sallow complexion, silvery hair in his prime, slovenly dress, and a seedy appearance" (Fred F. Endres, "Public Relations in the Jackson White House," *Public Relations Review* 2, No. 3[Fall 1976]: 5–12).

Like him or not, Barnum was a master publicist. In the 1800s, as owner of a major circus, Barnum generated article after article for his traveling show. He purposely gave his star performers short names—for instance, Tom Thumb, the midget, and Jenny Lind, the singer—so that they could easily fit into the headlines of narrow newspaper columns. Barnum also staged bizarre events, such as the legal marriage of the fat lady to the thin man, to drum up free newspaper exposure. And although today's practitioners scoff at Barnum's methods, some press agents still practice his techniques. Nonetheless, when today's public relations professionals bemoan the specter of shysters and hucksters that still overhangs their field, they inevitably place the blame squarely on the fertile mind and silver tongue of Phineas T. Barnum.

Emergence of the Robber Barons

The American Industrial Revolution ushered in many things at the turn of the century, not the least of which was the growth of public relations. The twentieth century began with small mills and shops, which served as the hub of the frontier economy, giving way to massive factories. Country hamlets, which had been the centers of commerce and trade, were replaced by sprawling cities. Limited transportation and communications facilities became nationwide railroad lines and communications wires. Big business took over, and the businessman was king.

The leaders who ran America's industries—and without exception they were all male—seemed more concerned with making a profit than with improving the lot of their fellow citizens. Railroad owners such as William Vanderbilt, bankers such as J. P. Morgan, oil magnates such as John D. Rockefeller, and steel impresarios such as Henry Clay Frick ruled the fortunes of thousands of others. Typical of the reputation acquired by this group of industrialists was the famous—and perhaps apocryphal—response of Vanderbilt when questioned about the public's reaction to his closing of the New York Central Railroad: "The public be damned!"

Little wonder that Americans cursed Vanderbilt and his ilk as robber barons who cared little for the rest of society. Although most who depended on these industrialists for their livelihood felt powerless to rebel, the seeds of discontent were being sprinkled liberally throughout the culture. It was just a matter of time before the robber barons would get their comeuppance.

Enter the Muckrakers

When the ax fell on the robber barons, it came in the form of criticism from a feisty group of journalists dubbed "muckrakers." The muck that these reporters and editors "raked" was dredged from the scandalous operations of America's business enterprises. Upton Sinclair's novel *The Jungle* attacked the deplorable conditions of the meat-packing industry. Ida Tarbell's *History of Standard Oil* stripped away the public facade of the nation's leading petroleum firm. Magazines such as *McClure's* struck out systematically at one industry after another. The captains of industry, so used to getting their own way and having to answer to no one, were wrenched from their environment of peaceful passivity and rolled out on the public carpet to answer for their sins. Journalistic shock stories soon led to a wave of sentiment for legislative reform.

As journalists and the public became more anxious, the government got more involved. Congress began passing laws telling business leaders what they could and couldn't do. Trustbusting then became the order of the day. Conflicts between employers and employees began to break out, and newly organized labor unions came to the fore. The Socialist and Communist movements began to take off. Ironically, it was "a period when free enterprise reached a peak in American history, and yet at that very climax, the tide of public opinion was swelling up against business freedom, primarily because of the breakdown in communications between the businessman and the public."[4]

For a time, these men of inordinate wealth and power found themselves limited in their ability to defend themselves and their activities against the tidal wave of public condemnation. They simply did not know how to get through to the public effectively. To tell their side of the story, the business barons first tried using the lure of advertising to silence journalistic critics; they tried to buy off critics by paying for ads in their papers. It didn't work. Next, they paid publicity people, or press agents, to present their companies' positions. Often, these hired guns painted over the real problems and presented their client's view in the best possible light. The public saw through this approach.

Clearly, another tack had to be discovered to get the public to at least consider the business point of view. Business leaders were realizing that a corporation might have capital, labor, and natural resources, yet be doomed to fail if it lacked intelligent management, particularly in the area of influencing public opinion. The best way to influence public opinion, as it turned out, was through the vehicles of honesty and candor. Such simple truths were the keys to the accomplishments of American history's first successful public relations counselor, Ivy Lee.

Ivy Lee: A Father of Modern Public Relations

Ivy Ledbetter Lee was a former Wall Street newspaper reporter who plunged into publicity work in 1903. Lee believed in neither Barnum's the-public-be-fooled approach nor Vanderbilt's the-public-be-damned philosophy. To Lee the key to business acceptance and understanding was that the public be informed. Lee firmly believed that the only way business could answer its critics convincingly was to present its side honestly, accurately, and forcefully.[5] Instead of merely appeasing the public, Lee thought a company should strive to earn public confidence and good will. Sometimes, this task meant looking further for mutual solutions. At other times, it even meant admitting that the company was wrong.* Hired by the anthracite coal industry in 1906, Lee set forth his beliefs in a Declaration of Principles to newspaper editors.

> This is not a secret press bureau. All our work is done in the open. We aim to supply news. This is not an advertising agency; if you think any of our matter ought properly to go to your business office, do not use it. Our matter is accurate. Further details on any subject treated will be supplied promptly, and any editor will be assisted most cheerfully in verifying any statement of fact. . . .
>
> In brief, our plan is frankly and openly, on behalf of business concerns and public institutions, to supply to the press and public of the United States prompt and accurate information concerning subjects which it is of value and interest to the public to know about.[6]

In 1914, John D. Rockefeller, Jr., who headed one of the most maligned and misunderstood of America's wealthy families, hired Lee. As Lee biographer Ray Eldon Hiebert has pointed out, Lee did less to change the Rockefellers' policies than to give them a public hearing.[7] For example, when the family was censured scathingly for its role in breaking up a strike at the Rockefeller-owned Colorado Fuel and Iron Company, the family hired a labor relations expert (at Lee's recommendation) to determine the causes of an incident that had led to several deaths. The end result of this effort was the formation of a joint labor-management board to mediate all workers' grievances on wages, hours, and working conditions. When the chairman of the Colorado company balked at the plan, John, Jr. (again on Lee's advice) personally toured the mines, listened to the miners' complaints, and even danced with the miners' wives at a social function. By the end of his visit, Rockefeller was not only a hero to the miners, but also a new man to the public. Years later, John, Jr., admitted that the public relations outcome of the Colorado strike "was one of the most important things that ever happened to the Rockefeller family."[8]

In working for the Rockefellers, Lee tried to "humanize" them, to feature them in real-life situations, such as playing golf, attending church, and celebrating birthdays. Simply, Lee's goal was to translate the Rockefellers

---

*Lee's dramatic influence on the standards of the emerging profession is obvious in an observation made in 1963 by Earl Newsom, prominent public relations counsel, who told a colleague, "The whole activity of which you and I are a part can probably be said to have had its beginning when Ivy Lee persuaded the directors of the Pennsylvania Railroad that the press should be given the facts on all railway accidents—even though the facts might place the blame on the railroad itself."[5]

into terms that every individual could understand and appreciate. Years later, despite their critics, the family came to be known as one of the nation's outstanding sources of philanthropic support.

Lee's contributions to the development of public relations went beyond his work with the Rockefellers. He urged the American Tobacco Company, for example, to initiate a profit-sharing plan. He advised the Pennsylvania Railroad to beautify its stations. He educated the American public about ocean travel to overcome the negative impressions of the *Titanic* and *Lusitania* disasters. In addition, he was instrumental in working with Admiral Richard Byrd and aviator Charles Lindbergh to combat the public's fear of flying.

Ironically, even Ivy Lee could not escape the glare of public criticism. In the late 1920s, Lee was asked to serve as advisor to the parent company of the German Dye Trust, which, as it turned out, was an agent for the policies of Adolf Hitler. When Lee realized the nature of Hitler's intentions, he advised the Dye Trust cartel to work to alter Hitler's ill-conceived policies of restricting religious and press freedom. For his involvement with the Dye Trust, Lee was branded a traitor and dubbed "Poison Ivy" by members of Congress investigating un-American activities. The smears against him in the press rivaled the most vicious against the robber barons.

Despite his unfortunate involvement with the Dye Trust, Ivy Lee is recognized as the individual who brought honesty and candor to public relations. Lee, more than anyone before him, lifted the field from a questionable pursuit (that is, seeking positive publicity at any cost) to a professional discipline designed to win public confidence and trust through communications based on candor and truth.

The Growth of Modern Public Relations

Ivy Lee helped to open the gate. After he established the idea that firms have a responsibility to inform their publics, the practice began to grow in every sector of American society.

Government

During World War I, as already noted, President Woodrow Wilson established the Creel Committee under journalist George Creel. It proved to be an effective force, mobilizing public opinion in support of the war effort and stimulating the sale of war bonds through Liberty Loan publicity drives. Not only did the war effort get a boost, but so did the field of public relations.

During World War II, the public relations field received an even bigger boost. With the Creel Committee as its precursor, the Office of War

Information (OWI) was established to convey the message of the United States at home and abroad. Under the directorship of Elmer Davis, a veteran journalist, the OWI laid the foundations for the United States Information Agency as the voice of America around the world.

World War II also saw a flurry of activity to sell war bonds, boost the morale of those at home, spur production in the nation's factories and offices, and, in general, support America's war effort as intensively as possible. By virtually every measure, this full-court public relations offensive was an unquestioned success.

The proliferation of public relations officers in World War II led to a growth in the number of practitioners during the peacetime that followed. This was probably a good thing, especially in light of the feisty, combative attitude of President Harry Truman toward many of the country's largest institutions. For example, in a memorable address over radio and television on April 8, 1952, President Truman announced that, as a result of a union wage dispute, "the government would take over the steel plants." The seizure of the steel mills touched off a series of historic events that reached into Congress and the Supreme Court and stimulated a massive public relations campaign, the likes of which had rarely been seen outside the government.[9] The steel conflict between the president and big business was the first of many such battles that have marked the government-business relationship over the years.

Counseling

The nation's first public relations firm, the Publicity Bureau, was founded in Boston in 1900 and specialized in general press agentry. The first Washington, DC, agency was begun in 1902 by William Wolff Smith, a former correspondent for the *New York Sun* and the *Cincinnati Inquirer*. Two years later Ivy Lee joined with George Parker to begin a public relations agency that was later dissolved. Lee reestablished the agency in New York in 1919 and brought in T. J. Ross as a partner.

John W. Hill entered public relations in 1927 after a dozen years as a journalist. Together with William Knowlton, Hill founded Hill & Knowlton, Inc., in Cleveland. Hill soon moved east, and Knowlton dropped out of the firm. However, the agency quickly became one of the largest public relations operations in the world, with 1,050 employees in 20 countries and 20 U.S. cities. Hill stayed active in the firm for half a century and mused about the field's beginnings.

> In 1927, public relations was just in its infancy. Think of the contrast of the present with fifty years ago. Less than a handful of counseling firms anywhere in the world and barely a handful of practitioners tucked away and lost in the offices of a very few large corporations—far removed from the executive suite.[10]

In addition to Hill, the Creel Committee associate chairman, Carl Byoir, launched his own public relations counseling firm in 1930. Ironically, 56 years later, Byoir's firm, Carl Byoir & Associates, merged with Hill & Knowlton to become the largest public relations company in the world.

Besides Byoir and Hill, Earl Newsom and Pendleton Dudley also founded early firms. Newsom, who began Newsom & Company in 1935, generally limited his public relations practice to counseling companies like Ford, General Motors, and Jersey Standard. In his otherwise critical treatment of public relations, *The Image Merchants,* author Irwin Ross paid tribute to Newsom's success.

> The goal of a good many public relations men is someday to attain the lonely eminence of Earl Newsom. His fees are high; his clients include some of the most august names in the corporate roster; and his work involves pure "consultation."[11]

Dudley, like Newsom, got started early and remained in public relations until his death in 1966 at age ninety. Dudley's firm later became Dudley-Anderson-Yutzy, one of the most admired agencies for introducing innovative techniques to win public approval.

Another early counselor, Harold Burson, emphasized marketing-oriented public relations, "primarily concerned with helping clients sell their goods and services, maintain a favorable market for their stock, and foster harmonious relations with employees."[12] Today, Burson-Marsteller ranks as one of the world's largest public relations agencies.

In the early 1990s, the counseling business saw the emergence of international super agencies. Hill & Knowlton, Burson-Marsteller, and the world's largest, Shandwick, all boasted worldwide networks with thousands of employees linked to serve clients with communications services throughout the globe.

Corporations

Problems in the perception of corporations and their leaders dissipated in the United States in the wake of World War II. Public opinion polls of that period ranked business in an esteemed position. People were back at work, and business was back in style.

Smarter companies—General Electric, General Motors, American Telephone & Telegraph (AT&T), for example—worked hard to preserve their good names through both words and actions. Arthur W. Page became AT&T's first public relations vice-president in 1927. Page was a pacesetter, helping to manage AT&T's reputation as a prudent and proper corporate

BETWEEN THE LINES

P. T. Barnum Revisited: The Days of Super Hype

Although most public relations professionals disagree with the publicity-seeking antics attributed to P. T. Barnum, publicity for publicity's sake is still very much in vogue, especially in the numerous national photo magazines. In a return to the kind of media hype that Barnum made famous over one hundred years ago, today's magazine journalists occasionally sacrifice everything—including objectivity and news judgment—to land a story about a hot personality or a hot project.

This is especially true in the case of Hollywood celebrities. For some reason, the public has an unquenchable thirst for stories, gossip, rumor, and innuendo about Hollywood. So personality journalism—also labeled "disposable journalism"—reigns supreme.

Hollywood publicists—cynics would call them "latter-day Barnums"—have carte blanche in the 1990s, pitting personality-oriented magazines against one another to gain "exclusive interviews" with their clients. Indeed, magazines from *Life* and *People* and *Us* to *Premiere* and *Interview* and *Entertainment* to *Time* and *Newsweek* will literally fall over themselves to land an exclusive with Bruce Willis or Tom Cruise or Madonna or Cher.

And right behind the magazines are the electronic interviewers, from Joan Rivers to Arsenio Hall to Sally Jesse Raphael to Phil Donahue to the irrepressible Geraldo Rivera.

Finally, down the "hype chain" lie the gossipy entertainment programs, from "Entertainment Tonight" to "A Current Affair" to "Life Styles of the Rich and Famous."

And finally come the dolls, video games, magazines, coloring books, lunch boxes, and assorted other merchandising spin-offs. Somewhere P. T. Barnum is beaming.

As *Newsweek* cultural affairs editor Charles Michener summarized the craze, "There's a great deal of public apathy toward news. The line is growing very blurred between news and entertainment. It's big business, and agents and PR people are now in the position of playing magazines off against each other in ways that they never could before. It obviously has to do with people seeking escape."

citizen. Indeed, Page's five principles of successful corporate public relations are as relevant now as they were in the 1930s.

1. To make sure management thoughtfully analyzes its overall relation to the public
2. To create a system for informing all employees about the firm's general policies and practices
3. To create a system giving contact employees (those having direct dealings with the public) the knowledge needed to be reasonable and polite to the public
4. To create a system drawing employee and public questions and criticism back up through the organization to management
5. To ensure frankness in telling the public about the company's actions[13]

Paul Garrett was another who felt the need to be responsive to the public's wishes. A former news reporter, he became the first director of public relations for General Motors in 1931. Garrett once reportedly explained that the essence of his job was to convince the public that the powerful auto company deserved trust, that is, "to make a billion-dollar company seem small."

Education

One public relations pioneer who began as a publicist in 1913 was Edward L. Bernays, nephew of Sigmund Freud and author of the landmark book *Crystallizing Public Opinion* (see page 50). Bernays was a true public relations scholar, teaching the first course in public relations in 1923. Bernays's seminal writings in the field were among the first to disassociate public relations from press agentry or publicity work. As Bernays wrote later,

> At first we called our activity "publicity direction." We intended to give advice to clients on how to direct their actions to get public visibility for them. But within a year we changed the service and its name to "counsel on public relations." We recognized that all actions of a client that impinged on the public needed counsel. Public visibility of a client for one action might be vitiated by another action not in the public interest.[14]

Historian Eric Goldman credited Bernays with "[moving] along with the most advanced trends in the public relations field, thinking with, around, and ahead of them."[15]

Bernays was also at least indirectly responsible for encouraging the development of another public relations phenomenon that would take on added impetus in the 1990s—the emergence of women in the field. Bernays's associate (and later, wife), Doris E. Fleischman, helped edit a leaflet, called *Contact,* that helped American leaders understand the underpinnings of the new profession Bernays represented. Fleischman's important assistance in spreading the Bernays doctrine was an early contribution to a field that, in the 1990s, showed women clearly in the majority among public relations professionals.

Other leading public relations educators included Milton Fairman, a Chicago news reporter and corporate public relations practitioner who later served as president of the Foundation for Public Relations Research and Education; Rex F. Harlow, who formed the American Council on Public Relations in 1939 and later presided over its merger with the Public Relations Society of America (PRSA) in 1947; and W. Howard Chase, a founding member of the PRSA, who advocated that public relations professionals should concern themselves with public issues management rather than with more narrow communications problems.

Public Relations Comes of Age

As noted earlier in this chapter, public relations really came of age as a result of the confluence of four general factors in our society: (1) the growth of large institutions and their sense of responsibility to the public; (2) the increased changes, conflicts, and confrontations among interest groups in society; (3) the heightened awareness of people everywhere brought about by increasingly sophisticated communications technology; and (4) the spread of global democracy.

Growth of Large Institutions

See p. 25

Ironically, the public relations profession received perhaps its most major forward thrust when business confidence suffered its most severe setback. The economic and social upheaval caused by the Great Depression of the 1930s provided the impetus for corporations to seek public support by telling their stories. Public relations departments sprang up in scores of major companies, among them Bendix, Borden, Eastman Kodak, Eli Lilly, Ford, General Motors, Standard Oil, Pan American, and U.S. Steel. The role that public relations played in helping regain post-Depression public trust in big business helped project the field into the relatively strong position it enjoyed during World War II.

Again, the Truman years marked a challenging period for public relations practitioners. That era was characterized by controls on information in the name of national security, Communist scares, and a general antagonism between government and big business. Nonetheless, as big business became more and more cognizant of the vulnerable public role it played in American society, so too did corporate managers become increasingly aware of the important role that could be played by skillful public relations practitioners.

BETWEEN THE LINES

Terrorism in the Satellite Era

Nowhere has new communications technology been more striking than in its use as a persuasive tool in the politics of war—particularly by terrorists. Using the 1979 capture of American embassy employees as the linchpin, Iranian militants in Tehran launched a massive, long-distance, nonstop media campaign to convince the world of their nation's mistreatment at the hands of the shah. Angry mobs of Iranian fanatics were beamed live and in blazing color to millions of Western homes on a nightly basis—only serving to infuriate viewers and further harden anti-Iranian feelings.

In the summer of 1982, hopelessly surrounded in the suburbs of West Beirut, Lebanon, by the Israeli army, Palestinian Liberation Organization Chief Yasir Arafat also tried to use the world media to slip out of his predicament. When a U.S. congressional delegation with an accompanying television camera crew visited him, Arafat signed a document in his bunker—in full view of the television cameras— ostensibly recognizing Israel's right to exist. Within an hour of Arafat's televised encounter with the congressmen, authoritative Palestinians in the West rushed to clarify that what their leader really meant in signing the document was that "Israel would be recognized when we get an independent Palestinian state."

Three years later, when Palestinian gunmen hijacked a TWA jetliner, murdered an American passenger, and terrorized all aboard, they also gleefully posed for international television with a gun at the head of the plane's pilot.

In 1990, Iraq's president, Saddam Hussein, invited American journalists, including perpetual presidential candidate Jesse Jackson, to interview him, to show the world that, contrary to his global persona, Saddam was a kind and benevolent soul.* Hussein's shocking and bizarre attempt to manipulate the world's airwaves was the latest reminder of the importance modern-day terrorists ascribe to manipulating the media.

---

*Evidently the Reverend Jackson's producers at his syndicated "Inside Edition" TV show had second thoughts about their man's association with the Bully of Baghdad. When asked later for a photo of Jackson and Hussein, "Inside Edition's" director of legal affairs told a certain textbook author, "I regret to inform you that we are not in a position to grant your request."

Change, Conflict, and Confrontation

Disenchantment with big institutions reached a head in the 1960s. The conflicts during the early part of the decade between private economic institutions—especially large corporations—and various disenfranchised elements of society arose from longstanding grievances. As one commentator put it, "Their rebellion was born out of the desperation of those who had nothing to lose. Issues were seen as black or white, groups as villainous or virtuous, causes as holy or satanic, and leaders as saints or charlatans."[16]

The social and political consternation of the 1960s dramatically affected many areas, including the practice of public relations. The Vietnam War fractured society. In addition, people began talking about the environment, the rights of minorities and consumers, and, once again, the ills perpetrated by big business. Assassinations of civil rights leaders, political heroes, and even the president of the United States—all magnified by the omnipresence of television—caused the American public to demand answers to society's ills.

Ralph Nader began to look pointedly at the inadequacies of the automobile industry. Women, long denied equal rights in the workplace and elsewhere, began to mobilize into activist groups, such as the National Organization of Women (NOW). Environmentalists, worried about threats to the land and water by business expansion, began to support groups such as the Sierra Club. Minorities—particularly blacks and Hispanics—began to petition and protest for their rights through such groups as the Congress on Racial Equality, the National Association for the Advancement of Colored People (NAACP), and the Student Nonviolent Coordinating Committee. Homosexuals, senior citizens, birth control advocates, and social activists of every kind began to challenge the legitimacy of large institutions. Not since the days of the robber barons had large institutions so desperately needed professional communications help.

Heightened Public Awareness

The 1970s brought a partial resolution of the problems that afflicted society in the 1960s. Many of those solutions came through the government in the form of affirmative action guidelines, senior citizen supports, consumer and environmental protection acts and agencies, aids to education, and a myriad of other laws and statutes.

As for society's large institutions—particularly big business—they began clearly to recognize their responsibilities as social creatures. Business began to contribute to charities. Managers began to consider community relations a first-line responsibility. The general policy of corporations confronting their adversaries was abandoned. In its place most large companies adopted a policy of conciliation and compromise.

This new policy of social responsibility became corporate gospel in the 1970s and has continued to the 1990s. Corporations have come to realize that their reputations are a valuable asset, to be protected, conserved, defended, nurtured, and enhanced at all times. In truth, institutions in the 1990s have had little choice but to get along with their publics. Largely because of increasingly sophisticated communications technology, the public at large is more aware and better informed than it was in any previous period.

For example, by 1991, 93 million American homes had television, with another 54 million wired for cable. The potential of two-way communications systems through cable, satellite, fax, computer, and video disc technologies promises to further revolutionize the information transmission and receiving process. As a result, publics have become much more segmented, specialized, and sophisticated. Public relations professionals have had to discard many of the traditional methods used to reach and influence these publics. Today companies face the new reality of instant communication through desktop video display terminals, instant file and retrieval through centralized data banks, and comprehensive management information systems.

Spread of Global Democracy

The spread of worldwide democracy in the 1990s underscored the impact of public opinion as a force in society. People everywhere in the '90s were "being heard." In Russia, for example, the totalitarian teachings of Karl Marx and Josef Stalin and Nikita Khrushchev were giving way to the more moderate, democratic dialogue of 1990 Nobel Peace Prize winner Mikhail Gorbachev. And while the world in the 1990s became more open to democratic ideas, the public relations challenge increased significantly.

Public Relations Education

As the practice of public relations has developed, so too has the growth of public relations education. In 1951, 12 schools offered major programs in public relations. Four years later there were 28, with 66 other schools offering some instruction in the subject. By 1964, more than 40 colleges and universities offered major programs or sequences in public relations, and another 280 institutions provided some classroom work in the field.

Today approximately 200 journalism or communication programs offer concentrated study in public relations with nearly 300 others offering at least one course dealing with the profession. Although few data are available on public relations programs in business schools, the numbers are increasing, especially those related to marketing.[17]

Even though discussion has continued about where public relations education should appropriately be housed—in journalism, business, or liberal arts—the profession's role as an academic pursuit has continued to gain strength.

Public Relations Today

Today, public relations is big business.

♦ The Public Relations Society of America, organized in 1947, boasts a growing membership of 15,000 in 100 chapters nationwide.

♦ The Public Relations Student Society of America, formed in 1968 to facilitate communications between students interested in the field and public relations professionals, has 5,700 student members at 171 colleges and universities.

♦ More than 5,400 U.S. companies have public relations departments.

♦ More than 1,800 public relations agencies exist in the United States, some billing hundreds of millions of dollars per year.

♦ More than 500 trade associations have public relations departments.

♦ Top communications executives at major companies and agencies draw salaries in six figures.

♦ At the University of Florida, public relations education has passed the half-century mark.

The scope of modern public relations practice is vast. Press relations, employee communications, public relations counseling and research, local community relations, audiovisual communications, contributions, and numerous other diverse activities fall under the public relations umbrella. Because of this broad range of functions, many public relations practitioners today seem preoccupied with the proper title for their calling—public relations, external affairs, corporate communications, public affairs, corporate relations, ad infinitum. They argue that the range of activities involved offers no hope that people will understand what the pursuit involves unless an umbrella term is used.[18]

Practitioners also worry that as public relations becomes more prominent, its function and those who purportedly practice it will be subject to increasingly intense public scrutiny.

♦ When former White House aides Michael Deaver and Lyn Nofziger were indicted for illegal lobbying violations in 1987, the public relations business was tarred by association.

♦ Public relations was skewered again when former White House press secretary Larry Speakes admitted in 1988 that he made up presidential quotes.

♦ In the same year, when the chief communications executive of Mobil Oil, Herb Schmertz, left his $640,000-per-year job, it was also national news.

♦ In 1988, when Attorney General Ed Meese fired the Justice Department's respected chief spokesman, Terry Eastland, conservative and liberal observers alike called for Meese's resignation.

♦ In 1990, when the public relations firm of Hill & Knowlton agreed to represent the U.S. Catholic Conference in an anti-abortion campaign, pro-abortion advocates from around the nation—including many Hill & Knowlton employees—protested loudly and publicly. (See the Case Study in Chapter 15.)

♦ With women now representing more than 50 percent of public relations professionals, practitioners worry about both the "feminization" of public relations and the paucity of women in management positions in the field. Others worry about the field's failure to attract minority practitioners, who represent only 7 percent of the public relations workforce.[19]

Summary

From its gradual beginnings, the practice of public relations has emerged in the 1990s as a potent, persuasive force in society. Clearly, the public relations field today—whatever it is called and by whomever it is practiced—is in the spotlight. Its professionals command higher salaries. Its counselors command increased respect. And its practice is taught in increasing numbers, not only in American colleges and universities but around the world.

With upward of 159,000 men and women in the United States alone practicing public relations in some form, the field has solidly entrenched itself as an important, influential, and professional component of our society.

DISCUSSION STARTERS

1. What societal factors have influenced the spread of public relations in society?
2. Why do public relations professionals think of P. T. Barnum as a "mixed blessing"?
3. What is the significance to the practice of public relations of American revolutionary hero Sam Adams?
4. What did the robber barons and muckrakers have to do with the development of public relations?
5. Why are Ivy Lee and Edward Bernays considered two of the "fathers" of public relations?

6. What impact did the Creel Committee and the Office of War Information have on the development of public relations?
7. What was the significance of Arthur Page to the development of corporate public relations?
8. Identify and discuss the significance of some of the earliest public relations counselors.
9. What are some of the yardsticks that indicate public relations has "arrived" in the 1990s?
10. What are some of the question marks that confront public relations in the 1990s?

NOTES

1. Scott M. Cutlip, Allen H. Center, and Glen M. Broom, *Effective Public Relations*, 6th ed. (Englewood Cliffs, NJ: Prentice-Hall, 1985), 23.
2. Edward L. Bernays, speech at the University of Florida Public Relations Symposium, Gainesville, FL, February 1, 1984.
3. Harold Burson, speech at Utica College of Syracuse University, Utica, NY, March 5, 1987.
4. Ray Eldon Hiebert, *Courtier to the Crowd: The Story of Ivy L. Lee and the Development of Public Relations* (Ames: Iowa State University Press, 1966).
5. Rex Harlow, "A Public Relations Historian Recalls the First Days," *Public Relations Review* (Summer 1981): 39–40.
6. Cited in Sherman Morse, "An Awakening in Wall Street," *American Magazine* 62 (September 1906): 460.
7. Hiebert, loc. cit.
8. Cited in Alvin Moscow, *The Rockefeller Inheritance* (Garden City, NY: Doubleday, 1977), 23.
9. John W. Hill, *The Making of a Public Relations Man* (New York: David McKay, 1963), 69.
10. John W. Hill, "The Future of Public Relations," speech delivered at the Seventh Public Relations World Congress, Boston, MA, August 14, 1976.
11. Irwin Ross, *The Image Merchants* (Garden City, NY: Doubleday, 1959), 85.
12. Burson, loc. cit.
13. Cited in Noel L. Griese, "The Employee Communications Philosophy of Arthur W. Page," *Public Relations Quarterly* (Winter 1977): 8–12.
14. Edward L. Bernays, "Bernays' 62 Years in Public Relations," *Public Relations Quarterly* (Fall 1981): 8.
15. David L. Lewis, "The Outstanding PR Professionals," *Public Relations Journal* (October 1970): 84.
16. S. Prakash Sethi, "Business and Social Challenge," *Public Relations Journal* (September 1981): 30.
17. James E. Grunig, "Teaching Public Relations in the Future," *Public Relations Review* (Spring 1989): 16.
18. "Diverse Titles Splinter Image of Field: Report of PRSA's Special Committee on Terminology," *Public Relations Reporter* (April 20, 1987): Tips & Tactics.
19. Marilyn Kern-Foxworth, "Status and Roles of Minority PR Practitioners," *Public Relations Review* (Fall 1989): 39.

TOP OF THE SHELF

Bernays, Edward L. *Crystallizing Public Opinion,* New York: Liveright Publishing Corp., 1961.

What *Casablanca* is to cinema, *Crystallizing Public Opinion* is to public relations literature—a classic. It defined for the first time public relations, principles, practices, and ethics and gave it recognition and professional status.

Ed Bernays' teachings are as relevant today as they were when he introduced them in 1923. His book covers the core aspects of the profession: the job of public relations counselors, the role of public opinion, and the techniques of public relations professionals. His writings on public opinion—"an ill-defined, mercurial, and changeable group of individual judgments"—are especially incisive. How are

attitudes formed? How are they modified through persuasion? How does public opinion interact with forces like the media? Bernays examines these and related issues. Also of interest is a revised preface that Bernays wrote in 1961. In it, he takes readers through a detailed history of public relations, beginning when he and his late wife coined the term for the business they opened in 1919.

Bernays' experiences and insights of those formative years are preserved in *Crystallizing Public Opinion.* As the original book on public relations, Bernays's work is essential reading for all who are fascinated by this field.

SUGGESTED READINGS

Bernays, Edward L. *The Later Years: PR Insights, 1956–1958.* Rhinebeck, NY: H & M, 1987 (44 W. Market St., P.O. Box 311 12572).

Burson, Harold. "A Decent Respect to the Opinions of Mankind." Speech delivered at the Raymond Simon Institute for Public Relations (Burson-Marsteller, 866 Third Ave., New York, NY), March 5, 1987. This speech highlights public relations activities that have influenced the United States from colonial times to the present day.

Dunn, S. W. *Public Relations: A Contemporary Approach.* Homewood, IL: Richard D. Irwin, 1986.

Olasky, Marvin H. "A Reappraisal of 19th Century Public Relations." *Public Relations Review* (Spring 1985): 3–11. The author calls for a return to the voluntarism and spirit of public enthusiasm that characterized public relations in the nineteenth century.

Phillips, Charles. *Secrets of Successful Public Relations.* Englewood Cliffs, NJ: Prentice-Hall, 1986.

Poppe, Fred. *50 Rules to Keep a Client Happy.* New York: Harper & Row, 1987.

PR Reporter (P.O. Box 600, Exeter, NH 03833–0600). Weekly.

Public Relations Career Directory. Hawthorne, NJ: Career Press, 1987 (62 Beverly Rd., P.O. Box 34 17507).

Public Relations Journal (PRSA, 33 Irving Place, New York, NY 10003). Monthly.

Public Relations News (127 E. 80 St., New York, NY 10021). Weekly.

Public Relations Quarterly (P.O. Box 311, Rhinebeck, NY 12572).

Public Relations Review (10606 Mantz Rd., Silver Spring, MD 20903).

Rogers, Henry. *One-Hat Solution: Strategy for Creative Middle Management.* New York: St. Martin's Press, 1986.

CASE STUDY   Watergate

> I felt sure that it was just a public relations problem that only needed a public relations solution.
>
> —Richard M. Nixon*

In 1972 Richard Nixon was elected president of the United States in a landslide. His opponent, Senator George McGovern, won only Massachusetts and the District of Columbia.

Two years later, on August 8, 1974, Nixon resigned in disgrace and humiliation. His administration had been tarnished by illegal wiretapping, illegal surveillance, burglary, and unlawful use of the law. The president and his men were toppled by the most profound political scandal in the nation's history, which grew out of a series of break-ins at the Democratic national headquarters in a Washington, DC, building named Watergate.

One notion raised in the aftermath of Watergate was that the president and his advisors were too concerned about public relations—about covering up the facts— and that this concern led to their downfall. This castigation of public relations for its supposed role in Watergate is ironic. Had Nixon or his aides been able to comprehend the broad ramifications and deal with them straightforwardly, they might have been judged with more compassion and spared

their severe and precipitous fall. (Although the field of public relations took the heat for the Watergate scandal, most of Nixon's key public relations advisors came from the field of advertising.)

As excerpts from transcripts indicate, neither the president nor his advisors knew much about good public relations. By ignoring virtually every elementary public relations principle, they destroyed any chance of many Americans understanding and forgiving them for their misjudgments.

Here are six of the more onerous miscalculations from the Watergate saga.

1. In late 1972, while rumors abounded that the administration was corrupt, the White House remained silent. As the president concluded in a conversation with top aides H. R. Haldeman and John Dean, "We take a few shots and it will be over. Don't worry." Evidently, Nixon felt the public would grow tired of the perpetual pounding on Watergate—thus his strategy, "Hang tough and ignore it."

2. The spotlight on Watergate intensified, and the media refused to let up. Nixon ordered Dean to prepare an enemies list of journalists and others who opposed the administration, saying, "I want the most comprehensive notes on all those who tried to do us in." Evidently, Nixon felt that going directly after particular individuals would stifle their efforts. This step, according to Dean, was to use

---

*Richard Nixon, *RN: The Memoirs of Richard Nixon* (New York: Grosset & Dunlap, 1978), 773.

"available federal machinery to screw our political enemies."

3. In early 1973, the Senate's investigation dominated national news. The president and his aides were invited to testify, but they declined on the grounds of executive privilege.

4. Like *executive privilege*, the term *national security* also received an extensive workout during the Watergate period. In March 1973, the president discussed with Haldeman and Dean the break-in at the office of the psychiatrist of Daniel Ellsberg, an administration enemy who had

leaked secret Pentagon papers to the *New York Times*. Dean suggested that the break-in be defended as national security. The president agreed, saying, "We had to get information on national security grounds. We had to do it on a confidential basis. Neither[the FBI nor the CIA] could be trusted." Several years later, both Dean and Haldeman were imprisoned, primarily because of their roles in the break-in.

5. In October 1973, Nixon had had enough of Archibald Cox, the special prosecutor he had appointed to get to the bottom of

FIGURE 2—2 Watergate's dubious cast of characters stimulated this takeoff on the promotional work done for the movie, *That's Entertainment*. *(Courtesy of Frankfurt, Gips, Balkind)*

the Watergate case. When Cox persisted in trying to secure the release of the president's confidential tapes, Nixon ordered Attorney General Elliot Richardson to fire him. Richardson refused and resigned. Deputy Attorney General William Ruckelshaus, the next in line, also refused and was fired. Finally, Solicitor General Robert Bork, the third person in line, fired Cox. In one fell swoop, Nixon's Saturday Night Massacre became a new cause célèbre, and the Watergate fires were reignited.

6. The president's relations with the media steadily deteriorated. About a major report by Dean on Watergate, Nixon told an aide, "We've got to keep our eye on the Dean thing—just give them some of it, not all of it . . . just take the heat."

Facing an audience of several hundred newspaper editors in November 1973, the president rambled, "In all of my years of public life, I have never obstructed justice. And I think too that I could say that in my years of public life, that I welcome this kind of examination, because people have got to know whether or not their president is a crook. Well, I am not a crook."

Later on, the president instructed Press Secretary Ronald Ziegler in responding to substantive press queries: "Just get out there and act like your usual cocky, confident self."†

---

†This case is adapted from one of the more significant analyses of Watergate as a study in public relations: Joseph T. Nolan, "Watergate: A Case Study in How Not to Handle Public Relations," *Public Relations Quarterly* (Summer 1975): 23–26. It is reprinted by permission. Also see Gladys Engle Lang and Kurt Lang, "Polling on Watergate: The Battle for Public Opinion," *Public Opinion Quarterly* 44 (Winter 1980) 530–547.

QUESTIONS

1. How sound was the early White House public relations strategy to hang tough in the midst of media flak?
2. Why didn't Watergate go away?
3. Why was the compilation of an enemies list a mistake?
4. Did the enemies list serve any purpose for Nixon?
5. Was invoking executive privilege justified in the administration's refusal to appear before the Senate Watergate Committee?
6. What were the public relations consequences of invoking executive privilege?
7. How would you have interpreted the Saturday Night Massacre if you were an objective observer?
8. What public relations/credibility problems might have been caused by the break-in at the office of Ellsberg's psychiatrist and the subsequent national security explanation defending it?
9. How would you assess Nixon's media relations philosophy?
10. If you had been Nixon's public relations counselor, what would you have recommended upon learning the full story about Watergate?

Helpful hint for answering the questions: British statesman Edmund Burke once said, "It is not what a lawyer tells me I may do, but what humanity, reason, and justice tell me I ought to do."

Tips from the Top

EDWARD L. BERNAYS

Edward L. Bernays is a public relations patriarch. A nephew of Sigmund Freud, Bernays pioneered the application of the social sciences to public relations. In partnership with his late wife, he advised presidents of the United States, industrial leaders, and legendary figures—from Enrico Caruso to Eleanor Roosevelt. Indeed, Edward Bernays himself is a legend in the field of public relations.

When you taught the first public relations class, did you ever envision the field growing to its present stature?
I gave the first course in public relations after *Crystallizing Public Opinion* was published in 1923. I decided that one way to give the term *counsel on public relations* status was to lecture at a university on the principles, practices, and ethics of the new vocation. New York University was willing to accept my offer to do so. But I never envisioned at that time that the vocation would spread throughout the United States and then throughout the free world.

What were the objectives of that first public relations course?
The objectives were to give status to the new vocation. Many people still believed the term *counsel on public relations* was a euphemism for publicity man, press agent,

flack. Even H. L. Mencken, in his book on the American language, ranked it as such. But in his *Supplement to the American Language*, published some years later, he changed his viewpoint and used my definition of the term.

What are the most significant factors that have led to the rise in public relations practice?
The most significant factor is the rise in people power and its recognition by leaders. Theodore Roosevelt helped bring this about with his Square Deal. Woodrow Wilson helped with his New Freedom, and so did Franklin Delano Roosevelt with his New Deal. And this tradition was continued as time went on.

Do you have any gripes with the way public relations is practiced today?
I certainly do. The meanings of words in the United States have the stability of soap bubbles. Unless words are defined as to their meaning by law, as in the case of professions—for instance, law, medicine,

architecture—they are in the public domain. Anyone can use them. Recently, I received a letter from a model agency offering to supply me with a "public relations representative" for my next trade fair at which we might exhibit our client's products. Today, any plumber or car salesman or unethical character can call himself or herself a public relations practitioner. Many who call themselves public relations practitioners have no education, training, or knowledge of what the field is. And the public equally has little understanding of the meaning of the two words. Until licensing and registration are introduced, this will continue to be the situation.*

What pleases you most about current public relations practice?
What pleases me most is that there are, indeed, practitioners who regard their activity as a profession, an art applied to a science, in which the public interest, and not pecuniary motivation, is the primary consideration; and also that outstanding leaders in society are grasping the meaning and significance of the activity.

What is the most significant problem that confronts the field?
The most significant problem confronting

---

*(Ed. Note: The always gracious Mr. Bernays, in the winter of his ninety-eighth year, gently reminded the author that, as this response implies, "a profession is not a business." Thus, in this interview, Mr. Bernays pointedly defined the practice of public relations as a "vocation" not a "profession.")

the field is this matter of definition by the state of what public relations is and does—defining it, registering and licensing practitioners through a board of examiners chosen from the field, and developing economic sanctions for those who break the code of ethics.

How would you compare the caliber of today's public relations practitioner with that of the practitioner of the past?
The practitioner today has more education in his subject. But, unfortunately, education for public relations varies with the institution where it is being conducted. This is due to the lack of a standard definition. Many institutions of higher learning think public relations activity consists of skillful writing of press releases and teach their students accordingly. This is, of course, not true. Public relations activity is applied social science to the social attitudes or actions of employers or clients.

Where do you think public relations will be twenty years from now?
It is difficult to appraise where public relations will be twenty years from now. I don't like the tendency of advertising agencies gobbling up large public relations organizations. That is like surgical instrument manufacturers gobbling up surgical medical colleges or law book publishers gobbling up law colleges. However, if licensing and registration take place, then the vocation is assured a long lifetime, as long as democracy's.

3

Public Relations Management, Strategy, and Tactics

In the decade of the 1990s, public relations, like most other organizational pursuits, must compete for its survival in an atmosphere of rising manpower costs, shrinking markets, and volatile public opinion. Management is insisting that public relations be run as a management process. Like other management processes, professional public relations work emanates from clear strategies and bottom-line objectives that flow into specific tactics, each with its own discrete budget, timetable, and allocation of resources. Stated another way, public relations today is much more a planned, persuasive social/managerial science than it is a knee-jerk, damage-control reaction to sudden flare-ups.

On the organizational level, as public relations has enhanced its overall stature, it has been brought increasingly into the general management structure of institutions. Indeed, the public relations function works most effectively when it reports directly to top management.

On the individual level, public relations practitioners are increasingly expected to have mastered a wide variety of technical communications skills, such as writing, editing, placement of articles, production of printed materials, and video programming. At the same time, by virtue of their relatively recent integration into the general management process, public relations professionals are expected to be fluent in management theory and technique. In other words, public relations practitioners themselves must be, in every sense of the word, managers.

Reporting to Top Management

In many organizations today, public relations is accorded a prominent role in management decision making. Frequently, the public relations director reports directly to top management—generally to the chief executive officer. The reason for this is simple. If public relations is to be the interpreter of management, then it must know what management is thinking at any moment on virtually every public issue. If public relations is made subordinate to any other discipline—marketing, advertising, legal, administration, whatever—then its independence, credibility, and, ultimately, value as an objective management counselor will be sacrificed.

Whereas marketing and advertising groups must, by definition, be defenders of their specific products, the public relations department has no such mandated allegiance. Public relations, rightfully, should be the corporate conscience. An organization's public relations professionals should enjoy enough autonomy to tell it to management "like it is," as sportscaster Howard Cosell might put it. If an idea doesn't make sense, if a product is flawed, if the general institutional wisdom is wrong, it is the duty of the public relations professional to challenge the consensus.

This is not to say that advertising, marketing, and all other disciplines shouldn't enjoy a close partnership with public relations. Clearly, they must. All disciplines must work to maintain their own independence while building long-term, mutually beneficial relationships for the good of the organization. However, public relations should never shirk its overriding responsibility to enhance the organization's credibility by ensuring that corporate actions are in the public interest.

Management Theory of Public Relations

In recent years public relations has developed its own theoretical framework as a management system. In particular, the work of communications professors James Grunig and Todd Hunt has done much to advance this development.[1] Grunig and Hunt suggest that public relations managers perform what organizational theorists call a boundary role; they function at the edge of an organization as a liaison between the organization and its external and internal publics. In other words, public relations managers have one foot inside the organization and one outside. Often, this unique position is not only lonely, but also precarious.

As boundary managers, public relations people support their colleagues by helping them communicate across organizational lines both within and outside the organization. In this way public relations professionals also become systems managers, knowledgeable of and able to deal with the complex relationships inherent in the organization.

- They must consider the relationship of the organization to its environment—the ties that unite business managers and operations support staff, for example, and the conflicts that separate them.

- They must work within organizational confines to develop innovative solutions to organizational problems. By definition, public relations managers deal in a different environment from that of their organizational colleagues. The amorphous world of perceptions, attitudes, and public opinion, in which public relations managers dwell, is alien to the more empirical, quantitative, concrete domain of other business managers. Public relations managers, therefore, must be innovative, not only in proposing communications solutions, but also in making them understandable and acceptable to colleagues.

- They must think strategically. Public relations managers must demonstrate their knowledge of the organization's mission, objectives, and strategies. Their solutions must answer the real needs of the organization. They must reflect the big picture. Business managers will care little that the company's name was mentioned in the morning paper unless they can recognize the strategic rationale for the reference.

- Public relations managers must also be willing to measure their results. They must state clearly what they want to accomplish, systematically set out to accomplish it, and measure their success. This means using such accepted business school techniques as management by objectives (MBO), management by objectives and results (MOR), and program evaluation and research technique (PERT).

- Finally, as Grunig and Hunt point out, in managing an organization's public relations system, practitioners must demonstrate a comfort with the various elements of the organization itself: (1) functions, the real jobs of organizational components; (2) structure, the organizational hierarchy of individuals and positions; (3) processes, the formal decision-making rules and procedures the organization follows; and (4) feedback, the formal and informal evaluative mechanisms of the organization.[2]

Such a theoretical overview is important to consider in properly situating the practice of public relations as a management system within an organization.

Planning for Public Relations

Like research, planning in public relations is essential not only to know where a particular campaign is headed, but also to win the support of top management. Indeed, one of the most frequent complaints about public relations is that it is too much a seat-of-the-pants activity, impossible to plan and difficult to measure. Clearly, planning in public relations must be given greater shrift. With proper planning, public relations professionals can indeed defend and account for their actions.

Before organizing for public relations work, practitioners must consider objectives and strategies, planning and budgets, and research and evaluation. The broad environment in which the organization operates must dictate overall business objectives. These, in turn, dictate specific public relations objectives and strategies. And once these have been defined, the task of organizing for a public relations program should flow naturally.

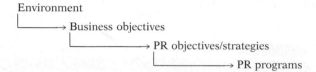

Setting objectives, formulating strategies, and planning are essential if the public relations function is to be considered of equal stature with other organizational components. Planning requires thinking. Planning a short-term public relations program to promote a new service may require less thought and time than planning a longer-term campaign to win support for a public policy issue. However, in each case, the public relations plan must include clear-cut objectives to achieve organizational goals, strategies to reach those objectives, tactics to implement the strategies, and measurement to determine whether the tactics worked.

Among the most important aspects of public relations practice is setting clear goals, objectives, and targets for the tactics applied. Public relations activities are meaningless unless designed to accomplish certain measurable goals.

For example, consider the following elementary Public Relations Plan:

I. *Environment*

We need to increase product sales in the local market. Currently we are number three in the market, running close behind the second-place supplier, but far behind the market leader.

II. *Business objectives*

Our goal is to build market share for our product in the local area. We seek to surpass the number-two provider and edge closer to number one.

III. *Public relations objectives*

   ◆ Confirm our company's solid commitment to local customers.
   ◆ Convince potential customers that our company offers the staff, expertise, products, and responsiveness that match their needs.
   ◆ Position our company as formidable competition to the two market leaders.

Planning the GE Plant Closing

Public relations planning must follow general organizational planning. Sometimes, as the saying goes, "It just don't work that way."

On April 16, 1985, the *Virginian-Pilot* newspaper published a page-one story stating that because of "poor sales and increased foreign competition, the General Electric Company might halt production of televisions and close its Suffolk, VA, manufacturing plant, eliminating 1,800 jobs." While GE spokesmen vociferously denied the speculation, the article quoted industry analysts and GE employees who suggested that the closing of the nineteen-year-old plant was "just a matter of time."

General Electric immediately cried foul and demanded a meeting with *Virginian-Pilot* editors. They complained that the newspaper's information came from unnamed sources—employees who might have misunderstood what they had been told by management in private meetings at the factory. They complained that the story allowed a perception that company executives had, in effect, "already made the decision to close the plant." This allegation, they argued, could significantly hurt GE's business.

In an internal memo distributed to its plant employees after the newspaper story, the company wrote: "The article regarding the Consumer Electronics Business Operations is unfortunate in that many employees are perceiving it as an announcement. In fact, no announcements have been made. No decisions have been reached."

Meanwhile, the *Virginian-Pilot* made two declarations: (1) it stood by its story, and (2) it invited GE's general manager to be interviewed to clarify the situation. The general manager declined, and the company remained silent.

In June, GE announced it would reduce its Suffolk workforce by 295 employees, adding, "Further cuts might be necessary." In October, the company announced that it was closing the Suffolk plant, eliminating all remaining jobs.

QUESTIONS

1. Assuming the company had a good idea in April that the Suffolk plant might soon be closed, how would you characterize its public relations planning for this eventuality?
2. What public relations options did the company have during the seven-month period of speculation? How did the firm handle this period?
3. Do you think the *Virginian-Pilot* handled the story responsibly?
4. In a public relations sense, how else might the company have planned for the eventual closing of its plant?

This case is based largely on Gerald P. Merrell, "Speculation on Plant Closing Leaves GE Angry, Silent," *Media Institute Forum* (Fall 1985): 1–6, 7.

IV. *Public relations strategies*

Position our company as the "expert" in the market, through company-sponsored surveys and research directed at local decision makers; media placement of company-related articles; speaking platforms of company executives; and company-sponsored seminars to demonstrate our expertise.

V. *Public relations programs/tactics*

◆ Seek media placements and by-lined articles discussing company products for local media.

◆ Solicit profile features and interviews with company officials on an "exclusive" basis with leading trade publications.

◆ Sponsor a quarterly survey of local companies. Mail the survey to local decision makers, focus on a current topic of concern, and offer information and comment from a customer view.

◆ Sponsor four seminars a year for emerging product-using companies in the local area. Tailor each seminar to particular audiences—women, minorities, small businesses, specific industries, not-for-profit, etc. Seminars should feature company experts and well-known outside speakers. Thus, they should reinforce our commitment to the local market and also stimulate publicity.

◆ Launch a Company Speakers Bureau, wherein company speakers address important groups throughout the area.

After the adoption of such public relations programs, evaluation of the success or failure of the campaign must be undertaken. In devising the public relations plan along these lines, an organization is assured that public relations programs will reinforce and complement its overall business goals.

Managing by Public Relations Objectives

An organization's goals must define what its public relations goals will be, and the only good goals are ones that can be measured. Public relations objectives and the strategies that flow from them, just like those in other business areas, must be results-oriented. As the old baseball pitcher Johnny Sain used to say, "Nobody wants to hear about the labor pains, but everyone wants to see the baby."

So, too, must public relations people think strategically. Strategies are the most crucial decisions of a public relations campaign. They answer the general question, "How will we manage our resources to achieve our goals?" The specific answers then become the public relations tactics used to implement the strategies. Ideally, strategies and tactics should profit from pretesting.

As for objectives, good ones stand up to the following questions:

♦ Do they clearly describe the end result expected?
♦ Are they understandable to everyone in the organization?
♦ Do they list a firm completion date?
♦ Are they realistic, attainable, and measurable?
♦ Are they consistent with management's objectives?[3]

Increasingly, public relations professionals are managing by objectives, adopting MBO and MOR techniques to help quantify the value of public relations in an organization. The two questions most frequently asked by general managers of public relations practitioners are "How can we measure public relations results?" and "How do we know whether the public relations program is making progress?" Management by objectives can provide public relations professionals with a powerful source of feedback. MBO and MOR tie public relations results to management's predetermined objectives. Even though procedures for implementing MBO programs differ, most programs share four points.

1. Specification of the organization's goals with objective measures of the organization's performance
2. Conferences between a superior and a subordinate to agree on achievable goals
3. Agreement between the superior and the subordinate on objectives consistent with the organization's goals
4. Periodic reviews by the superior and the subordinate to assess progress toward achieving the goals

Again, the key is to tie public relations goals to the goals of the organization and then to manage progress toward achieving those goals. The goals themselves should be clearly defined and specific, practical and attainable, and measurable.

The key to using MBO effectively in public relations work can be broken down into seven critical steps.

1. Defining the nature and mission of the work
2. Determining key result areas in terms of time, effort, and personnel
3. Identifying measurable factors on which objectives can be set
4. Setting objectives/determining results to be achieved
5. Preparing tactical plans to achieve specific objectives, including

   ♦ Programming to establish a sequence of actions to follow
   ♦ Scheduling to set time requirements for each step

◆ Budgeting to assign the resources required to reach the goals
◆ Fixing individual accountability for the accomplishment of the objectives
◆ Reviewing and reconciling through a testing procedure to track progress

6. Establishing rules and regulations to follow
7. Establishing procedures to handle the work[4]

Budgeting for Public Relations

Like any other business activity, public relations programs must be bolstered with sound budgets and principles of cost control. After identifying objectives and strategies, the public relations practitioner must detail the particular tactics that will help deliver those objectives. At that point the practitioner should also begin to estimate costs. The key to budgeting may lie in performing these two steps: (1) estimating the extent of the resources—both manpower and purchases—needed to accomplish each activity; and (2) estimating the cost and availability of those resources.[5] With this information in hand, the development of a budget and monthly cash flow for a public relations program becomes easier. Such data also provide the milestones necessary to audit program costs on a routine basis and to make adjustments well in advance of budget crises.

Most public relations programs operate on limited budgets. Therefore, whenever possible, adaptable programs—ones that can be readily recycled and redesigned to meet changing needs—should be considered. For example, television, magazine, and newspaper advertising generally are too expensive for most public relations budgets. On the other hand, special events, personalized literature, direct mail, personal contacts, and promotional displays are the kinds of inexpensive communications vehicles that can be easily duplicated.[6]

Budgeting in public relations is, by definition, somewhat arbitrary. For example, if you need to budget for a recruiting brochure, you must first decide how many copies, colors, and pages are needed and how elaborate you want the document to be. A brochure can be produced for $2,500 as well as $10,000. But the difference in quality between a $.50-per-copy document and a $2-per-copy one is substantial. Estimates for material costs should be sought from several suppliers before settling on a specific budget. In addition, public relations budgets should be reasonable—ordinarily a fraction of advertising budgets—and flexible enough to withstand midcourse corrections.

Most public relations agencies treat client costs in a manner similar to that used by legal, accounting, and management consulting firms: the client pays only for services rendered, often against an established monthly minimum for staff time. Time records are kept by every employee—from chairperson to mail clerk—on a daily basis, to be sure that agency clients know exactly what they are paying for.

Preparing the Public Relations Campaign Plan

The public relations campaign puts all of the aspects of public relations planning—objectives, strategies, research, tactics, and evaluation—into one cohesive whole. The plan specifies a series of "whats" to be done and "hows" to get them done—whatever is necessary to reach the objectives.

The skeleton of a typical public relations campaign plan resembles the following:

1. **Backgrounding the problem** This is the so-called situation analysis, background, or case statement that specifies the major aims of the campaign. It can be a general statement that refers to audiences, known research, the organization's positions, history, and the obstacles faced in reaching the desired goal. A public relations planner should divide the overriding goal into several subordinate objectives, which are the "whats" to be accomplished.

2. **Preparing a proposal** The second leg of the campaign plan sketches broad approaches to solve the problem at hand. It outlines the strategies, the "hows," and the public relations tools to be used to fulfill the objectives. The elements of the public relations proposal may vary depending on subject matter but generally include the following:

◆ *Situational analysis*—description of the challenge as it currently exists, including background on how the situation reached its present state
◆ *Scope of assignment*—description of the nature of the assignment—what the public relations program will attempt to do
◆ *Target audiences*—specific targets identified and apportioned into manageable groups
◆ *Research methods*—specific research approach to be used
◆ *Key messages*—specific selected appeals: What do we want to tell our audiences? How do we want them to feel about us? What do we want them to do?
◆ *Communications vehicles*—tactical communications devices to be used
◆ *Project team*—key players who will participate in the program
◆ *Timing and fees*—a timetable with proposed costs identified

The specific elements of any proposal depend on the unique nature of the program itself. When an outside supplier submits a proposal, additional elements—such as cancellation clauses, confidentiality of work, and references—should also be included.

3. **Activating the plan** The third stage of a campaign plan details operating tactics. It may also contain a time chart, specifying when each action will take place. Specific activities are defined, people are assigned to them, and deadlines are established. This stage forms the guts of the campaign plan.

4. **Evaluating the campaign** To find out whether the plan worked, evaluation methods should be spelled out here. Pretesting and posttesting of audience attitudes, quantitative analysis of event attendance, content analysis of media success, surveys, sales figures, staff reports, letters to management, and feedback from others—the specific method of evaluative testing is up to the practitioner. But the inclusion of a mechanism for evaluation is imperative.[7]

A public relations campaign plan should always be spelled out—in writing—so that planners can keep track of progress and management can assess results. And although planning in public relations is important and should be taken more seriously than it presently is by public relations professionals, the caveat of the management gurus of the mid-1980s, Thomas Peters and Robert Waterman, must always be considered: "The problem is that the planning becomes an end in itself."[8] In public relations this occurrence cannot be allowed. No matter how important planning may be, public relations is assessed principally in terms of its action, performance, and practice.

Public Relations Tactics

The duties and responsibilities of public relations practitioners are as diverse as the publics with whom different institutions deal. For example, here is a partial list of potential public relations duties.

1. **Reaching the employees** through a variety of internal means, including newsletters, television, and meetings. Traditionally, this role has emphasized news-oriented communications rather than benefits-oriented ones, which are usually the province of personnel departments.

2. **Coordinating relationships with the print and electronic media,** which includes arranging and monitoring press interviews, writing news releases and related press materials, organizing press conferences, and answering media inquiries and requests. A good deal of media relations work is spent attempting to gain favorable news coverage for the firm.

3. **Coordinating activities with legislators** on local, state, and federal levels. This includes legislative research activities and public policy formation.

The Perfect Public Relations Manager

Robert Cushman, chairman and chief executive officer of the Norton Company of Worcester, MA, is one executive who knows what he wants in a public relations manager. Here are his nine requisites for perfect public relations managers.

1. They should be students of public attitudes and perceptions, who understand that communications is not just what you say, but also what others hear.
2. They must understand a variety of different publics and the things that make them tick—from security analysts to hard hats, from state senators to Mexican Americans.
3. They must have ideologies, yes—but with enough flexibility and empathy to understand conflicting views and the role of trade-offs.
4. They must be honest, open, and accessible.
5. They must hold a deep interest in what's going on in the world; they should be concerned about Iran, Afghanistan, an election, energy, inflation, education, tax reform, the capital problems of business, new economic philosophies, and new trends in art, music, and public tastes. In short, they should be Renaissance people.
6. They must have ideas and be responsive to the ideas of others.
7. They must be good writers.
8. They must be in touch with the real world and protect senior managers from insulating themselves from what is happening out there.
9. Most of all, they must talk straight to members of management. We don't want to be patronized. We don't want sycophants. We want advisors who will advocate, debate, and defend their thinking and proposals.[9]

4. **Orchestrating interaction with the community,** perhaps including open houses, tours, and employee volunteer efforts designed to reflect the supportive nature of the organization to the community.
5. **Managing relations with the investment community,** including the firm's present and potential stockholders. This task emphasizes personal contact with securities analysts, institutional investors, and private investors.
6. **Supporting activities with customers and potential customers,** with

activities ranging from hard-sell product promotion activities to "soft" consumer advisory services.

7. **Coordinating the institution's printed voice to its publics** through reprints of speeches, annual reports, quarterly statements, and product and company brochures.

8. **Coordinating relationships with outside specialty groups,** such as suppliers, educators, students, nonprofit organizations, and competitors.

9. **Managing the institutional—or nonproduct—advertising image,** as well as being called on increasingly to assist in the management of more traditional product advertising.

10. **Coordinating the graphic and photographic services** of the organization. To do this task well requires knowledge of typography, layout, and art.

11. **Conducting opinion research,** which involves assisting in the public policy formation process through the coordination and interpretation of attitudinal studies of key publics.

12. **Managing the gift-giving apparatus,** which ordinarily consists of screening and evaluating philanthropic proposals and allocating the organization's available resources.

13. **Coordinating special events,** including travel for company management, corporate celebrations and exhibits, dinners, ground-breakings, and grand openings.

14. **Management counseling,** which involves advising administrators on alternative options and recommended choices in light of public responsibilities.

Organizing the Public Relations Department

Once an organization has analyzed its environment, established its objectives, set up measurement standards, and thought about appropriate programs and budgets, it is ready to organize a public relations department. Departments range from one-person operations to firms such as that of General Motors, with a staff of more than 200 persons (half professionals and half support staff) responsible for relations with the press, investors, civic groups, employees, and governments around the world.

Typically, most departments begin as small operations and grow as the business environment changes. For example, the increasing importance of public relations with investors, employees, and minority groups has created new areas for department expansion. As an exhaustive study by the Conference Board pointed out, there is no one best way to organize for public or external relations.[10] Some firms use decentralized organizational

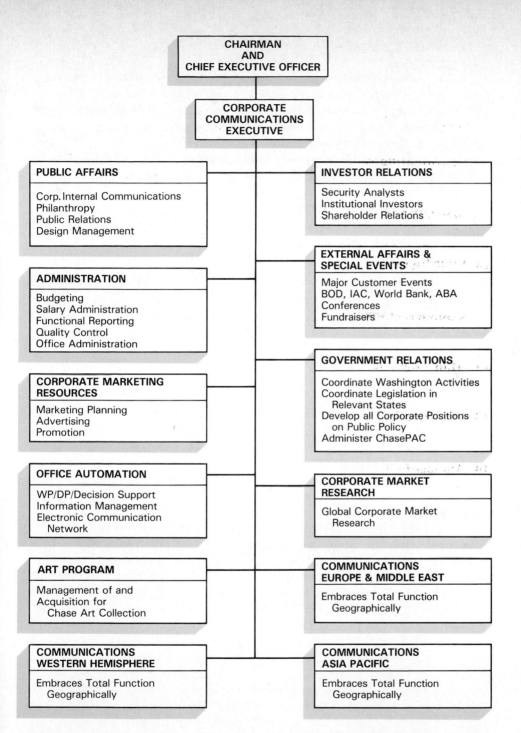

CHAIRMAN AND CHIEF EXECUTIVE OFFICER

CORPORATE COMMUNICATIONS EXECUTIVE

PUBLIC AFFAIRS

Corp. Internal Communications
Philanthropy
Public Relations
Design Management

INVESTOR RELATIONS

Security Analysts
Institutional Investors
Shareholder Relations

ADMINISTRATION

Budgeting
Salary Administration
Functional Reporting
Quality Control
Office Administration

EXTERNAL AFFAIRS & SPECIAL EVENTS

Major Customer Events
BOD, IAC, World Bank, ABA
Conferences
Fundraisers

CORPORATE MARKETING RESOURCES

Marketing Planning
Advertising
Promotion

GOVERNMENT RELATIONS

Coordinate Washington Activities
Coordinate Legislation in
   Relevant States
Develop all Corporate Positions
   on Public Policy
Administer ChasePAC

OFFICE AUTOMATION

WP/DP/Decision Support
Information Management
Electronic Communication
   Network

CORPORATE MARKET RESEARCH

Global Corporate Market
   Research

ART PROGRAM

Management of and
Acquisition for
   Chase Art Collection

COMMUNICATIONS EUROPE & MIDDLE EAST

Embraces Total Function
   Geographically

COMMUNICATIONS WESTERN HEMISPHERE

Embraces Total Function
   Geographically

COMMUNICATIONS ASIA PACIFIC

Embraces Total Function
   Geographically

FIGURE 3–1 Chase Manhattan Bank's communications operation is headquartered in the Corporate Communications Group, reporting to the bank's chief executive officer. Corporate Communications is composed of 100 professionals, who perform a variety of discrete functions. *(Courtesy of Chase Manhattan Bank)*

structures, with public relations reporting to a communications professional, public affairs reporting to a legal professional, and investor relations reporting to the head accountant. In other companies the public relations or communications function is organized centrally, under one executive who is responsible for dealing with many of the firm's key publics.

In government, public relations professionals typically report directly to department heads. In universities, the public relations function is frequently coupled with fund-raising and development activities. In hospitals, public relations is typically tied to the marketing function.

As for the names of the departments in which public relations is housed, organizations use a wide variety of names for the function. Ironically, the trend in the 1990s seems to be away from use of the traditional term *public relations* and toward *corporate communications*. In one comprehensive analysis, about 30 percent of the organizations surveyed still used *public relations*, whereas *corporate communications* or just plain *communications* was used by nearly 20 percent. About 8 percent used *public affairs*, and another 8 percent used *advertising/public relations*. Among the other titles in use were *corporate relations* and *public information*.[11]

Organizing the Public Relations Agency

The biggest difference between an external agency and an internal department is perspective. The former is outside looking in; the latter is inside looking out (often for itself, quite literally). Sometimes the use of an agency is necessary to escape the tunnel-vision syndrome that afflicts some firms, in which a detached viewpoint is desperately needed. An agency unfettered by internal corporate politics might be better trusted to present management with an objective reading of the concerns of its publics.

An agency has the added advantage of not being taken for granted by a firm's management. Unfortunately, management sometimes has a greater regard for an outside specialist than for an inside one. This attitude frequently defies logic but is nonetheless often true. Generally, if management is paying (sometimes quite handsomely) for outside counsel, it tends to listen carefully to the advice.

Agencies may also fit an organization's certain unique needs. A company may need a technically complex speech, a specially targeted consumer program, or a particularly pointed financial relations project. Such needs may be filled quickly and professionally by outside counsel.

Public relations counsel is, by definition, a highly personalized service. A counselor's prescription for a client depends primarily on what the counselor thinks a client needs and how that assessment fits the client's own perception of those needs. Often, an outsider's fresh point of view is helpful

Not For Sale!

You cannot pick up a business publication nowadays without reading about a new acquisition in the public relations business. Ad agencies buy public relations firms; big public relations agencies buy little ones; little ones buy each other; and every few days some British holding company buys anything that moves. I can see the headline now: "All Public Relations Firms Finally Bought."

Well, it ends here. We are not for sale. This company has been around for 30 years and, Lord willing, we'll be here a few more. And it's not that we don't have the opportunities. We've had our share; some real, some frivolous, a few even kind of insulting. But we turned them down and we will continue to do so.

There are many reasons for this, some practical, some emotional and some that defy category -- scoffers might call it stubbornness. But whatever label you give it, I think it is because we're something wonderfully special. Let me tell you why.

When this company was formed, I was pretty young -- at least, 29 seems pretty young to me now. I had been out of the Air Force for only a year and a half, and during that time I worked as a writer and editor for a couple of big companies. What bothered me at all of them was that what I did (or didn't do) didn't really much matter. I thought then, and I think now, that if you succumb to bus fumes on the way to work, you should leave a void in your chosen profession.

I must admit that there was an awful lot about public relations that I didn't know then. What I did know was that hard work and a concern about excellence might lead to success.

I thought that a company should provide an environment in which a thought process did not have to be politically sensitive. Where an idea -- even a lousy one -- is a thing of majesty. I thought that bright, eager people would want to work in an agency that let them pursue their vocational dreams and demons as far as their talents and energies would allow.

I thought if we did these things, we would attract clients who wanted their stories told with intelligence, flair and sensitivity, and who would appreciate an agency that prized laughter more than fear.

I also thought it would pay the mortgage on the house and educate my three sons.

Fortunately, I was right on just about all counts.

As we grew and learned, we tried not to forget the important things that brought us here.

For one thing, creativity isn't something you demand by executive fiat. It's a personal and strange thing that appears mysteriously from some inner wellspring of ideas. It's the ability to take a couple of ordinary things and turn them into something new and wonderful. It's the peculiar talent of seeing things from a secret vantage that no one else can share.

I don't suggest we have a monopoly on these things. I do think that we let minds roam freely over the landscape of thought -- where nothing is too silly to contemplate.

It is no secret that some clients prefer large service organizations -- giant law firms, big eight accountants, international advertising agencies, and public relations companies with branches everywhere but the moon. And who can fault them? After all, bigness, well. . . it means big.

It may not mean extraordinary management skills, nor even success. What it does mean is safety. "You can't blame me. I hired big."

I will admit that there are times -- usually about 3 in the morning -- when I wish we too were big. Then a few minutes after getting to the office the next morning, I look around. I see some 50 odd (Do I dare say some odder than others? Of course, I do!) people of wide range of ages and experience who think their work is fun and exciting.

There, amidst the space-age click of word processors, and the strange buzzing sound that has replaced the telephone ring, you know that you are in a place that has a special character. And even though you may not fully be able to define it, you can feel its essence, its drama and its hunger somewhere between your heart and your mind.

On occasion, we are still approached with enticing and complex financial offers, accompanied with the ultimate promise of bigness.

Understand now, we're not exactly tiny. We're about the 8th largest independent in the country. But that's not enough for our suitors. "Sell to us and your company will be bigger," they say.

Well, this company is bigger in the things that count to us. We're bigger in spirit, we're bigger in caring, we're bigger in service, we're bigger in ideas, we're bigger in fun. And we're bigger in being better.

Sell? Hell, no.

John Softness

THE SOFTNESS GROUP, INC.
250 Park Avenue South
New York, NY 10003
212·674·7600 Fax 212·995·2837

FIGURE 3–2 In the late '80s and early '90s, independent public relations firms were gobbled up by U.S. and British advertising and full-service communications organizations. One exception was the fiercely independent Softness Group, whose chairman took out this ad to let the world know he wasn't "for sale!" *(Courtesy of the Softness Group)*

in focusing a client on particular problems and opportunities and on how best to conquer or capitalize on them.

On the other hand, because outside agencies are just that—outside— they are often unfamiliar with details affecting the situation of particular companies and with the idiosyncrasies of company management. The good external counselor must constantly work to overcome this barrier. The best client-agency relationships are those with free-flowing communications between internal and external public relations groups, so that both resources are kept informed about corporate policies, strategies, and tactics. A well-oiled, complementary department/agency relationship can result in a more positive communications approach for an organization.

Table 3–1

Comparison of 1989 and 1988 median salaries of public relations/public affairs practitioners in the United States and Canada.

Age Groups	Percent of Total	Percent Men	Percent Women	Median Salary Overall	Median Salary Men	Median Salary Women
All (US & Canada)		44.4	55.6	$46,000	$54,000	$40,000
24 & under	0.1	0.0	100.0	____*	____*	____*
25–29	11.8	20.5	79.5	$30,000	$28,000	$30,000
30–34	14.0	29.5	69.9	$37,950	$42,750	$36,400
35–39	17.9	37.7	61.8	$45,000	$48,000	$43,000
40–49	32.7	50.8	48.9	$52,000	$59,500	$46,540
50–59	16.4	63.4	36.1	$60,000	$68,000	$50,000
60–64	4.4	64.6	35.4	$51,500	$60,750	$45,000
65+	1.5	47.1	52.9	$65,000	$70,000	$57,000
No Response	1.2	14.3	85.7			

SOURCE: PR Reporter (October 1, 1990): 2.
*Sample size too small too compute valid median

What's It Pay?

Without question the communications function has increased in importance and clout. Top communications professionals in many large corporations today draw compensation packages well into six figures. Entry-level jobs for writers and editors generally fall into the $20,000–$30,000 range. Managers of public relations units, press relations, consumer relations, financial communications, and the like may earn anywhere from $40,000 to $100,000. Public relations directors may range in salary from $30,000 to upward of $200,000 (Table 3–1, p. 00). Public relations agency salaries may be a bit higher in some cases than corporate staff salaries because account executives are on the line earning income for the firm (Table 3–2, p. 00). But job security in an agency is usually less than that offered by a corporation.

What Manner of Man/Woman?

What kind of individual does it take to become a competent public relations professional?

In order to make it, a public relations professional ought to possess a set of specific, technical skills, as well as an appreciation of the proper attitudinal approach to the job. On the technical side, these six skills are important:

Table 3–2

Fifty largest U.S. public relations operations, independent and ad agency affiliated, for the year ending December 31, 1990

Public Relations Operation	1990 Net Fees	Employees	% Fee Change from 1989
1. Shandwick	$200,000,000+	2,000 +	—
2. Hill & Knowlton (A)	190,000,000+	1,900 +	—
3. Burson-Marsteller (A)	190,000,000+	2,000 +	—
4. Ogilvy Public Relations Group (A)	62,341,000	759	+7.9
5. Omnicom PR Network (A)	61,849,214	761	+27.5
6. Edelman Public Relations Worldwide	45,970,535	495	+28.7
7. Fleishman-Hillard	45,858,000	509	+20.6
8. Ketchum Public Relations (A)	42,300,000	401	+18.4
9. Manning, Selvage & Lee (A)	29,322,000	303	+9.6
10. Ruder Finn	25,294,808	296	+19.4
11. GCI Group (A)	21,949,740	267	+35.0
12. Robinson, Lake, Lerer & Montgomery (A)	20,484,000	146	+10.0
13. Cohn & Wolfe (A)	14,998,000	122	+29.0
14. Financial Relations Board	9,540,626	110	+8.0
15. Corporate Communications (U.S.)	8,428,124	73	+9.7
16. The Kamber Group	7,422,129	100	+23.9
17. Gibbs & Soell	7,195,723	81	+4.5
18. Stoorza, Ziegaus & Metzger	6,232,017	78	+27.5
19. Earle Palmer Brown Cos. (A)	5,665,104	62	+17.6
20. E. Bruce Harrison Co.	5,618,403	49	+28.3
21. Dix & Eaton	4,800,731	47	+15.1
22. Padilla Speer Beardsley	4,481,600	49	+18.9
23. Dewe Rogerson (U.S.)	4,444,000	43	+83.0
24. Jay Rockey Public Relations	4,255,381	56	+5.0
25. Cone Communications	4,228,784	46	+9.3
26. Nelson Communications Group	4,154,413	44	+38.4
27. Aaron D. Cushman and Assocs.	3,775,848	47	−6.6
28. Lobsenz-Stevens	3,700,000	40	+5.0
29. Morgen-Walke Assocs.	3,638,767	32	+16.4
30. Cunningham Communications	3,475,945	34	+38.9
31. Edward Howard & Co.	3,452,700	37	+11.0
32. Bader Rutter & Assocs. (A)	3,325,099	40	+24.2
33. Makovsky & Co.	3,300,000	40	+12.0
34. Public Communications	3,265,534	40	−2.1
35. KCS&A Public Relations	3,243,000	34	−1.6
36. Dye, Van Mol & Lawrence	3,060,571	56	+11.9
37. Clarke & Co. (A)	3,054,234	33	+17.0
38. DeVries Public Relations	3,038,701	38	+12.1
39. BMc Strategies	2,802,906	19	−8.6

Table 3-2

Fifty largest U.S. public relations operations, independent and ad agency affiliated, for the year ending December 31, 1990 *(continued)*

Public Relations Operation	1990 Net Fees	Employees	% Fee Change from 1989
40. Cerrell Associates	2,674,271	29	+18.8
41. Pacific West Communications Group	2,655,652	28	+104.0
42. Creswell, Munsell, Fultz & Zirbel (A)	2,640,717	26	−9.2
43. Charles Ryan Associates	2,526,767	39	−2.0
44. Gross Townsend Frank Hoffman (A)	2,500,000	32	+39.0
45. Bob Thomas & Associates (A)	2,500,000	30	+47.0
46. Holt, Ross & Yulish	2,495,355	31	−6.7
47. PRx	2,475,109	30	+19.0
48. M. Silver Associates	2,430,918	23	+29.9
49. Franson, Hagerty and Assocs.	2,423,000	20	+5.0
50. MWW Strategic Communications	2,399,245	18	+58.8

1. **Knowledge of the field**—an understanding of the underpinnings of public relations, culture and history, philosophy, and social psychology
2. **Communications knowledge**—an understanding of the media and the ways in which they work, of communications research, and, most importantly, of the writing process
3. **Knowledge of what's going on around you**—an understanding of the current events and factors that influence society: literature, language, politics, economics, and all the rest—from the Polisarios in Morocco to the politics in Manila; from a unified Germany to a divided Lebanon; from David Souter to Bruce Springsteen; from John Major to Milli Vanilli. A public relations professional must be, in the truest sense, a Renaissance man or woman
4. **Business knowledge**—an understanding of how business works, a bottom-line orientation, and a knowledge of one's company and industry
5. **Knowledge of bureaucracy**—an understanding of how to get things done in a bureaucratic organization, how to use and gain power for the best advantage, and how to maneuver in a politically charged environment
6. **Management knowledge**—an understanding of how public policy is shaped and an appreciation of the various pressures on and responsibilities of senior managers

In terms of attitude, public relations professionals ought to possess the following four characteristics:

1. **Communications orientation**—a bias toward disclosing rather than withholding information. Public relations professionals should *want* to communicate with the public. They should practice the belief that the public has a right to know.

2. **Advocacy**—a desire to be advocates for their employers. Public relations people must stand up for what their employers stand for. Although they should never distort, lie, or hide facts, occasionally it may be in an organization's best interest to avoid comment on certain issues. If practitioners don't believe in the integrity and credibility of their employers, their most honorable course is to quit.

3. **Counseling orientation**—a compelling desire to advise senior managers. As noted, top executives are used to dealing in tangibles, such as balance sheets, costs per thousand, and cash flows. Public relations practitioners understand the intangibles, such as public opinion, media influence, and communications messages. Practitioners must be willing to support their beliefs—often in opposition to lawyers or personnel executives. They must even be willing to disagree with management at times. Far from being yes men, public relations practitioners must have the gumption to counsel no.

4. **Personal confidence**—a strong sense of honesty and ethics, a willingness to take risks, and, not unimportantly, a sense of humor. Public relations professionals must have the courage of their convictions and the personal confidence to represent proudly a curious—yet critical—role in any organization.

In recent years many more women have joined the public relations ranks. Women now account for just under half of all practitioners but still earn substantially less than men. For example, the median salary of public relations professionals, according to one survey, was $55,000 for men but only $39,000 for women.[12]

The issue of increased "feminization," as noted, is a particularly thorny one for the practice of public relations. University public relations sequences across the country report a preponderance of female students, outnumbering males by as much as 80 percent. In public relations practice, too, women now outnumber men. However, the ranks of women executives in public relations, as opposed to their male counterparts, are still woefully thin. So the double-edged sword of, on the one hand, public relations becoming a "velvet ghetto" of women workers, and on the other hand, women not achieving upper-management status, is very much of front-burner concern to the profession.

In addition to gender-gap problems, there is the issue of minority public relations professionals. According to the Bureau of Labor Statistics, only 7 percent of public relations professionals are minorities—one-third less than the national average for minorities in professional fields. To help more minorities enter the field, in 1990 the Public Relations Society of America announced a program of scholarships and internships at public relations agencies for minority professionals.

Summary

In recent years, the practice of public relations has become accepted, not only as part of the marketing mix, but as part of the management process of any well-run organization.

Public relations objectives and goals, strategies, and tactics must flow directly from the organization's overall goals. Public relations strategies must reflect organizational strategies. And public relations tactics must be designed to realize, ultimately, the organization's business objectives.

So despite its stereotypes and demographic idiosyncrasies, public relations takes neither a false smile nor a glad hand. Rather, it takes a solid grounding in all aspects of professional communications, human relations, and judgmental and learning skills. Most of all, it takes hard work.

DISCUSSION STARTERS

1. Describe the elements of a public relations plan.
2. How does MBO relate to public relations?
3. How are public relations objectives derived?
4. What elements go into framing a public relations budget?
5. What are the four general steps in preparing a public relations campaign plan?
6. What activities are included in the scope of public relations practice?
7. What is the ideal "reporting relationship" for a director of public relations?
8. What are the technical skills that a public relations professional should possess?
9. What kinds of attitudinal characteristics should a public relations professional possess?
10. What is meant by "velvet ghetto"?

NOTES

1. James E. Grunig and Todd Hunt, *Managing Public Relations* (New York: Holt, Rinehart and Winston, 1984), 89–97.
2. Ibid.
3. Richard H. Truitt, "Wanted: Hard-Headed Objectives," *Public Relations Journal* (August 1969): 12, 13.
4. George L. Morrisey, *Management by Objectives and Results for Business and Industry*, 2d ed. (Reading, MA: Addison-Wesley, 1977), 9.
5. Jack Tucker, "Budgeting and Cost Control: Are You a Businessman or a Riverboat Gambler?" *Public Relations Journal* (March 1981): 15.
6. Donald T. Mogavero, "When the Funds Come Tumbling Down," *Public Relations Journal* (October 1981): 13.
7. Anthony Fulginiti, "How to Prepare a Public Relations Plan," *Communication Briefings* (May 1985): 8a, b.
8. Thomas J. Peters and Robert H. Waterman, Jr., *In Search of Excellence* (New York: Harper & Row, 1982), 40.

9. Robert Cushman, speech before the New England Chapter of the Public Relations Society of America, February 27, 1980, Boston, Ma.
10. "Managing Corporate External Relations: Changing Perspectives and Responses," Report 679, New York: Conference Board, 1976.
11. Jack O'Dwyer, *O'Dwyer's Directory of Corporate Communications* (New York: J. R. O'Dwyer, 1985), 2.
12. "25th Annual Survey of the Profession, Part 1: Salaries and Demographics," *PR Reporter* (October 16, 1989): 1.

TOP OF THE SHELF

Wood, Robert J. *Confessions of a PR Man.* Scarborough, Ontario. The New American Library of Canada Limited, 1988.

In *Confessions of a PR Man,* Bob Wood describes the principles and practices that made him one of the most respected counselors in the business.

From his public relations days in the U.S. Air Force to his 37 years at Carl Byoir & Associates, Wood distinguished himself in all areas of the field. He illustrates his crisis-management expertise with revealing case studies that include high-profile companies such as Woolworth and A&P. In media relations, Wood recounts how he finessed problems for clients like Howard Johnson, and he addresses how to deal with particularly thorny media issues in the chapter, "Good Silences and Bad." Wood's advice on public relations planning is instructive. To wit: "Always have clear objectives and measure how well they have been achieved." He also provides instruction on public opinion and legislation and on the value of briefing clients before they face the media.

Wood's candor, supported by 65 "war stories," makes *Confessions of a PR Man* a rich source of public relations knowledge. Students should consider this to glean the key ingredients of a successful public relations career.

Block, Edward M. "Strategic Communications: Practicing What We Preach." Speech at PRSA Annual Convention, November 8, 1987. New York: Burson-Marsteller (230 Park Ave. South 10003).

Brief, Arthur, and Gerald Tomlinson. *Managing Smart.* Lexington, MA: Lexington Books, 1987.

Brody, E. W. *Public Relations Programming and Production.* New York: Praeger, 1988.

Brody, E. W. *Professional Practice Development.* New York: Praeger, 1989.

Burson, Harold. *What Works for Me.* New York: Random House, 1987.

Careers in Public Relations. New York: PRSA (33 Irving Place 10003).

Cluff, Susan. "The Changing Face of Corporate Communication." *Communication World* (May 1987): 27–31. (IABC, 870 Market St., San Francisco, CA 94102)

SUGGESTED READINGS

Fraser, Bruce W. "How to Be a Freelance Public Relations Professional . . . and Survive." Tips & Tactics, a supplement of *Public Relations Reporter* 25, no. 9 (June 22, 1987). The author discusses the pros and cons of freelancing.

Hamilton, Seymour. *A Communications Audit Handbook: Helping Organizations Communicate.* White Plains, NY: Longman, 1987.

Hendrix, Jerry A. *Public Relations Cases.* Belmont, CA: Wadsworth, 1988.

Hills, Curtis. *How to Save Your Clients from Themselves.* Phoenix, AZ: Olde & Oppenheim, 1988.

Hitt, Michael A., et al. *Management: Concepts and Effective Practice.* 2nd ed. St. Paul, MN: West, 1986.

Jackson, Patrick. "Tomorrow's Public Relations." *Public Relations Journal* (March 1985): 24–25. By raising our sights, embracing research, and learning without end, today's practitioners will be able to meet future world challenges, Jackson advises.

Jefkins, Frank. *P.R. Techniques.* Portsmouth, NH: William Heinemann, 1988.

Martin, Dick. *Executive's Guide to Handling a Press Interview.* Babylon, NY: Pilot Books, 1985.

Monsanto Decentralizes & Downsizes Without Losing on Public Affairs. New York: Business International October 19, 1987. 215 Park Avenue South, 10003.

Nager, Norman R., and Allen T. Harrell. *Public Relations Management by Objectives.* New York: Longman, 1984.

National Directory of Corporate Public Affairs, 1990. Washington, DC: Columbia Books (1350 New York Ave., NW 20005).

Rogers, Henry. *Rogers' Rules for Success.* New York: St. Martin's Press, 1986.

Safire, Bill. "Twenty-First Annual Survey of the Profession." *PR Reporter* (September 30, 1985): 1–6.

Simon, Raymond. *Public Relations Management: Casebook.* 3rd ed. Columbus, OH: Publishing Horizons, 1986.

Sullivan, Michael. *Management Audit for Public Relations Firms.* Palo Alto, CA.: Sullivan Associates, 1987.

Theus, Kathryn T. "Gender Shifts in Journalism and Public Relations." *Public Relations Review* (Spring 1985): 42–50. This article discusses the increased female enrollment in journalism and communications schools, which graduate classes of up to 60 percent women.

Timpe, A. Dale. *Productivity.* New York: Facts on File, 1989.

Walton, Wesley, and Charles Brissman. *Corporate Communications Handbook.* New York: Clark Boardman, 1989.

Wilcox, Dennis L., Phillip H. Ault, and Warren K. Agee. *Public Relations: Strategies & Tactics.* 2nd ed. New York: Harper & Row, 1989.

CASE STUDY   Regaining the Fizz at Perrier

"It's perfect. It's Perrier."

This advertising slogan symbolized the status symbol in the chic green bottle for an entire generation of yuppies. Perrier was the epitome of freshness, purity, and perfection.

Then, in February of 1990, the sparkling spring water burst its bubbly.

The scare started when a lab in North Carolina picked up traces of benzene, a carcinogen, in a bottle of Perrier. Upon hearing the news, the president of Perrier Group of America, Inc., Ronald V. Davis, didn't hesitate. He ordered Perrier removed from distribution in North America.

Mr. Davis relied on instinct in ordering the recall of every single Perrier bottle in the United States. "I feel like my family has been attacked," he said in describing his reaction to the worst problem the company had ever faced.

At first, Perrier officials were uncertain as to what had caused the benzene contamination. Some speculated that sabotage was responsible. Another suspicion was that an employee had used a solution containing benzene to clean grease from bottling machinery. Later it was revealed that an employee had failed to clean filters that remove impurities, including benzene, that occur naturally in the water.

Company officials also swore that the benzene had tainted only a few bottles shipped from France to the United States. But then, according to French press reports, distributors in Denmark, the Netherlands, and Japan reported problems with Perrier.

Despite its initial uncertainty, when faced with an expanding crisis, Perrier didn't hesitate. From Paris, the company's seventy-five-year-old chief executive, Gustav Leven, announced, before a packed press conference, that Perrier would immediately launch a worldwide recall of its bottled water.

Said Mr. Leven, "We don't want the slightest doubt to weigh on Perrier." Mr. Leven then served bottles of Perrier to the throng of reporters on hand for the press conference.

The recall of 160 million bottles of Perrier cost the company $30 million after taxes. Even worse, the company wasn't certain how long it would take before shelves could

be restocked with new Perrier. Reports varied from three weeks to three months.

In the face of the confusion, one analyst predicted, "The recall is definitely going to hurt Perrier because this is the kind of stuff that breeds press sensationalism."

In the wake of the water company's problems, industry analysts speculated that Perrier had done significant damage. "It's a product based purely on confidence," said another analyst, pointing out that Perrier had little else going for it other than its purity. A fellow beverage analyst said the public, in a subliminal sense, would be aware that Perrier was once contaminated, would question where it was bottled, and would likely wonder, "Maybe the filter works and maybe it doesn't."

Perrier's naysayers were all over. They predicted, in essence, the product would have real trouble reestablishing its credibility and clout.

As it turned out, Perrier kept its product off the shelves for three months, while it made sure its processes were corrected.

But while it was "correcting" its processes, the usually closed-mouthed company became more vocal. It launched a $25-million advertising campaign—the biggest in its history—to acknowledge and apologize for the benzene contamination and announce the imminent reintroduction of Perrier sparkling water. The ads played down the contamination, even using humor to try to make light of the Perrier recall.

At the same time, Perrier stepped up its sports sponsorships and product sampling and couponing, and hired public relations firm Burson-Marsteller to help it out. Prior to its relaunch, Perrier began dropping coupons for a free bottle of the "new" product in select markets.

In April, Perrier returned.

Miraculously, in but one month back on the shelves, Perrier sales totaled almost 70 percent of what they had equaled the year before—far above the company's expectation. Distribution in bars, restaurants, and hotels also quickly resumed. By the winter of 1990, Perrier sales had plateaued at about 60 percent of pre-recall levels, with Evian replacing it as America's leading imported bottled water.

While Perrier research confirmed that memory of the benzene incident had all but faded by January 1991, nonetheless the contamination crisis forced consumers to sample other bottled waters. Thus consumers got out of the habit of seeing Perrier and began to seek alternatives.

So while Perrier still faced a significant marketing challenge, company executives at the start of 1991 were optimistic that the product was back on the road to recovery.

Said Perrier's marketing director, "Being private sort of became a way of life to us . . . obviously what's happened in the last couple of months has kind of blown that all out of the water. It's pretty hard to stay private with what's happened with Perrier, and so I think there's a much greater willingness on our part, after what we've been through, to talk to people and share it."

Summarized Perrier president Davis, "You can't be trained for an event like this.

by Kim E. Jeffery
Senior Vice President
Sales & Marketing

Just a few short weeks ago I was living a marketer's dream. I had the premier brand in a growing market. And a seemingly unlimited supply of naturally pure product produced by mother nature.

The funny thing is, I still have all those things.

Perrier is still the best known brand of mineral water.

The market is still growing.

And the spring source in Vergèze, France, is just as pure and as bountiful as ever.

The only thing I *don't* have is sales. And I have to admit, I sort of miss them.

It's not as if people have forgotten about us. Johnny Carson remembers us. All the talk show hosts seem to remember us. In fact, we've been top-of-mind with virtually every comic and cartoonist in the country.

If one-liners were sales, we'd be outselling milk.

I have to take as my prototype the Zen archers of the Orient. Every day they diligently practice. They carefully draw a non-existent arrow from a non-existent quiver, pull a non-existent bow and release.

The result, of course, is a bullseye. Every time. They contend that the visualization is as important as the tangible reality.

Me? Well, I still sort of miss those sales. And so does my boss.

That's why I promise you, we'll be back as soon as possible. In the meantime, thanks for your patience.

I've got to go now and meet with my new Perrier brand manager.

He's a very large rabbit named Harvey.

perrier®

Worth waiting for.

We're coming! Wish we were here, but it's not easy restocking an entire thirsty world. We have to go city by city, in orderly French fashion, with total Gallic logic.

But we make you this promise: we'll be back in the same restaurants, hotels and grocery stores where you've always found us. Just as soon as we possibly can. The same green bottle. The same pure mineral water. Just as it has been for thousands of years.

Eau boy!

Worth waiting for.

FIGURE 3–3   *(Courtesy of Burson-Marsteller)*

When a product's whole reason for being is quality and purity, the costs of not doing what we did would have been borne for the next 100 years."

QUESTIONS

1. Do you think Perrier did the right thing in managing its public relations crisis? What other options did the company have?

2. Would you take issue with any aspects of the Perrier advertising/public relations campaign?

3. How damaging were the company's initial uncertainties on the cause of the contamination and the timing of Perrier's return? Could they have been avoided?

4. What else could Perrier have done to help bolster consumer confidence in its product?

Tips from the Top

HAROLD BURSON

Harold Burson is chairman of Burson-Marsteller, a worldwide public relations firm with 2,500 employees and fifty offices in twenty-seven countries. He was chief executive officer of Burson-Marsteller from its founding in 1953 until January 1988. Burson is a legendary public relations practitioner and lecturer, the recipient of virtually every major honor awarded by the profession.

How has the business of public relations changed over time?
Public relations has, over time, become more relevant as a management function for all manner of institutions, public and private sector, profit and not-for-profit. CEOs increasingly recognize the need to communicate to achieve their organizational objectives. Similarly, they have come to recognize public relations as a necessary component in the decision-making process. This has enhanced the role of public relations both internally and for independent consultants.

How can a public relations firm influence public opinion?
The public relations function can be divided into two principal classes of activity: the strategic and the implementing. Public relations firms play a major role on behalf of clients in both areas. In the realm of the strategic, a public relations firm brings to

a client an independent perspective based on broad organizational experience with a wide spectrum of clients and problems. The public relations firm is not encumbered with the many internal considerations that frequently enter into the corporate or institutional decision-making process. In implementing programs, the public relations firm has a broad range of resources, both functional and geographic, that can be brought to bear on a client's problem. Furthermore, the public relations firm can usually be held to more specific accountability—both in terms of results and costs.

What constitutes the ideal public relations man or woman?
Public relations today covers so broad a range of activity that it is difficult to establish a set of specifications for all the kinds of people wearing the public relations mantle. Generally, I feel four primary characteristics apply to just about every successful public relations person I know.

1. They're smart—bright, intelligent people; quick studies. They ask the right

questions. They have that unique ability to establish credibility almost on sight.

2. They know how to get along with people. They work well with their bosses, their peers, their subordinates. They work well with their clients and with third parties like the press and suppliers. They are emotionally stable—even (especially) under pressure. They use the pronoun *we* more than *I*.

3. They are motivated, and part of that motivation involves an ability to develop creative solutions. No one needs to tell them what to do next; instinctively, they know. They don't fear starting with a blank sheet of paper—to them the blank sheet of paper equates with challenge and opportunity.

4. They can write; they can articulate their thoughts in a persuasive manner.

What are the primary attributes you look for in a subordinate?

Presumably this pertains to character traits. If so, it's difficult to avoid those textbook traits present on any list. But so be it! Here are some of those that mean the most to me.

♦ **Integrity**—not only if he/she can be trusted with the cash box. Perhaps most important, can that person be trusted to be totally truthful and open in reporting the negative as well as the positive—and in a timely fashion? Is he/she willing to say, "I don't know the answer," and ask for help?

♦ **A strong work ethic**—those in higher management (and we at Burson-

Marsteller like to think all our hires are capable of becoming higher management) set the pace for those who work for and with them. I prefer a fast pace with high productivity.

♦ **Be a team player**—in building an organization, we have developed our share of stars, even superstars. But those achieving that distinction have invariably reached it because they got help from others along the way. We say we are a sharing organization. Team players share and welcome help.

♦ **Commitment**—to Burson-Marsteller and to our clients alike. An early associate of mine once said, "When my client gets stuck with an ice pick, I bleed." Clients are quick to sense that kind of commitment, and so do those who work alongside that kind of person.

♦ **A willingness to take responsibility**—someone who seeks rewards and accepts penalties for being in charge.

How do ethics apply to the public relations function?

In a single word, pervasively. Ethical behavior is at the root of what we do as public relations professionals. We approach our calling with a commitment to serve the public interest, knowing full well that the public interest lacks a universal definition and knowing that one person's view of the public interest differs markedly from that of another. We must therefore be consistent in our personal definition of the public interest and be prepared to speak up for those actions we take.

4

The Court of Public Opinion

Public opinion is an elusive and fragile commodity. One day you're a hero, the next a villain. Just ask Al Campanis and Victor Kiam.

♦ Mr. Campanis, for forty years a player, coach, and executive of first the Brooklyn and then the Los Angeles Dodgers, saw his career capsize with 40 seconds of ill-chosen words during a live interview with Ted Koppel on *Nightline*. Mr. Campanis hit the skids with a convoluted and offensive explanation of why black people don't get front-office jobs in baseball.[1]

♦ Mr. Kiam, the successful owner of both a shaving products company and the New England Patriots football team, created a national furor in the fall of 1990, when he reportedly called a woman reporter, "a classic bitch," after she claimed sexual harassment in the team's locker room. (Mr. Kiam, after hiring a public relations consultant, later denied the "classic bitch" remark.) As a result of the controversy, Mr. Kiam—and worse, his Lady Remington shaver—were excoriated by women everywhere.[2]

Such are the vicissitudes of public opinion.

But the galvanizing nature of the remarks of Messrs. Campanis and Kiam are the exception (unfortunate for them!) rather than the rule. Usually it's difficult to move people toward a strong opinion on anything. It's even harder to move them away from an opinion once they reach it. Recent research, in fact, indicates that mass media appeals may have little immediate effect on influencing public opinion.

Nonetheless, the heart of public relations work lies in attempting to affect the public opinion process. Most public relations programs are designed either to (1) *persuade* people to change their opinion on an issue, product, or organization, (2) *crystalize* uninformed or undeveloped opinions, or (3) *reinforce* existing opinions.

So public relations professionals must understand how public opinion is formed, how it evolves from people's attitudes, and how it is influenced by communication. This chapter discusses attitude formation and change and public opinion creation and persuasion.

What Is Public Opinion?

Public opinion, like *public relations*, is not easily defined. Newspaper columnist Joseph Kraft called public opinion "the unknown god to which moderns burn incense." Edward Bernays called it "a term describing an ill-defined, mercurial, and changeable group of individual judgments."[3] And Princeton professor Harwood Childs, after coming up with no fewer than forty different, yet viable definitions, concluded with a definition by Herman C. Boyle: "*Public opinion* is not the name of something, but the classification of a number of somethings."[4]

Splitting public opinion into its two components, *public* and *opinion*, is perhaps the best way to understand the concept. Simply defined, *public* signifies a group of people who share a common interest in a specific subject—stockholders, for example, or employees or community residents. Each group is concerned with a common issue—the price of the stock, the wages of the company, or the building of a new plant.

An opinion is the expression of an attitude on a particular topic. When attitudes become strong enough, they surface in the form of opinions. When opinions become strong enough, they lead to verbal or behavioral actions.

A corporate executive and an environmentalist from the Sierra Club might differ dramatically in their attitudes about the relative importance of pollution control and continued industrial production. Their respective opinions on a piece of environmental legislation might also differ radically. In turn, how their organizations respond to that legislation—by picketing, petitioning, or lobbying—might also differ.

Public opinion, then, is the aggregate of many individual opinions on a particular issue that affects a group of people. Stated another way, public opinion represents a consensus. And that consensus, deriving as it does from many individual opinions, really begins with people's attitudes toward the issue in question. Trying to influence an individual's attitude—how he or she thinks on a given topic—is a primary focus of the practice of public relations.

If an opinion is an expression of an attitude on a particular topic, what then is an attitude? Unfortunately, that also is not an easy question to answer. It had been generally assumed that attitudes were predispositions to think a certain way about a certain topic. But recent research has indicated that attitudes may more likely be evaluations people make about specific problems or issues. These conclusions are not necessarily connected to any broad attitude.[5] For example, an individual might favor a company's response to one issue but disagree vehemently with its response to another. Thus, that individual's attitude may differ from issue to issue.

Attitudes are based on a number of characteristics.

1. **Personal**—the physical and emotional ingredients of an individual, including size, age, and social status.
2. **Cultural**—the environment and life-style of a particular geographic area, such as Japan versus the United States or rural America versus urban America. National political candidates often tailor messages to appeal to the particular cultural complexions of specific regions of the country.
3. **Educational**—the level and quality of a person's education. To appeal to the increased number of college graduates in the United States today, public communication has become more sophisticated.
4. **Familial**—people's roots. Children acquire their parents' tastes, biases, political partisanships, and a host of other characteristics. Some pediatricians insist that children pick up most of their knowledge in the earliest years, and few would deny the family's strong role in helping mold attitudes.
5. **Religious**—a system of beliefs about God or the supernatural. Religion is making a comeback. In the 1960s many young people turned away from formal religion. In the 1990s, even after the evangelical scandals of the 1980s, religious fervor has reemerged. From followers of traditional Christianity and Judaism to disciples of Hare Krishna and the Reverend Sun Myung Moon to believers in the various fundamentalist sects of the Bible Belt, religion is back, influencing attitudes.
6. **Social class**—position within society. As people's social status changes, so do their attitudes. For example, college students unconcerned with making a living may dramatically change their attitudes about such concepts as big government, big business, wealth, and prosperity after entering the job market.
7. **Race**—ethnic origin, which today increasingly helps shape people's attitudes. The history of blacks and whites in America has been a stormy one, with peaceful coexistence often frustrated. Nonetheless, minorities in our society, as a group, continue to improve their standard of living.

And in so doing, African-Americans, Chicanos, Puerto Ricans, and others have retained distinct racial pride in and allegiance to their cultural heritage.

These characteristics help influence the formation of attitudes. So, too, do other factors, such as experience, economic class, and political and organizational memberships. Again, recent research has indicated that attitudes and behaviors are situational—influenced by specific issues in specific situations. Nonetheless, when others with similar attitudes reach similar opinions, a consensus, or public opinion, is born.

How Are Attitudes Influenced?

Strictly speaking, attitudes are positive, negative, or nonexistent. A person is for something, against it, or couldn't care less. Studies show that most people don't care much one way or the other. For any one issue, a small percentage of people express strong support, and another small percentage express strong opposition. The vast majority are right smack in the middle—passive, neutral, indifferent. Former Vice-president Spiro T. Agnew called them "the silent majority." In many instances—political campaigns being a prime example—this silent majority holds the key to success because they are the most readily influenced by a communicator's message.

It's hard to change the mind of a person who is staunchly opposed to a particular issue or individual. Likewise, it's easy to reinforce the support of a person who is wholeheartedly in favor of an issue or an individual. Social scientist Leon Festinger discussed this concept when he talked about cognitive dissonance. He believes that individuals tend to avoid information that is dissonant or opposed to their own points of view and tend to seek out information that is consonant with, or in support of, their own attitudes.[6] In other words, one who regularly reads the liberal *Village Voice* probably wouldn't read the conservative *National Review*, and vice versa. In effect, this example is cognitive dissonance in action.

As Festinger's theory intimates, the people whose attitudes can be influenced most readily are those who have not yet made up their minds. In politics, as noted in Chapter 1, this group is often referred to as the swing vote. Many elections have been won or lost on last-minute appeals to these politically undecided voters. In addition, it is possible to introduce information that may cause dissonance in the mind of a receiver.

Understanding this theory and its potential for influencing the silent majority is extremely important for the public relations practitioner, whose objective is to win support through clear, thoughtful, and persuasive communication. Moving a person from a latent state of attitude formation to a more aware state and finally to an active one becomes a matter of motivation.

Motivating Attitude Change

People are motivated by different factors, and no two people are apt to respond exactly the same way to the same set of circumstances. Each of us is motivated by different drives and needs.

The most famous delineator of what motivates people was Dr. Abraham Maslow. His hierarchy of needs helps define the origins of motivation, which, in turn, help explain attitude change. Maslow postulated a five-level hierarchy.

1. The lowest order is physiological needs: a person's biological demands— food and water, sleep, health, bodily needs, exercise and rest, and sex.
2. The second level is safety needs: security, protection, comfort and peace, and orderly surroundings.
3. The third level is love needs: acceptance, belonging, love and affection, and membership in a group.
4. The fourth level is esteem: recognition and prestige, confidence and leadership opportunities, competence and strength, intelligence and success.
5. The highest order is self-actualization, or simply becoming what one is capable of becoming. Self-actualization involves self-fulfillment and achieving a goal for the purposes of challenge and accomplishment.[7]

According to Maslow, the needs at all five levels compose the fundamental motivating factors for any individual or public.

In the 1990s, as people once again "get involved" with causes—from abortion to animal rights to environmentalism—motivating attitude change becomes more important. Many activist groups, in fact, borrow heavily from psychological research on political activism to accomplish attitude change. Six cardinal precepts of political activism are instructive in attempting to change attitudes:

1. *Don't use graphic images unless they are accompanied by specific actions people can execute.* Many movements—the nuclear freeze campaign for one and the anti-abortion movement for another—began by relying heavily on graphic images of death and destruction. But such images run the risk of pushing people away rather than drawing them in. Disturbing presentations rarely lead to a sustained attitude change.
2. *Go to the public instead of asking the public to come to you.* Most people will never become directly involved in an activist campaign. They will shy away. But by recognizing the limits of public interest and involve-

ment, you can develop realistic strategies to capitalize on public goodwill without demanding more than people are willing to give.

3. *Don't assume that attitude change is necessary for behavior change.* A large body of psychological research casts doubt on the proposition that the best way to change behavior is to begin by changing attitudes. Indeed, the relationship between attitudes and behavior is often quite weak. Therefore, informing smokers of the link between cigarettes and cancer is far easier than getting them to kick the habit.

FIGURE 4–1 In 1989, the popular musical group the Grateful Dead was so concerned with "public opinion" that it began mailing letters to fans asking them to "shape up or the band might have to ship out." The Dead, in its third decade of existence, was worried when thousands of people began showing up at its sold-out concerts without tickets. Clashes with police and public disorder became common. "We're running out of places to play, and we're running out of ways to say the obvious," wrote the Dead. The group beseeched its loyal Deadheads to leave "nothin' but footprints" in blazing a new, more refined image. *(Courtesy of Grateful Dead Productions)*

4. *Use moral arguments as adjuncts, not as primary thrusts.* Moral views are difficult to change. It is much easier to gain support by stressing the practical advantages of your solution rather than the immorality of your opponent's. For example, it is easier to convert people to a meatless diet by discussing the health benefits of vegetables than by discussing whether the Bible gives people dominion over animals.

5. *Embrace the mainstream.* In any campaign, people from all walks of like are necessary to win widespread approval. No campaign can be won if it is dubbed "radical" or "faddish." That is why the involvement of *all* people must be encouraged in seeking attitude change.

6. *Don't offend the people you seek to change.* Research on persuasion shows that influence is usually strongest when people like the persuader and see the persuader as similar to themselves. It is impossible to persuade someone whom you have alienated. Or, as my mother used to say, "You can attract more flies with honey than you can with vinegar." The same applies to people.[8]

Power of Persuasion

Perhaps the most essential element in influencing public opinion is the principle of persuasion. Persuading is the goal of the vast majority of public relations programs. Persuasion theory has myriad explanations and interpretations. Basically, persuasion means getting another person to do something through advice, reasoning, or just plain arm-twisting. Books have been written on the enormous power of advertising and public relations as persuasive media.

Researchers in recent years have questioned whether we really can be persuaded—particularly through the mass media. In the late 1940s and 1950s, evidence mounted that such communication rarely has a persuasive effect. Most evidence came from voting studies and studies of information flow from the media to individuals, as researched by Elihu Katz and Paul Lazarsfeld. The studies of Carl Hovland and his colleagues at Yale University also demonstrated that the credibility of a source exercised a prime influence on the persuasiveness of the message being delivered.

Social scientists and communications scholars take issue with the view of many public relations practitioners that a story on network news or the front page of the *New York Times* has a tremendous persuasive effect. Scholars argue that the media have a limited effect on persuasion—doing more to reinforce existing attitudes than to persuade toward a new belief. There is little doubt, however, that the persuasiveness of a message can be increased when it arouses or is accompanied by a high level of personal involvement. In other words, an individual who cares about something and is in fundamental agreement with an organization's basic position will tend to be persuaded by a message supporting that view.

Following this belief is the persuasion theory of Michael Ray—the hierarchies of effects.[9] According to this theory, there are at least three basic orderings of knowledge, attitude, and behavior relative to persuasion.

1. When personal involvement is low and little difference exists between behavioral alternatives, knowledge changes are likely to lead directly to behavioral changes.

2. When personal involvement is high but behavioral alternatives are indistinguishable, behavioral change is likely to be followed by attitudinal change, similar to Festinger's cognitive dissonance approach.

3. When personal involvement is high and clear differences exist among alternatives, people act in a more rational manner. First, they learn about the issue. Second, they evaluate the alternatives. Then they act in a manner consistent with their attitudes and knowledge.

The application of Ray's hierarchy to public relations rests in the ability of a practitioner to involve a target personally in an organization, issue, or idea and then to argue rationally for a particular alternative.

To these complex theories of persuasion is added the simpler, yet no less profound notion of former Secretary of State Dean Rusk: "One of the best ways to persuade others is to listen to them." No matter how one characterizes persuasion, the goal of most communications programs is, in fact, to influence a receiver to take a desired action.

Influencing Public Opinion

Public opinion is a lot easier to measure than it is to influence. However, a thoughtful public relations program can crystallize attitudes, reinforce beliefs, and occasionally change public opinion. First, the opinions to be changed or modified must be identified and understood. Second, target publics must be clear. Third, the public relations professional must have in sharp focus the "laws" that govern public opinion—as amorphous as they may be.

In that context, the 15 "Laws of Public Opinion," developed many years ago by social psychologist Hadley Cantril, remain pertinent.

1. Opinion is highly sensitive to important events.

2. Events of unusual magnitude are likely to swing public opinion temporarily from one extreme to another. Opinion doesn't become stabilized until the implications of events are seen in some perspective.

3. Opinion is generally determined more by events than by words—unless those words are themselves interpreted as an "event."

4. Verbal statements and outlines of courses of action have maximum importance when opinion is unstructured and people are suggestible and seek some interpretation from a reliable source.

5. By and large, public opinion doesn't anticipate emergencies—it only reacts to them.

6. Opinion is basically determined by self-interest. Events, words, or any other stimuli affect opinion only insofar as their relationship to self-interest is apparent.

7. Opinion doesn't remain aroused for any long period of time unless people feel their self-interest is acutely involved or unless opinion—aroused by words—is sustained by events.

8. Once self-interest is involved, opinions aren't easily changed.

9. When self-interest is involved, public opinion in a democracy is likely to be ahead of official policy.

10. When an opinion is held by a slight majority or when opinion is not solidly structured, an accomplished fact tends to shift opinion in the direction of acceptance.

11. At critical times people become more sensitive to the adequacy of their leadership. If they have confidence in it, they are willing to assign more than usual responsibility to it; if they lack confidence in it, they are less tolerant than usual.

12. People are less reluctant to have critical decisions made by their leaders if they feel that somehow they, themselves, are taking some part in the decision.

13. People have more opinions and are able to form opinions more easily on goals than on methods to reach those goals.

14. Public opinion, like individual opinion, is colored by desire. And when opinion is based chiefly on desire, rather than on information, it is likely to shift with events.

15. By and large, if people in a democracy are provided with educational opportunities and ready access to information, public opinion reveals a hard-headed common sense. The more enlightened people are to the implications of events and proposals for their own self-interest, the more likely they are to agree with the more objective opinions of realistic experts.[10]

When Hutton Talked . . .

By 1985, E. F. Hutton & Company had become the fifth largest retail brokerage house in the United States, with revenues approaching $3 billion. Its advertising slogan—"When E. F. Hutton talks, people listen"—was well known. But midway through that year, people began listening to Hutton in a way the firm found most embarrassing. In May, Hutton pleaded guilty to 2,000 felony counts resulting from an illegal check overdraft scheme that involved approximately

E.F. Hutton Talks...

"Thank you."

That's the most important thing we can say to our 17,500 employees and our thousands of customers and clients. The loyalty and support of our clients and the commitment to excellence and integrity of our employees is what built our reputation over 81 years and what has seen us through the trying times of these past few weeks. You are the best.

To those in government and industry who look on with concern, we simply say, if you judge us on our merits, we are confident of your conclusions.

We will continue to meet the investment needs of our clients in more than 500 local communities and we are proud to say "When E.F. Hutton Talks, People Listen."

Sincerely,

Robert Fomon

Robert Fomon
Chairman and
Chief Executive Officer

100 of its nearly 400 branches nationwide, from 1980 to 1982. The firm agreed to pay $2.75 million in fines and set up an $8 million fund to reimburse the banks.

The Justice Department did not bring charges against individuals. It said that only two mid-level individuals could be charged in a criminal sense and that the plea agreement was preferable because it established new law in cash management and sent a strong signal to other corporations. The media and a congressional subcommittee, however, sharply criticized Hutton and the Justice Department, saying that top executives should have been punished. Cartoonists and headline writers around the country had a field day with Hutton's slogan; one of many parodies read, "When E. F. Hutton talks, it says 'Guilty.'"

In a move to settle the matter, Hutton retained former Attorney General Griffin Bell, who led a team of fourteen lawyers in a summer-long investigation into individual wrongdoing. As a result of the inquiry, three senior executives resigned or retired, six branch managers were fined $25,000 each, and three regional executives were suspended for thirty days without pay.

Under siege, Hutton conducted an extensive internal and external information program to present its positions to employees, clients, and the media. It suspended advertising briefly but did not abandon its fifteen-year-old slogan. In July, the company ran the ad shown here in several papers to help boost employee morale; and in the fall it launched a new national TV advertising campaign, using Olympic athletes to personify the quest for excellence.

Alas, in 1988, Hutton was sold to Shearson Lehman Brothers, which ultimately dropped the Hutton name.

QUESTIONS

1. If you were Hutton's public relations director, what steps would you take to assess the damage?
2. Should Hutton have retained its advertising slogan in the wake of its well-publicized problems?
3. What measures might you have adopted to resurrect Hutton's corporate image?

Polishing the Corporate Image

Most organizations today and the people who manage them are extremely sensitive about the way they are perceived by their critical publics. In one nationwide survey of one hundred top executives, more than half considered it "very important to maintain a good public image."[11] As a result, some corporate managements today are reluctant to stick their collective necks out. As former General Motors executive John DeLorean described the executive thinking at his alma mater, "General Motors management feels that the corporation simply draws the lion's share of criticism. The best way

**Brighten
Your Corner**

Have you
noticed the
great difference
between the
people you
meet?
Some are as
sunshiny as
a handful of
forget-me-nots.
Others come on
like frozen mackerel.
A cheery, comforting
nurse can
help make a
hospital stay
bearable.
An upbeat secretary
makes visitors
glad they came
to see you.
Every corner of the
world has its clouds,
gripes, complainers,
and pains in the
neck—because many
people have
yet to
learn that
honey works better
than vinegar.
You're in control
of *your* small
corner of the
world.
Brighten it. . .
You *can.*

FIGURE 4–2   Although many companies attempted to construct a differentiable corporate image through advertising, few succeeded as well as United Technologies, which kept its messages succinct, savvy, and sparkling. *(Courtesy of United Technologies Corporation, Hartford, CT)*

to reduce this inevitable criticism, as top management sees it, is to keep a low, faceless profile."[12] Ironically, in the case of General Motors, the company was one of the first U.S. corporations to adopt a high-profile, industrial statesman approach to public affairs.* Indeed, few firms today can afford to keep a low profile.

Consider the following:

◆ Procter & Gamble voluntarily recalled and permanently removed from the market its successful Rely tampons when it was suspected that they contained carcinogenic agents.

◆ McDonald's reluctantly went public to defuse a quickly spreading rumor that ground worms were among the tasty ingredients in its patented hamburger.

◆ J. P. Stevens, the nation's second-largest textile manufacturer, reluctantly agreed to reconsider its labor practices when a group of activists successfully focused national media attention on the firm's treatment of its employees.

◆ Ernest and Julio Gallo and their E&J Gallo Winery sued and won a 1990 lawsuit to keep their younger brother, Joseph, from using his own name as the name of his new cheese—so concerned were the Gallo brothers that their sibling would tarnish the family's reputation.

◆ Computer giant IBM, known affectionately as "Big Blue," sent a stinging legal letter to a small Long Island computer-equipment company, Big Blue Products Inc., in 1990, giving it thirty days to drop "Big Blue" from its title—or else.

Most organizations today understand clearly that it takes a great deal of time to build a favorable image for a corporation but only one slip to create a negative public impression. In other words, the corporate image is a fragile commodity. Yet, most firms also believe that a positive corporate image is essential for continued long-term success.

As Ray D'Argenio, the former communications director of United Technologies, put it, "Corporate communications can't create a corporate character. A company already has a character, which communications can reinforce."[13]

Discovering the Corporate Image

Helping an organization discover its own special and distinct corporate image is an important function of the public relations practitioner. In the process, the practitioner must ask the following basic questions:

---

*Also ironically, John DeLorean was arrested—and subsequently acquitted—in a 1983 blaze of publicity for attempted cocaine smuggling.

FIGURE 4–3 The key to a corporate image that gets through to people is a combination of simplicity, unity, and balance. These excerpts from the corporate identity manual of David's lemonade, the creation of Fulton + Partners, Inc., are examples of a clear corporate image. *(Courtesy of Sanders Printing Corporation)*

The Corporate Signature

Our signature is an arrangement of our mark and logotype. It is considered as one design element in any layout or application situation. A complete corporate signature must be used whenever identification is necessary. Each authorized arrangement has an established relationship between the mark and logotype. This relationship is not to be altered or changed in any way.

Preferred form
for vertical format

Preferred form
for horizontal format

Alternate form
for horizontal format

♦ **What is the firm's present corporate image?** How does the public perceive the company? Does this perception differ from management's? Often research turns up significant discrepancies. For example, one computer company, which prided itself on its frequent communication with Wall Street analysts, was surprised to learn that it was perceived by analysts as pushy. In another example a food chain that considered its new menu to be up-to-date discovered that everyone under forty still thought of the firm as old and stodgy. One public utility, active in community affairs, was amazed to discover that few in the community appreciated the full extent of the firm's public service activities.

♦ **What corporate image does the firm want?** An organization can't be all things to all people. One department store might decide, for instance, that its market is the upper middle class. Another store might shoot for an even more elite market. Still another might wish to project the image of a discount merchant, servicing the less well-to-do. Before an organization can take action in achieving a new corporate image, it must first decide the specific kind of image it wants to attain (Figure 4–3).

Logo

♦ **How do the company's various entities—products and/or services— affect the image of the company? Does this vary by audience?** Many times, a company's divisions, subsidiaries, or products have a completely different image from that of the rest of the firm. Often this is a good idea, but sometimes it isn't. If a firm wants to be looked on as a consistently high-class/high-quality operation, a profitable, yet low-class/low-quality area within that corporation might be detrimental to the overall corporate image. This is the kind of tough issue with which an organization must grapple if it wishes to convey a cohesive corporate image among all of its parts. Then, too, different audiences associated with different elements of an organization may perceive the firm's image to be completely different. Often, this is exactly what the organization wants.

♦ **What must a firm do to win a new corporate image?** Often, the process starts with changing the internal culture. The company's procedures might need revision. Product lines might require reexamination. If the firm truly wishes to change, corporate philosophies might have to be adjusted. Sometimes the very name of the company needs to be changed to shed an old image and don a new one.

Beware the Traps of Public Opinion

Analyzing public opinion is not as easy as it looks. Once a company wins favorable public opinion for a product or an idea, the trick is to maintain it. The worst thing to do is sit back and bask in the glory of a positive public image—that's a quick route to image deterioration.

Public opinion is changeable, and in assessing it, communicators are susceptible to a number of subtle, yet lethal traps.

◆ **Cast in stone** This fallacy assumes that just because public opinion is well established on a certain issue, it isn't likely to change. Not true. Consider an issue such as women's liberation. In the early 1960s, people laughed at the handful of women raising a ruckus about equal rights, equal pay, and equal treatment. By the early 1970s, women's liberation pervaded every sector of our culture, and nobody laughed. In the space of a decade, public opinion about the importance of this issue had shifted substantially.

◆ **Gut reaction** This fallacy assumes that if management feels in its corporate gut that the public will feel strongly in a certain direction, then that must be the way to go. *Be careful.* Some managements are so cut off

FIGURE 4–4 The Xerox Company has a unique name and logo problem. The Xerox name is so widely used that it must fight a continual battle to have the name treated as a proper adjective with a capital X, rather than a verb with a lowercase x—thus the frustration expressed in this ad. *(Courtesy of Xerox Corporation)*

from the real world that their knee-jerk reactions to issues often turn out to be more jerk than anything else. One former auto company executive, perhaps overstating the case, described the problem this way: "There's no forward response to what the public wants today. It's gotten to be a total insulation from the realities of the world." Certainly, management's instincts in dealing with the public may be questionable at times. Generally, gut-reaction judgments should be avoided in assessing public opinion.

◆ **General public**   There may well be a public at large, but there's no such thing as the general public. Even the smallest public can be subdivided. No two people are alike, and messages to influence public opinion should be as pointed as possible rather than scattershot. Sometimes individuals may qualify as members of publics on both sides of an issue. In weighing the pros and cons of lower speed limits, for example, many people are both drivers and pedestrians. Categorizing them into one general group can be a mistake.

B E T W E E N   T H E   L I N E S

Love That Sara Lee Underwear

Talk about clarifying the corporate image . . . In 1985, Consolidated Foods Corporation learned that 98 percent of 800 people surveyed were aware of the products of its subsidiary, Sara Lee. At the same time the company was unhappy that its own Consolidated Foods name didn't give consumers and investors an accurate picture of the broad range of the company's products—from foods to vacuum cleaners to underwear.

So . . . dismissing several alternative names recommended by consultants and defying all logic, corporation executives decided to rename the firm to take advantage of the high recognition level of the subsidiary responsible for only 8 percent of its products. Thus, the Sara Lee Corporation was born, complete with a line of underwear. As Yogi Berra said when they told him the people of Dublin had just elected a Jewish mayor, "Only in America!"

CONSOLIDATED
FOODS CORPORATION

SARA LEE CORPORATION

♦ **Words move mountains** Perhaps they do, sometimes; but public opinion is usually influenced more by events than by words. For example, in 1979, nuclear power foes lacked a solid political base until an accident at Pennsylvania's Three Mile Island plant rallied public sentiment against the proponents of nuclear power.

♦ **Brother's keeper** It's true that most people will rise up indignantly if a fellow citizen has been wronged. But they'll get a lot more indignant if they feel they themselves have been wronged. In other words, self-interest often sparks public opinion. An organization wishing to influence public opinion might be well advised to ask initially, "What's in this for the people whose opinion we're trying to influence?"

Summary

Influencing public opinion remains at the heart of professional public relations work. Perhaps the key to realizing this objective is anticipating or keeping ahead of trends in our society. Anticipating trends is no easy task. But in the 1990s, trend watching has developed into a veritable cottage industry. One self-styled prognosticator riding the crest of trend analysis was John Naisbitt, whose book *Megatrends 2000* claimed to predict the new directions that would influence American lives in the next decade. Among them are

♦ Inflation and interest rates will be held in check.

♦ There will be a shift from welfare to workfare.

♦ There will be a shift from public housing to home ownership.

♦ There will be a shift from sports to the arts as the primary leisure preference.

♦ Consumers will demand more customized products.

♦ The media will amplify bad economic news.

♦ The rise of the Pacific Rim will be seen in terms of economic dominance. Asia will add 80 million more people.

♦ CEOs in a global economy will become more important and better known than political figures.[14]

Some might argue that there is nothing very revolutionary in these megatrends (and they might well be right). Nonetheless, such trends deserve to be scrutinized, analyzed, and evaluated by organizations in order to deal more effectively with the future.

As public relations counselor Philip Lesly has pointed out, "The real problems faced by business today are in the outside world of intangibles and public attitudes."[15] To keep ahead of these intangibles, these public

FIGURE 4–5   The Court of Public Opinion is indeed a fickle and ruthless judge. Witness the contribution of No Excuses, the irreverent jeans company, with its list of those who fell farthest from grace in public opinion terms at the close of the 1980s. *(Courtesy of No Excuses)*

attitudes, and these kernels of future public opinion, managements will turn increasingly to professional public relations practitioners for guidance.

1. What is public opinion?
2. What are attitudes, and upon what characteristics are they based?
3. How are attitudes influenced?
4. What is Maslow's hierarchy of motivation?
5. Explain the law of cognitive dissonance.
6. How difficult is it to change a person's behavior?
7. What are Cantril's Laws of Public Opinion?
8. How might an organization go about discovering its own "corporate image"?

DISCUSSION STARTERS

9. What was the approach of Mobil Oil in terms of public opinion in the 1970s, and why is it significant?
10. What are the "traps" of public opinion?

_____
NOTES
_____

1. Joanne Desmond, "Managing Your Media Relations," *Physician Executive,* (September–October 1989): 24.
2. Carol Stuart, "Kiam Buys Ad Space to Reiterate Apology," *USA Today* (October 1, 1990): 2C.
3. Cited in Edward L. Bernays, *Crystallizing Public Opinion* (New York: Liveright Publishing Corp., 1961), 61.
4. Cited in Harwood L. Childs, *Public Opinion: Nature, Formation, and Role* (Princeton, NJ: Van Nostrand, 1965), 15.
5. James E. Grunig and Todd Hunt, *Managing Public Relations* (New York: Holt, Rinehart & Winston, 1984), 130.
6. Leon A. Festinger, *A Theory of Cognitive Dissonance* (New York: Harper & Row, 1957), 163.
7. Abraham Maslow, *Motivation and Personality* (New York: Harper & Row, 1954).
8. S. Plous, "Toward More Effective Activism," *The Animal's Agenda* (December 1989): 24–26.
9. John V. Pavlik, *Public Relations: What Research Tells Us* (Newbury Park, CA: Sage Publications, 1987), 74.
10. Hadley Cantril, *Gauging Public Opinion* (Princeton, NJ: Princeton University Press, 1972), 226–230.
11. "Image Is a Priority to 53% of Executives Surveyed," *Wall Street Journal,* 23 July 1981.
12. J. Patrick Wright, *On a Clear Day You Can See General Motors* (New York: Avon Books, 1980), 279.
13. Ray D'Argenio, speech at the Communications Executive of the Year Luncheon, sponsored by Corpcom Services, December 10, 1981.
14. John Naisbitt and Patricia Aburdene, *Megatrends 2000* (New York: Morrow, 1990).
15. Philip Lesly, "How the Future Will Shape Public Relations—and Vice Versa," *Public Relations Quarterly* (Winter 1981–82): 7.

_____
SUGGESTED READINGS
_____

A.R.3: The Complete Annual Report & Corporate Image Planning Book. New York: Macmillan, 1988.
Axtell, Roger E., ed.,   *Do's and Taboos Around the World.* New York: The Benjamin Co., 1985.
Bennett, Amanda.   "What Went Wrong: Experts Look at the Sudden Upheaval at Allegis," *The Wall Street Journal,* 24 June 1987, 29.
Fink, Steven.   *Crisis Management: Planning for the Inevitable.* New York: AMA-COM, 1986 (135 W. 50th St.).
Garbett, Thomas F.   *How to Build a Corporation's Identity and Project Its Image.* Lexington, MA: Lexington Books, 1988.
Gilbert, Dennis A.   *Compendium of American Public Opinion.* New York: Facts on File, 1988.
Gray, James G., Jr.   *Managing the Corporate Image: The Key to Public Trust.* Westport, CT: Greenwood, 1986.

TOP OF THE SHELF

The New York Times. New York: The New York Times Company; and *The Wall Street Journal.* New York: Dow Jones & Company, Inc.

Public relations can be practiced only by understanding public opinion, and the best forums in which to study it are *The New York Times* and *The Wall Street Journal.* Their pages daily reveal the diverse views of pundits, politicians, and plain people.

Both papers, through their opinion pages and in-depth stories, express the attitudes of leaders in politics, business, science, education, journalism and the arts, on topics from abortion rights to genetic engineering to race relations. Occasionally, the *Times* and the *Journal* will supplement their usual coverage with public opinion polls to gauge attitudes and beliefs on particularly hot issues. *The Sunday Times,* with features that include the magazine section, "Week in Review" and "Business Forum," is an important resource for public relations professionals.

To influence public opinion, counselors must first understand it. Two excellent sources with which to begin the quest are *The New York Times* and *The Wall Street Journal.* Read these papers daily, and you'll keep abreast of popular thought on major issues and trends.

Idea Bank for Annual Reports. New York: Corporate Shareholder Press, 1987 (271 Madison Ave.).

Irvine, Robert B.   *When You Are the Headline: Managing a News Story.* Homewood, IL: Dow Jones-Irwin, 1987.

Leff, Suzanne.   "10 Dos and Don'ts of Naming. *Public Relations Journal* (December 1987): 37, 38. This checklist gives guidelines for coining memorable company or product names for effective promotion.

Lerbinger, Otto.   *Managing Corporate Crises: Strategies for Executives.* Boston, MA: Barrington Press, 1986 (P.O. Box 291, Boston University Station 02109).

Lipset, Seymour Martin, and William Schneider.   *The Confidence Gap: Business, Labor and Government in the Public.* New York: Free Press, 1987.

McGill, Michael.   *American Business and the Quick Fix.* New York: Holt & Co., 1988.

Mercer, Laurie, and Jennifer Singer.   *Opportunity Knocks: Using PR.* Radnor, PA: Chilton, 1989.

Meyers, Gerald.   *When It Hits the Fan.* Scarborough, Ontario: The New American Library of Canada, Limited, 1987.

Nager, Norman, and Richard Truitt.   *Strategic Public Relations Counseling.* White Plains, NY: Longman, 1987.

Napoles, Veronica.   *Corporate Identity Design.* New York: Von Nostrand Reinhold, 1987.

Olasky, Marvin N. *Corporate Public Relations & American Public Enterprise.* Hillsdale, NJ: Erlbaum, 1987.

Paluszek, John. *Business and Society: 1976–2000.* Ann Arbor, MI: Books on Demand.

Pinsdorf, M. *Communicating When Your Company Is Under Siege.* Lexington, MA: Lexington Books, 1986.

Sauerhaft, Stan, and Chris Atkins. *Image Wars.* New York: John Wiley, 1989.

Selame, Elinor, and Joseph Selame. *The Company Image: Building Your Identity & Influence in the Marketplace.* New York: John Wiley, 1988.

Sonnenfeld, Jeffrey. *The Hero's Farewell: What Happens When CEOs Retire.* New York: Oxford University Press, 1988.

Stevens, Art. *The Persuasion Explosion.* Washington, DC: Acropolis Books, 1985.

Toper, Robert. *Institutional Image: How to Define, Improve, Market It.* Washington, DC: Case, 1986 (11 Dupont Circle 20036).

Welch, Susan, and John Comer, eds., *Public Opinion: Its Formation, Measurement, and Impact.* 2d ed. Chicago: Dorsey Press, 1987.

CASE STUDY   Coke Are It

For 99 years the Coca-Cola Company—with a product that had become more American than apple pie—knew only the sweet taste of success. Then midway through 1985, because of a colossal management misjudgment based primarily on faulty research, disaster struck. In late April, Coke's hard-driving chairman, Roberto Goizueta, announced that the company would scrap the original, ninety-nine-year-old secret formula for Coca-Cola. Amid great fanfare, Goizueta introduced the new Coke with its "smoother, rounder, yet bolder—more harmonious flavor."

The reason for Coke's decision to retire the old formula was that its primary product was losing its market share to arch-competitor Pepsi-Cola and the youth-oriented "Pepsi generation" promotional campaigns. Coke needed to increase its appeal to the young, so it decided to sweeten the old recipe, bringing it closer to Pepsi.

Subsequent criticism to the contrary, Coca-Cola did not move precipitously to change the formula. In fact, it moved cau-

tiously, relying on extensive research to see whether the switch made sense. Specifically, the company spent about $4 million over 4½ years to taste-test the new soda pop on nearly 200,000 consumers. Tests took many forms. Some were blind tests without the emotion-laden brand name attached to them. Others posed such questions as, "What if this were a new Coke taste?"

The company learned from all this testing that more people liked the new, sweeter formula than liked the old. This was good news to Coke, which had consistently lost out to Pepsi in head-to-head taste tests over the years. However, Coke neglected in its research to disclose to interviewees that the product they were sipping would ultimately replace their old favorite entirely. And this, as it turned out, was a tragic research oversight.

Immediately after Goizueta's announcement, Coke launched a multimillion dollar advertising campaign to introduce the new Coke. In the first month after its introduction, new Coke showed every sign of ful-

FIGURE 4–6

filling the chairman's declaration that the decision was "one of the easiest we ever made." Indeed, shipments to Coke bottlers during that May rose by the highest percentage in five years. New Coke was tried by a record number of people for any product, and more than three-quarters of those who tried it indicated they would eagerly buy it again.

Then, without warning, the roof caved in. Articles began appearing across the country about the angry old Coke loyalists who wanted original Coke returned. Coca-Cola headquarters was flooded with thousands of angry phone calls and sacks of nasty mail. Bottlers, Coke's front-line contact with consumers, began to feel the heat, and a petition was circulated among bottlers demanding the return of the old formula.

Coca-Cola management turned again to research to find out what was going on.

■ When they polled 900 consumers about which Coke they liked better, 60 percent said old and only 30 percent said new.
■ When they followed up with a survey of another 5,000 consumers, the results only further confirmed the bad news.

■ When they held smaller, focus-group sessions to observe how consumers thought the company should deal with the problem, they kept getting the same answer: "Bring back old Coke."

So, in early July, three months after the introduction of new Coke, an embarrassed Coca-Cola president, Donald Keough, announced that the company was bringing back its old formula, now dubbed Classic Coke. New Coke, the company said, would be marketed separately to see whether it could or couldn't survive. At his press conference, Keough read from complaint letters comparing the switch in formulas to "burning the flag" and "God making the grass purple." Said Keough, "All of the time and money and skill that we poured into consumer research could not reveal the depth of feeling for the original taste of Coca-Cola."

Others agreed. One researcher told *Fortune* magazine, "Taste tests don't take into account the emotional tie-in with the old brand, which is all wrapped up with people's childhoods. Now that consumers are drinking out of cans labeled 'new' Coke, naturally there is an emotional backlash."

In 1990, five years after its ill-fated attempt to introduce New Coke, the company was ready to try again. Only this time, learning from its earlier blunder, Coca-Cola would call its new attempt "Coke II," clearly indicating that this wouldn't be another attempt to replace its cherished, best-selling, century-old formula.*

*Among the most comprehensive analyses of the new Coke saga are Ann E. B. Fisher, "Coke's Brand-Loyalty Lesson," *Fortune* (August 5, 1985): 44–46; John Koten and Scott Kilman, "How Coke's Decision to Offer two Colas Undid Four and a Half Years of Planning," *Wall Street Journal*, 15 July 1985, 1; Eric Gelman, "Hey America, Coke Are It!" *Newsweek* (July 22, 1985): 40–42; and Mark Potts, "New Coke to Try a New Name in Test," *Washington Post*, 7 March 1990, C1, C4.

QUESTIONS

1. In terms of attaining a younger image, what alternatives did the Coca-Cola Company have besides changing the original formula?
2. How could new Coke have been introduced more quietly?
3. Ultimately, why did the research that indicated consumers would enjoy new Coke backfire?
4. How do you explain the research phenomenon that 94 percent of those who hadn't tried new Coke preferred the old?
5. What does this case indicate about the vulnerability of research findings?

Tips from the Top

ROBERT L. DILENSCHNEIDER

Robert L. Dilenschneider is president and chief executive officer of Hill & Knowlton, Inc., probably the world's best-known public relations firm. He joined the firm in 1967 and led H&K's Chicago office, before returning to New York to head the worldwide, 60-office Hill & Knowlton empire. Dilenschneider has personally counseled executives in some of history's best-known crises, has been the subject of numerous magazine profiles, and is widely published. His most recent book, *Power and Influence: Mastering the Art of Persuasion,* was published in 1990 by Prentice-Hall.

Is public opinion of business tainted by ethical failure?

The failures of ethical standards in business are rarely known outside headquarters offices, unless they involve law breaking that becomes public knowledge. Obviously, the decade of the 1980s will not be recorded in history as the purest in the annals of American business. The widely publicized cases of fraud in securities dealing, mismanagement of savings and loan institutions, and the use of questionable tactics by some in takeover situations are evidence of an ethical lapse in a part of the financial world.

However, we have experienced little of it in our dealings with clients and potential clients, and that leads me to believe that corporate ethics remain at a reasonably high level.

What is the public opinion of government today?

Scandalous behavior has most frequently been traceable to bad executive appointments, rather than to low ethical behavior throughout the federal establishment. Lately we have experienced a bulge of ousters, resignations, and accusations in the Congress itself, which has undertaken reforms as a result. Throughout the political world, negative campaigning has become so common as to threaten the faith of voters in the electoral system itself.

Government is the one area of American life that is under constant inspection by the citizens and suspicion by the media. Instances of wrong-doing are usually conspicuous and widely publicized. But I believe, considering that we are served by hundreds of thousands of men and women, the ethical standards are generally good.

105

What is the general state of public relations practice today?
Over my more than 20 years in public relations, the field of counseling has evolved from a disparate group—that included scoundrels, fakes, pretenders, and rank amateurs, as well as legitimate firms—into a solid and reasonably trustworthy business.

As the charlatans dropped out of the business and newcomers entered it—many trained in communications, public relations, social studies, and other specialties—the function became much more professional. By any standards of ethics, it also became much more admirable.

Are there clients with whom you would refuse to do business?
We have refused Ivan Boesky, General Noriega, and others.

How would you assess the future of the practice of public relations?
I expect growth of 20 to 30 percent per year for the counseling branch of the public relations business, during the next few years at least. For public relations professionals working for other employers, my guess is a slower pace of growth can be anticipated.

This is not to say that the future is without risk for public relations practitioners and for the specialty itself. Our growing importance throughout society is rivaled by the ambitions of law, management consulting, and financial institutions, each of them claiming some expertise in our rather broad scope of practice. The relatively lower stature of public relations in many sectors, in respect to theirs, makes any threat from them hazardous to our health.

Yet, it is most encouraging that the public relations function is still forging ahead in both recognition by astute executives of every sort, and in stature—although we still have far to go.

Ethics

A few years ago, sociologist Raymond Baumhart asked businesspeople, "What does ethics mean to you?" Among their replies:

> Ethics has to do with what my feelings tell me is right or wrong.
> Ethics has to do with my religious beliefs.
> Being ethical is doing what the law requires.
> Ethics consists of the standards of behavior our society accepts.
> I don't know what the word means.[1]

The meaning of "ethics" is hard to pin down, and the views many people have about ethics are uncertain. Nonetheless, ethical dilemmas are all around us. In many sectors of society in the '90s, institutions are sending out mixed signals about the value of moral conduct.

Consider the following:

♦ Neil Bush, eldest son of the president of the United States, is charged with "ethical myopia" for recommending huge loans to two business associates, while he was director of a Denver savings & loan that ultimately went bankrupt.

♦ The American Express Company, among the world's largest and most prestigious corporations, contributes $8 million to settle a dispute with a former top executive, after acknowledging the corporation tried to discredit the man by linking him to illegal activities. (See the case study at the end of this chapter.)

♦ Hertz Corporation overcharges consumers and insurers $13 million for repairs to damaged rental cars.

♦ Beech-Nut Company is found guilty of secretly diluting apple juice for babies.

♦ The president of the Public Relations Society of America is forced to resign when it is revealed that he has profited from an insider-trading scheme.

What is going on here?

There may be no obvious solution that is right or that does not cause some harm. Ethical guidelines are just that—guidelines. They don't necessarily provide right answers, just educated guesses. And reasonable people can and do disagree about what is moral, ethical, and right in a given situation.

Nonetheless, when previously respected business, government, and religious leaders, as well as other members of society, are exposed as cheaters, con artists, and even crooks, those who would look up to and be influenced by such people are correctly appalled. Little wonder then that societal pressure in the area of ethics has never been more intense. In public relations no issue is more critical than ethics—of both the practice and the practitioner.

The bigness of most institutions in the 1990s—companies, schools, hospitals, associations, news organizations, and even professions like public relations—immediately makes them suspect. All have become concerned about their individual cultures—the values, ideals, principles, and aspirations that underlie their credibility and viability. As the internal conscience of many organizations, the public relations department has become a focal point for the institutionalization of ethical conduct. Increasingly, management has turned to public relations officers to lead the internal ethical charge, to be the keeper of the organizational ethic.

Ethics in Society

What exactly are *ethics?* Roughly translated, an individual's or organization's ethics come down to the standards that are followed in relationships with others—the real integrity of the individual or organization.

Public relations people, in particular, must be ethical. They can't assume that ethics are strictly personal choices without relevance or related methodology for resolving moral quandaries. Rather, as the Code of Professional Standards of the Public Relations Society of America states (Appendix A), practitioners must be scrupulously honest and trustworthy, acting at all times in the public interest, which, by definition, also represents the best interests of individual organizations. Indeed, if the ultimate goal of the public relations professional is to enhance public trust of an organization, then only the highest ethical conduct is acceptable.

The essence of the PRSA Code of Standards and that of the International Association of Business Communicators (Figure 5–7) is that *honesty* and *fairness* lie at the heart of public relations practice. In light of the field's public nature, the PRSA code underscores the importance of members promoting and maintaining "high standards of public service and ethical conduct." Inherent in these standards of the profession is the understanding that ethics have changed and continue to change as society changes. Over time, views have changed on such areas as minority discrimination, double standards in the treatment of women, pollution of the environment, destruction of endangered species and natural resources, lack of concern for human rights, and on and on. Again, honesty and fairness are two critical components that will continue to determine the ethical behavior of public relations professionals.[2]

Many in public relations have called into question the standards and values practiced by some today in a society that often demonstrates a low regard for ethics.

◆ Faced with dwindling resources, increased competition, and rising threats of acquisition by unfriendly suitors, businesses have, in alarming numbers, been exposed in their sacrifice of the ethical for the expedient. Clearly this was the case in the summer of 1988, when several of the nation's largest defense contractors were investigated for bribery and fraud involving government military contracts.

◆ Government ethics have become debatable. When executive branch officials at the highest levels of the Reagan administration, from Budget Director David Stockman to White House Press Secretary Larry Speakes (see box on pp. 118–120) to Presidential Chief of Staff Donald Regan, author kiss-and-tell memoirs that reap publishing windfalls at the expense of the president they served, are they really doing it because of the public's right to know? Even more serious, President Reagan's one-time national security advisor, John Poindexter, and his assistant, Oliver North, admit to lying to the Congress about the details of Iranscam—an Iran-Nicaragua connection that skirted U.S. law.

◆ In the legislative branch, the highest-ranking official in the House of Representatives, Speaker James Wright, is paraded before the House Ethics Committee for improperly intervening for constituents, accepting abnormally high royalties from supporters, and generally bending the rules. Several other members are accused of sexual indiscretions with members of their own and the opposite sex. In the Senate, Minnesota Republican David Durenberger is censured by his colleagues for what amounts to "stealing" from the public. Five other senators are linked inextricably to Charles Keating, one of the kingpins in the savings and loan scandal, who is also being investigated by an ethics panel.

In journalism, syndicated columnist and TV commentator Pat Buchanan is linked to anti-Semitism. Earlier, a Pulitzer Prize is won by a *Washington Post* reporter, Janet Cooke, whose heart-rending description of an impoverished young drug addict turns out to be a total fabrication. And when best-selling author Joe McGinnes promises to write a "sympathetic" treatise about accused family murderer Jeffrey MacDonald, the author proceeds to slam his trusting subject in the subsequent best seller.

♦ In the ministry, so-called televangelists, like Jim Bakker and Jimmy Swaggert, are called to task for their hypocritical "sins of the flesh."

♦ Even the United Transportation Union in New York City is exposed as a front for the Philip Morris cigarette company; the union's Open Letter advertising campaign against a proposed smoking ban on commuter trains turns out to be clandestinely written and paid for by Philip Morris.

Ethical violations are certainly not new in society: the 1919 Black Sox scandal in baseball, the 1950s salad oil scandal in business, and numerous government scandals over the years are cases in point. Nonetheless, people today are legitimately concerned about the increasing incidence of ethical violations in a seemingly value-free, self-indulgent society. Nowhere is the push for higher ethical standards more pronounced than in the areas of business, journalism, and public relations.

Ethics in Business

For many people today, regrettably, the term *business ethics* is an oxymoron. Its mere mention stimulates thoughts of unscrupulous financiers like Ivan Boesky and Michael Milken illegally raking in millions of dollars with insider stock tips or of companies like Rockwell International being indicted by a federal grand jury for defrauding the U.S. Air Force.

Fraud, price-gouging, runaway pollution—all these allegations have made headlines in recent years. And American business, perhaps the most ethical business system in the world, has been shocked—so much so that in 1987 the former Securities and Exchange Commission chairman, John Shad, donated $23 million to begin a program at Harvard Business School to make the study of ethics an integral part of the curriculum.*

Mr. Shad is not alone. Fearing public and government retribution, companies are

♦ developing ethical codes and credos in the form of handbooks, policy statements, and guidelines.

♦ conducting training sessions, preferably by line managers, on ethical conduct.

*Ironically Mr. Shad, himself, was the subject of an embarrassing ethical dilemma. He was called in to head Drexel Burnham Lambert, after the firm was fined and discredited for junk-bond indiscretions, led by Milken. Shad was duly mortified when Drexel Burnham went belly up in 1989.

◆ creating ethics committees that report to top management or the board of directors.

◆ providing toll-free numbers or other means for employees to blow the whistle on ethics violators.

◆ conducting surveys to ensure ethical compliance.

◆ demonstrating enforcement by punishing ethics violators.[3]

In one significant 1988 study, a leading business group, the Business Roundtable, pointed out the "crucial role of the chief executive officer and top managers in establishing a strong commitment to ethical conduct and in providing constant leadership in tending and reviewing the values of the organization."[4] The Roundtable study debunked the myth that there is an inherent contradiction between ethics and profits. On the contrary, it emphasized that there is a strong relationship between acting ethically, maintaining a good reputation for fair and honest business, and making money.

Another 1988 study of key business leaders, conducted by the accounting firm Touche Ross, corroborated the notion that a majority of business leaders—63 percent—"believe that a business enterprise actually 'strengthens' its competitive position by maintaining high ethical standards." Only 14 percent said that a company with high ethical standards was a "weaker competitor."[5] The Touche Ross research on more than 1,000 business leaders also turned up other interesting findings about the current state of business ethics.

◆ Intense concentration on short-term earnings is a major threat to American business ethics today. Respondents ranked this threat almost equal to that posed by decay in cultural and social institutions.

◆ Respondents ranked the United States as having higher standards of business ethics than any other country—noting high standards also in the United Kingdom, Canada, Switzerland, and Germany.

◆ Among industries, respondents ranked commercial banking, utilities, and drugs, pharmaceuticals, and cosmetics as the three most ethical.

◆ Among all professions, respondents ranked the clergy, teachers, engineers, and accountants as the four most ethical.[6]

One business problem that leads to ethical abuses is the murkiness of the law, from insider-trading regulations to the laws that govern access to personal records via computers. An activity that is legal is not necessarily ethical. Regrettably, the wave of ethics violations in business has stimulated a rash of so-called white-collar crime, such as stealing company secrets and equipment. The power of computers has exacerbated the problem. And if business is not quick to reverse this trend, an antibusiness backlash is sure to follow.

In response, a more positive peer pressure among business leaders and companies is emerging. When Niels Hoyvald of Beech-Nut Nutrition Corporation was found guilty in 1988 of 351 counts of violating the Food, Drug and Cosmetic Act—his company misrepresented as pure apple juice a product it distributed to babies—Hoyvald's lawyers came up with a unique proposition to spare him from a prison sentence. Specifically, said his lawyer, Brendan V. Sullivan (who also served as Oliver North's attorney), let Mr. Hoyvald teach ethics to business students: "Business students undoubtedly hear this principle regularly in their ethics classes. But the impact of the message would be far clearer coming from Niels Hoyvald, whose career has been shattered because he did not heed it, than it could ever be coming from a textbook or a professor." The judge rejected the lawyer's appeal.

Corporate Codes of Conduct

In addition to corporate executives becoming ethics teachers, another manifestation of the increased attention to corporate ethics is the growth of internal codes of conduct. Codes of ethics, standards of conduct, and similar statements of corporate policies and values have proliferated in recent years.

The reasons corporations have adopted such codes vary from company to company.

♦ **To increase public confidence** The scandals concerning overseas bribery and domestic political campaign contributions during the 1970s led to a decline of public trust and confidence in business. Many firms responded with written codes of ethics.

♦ **To stem the tide of regulation** As public confidence declined, government regulation of business increased. Some estimated the cost to society of compliance with regulations at $100 billion per year. Corporate codes of conduct, it was hoped, would serve as a self-regulation mechanism.

♦ **To improve internal operations** As companies became larger and more decentralized, management needed consistent standards of conduct to assure that employees were meeting the business objectives of the company in a legal and ethical manner.

♦ **To respond to transgressions** Frequently when a company itself was caught in the web of unethical behavior, it responded with its own code of ethics. For example, the McCormick Company instituted an ethics plan after it was revealed that its grocery products division had inflated sales and earnings figures, which ultimately required the company to restate its earnings over a five-year period.[7]

Ralph Waldo Emerson once wrote that "an organization is the lengthened shadow of a man." By the 1990s, many corporate executives realized that just as an individual has certain responsibilities as a citizen, so, too, does a corporate citizen have responsibilities to the society in which it is privileged to operate (Figure 5–1).

Corporate codes of conduct are not without their critics. Some ethics specialists say that what is contained in the codes doesn't really address ethics in general. A Washington State University study of ethical codes at 200 Fortune 500 companies found that while 75 percent failed to address

Our Guiding Principles

Over our long history we have evolved standards and values guiding the management of the company that comprise an unwritten creed. These beliefs are central to conducting our affairs responsibly in fulfilling our obligations to shareowners, employees, customers and the communities in which we work.

Two contemporary developments suggest that a more formal statement of the company's principles is in order. One, the substantial increase in the size and geographic breadth of the company, and, two, the growing interest of the public in the ethical practices and social commitments of business. To be responsive to these new needs, our Board of Directors two years ago approved a written declaration of the canons that have guided this company's operations for so many years.

Since these are not static rules to be filed, but active principles to be practiced, they have recently been reviewed and again endorsed.

Implicit in the responsible conduct of the affairs of the company is one fundamental consideration — our consistent compliance with all pertinent laws, regulations and ethical standards.

These principles are personal and important to us. Obviously, they are not unique. We share many of them with other responsible and successful members of the business community.

We set forth these guiding principles looking ahead to continued growth for our company, improvement in the quality of life of our people and continued constructive relationships with the communities closest to us.

T M Ford
Chairman and President

FIGURE 5–1   The principles enumerated here by the chief executive of the Emhart Corporation represent the obligations the company believes it has to its corporate community. *(Courtesy of Emhart Corporation)*

the company's role in civic and community affairs, consumer relations, environmental safety, and product safety, more than 75 percent dealt with conflicts of interest—which can affect the bottom line.[8] Such skepticism notwithstanding, formal ethical codes, addressing such topics as confidentiality of corporate information, misappropriation of corporate assets, bribes and kickbacks, and political contributions, have become a corporate fact of life in the 1990s.

YOU MAKE THE CALL

The Bank's South Africa Policy

To: Barrie Clem, Bigge Bank Public Affairs Director
From: I. M. DeLaw, Chairman of the Board
Re: South Africa Policy

My office has just learned that next Tuesday, the day of our annual shareholders' meeting, a group of community activists, politicians, religious leaders, and Harvard University students will convene on the plaza surrounding headquarters to demonstrate against our involvement in South Africa. The group refers to itself as Foes of Apartheid Policy, or simply FAP.

Basically, FAP is attacking us because of our current policy with respect to South Africa. They are demanding that we do the following:

- Immediately cease lending money to the government of South Africa, its parastatal institutions, Namibia, or the Homelands
- Immediately cease lending money to the private sector in South Africa
- Close down our office in Johannesburg and fire the 20 staff members working there
- Publicly excoriate the policy of apartheid

As you know, for the last 30 years our bank has loaned money to the government of South Africa. Last year, we barely broke even on these loans. However, we made $10 million on loans to the private sector in South Africa. As you also know, we regularly contribute to South African nonprofit institutions, including $400,000 over the years to institutions active in educational, community development, and legal efforts—all of which help nonwhites.

Our bank has also been a signer of the Sullivan Principles, the generally accepted criterion for measuring corporate behavior in South Africa. We also have felt that lending to firms in South Africa who support black employment is in everyone's best interests. And 6 of our 20 Johannesburg staffers are nonwhite.

Nonetheless, we've got a real problem here. For one thing, the city council has proposed a bill prohibiting the city from depositing funds in banks that make loans to the South African government and its agencies. As you know, we do a *lot* of business with the city.

Furthermore, I understand that Columbia University, Fairleigh Dickinson University, and Purdue University, among others, all have decided to divest themselves of stock holdings in banks that loan to the government of South Africa. As you know, these universities have a goodly number of Bigge Bank shares.

With these FAPs running around, we'll clearly need to respond at the annual meeting with answers to their most pressing questions.

I need your help. We don't have much time. Please be back to me shortly on how we should handle these hot potatoes.

Thank you and Godspeed.

I. M. D.

QUESTIONS

1. If you were Clem, would you suggest that the bank continue lending to the government of South Africa and related institutions?
2. Should the bank continue lending to the private sector in South Africa?
3. Should the bank remove its Johannesburg office?
4. What should be the bank's South Africa policy?

Corporate Social Responsibility

Closely related to the ethical conduct of an organization is its social responsibility, which has been defined as a social norm. This norm holds that any social institution, including the smallest family unit and the largest corporation, is responsible for the behavior of its members and may be held accountable for their misdeeds.

In the late 1960s, when this idea was just emerging, initial responses were of the knee-jerk variety. A firm that was threatened by increasing legal or activist pressures and harassment would ordinarily change its policies in a hurry. Today, however, organizations and their social responsibility programs are much more sophisticated. Social responsibility is treated just like any other management discipline—you analyze the issues, evaluate performance, set priorities, allocate resources to those priorities, and implement programs that deal with issues within the constraints of your resources.

Many companies have created special committees to set the agenda and target the objectives. The primary concerns of the Corporate Responsibility Committee of Chase Manhattan Bank are illustrative.

1. To continue Chase's leadership in equal opportunity employment, both at home and abroad
2. To foster a broader and healthier economic base in New York City and other areas served by the bank
3. To encourage housing and community development facilities
4. To improve the physical and cultural environment of the bank's community

B E T W E E N   T H E   L I N E S

The $100,000 Lesson Plan

In 1987, when the Columbia Business School asked Asher B. Edelman, an expert on corporate takeovers, to teach a course on corporate raiding, Dean John C. Burton thought students would gain some valuable lessons. Exactly how valuable he was soon to learn. As a final exam, Mr. Edelman offered a finder's fee of $100,000 to the student who could identify a corporate takeover candidate that the professor would actually decide to buy.

When the *New York Times* and others publicized the $100,000 student assignment, Dean Burton rescinded the offer. "We felt that the linkage between direct economic incentive and what goes on in the classroom—especially an incentive of this magnitude—would bias the academic environment," Dean Burton said. Mr. Edelman did not agree, citing "a violation of the integrity of the classroom, of my right to teach after I was hired, and of the students' right to learn."

Reaction to Dean Burton's squelching of the deal was generally applauded. Said the publisher of Columbia's campus newspaper, "Business school professors should teach students how to be ethical and how to be good managers, not how to be millionaires." Most periodicals and other business school leaders also applauded Dean Burton's action. But there was at least one disgruntled group—Professor Edelman's students. In a poll taken by the professor after the dean's declaration, only one of 14 students backed the dean. The rest saw nothing wrong with the incentive. Said one, "When money is introduced, your energy is channeled into areas where it ordinarily wouldn't be. With $100,000 you have to ask, 'Can I afford *not* to concentrate on that?' "*

*Also see Leslie Wayne, "Columbia Gives 'F' to a $100,000 Lesson Plan," *New York Times*, 14 October 1987, A1, D6; Nancy J. Perry, "Edelman's Art of Reward," *Fortune* (November 9, 1987): 159; and Barbara Kantrowitz and Tessa Namuth, "A $100,000 Question Stirs up Columbia," *Newsweek* (October 26, 1987): 76.

5. To initiate comprehensive international social responsibility programs

Social responsibility touches practically every level of organizational activity, from marketing to hiring, from training to work standards. A partial list of social responsibility categories might include the following:

- **Product lines**—dangerous products, product performance and standards, packaging, and environmental impact
- **Marketing practices**—sales practices, consumer complaint policies, advertising content, and fair pricing
- **Employee services**—training, counseling and placement services, transfer procedures, and educational allowances
- **Corporate philanthropy**—contribution performance, encouragement of employee participation in social projects, and community development activities
- **Environmental activities**—pollution-control projects, adherence to federal standards, and evaluation procedures of new packages and products
- **External relations**—support of minority enterprises, investment practices, and government relations
- **Employment of minorities and women**—current hiring policies, advancement policies, specialized career counseling, and opportunities for special minorities, such as the physically handicapped
- **Employee safety and health**—work environment policies, accident safeguards, and food and medical facilities

More often than not, organizations have incorporated social responsibility into the mainstream of their practice. Most firms recognize that social responsibility, far from being an add-on program, must be a corporate way of life. Beyond this, some studies have indicated that those organizations that practice social responsibility over time rank among the most profitable and successful firms in society.

Ethics in Government

Politics has never enjoyed an unblemished reputation. But lately, American politics has gotten downright sleazy. The savings and loan scandal of the early '90s implicated everyone from longstanding U.S. senators to the son of the president of the United States. Neil Bush, the president's eldest son, doggedly defended himself against improprieties while he was a director of Colorado's Silverado Banking, Savings and Loan Association. But prior to Silverado's collapse late in 1988, Bush recommended that Silverado loan significant cash to two of his business partners. This despite the fact, according to allegations, that Bush failed adequately to disclose his business relationship with the borrowers. Silverado's collapse subsequently cost taxpayers $1 billion.

BETWEEN   THE   LINES

Larry Speakes No More

The sad saga of former White House press secretary Larry Speakes is as pointed an example of an ethical dilemma as any in recent public relations history. By all accounts, Speakes served President Ronald Reagan as an able and respected spokesperson. His credo seemed to be to tell the truth, no matter what. Indeed, Speakes was interviewed for the third edition of *The Practice of Public Relations* shortly after leaving the White House and offered the following observations:

What is the biggest problem of the president's press secretary?
It is impossible to identify something as the "biggest" problem. One of the greatest frustrations of the job was the fact that most reporters automatically assumed the government was lying. This was the aftermath of Watergate, but it was inappropriately and unfairly applied to the Reagan administration. We told the truth; I was always a bit disadvantaged when I was forced to convince people I was doing so.

What is the overriding objective of the president's chief spokesman?
My overriding objective as the president's chief spokesman was to tell the truth.

What advice would you give to the public relations practitioners of the future?
I would advise practitioners to do two things: (1) tell the truth, and (2) understand that journalists have a job to do and be as considerate of their professional needs as you expect them to be of yours.*

Such words would come back to haunt the former press secretary. In mid-1988, having become communications director of Merrill Lynch, Speakes revealed in his book *Speaking Out* that he had manufactured quotes and had attributed them to President Reagan. For example, when Reagan and Soviet leader Mikhail Gorbachev held their historic first meeting in Geneva in 1985, according to Speakes White House officials found Mr. Gorbachev to be a master at handling the press "while Reagan was very tentative and stilted." Consequently, Speakes told reporters that the president had said, "There is much that divides us, but I believe the world breathes easier because we are talking

*Fraser P. Seitel, *The Practice of Public Relations*, 3d ed. (Columbus, OH: Merrill Publishing Company, 1987), 137.

together," and the quote was widely reported by American news organizations, even though the president hadn't really said it. In his book, Speakes conceded in retrospect that it was "clearly wrong to take such liberties," even though the president would not have disavowed the words—until Speakes's book came out, that is.

In a ringing denunciation Larry Speakes's successor at the White House, Marlin Fitzwater, characterized his predecessor's actions as a "damn outrage." Merrill Lynch wasn't particularly happy either, reportedly alarmed that Speakes's admissions might tarnish its new ad campaign, "A Tradition of Trust." Two weeks after his book's publication, Speakes resigned from his Merrill Lynch job.

And the lesson in all of this? Frankly, despite the self-righteous indignation of the media, the lesson isn't at all clear. Like it or not, public relations people do indeed fabricate statements for their employers—it goes with the territory. And if such statements are approved by employers in advance, ethical questions are less pertinent. However, public relations people rarely announce or even acknowledge that they have authored such statements. Ironically, then, in violating the confidence of the president by retrospectively telling the truth about the bogus quotes, Larry Speakes may have committed his most costly misstep.

President Bush's troubles followed President Reagan's numerous ethical dilemmas, including a scandal in his Housing and Urban Development department; the secret Iran-Contra negotiations of national security advisor John Poindexter and Colonel Oliver North; and the lobbying violations of presidential assistants Lynn Nofziger and Mike Deaver.

On Capitol Hill, the sleaze factor was strictly bipartisan. The Democratic speaker of the house, Jim Wright, reportedly intervened for the late Egyptian President Anwar Sadat on behalf of a business friend seeking oil rights in Egypt and intervened similarly at the Interior Department to influence the award of gas leases to a company in which Wright had a $15,000 investment. Wright also received an unheard-of royalty of 55 percent on sales of an alleged book of his thoughts, published by a wealthy supporter. To top things off, Wright's principal aide was forced to resign in 1989 when news coverage revealed that he had brutally attacked a young woman 16 years earlier and received a jail sentence.

Finally, in the winter of 1990, the public was "treated" to the spectacle of five U.S. senators—Democrats and Republicans—accused of ethical violations in support of Charles Keating, a notorious S&L operator. The senators ranted and raved about the unfairness of the highly publicized hearings. But like it or not, the "Keating Five," in the eyes of most of their countrymen, stood guilty of a special degree of ethical ignominy.

The sleaze factor in government is, of course, nothing new. In 1976, when the shah of Iran was petitioning Congress for financial aid, the wife of influential New York Senator Jacob Javits was drawing down $500,000 from Iran as a public relations representative for the country. However, society today seems increasingly less willing to tolerate such violations from those whose livelihood depends on public trust. In the 1990s, it is likely that ethics in government will become an even more important issue, as fed-up voters insist on representatives who are honest, trustworthy, and clean.

Ethics in Journalism

The Society of Professional Journalists, Sigma Delta Chi, is quite explicit on the subject of ethics (Figure 5–2).

> Journalists at all times will show respect for the dignity, privacy, rights and well-being of people encountered in the course of gathering and presenting the news.

THE SOCIETY OF PROFESSIONAL JOURNALISTS,
SIGMA DELTA CHI

Code
of Ethics

THE SOCIETY of Professional Journalists, Sigma Delta Chi believes the duty of journalists is to serve the truth.
WE BELIEVE the agencies of mass communication are carriers of public discussion and information, acting on their Constitutional mandate and freedom to learn and report the facts.
WE BELIEVE in public enlightenment as the forerunner of justice, and in our Constitutional role to seek the truth as part of the public's right to know the truth.
WE BELIEVE those responsibilities carry obligations that require journalists to perform with intelligence, objectivity, accuracy and fairness.

To these ends, we declare acceptance of the standards of practice here set forth:

RESPONSIBILITY:
The public's right to know of events of public importance and interest is the overriding mission of the mass media. The purpose of distributing news and enlightened opinion is to serve the general welfare. Journalists who use their professional status as representatives of the public for selfish or other unworthy motives violate a high trust.

FREEDOM OF THE PRESS:
Freedom of the press is to be guarded as an inalienable right of people in a free society. It carries with it the freedom and the responsibility to discuss, question and challenge actions and utterances of our government and of our public and private institutions. Journalists uphold the right to speak unpopular opinions and the privilege to agree with the majority.

ETHICS:
Journalists must be free of obligation to any interest other than the public's right to know the truth.
1. Gifts, favors, free travel, special treatment or privileges can compromise the integrity of journalists and their employers. Nothing of value should be accepted.
2. Secondary employment, political involvement, holding public office and service in community organizations should be avoided if it compromises the integrity of journalists and their employers. Journalists and their employers should conduct their personal lives in a manner which protects them from conflict of interest, real or apparent. Their responsibilities to the public are paramount. That is the nature of their profession.

3. So-called news communications from private sources should not be published or broadcast without substantiation of their claims to news value.
4. Journalists will seek news that serves the public interest, despite the obstacles. They will make constant efforts to assure that the public's business is conducted in public and that public records are open to public inspection.
5. Journalists acknowledge the newsman's ethic of protecting confidential sources of information.

ACCURACY AND OBJECTIVITY:
Good faith with the public is the foundation of all worthy journalism.
1. Truth is our ultimate goal.
2. Objectivity in reporting the news is another goal, which serves as the mark of an experienced professional. It is a standard of performance toward which we strive. We honor those who achieve it.
3. There is no excuse for inaccuracies or lack of thoroughness.
4. Newspaper headlines should be fully warranted by the contents of the articles they accompany. Photographs and telecasts should give an accurate picture of an event and not highlight a minor incident out of context.
5. Sound practice makes clear distinction between news reports and expressions of opinion. News reports should be free of opinion or bias and represent all sides of an issue.
6. Partisanship in editorial comment which knowingly departs from the truth violates the spirit of American journalism.
7. Journalists recognize their responsibility for offering informed analysis, comment and editorial opinion on public events and issues. They accept the obligation to present such material by individuals whose competence, experience and judgment qualify them for it.
8. Special articles or presentations devoted to advocacy or the writer's own conclusions and interpretations should be labeled as such.

FAIR PLAY:
Journalists at all times will show respect for the dignity, privacy, rights and well-being of people encountered in the course of gathering and presenting the news.
1. The news media should not communicate unofficial charges affecting reputation or moral character without giving the accused a chance to reply.
2. The news media must guard against invading a person's right to privacy.
3. The media should not pander to morbid curiosity about details of vice and crime.
4. It is the duty of news media to make prompt and complete correction of their errors.
5. Journalists should be accountable to the public for their reports and the public should be encouraged to voice its grievances against the media. Open dialogue with our readers, viewers and listeners should be fostered.

PLEDGE:
Journalists should actively censure and try to prevent violations of these standards, and they should encourage their observance by all newspeople. Adherence to this code of ethics is intended to preserve the bond of mutual trust and respect between American journalists and the American people.

FIGURE 5–2 The Society of Professional Journalists, Sigma Delta Chi, has elaborated in some detail on the ethical guidelines that should govern reporters and editors.

1. The news media should not communicate unofficial charges affecting reputation or moral character without giving the accused a chance to reply.
2. The news media must guard against invading a person's right to privacy.
3. The media should not pander to morbid curiosity about details of vice and crime.

And so on.

Unfortunately, what is in the code often doesn't reflect what appears in print or on the air. More often than not, journalistic judgments run smack into ethical principles.

♦ In 1984, when presidential candidate Jesse Jackson held a background breakfast with some reporters, his words were supposed to be unattributable to him in print. One attendee, Milton Coleman of the *Washington Post,* later told a colleague that the candidate had referred to Jews as "Hymie" and to New York as "Hymietown." Although Coleman never used the material in the *Post,* his colleague did, and Jackson's relations with the Jewish community suffered irreparably.

♦ That same year, when Senator Gary Hart became the Democratic front-runner for the presidential nomination, *Miami Herald* reporters staked out his Washington home long enough to notice that an attractive blond visitor came in one day and didn't leave until early the next. The resulting scandal cost Hart not only the nomination, but also the remainder of his political career. *Miami Herald* executives argued that surreptitiously trailing Hart was ethical because the public had a right to know.

♦ In 1988, when a Steele County, Minnesota, woman's description of a bloody fight between two men was broadcast over the police radio band, she begged an *Owatonna People's Press* reporter not to use her name. She feared reprisal from either or both of the men. The next day's story reported her name, address, and an account of what she had seen. The following day one of the men was found stabbed to death, and the other was arrested not far from the woman's home.

♦ In 1990, the banking reporter and business editor of the *St. Petersburg (FL.) Times* resigned under pressure when it was disclosed that they dealt in the stocks of companies they wrote about. Because the *Times'* policy cautions reporters to "avoid even the appearance of a conflict and to ask their supervisors if they have doubts about an investment," the two men were let go.

These examples—all of questionable ethics—illustrate the difficulty of living up to journalistic codes of ethics. A journalist's job is to get the story. Often that means trampling over the personal privacy and trust of the subject.

Once this man held a flaming torch...now he wants to hold office..

You're an editor. One of your reporters learns that a candidate for public office once was a member of the Ku Klux Klan. But, on further investigation, she finds out that the man was actually a federal informant. To reveal his name could mean death for him and his family. Do you print the whole story? Part of it? Or suppress it?

As reported in FineLine, this real life ethical dilemma raises tough questions about the right of privacy and the public's right to know. If you've faced similar situations, FineLine would like you to share them with us and your colleagues.

And we'll pay you $500 for every accepted article.

For more information on how you can be a contributor or to subscribe contact ...

FineLine™

The Newsletter On Journalism Ethics

600 E. Main Street, Louisville, Kentucky 40202 • 502/584-8182 • Robin Hughes, Editor • Barry Bingham, Jr., Publisher

FIGURE 5–3 The topic of journalistic ethics in the 1990s has become such an important one that newsletters like this one have begun to emerge. *(Courtesy of Fine-Line)*

Many times the ethical decisions faced by journalists are subtle ones. For example, a journalist quoting an anonymous source in a news story runs up against an ethical dilemma; most of the time such sources have a bias toward the issue on which they are commenting—an anonymous Democrat talking about a Republican program, a competitor talking about a rival firm's product, or a securities analyst talking about a favorite or a despised stock. Clearly, journalists and editors can't be totally objective, but they should always strive to be fair. That involves being aware of the biases and hidden agendas of news sources and understanding the ethical questions raised by quoting such sources.

The point is that a sense of ethics helps an individual make moral decisions, and journalists have to make their decisions with speed and certainty. They can't usually afford to say maybe, and they can never say, "We'll have time to get back to this when the dust settles." Their decisions must meet a deadline. Usually, the principles, values, and ideals that get reported depend largely on the individual doing the reporting.

Ethics In Public Relations

In light of numerous misconceptions about what the practice of public relations is or isn't, it is imperative that practitioners emulate the highest standards of personal and professional ethics. Within an organization, public relations practitioners must be the standard bearers of corporate ethical initiatives. By the same token, public relations consultants must always counsel their clients in an ethical direction—toward accuracy and candor and away from lying and hiding the truth.

The Public Relations Society of America has been a leader in the effort to foster a strong sense of ethics among its membership. Its Code of Professional Standards is a model in the attempt to promulgate high standards of public service and ethical conduct. In recent years, the PRSA code has been tested on a variety of issues, ranging from noncompetition agreements with the employees of a public relations firm, to the protection of public relations campaign proposals to prospective clients, to paying employees and consultants finder's fees to obtain new accounts.

In 1987, a study by the Foundation for Public Relations Research and Education, covering the years 1950 to 1985, revealed a strong adherence in the field to the ethical code originally adopted in 1950. During that period of time, 168 issues and complaints were registered and investigated. Articles of the code most frequently cited were these:

♦ A member shall deal fairly with clients or employers—past, present, and potential—with fellow practitioners, and with the general public.

◆ A member shall adhere to truth and accuracy and to generally accepted standards of good taste.

◆ A member shall conduct his or her professional life in accord with the public interest.

◆ A member shall not intentionally communicate false or misleading information and is obligated to use care to avoid communication of false or misleading information.

◆ A member shall not engage in any practice that tends to corrupt the channels of communication or the processes of government.

The foundation concluded that the code, with its enforcement provisions, is a good one: "It has been, can be, and will be improved. It is a vibrant, living document that depends, as our future and that of public relations depends, on constant understanding and application by the society's members."[9]

Ironically, in 1986, the president of the Public Relations Society of America, Anthony M. Franco, abruptly resigned after signing an SEC consent decree following charges of insider-trading violations. Even more ironic, Franco said in his defense, "I had legal advice but no outside public relations counsel, which I should have gotten."[10]

Although the Franco case embarrassed the public relations field, the Public Relations Society didn't shrink from the ethical challenge in subsequent years. When Speakes had his fabricated quotes problem in 1988, PRSA President Dwayne Summar was quick to renounce that conduct as "inconsistent with the Public Relations Society of America's Code of Standards for the Practice of Public Relations." Summar went on to point out that Speakes didn't join PRSA until after he left his position as the president's chief spokesman. "In becoming a member, he pledged to uphold the code," Summar said.[11] At the World Congress of Public Relations in Melbourne, Australia, that same year, Summar reported that the PRSA was organizing a common code of ethics that could be adopted by public relations associations around the world. One such code of ethics was that adopted by the International Association of Business Communicators (Figure 5–4).

Among the general public, the relatively strong state of public relations ethics apparently is being recognized more. In a 1989 ethics survey of The Pinnacle Group, businesspersons ranked public relations practitioners fifth among occupations in terms of ethics. Public relations counselors ranked ahead of lawyers, funeral home operators, and advertising professionals. In the same survey, senior high school students ranked public relations professionals seventh in terms of ethics, with doctors, dentists, accountants, and yes, even lawyers, outpacing public relations people.[12]

IABC CODE OF ETHICS

The IABC Code of Ethics has been developed to provide IABC members and other communication professionals with guidelines of professional behavior and standards of ethical practice. The Code will be reviewed and revised as necessary by the Ethics Committee and the Executive Board.

Any IABC member who wishes advice and guidance regarding its interpretation and/or application may write or phone IABC headquarters. Questions will be routed to the Executive Board member responsible for the Code.

Communication and Information Dissemination

1. Communication professionals will uphold the credibility and dignity of their profession by encouraging the practice of honest, candid and timely communication.

The highest standards of professionalism will be upheld in all communication. Communicators should encourage frequent communication and messages that are honest in their content, candid, accurate and appropriate to the needs of the organization and its audiences.

2. Professional communicators will not use any information that has been generated or appropriately acquired by a business for another business without permission. Further, communicators should attempt to identify the source of information to be used.

When one is changing employers, information developed at the previous position will not be used without permission from that employer. Acts of plagiarism and copyright infringement are illegal acts; material in the public domain should have its source attributed, if possible. If an organization grants permission to use its information and requests public acknowledgment, it will be made in a place appropriate to the material used. The material will be used only for the purpose for which permission was granted.

Standards of Conduct

3. Communication professionals will abide by the spirit and letter of all laws and regulations governing their professional activities.

All international, national and local laws and regulations must be observed, with particular attention to those pertaining to communication, such as copyright law. Industry and organizational regulations will also be observed.

4. Communication professionals will not condone any illegal or unethical act related to their professional activity, their organization and its business or the public environment in which it operates.

It is the personal responsibility of professional communicators to act honestly, fairly and with integrity at all times in all professional activities. Looking the other way while others act illegally tacitly condones such acts whether or not the communicator has committed them. The communicator should speak with the individual involved, his or her supervisor or appropriate authorities – depending on the context of the situation and one's own ethical judgment.

Confidentiality/Disclosure

5. Communication professionals will respect the confidentiality and right-to-privacy of all individuals, employers, clients and customers.

Communicators must determine the ethical balance between right-to-privacy and need-to-know. Unless the situation involves illegal or grossly unethical acts, confidences should be maintained. If there is a conflict between right-to-privacy and need-to-know, a communicator should first talk with the source and negotiate the need for the information to be communicated.

6. Communication professionals will not use any confidential information gained as a result of professional activity for personal benefit or for that of others.

Confidential information can be used to give inside advantage to stock transactions, gain favors from outsiders, assist a competing company for whom one is going to work, assist companies in developing a marketing advantage, achieve a publishing advantage or otherwise act to the detriment of an organization. Such information must remain confidential during and after one's employment period.

Professionalism

7. Communication professionals should uphold IABC's standards for ethical conduct in all professional activity, and should use IABC and its designation of accreditation (ABC) only for purposes that are authorized and fairly represent the organization and its professional standards.

IABC recognizes the need for professional integrity within any organization, including the association. Members should acknowledge that their actions reflect on themselves, their organizations and their profession.

Printed with the assistance of the Mead Corporation and Brown & Kroger Printing, Dayton, OH

FIGURE 5–4 The International Association of Business Communicators adopted these seven tenets to guide the professional behavior of its members.

The success of public relations in the 1990s and beyond will depend to a large degree on how the field responds to the issue of ethical conduct. Public relations professionals must have credibility in order to practice. They must be respected by the various publics with whom they interact. To be credible and to achieve respect, public relations professionals must be ethical. It is that simple.

Corporations in the '90s will be buffeted by ethical dilemmas in all aspects of their business. For example, in 1990, when the Planned Parenthood Foundation became more outspoken in the national debate over abortion, American Telephone & Telegraph Co. halted its sizable donation—for the first time in 25 years. AT&T decided that it didn't want to be associated with the political fight over abortion. This touched off a firestorm among AT&T employees and other corporate givers, with a few major contributors quietly joining AT&T on the Planned Parenthood sidelines. It also triggered a strong rebuttal from Planned Parenthood (see Figure 5–5).

The media, too, are confronting significant ethical questions. In this post-Watergate era of journalism, reporting the facts sometimes is less important than finding a hook that is controversial. Television journalism, in particular, has been confronted with disturbing ethical dilemmas. Today, when hostages are seized or terrorists spring to power, more often than not, television journalists rush headlong to broadcast as much of the story as quickly as possible. Often, in recent years, this rush has nurtured terrorist purposes. Television reached perhaps its lowest ebb in the summer of 1985, when a TWA commercial aircraft was hijacked in the Middle East and "the hostages' survival was the terrorists' admission ticket for on-going access to the media—and world opinion."[13]

In 1990, likewise, television networks were criticized by the Bush administration for giving Iraq's Saddam Hussein freedom to dominate the U.S. airwaves whenever he chose. The CIA, on the other hand, evidently welcomed Saddam's network access because it helped the agency piece together the dictator's battle plans. In any event, media excesses regarding terrorist actions have brought into question Edward R. Murrow's warning that terrorists shouldn't be permitted to "shoot their way onto our air."

To be sure, it's difficult—for the media or anyone else—to act ethically when working with unethical mandates. For the public relations profession in general and individual public relations practitioners in particular, credibility in the years ahead will depend on how scrupulously they observe and apply ethical principles in everything they do.

CAVING IN TO EXTREMISTS, AT&T HANGS UP ON PLANNED PARENTHOOD.

In March, AT&T announced it was cutting off twenty-five years of philanthropic support to Planned Parenthood.

For the record, AT&T's annual grant was devoted to preventing teen pregnancy.

It did not pay for abortion services.

Nor did it aid Planned Parenthood's efforts to protect the health of women by keeping abortion safe and legal.

In fact, AT&T was helping *us* avert abortion by teaching teenagers how to avoid unintended pregnancies.

Yet AT&T caved in to anti-choice extremists, just weeks before the annual meeting at which the question was to be openly discussed and voted on by shareholders.

And decided to leave teens at risk.

The free exchange of information is basic to AT&T's communications business.

By catering to a closed-minded minority intolerant of differing ideas, AT&T is working against its own best interests.

It only encourages those who use bullying tactics to stop women of all ages from getting the information they need to make their own personal, private decisions.

The saddest part of this shameful episode is that AT&T's action has only made abortions more likely.

Indeed, in a panic to distance itself from Planned Parenthood, AT&T has sent a message that education and family planning — the only safe and sure ways to reduce abortion — are unworthy of support.

That's precisely what the anti-choice extremists want. To see their threats succeed. To silence discussion. And take away *all* our choices, one by one.

This time, family planning was the target.

But what's next on their hit list? And who will have the integrity to stand fast?

We urge you to send a message back by mailing the coupons below.

AT&T advertises itself as "the right choice."

It's time to remind the company what the word really means.

TO: Robert E. Allen, Chairman and CEO,
AT&T
550 Madison Avenue, New York, NY 10022-3297

As a [ ] stockholder, [ ] customer, [ ] employee of AT&T, I'm shocked that you have caved in to a small group of extremists and cut off support for Planned Parenthood. This isn't a case of being "caught in the middle." You were unwilling to stand by a worthy organization being attacked for defending values fundamental to our way of life. I urge you to reconsider this shameful action.

NAME

ADDRESS

CITY   STATE   ZIP

I want to help make up for AT&T's corporate cowardice and help Planned Parenthood fight back. [ ] I'm enclosing my cash contribution to all of Planned Parenthood's programs encouraging responsible decision-making: __ $15 __ $35 __ $50 __ $100 __ $500 __ other. [ ] I'm making my contribution in the form of AT&T [ ] shares or [ ] proxies.

NAME

ADDRESS

CITY   STATE   ZIP

Planned Parenthood®
Federation of America

810 Seventh Ave., N.Y., N.Y. 10019-5882

A copy of our latest financial report is available from the New York Department of State, Office of Charities Registration, Albany, New York 12231, or from Planned Parenthood Federation of America, 810 Seventh Avenue, New York, New York 10019. Please write PPFA for a description of our program and activities and/or a list of the organizations to which PPFA has contributed in the last year. © 1990 PPFA, Inc. This ad was paid for with private contributions.

FIGURE 5–5 In 1990, the outspokenness of Planned Parenthood on the issue of abortion caused some companies to reevaluate their philanthropic gifts to the organization. In a controversial decision, AT&T decided not to give its normal $50,000 donation, triggering this spirited response from Planned Parenthood. *(Reprinted by permisson. Planned Parenthood® Federation of America, Inc.)*

FIGURE 5—6 In 1987, a provocative series of three Associated Press photographs showed Pennsylvania treasurer R. Budd Dwyer motioning to reporters, putting a pistol in his mouth, and actually firing the shot that claimed his life. The first picture in the series is shown here; however, the other two are so graphic that ethical standards—not to mention good taste—precluded their presentation in this text. *(Courtesy AP/Wide World Photos)*

DISCUSSION STARTERS

1. How would you define "ethics"?
2. How would you describe the state of ethics in society—in business, government, journalism?
3. How important are "ethics" in the practice of public relations?
4. What two concepts underscore ethical conduct in public relations?
5. Compare the ethical codes of the Society of Professional Journalists and the Public Relations Society of America.
6. What is corporate social responsibility?
7. What are corporate codes of conduct?
8. What was the ethical dilemma in the case of Larry Speakes?
9. What was the ethical debate in AT&T's reaction to Planned Parenthood?
10. What is the significance, in terms of ethical practice, of Neil Bush, Mike Milken, Janet Cooke?

NOTES

1. "What is Ethics?" *Issues in Ethics,* Center for Applied Ethics (October 1987): 2.
2. See Melvin L. Sharpe, "Exploring Questions of Media Morality," *Journal of Mass Media Ethics,* Vol. 4, No. 1 (1989): 113–115.
3. John A. Byrne, "Businesses Are Signing up for Ethics 101," *Business Week* (February 15, 1988): 56–57.
4. "An Overview of a Landmark Roundtable Study of Corporate Ethics," *Roundtable Report* (February 1988): 1.
5. "Ethics in American Business," Touche Ross (January 1988).
6. Ibid.
7. Brian Sullam, "Ethics Codes Becoming Standard for Business," *Baltimore Sun,* 27 March 1983.
8. Amanda Bennett, "Ethics Codes Spread Despite Skepticism," *The Wall Street Journal,* 15 July 1988, 18 19.
9. Public Relations Society of America, study of ethical files, 1950–85, Foundation for Public Relations Research and Education, April 17, 1987, New York, NY.
10. "Franco Speaks Publicly for First Time About His Case," *Public Relations Reporter* (13 April 1987): 2.
11. Public Relations Society of America, news release, 15 April 1988.
12. *Business Ethics Survey,* Minneapolis, MN.: The Pinnacle Group, Inc., (September 27, 1989).
13. "Some Ethical Questions," address by David C. Venz, director of corporate communications for Transworld Airlines, before the Society of American Travel Writers, New York City, September 7, 1985.

SUGGESTED READINGS

Beauchamp, Tom, and Norman E. Bowie, eds.   *Ethical Theory and Business.* 3rd ed. Englewood Cliffs, NJ: Prentice-Hall, 1988.

Behrman, Jack N.   *Essays on Ethics in the Business and the Professions.* Englewood Cliffs, NJ: Prentice-Hall, 1988.

Biddle, Wayne.   "Ethics According to General Dynamics," *New York Times,* 16 August 1985, A12.

Bishop, Nancy.   "New Ethics Policies Spell Out Worker No-No's," *Dallas Morning News,* 12 February 1985.

Corporate Ethics: A Prime Business Asset. New York: Business Roundtable, February 1988 (200 Park Ave. 10166). Members of TBR supplied information to develop this report on policy and practice in company conduct.

TOP OF THE SHELF

Dilenschneider, Robert L. *Power and Influence: Mastering the Art of Persuasion.* New York: Prentice-Hall, 1990.

Bob Dilenschneider delivers an insider's look at ethics and public relations in this book.

Dilenschneider, CEO of Hill & Knowlton, draws on two decades of experience at the firm to assemble a collection of insights that illuminate public relations areas from crisis communications to community relations to media relations. While he suggests how one can gain influence, wield it, and protect it, some of his more memorable words are in "Influence and Integrity," a chapter in which he advises readers to "Make high ethical standards evident in everyday business decisions." Dilenschneider argues that some public relations problems, such as Three Mile Island, could have been minimized if executives had been truthful from day one. In short, Dilenschneider says that "Bad ethics is Bad Business."

Dilenschneider's *Power and Influence* is packed with compelling advice straight from the front lines of public relations. He teaches how to practice the profession— and how to do it with honesty and integrity.

Cross, Robert. "Corporate Conscience: Putting Big Business on Its Best Behavior." *Chicago Tribune,* 3 January 1985, 1, sect. 2.

Ethics in American Business. New York: Deloitte & Touche, January 1988 (1633 Broadway 10019). This report on ethical behavior is based on a poll of key business leaders.

Fink, Conrad. *Media Ethics.* New York: McGraw-Hill, 1988.

Foundation for Public Relations. (310 Madison Ave., New York, NY 10017). The foundation issued a report on an ethics and standards study conducted by PRSA in 1987 to determine adherence to PRSA's code.

Jones, Donald G., and Patricia Bennett. *A Bibliography of Business Ethics 1981–1985.* Lewiston, NY: Edwin Mellen, 1986.

"An Overview of a Landmark Roundtable Study of Corporate Ethics." *Roundtable Report.* New York: Business Roundtable (Suite 2222, 200 Park Ave. 10166).

Posner, Ari. "The Culture of Plagiarism." *New Republic* (18 April 1988): 19–24.

"PR Groups Combine on Code of Ethics." *Jack O'Dwyer's Newsletter.* New York: J. R. O'Dwyer Co., May 18, 1988 (Rm. 600, 271 Madison Ave. 10016).

Sevareid, Eric. "Ethics and the Media." *Across the Board.* New York: Conference Board, May 1988, pp. 12, 13 (845 Third Ave. 10022).

Walton, Clarence. *The Moral Manager.* New York: Ballinger, 1988.

Ward, Gary. *Developing and Enforcing a Code of Business Ethics.* Babylon, NY: Pilot, 1989.

Weaver, Paul H. *The Suicidal Corporation.* New York: Simon and Schuster, 1988. A former Ford Motor Company public affairs staffer says that Ford is not the place to be entirely honest with one's publics.

The Xerox Policy on Business Ethics. Stamford, CT: Xerox Corporation (P.O. Box 1600 06904).

CASE STUDY   The Safra Smears of American Express

Few companies were as well-known for gold-plated integrity as the American Express Company. Chairman James Robinson cut a dashing swath in Washington, New York, and world capitals as a concerned, caring, and committed corporate leader.

The business community was therefore shocked to read, in a stunning disclosure in late 1989, that American Express admitted engaging in a covert campaign to ruin the reputation of a former colleague, Edmond Safra, by spreading rumors and stimulating articles in the international press. The company made a painful, public apology for what its chairman called an "unauthorized and shameful effort," and paid $8 million to Mr. Safra and charities he selected. As part of the agreement, details of the "shameful effort" were to remain secret. Eventually, however, as inevitably happens to public citizens today, the events involving American Express and Mr. Safra did indeed become very public.

American Express's problems with Mr. Safra began in the early 1980s, when it bought one of his former banks and hired Mr. Safra to manage it. But Mr. Safra soon tired of the corporate structure of American Express, and he resigned as chairman and chief executive officer of American Express International Banking Corp. at the end of 1984.

The international banker then turned his attention to his other principal holding, Republic New York Corp., an American Express competitor. Accordingly, he began hiring international bankers away from American Express, ending up with as many as 23 American Express alumni over the next four years.

Apparently fearing that wealthy clients would abandon it, American Express formally opposed Mr. Safra's plans to seek a Swiss license and also hired an investigator to gather information on its former colleague. Mr. Safra's successor at American Express allegedly put it this way, "If the son of a bitch competes with us, we'll turn him in to the IRS."

After Mr. Safra's Swiss license was approved in 1988, strange stories about him began appearing in the international press. One French newspaper linked him to the Mafia, South American drug traffickers, the CIA, and the Iran-Contra scandal.

And this was just the beginning. In the months that followed, articles appeared in papers throughout the world. One front-page profile from Peru linked Mr. Safra and his banks to drug-money laundering, as the pawns of drug traffickers in New York.

The articles posed a potentially devastating attack on Safra's reputation for honesty and discretion. Private banking customers would be reluctant to deal with him. And just as Safra and his people debated what to do about the spate of nasty articles, a bombshell hit.

In Paris, a right wing, anti-Semitic newspaper charged that the Jewish Mr. Safra was actively involved with cocaine importers and the Mafia. "Billionaire of the White Stuff," the headline read.

Clearly, Mr. Safra concluded, there must be an organized campaign "out to get him." Mr. Safra had to find out who was behind it. So he sued the French paper.

As part of its documentation of Mr. Safra's underworld involvement, the paper produced a copy of a fax of an article dealing with the Mafia. The fax revealed in tiny lettering in one corner that it had been sent from the corporate communications department of the American Express Company in New York.

Upon learning of the American Express involvement, Mr. Safra hired street-fighting New York attorney Stanley Arkin to get to the bottom of the smear campaign. "Get to the bottom" he did.

Arkin accused the American Express director of communications, a close associate of Mr. Robinson's for many years, of hiring a former ABC News investigative producer as a "secret weapon" against Safra. Her job, according to reports revealed later, was to influence the placement of anti-Safra articles in international publications.

By the spring of 1989, Safra had had enough. He met with Mr. Robinson, who reportedly said he would be "dumbfounded" if Safra's reports about an American Express smear campaign were true.

Arkin then turned up the heat on American Express. In his regular column for the *New York Law Journal,* he wrote a hypothetical story of a corporate executive, who "cherishes his Boy Scout image" but whose "aides had spread rumors" that a competitor was involved in the drug business. "Spreading false or malicious rumors or flat-out lies may well amount to a criminal fraud," author Arkin summarized in his column.

Mr. Robinson got the message.

American Express lawyers began negotiating a settlement with Arkin. Soon thereafter, Robinson issued the American Express apology to Safra and agreed to pay $8 million to Safra and charities he selected. Within a week of the apology, the American Express communications director announced his retirement and accepted "executive responsibility" for the campaign against Safra.

As a postscript to the unseemly affair, a year after its apology, American Express still denied that any of its employees knowingly spread false information. The company steadfastly declined to discuss details of the matter. Its attorney even went to the bizarre extreme of notifying *The Wall Street Journal* that he would "urge the company to sue" if it published defamatory statements about the anti-Safra campaign. The *Journal* responded with the longest article in its history, which dissected the whole sordid mess.

The *Journal* summarized, "For American Express, a company that has enjoyed a virtually unrivaled reputation for integrity, the Safra affair reveals a willingness to engage in unseemly corporate revenge when confronting a rival and, at the very least, a jarring lack of oversight on the part of top company officials."

QUESTIONS

1. How would you describe the "ethical implications" of the American Express-Safra controversy?
2. How would you characterize the American Express "settlement" with Mr. Safra?
3. What is your view of the reaction of American Express and its lawyers to *The Wall Street Journal's* 1990 inquiry of the case?
4. How does this case reflect on the ethics of the company, its chairman, its communications department?

This case was largely based on Bryan Burrough, "How American Express Orchestrated a Smear of Rival Edmond Safra," *The Wall Street Journal,* 24 September 1990, A1, A27–28; Jeffrey A. Trachtenberg, "American Express Makes Apology to Safra," *The Wall Street Journal,* 31 July 1989, A3; and Jeffrey A. Trachtenberg, "Top American Express Official to Quit, Takes Responsibility for Safra Campaign," *The Wall Street Journal,* 4 August 1989, A3.

Tips from the Top

BARBARA LEY TOFFLER

Barbara Ley Toffler is one of the nation's best-known authorities on the subject of ethics. A founding partner of Resources for Responsible Management in Boston, Toffler served on the faculty of the Graduate School of Business Administration at Harvard University for eight years. She lectures on the subject of ethics and is the author of *Tough Choices: Managers Talk Ethics*, published in 1986.

Are there any absolutes in dealing with ethics?

In the United States one has to start with the Judeo-Christian tradition. We believe that truth telling is an absolute. But, unfortunately, life today is a complicated exercise. For instance, what if telling the truth is harmful to someone else's sense of self-esteem? In most situations we're faced with competing claims—loyalty to an organization *vs.* responsibility to the public, for example. Sometimes fulfilling one claim means having to compromise another. I dislike the negative implications of the term *situational ethics*, but, in reality, that's what usually applies.

What is the state of ethics in business?

Private industry clearly is struggling with ethical issues. Many companies are paying serious attention to creating an ethical en-

vironment in their firms and encouraging employees to act with integrity. I'm not certain that all of the firms engaged in these activities are truly committed to resolving the tough ethical problems that face them. However, the smart companies are those that take ethics seriously and realize that ethics can't be tacked on. It must be integrated into business goals, business practices, and the way that employees conduct themselves.

How do you solve an ethical problem in an organization?

First, you've got to talk to the key people, those who run the organization. Next, you must meet with other groups and elicit their views on issues and problems in the organization. Then you must consider the environment in which the organization operates and what issues loom on the horizon. Then, like a doctor, you've got to diagnose the company and its problems so that you can both suggest preventive medicine and design and implement responses to existing conditions. Such a study of ethics in an organization isn't at all "glitzy" and doesn't necessarily make good press. It takes intensive and extensive commitment throughout the organization, and most of all, it takes a lot of hard work.

What is the state of ethics in government?

I wouldn't say the public sector is less ethical than others. But one of the most fascinating things I've noticed is that the public sector managers with whom I've dealt don't tend to think about ethics in terms of their own behavior. Rather, they think first about the constituencies they serve. A private sector manager, by contrast, focuses first on his or her behavior and is therefore more self-reflective. The reason that public sector people run into more difficulty in this area is not that they are less ethical, but rather they often don't know where to look.

What is the state of ethics in religion?

People who do pastoral counseling today struggle terribly with ethics and probably have the most difficulty in dealing successfully with ethical problems in complex situations. As professionals in religion, they feel obligated to enact that which is absolutely ethical. The stresses of dealing in a complex world make this particular charge difficult, if not impossible. A theologian might say, "I don't like any of the choices, so I won't decide." Well, often neither do we like our choices, but we *must* make a decision. A manager must always decide

and act, and therein lies the ethical dilemma.

What is the state of ethics in public relations?

Public relations people have as difficult a job as anyone in society. Their role is to manage all of the boundaries between the organization and the outside world and within the organization itself. Consequently, they struggle mightily with difficult ethical problems all the time. If anything, they tend to err on the side of loyalty to and protection of the organization, which is their primary charge. Is that unethical? Again, it all depends.

How does one begin to act ethically?

First, spend time thinking about how others view the world. One critical word in ethics is *respect*. In fact, the Golden Rule falls a bit short. What it should say is, "Do unto others as you would have them do unto you—*if you were they.*" It takes empathy and understanding to settle conflicts. Another key word is *competence*. A manager can't be ethical unless he or she is also competent. Frankly, a great deal of unethical behavior in our society is attributable to incompetent people. Finally, because most ethical situations involve competing claims and complex situations where people can't simply apply what they believe, acting ethically also demands imagination. In public relations, when you consider a complicated situation where you must defend the organization, act fairly with respect to the public, and explain your actions to the press, you must have the imagination to think through various scenarios to arrive at positive solutions. By imagination I don't mean creat-ing stories to cover things up. Rather I mean using an active, creative imagination to arrive at positive solutions that are also ethical.

Research

In the 1980s, the Sperry Corporation advertised a basic strength in a unique and most effective manner. "We listen" was the company's simple, yet profound theme (Figure 6–1). In the 1990s, public relations professionals, too, have begun to listen—both inside and outside their organizations. Indeed, the element of listening has become an increasingly important part of the public relations practitioner's job.

Another name for listening in public relations work is *research*, particularly the kind that involves public opinions, attitudes, and reactions to the policies and practices of an organization. Research has become essential in the practice of modern public relations. Instinct, intuition, and "gut-feelings" all remain important in the conduct of public relations work; but management today demands more—measurement, analysis, and evaluation at every stage of the public relations process. In an era of scarce resources, management wants facts and statistics from public relations professionals, to show that their efforts contribute not only to overall organizational effectiveness, but also to the bottom line. Why should we introduce a new employee newspaper? What should it say and cost? How will we know it's working? Questions like these must be answered through research.

Research should be applied in public relations work both at the initial stage, prior to planning a campaign, and at the final stage, to evaluate a program's effectiveness. Early research helps to determine the current situation, prevalent attitudes, and difficulties that the program is up against. Later research examines the program's success, along with what else still needs to be done. Research at both points in the process is critical.

Even though research does not necessarily provide unequivocal proof of a program's effectiveness, it does allow a means for public relations

Jean Smith

137

138

**AT SPERRY,
LISTENING IS NOT
A 9 TO 5 JOB.**

A listener loose in a world of
talkers has one unbeatable edge: the
flow of new ideas through his ears
to his mind never stops.

It's been said there's at least one
thing to learn from everyone one
meets. Provided one bothers to listen.

Unfortunately for most people,
no one ever bothered to teach us how.
Which is why listening training
is available to Sperry employees,
worldwide.

Helping our people become better
listeners helps make us a better
corporation.

For one thing, it eliminates the
enormous costs of simple listening
errors.

But more than that, it's making
our employees better thinkers. Better
problem solvers. And ultimately,
more open to the original and
unexpected.

That's the most compelling reason
of all for learning to listen.

You never know where the next
great idea is coming from.

⇑ SPERRY

We understand how important it is
to listen.

Sperry is Sperry Univac computers, Sperry New Holland
farm equipment, Sperry Vickers fluid power systems,
and guidance and control equipment from Sperry division
and Sperry Flight Systems.

Dept.   To learn more about listening, write to Sperry,
         1290 Avenue of the Americas, New York, N.Y. 10104

FIGURE 6–1   At Sperry, the theme for the 1980s was "We listen." *(Courtesy of Sperry Corporation)*

professionals to support their own intuition. It's little wonder, then, that the idea of measuring public relations work has steadily gained acceptance.[1]

What Is Research?

Research is the systematic collection and interpretation of information to increase understanding (Figure 6–2).[2] Most people associate public relations with *conveying* information, and although that association is accurate, research must be the obligatory first step in any project. A firm must acquire enough accurate, relevant data about its publics, products, and programs to answer these kinds of questions:

◆ How can we identify and define our constituent groups?
◆ How does this knowledge relate to the design of our messages?
◆ How does it relate to the design of our programs?
◆ How does it relate to the media we use to convey our messages?

FIGURE 6–2   An early research effort, albeit a futile one, was the return of the biblical scouts sent by Moses to reconnoiter the land of Cannan. They disagreed in their reports, and the Israelites believed the gloomier versions. This failure to interpret the data correctly caused them to wander another 40 years in the wilderness. (An even earlier research effort was Noah's sending the dove to search for dry ground.) *(Courtesy of Trout & Ries)*

♦ How does it relate to the schedule we adopt in using our media?

♦ How does it relate to the ultimate implementation tactics of our program?

It is a difficult task to delve into the minds of others, whose backgrounds and points of view may be quite different from one's own, with the purpose of understanding why they think as they do. Research skills are partly intuitive, partly an outgrowth of individual temperament, and partly a function of acquired knowledge. There is nothing mystifying about them. Although we tend to think of research in terms of impersonal test scores, interviews, or questionnaires, they are only a small part of the process. The real challenge lies in using research—knowing when to do what, with whom, and for what purpose.

Types of Public Relations Research

In general, research is conducted to do three things: (1) describe a process, situation, or phenomenon; (2) explain why something is happening, what its causes are, and what effect it will have; and (3) predict what probably will happen if we do or don't take action. Most research in public relations is either theoretical or applied. Applied research solves practical problems; theoretical research aids understanding of a public relations process.

Applied Research

In public relations work, applied research can be either strategic or evaluative. Both applications are designed to answer specific practical questions.

♦ **Strategic research** is used primarily in program development, to determine program objectives, develop message strategies, or establish benchmarks. It often examines the tools and techniques of public relations. For example, a firm that wants to know how employees rate its candor in internal publications would first conduct strategic research to find out where it stands.

♦ **Evaluative research,** sometimes called summative research, is conducted primarily to determine whether a public relations program has accomplished its goals and objectives. For example, if changes are made in the internal communications program to increase candor, evaluative research can determine whether the goals have been met. Formative research, a variant of evaluation, can be applied during a program to monitor progress and indicate where modifications might make sense.

Theoretical Research

Theoretical research is more abstract and conceptual than applied research. It helps build theories in public relations work in areas such as why people communicate, how public opinion is formed, and how a public is created. Knowledge of theoretical research is important as a framework for persuasion and a base for understanding why people do what they do.

Some knowledge of theoretical research in public relations and mass communications is essential for practitioners to understand the limitations of communication as a persuasive tool. Attitude and behavior change have been the traditional goals in public relations programs, yet theoretical research indicates that such goals may be difficult or impossible to achieve through persuasive efforts. According to such research, other factors are always getting in the way.

Researchers in the 1980s found that communication is most persuasive when it comes from multiple sources of high credibility. Credibility itself is a multidimensional concept that includes trustworthiness, expertise, and power. Others have found that a message generally is more effective when it is simple because it is easier to understand, localize, and make personally relevant. According to still other research, the persuasiveness of a message can be increased when it arouses or is accompanied by a high level of personal involvement in the issue at hand. The point here is that knowledge of theoretical research can help practitioners not only understand the basis of applied research findings, but also temper management expectations of attitude and behavioral change resulting from public relations programs.

In public relations, then, research may be applied to determine, in advance of a communications program, the attitudes and beliefs of a public. It can be used to monitor the performance of a public relations program in process and as an evaluative mechanism to determine a program's progress, success, and suggested modifications. When limited information is available, public relations research can also help clarify issues. For example, attitudes are often fuzzy, and people may say they like something without being specific about the particular characteristics they admire. Research can probe deeper to determine the specifics. Frequently, research may also confirm assumptions about public opinion. Intuition may be accurate, but research corroborates the validity of the public relations program.

Methods of Public Relations Research

Observation is the foundation of modern social science. Scientists, social psychologists, and anthropologists make observations, develop theories, and, hopefully, increase understanding of human behavior. Public relations research, too, is founded on observation. The three primary forms of public relations research are methods, mostly indirect, of observing human behavior.

◆ **Surveys** are designed to reveal attitudes and opinions—what people think about certain subjects.

◆ **Communication audits** are often designed to reveal disparities between real and perceived communications between management and target audiences. Management may make certain assumptions about its methods, media, materials, and messages, whereas its targets may confirm or refute those assumptions.

◆ **Unobtrusive measures**—such as fact finding, content analysis, and readability studies—enable the study of a subject or object without involving the researcher or the research as an intruder.

Each method of public relations research offers specific benefits and should be understood and used by the modern practitioner.

Surveys

Survey research is one of the most frequently used research methods in public relations. Surveys can be applied to broad societal issues, such as determining public opinion about a political candidate, or to the most minute organizational problem, such as whether shareholders like the quarterly report. Surveys come in two types.

1. **Descriptive surveys** offer a snapshot of a current situation or condition. They are the research equivalent of a balance sheet—capturing reality at a specific point in time. A typical public opinion poll is a prime example.

2. **Explanatory surveys,** on the other hand, are concerned with cause and effect. Their purpose is to help explain why a current situation or condition exists and to offer explanations for opinions and attitudes. Frequently, such explanatory or analytical surveys are designed to answer the question "Why?" Why are our philanthropic dollars not being appreciated in the community? Why are employees not believing management messages? Why is our credibility being questioned?

Surveys generally consist of four elements: (1) the sample, (2) the questionnaire, (3) the interview, and (4) the analysis of results. (Direct mail surveys, of course, eliminate the interview step.) Because survey research is so critical in public relations, we will examine each survey element in some detail.

The Sample

The sample, or selected target group, must be representative of the total public whose views are sought. Once a survey population has been determined, a researcher must select the appropriate sample or group of respondents from whom to collect information. Sampling is tricky. A

B E T W E E N   T H E   L I N E S

Pay Attention To What I Do, Not What I Say

Public relations professionals must always keep in mind that, as most research has shown, attitudes are not a reliable predictor of behavior. In other words, people often talk one way but act another.*

- Ask American adults whether they're satisfied with their jobs, and 88 percent will answer yes. But only 30 percent of those adults expect to have the same job in five years. Another 31 percent of them plan to quit their jobs, and 25 percent don't know where they will be working in five years.

- A whopping 76 percent of American adults vow they exercise regularly, and 33 percent will tell you that they exercise strenuously three or more times a week. But when those self-proclaimed fitness fans waddle over to the scales, the truth comes out. Fully 59 percent of all U.S. adults—about 105 million people—are overweight.

- Another 65 percent of adults claim they are making a real effort to eat more brussels sprouts and cauliflower; 59 percent try hard to eat enough fiber; 56 percent claim they avoid eating too much fat; 57 percent say they are cutting down on salt; and 46 percent steer clear of high-cholesterol foods. But the number of adults who would like to see more all-you-can-eat specials in restaurants increased from 30 to 37 percent during the last decade. By contrast, the number who want more dieter's specials declined from 18 to 16 percent over the same period.

What's the point? People sometimes tell you what they think you want to hear, rather than what they really believe. So be wary of even the most buttoned-up research.

*Joe Schwartz, "Do As I Say," *U.S. Demographics* (April 1988).

researcher must be aware of the hidden pitfalls in choosing a representative sample, not the least of which is the perishable nature of most data. Survey findings are rapidly outdated because of population mobility and changes in the political and socioeconomic environment. Consequently, sampling should be completed quickly.

Two approaches are used in obtaining a sample: probability sampling and nonprobability sampling. The former is more scientific; the latter, more informal.

Probability Sampling In probability sampling, each member of a population has a known chance of being selected. Probability sampling is based on a mathematical criterion that allows generalizations from the sample to be made to the total population. There are four types of probability samples.

1. **Simple random sampling** gives all members of the population an equal chance of being selected. First, all members of the population are identified, and then as many subjects as are needed are randomly selected—usually with the help of a computer. Election polling uses a random approach; although millions of Americans vote, only a few thousand are ever polled on their election preferences. The Nielson national television sample, for example, consists of 4,000 homes. The Census Bureau uses a sample of 72,000 out of 93 million households to obtain estimates of employment and other population characteristics.

   How large should a random sample be? The answer depends on a number of factors, one of which is the size of the population. In addition, the more similar the population elements are in regard to the characteristics being studied, the smaller the sample required. In most random samples, the following population-to-sample ratios apply, with a 5 percent margin of error:[3]

Population	Sample
1,000	278
2,000	322
3,000	341
5,000	355
10,000	370
50,000	381
100,000	383
500,000	383
Infinity	384

Random sampling owes its accuracy to the laws of probability, which are best explained by the example of a barrel filled with 10,000 marbles—5,000 green ones and 5,000 red ones. If a blindfolded person selects a certain number of marbles from the barrel—say 400—the laws of probability suggest that the most frequently drawn combination will be 200 red and 200 green. These laws further conjecture that with certain margins of error (discussed on p. 000 under "Analysis"), a very few marbles can represent the whole barrel, which can correspond to any size—city, state, or nation.

2. **Systematic sampling** is closely related to simple random sampling, but it uses a random starting point in the sample list. From then on, the researcher selects every nth person in the list. Because each member of the population does not have an equal probability of being selected, this type of sampling is less reliable than simple random sampling. It is also cheaper and easier to perform.

3. **Stratified sampling** is used to survey different segments or strata of the population. For example, if an organization wants to determine the relationship between years of service and attitudes toward the company, it may stratify the sample to ensure that the breakdown of respondents accurately reflects the population makeup. In other words, if more than half of the employees have been with the company more than 10 years, more than half of those polled should also reflect that level of service. By stratifying the sample, the organization's objective can be achieved.

4. **Cluster sampling** involves first breaking the population down into small heterogeneous subsets, or clusters, and then selecting the potential sample from the individual clusters or groups. A cluster may often be defined as a geographic area, such as an election district.

Nonprobability Sampling   Nonprobability samples come in two types, the convenience sample and the purposive sample.

1. **Convenience samples** are relatively unstructured, rather unsystematic, and designed to elicit ideas and points of view. Journalists use convenience samples when they conduct man-on-the-street interviews. The most common type of convenience sample in public relations research is the focus group. Focus groups generally consist of 8 to 12 people, with a moderator encouraging in-depth discussion of a specific topic. Focus groups generate concepts and ideas rather than validate hypotheses.

2. **Purposive sampling**—often called quota sampling—permits a researcher to choose subjects on the basis of certain characteristics. For example, the attitudes of a certain number of women, men, blacks, whites, rich, or poor may need to be known. Quotas are imposed in proportion to each group's percentage of the population. The advantage of quota sampling is that it increases homogeneity of a sample population, thus enhancing the validity of a study. However, it is hard to

classify interviewees by one or two discrete demographic characteristics. For example, a particular interviewee may be black, Catholic, female, under twenty-five, and a member of a labor union all at the same time, making the lines of demographic demarcation pretty blurry.

The Questionnaire

Before creating a questionnaire, it's wise to talk informally with the type of people the study is designed to reach. These talks should yield insights into how target publics think. In addition, because everybody today receives questionnaires, researchers should follow these tips in their design process.

1. Keep it short, probably under 20 questions. It's terrific if the questionnaire can be answered in five minutes.

2. Use structured, not open-ended, questions. People would rather check a box or circle a number than write an essay. But leave room at the bottom for general comments or "Other." Also, start with simple, nonthreatening questions before getting to the more difficult, sensitive ones. This approach will build respondent trust as well as commitment to finishing the questionnaire.

3. Measure intensity of feelings. Let respondents check "very satisfied," "satisfied," "dissatisfied," or "very dissatisfied," rather than "yes" or "no." One popular approach is the semantic differential technique in Figure 6–3.

4. Don't use fancy words or words that have more than one meaning. If you must use big words, make the context clear.

5. Don't ask loaded questions. "Is management doing all it can to communicate with you?" is a terrible question. The answer is always no.

6. Don't ask double-barreled questions. "Would you like management meetings once a month, or are bimonthly meetings enough?" is another terrible question.

7. Pretest. Send your questionnaire to a few colleagues, and listen to their suggestions.

8. Attach a letter explaining how important the respondents' answers are, and let recipients know they will remain anonymous. Respondents will feel better if they think the study is significant and their identities are protected. Also, specify how and where the data will be used.

9. Hand-stamp the envelopes—preferably with unique commemorative stamps. Metering an envelope indicates assembly-line research, and researchers have found that the more expensive the postage, the higher the response rate. People like to feel special.

10. Follow up your first mailing. Send a reminder postcard three days after the original questionnaire. Then wait a few weeks and send a second questionnaire, just in case they've lost the first.

Dictaphone

1	2	3	4	5
High price				Low price

1	2	3	4	5
Not reliable				Reliable

1	2	3	4	5
Bulky				Compact

1	2	3	4	5
Inconvenient				Convenient

1	2	3	4	5
Bad service				Good service

1	2	3	4	5
Not likely to buy				Likely to buy

Stowe

1	2	3	4	5	6	7	8	9	10
Hard to get to									Easy to get to

1	2	3	4	5	6	7	8	9	10
Severe weather									Moderate weather

1	2	3	4	5	6	7	8	9	10
Few levels of skiing									Many levels of skiing

1	2	3	4	5	6	7	8	9	10
Relatively easy trails									Very difficult trails

1	2	3	4	5	6	7	8	9	10
Poor trail grooming									Excellent trail grooming

1	2	3	4	5	6	7	8	9	10
Long liftlines									Short liftlines

1	2	3	4	5	6	7	8	9	10
Few apres-ski activities									Many apres-ski activities

1	2	3	4	5	6	7	8	9	10
Poor lodging facilities									Excellent lodging facilities

1	2	3	4	5	6	7	8	9	10
Poor overall resort value									Excellent overall resort value

FIGURE 6–3 In questionnaires, one common device to measure intensity of feelings is the semantic differential technique, which gives respondents a scale of choices from the worst to the best. These semantic differential scales for portable dictating equipment and for ski lodges are typical. *(Courtesy of Trout & Ries)*

11. Send out more questionnaires than you think necessary. The major weakness of most mail surveys is the unmeasurable error introduced by nonresponders. You're shooting for a 50 percent response rate; anything less tends to be suspect.
12. Enclose a reward. There's nothing like a token gift of merchandise or money—a $2 bill works beautifully—to make a recipient feel guilty for not returning a questionnaire.

Figure 6–4 illustrates an internal survey using a questionnaire with a simple rating format. Appendix B gives an example of a more elaborate questionnaire.

The Interview

Research interviews can provide a more personal, firsthand feel for public opinion. Interviews can be conducted in a number of ways, including fact-to-face, telephone, mail, and drop-off techniques.

Focus Groups This approach is probably the most common form of research in public relations today. Such interviews can be conducted one-to-one or through survey panels. These panels can be used, for example,

The Chase Manhattan Bank, N.A.
1 Chase Manhattan Plaza
New York, New York 10015

May 11, 1977

TO ALL STAFF MEMBERS

We are currently in the midst of revitalizing our corporate internal communications programs and practices. At this point, however, to move forward and to do the job right, we need some information from you.

To begin with, we need to know what you think about the various corporate internal communications programs already in place. We also need to know what kinds of information you need to keep in tune with Chase and its overall directions. And, finally, we need to know what information you feel is necessary if you are to do the best possible job in fulfilling your particular responsibilities.

The ideal way to get this information would be to talk with each of you directly, but this is obviously unrealistic. But we can speak with many of you indirectly through the survey that we are conducting.

We are extremely interested in having your opinion on this critical matter, and therefore urge you to take the time to give us serious, thoughtful answers to the questions that are attached.

We are firmly committed to establishing a vital internal communications program which is responsive to your information needs. You can be sure that we'll be listening to what you have to say.

Sincerely,

---

1. In general, would you say that the information Chase gives its employees keeps you:

   1) Very well informed
   2) Reasonably well informed
   3) Somewhat informed
   4) Not too well informed
   5) Not informed at all

2. Generally, when Chase gives information to employees, how do you feel about it?

   1) Always believe it
   2) Usually believe it
   3) Believe it about half the time
   4) Seldom believe it
   5) Never believe it

3. Overall, how would you rate the timeliness of the information you receive about the bank and your job?

   1) Very good
   2) Good
   3) So-So
   4) Poor
   5) Very poor

Please rate the *importance* of each of the following as a *source of information.*

	VERY IMPORTANT	IMPORTANT	SOMEWHAT IMPORTANT	NOT TOO IMPORTANT	NOT AT ALL IMPORTANT	NEVER RECEIVED INFORMATION FROM THIS SOURCE
4. Your Supervisor	1	2	3	4	5	9
5. Chase Manhattan News	1	2	3	4	5	9
6. Staff Bulletin	1	2	3	4	5	9
7. Benefits News	1	2	3	4	5	9
8. Recorded Message Service	1	2	3	4	5	9
9. Annual Report	1	2	3	4	5	9
10. Chase Quarterly	1	2	3	4	5	9
11. Bulletin Boards	1	2	3	4	5	9
12. Consumer Sense	1	2	3	4	5	9
13. Benefits Booklets	1	2	3	4	5	9
14. Orientation	1	2	3	4	5	9
15. Other Chase Employees (The grapevine)	1	2	3	4	5	9

Have you any comments on your answers to questions 4-15? Include suggestions for improvement in any of the above sources of information. PLEASE WRITE IN SPACE PROVIDED BELOW:

FIGURE 6–4 In the area of internal communications and morale, companies constantly devise questionnaires to seek employee opinions about current communications channels. This figure shows the introduction to and first portion of a survey distributed to a random sampling of Chase Manhattan Bank employees. *(Courtesy of Chase Manhattan Bank)*

to measure buying habits or the impact of public relations programs on a community or organizational group. They can also be used to assess general attitudes toward certain subjects, such as new products or advertising.

With the focus group technique, a well-drilled moderator leads a group through a discussion of opinions on a particular product, organization, or idea. Participants represent the socioeconomic level desired by the research sponsor—from college students to office workers to millionaires. Almost always, focus-group participants are paid for their efforts. Sessions are frequently videotaped and then analyzed, often in preparation for more formal and specific research questionnaires.

Focus groups should be organized with the following guidelines in mind:

1. **Define objectives and audience.** The more tightly you define your goals and your target audience, the more likely you are to gather relevant information. In other words, don't conduct a focus group with friends and family members, hoping to get a quick and inexpensive read. Nothing of value will result.

2. **Recruit your groups.** Recruiting participants takes several weeks, depending on the difficulty of contacting the target audience. Contact is usually made by phone, with a series of questions to weed out those who don't fit specifications, competitors' employees, and members of the news media (to keep the focus group from becoming a news story). "Professional" participants who have participated in a group in the past year should also be screened out; they may be more interested in the money than in helping you find what you're looking for.

3. **Choose the right moderator.** Staff people who may be magnificent conversationalists are not necessarily the best focus-group moderators. The gift of gab is not enough. Professional moderators know how to establish rapport quickly, how and when to probe beyond the obvious, how to draw comments from reluctant participants, how to keep a group on task, and how to interpret results validly.

4. **Conduct enough focus groups.** One or two focus groups are usually not enough. Four to six are better to uncover the full range of relevant ideas and opinions. Regardless of the number of groups, however, you must resist the temptation to add up responses; that practice gives the focus group more analytical worth than it deserves.

5. **Use a discussion guide.** This is a basic outline of what you want to investigate. It will lead the moderator through the discussion and keep the group on track.

6. **Choose proper facilities.** The discussion room should be comfortable, with participants sitting around a table that affords observers a good view of all members. Observers can use closed-circuit TV and two-way mirrors, but participants should always be told when they are being observed.

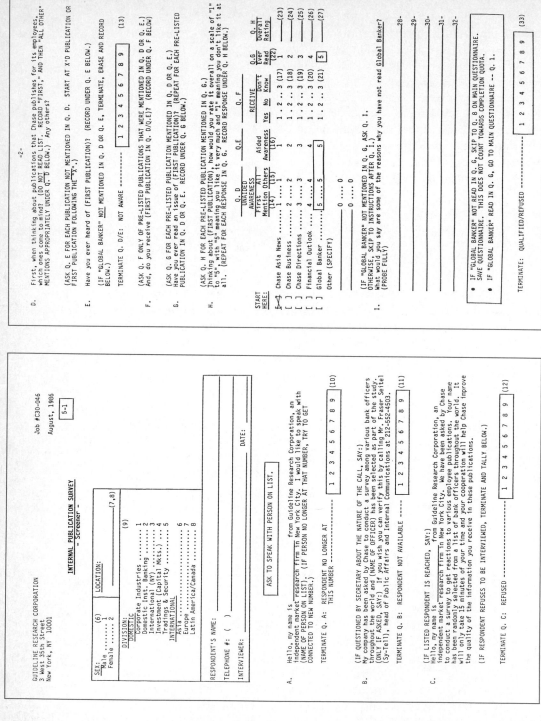

FIGURE 6–5 Telephone interviewers must be guided by this kind of prepared script, to ensure that appropriate responses are achieved for the whole question-naire. *(Courtesy of Guideline Research Corporation)*

7. **Keep a tight rein on observers.** Observers should rarely be in the same room with participants; the two groups should ordinarily be separated. Observers should view the proceedings seriously; this is not "dinner and a show."

8. **Consider using outside help.** Setting up focus groups can be time-consuming and complicated. Often the best advice is to hire a firm recommended by the American Marketing Association or the Marketing Research Association, so the process, the moderator, and the evaluation are as professional as possible.[5]

Telephone Interviews   In contrast to personal interviews, telephone interviews suffer from a high refusal rate. Many people just don't want to be bothered. Such interviews may also introduce an upper-income bias because lower-income earners may lack telephones. However, the increasing use of unlisted numbers by upper-income people may serve to mitigate this bias. Telephone interviews must be carefully scripted, so that interviewers know precisely what to ask, regardless of a respondent's answer. Calls should be made at less busy times of the day, such as early morning or late afternoon (Figure 6–5).

With both telephone and face-to-face interviews, it is important to establish rapport with the interview subject. It may make sense to begin the interview with nonthreatening questions, saving the tougher, more controversial ones—on income level or race, for example— until last. Another approach is to depersonalize the research by explaining that others have devised the survey and that the interviewer's job is simply to ask the questions.

Mail Interviews   These constitute the least expensive approach, but they often suffer from low response rates. You are aiming for a 50 percent response rate. Frequently, those who return mail questionnaires are people with strong biases either in favor of or, usually, in opposition to the subject at hand. As noted, one way to generate a higher response from mail interviews is through the use of self-addressed, stamped envelopes or enclosed incentives, such as dollar bills or free gifts.

Drop-Off Interviews   This approach combines face-to-face and mail interview techniques. An interviewer personally drops off a questionnaire at a household, usually after conducting a face-to-face interview. Because the interviewer has already established some rapport with the interviewee, the rate of return with this technique is considerably higher than it is for straight mail interviews.

Analysis

After selecting the sample, drawing up the questionnaire, and interviewing the respondents, the researcher must analyze the findings. Often, a great deal of analysis is required to produce meaningful recommendations.

B E T W E E N   T H E   L I N E S

Figures Lie

If you don't believe the old maxim, "figures lie and liars figure," consider the following sources of error that can throw off research findings:

- *The skewed sample.* Women answer the phone 70 percent of the time. A telephone poll that doesn't take that into account by making extra calls to get enough men is likely to be slanted.
- *The ignorance factor.* Not many people want to appear unpatriotic, uninformed, or socially unacceptable. Therefore, when the pollster calls, they say they intend to vote when they don't, offer what they believe are less controversial opinions, or express a view—any view—to cover up their ignorance of an issue. One study found that almost a third of respondents offered strong opinions on a nonexistent piece of legislation.
- *The "pseudo poll."* The least-reliable polls are not even polls at all—experts call them "pseudo polls" because they don't make an attempt at surveying a random sample. TV stations ask viewers to call a number to register a yes vote, another for a no. The results are then tallied and aired. The trouble is that only those who feel strongly enough to spend the 50 cents the phone company charges for each call are likely to phone in—hardly a representative sample.
- *Loaded questions.* Even polls taken at the same time can produce dramatically different results, depending on how the questions are phrased.*

    For example, 67 percent of the public polled in 1990 was against a "Constitutional amendment prohibiting abortions." But 50 percent were for a "Constitutional amendment protecting the life of the unborn." By the same token, while 91 percent were for "waiting periods and background checks before guns can be sold," 61 percent were against "national gun registration programs costing about 20 percent of all dollars spent on crime control."

    In other words, figures lie and liars figure.

---

*Stephen Budiansky, with Art Levine, "The Numbers Racket: How Polls and Statistics Lie," *U.S. News & World Report* (July 11, 1988): 44–47.

The objective of every sample is to come up with results that are valid and reliable. A margin of error explains how far off the prediction may be. A sample may be large enough to represent fairly the larger universe; yet depending on the margin of sampling error, the results of the research may not be statistically significant. That is, the differences or distinctions detected by the survey may not be sizable enough to offset the margin of error. Thus, the margin of error must always be determined.

This concept is particularly critical in political polling, where pollsters are quick to acknowledge that their results may accurately represent the larger universe—but normally with a 2 or 3 percent margin of error. Thus, the results could be as much as 3 percent more or less for a certain candidate. Consequently, a pollster who says a candidate will win with 51 percent of the vote really means that the candidate could win with as much as 54 percent or lose with as little as 48 percent of the vote.

Political polls are fraught with problems. They cannot scientifically predict outcomes. Rather, they freeze attitudes at a certain point in time, and people's attitudes obviously change with the tide of events. Perhaps the most notorious political poll was that of the *Literary Digest* in 1936, which used a telephone polling technique to predict that Alf Landon would be the nation's next president. Landon thereupon suffered one of the worst drubbings in American electoral history at the hands of Franklin Roosevelt. It was probably of little solace to the *Literary Digest* that most of its telephone respondents, many of whom were Republicans wealthy enough to afford phones, did vote for Landon.

The point here is that in analyzing results, problems of validity, reliability, and levels of statistical significance associated with margins of error must be considered before recommendations based on survey data are offered.

Communication Audits

The second primary method in public relations research is the communication audit, which frequently evaluates how an organization is doing with respect to a particular constituent group. Communication audits are typically used to analyze the standing of a company with its employees or community neighbors; assess the readership of routine communication vehicles, such as annual reports and news releases; or examine an organization's performance as a corporate citizen. Communication audits often provide benchmarks against which future public relations programs can be applied and measured.

More recently, communication audits have been used to provide information on how to solve

◆ bottlenecked information flows
◆ uneven communication workloads

◆ employees working at cross-purposes
◆ hidden information within an organization that is not being used, to the detriment of the institution
◆ conflicting or nonexisting notions about what the organization is and does[6]

The most effective communication audits start with a researcher who (1) is familiar with the public to be studied, (2) generally understands the attitudes of the target public toward the organization, (3) recognizes the issues of concern to the target public, and (4) understands the relative power of the target public vis-à-vis other publics (Figure 6–6).

Unobtrusive Methods

Of the various unobtrusive methods of data collection available to public relations researchers, probably the most widely used is simple fact finding. Facts are the bricks and mortar of public relations work; no action can be taken unless the facts are known, and the fact-finding process is continuous.

Each organization must keep a fact file of the most essential data with which it is involved. For example, such items as key organization statistics, publications, management biographies and photos, press clippings, media lists, competitive literature, pending legislation, organizational charters and bylaws—all should be kept on file and updated. Even better, computerized listings of such facts offer easier access when research is called for in these areas.

Another unobtrusive method is content analysis, the primary purpose of which is to describe a message or set of messages. For example, an organization with news releases that are used frequently by local newspapers can't be certain, without research, whether the image conveyed by its releases is what the organization seeks. By analyzing the news coverage, the firm can get a much clearer idea of the effectiveness of its communications. Such content analysis might be organized along the following specific criteria:

◆ **Frequency of coverage**   How many releases were used?
◆ **Placement within the paper**   Did releases appear more frequently on page 1 or 71?
◆ **People reached**   What was the circulation of the publications in which the releases appeared?
◆ **Messages conveyed**   Did the releases used express the goals of the organization, or were they simply informational in content?
◆ **Editing of releases**   How much did the newspaper edit the copy submitted? Were desired meanings materially changed?

BANZAI HOSPITAL AUDIT
January 5, 1990

GUIDELINES

1. All interviews are confidential. Assure those you interview that their statements will be held in confidence so that the source of their remarks will not be identifiable.
2. Copy all of your interview notes within 24 hours after each interview is completed, to protect against possible loss of your notes.
3. Use an informal interview style, referring to the question sheets as little as possible. Have the questions in mind before the interview so that they can come up during conversation.
4. Type up your notes, using direct quotes as much as possible.

INTERVIEW CATEGORIES

Board members
Executive staff
Medical staff
Volunteers
Community leaders
Residents and tenants

Families of residents and tenants
Financial supporters
Business leaders
News media
General public

BANZAI COMMUNICATION AUDIT

Board members
1. How did you become involved with Banzai?
2. How do you perceive your role with Banzai? Are your assignments and responsibilities clear?
3. What are the strengths of Banzai today? weaknesses?
4. If it was in your power to do so, what would you change about Banzai?

Medical staff
1. How would you describe your relationship with the institution?
2. Is communications a factor in your relationship? How? Is there a need for improvement? What suggestions do you have?
3. How do you think the institution is perceived in the community? Why? Any suggestions for community programs that should be undertaken?
4. Do you believe this institution provides adequate patient information?

Volunteers
1. How do you get information about what is happening in the institution? What are your best sources? Do you think you get enough information? If not, what else would you like to know?
2. Is there an effective way for you to communicate upward? Do you take advantage of it? What type of information do you pass along?
3. How do you think the institution is perceived in the community? Why?

Community leaders
1. What do you know about the institution?
2. What are your sources of information? Which do you consider the most reliable?
3. How do you value the institution? Does the community perceive the institution in the same light?
4. What recommendations do you have that would help the institution respond to community needs?

BUDGET

The audit will take approximately 120 days. Budget will be kept to the lowest possible figure but will be in the $12,000 to $15,000 range for professional services and about $5,000 for out-of-pocket expenses.

PROCEDURE

A preliminary audit report will be prepared following completion of the interviews. This draft will be reviewed with appropriate members of Banzai staff to uncover possible misconceptions, misinterpretations, or errors. A final audit report will follow in 15 days.

FIGURE 6—6 A typical communication audit will gather subjective information on how an organization is perceived by its major constituencies. It determines which communications systems are being used, which are the most effective, and whether the information being transmitted is regarded as sufficient by recipients.

♦ **Attitude conveyed**   Was the reference positive, negative, or neutral to the organization?

Another unobtrusive method, the readability study, helps a communicator determine whether messages are written at the right educational level for the audience. Typical measures include the Flesch Formula, the FOG Index, and the SMOG Index—all based on the concept that the greater the number of syllables in a passage, the more difficult and less readable the text.[7]

Clearly, there is nothing particularly mysterious or difficult about unobtrusive methods of research. Such methods are relatively simple to apply, yet they are essential for arriving at appropriate modifications for an ongoing public relations program.

Evaluation

No matter what type of public relations research is used, results of the research and the research project itself should always be evaluated. In evaluating after-the-fact, researchers can learn how to improve future efforts. Were the target audiences surveyed the right ones? Were the research assumptions applied to those audiences correct? Were questions from research tools left unanswered?

Research results can be evaluated in a number of ways. Perhaps the most common in public relations is a seat-of-the-pants evaluation, where anecdotal observation and practitioner judgment are used to estimate the effectiveness of the public relations program. Such evaluation might be based on feedback from members of a key public, personal media contacts, or colleagues, but the practitioner alone evaluates the success of the program with subjective observation.

More scientific evaluation results from public relations opinion polls and surveys and fact-finding research, such as content analysis, where the numerical tabulation of results is evaluated and often combined with seat-of-the-pants observation. One of the most effective evaluative techniques to determine the success of a program is to pretest target audiences prior to the implementation of the public relations program and then posttest after the program's completion. A comparison of the results of the two tests enables a more scientific assessment of the program's success.

An on-going system for monitoring public relations activities is yet another way to evaluate programs. Monitoring a public relations campaign, for example, may indicate necessary changes in direction, reallocation of resources, or redefinition of priorities. Another way to evaluate is to dissect public programs after-the-fact. Such postmortem evaluation can provide objective analysis when a program is still fresh in one's mind. This can be extremely helpful in modifying the program for future use.

The evaluation of most public relations research is by no means foolproof. One 1986 study revealed that few public relations research efforts satisfied generally accepted criteria for establishing causality: (1) time ordering—implementation of the campaign before changes are observed, (2) correlation—relationship between campaign objectives and observed changes, and (3) parsimoniousness—an economical research design that rules out all alternative explanations (in other words, being sure the public relations campaign caused the change).[8]

Using Outside Research Help

Despite its occasional rough spots, public relations research has made substantial gains in recent years in quantifying the results of public relations activities. Counseling firms have even organized separate departments to conduct attitude and opinion surveys, as well as other types of research projects.

Ketchum Public Relations, for example, has devised a computer-based measurement system that evaluates public relations results on both a quantitative and qualitative basis. The Ketchum system focuses on the differences in placement of publicity—that is, where in a periodical publicity has a better chance of being noticed. Although the Ketchum system cannot predict attitudinal or behavioral change, it nonetheless is a step forward in providing practitioners with a mechanism to assess the extent to which their publicity has been seen.

It often makes sense to use outside counsel for research assistance. In evaluating the performance of outside consultants, practitioners should ask the following questions:[9]

1. From what population is the sample drawn, and is it the right population?
2. Are random sampling techniques used?
3. Is the sample size adequate?
4. Has the researcher specified the margin of error?
5. If data are broken into subcategories, are the margins of error for each category specified, and are they adequate?
6. Is the method of contact—telephone, mail, or personal interview—justified?
7. Are interviewers professionally trained?
8. Is the timing of interviews right; have results been contaminated by external events?

The Cuyhoda County Questionnaire

Patty Kay is director of public information for Cuyhoda County. In anticipation of the county's attempt to attract industry from other parts of the region, Kay plans an attitude survey of Cuyhoda County residents to reveal the benefits they see in living in the county. She hopes to discover the qualities that make Cuyhoda County attractive to most people, as well as any unattractive qualities that may annoy residents.

Here's her survey.

1. Do you enjoy living in Cuyhoda County?
   (Very much, considerably, not at all)
2. What is the most attractive quality about the county?
   (Schools, transportation access, recreation)
3. What is the most unattractive quality of the county?
   (Crime, climate, racial mix)
4. On the whole, how would you rate Cuyhoda County as a place to work?
   (Excellent, good, poor)
5. How important to you is continued industrial development in the county?
   (Very important, not very important, no opinion)
6. On a scale of 1 to 5, how would you rate your enthusiasm toward Cuyhoda County?
   (1, 2, 3, 4, 5)
7. If you were asked to list the major benefit that a new resident could expect by moving to Cuyhoda County, what would it be?

Thank you.

QUESTIONS

1. Do you think Kay will be able to derive meaningful results from the data she collects?
2. How would you rate her questions in terms of specificity?
3. Will each question evoke only one answer?
4. What problems are raised by the format of the questionnaire? by the wording of the questions? by the choice of language?

9. Are the survey questions precise, objective, and clear?
10. Does the researcher have a vested interest in the survey results? For example, when Pete Dawkins ran for the U.S. Senate in New Jersey in

1988, he sent out a questionnaire that asked voters to answer yes or no on the following "objective" survey questions concerning the two candidates:

◆ Can you cite one specific accomplishment made by Frank Lautenberg since he became our U.S. senator?
◆ Were you aware that Frank Lautenberg has voted to increase taxes 12 times?
◆ Were you aware that Frank Lautenberg voted for a pay increase for senators less than six months after he was elected?
◆ Pete Dawkins was in the top of his West Point class, a Heisman Trophy winner, a Rhodes Scholar, earned a Master's and Ph.D. from Princeton, and became the youngest general in the U.S. Army, followed by success in the world of business. Do you feel Pete Dawkins has the leadership we need for New Jersey in the U.S. Senate?

Often, before turning to outside consultants, the best first step is to determine whether research has already been done on your topic. Because research assistance is expensive, it makes little sense to reinvent the wheel. It is much wiser to piggyback on existing research.

Future of Public Relations Research

Because today's management wants proof that public relations departments are worth what they're paid, research in the field will undoubtedly continue to increase in importance. To be sure, it has a ways to go. In the spring of 1988, Ketchum Public Relations conducted a comprehensive nationwide survey on public relations research, measurement, and evaluation among 253 public relations executives, counselors, and academicians. The results were revealing.

◆ First, 32 percent agreed strongly and 44 percent agreed somewhat that research is an essential component of the public relations planning, program development, and evaluation process. Only 24 percent disagreed.
◆ However, 93 percent said that "in actual fact, research is still talked about much more in public relations than it is actually being done." Of those interviewed, 54 percent agreed strongly with that statement.
◆ Only 57 percent thought it is possible to measure public relations outcome, impact, and effectiveness in precise terms; 43 percent believed it is not possible to measure public relations outcomes precisely.

♦ By a 71 percent-to-28 percent margin, respondents thought that most public relations research is for the planning of programs and activities, rather than for measuring and evaluating public relations effectiveness.

Summary

The intelligent use of research represents a technology for both defining problems and evaluating solutions. The day of the seat-of-the-pants practitioner is over. Even though intuitive judgment remains a coveted and important skill, management must see measurable results.

Nonetheless, informed managements recognize that public relations may never reach a point where its results can be fully quantified. Management confidence is still a prerequisite for active and unencumbered programs. However, such confidence can only be enhanced as practitioners become more adept in using research.

DISCUSSION STARTERS

1. Why is research important in public relations work?
2. What are several methods of public relations research?
3. What are the four elements of a survey?
4. What is the difference between random and stratified sampling?
5. What are the keys to designing an effective questionnaire?
6. What are the several rules-of-thumb in organizing focus groups?
7. What is a communication audit?
8. What is the most widely used unobtrusive method of public relations research?
9. Why is the element of evaluation important in public relations research?
10. How essential do you think research will be in the future for public relations practice?

NOTES

1. Ray Chapman, "Measurement: It Is Alive and Well in Chicago," *Public Relations Journal* (May 1982): 28.
2. John V. Pavlik, *Public Relations: What Research Tells Us* (Newbury Park, CA: Sage Publications, 1987), 16.
3. Walter K. Lindenmann, "Opinion Research: How It Works; How to Use It," *Public Relations Journal* (January 1977): 13.
4. Walter K. Lindenmann, *Attitude and Opinion Research: Why You Need It/How to Do It*, 3d ed. (Washington, DC: Council for Advancement and Support of Education, 1983), 35–38.
5. David L. Nasser, "How to Run a Focus Group," *Public Relations Journal* (March 1988): 33–34.
6. Seymour Hamilton, "Selling the CEO on a Communication Audit," *IABC Communication World* (May 1988): 33.
7. Pavlik, op. cit., 39.
8. Ibid.
9. Michael Ryan, "Ten Criteria for Getting Good Research," *Public Relations Journal* (July 1983): 18–19.

TOP OF THE SHELF

Broom, Glen M., and David M. Dozier. *Using Research in Public Relations: Applications to Program Management.* Englewood Cliffs, NJ: Prentice-Hall, 1990. Pavlik, John V. *Public Relations: What Research Tells Us.* Newbury Park, CA: Sage Publications, 1987.

Research is an essential component of any communications program. Two texts that contribute to the understanding of this important public relations function are *Using Research in Public Relations: Applications to Program Management* and *Public Relations: What Research Tells Us.*

In *Using Research in Public Relations,* Glen Broom and David Dozier, leading public relations researchers, explain the value of conducting basic quantitative and qualitative analyses to help achieve communications goals. Such research, they contend, can substantiate a practitioner's hunches and enhance the credibility of the profession. The authors also present the research methods counselors employ: statistical inference, focus groups, sampling, and content analysis, among others. To show how these tools influence and enhance

public relations work, Broom and Dozier engage several case studies.

In similar fashion, John Pavlik, a communications professor at Penn State University, explores the uses of research in the profession, as well as common research techniques. He also examines what methodical research can reveal about the profession itself—that is, what scientific evidence discloses about the field and its effects on the journalism people consume. Pavlik discusses these and similar issues by citing numerous media studies.

Sound research can yield benefits to public relations strategies at all phases, from development to execution to evaluation. For expert instruction on the public relations/research relationship, read *Using Research in Public Relations,* and *Public Relations: What Research Tells Us.*

SUGGESTED READINGS

Attitude and Opinion Research: Why You Need It/How to Do It. 3rd ed. Washington, DC: Case (11 Dupont Circle, 20036), 1983.

Awards, Honors, Prizes. Detroit: Gale Research Co. (Book Tower 835 Penobscott Bldg. 48226), 1990.

Babbie, Earl R. *The Practice of Social Research.* 4th ed. Belmont, CA: Wadsworth, 1986.

Bradburn, Norman, and Seymour Sudman. *Polls and Surveys.* San Francisco: Jossey-Bass, 1988 (350 Sansome St. 94104).

Breen, George, and A. B. Blakenship. *Do-It-Yourself Marketing Research.* 3rd ed. New York: McGraw-Hill, 1989.

Brody E. W., and Gerald C. Stone. *Public Relations Research.* New York: Praeger, 1989.

Brownstone, D. M. *Where to Find Business Information: A Worldwide Guide for Everyone Who Needs the Answers to Business Questions.* New York: John Wiley, 1982.

Duro, Robert, and Bjorn Sandstro. *The Basic Principles of Marketing Warfare.* New York: John Wiley, 1987.

Druck, Kalman B., Merton Fiur, and Don Bates. *New Technology in Public Relations.* New York: Foundation for Public Relations Research and Education, 1987.

Emmert, Philip, and Larry Baker. *Measurements of Communication Behavior.* White Plains, NY: Longman, 1989.

Fink, Arlene, and Jacqueline Kosecoff. *How to Conduct Surveys.* Newbury Park, CA: Sage Publications, 1985.

FORTUNE 500 Directory (250 W. 49th St., New York, NY 10019).

The Foundation Directory. New York: The Foundation Center, 1988 (79 5th Ave. 10003).

Francese, Peter. *Capturing Consumers.* Ithaca, NY: American Demographics, 1989 (P.O. Box 68 14851).

Fuld, Leonard. *Monitoring the Competition: Finding Out What's Really Going on Over There.* New York: John Wiley, 1988.

Grunig, James, and Larissa Grunig. *Public Relations Research Annual.* Hillsdale, NJ: Earlbaum, 1989 (365 Broadway 07642).

Hamilton, Seymour. "Selling the CEO on a Communication Audit." *Communication World* (May 1988): 33, 34. (IABC, 870 Market St., San Francisco, CA 94102).

How to Find Business Intelligence in Washington. Washington, DC: Researchers Publishing Co., 1988.

International Directory of Special Events & Festivals. Special Events Reports (213 W. Institute Place, Chicago)

Investor Relations Almanac/Resource Directory. Corporate Shareholder Press (271 Madison Ave., New York, NY).

Lowery, Shearon, and Melvin DeFleur. *Milestones in Mass Communications Research.* 2nd ed. White Plains, NY: Longman, 1987.

Makower, J., and A. Green, eds. *Instant Information.* Englewood Cliffs, NJ: Prentice-Hall, 1987.

Martel, Myles. *Mastering the Art of Q&A.* Homewood, IL: Dow Jones-Irwin, 1988.

Nasser, David L. "How to Run a Focus Group," *Public Relations Journal* (March 1988): 33, 34.

New Technology & Public Relations. New York: Institute for PR Research and Education, 1988 (310 Madison Ave.).

Newsletter on Newsletters (P.O. Box 311, Rhinebeck, NY 12572). Weekly.

Palshaw, John L. "Full Service Research." Pebble Beach, CA: *Palshaw Measurement,* September/October 1987 (P.O. Box 1439).

Palshaw, John L. "The Planning of Research." Pebble Beach, CA: *Palshaw Measurement,* November/December 1987 (P.O. Box 1439). The author points out those items that must be considered to make a research plan work.

Professional's Guide to Public Relations Services. New York: R. Weiner, 1986 (888 7th Ave.).

Public Interest Profiles (250 activist groups). Foundation for Public Affairs (1255 23rd St., NW, Washington, DC).

Shaw, Robert, and Merlin Stone. *Database Marketing.* New York: John Wiley, 1989.

Soares, Eric. *Cost-Effective Marketing Research.* Westport, CT: Quorum, 1988.

Television & Cable Factbook. 2 vols. TV Digest, (2115 Ward Court, NW, Washington, DC) 20037.

Toth, Elizabeth L. "Broadening Research in Public Affairs." *Public Relations Review* (Summer 1986): 27–36.

Wickman, Penelope. *Insider's Guide to Demographic Know-how.* Ithaca, NY: American Demographics, 1988 (P.O. Box 68 14851).

CASE STUDY   Researching a Position for Alan Louis General

The administrator at Alan Louis General Hospital confronted a problem that he hoped research could help solve. Alan Louis General, although a good hospital, was smaller than most of Bangor's other hospitals and less well known. In its area alone, it competed with 20 other medical facilities. Alan Louis needed a "position" that it could call unique, to attract patients to fill its beds.

For a long time, the Alan Louis administrator, Sven Rapcorn, had believed in the principle that truth will out. Build a better mousetrap, and the world will beat a path to your door. Erect a better hospital, and your beds will forevermore be 98 percent filled. Unfortunately, Rapcorn learned, the real world seldom recognizes truth at first blush.

In the real world, more often than not, perception will triumph. And because people act on perceptions, those perceptions become reality. Successful positioning, Rapcorn learned, is based on recognizing and dealing with people's perceptions. And so Rapcorn set out with research to build on existing perceptions about Alan Louis General.

In the first step, Rapcorn talked to his own doctors and trustees to gather data about their perceptions, not only of Alan Louis General, but also of other hospitals in the community. From this data gathering, pictures of each major competitor began to emerge. For example, the University Health Center had something for everybody—exotic care, specialized care, and basic, bread-and-butter care. Bangor General was a huge, well-respected hospital, whose reputation was so good that only a major tragedy could shake its standing in the community. Mercy Hospital was known for its trauma center. And so on. As for Alan Louis itself, doctors and trustees said that it was a great place to work, that excellent care was provided, and that the nursing staff was particularly friendly and good. The one problem, everyone agreed, was that "nobody knows about us."

The second step in Rapcorn's research project was to test attributes important in health care. Respondents were asked to rank eight factors in order of importance and tell Rapcorn and his staff how each of the surveyed hospitals rated on those factors. The research instrument used a semantic differential scale of 1 to 10, with 1 the worst and 10 the best possible score. Questionnaires were sent to two groups: 1,000 area residents and 500 former Alan Louis patients.

The third step in the research was to tabulate results. Among area residents responding, the eight attributes were ranked accordingly:

1. Surgical care—9.23
2. Medical equipment—9.20
3. Cardiac care—9.16
4. Emergency services—8.96
5. Range of medical services—8.63
6. Friendly nurses—8.62
7. Moderate costs—8.59
8. Location—7.94

After the attributes were ranked, the hospitals in the survey were ranked for each attribute. On advanced surgical care, the most important feature to area residents, Bangor General ranked first, with University Health Center a close second. Alan Louis was far down on the list. The same was true on virtually every other attribute. Indeed, on nursing care, an area in which its staff thought Alan Louis excelled, the hospital came in dead last in the minds of area residents. Rapcorn was not surprised. The largest hospitals in town scored well on most attributes; Alan Louis trailed the pack.

However, the ranking of hospital scores according to former Alan Louis patients revealed an entirely different story. On surgical care, for example, although Bangor General still ranked first, Alan Louis came in a close second. And its scores improved similarly on all other attributes. In fact, in nursing care, where Alan Louis came in last on the survey of area residents, among former patients its score was higher than that of any other hospital. It also ranked first in terms of convenient location and second in terms of costs, range of services, and emergency care.

The fourth step in Rapcorn's research project was to draw some conclusions. He concluded three things.

1. Bangor General was still number one in terms of area hospitals.
2. Alan Louis ranked at or near the top on most attributes, according to those who actually experienced care there.
3. Former Alan Louis patients rated the hospital significantly better than the general public did.

In other words, thought Rapcorn, most of those who try Alan Louis like Alan Louis. The great need was to convince more people to try the hospital.

But how could this be accomplished with a hospital? Other marketers generate trial by sending free samples in the mail, offering cents-off coupons, holding free demonstrations, and the like. Hospitals are more limited in this area. Rapcorn's challenge was to launch a communications campaign to convince prospects to see other area hospitals in a different, less favorable light and/or to give people a specific reason to think about trying Alan Louis. In other words, he needed to come up with a communications strategy that clearly differentiated Alan Louis—admittedly among the smallest hospitals in the area—from the bigger, less personal hospitals in town. Rapcorn was confident that the data he had gathered from the research project were all he needed to come up with a winning idea.

QUESTIONS

1. What kind of communications program would you launch to accomplish Rapcorn's objectives?
2. What would be the cornerstone—the theme—of your communications program?
3. What would be the specific elements of your program?
4. In launching the program, what specific steps would you follow—both inside and outside the hospital—to build support?

Tips from the Top

WALTER K. LINDENMANN

Walter K. Lindenmann, senior vice-president and director of research at Ketchum Public Relations, is among the foremost authorities in public relations research. Mr. Lindenmann is a former manager of the New York office of Opinion Research Corporation and was president of Group Attitudes Corporation, the Hill & Knowlton survey research subsidiary. A sociologist by training, Dr. Lindenmann has supervised more than 500 marketing, public relations, and advertising research projects. He is a frequent lecturer on public opinion research and a visiting adjunct professor at the Syracuse University Newhouse School for Public Communications.

How important is research in public relations practice?
Extremely important. Public relations cannot be carried out effectively without some type of research being conducted. Research is essential for public relations planning, for program development, and for evaluation. It also is quite crucial when an organization needs to obtain information quickly in order to deal with a crisis. If public relations activities are carried out without any research at all, then the public relations practitioner ends up operating in the dark, without any insights and without necessary background information.

What is the "state-of-play" in public relations research today?
Mixed. More practitioners are carrying out research today than ever before, yet there is still a sizable segment of the field that does either no research at all, or does research at a very superficial level.

Can you really measure public relations success?
Most definitely, if you set clear and precise targeted goals and objectives in advance of a public relations project or activity. It is impossible to assess the success or failure of anything, unless you have something specific to measure that success or failure against. If a public relations practitioner were to set a vague goal of hoping to have people somehow become better informed about his or her organization, the success or failure of trying to achieve that is very hard to measure. However, if the practitioner knows—through research—that perhaps only 40 percent of a given audience segment is well informed about something related to his or her organization and

wants to improve that "well-informed" portion to, say 50, percent, then it *is* possible to measure the success or failure of reaching that specific objective.

It is not at all difficult to measure individual components of public relations, such as whether a publicity campaign has succeeded or failed; the effectiveness of a community relations program; or how well an investor relations activity is working, or a speakers' program. If goals and objectives are well defined in advance and are spelled out as precisely as possible, then measurement of results is always possible.

How do you answer practitioners who challenge the necessity of research in public relations work?
I tell them that trying to carry out public relations activities without the benefit of research is a little like trying to walk down a crowded street blindfolded. How can you possibly do effective public relations if you cannot "see" precisely where you are heading, how you are proceeding, and where you have been? Relying on your "instincts" is, of course, of some value, but if that's all you rely on—if you don't obtain necessary facts and opinions about issues or topics important to you or your organization— eventually you are going to miss the mark, go astray, and end up with a disaster.

What is the future of research in public relations?
Extremely promising. As the field of public relations matures, as practitioners engage more and more in strategic planning activities, and as they seek to respond to pressures from senior management to be more "accountable" for what they do, research will grow in importance during the 1990s.

7

Communication: The Backbone of Public Relations

Wall Street acquisitions expert Henry Kravis may be one of the world's savviest financiers, but he had his head handed to him in the spring of 1990 when he tried to get cute with language. In a speech before a sold-out luncheon, sponsored by New York's Financial Women's Association, Kravis greeted his mostly female audience with an apology that his fashion-designer wife couldn't be there: "She could have gotten up and talked about what's probably of much more interest to you—fashion." The boos and hisses were unrelenting.[1] Kravis learned the hard way that, in the 1990s, communications must be handled with great care.

The public relations practitioner is a professional communicator. Above all others in an organization, the practitioner must know how to communicate. This knowledge sets the public relations professional apart from the others.

Fundamentally, communication is a process of exchanging information, imparting ideas, and making oneself understood by others. It also, importantly, includes understanding others in return. Indeed, understanding is critical to the communications process. If one person sends a message to another, who disregards or misunderstands it, then communication hasn't taken place. But if the idea received is the one intended, then communication has been accomplished. Thus, a boss who sends subordinates mountains of memos isn't necessarily communicating with them. If the idea received is not the one intended, then the sender has done little more than convert personal thoughts to words—and there they lie.

Although all of us are endowed with some capacity for communicating, the public relations practitioner must be better than most. Indeed, the effectiveness of public relations professionals is determined by their own ability to communicate and to counsel others on how to communicate. Before public relations practitioners can earn the respect of management and become trusted advisors, they must demonstrate a mastery of many communications skills—writing, speaking, listening, promoting, and counseling. Just as the controller is expected to be an adept accountant and the legal counsel is expected to be an accomplished lawyer, so, too, is the public relations professional expected to be an expert communicator.

Communications Theory

Books have been written on the subject of communications theory. Theoretical explanations of how people communicate vary as much as do the definitions of public relations itself. In its most basic sense, communication commences with a source, who sends a message through a medium to a receiver.

One early theory of communication, the *two-step flow theory*, had it that an organization would beam a message first to the mass media, which would then deliver that message to the great mass of readers, listeners, and viewers for their response. This theory, as noted in Chapter 4, may have given the mass media too much credit. People today are influenced by a variety of factors, of which the media may be one, but not necessarily the dominant one. Another theory, *the concentric-circle theory*, developed by pollster Elmo Roper, assumed that ideas evolve gradually to the public-at-large, moving in concentric circles from Great Thinkers to Great Disciples to Great Disseminators to Lesser Disseminators to the Politically Active to the Politically Inert. Broken down, as rapper M. C. Hammer would say, this theory suggests that people pick up and accept ideas from leaders, whose impact on public opinion may be greater than that of the mass media. The overall study of how communication is used for direction and control is called cybernetics.

Although there are numerous models of communication, one of the most fundamental is the S-M-R approach. This model suggests that the communication process begins with the source, who issues a message to a receiver, who then decides what action to take, if any, relative to the communication. This element of receiver action, or feedback, underscores that good communication always involves dialogue between two or more parties.

The S-M-R model has been modified to include additional elements: (1) an encoding stage, in which the source's original message is translated and conveyed to the receiver; and (2) a decoding stage, in which the receiver interprets the encoded message and takes action. This evolution from the traditional model has resulted in the S-E-M-D-R method, which illustrates graphically the role of the public relations function in modern communications; both the encoding and the decoding stages are of critical importance in communicating any public relations message.

The Source

The source of a message is the central person or organization doing the communicating. The source could be a politician giving a campaign speech, a school announcing curriculum changes, or even, as one superior court judge in Seattle ruled, a topless go-go dancer in the midst of gyrating.

Although the source usually knows how it wants the message to be received, there is no guarantee that it will be understood that way by the receiver. In many cases—a public speech, for example—the speaker is relatively limited in the ability to influence the interpretation of the message. Gestures, voice tone, and volume can be used to add special importance to certain remarks, but whether the audience understands what is intended may ultimately depend on other factors, particularly the encoder.

The Encoder

What the source wants to relate must be translated from an idea in the mind to a communication. In the case of a campaign speech, a politician's original message may be subject to translation or reinterpretation by at least three independent encoders.

1. The politician may consult a speech writer to help put ideas into words on paper. Speech writers become encoders in first attempting to clearly understand the politician's message and then effectively translating that message into language that an audience will understand and, hopefully, accept.
2. Once the speech is written, it may be further encoded into a news release. In this situation, the encoder—perhaps a different individual from the speech writer—selects what seem to be the most salient points of the speech and provides them to media editors in a fairly brief format.
3. A news editor may take the news release and retranslate it before reporting it to the voters, the ultimate audience of the politician's message.

Thus, the original message in the mind of the politician has been massaged three separate times before it ever reaches the intended receivers.

Each time, in all likelihood, the particular encoder has added new subjective shadings to the politician's original message. The very act of encoding depends largely on the encoder's own personal experience.

Words/Semantics   Words are among our most personal and potent weapons. Words can soothe us, bother us, or infuriate us. They can bring us together or drive us apart. They can even cause us to kill or be killed. Words mean different things to different people, depending on their backgrounds, occupations, education, or geographic locations. What one word means to you might be dramatically different from what that same word means to your neighbor. The study of what words really mean is called semantics, and the science of semantics is a peculiar one indeed.

Words are perpetually changing in our language. What's in today is out tomorrow. What a word denotes according to the dictionary may be thoroughly dissimilar to what it connotes in its more emotional or visceral sense. Even the simplest words—*liberal, conservative, profits, consumer activists*—can spark semantic skyrockets. Many times, without knowledge of the territory, the semantics of words may make no sense. Take the word *cool.* In American vernacular a person who is cool is good. A person who is "not so hot" is bad. So *cool* is the opposite of "not so hot." But wait a minute; "not so hot" must also be the opposite of *hot.* Therefore, in a strange and convoluted way, cool must equal hot.

In the 1990s, public relations professionals must constantly be alert to alterations in the language. In 1990, when the august New York Jockey Club restaurant offered a breakfast called the "Central Park Jogger"—a term widely used as the identification of a woman brutally attacked the year before in a well-publicized rape case—the menu was reprinted. On the other hand, when the term *couch potato* came into vogue to signify an inveterate television watcher, a Pennsylvania potato chip maker was quick to capitalize (Figure 7–1).

Even more confusing is the language used by various special publics in society, which seems foreign to the uninitiated.

◆ To a computer analyst, a bit and a bomb and a chip are commonplace. The rest of us might have a hard time discerning that a bit is the smallest binary number, a bomb is a piece of computer equipment that ceases to function, and a chip is a tiny wafer of silicon or an equally tiny complete circuit.

◆ To a human resources manager, a 401(k) is a salary deferral plan. A Gantt chart is a bar chart used in project planning and scheduling. And COBRA, of course, is the Consolidated Omnibus Budget Reconciliation Act covering employers of 20 or more who offer group health plans.

◆ And then there are teenagers, whose vocabularies defy description. Sure, *they* know what they're talking about; but do the rest of us have any idea

FIGURE 7–1 Pennsylvania snack food maker Snyder of Berlin was quick to take advantage of the pervasive use of the term *couch potato* by cooking up a "potato couch" for use in a promotion for Thunder Crunch, its newest line of potato chips. The spud sofa was a most "ap-peeling" promotion. (Sorry.) *(Courtesy of Marcus Public Relations)*

that *fresh* means cool, *dweeb* means nerd, *gleek* means spitting, *deaf* means the same thing as *fresh,* and *biter* is another name for *dweeb*?

Finally, there are the dozen words—important for communicators to know—that, according to Yale University, are the most persuasive in the English language: *discovery, easy, new, proven, guarantee, health, love, money, results, safety, save,* and *you.*

The point here is that the words used in the encoding stage have a significant influence on the message conveyed to the ultimate receiver. Thus, the source must depend greatly on the ability of the encoder to accurately understand and effectively translate the true message—with all its semantic complications—to the receiver.

The Message

Once an encoder has taken in the source's ideas and translated them into terms a receiver can understand, the ideas are then transmitted in the form of a message. The message may be carried in a variety of communications media: speeches, newspapers, news releases, press conferences, broadcast reports, and face-to-face meetings. Communications theorists differ on what exactly constitutes the message, but here are three of the more popular explanations.

B E T W E E N   T H E   L I N E S

Are You Sure It Means What You Think It Means?

Words can get you in a lot of trouble. Public relations professionals, who deal on a daily basis with the arcane province of semantics, must be aware of and sensitive to the potential explosiveness of words and phrases. The following random list of culturally biased phrases is a case in point. How many of these can you adequately define? Are you sure?

- Over the hill
- Cool your jets
- Catch-22
- Out of the blue
- Go for it
- Stonewall it
- A "10"
- We blew it
- A boo-boo
- Get it together
- Jive turkey
- Shot full of holes
- Flipped out
- Circular file
- Deep six it
- Put it on the back burner
- The bottom fell out
- Wasted
- Workhorse
- Taking care of business (TCBing)

---

1. **The content is the message.** According to this theory, which is far and away the most popular, the content of a communication—what it says—constitutes its message. According to this view, the real importance of a communication—the message—lies in the meaning of an article or in the intent of a speech. Neither the medium through which the message is being communicated nor the individual doing the communicating is as important as the content.

2. **The medium is the message.** Other communications theorists—the late Canadian professor Marshall McLuhan being the best known—argue that the content of a communication is not the message at all. According to McLuhan, the content is less important than the vehicle of communication.

   McLuhan's argument stemmed largely from the fact that many people today watch television. He said that television is a "cool" medium—that is, someone can derive meaning from a TV message without working too hard. On the other hand, reading involves hard work to grasp an idea fully; thus, newspapers, magazines, and books are "hot" media. Furthermore, McLuhan argued, a television viewer can easily become part of that which is being viewed.

One direct outgrowth of this medium-is-the-message theory was the mid-1970s development of the friendly-team style of local television news reporting. Often called the eyewitness approach, this format encouraged interaction among TV newscasters in order to involve viewers as part of the news team family.

The medium of television has become particularly important to the president of the United States. John F. Kennedy literally won the presidential election on the strength of his TV debate performance against Richard Nixon. President Gerald Ford, although not particularly well known for his public speaking presence, rehearsed assiduously for TV appearances and performed well. President Jimmy Carter also took pains with his TV image, occasionally dressing casually—in cardigan sweaters rather than dark suits—to convey subtly a message of confidence, informality, and the antithesis of the imperial presidency.

In recent years, the best use of television to its maximum advantage for the White House was made by Ronald Reagan. Clearly, he had the most experience in the medium, having begun as a movie actor and later been a media spokesman for General Electric. Just how good Reagan was on television was underscored in his debates with 1984 Democratic candidate Walter Mondale; Reagan revealed himself as a witty, articulate, unflappable performer. During his term, President Reagan used television to boost virtually every important administration program, from budget cuts to strategic defense to relations with the Soviets.

George Bush, well schooled in the political art, picked up where Reagan left off. Bush frequently held news conferences for television consumption, and with Cable News Network broadcasting live from the White House, the president had a ready live audience. Although the chief executive got in some trouble with his peculiar speaking phrases—"read my lips," "lighten up," and the inimitable "blah blah blah"—he nonetheless became every bit the television force his predecessor was.

3. **The person is the message.** Still other theorists argue that it is neither the content nor the medium that is the message, but rather the speaker. For example, Hitler was a master of persuasion. His minister of propaganda, Josef Goebbels, used to say, "Any man who thinks he can persuade, can persuade." Hitler practiced this self-fulfilling communications prophecy to the hilt. Feeding on the perceived desires of the German people, Hitler was concerned much less with the content of his remarks than with their delivery. His maniacal rantings and frantic gestures seized public sentiment and sent friendly crowds into a frenzy. In every way, Hitler himself was the primary message of his communications.

Today, in a similar vein, we often refer to a leader's charisma. Frequently, the charismatic appeal of a political leader may be more important than what that individual says. President John F. Kennedy, for example, could move an audience by the very inflection of his words. Jesse Jackson can bring a group to its feet, merely by shaking a fist or raising the pitch of his voice.

Often, people cannot distinguish between the words and the person who speaks them. The words, the face, the body, the eyes, the attitude, the timing, the wit, the presence—all form a composite that, as a whole, influences the listener. As communications consultant Roger Ailes has put it, it comes down to the "like" factor in communication. Ailes points out that some candidates get votes just because people like them. "They forget that you're short, or you're fat, or you're bald . . . they say 'I like that guy.' "[2] In such cases, the source of the communication becomes every bit as important as the message itself.

B E T W E E N   T H E   L I N E S

Are You Sure You Saw What You Thought You Saw?

First, read the sentence that follows:

FINISHED FILES ARE THE RESULT OF YEARS OF SCIENTIFIC STUDY COMBINED WITH THE EXPERIENCE OF MANY YEARS.

Now, count the *Fs* in the sentence. Count them only once, and do not go back and count them again.

QUESTION
How many *Fs* are there?

ANSWER
There are six *Fs*. However, because the capital *F* in *OF* sounds like a capital *V,* it seems to disappear. Most people perceive only three *Fs* in the sentence. Our conditioned, habitual patterns (mental blocks) restrict us from being as alert as we should be. Frequently, we fail to perceive things as they really are.

The Decoder

After a message has been transmitted, it must be decoded by a receiver before action can be taken. This stage is like the encoding stage in that the receiver takes in the message and translates it into his own common terms. Obviously, language again plays a critical role. The decoder must fully understand the message before acting on it; if the message is unclear or the decoder is unsure of its intent, there's probably little chance that the action taken by the receiver will be the action desired by the source. Messages must be in common terms.

A good example of the problem of uncommon terms is the following fictitious exchange between the Bureau of Standards of the U.S. Department of Commerce and a New York plumber. The plumber had written the bureau to say that she had found hydrochloric acid to be a good drain cleaner and to ask whether the acid was harmless for this purpose.

Washington replied, "The efficacy of hydrochloric acid is indisputable,

---

BETWEEN THE LINES

Decoding Language at the Pension Office

These 11 extracts supposedly emanate from genuine letters sent to the pensions office of some company, somewhere, some time. Although crude, they were written in good faith by their authors. Try to decode them.

1. I can't get sick pay. I have six children. Can you tell me why this is?
2. This is my eighth child. What are you going to do about it?
3. Mrs. Morris has no clothes and has not had any for a year. The clergy have been visiting her.
4. Unless I get my husband's money quickly, I shall be forced to lead an immortal life.
5. I am sending you my marriage certificate and six children. I had seven and one died, which was baptized on a half sheet of paper by the Rev. Thomas.
6. In answer to your letter, I have given birth to a little boy weighing 10 pounds. Is this satisfactory?
7. You have changed my little girl into a little boy. Will this make any difference?
8. I have no children as my husband is a bus driver and works all day and night.
9. Milk is wanted for my baby as the father is unable to supply it.
10. I want money as quick as you can send it. I have been in bed with my doctor all week, and he does not seem to be doing me any good.
11. Sir, I am glad to say that my husband, reported missing, is now dead.

but the chlorine residue is incompatible with metallic permanence."

The plumber, unfamiliar with scientific terminology, replied that she was mighty glad that the bureau agreed with her.

The bureau answered with a note of alarm: "We cannot assume responsibility for the production of toxic and noxious residues with hydrochloric acid and suggest that you use an alternate procedure."

The plumber replied that she was happy that the bureau still agreed with her.

The bureau finally exploded: "Don't use hydrochloric acid, you jackass. It eats the hell out of your pipes."

Perception

How a receiver decodes a message depends greatly on that person's own perception. How an individual looks at and comprehends a message is a key to effective communications (Figure 7–2). Remember that everyone is biased; no two people perceive a message identically. Personal biases are

What do you see: Fish or fowl?

FIGURE 7–2   Often what we see may not be what others see. (Hint: there are both white fish and black fowl.) *(Courtesy of Trout & Ries)*

nurtured by many factors, including stereotypes, symbols, semantics, peer group pressures, and—especially in today's culture—the media.

Stereotypes   Everyone lives in a world of stereotypical figures. Ivy Leaguers, Midwesterners, feminists, bankers, politicians, PR types, and thousands of other characterizations cause people to think of certain specific images. Public figures, for example, are typecast regularly. The dumb blond, the bigoted blue-collar worker, and the shifty used-car salesman are the kinds of stereotypes our society—particularly television—perpetuates.

Consider the plight of the poor businessman. As syndicated cartoonist Charles Saxon wrote, "The big problem for cartoonists is that most businessmen don't fall into comfortable stereotypes."[3] Nonetheless, cartoonists are obligated to come up with stereotypes. Therefore, the ubiquitous businessman caricature is middle-aged, looks like he might be posing for a portrait in *Fortune*, rarely relaxes his facial features, and, in general, looks overblown and pompous.

Like it or not, most of us are victims of such stereotypes. For example, research indicates that a lecture delivered by a person wearing glasses will be perceived as "significantly more believable" than the same lecture delivered before the same audience by the same lecturer without glasses. The stereotyped impression of people with glasses is that they are more trustworthy and more believable.

BETWEEN THE LINES

What's in a Name?

Stereotypes apply most especially to our own names.

In one study, a pair of psychologists showed that a grade-school essay titled "What I Did Last Sunday," when said to have been written by a "David" or a "Lisa," consistently got a better grade from teachers than an identical composition said to have been written by an "Elmer" or a "Bertha."

Another study of the effect of women's first names on how others perceive their attractiveness tested three "desirable" names (Kathy, Jennifer, and Christine) against three "undesirable" names (Ethel, Harriet, and Gertrude). The names were attached to photographs of six women who, in an earlier study, were judged to be equally attractive. People at random were asked to choose a local beauty queen from the six. Ethel, Harriet, and Gertrude lost four out of five times.

Neil Spitzer, "What's in a Name?" *Atlantic Monthly* (August 1988): 14, 16.

NAMES

Symbols   The clenched fist salute, the swastika, and the thumbs-up sign all leave distinct impressions with most people. Marshaled properly, symbols can be used as effective persuasive elements. The Statue of Liberty, the Red Cross, the Star of David, and many other symbols have been used traditionally for positive persuasion. Indeed, in the Falkland Islands invasion by Argentina in 1982, England used the symbol of its queen—and the honor of the crown—to stimulate public sentiment behind the war effort to win the islands back. Later that same year, a disgruntled antinuclear activist tried to hold the Washington Monument hostage as a symbol of a threatened nation. In the Mideast in 1990, Iraqis burned the American flag as a symbol of the American "satan."

Semantics   Public relations professionals make their living largely by knowing how to use words effectively to communicate desired meanings. Occasionally, this is tricky because the same words may hold contrasting meanings for different people. Especially vulnerable are popular and politically sensitive phrases such as "capital punishment," "law and order," "liberal politician," "right winger," and on and on, until you reach the point where the Oakridge Mall in San Jose, California, demanded that the gourmet hamburger restaurant on its premises, with a logo depicting a smiling hamburger with a monocle and top hat, either change its "suggestive name" or leave the mall. The restaurant's name? Elegant Buns.

In the 1990s, the label *terrorist,* a misnomer that the media have bestowed on those who hijack planes and blow up airport terminals, may play right into the hands of those who attack innocent civilians. Because behavioral science studies show that such people seek the aura of power, calling them terrorists concedes that they are, in fact, achieving their aims. One semanticist argued that such criminals should be called condemned barbarians or savages, rather than terming "a puny misfit as a great terrorist."[4]

Semantics must be handled with extreme care because language and the meanings of words change constantly. Good communicators always consider the consequences of the words they plan to use *before* using them.

Peer Groups   In one famous study, students were asked to point out, in progression, the shortest of three lines.

A _____

B _____

C _____

Although Line B is obviously the shortest, each student in the class except one was told in advance to answer that Line C was the shortest. The object of the test was to see whether the one student would agree with his peers.

Results generally indicated that, to a statistically significant degree, all students, including the uncoached one, chose C. Peer pressure prevails.

Media   The power of the media—particularly as an agenda setter or reinforcement mechanism—is also substantial. A common complaint among lawyers is that their clients cannot receive fair trials because of pretrial publicity leading to preconceived verdicts among potential jurors who read newspapers and watch television.

In one famous case in North Carolina, Army officer Jeffrey MacDonald was put on trial for the savage killing of his wife and two children. The officer claimed that he was innocent and that a band of hippies had stabbed him and killed his family. State newspapers publicized the case extensively, running photographs of the soldier and commentary about the circumstances of the murders. Neither the soldier nor his lawyer would talk to the press. A random telephone survey, taken a week before the trial, indicated that most people thought the soldier was guilty. Several weeks later, however, the Army dropped murder charges against him when it couldn't make a case. Ironically, nine years later the man was convicted of those murders, subsequently released, and then found guilty on appeal. In 1985, MacDonald's story was the subject of a scathing book and a television docudrama, *Fatal Vision*, after which subsequent appeals were flatly rejected.

The point remains that people often base perceptions on what they read or hear without bothering to dig further to elicit the facts of the situation. Although appearances are sometimes revealing, they are often deceiving.

The Receiver

You really aren't communicating unless someone is at the other end to hear and understand what you're saying. This situation is analogous to the old mystery of the falling tree in the forest: does it make a noise when it hits the ground if there's no one there to hear it? Regardless of the answer, communication doesn't take place if a message doesn't reach the intended receivers and exert the desired effect on those receivers.

Even if a communication is understood clearly, there is no guarantee that the motivated action will be the desired one. In fact, a message may trigger several different effects.

1. **It may change attitudes.** This result, however, is very tough to accomplish and rarely happens.
2. **It may crystallize attitudes.** This outcome is much more common. Often a message will influence receivers to take actions they might already have been thinking about taking but needed an extra push to accomplish. For example, a receiver might want to contribute to a

The Erring Encoder

To swing the election, Representative Rankle desperately needed the votes of the Booneville Urban League chapter. "It's up to you, Herby," Rankle confided to his chief speech writer, Herbert Mertz, "to make sure we get the key points across in my speech tonight, to let 'em know I'm up to speed on the issues—particularly campaign contributors and busing." On the former issue, Rankle was well aware of rumors that his campaign was subsidized by several underworld figures. On the latter issue, Rankle knew that the recent burning of a school bus had created an enormous amount of tension among Urban League members.

"Make it clear, Herby, that I am against revealing the names of campaign contributors because I believe in protecting an individual's right to privacy, and I don't intend to focus the spotlight of public attention on those who have contributed to my campaign. I wouldn't like it if I were they, and I know they wouldn't either. As far as busing, let 'em know that I know the debate is a hot one, but that I simply will not accept the old, pat answers. I intend to seek revolutionary solutions on this issue of heated debate."

"I understand perfectly, Congressman," Mertz smiled. "Just leave the writing to me."

Regrettably for Rankle, that's exactly what he did. It took only a few sentences to convince the audience that Rankle was either crooked, stupid, insensitive, or a combination of all three. Here's how his speech began: "I intend tonight, ladies and gentlemen, to address two subjects that I know are on your minds—campaign contributors and busing. On the former, I believe quite strongly that a candidate should never disclose the names of his campaign contributors. I know my contributors well, and I know that such disclosure would frankly embarrass them. Were I in their position, I have no doubt that I, too, would be embarrassed.

"Let me be equally frank on school busing—indeed, another burning issue in our community. Neither I nor my running mates will sit by when others call for the old pat solutions. We will fight their every move. In a word, my colleagues and I are revolting! Tonight, I intend to prove it."

QUESTIONS

1. Where did Mertz go wrong in encoding the message?
2. Might Mertz have believed his encoding was correct?
3. How many faux pas did Rankle commit in his remarks? Might they be enough to cost him the election?
4. Had you been Mertz, what would you have done differently in encoding the speech?

certain charity, but seeing a child's photo on a contribution canister might crystallize the attitude sufficiently to trigger action.

3. **It might create a wedge of doubt.** Communication can sometimes force receivers to modify their points of view. A persuasive message can cause receivers to question their original thinking on an issue.
4. **It may do nothing.** Often, communication results in no action at all. When the American Cancer Society waged an all-out effort to cut into cigarette sales, the net impact of the communication campaign was hardly significant.

Feedback

Feedback is critical to the process. A communicator must get feedback from a receiver to know what messages are or are not getting through and how to structure future communications. Occasionally, feedback is ignored by professional communicators, but this is always a mistake.

Whether the objectives of a communication have been met can often be assessed by such things as the amount of sales, number of letters, or number of votes obtained. If individuals take no action after receiving a communication, feedback must still be sought. In certain cases, although receivers have taken no discernible action, they may have understood and even passed on the message to other individuals. This person-to-person relay of received messages creates a two-step flow of communications: (1) vertically from a particular source and (2) horizontally from interpersonal contact. The targeting of opinion leaders as primary receivers is based on the hope that they will distribute received messages horizontally within their own communities.

In any event, it's always a sound investment to research how many people saw or heard a message, how many agreed with it, how many acted on it, and what action they took. Without measurement, an organization is communicating blindly.

Making a Message Count

Public relations practitioners should be familiar with the variety of communication approaches available, from interpersonal to small group to mass audience. The media available for such communications are myriad—everything from interpersonal speech to visual aids to skywriting. In recent years, innovations—electronic technology, electronic mail, electronic conferencing, desktop publishing, and the like—have speeded public relations messages.

The ultimate communication is influenced by many factors: emotional reactions, superstitions, physical conditions, prejudices, indifference to the message, and numerous others. A smart communicator must be aware of the common mistakes that people make when they communicate.

♦ **Failing to listen well**   Most people are poor listeners. If you're doing more than half the talking when you're in a meeting with others, then you should improve your listening skills. Listeners should be active.

♦ **Failing to use the "you" approach**   People are interested in what's in it for them, not what you or the organization desires. A "you" approach communicates to the recipient that the speaker cares about the recipient's needs.

♦ **Sending the wrong nonverbal signals**   Experts say that 65 percent of a message is conveyed nonverbally in face-to-face communication. People look for such things as body position and movement, gestures, facial expression, eye contact, silence, use of space and time, and so on.

♦ **Failing to write to be understood**   Many people write to *im*press, not to *ex*press. They use long, pompous words in the mistaken belief that such words add dignity and strength to their messages. They don't.

♦ **Lacking knowledge of audiences**   Communicators must relate their messages to the specific characteristics, needs, and interests of their audiences. They should know such things as educational levels and occupations, beliefs and attitudes, group loyalties and norms, and the disposition of the audience—friendly, hostile, or indifferent.

B E T W E E N   T H E   L I N E S

Whaaat?

Extra credit for anyone who can decode the following sentence:

> We respectfully petition, request, and entreat that due and adequate provision be made, this day and the date herein after subscribed, for the satisfying of this petitioner's nutritional requirements and for the organizing of such methods as may be deemed necessary and proper to assure the reception by and for said petitioner of such quantities of baked products as shall, in the judgment of the aforesaid petitioner, constitute a sufficient supply thereof.*

Whaaat?

*Give us this day our daily bread.

◆ **Failing to realize that communication is a two-way process** Many think communication is finished when information is imparted. They fail to consider that communication involves getting feedback and evaluating it.

◆ **Failing to observe common courtesies** If communicators come across as impersonal or rude, their ability to communicate with people will suffer. On the other hand, if they are respectful of others and treat them courteously, their audiences will listen to what is said. More importantly, they are apt to understand and appreciate the message.[5]

Summary

In the 1990s, some communications consultants believe the future of communication may be a "step back in time." The advent of narrowcasting and communicating to more targeted, smaller audiences will mean a return to more direct communication between people. By combining the new technology—cable, videocassettes, telemarketing, floppy disks, and all the rest—people will need the help of public relations professionals to communicate effectively.[6]

There really is no trick to effective communication. Other than some facility with techniques, hard work and common sense are the basic guiding principles. Naturally, communication must follow performance; organizations must back up what they say with action. Slick brochures, engaging speeches, intelligent articles, and a good press may capture the public's attention, but in the final analysis the only way to obtain continued public support is through proper performance.

DISCUSSION STARTERS

1. Above all else, the public relations practitioner is what?
2. Describe the "process" of communication.
3. Why do words like *liberal, conservative, profits,* and *consumer activist* spark semantic skyrockets?
4. What communications vehicle did President Reagan and President Bush use to maximum effectiveness?
5. Describe the S-E-M-D-R approach to communication.
6. Give an example of an encoder, a decoder.
7. How does perception influence a person's decoding?
8. Why is feedback critical to the communications process?
9. What common mistakes do people make when they communicate?
10. Why do some communications consultants believe the future of communications in the 90s may be a "step back in time"?

NOTES

1. Susan Antilla, "An Unfashionable Miscue by Kravis," *USA Today,* 7 March 1990, 2B.
2. "The 'Like Factor' in Communications," *Executive Communications* (February 1988): 1.

3. Charles Saxon, "How to Draw a Businessman," *New York Times,* 28 March 1982, 2F.

4. "Semantics Power," *Public Relations Reporter* (April 4, 1988): 4.

5. Frank Grazian, "Common Mistakes People Make When They Communicate," *Communication Briefings* (August 1987): 8A, B.

6. Communication May Step Back in Time '90s," *IABC Communication World* (February 1990): 9.

TOP OF THE SHELF

Ailes, Roger, and Jon Kraushar. *You Are the Message.* Homewood, IL: Dow Jones-Irwin, 1988.

Some rules to follow when speaking are relax, think clearly, exhibit emotion, and most important, be yourself. So advises *You Are the Message,* which builds on people's natural communications abilities to help them inform, persuade, and entertain.

Roger Ailes, a communications consultant whose clients have included U.S. presidents and Fortune 500 CEOs, shares his public speaking acumen in this useful book. Above all, he urges, play to your strengths when talking, whether you're at meetings, client presentations or job interviews. That means cleverly employing facial expressions, body movement, vocal pitch, humor, tone, and volume. Once you've mastered

these cues, Ailes suggests incorporating them into his "four essentials of a great communicator": be prepared, make others comfortable, be committed, and be interesting. Ailes says that if you consider these guidelines and are likeble—the "magic bullet"—you, too, can become a polished communicator. Your verbal and nonverbal skills will work together to produce crisp and lively speech.

Ailes suggests that communicating well counts more than on-the-job performance when it comes to moving up the corporate ladder. To help your climb, pay close attention to *You Are the Message.*

SUGGESTED READINGS

Agee, W. *Introduction to Mass Communication.* 9th ed. New York: Harper & Row, 1988.

Baldridge, L. *Complete Guide to Executive Manners.* New York: Rawson Associates, 1985.

Bateman, David, and Norma Sigband. *Communicating in Business.* 3rd ed. Glenview, IL.: Scott-Foresman, 1989.

Bittner, John. *Mass Communications.* 5th ed. Englewood Cliffs, NJ: Prentice-Hall, 1989.

Crable, Richard, and Steven Vibbert. *Public Relations as Communication Management.* Edina, MN: Burgess International Group, 1986.

Degan C. *Understanding & Using Video: Guide for the Organizational Communicator.* White Plains, NY: Longman, 1985.

Didsbury, Howard. *Communications and the Future.* Bethesda, MD: World Future Society, 1986 (4916 St. Elmo Ave. 20814).

Fraser, Edith A. *Glossary of Common Acronyms and Terms of Modern Human Resource Management.* Orangeburg, NY: Implementation Support Associates (100 Dutch Hill Road 10962).

Goldhaber, Gerald. *Organizational Communication.* 4th ed. Dubuque, IA: W. C. Brown Co., 1986.

Grazian, Frank. *Common Mistakes People Make When They Communicate.* Blackwood, NJ: *Communication Briefings* August 1987 (806 Westminster Blvd. 08012). To help people identify areas that could be improved, the author brings some serious communication errors to light. This sheet is a "must read."

Hilton, J. *Straight Talk About Videoconferencing.* Englewood Cliffs, NJ: Prentice-Hall, 1986.

International Encyclopedia of Communication. New York: Oxford University Press, 1989, Vol. 4.

Kreps, Gary L. *Organizational Communications.* White Plains, NY: Longman, 1986.

Murphy, Kevin. *Effective Listening.* New York: Bantam, 1987.

Murphy, Kevin. *What Did You Say?* New York: Bantam, 1987.

Petty, Richard, and John T. Capioppo. *Communication & Persuasion.* New York: Springer-Verlag, 1986.

Ragan Report (Ragan Communications, 407 S. Dearborn, Chicago, IL 60605). Weekly.

Reardon, Kathleen. *Interpersonal Communication.* Belmont, CA: Wadsworth, 1987.

Severin, Werner, and James Tankard. *Communication Theories: Origins, Methods, Uses.* White Plains, NY: Longman, 1987.

Stevens, Art. *The Persuasion Explosion.* Washington, DC: Acropolis Books, 1985.

Winett, Richard. *Information & Behavior: Systems of Influence.* Hillsdale, NY: Erlbaum, 1986.

CASE STUDY   The IUD Notice "Mumbo Jumbo"

For over a decade, the A. H. Robins Company was plagued with health claims arising from its Dalkon Shield birth control device. The company began marketing the device in early 1971, only to be implicated three years later in the deaths of four women who had become pregnant while wearing the Dalkon Shield and had suffered septic abortions from infection in the uterus. By June 1974, Robins had suspended distribution and sale of the Dalkon Shield, and by January 1975, the product was permanently removed from the market.

Nonetheless, the damage had been done. In 1979, a federal court awarded $6.8 million to a Colorado woman who charged that the use of a Dalkon Shield had caused a miscarriage that almost killed her. Late in 1980, Robins recommended to doctors that they recall all Dalkon Shields.

Late in 1984, Robins started an advertising campaign aimed at convincing women still wearing the device to have it removed. Claims paid by Robins and its insurers at the time amounted to more than $244 million in 7,600 suits involving the device. Midway through 1985, Robins set aside $615 million to settle legal claims from women who had used its Dalkon Shields. But in August, realizing its reserve fund would not be enough to pay the legal expenses for the now 15,500 suits and claims it faced, Robins filed for bankruptcy protection from its creditors.

Shortly thereafter, Robins proposed an international publicity and advertising campaign setting an end-of-the-year deadline for women wishing to file claims against the company. Robins worded its announcement in the following manner:

> Any claims filed after December 30, 1985, shall be disallowed. Any person or entity that is required to file a proof of claim and that fails to do so by December 30, 1985, shall not be treated as a creditor for purposes of voting or distribution, and any claim of such person or entity shall be forever barred; provided, however, that a proof of claim for any claim against A. H. Robins, Incorporated, arising out of the rejection by A. H. Robins Company, Incorporated, of a voidable transfer as described in Bankruptcy Code Section 502(g) and 502(h), must be filed on or before the later of December 30, 1985, and 30 days after the entry of an order authorizing the rejection of the executory contract or unexpired lease, or 30 days after the entry of an order or judgment avoiding the transfer.

IMPORTANT NOTICE
REGARDING THE
DALKON SHIELD INTRAUTERINE
BIRTH CONTROL DEVICE (IUD) AND
A. H. ROBINS COMPANY, INCORPORATED

On August 21, 1985, A. H. Robins Company, Incorporated, the maker of the Dalkon Shield, filed a case under Chapter 11 of the United States Bankruptcy Code.

If you: (a) may have been injured because you used the Dalkon Shield; or

     (b) may have used the Dalkon Shield but have not as yet experienced an injury; or

     (c) may have been injured because of another person's use of the Dalkon Shield

and if you wish to assert a claim against the A. H. Robins Company, Incorporated, the United States Bankruptcy Court for the Eastern District of Virginia must receive your claim in writing at the Clerk's office or at the address below **on or before April 30, 1986, or you will lose your right to make a claim.** Receipt of a simple statement containing your full name and complete mailing address and the fact that you are making a Dalkon Shield claim will register your claim.

Mail your statement with your full name and complete mailing address to:

    Dalkon Shield
    P. O. Box 444
    Richmond, VA 23203
    U.S.A.

Mail your claim promptly. Each claimant is required to file a separate claim. You do not need a lawyer to file a claim.

After your claim is registered, you will be sent a questionnaire with additional instructions. You must complete this questionnaire and return it or your claim may be disallowed. Claimants residing in the United States must return the questionnaire by June 30, 1986. Claimants residing outside the United States must return the questionnaire by July 30, 1986.

If you have already filed a claim with the United States Bankruptcy Court for the Eastern District of Virginia, do not file a second claim as your claim is already registered. You also will be sent a formal questionnaire with additional instructions with which you must comply.

An Important Health Warning To Women Using An IUD

If you are still using an intrauterine birth control device (IUD) inserted in the early to mid 1970s, this message is for you. Many women had an IUD called the Dalkon Shield inserted during that time. It is important that each Dalkon Shield be removed, since there is substantial medical opinion that its continued use may pose a serious personal health hazard. If you are still using a Dalkon Shield, A. H. Robins Company will pay your doctor or clinic to remove it.

A. H. Robins ceased distribution of the Dalkon Shield in 1974. Many claims have been made that the device causes health problems, including pelvic infections, that may result in serious injury or death. In 1980, A. H. Robins advised doctors to remove the Dalkon Shield from any woman still using it. In 1983, the U.S. Food and Drug Administration and other

The Dalkon Shield

government agencies issued the same advice based on their concern about pelvic infections among Dalkon Shield users.

A. H. Robins will pay your doctor or clinic for any examination needed to find out if you are using the Dalkon Shield. If you are, A. H. Robins will pay the cost of having it removed.

WHAT TO DO

If you know you are using a Dalkon Shield IUD, or if you are using an IUD inserted in the early to mid 1970s and are unsure of the kind, call your doctor or health clinic for an appointment. Your call will be in confidence, and there will be no cost to you.

If you have further questions, please call A. H. Robins Company toll free. The number is **1-800-247-7220.** (In Virginia call collect **804-257-2015.**)

A·H·ROBINS
1407 Cummings Drive, Richmond, Virginia 23220

FIGURE 7–3   *(Courtesy of A. H. Robins Co.)*

In October, a federal judge ordered the company to simplify the notice because it was written in "legal mumbo jumbo" and not in plain English.

In January 1986, the company's revised, plain-English advertising and publicity campaign began with a new claims deadline set for April 30, 1986 (Figure 7.3). At the end of the year, the company faced more than 300,000 claims on behalf of women charging that the Dalkon Shield had caused infertility, involuntary abortions, pelvic disease, and, in some cases, death.

In December 1987, a federal judge said that A. H. Robins would have to set aside about $2.5 billion in its bankruptcy reorganization plan to compensate the women injured by the Dalkon Shield. The judge's estimate was more than double the sum Robins had projected at a hearing the prior month. The company said it would "try to meet the demands" that the judge had set.

QUESTIONS

1. Does it appear to you that Robins acted in good faith throughout the Dalkon Shield controversy?
2. Does the fact that Robins insisted that its product "posed no greater risk to its users than any other intrauterine device" change your answer to question 1?
3. Do you think the judge was justified in making the company revise the wording of its deadline announcement?
4. How might you have worded the ultimate announcement?

For further information about the Dalkon Shield controversy, see Christopher Policano, "A. H. Robins and the Dalkon Shield," *Public Relations Journal* (March 1985): 17–21; Stuart Diamond, "Robins in Bankruptcy Filing Cites Dalkon Shield Claims," *The New York Times*, 22 August 1985, 1; and Francine Schwadel, "Robins and Plaintiffs Face Uncertain Future," *The Wall Street Journal*, 23 August 1985, 4.

Tips from the Top

FRANKIE A. HAMMOND

Frankie Hammond is associate professor of public relations in the College of Journalism and Communications at the University of Florida, where she has taught since 1974. During a five-year period as director of development and placement for the college, Professor Hammond helped more than 1,000 graduates launch their professional careers in public relations, advertising, journalism, and broadcasting. A former reporter and editor, Professor Hammond has also served as acting associate chairman for the University of Florida's Department of Advertising and Public Relations.

How would you describe today's public relations students?
Today's students appear to be more career-driven than their earlier counterparts. They are ambitious and eager to join the workforce. But at the same time, they exhibit more altruism; they want to give something back to society. Current students' interests expand beyond the workplace, and money no longer seems to be a prime motivator.

What advice do you give those who want to become public relations practitioners?
Learn anything you can about everything you can. Then write. Rewrite. And rewrite some more. Sharpen your problem-solving capabilities. Get practical experience while you're in school and during the summers. Participate in the Public Relations Student Society of America. Take advantage of every opportunity to improve yourself and your skills.

Why should a student be interested in a career in public relations?
Public relations is such a multifaceted endeavor that any individual should be interested in it. The opportunities for personal and professional growth offer a lifetime of interesting work, interesting people, and a lot of enjoyment.

How does one land a job in the field?
Solid writing ability, common sense, and good judgment are always in demand. There are many entry-level jobs for well-rounded, enthusiastic, skilled, and persistent new graduates.

What distinguishes a good public relations practitioner?
Judgment and ethics, backed by communications skills and a familiarity with the so-

cial and behavioral forces that make people tick. An understanding of the public relations process and how it impacts on and is impacted by society is a must. The ability to view problems as opportunities and having a good sense of humor are also important.

What is the most significant challenge confronting public relations today?
The constant change in the environment in which public relations operates, and therefore the constant change in its practice, is undoubtedly the most significant challenge today. The successful practitioner must adapt to meet the societal, economic, and political changes in the world or become an anachronism.

If you had your career to start over again, what would you do?
Basically, I would do what I have done. I have had a variety of interesting experi-

ences as the result of a willingness to take advantage of opportunities and new directions as they came up. It's added a broader perspective to my thinking, as well as being a lot of fun.

What will the state of public relations be like in the year 2000?
Virtually every organization will have a public relations effort because the organization's survival will depend on it. The need for and appreciation of public relations will increase as the field continues its shift from primarily communications toward more emphasis on counseling and advising. The number of practitioners in top-level jobs will increase by the turn of the century, with more and more CEOs named from the ranks of practitioners.

8

Fundamentals of Public Relations Writing

The ability to write easily, coherently, and quickly distinguishes the public relations professional from others in an organization. It's not that the skills of counseling and judgment aren't just as important; some experts argue that these skills are far more important than knowing how to write. Maybe. But not knowing how to write—how to express ideas on paper—may reduce the opportunities to ascend the public relations success ladder.

General managers usually come from finance, legal, engineering, or sales backgrounds, where writing is not stressed. But when they reach the top, they are expected to write articles, speeches, memos, and testimony. Here they need advisors, who are often their trusted public relations professionals. That's why it's imperative that public relations students know how to write. Even beginning public relations professionals are expected to have mastery over the written word. Chapters 8, 9, and 10 will focus on what public relations writing is all about.

What does it take to be a public relations writer? For one thing, it takes a good knowledge of the basics. Although practitioners probably write for a wider range of purposes and use a greater number of communications methods than do other writers, the principles remain the same, whether writing an annual report or a case history, an employee newsletter or a public speech. This chapter and the two that follow will explore the fundamentals of writing: (1) discussing public relations writing in general and news releases in particular; (2) reviewing writing for reading; and (3) discussing writing for listening.

Writing for the Eye and the Ear

Writing for a reader differs dramatically from writing for a listener. A reader has certain luxuries a listener does not have. For example, a reader can scan material, study printed words, dart ahead, and then review certain passages for better understanding. A reader can check up on a writer; if the facts are wrong, for instance, a reader can find out pretty easily. To be effective, writing for the eye must be able to withstand the most rigorous scrutiny.

On the other hand, a listener gets only one opportunity to hear and comprehend a message. If the message is missed the first time around, there's usually no second chance. This situation poses a special challenge for the writer—to grab the listener quickly. A listener who tunes out early in a speech or a broadcast is difficult to draw back into the listening fold.

Public relations practitioners—and public relations students—should understand the differences between writing for the eye and the ear. Although it's unlikely that any beginning public relations professional would start by writing speeches, it's important to understand what constitutes a speech and how it's prepared and then be ready for the assignment when opportunity strikes. Because writing lies at the heart of the public relations equation, the more beginners know about writing, the better they will do. Any practitioner who doesn't know the basics of writing and doesn't know how to write is vulnerable and expendable.

Fundamentals of Writing

Few people are "born writers." Like any other discipline, writing takes patience and hard work. The more you write, the better you should become, provided you have mastered the basics. Writing fundamentals do not change significantly from one form to another.

What are the basics? Here is a foolproof, three-part formula for writers, from the novice to the novelist.

1. **The idea must precede the expression.** Think before writing. Few people can observe an event, immediately grasp its meaning, and sit down to compose several pages of sharp, incisive prose. Writing requires ideas, and ideas require thought. Ideas must satisfy four criteria.

   ♦ They must relate to the reader.
   ♦ They must engage the reader's attention.
   ♦ They must concern the reader.
   ♦ They must be in the reader's own self-interest.

   Sometimes ideas come quickly. At other times they don't come at all. But each new writing situation does not require a new idea. The trick in coming up with clever ideas lies more in borrowing old ones than in creating new ones. An old idea, refined to meet a specific communications objective, can be most effective. Stated another way, never underestimate the importance of maintaining good files.

2. **Don't be afraid of the draft.** After deciding on an idea and establishing the purpose of a communication, the writer should prepare a rough draft. It is a necessary and foolproof method for avoiding a mediocre and half-baked product.

   Writing, no matter how good, can usually be improved with a second look. The draft helps you organize ideas and plot their development before you commit them to a written test. It often enhances writing clarity if you know where you will stop before you start. Organization should be logical; it should lead a reader in a systematic way through the body of the text. Sometimes, especially on longer pieces, an outline should precede the draft.

3. **Simplify, clarify, aim.** In writing, the simpler the better. The more people who understand what you're trying to say, the better your chances for stimulating action. Shop talk, jargon, and "in" words should be avoided. Clear, normal English is all that's required to get an idea across. In practically every case, what makes sense is the simple rather than the complex, the familiar rather than the unconventional, and the concrete rather than the abstract.

   Clarity is another essential in writing. The key to clarity is tightness; that is, each word, each passage, each paragraph must belong. If a word is unnecessary, a passage redundant, a paragraph vague—get rid of it. Writing requires judicious editing; copy must always be reviewed with an eye toward cutting.

   Finally, writing must be aimed at a particular audience. The writer must have the target group in mind and tailor the message to reach them. To win the minds and deeds of a specific audience, one must be willing to sacrifice the understanding of certain others. Writers, like companies, can't expect to be all things to all people.

   Television journalist Bill Moyers offers this advice for good writing:

   > Strike in the active voice. Aim straight for the enemy: imprecision, ambiguity, and those high words that bear semblance of worth, not substance. Offer no quarter to the tired phrase or overworn idiom. Empty your knapsack of all adjectives, adverbs, and clauses that slow your stride and weaken your pace. Travel light. Remember the most memorable sentences in the English language are also the shortest: "The King is dead" and "Jesus wept."[1]

Flesch Readability Formula

Through a variety of writings, the late Dr. Rudolf Flesch staged a one-man battle against pomposity and murkiness in writing.* According to Flesch,

---

*Among the more significant of Flesch's books are *Say What You Mean, The Art of Plain Talk, The Art of Readable Writing,* and *How to Be Brief: An Index to Simple Writing.*

anyone can become a writer. He suggests that people who write like they talk will be able to write better. In other words, if people were less inclined to obfuscate their writing with 25-cent words and more inclined to substitute simple words, then not only would communicators communicate better, but receivers would receive more clearly.

In responding to a letter, Flesch's approach in action would work like this: "Thanks for your suggestion, Tom. I'll mull it over and get back to you as soon as I can." The opposite of the Flesch approach would read like this: "Your suggestion has been received; and after careful consideration we shall report our findings to you." See the difference?

There are countless examples of how Flesch's simple dictum works.

◆ Few would remember William Shakespeare if he had written sentences like "Should I act upon the urgings that I feel or remain passive and thus cease to exist?" Shakespeare's writing has stood the test of centuries because of sentences such as "To be or not to be?"

◆ A scientist, prone to scientific jargon, might be tempted to write, "The biota exhibited a 100 percent mortality response." But, oh, how much easier and infinitely more understandable to write, "All the fish died."

◆ One of President Franklin D. Roosevelt's speech writers once wrote, "We are endeavoring to construct a more inclusive society." FDR changed it to "We're going to make a country in which no one is left out."

◆ Even the most famous book of all, the Bible, opens with a simple sentence that could have been written by a twelve-year-old: "In the beginning, God created the heaven and the earth."

Flesch gave seven suggestions for making writing more readable.

1. Use contractions, like *it's* or *doesn't*.
2. Leave out the word *that* whenever possible.
3. Use pronouns like *I, we, they,* and *you*.
4. When referring back to a noun, repeat the noun, or use a pronoun. Don't create eloquent substitutions.
5. Use brief, clear sentences.
6. Cover only one item per paragraph.
7. Use language the reader understands.

To Flesch the key to all good writing was getting to the point.

Espousing—only slightly tongue-in-cheek—the opposite of the Flesch view was real estate communicator Barrie Doyle, who offered the following seven suggestions on "How to Write Good:"

1. Prepositions are not words to end sentences with.
2. Avoid cliches like the plague. They're old hat.
3. Parenthetical remarks (however relevant) are unnecessary.

BETWEEN THE LINES

The Flesch 60-Word Blacklist

In his book *Say What You Mean*, Rudolf Flesch expressed particular loathing for the following words. He contended they could easily be replaced by the words in parentheses.

1. advise (write)	31. insufficient (not enough)
2. affirmative (yes)	32. in the event that (if)
3. anticipate (expect)	33. locate (find)
4. appear (seem)	34. negative (no)
5. ascertain (find out)	35. obtain (get)
6. assist (help)	36. personnel (people)
7. complete (fill out)	37. pertaining to (of, about)
8. comply (follow)	38. presently (now)
9. constitute (be)	39. prior to (before)
10. cooperate (help)	40. prohibit (forbid)
11. deceased (dead)	41. pursuant to (under)
12. deem (think)	42. provide (give, say)
13. desire (want)	43. represent (be)
14. determine (figure, find)	44. request (ask for)
15. disclose (show)	45. require (need)
16. effect (make)	46. residence (home, address)
17. elect (choose, pick)	47. reveal (show)
18. endeavor (try)	48. review (check)
19. ensue (follow)	49. spouse (wife, husband)
20. execute (sign)	50. state (say)
21. experience (have)	51. submit (give, send)
22. facilitate (make easy)	52. subsequent (later)
23. failed to (didn't)	53. substantial (big, large, great)
24. forward (send)	54. sufficient (enough)
25. furnish (send)	55. supply (send)
26. inasmuch as (since)	56. sustain (suffer)
27. inconvenience (trouble)	57. terminate (end, stop)
28. indicate (say, show)	58. thus (so, that way)
29. initial (first)	59. transpire (happen)
30. in lieu of (instead of)	60. vehicle (car, truck)

4. Comparisons are as bad as cliches.
5. Be more or less specific.
6. Exaggeration is a billion times worse than understatement.
7. Don't be redundant; don't use more words than necessary; it's highly superfluous.[2]

In addition to Flesch, a number of other communications specialists have concentrated on how to make writing more readable. Many have developed their own instruments to measure readability. The most prominent, the Gunning Fog Index, designed by Robert Gunning, measures reading ease through the number of words and their difficulty, the number of complete thoughts, and the average sentence length in a piece of copy. The point is that good writing can't be confusing or unclear. It must be understandable.

The Secret of the Inverted Pyramid

Newspaper writing is the Flesch formula in action. Reporters learn that words are precious and are not to be wasted. In their stories every word counts. If readers lose interest early, they're not likely to be around at the end of the story.

That's where the inverted pyramid comes in. Newspaper story form is the opposite of that for a novel or short story. Whereas the climax of a novel comes at the end, the climax of a newspaper story comes at the beginning. A novel's important facts are rolled out as the plot thickens, but the critical facts in a newspaper story appear at the start. In this way, if readers decide to leave a news article early, they have already gained the basic ideas.

Generally, the first tier, or lead, of the inverted pyramid is the first one or two paragraphs, which include the most important facts. From there, paragraphs are written in descending order of importance, with progressively less important facts presented as the article continues—thus, the term *inverted pyramid.* (See Figure 8–1 for an exception to the inverted pyramid style.)

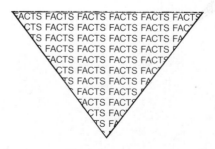

Palm Coast™

ITT COMMUNITY DEVELOPMENT CORPORATION
CORPORATE RELATIONS
PALM COAST, FLORIDA 32051
(904) 445-5000

NEWS RELEASE

ITT

105**88   FOR IMMEDIATE HOLIDAY ENJOYMENT

CONTACT: CAL MASSEY 904/445-2653

(Individual versions sent to media contacts)

<u>Linda Chase and Family</u>

TO ENJOY HAPPY HOLIDAY SEASON

　　　PALM COAST, FL -- Palm Coast media relations guy Cal Massey introduced the
world's first (possibly not) sing-along press release today, in order to wish
Linda Chase and family happiness during the holidays and new year, and in order
to embarrass himself and his profession for the fifth consecutive holiday
season.

(Sung to the tune of "Jingle Bell Rock")

　　　　　　Writer's block/writer's block/writer's block rock...
　　　　　　The brain said goodbye/and left nothing but schlock...
　　　　　　Norm-al-ly you get/a witty release...
　　　　　　But this year/the PR guy's blocked!

　　　　　　　　Dum-de-dum-dum...

　　　　　　Writer's block/writer's block/writer's block rock...
　　　　　　Hope your holiday's fun/and you get more than socks...
　　　　　　Rhy-ming is tough/when there's nothing but -ock...
　　　　　　But this year/it's all that we've got!

　　　　　　　　A little as-son-ance...

　　　　　　Writer's block/writer's block/writer's block rock...
　　　　　　It's been a great year/with good news 'round the clock...
　　　　　　Palm Coast is growing/and not without thought...
　　　　　　Except for/the PR guy, BLOCKED!

　　　　　　　　Big finish, now...

　　　　　　Writer's block/writer's block/writer's block rock...
　　　　　　I'm taking a few days/so don't be too shocked...
　　　　　　If very soon/you receive in your mail...
　　　　　　Next year's/release in a box!

　　　　　　　　My brain's rested...

　　　　　Dum-de-dum/dum-de-dum/dum-de-dum-dum...

The final refrain: I hope the media representatives I have had the pleasure of
working with over the years enjoy a relaxing holiday and new year graced by a
light touch --- Cal Massey/Manager, Media Services/ITT Community Development
Corporation.

FIGURE 8–1　As a holiday exception to the inverted pyramid news release, Palm
Coast Media Services manager Cal Massey dispatched this sing-along press release, tailored to each of his primary media contacts. *(Courtesy of ITT Community Development Corporation)*

The lead is the most critical element, usually answering who, what, why, when, where, and occasionally how. For example, the following lead effectively answers most of the initial questions a reader might have about the subject of the news story.

> Rock Hudson, movie idol of millions, died yesterday in Hollywood after suffering from AIDS.

That sentence tells it all; it answers the critical questions and highlights the pertinent facts. It gets to the point quickly without a lot of extra words. In only 14 words it captures and communicates the essence of what the reader needs to know.

This same style of easy and straightforward writing forms the basis for the most fundamental and ubiquitous of all public relations tools—the news release.

The News Release

The news release, a valuable but much-maligned device, is the granddaddy of public relations writing vehicles. Most public relations professionals swear by it. Some newspaper editors swear about it. But everyone uses the release as the basic interpretive mechanism to let people know what an organization is doing. That's why the news release deserves special attention as a public relations writing vehicle.

A news release may be written as the document of record to state an organization's official position—for example, in a court case or in announcing a price or rate increase. More frequently, however, releases have one overriding purpose: to influence a publication to write favorably about the material discussed. Each day, in fact, professionals send releases to editors in the hopes of stimulating favorable stories about their organizations.

Most of the time, news releases are not used verbatim. Rather, they may tip off editors to potential stories or serve as editorial reminders about coming stories. In both instances, the news release forms the point of departure for an original newspaper or magazine story. Unfortunately, as one hardened newspaper editor put it, "Few [releases] are worth the paper they are printed on . . . particularly in this day of escalating paper costs."[3] Much of the editorial criticism of news releases revolves around the apparent shoddiness with which releases are planned and executed. In one survey of newspaper editors, six factors in particular goaded editors about news releases. They are arranged here in order of onerousness.

1. Information isn't localized.
2. Information isn't newsworthy.

3. Release contains too much advertising puffery.
4. Release is too long and cumbersome.
5. Release arrived too late to be useful.
6. Release was poorly written.[4]

Faced with paper shortages, spiraling production costs, shrinking news holes, and intense deadline pressures, editors simply don't have time to wade through masses of poorly written, self-serving pap. They're looking for news. According to most editors, most releases just don't contain much news. As one city editor, who claimed to receive hundreds of releases daily, scornfully put it,

> Most press releases are written for clients and not for reporters. The people who write them must know this, so I don't imagine they will be persuaded to change their practices, which they must feel serve a useful purpose. The fact that it is not a news purpose or even a public relations purpose is probably irrelevant to them. It keeps the fees or the paychecks coming.[5]

These editorial comments are instructive to public relations professionals as a reminder of what news-release writing should be all about—releasing news. The writer's first question must be, "What in our announcement is newsworthy?" The most newsworthy facts must be extricated, segregated, and arrayed in the news release to interest the editor and, by extension, the publication's readers. At the same time, the release writer must keep in mind the particular message that the writer's employer would like to get across. Such allusions should never be blatant, but rather subtle enough to qualify generally as part of the news (Figure 8–2).

Understandably, editors are proud people who don't readily admit to borrowing other people's ideas, particularly those of public relations people. Nevertheless, public relations ideas and releases are used regularly in most publications and serve as an integral part of newspaper content. If a release pierces the print barrier verbatim in a newspaper or magazine, the sponsor's message takes on the heightened stature associated with objective news reporting (Figure 8–3).

Format

The format of a news release is important. Because the release is designed to be used in print, it must be structured for easy use by an editor. Certain mechanical rules of thumb should be followed.

♦ **Spacing** News releases should always be typed and double-spaced on one side only of 8½' by 11" paper. No editor wants to go rummaging through a handwritten release or a single-spaced, oversized piece of paper with typing on both sides.

PUBLIC AFFAIRS DEPARTMENT
277 Park Avenue, New York, N.Y. 10172

RELEASE
ON RECEIPT

Contact: Nicholas R. Iammartino
212-573-4131

BORDEN COMPLETES THREE SNACK ACQUISITIONS
Purchase of Sooner Snacks Marks Entry into U.K. Market

NEW YORK, April 7, 1988 -- Borden, Inc. (NYSE: BN) today announced the completion of three acquisitions that strengthen its positions as a leader in worldwide snacks, a strategic growth area that should contribute an estimated $1.15 billion to Borden's projected 1988 sales of $7.3 billion. The acquisitions, totaling about $88 million in estimated full-year sales, are:

o Sooner Snacks Limited, a major U.K. producer and marketer of potato
   chips and other snacks;

o Nuschelberg, a West German chain of retail bakeries; and

o The Crane potato chip brand name and other selected assets from
   Illinois Snack Foods, Inc.

"The Sooner Snacks purchase not only is the largest of the three, but also marks our entry into the important U.K. snack market," said R. J. Ventres, Borden chairman and chief executive officer. "We are already the second-largest salty snack producer in the United States and the world. We enhanced our international position just two months ago by acquiring Humpty Dumpty Foods Ltd. in Canada, and we have snack units in Spain, Ecuador and Malaysia as well.

"Nuschelberg adds to the number one position we hold in West Germany in another type of snacks, namely, sweet baked snacks and specialty breads," Mr. Ventres continued. "That's a category with $6 billion per year in national sales, more than a dozen times larger than salty snacks in Germany."

- more -

FIGURE 8-2 Borden's announcement easily qualifies as news. The company's first-paragraph reference to its position "as a leader in worldwide snacks" is an attempt to subtly publicize a message that Borden would like to see in print.

David Rockefeller Optimista Sobre Aumento Economía P.R.

(393)
EL DIARIO-LA PRENSA
NEW YORK, N.Y.
D. 90,000

APR 3 0 1978

David Rockefeller, presidente del Chase Manhattan Bank, citó como un ingrediente principal en la continuada recuperación económica de Puerto Rico, su habilidad para mantener la clase de clima comercial que continuará señalando la isla como un sitio que invita a la inversión exterior.

En un discurso ante la Cámara de Comercio de Puerto Rico en los Estados Unidos, el banquero neoyorquino señaló que eliminando cualquier error serio en la estrategia económica, la economía de Puerto Rico deberá generalmente crecer paralelamente con la economía de los Estados Unidos.

Específicamente Rockefeller declaró que es razonable esperar que Puerto Rico aumente su economía alrededor de un 4%, durante los próximos cuatro años asumiendo que la de los Estados Unidos aumentará también de 4 a 4½ por ciento.

Rockefeller añadió que se sentía entusiasmado por los recientes desarrollos económicos positivos registrados en Puerto Rico, entre los que señaló que el empleo está emergiendo de los bajos niveles de la recesión.

A tales efectos señaló que el total de empleados en la isla está aumentado en una tasa anual de alrededor del 4½ por ciento.

Dijo también que el gobierno puertorriqueño desarrolla un programa para consolidar la deuda pública en un corto término y además reducir sus planes de préstamos, así como los de pertenecientes a las corporaciones públicas.

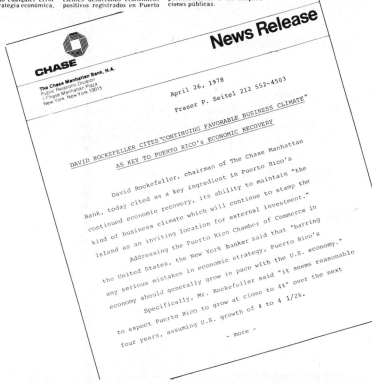

(704)
SAN JUAN STAR
SAN JUAN, PUERTO RICO
D. 51,000 SUN. 83,000

APR 2 8 1978

4% growth in island's economy foreseen by David Rockefeller

NEW YORK (UPI) — David Rockefeller, chairman of the Chase Manhattan Bank, Thursday cited as a key ingredient in Puerto Rico's continued economic recovery the island's ability to maintain "the kind of business climate which will continue to stamp it as an inviting location for external investment."

Addressing the Puerto Rico Chamber of Commerce in the United States, the New York banker said that "barring any serious mistakes in economic strategy, Puerto Rico's economy should generally grow in pace with the U.S. economy."

Specifically, Rockefeller said "it seems reasonable to expect Puerto Rico to grow at close to 4 percent" over the next four years, assuming U.S. growth of 4 to 4½ percent.

Rockefeller said he was "encouraged" by a number of positive recent economic developments in Puerto Rico, including:

—Continued emphasis of the Government Development Bank on sound and conservative practices of debt management. "The government has now embarked on a program to consolidate short-term debt and reduce its own borrowing plans and those of its public corporations," Rockefeller said.

—Employment seems to be re-emerging from the dismal levels of the recession. Rockefeller said the total number of people employed on the island is increasing at an annual rate of about 4½ percent.

Further, he said, while unemployment in March was still high at 17 percent, "when you compare this with the level of 19 percent in February and 20 percent in December, it suggests real improvement."

—Another area of encouragement is agriculture, where the government has begun to promote the development of import substitution crops such as rice and vegetables and the production of beef and poultry.

Rockefeller added that recent economic statistics in Puerto Rico's construction industry, which was hard hit by the recession, are also encouraging. However, he said, "the private sector is advancing at a much slower pace" than renewed construction activity in the public sector.

The Journal of Commerce
NEW YORK, N.Y.
D. 25,825

APR 2 8 1978

Business Climate 'Aids' Puerto Rico

David Rockefeller, chairman of the Chase Manhattan Bank, Thursday cited as a key ingredient in Puerto Rico's continued economic recovery, its ability to maintain "the kind of business climate which will continue to stamp the island as an inviting location for external investment."

Addressing the Puerto Rico Chamber of Commerce in the United States, the New York banker said that "barring any serious mistakes in economic strategy, Puerto Rico's economy should generally grow in pace with the U.S. economy."

Specifically, Mr. Rockefeller said "it seems reasonable to expect Puerto Rico to grow at close to 4 percent" over the next four years, assuming U.S. growth of 4 to 4½ percent.

Mr. Rockefeller said he was "encouraged" by a number of positive recent economic developments in Puerto Rico, including:

Continued emphasis of the Government-Development Bank on sound and conservative practices of debt management.

"The government has now embarked on a program to consolidate short-term debt and reduce its own borrowing plans and those of its public corporations," Mr. Rockefeller said.

Employment seems to be re-emerging from the dismal levels of the recession.

Mr. Rockefeller said the total number of people employed on the island is increasing at an annual rate of about 4½ percent. Further, while unemployment in March was still high at 17 percent, "when you compare this with the level of 19 percent in February and 20 percent in December, it suggests real improvement."

FIGURE 8–3 Although editors don't like to admit it, once in a while news releases score with point-blank accuracy. In this case, a news release was picked up verbatim by a wire service, translated into Spanish, and given wide circulation in the sponsor's target markets. *(Courtesy of Chase Manhattan Bank)*

- ♦ **Paper** Inexpensive paper stock should be used. Reporters win Pulitzer Prizes with stories written on plain copy paper. Nothing irritates an editor more than seeing an expensively embossed news release while watching newspapers die from soaring newsprint costs.

- ♦ **Identification** The name, address, and telephone number of the release writer should appear in the upper part of the release in case an editor wants further information. It's a good idea to list two names, with office and home telephone numbers.

- ♦ **Release date** Releases should always be dated, either for immediate use or to be held until a certain later date, often referred to as an embargoed date. In this day of instant communication, however, newspapers frown on embargoes. And only in the most extreme cases—for example, proprietary or confidential medical or government data—will newspapers honor them. Frequently, a dateline is used on releases; it is the first line of the release and tells where the story originated.

- ♦ **Margins** Margins should be wide enough for editors to write in, usually about 1 to 1½ inches.

- ♦ **Length** A news release is not a book. It should be edited tightly so that it is no more than two pages long. Words and sentences should be kept short.

- ♦ **Paragraphs** Paragraphs should also be short, no more than six lines at most. A single sentence can suffice as a paragraph. Because typographical composers may type exactly what they see in front of them, syllables should not be split from one line to the next. Likewise, paragraphs should be completed before a new page is begun, to ensure that a lost page in the news or composing rooms will not disrupt a particular thought in the release.

- ♦ **Slug lines** Journalistic shorthand, or slug lines, should appear on a release—such things as "more" at the bottom of a page when the release continues to another page and "30" or "###" to denote the end of the release. Page numbers and one-word descriptions of the topic of the release should appear on each page for quick editorial recognition.

- ♦ **Headlines** Headlines are optional. Often, headlines are avoided, and releases are begun one-third of the way down the page to allow editors to devise original headlines. Some practitioners prefer headlines to presell an editor on the gist of the news release that follows.

- ♦ **Proofreading** Grammar, spelling, and typing must be perfect. Misspellings, grammatical errors, or typos are the quickest route to the editorial wastebasket.

- ♦ **Timing** News-release writers must be sensitive to editorial deadlines. Newspapers, magazines, and broadcast stations work under constant

Chester Burger Company

NEWS RELEASE

For Immediate Release
CONTACT: Jim Horton
(212) 725-0000

NEW STUDY OF TOP 50 PR FIRMS EXPLORES CHALLENGES SHAPING INDUSTRY

New York, May 22, 1989 -- A new study, widely praised by industry opinion leaders, targets major issues and trends affecting the growth of the $900 million fee based public relations industry.

The report, ISSUES AND TRENDS 1989: Top 50 PR Firms, was developed from confidential, open-ended interviews with senior executives of 26 of the Top 50 PR agencies conducted by Chester Burger Company.

Chester Burger Company, founded in 1963, is the oldest and largest management consulting firm specializing in communications issues. The firm's expertise is in defining objectives, developing strategies and organizing communications functions.

"The future of public relations is bright," said James E. Arnold, president of the firm.

ISSUES AND TRENDS reports that the public relations industry is healthy, with a compound growth rate of 20 percent per year among the Top 50 agencies over the last five years.

"Combined fee billings of the industry should pass the billion dollar mark by the end of this year," said Arnold.

The study exposes an apparent split of Top 50 PR agencies based on the industry standard of fee billings into three categories: a "Bulge Bracket" of giants, a "Big Middle" of 14 firms all trying to be among the Top 10 agencies, and "Entrepreneurs," who are scrambling to reach from $4-10 million in fees.

Further, it brings to light the inherently different approaches of agencies in each category to top the next rung or hold their position.

--more--

Communications	171 Madison Avenue	A Division of
Management Consultants	New York, New York 10016	CommuniCorp, Inc.
	212 725-0000	
	212 684-4357 (FAX)	

FIGURE 8–4   This release about the future of public relations illustrates proper news-release format, from the spacing to the identification, from the margins to the headlines, from the slug lines to the overall appearance. *(Courtesy of Chester Burger Company)*

deadline pressure. A general-interest release should arrive at an editor's desk a week to 10 days in advance of the paper's deadline. Because stale news is no news, a release arriving even just a little late may just as well never have been mailed.

Style

The style of a news release is almost as critical as its content. Sloppy style can break the back of any release and ruin its chances for publication. Style must also be flexible and evolve as language changes.

One element of style that has evolved over the years relates to sexism in writing. Dealing with gender has become more important for a writer and also more difficult. No matter how hard a writer tries to be evenhanded in treating men and women in print, he—or she—is bound to offend someone. The Washington Press Club has published guidelines for the elimination of sexual bias in the media. Among its highlights are these rules:

1. Terms referring to a specific gender should be avoided when an alternative term will do. Use *business executive* instead of *businessman* and *city council member* for *councilman*.

2. Where neither a gender-free term nor any term accurately designating gender is yet in common use, continue to employ the old terminology— for example, *Yeoman* First Class Betty Jones or Mary Smith, a telephone company *lineman*.

3. No occupational designation should include a description of the person's gender unless the sex of the individual is pertinent to the story. For example, don't use *woman lawyer* or *male nurse*.

4. Avoid terms like *man-made* for synthetic, *man-on-the-street* for ordinary citizen, *manpower* for workforce, *man and wife* for husband and wife, and *co-ed* for student.

Despite such attempts to eliminate sexism in writing style, satisfying everyone is a nearly impossible task for any writer.

Most public relations operations follow the style practiced by major newspapers and magazines, rather than that of book publishers. This news style is detailed in various guides published by such authorities as the Associated Press, United Press International, and the *New York Times*.

Because the press must constantly update its style to conform to changing societal concepts, news-release style is subjective and everchanging. However, a particular firm's style must be consistent from one release to the next. The following are examples of typical style rules:

♦ **Capitalization**   Most leading publications use capital letters sparingly; so should you. Editors call this a down style, because only the most important words begin with capital letters.

♦ **Abbreviations** Abbreviations present a many-faceted problem. For example, months, when used with dates, should be abbreviated, such as Sept. 2, 1992. But when the day of the month is not used, the month should be spelled out, such as September 1992. Days of the week, on the other hand, should never be abbreviated. In addition, first mention of organizations and agencies should be spelled out, with the abbreviation in parentheses after the name, such as Securities and Exchange Commission (SEC).

♦ **Numbers** There are many guidelines for the spelling out of numbers, but a general rule is to spell out numbers up through nine and use figures for 10 and up. Yet, figures are perfectly acceptable for such things as election returns, speeds and distances, percentages, temperatures, heights, ages, ratios, and sports scores.

♦ **Punctuation** The primary purpose of punctuation is to clarify the writer's thoughts, ensure exact interpretation, and make reading and understanding quicker and easier. Less punctuation rather than more should be the goal. The following are just some of the punctuation marks a public relations practitioner must use appropriately.

1. The colon introduces listings, tabulations, and statements and takes the place of an implied "for instance."
2. The comma is used in a variety of circumstances, including before connecting words, between two words or figures that might otherwise be misunderstood, and before and after nonrestrictive clauses.
3. In general, exclamation points should be resisted in releases. They tend to be overkill!
4. The hyphen is often abused and should be used carefully. A single hyphen can change the meaning of a sentence completely. For example, "The six-foot man eating tuna was killed" means the man was eating tuna; it should probably be punctuated "The six-foot, man-eating tuna was killed."
5. Quoted matter is enclosed in double or single quotation marks. The double marks enclose the original quotation, whereas the single marks enclose a quotation within a quotation.

♦ **Spelling** Many words, from *adviser* to *zucchini*, are commonly misspelled. The best way to avoid misspellings is to have a dictionary always within reach. When two spellings are given in a dictionary, the first spelling is always preferred.

These are just a few of the stylistic stumbling blocks that writers must consider. In the news release, style should never be taken lightly. The style, as much as any other part of the release, lets an editor know the kind of organization that issued the release and the competency of the professional who wrote it.

Content

The cardinal rule in release content is that the end product be newsworthy. The release must be of interest to an editor and readers. Issuing a release that has little chance of being used by a publication serves only to crush the credibility of the writer.

When a release is newsworthy and of potential interest to an editor, it must be written clearly and concisely, in proper newspaper style. It must get to the facts early and answer the six key questions. From there it must follow inverted pyramid structure to its conclusion. For example, the following is not a proper lead for a release:

> CLEVELAND, OHIO, MARCH 7, 1991—Chief Justice William Rehnquist will speak tomorrow in Cleveland. He will speak at 8 P.M. He will address the convention of the American Bar Association. His address will be a major one and will concern the topic of capital punishment.

Why would an editor discard this lead? In the first place, it does not get to the heart of the issue—the topic of the speech—until the very end. Second, it's wordy. If the editor decided to use it at all, he'd have to rewrite it. Here's what should have been submitted:

> Chief Justice William Rehnquist will deliver a major address on capital punishment at 8 P.M. tomorrow in Cleveland before the American Bar Association convention.

Even though the second sample cut the verbiage in half, the pertinent questions still got answered: who (Chief Justice William Rehnquist), what (a major address on capital punishment), where (Cleveland), when (tomorrow at 8 P.M.), and why (American Bar Association is holding a convention). In this case how is less important. But whether the reader chooses to proceed further into the release or not, the story's gist has been successfully communicated in the lead.

To be newsworthy, news releases must be objective. All comments and editorial remarks must be *attributed* to organization officials. The news release can't be used as the private soapbox of the release writer. Rather, the release must appear as a fair and accurate representation of the "news" that the organization wishes to be conveyed.

News releases can be written about almost anything, but three frequent subjects are product and institutional announcements, management changes, and management speeches.

The Announcement

Frequently, practitioners want to announce a new product or institutional development, such as construction plans, earnings, mergers, acquisitions, or company celebrations. The announcement release should have a catchy, yet significant lead to stimulate an editor to capitalize on the practitioner's creative idea. The following are two examples:

> "Tennis whites," the traditional male court uniform, will yield to bright colors and fashion styling this spring as Jockey spearheads a new wave in tennis fashion with the introduction of a full line of tennis wear for men.

> The creation of the first manufacturing joint-venture company in Romania, involving a Romanian company and an American firm, was announced today by the Romanian Ministry of Machine Tools and Electro Techniques and Control Data Corporation.

Typically in an announcement release, after the lead identifies the significant aspects of the product or development, a spokesperson is quoted

Bungling the Bromo News Release

Bromo Corporation

CONTACT: Lance Ravenoo

Release date: Hold for Sept. 20, 1991

Bromo Company Announces Revolutionary Digital Clock

LINCOLN, SEPT. 21, 1991—Gromo Corporation today announced they would begin marketing immediately a revolutionary digital wristwatch, capable of withstanding more pressure than any other digital watch on the market.

The new watch, described by scientists as "an amazing piece of modern machinery," was produced in Bromo's Lincoln, Texas, plant. The watch was market-tested in the Lincoln, Nebraska, area and was universally applauded by test participants.

"I've never seen a watch absorb so much punishment," was the response of one participant.

According to Lance Ravenoo, Bromo's director of marketing, "We believe this watch will outpace any other timepiece on the market. It's capacity to withstand abuse is simply unvelievable."

The Bromo watch, which is also waterproof, comes in two styles: a "nautical" that retails for $37.50 and the "free spirit" which retails for $380.0.

QUESTIONS

1. If you were an editor, would you use the Bromo news release?
2. How many errors can you spot?

for additional product information. Editors appreciate the quotes because they then do not have to interview a company official.

> The new, lightweight plastic bottle for Coca-Cola began its national rollout today in Spartanburg, S.C. This two-liter package is the nation's first metric plastic bottle for soft drinks.
> "We are very excited about this new package," said John H. Ogden, president, Coca-Cola U.S.A. "Our two-liter plastic bottle represents an important advancement. Its light weight, toughness, and environmental advantages offer a new standard of consumer benefits in soft drink packaging."

The subtle product "plug" included in this release is typical of such announcements. Clearly, the organization gains if the product's benefits are described in a news story. But editors are sensitive to product puffery, and the line between legitimate information and puffery is thin. One must always be sensitive to the needs and concerns of editors. A professional avoids letting the thin line of product information become a short plank of puffery.

The Management Change

Newspapers are often interested in management changes, but editors frequently reject releases that have no local angle. For example, the editor of the Valdosta, Georgia, *Citizen* has little reason to use this announcement:

> NEW YORK, NY, SEPT. 5, 1992—Jeffrey O. Schultz has been named manager of the hosiery department at Bloomingdale's Paramus, NJ, store.

On the other hand, the same release, amended for local appeal, would almost certainly be used by the *Citizen*.

> NEW YORK, NY, SEPT. 5, 1992—Jeffrey O. Schultz, son of Mr. and Mrs. Siegfried Schultz of 221 Starting Lane, Valdosta, has been named manager of the hosiery department at Bloomingdale's Paramus, NJ, store.

Sometimes one must dig for the local angle. For example, suppose Mr. Schultz was born in Valdosta but went to school in Americus, Georgia. With this knowledge, the writer might prepare the following release, which would have appeal in the newspapers of both Georgia cities.

> NEW YORK, NY, SEPT. 5, 1992—Jeffrey O. Schultz, son of Mr. and Mrs. Siegfried Schultz of 221 Starting Lane, Valdosta, and a 1976 graduate of Americus High School, was named manager of the hosiery department of Bloomingdale's Paramus, NJ, store.

Penetrating local publications with the management change release is relatively easy once the local angle has been identified, but achieving publication in a national newspaper or magazine is much harder. The *Wall*

Street Journal, for example, will not use a management change announcement unless the individual has attained a certain level of responsibility, usually corporate vice-president or higher, in a major firm. In other words, if a release involves someone who has not attained senior executive status at a listed company, forget it, at least as far as the *Wall Street Journal* is concerned.

For national consumption it is the importance or uniqueness of the individual or company that should be emphasized. For example, an editor might not realize that the following management change is unique:

> WASHINGTON, DC, JUNE 6, 1991—Yolanda King of Sacramento, CA, today was promoted to the rank of admiral in the United States Navy.

However, the same release stands out clearly for its news value when the unique angle is played up.

> WASHINGTON, DC, JUNE 6, 1991—Yolanda King of Sacramento, CA, today was named the first woman admiral in the history of the United States Navy.

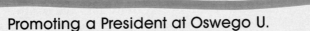

YOU MAKE THE CALL

Promoting a President at Oswego U.

As public information director of Oswego University, you are advised that the university's board of trustees has selected the fifteenth president in the school's history. He is Wilson W. Waters, a 1952 graduate of Oswego, who has most recently served as the school's dean of students. In researching Waters's background, you uncover a few other interesting facts.

- He is 60 years old and married to the former Renee Siggerson of Yankton, South Dakota.
- He was born in Oswego and spent the first 21 years of his life there.
- He has a master's degree from Brown University and a Ph.D. from Harvard.
- He is 6'9", Jamaican, and played 15 years in the National Basketball Association.
- He had been dean of students at Oswego for 10 years.

Your assignment, according to the board, is to publicize the Waters announcement as extensively as possible in local and national media.

QUESTIONS

1. Are these facts sufficient to write a news release about the new Oswego president? What additional information would help?
2. From the data given, what angle would you pursue for local Oswego editorial consumption?
3. What would your lead be for national media consumption?
4. Are there any facts given that you wouldn't use in the release?

One can never go wrong being straightforward in a news release, but a local or unique angle to help sell the story to an editor should always be investigated.

The Management Speech

Management speeches are another recurring source of news releases. The key to a speech news release is selecting the most significant portion of the talk for the lead. A good speech generally has a clear thesis, from which a lead naturally flows. Once the thesis is identified, the remainder of the release simply embellishes it.

> BOONEVILLE, MO, OCT. 18, 1991—Booneville Mining Company is "on the verge of having several very profitable years," Booneville Mining President Marsha Mulford said today.
>
> Addressing the Booneville Chamber of Commerce, the Missouri mining company executive cited two reasons for the positive projections: the company's orders are at an all-time high, and its overseas facilities have "turned the corner" on profitability in the current year.

Normally, if the speech giver is not a famous person, the release should not begin with the speaker's name but with the substance of the remarks. If the speaker is a well-known individual, leading with a name is perfectly legitimate.

> Federal Reserve Chairman Alan Greenspan called today for a "new attitude toward business investment and capital formation."

The body copy of a speech release should follow directly from the lead. Often, the major points of the speech must be paraphrased and consolidated to conform to a two-page release. In any event, it is frequently a significant challenge to convert the essence of a management speech to news-release form (Figure 8–5).

The Importance of Editing

Editing is the all-important final touch for the public relations writer. In a news release, a careful self-edit can save the deadliest prose. An editor must be judicious. Each word, phrase, sentence, and paragraph should be weighed carefully. Good editing will "punch up" dull passages and make them sparkle. For instance, "The satellite flies across the sky" is dead. But "The satellite roars across the sky" comes alive.

33434 Eighth Avenue South
Federal Way, Washington 98003
206 941 6700

Washington Education Association   **News Release**

March 31, 1989

For more information: Teresa Moore, Washington Education
                     Association, (206) 941-6700

FOR IMMEDIATE RELEASE

'GIVE OUR KIDS ROOM TO GROW' CAMPAIGN STARTS

FEDERAL WAY, WA -- What do sardines in a can and many of
Washington's public school children have in common? They're both
in a tight spot.

"Overcrowded classrooms are making it more and more difficult
for kids to learn," said Terry Bergeson, President of the
Washington Education Association. "Washington has the 4th largest
class size in the nation. Our children are too important to the
future of the state to allow this overcrowding to continue."

Bergeson's comments were made as the W.E.A. launched a media
campaign to heighten awareness statewide about school
overcrowding.

"We're taking our message to the streets, into people's
homes," Bergeson said. "When the people become aware of just how
large many classes are, they'll demand that our kids be given room
to grow."

One year ago, W.E.A. members agreed to sponsor and raise
funds for a statewide information campaign about Washington's K-12
public schools.

more ... more

WEA 3

Packed like sardines
Page 2

The campaign began April 3, 1989, breaking on television and
radio and in newspapers throughout the state.

"We used a real class in our ads," Bergeson said. "Carol
Lake's fourth grade class at Kimball Elementary in Seattle is one
of the largest - 31 children in one class."

"With so many kids it's hard to meet individual needs," said
Lake, Kimball Elementary teacher. "I teach kids with limited
English proficiency, kids with learning disabilities, kids with
high I.Q.'s. If I had fewer in the class, I could give the kind
of individualized attention that would really make a difference."

Lake's class took a field trip to the studio of Northwest
Video Communications as van Ackeren Productions and Stewart Tilger
Photography produced the material to be used in the ads.

The advertisements show kids packed in a can like sardines.
The theme of the campaign is "How can kids learn in classrooms
like this? Give our kids room to grow."

"There are so many kids in the class we have to be squished
at tables," student Julie Eisenberg said. "There's no room for
books or anything else."

Bergeson said, "This campaign is just the beginning. We're
going to tell our own story, directly to the people."

Celebrating its centennial year, the W.E.A. is comprised of
approximately 45,000 K-12 teachers, 6,000 support personnel and
over 1,000 higher education personnel and is headquartered in
Federal Way.

#   #   #

FIGURE 8–5   A news release, derived from a
speech by the president of the Washington Education Association on classroom overcrowding, was
complemented by this provocative advertisement.
(Courtesy of Sharp Hartwig Communications)

In the same context, good editing will get rid of passive verbs. Invariably, this will produce shorter sentences. For example, "The cherry tree was chopped down by George Washington" is shorter and better as "George Washington chopped down the cherry tree."

A good editor must also be gutsy enough to use bold strokes—to chop, slice, and cut through unnecessary verbiage, bad grammar, misspellings, incorrect punctuation, poorly constructed sentences, misused words, mixed metaphors, non sequiturs, cliches, redundancies, circumlocutions, and jargon. Sentences like "She is the widow of the late Nelson Apfelbaum" and "The present incumbent is running for reelection" are intolerable to a good editor.

Probably the two most significant writing and editing supports for a practitioner are a good unabridged dictionary and a thesaurus. To these might be added *Bartlett's Familiar Quotations, the World Almanac,* and an encyclopedia.

BETWEEN THE LINES

Tighten Up

Knowledgeable experts say that you should never, ever use redundant words and phrases and excess verbiage in your writing.

Ahem.

See if you can "tighten up" this list of verbosities with surgical editing.

- serious danger
- climb up
- past history
- revert back
- new record
- joined together
- pink in color
- commute back and forth
- merged together
- major breakthrough
- mutual cooperation
- personal friend
- completely filled
- completely unanimous
- absolutely necessary
- total destruction
- basic fundamentals
- unexpected emergency
- original source
- cease and desist

Editing should also concentrate on organizing copy. One release paragraph should flow naturally into the next. Transitions in writing are most important. Sometimes it just takes a single word to unite two adjoining paragraphs. Such is the case in the following example, which uses the word *size*.

> The machine works on a controlled mechanism, directed by a series of pulleys. It is much smaller than the normal motor, requiring less than half of a normal motor's components.
> Not only does the device differ in size from other motors, but it also differs in capacity.

Writing, like fine wine, should flow smoothly and stand up under the toughest scrutiny. Careful editing is a must.

Summary

Writing is the very essence of public relations practice. The public relations professional, if not the best writer in his or her organization, must at least be one of the best. Writing is the communications skill that differentiates public relations professionals from others.

Some writers are, as they say, "born." But writing can be learned by understanding the fundamentals of what makes interesting writing, by practicing different written forms, and by working constantly to improve and edit and refine the written product.

When an executive needs something written well, one organizational resource should pop immediately into his or her mind—public relations.

DISCUSSION STARTERS

1. What is the difference between writing for the ear and for the eye?
2. What are several of the "writing fundamentals" one must consider?
3. What is the essence of the Flesch method of writing?
4. What is the inverted pyramid and why does it work?
5. What is the essential written communications vehicle used by public relations professionals?
6. Why is the format of a news release important to a public relations professional and the organization?
7. What are common purposes of news releases?
8. Should a news release writer try to work his own editorial opinion into the release?
9. What is the key to writing a release on a management speech?
10. What is the purpose of editing?

NOTES

1. Bill Moyers, "Watch Your Language," *The Professional Communicator* (August-September 1985): 6.
2. "How to Write Good," *Public Relations Strategies* (January 1989): 10.

3. Charles Honaker, "News Releases Revisited," *Public Relations Journal* (April 1981): 25.
4. Bill L. Baxter, "The News Release: An Idea Whose Time Has Gone?" *Public Relations Review* (Spring 1981): 30.
5. Honaker, loc. cit.

TOP OF THE SHELF

Bivins, Thomas. *Handbook for Public Relations Writing.* Lincolnwood, IL: National Textbook Company, 1988.

Practitioners can't do their jobs well unless they can write, and one of the best guides to using the written word correctly is *Handbook for Public Relations Writing.*

Tom Bivins presents the basics of sound public relations writing in eight pertinent chapters, beginning with the characteristics that define good press releases, broadcast announcements, advertising copy, brochures, and newsletters. His section on speeches outlines the steps to composing well-organized presentations that inform, persuade, and entertain. Bivins also covers the rules of grammar, helping those who may have forgotten where to place prepositions, modifiers, linking verbs, and the like. He concludes with the fundamentals of style that make writing clear, crisp, and concise. Practical examples complement the instruction.

Whatever your ultimate communications goal, whether your writing is geared to newspapers or broadcasting, *Handbook for Public Relations Writing* should be kept at the ready. It is a most useful guidebook.

SUGGESTED READINGS

Beach, Mark. *Editing Your Newsletter.* 3rd ed. Portland, OR: Coast to Coast Books, 1988 (2934 N.E. 16th Ave.).

Beach, Mark. *Getting It Printed: How to Work with Printers/Graphic Art Services.* Portland, OR: Coast to Coast Books, 1986 (2934 N.E. 16th Ave.).

Bennett, David. *The Publication Marketing Plan.* Kirkwood, MO: Bennett Communications, 1988.

Berg, Karen, and Andrew Gilman. *Get to the Point.* New York: Bantam, 1989.

Bivins, Thomas. *Handbook for Public Relations Writing.* Lincolnwood, IL: National Textbook Company, 1988.

Block, Mervin. *Writing Broadcast News—Shorter, Sharper, Stronger.* Chicago, IL: Bonus Books, 1987.

Cohen, Paula M. *A Public Relations Primer: Thinking and Writing in Context.* Englewood Cliffs, NJ: Prentice-Hall, 1987.

Diving into Desktop Publishing. Gillian/Craig Associates (165 Eighth St., 301, San Francisco, CA:).

Matthews, Downs. *How to Manage Employees Publications.* Bartlesville, OK: Joe Williams Communications, 1988.

Iapoce, Michael. *A Funny Thing Happened on the Way to the Boardroom.* New York: John Wiley, 1988.

MacDonald, R. H. *Broadcast News Manual of Style.* White Plains, NY: Longman, 1987.

Meyer, Herbert, and Jill Meyer. *How to Write.* Washington, DC: Storm King Press, 1986 (P.O. Box 3566 20007).

Moyers, Bill. "Watch Your Language." *Professional Communicator* (August–September 1985): 4–6.

Newsom, Douglas, and Bob Carrell. *Public Relations Writing: Form and Style.* 2nd ed. Belmont, CA: Wadsworth, 1986.

Newsom, Douglas, and James A. Wollert. *Media Writing: Preparing Information for the Mass Media.* Belmont, CA: Wadsworth, 1988.

Publishing Newsletters. Newsletter Clearinghouse (P.O. Box 311, 12572, Rhinebeck, NY).

Standard Periodical Directory. New York: Oxbridge Communications, 1988.

Success in Newsletter Publishing & Hotline. Newsletter Association (1341 G St., NW, Washington, DC). Biweekly.

Strunk, W., and E. B. White. *Elements of Style.* New York: Macmillan, 1979.

Tilden, Scott, Anthony Fulginiti, and Jack Gillepsie. *Harnessing Desktop Publishing.* Pennington, NJ: Scott Tilden, 1987 (4 W. Franklin Ave. 08534-2211).

Tucker, Kerry, and Doris Derelian. *Public Relations Writing: A Planned Approach for Creating Results.* Englewood Cliffs, NJ: Prentice-Hall, 1988.

Video Monitor (10606 Mantz Rd., Silver Spring, MD 20903). Monthly.

Walsh, Frank. *Public Relations Writer in the Computer Age.* Englewood Cliffs, NJ: Prentice-Hall, 1986.

CASE STUDY   The Raina News Release

Background: The Raina, Inc. carborundum plant in Blackrock, Iowa, has been under pressure in recent months to remedy its pollution problem. Raina's plant is the largest in Blackrock, and even though the company has spent $1.3 million on improving its pollution-control equipment, black smoke still spews from the plant's smokestacks, and waste products are still allowed to filter into neighboring streams. The pressure on Raina has been intense of late.

■ On September 7, Andrew Laskow, a private citizen, called to complain about the "noxious smoke" befouling the environment.

■ On September 8, Mrs. Lizzy Ledger of the Blackrock Garden Club called to protest the "smoke problem" that was wreaking havoc on the zinnias and other flowers in the area.

■ On September 9, Clarence "Smoky" Salmon, president of the Blackrock Rod and Gun Club, called to report that 700 people had signed a petition against the Raina plant's pollution of Zeus Creek.

■ On September 10, WERS-radio editorialized that "the time has come to force area plants to act on solving pollution problems."

■ On September 11, the Blackrock City Council announced plans to enact an air and water pollution ordinance for the city. The council invited as its first witness before the public hearing Leslie Sludge, manager of the Raina carborundum Blackrock plant.

News Release Data

1. Leslie Sludge, manager of Raina's carborundum Blackrock plant, appeared at the Blackrock City Council hearing on September 11.

2. Sludge said Raina already has spent $1.3 million on a program to clean up pollution at its Blackrock plant.

3. Raina received 500 complaint calls in the past three months protesting its pollution conditions.

4. Sludge said Raina was "concerned about environmental problems, but profits are still what keeps our company running."

5. Sludge announced that the company had decided to commit another $2 million for pollution-abatement facilities over the next three months.

6. Raina is the oldest plant in Blackrock and was built in 1900.

7. Raina's Blackrock plant employs 10,000 people, the largest single employer in Blackrock.

8. Raina originally scheduled its pollution-abatement program for 1995 but speeded it up because of public pressure in recent months.

9. Sludge said that the new pollution-abatement program would begin in October and that the company projected "real progress in terms of clean water and clean air" as early as June 1992.

10. In 1986, Raina, Inc. received a Presidential Award from the Environmental Protection Agency for its "concern for pollution abatement."

11. An internal Raina study indicated that Blackrock was the "most pollutant laden" of all Raina's plants nationwide.

12. Sludge formerly served as manager of Raina's Fetid Reservoir plant in Fetid Reservoir, New Hampshire. In two years as manager of Fetid Reservoir, Sludge was able to convert it from one of the most pollutant-laden plants in the system to the cleanest, as judged by the Environmental Protection Agency.

13. Sludge has been manager of Blackrock for two months.

14. Raina's new program will cost the company $2 million in all.

15. Raina will hire 100 extra workers especially for the pollution abatement program.

16. Sludge, thirty-five, is married to the former Polly Usion of Wheeling, West Virginia.

17. Sludge is author of the book *Fly Fishing Made Easy*.

18. The bulk of the expense for the new pollution-abatement program will be spent on two globe refractors, which purify waste destined to be deposited in surrounding waterways, and four hyperventilation systems, which remove noxious particles dispersed into the air from smokestacks.

19. Sludge said, "Raina, Inc. has decided to move ahead with this program at this time because of its longstanding responsibility for keeping the Blackrock environment clean and in response to growing community concern over achieving the objective."

20. Former Blackrock plant manager Fowler Aire was fired by the company in July for his "flagrant disregard for the environment."

21. Aire also was found to be diverting Raina funds from company projects to his own pockets. In all, Aire took close to $10,000, for which the company was not reimbursed. At least part of the money was to be used for pollution control.

22. Aire, whose whereabouts are presently not known, is the brother of J. Derry Aire, Raina's vice-president for finance.

23. Raina's Blackrock plant has also recently installed ramps and other special apparatus to assist handicapped employees. Presently, 100 handicapped workers are employed in the Raina Blackrock plant.

24. Raina's Blackrock plant started as a converted garage, manufacturing plate glass. Only 13 people worked in the plant at that time.

25. Today, the Blackrock plant employs 10,000, covers 14 acres of land, and is the largest single supplier of plate glass and commercial panes in the country.

26. The Blackrock plant was slated to be the subject of a critical report from the Private Environmental Stabilization Taskforce (PEST), a private environmental group. PEST's report, "The Foulers," was to discuss "the 10 largest manufacturing polluters in the nation."

27. Raina management has been aware of the PEST report for several months.

QUESTIONS

1. If you were assigned to draft a news release to accompany Sludge to the Blackrock City Council meeting on September 11, which items would you use in your lead (i.e., who, what, why, where, when, how)?

2. Which items would you avoid using in the news release?

3. If a reporter from the *Blackrock Bugle* called and wanted to know what happened to former Blackrock manager Fowler Aire, what would you tell him?

Tips from the Top

ROBERT A. WILLIAMS

Robert A. Williams is president of Showtime Communications, a New York City public relations firm specializing in theatrical promotion, and the publisher of *Showtime Magazine*. Previously, he was public relations director of the Greater New York Council of the Boy Scouts of America, the country's largest boy scout unit. He also has had extensive experience as a public relations account executive and newspaper reporter, having served as a by-lined contributor to *The New York Times* since 1972. His reporting and writing have earned him awards for journalistic excellence from a variety of press associations. Williams is also an adjunct associate professor of communications arts at St. John's University in New York, where he teaches public relations and journalism.

How important is writing in public relations?
Clear, concise writing is probably the most important tool of the public relations practitioner.

Words on paper continue to be the principal conduit by which a person transmits information to another person. We in the writing business use words to tug at the emotions: we can make readers laugh, cry, even march off to war. Crisp writing—

words that dance off a page—should be at the head of everyone's list.

Are writers born or made?
The question reminds me of people I meet who squeal, "Oh, you're a *writer*? I just l-l-l-love to write, too!"

Don't we all. Plopping words on paper is easy. Everyone's a writer, right? But searching for the precise words to say the precise thing is the challenge.

I remember a cub reporter at a newspaper at which I worked. The initial stories he wrote were horrendous: half truths, not enough facts, sloppy construction. You name the shortcoming, his story contained it. But he continued to write. And editors continued to polish and restructure his work. Before long he developed into one of our best writers.

So you see, anyone born with an interest in writing can be made into a good writer.

How do you approach each writing assignment?
Now you're asking for my secrets. Okay, I'll come clean.

When I receive a writing assignment—whether it's for a news release, newspaper story, or magazine feature—the first thing I do is make sure my interviewing has brought me all the facts. Not *most* of the facts—*all* the facts. I keep talking to people until I'm satisfied I have accumulated the information I need to begin to write. Interviewing and research, you see, are essential parts of writing.

How would you assess the state of writing among public relations practitioners today?

Overall, it's poor. This is not to say that good writing doesn't exist in the public relations field. But the quality of most of the writing I see is embarrassingly inferior.

Many people entering our field really haven't mastered the basics. Not only can't Johnny read, he can't write correctly, either. This shortcoming hurts even more when people who are in the business of language and words, in fact, haven't mastered the craft. The answer? As I see it, our educational systems across the country—I'm talking grammar school, high school, and, yes, even college—have got to get back to basics.

Is the news release dead?

Is the nickel cigar history? Are high-buttoned shoes passé? Are the raccoon coat, straw hat, and swell expressions, such as "Oh voe dee oh doe," outdated on college campuses? Of course, they are!

But the news release, on the other hand, is as strong as ever!

In our society the written word remains the best way for us to transmit information. Sure, the methods may change—many of us now send information by computer instead of via a news release in an envelope—but everything still boils down to the written word. A news release is still the ideal way for a public relations practitioner to communicate with the media.

Incidentally, if you're wondering what "Oh voe dee oh doe" means, look it up—or ask your grandparents. They probably used the expression all the time.

What's the best advice you can give to practitioners just starting out?

First, read everything you can get your hands on: newspapers, magazines, books—even pulp novels. If you intend to be a wordsmith, you must understand the language inside out. Reading will help you develop your skills.

Next, go out and do it. The best way to learn how to write is to write. Over and over, day in and day out. There simply is no substitute. The more you write, the more you learn, and the easier it should become.

Finally, if you're not on the staff of your college newspaper, make tracks to the editor as soon as you finish reading this interview. Write as much as you can while you're in college. This will afford you a valuable opportunity to see what writing is all about, and to feel what it's like to be a writer.

Anything Else?

Yes. Don't be afraid to make a mistake.

The field of public relations is constantly changing, and practitioners tend to become unsure of which course of action to take in handling a project. If you plan to enter our profession, you must become results-oriented. The best way for you to accomplish your goals, then, is to go out and do it. In short, go for the gold!

9

Writing for the Eye

Writing for reading was traditionally among the strongest areas for public relations professionals. Most practitioners entered public relations through the field of print journalism. Accordingly, they had been schooled in the techniques of writing for the eye, not the ear. Today, of course, a background in the print media is not particularly necessary to practice public relations work. Indeed, as already noted, public relations professionals today gravitate to the field from a variety of backgrounds—law, television, general management, political science, and education. Nonetheless, demonstrating a facility for writing that is to be read continues to be a requirement for public relations work.

Although the news release is the most frequently used communications vehicle designed to be read, additional written tools are possible, each with its own purpose and style. This chapter will review the biography, the backgrounder, the feature story, the case history, the by-liner, the memorandum, and the pitch letter. Each of these may stand alone as an individual communication. Often, however, several are combined as limited elements in a media kit, which can provide editors with story ideas. The practitioner must know when each particular vehicle is appropriate.

The Media Kit

Media kits are often distributed in conjunction with an announcement. They incorporate several communications vehicles, including graphic elements, for potential use by newspapers and magazines. A bare-bones media kit consists of a news release plus one or two other elements, such as a biography or backgrounder, both of which will be discussed shortly. The

FROM: KETCHUM PUBLIC RELATIONS
55 Union Street
San Francisco, CA 94111
Hilary Hanson
(415) 984-6385
David Emanuel
(415) 984-6326

FOR IMMEDIATE RELEASE

CELEBRATED CALIFORNIA DANCING RAISINS HIT THE ROAD THIS SUMMER
ON ACTION-PACKED SUMMER VACATION

FRESNO, Calif. -- Guess who's packing their bags for a summer vacation across America?

Rumor has it through the grapevine that it's not Chevy Chase filming a new sequel. . .It's the California Dancing Raisins -- those entertaining characters who have captured the hearts of Americans and become celebrities overnight since their top-rated commercials began airing two years ago. The Raisins are planning a whirlwind 6,500-mile road trip stopping in 27 U.S. cities this summer to visit America's favorite landmarks, receive keys to major cities, inform fans of their new national fan club and entertain young and old alike with their famous Grapevine dance.

(more)

55 Union Street ▪ San Francisco, CA 94111

FACT SHEET

CALIFORNIA RAISIN ADVISORY BOARD

The Ad Campaign

- The California Dancing Raisin campaign was voted the most popular television commercial in 1987 by consumers, according to research by Video Storyboard Tests, Inc.

- Three Claymation raisin commercials have been produced since 1986: "Lunch Box," "Late Show" and "Playing With Your Food." A fourth television ad will premiere this fall, airing nationwide beginning in October, starring Ray Charles and a hip new cast of Claymation Raisins.

- A 30-second commercial featuring the Claymation Raisin characters takes an average of three months to produce; it takes one full day of work to create one second of footage. Claymation is the process of creating animation with clay. Produced by Will Vinton, Claymation requires 25 frames of film or individual pictures to create one second of a commercial.

The Raisin Industry

- Approximately 350,000 tons of raisins are produced annually, generating $400 million dollars in sales.

- The California Raisin Advisory Board (CALRAB) represents the U.S. raisin industry, which is composed of 23 raisin packers and more than 5,000 raisin growers in the San Joaquin Valley.

- The California Raisin industry produces virtually the entire domestic supply and almost one-third of the world's supply of raisins.

- Raisins are harvested in late August. Skilled farm workers carefully hand-pick the grapes and place them on clean paper trays in the fields between the rows of vines. They are allowed to dry naturally for days in the sun. After about three weeks of exposure, the grapes become delicious and nutritious juicy raisins.

(more)

55 Union Street ▪ San Francisco, CA 94111

FIGURE 9–1 When the California Raisin Advisory Board wanted to promote its product across the country, it launched a nationwide tour of the beloved California Raisins, announced via this media kit. *(Courtesy of Ketchum Public Relations)*

kit is designed to be all the media need to understand and portray an announcement.

Media kits might also require Fact Sheets or Q & A (Question-and-Answer) sheets. The public relations professional must weigh carefully how much information is required in the media kit. Journalists don't appreciate being overwhelmed by too much copy and too many photos.

In preparing a media kit, public relations professionals must keep the following points in mind:

♦ Be sure the information is accurate and thorough and will answer a journalist's most fundamental questions.

♦ Provide sufficient background information material to allow the editor to select a story angle.

♦ Don't be too commercial. Offer balanced, objective information.

♦ Confine opinions and value judgments to quotes from credible sources.

♦ Never lie. That's tantamount to editorial suicide.

♦ Visually arresting graphics may mean the difference between finding the item in the next day's paper or in the same day's wastebasket.

Figure 9–1 shows the press kit used to launch the nationwide tour of one of our country's "most critical natural resources," the California Raisins.

The Biography

Next to the news release, the most popular tool is the biography, often called the biographical summary, or just plain bio. The bio recounts pertinent facts about a particular individual. Most organizations keep a file of bios covering all top officers. Major newspapers and wire services prepare standby bios on well-known people for immediate use on breaking news, such as sudden deaths.

Straight Bios

The straight bio lists factual information in a straightforward fashion in a descending order of importance, with company-oriented facts preceding more personal details.

> David Rockefeller became chairman of the board of directors and chief executive officer of the Chase Manhattan Bank, N.A. in New York on March 1, 1969, and of the Chase Manhattan Corporation upon its formation on June 4, 1969.
>
> During his career with Chase Manhattan, Rockefeller gained a worldwide reputation as a leading banker and spokesman for the business community. He spearheaded the bank's expansion both internationally and throughout the

metropolitan New York area and helped the bank play a significant role as a corporate citizen.

Rockefeller joined the Chase National Bank as an assistant manager in the foreign department in 1946. He was appointed an assistant cashier in 1947, second vice-president in 1948, and vice-president in 1949.

From 1950 to 1952, he was responsible for the supervision of Chase's business in Latin America, where, under his direction, new branches were opened in Cuba, Panama, and Puerto Rico, plus a representative office in Buenos Aires.

Narrative Bios

The narrative bio, on the other hand, is written in a breezier, more informal way. This style gives spark and vitality to the biography to make the individual come alive.

David Rockefeller, who has been described as a man possessed of "a peculiar blend of enterprise, prudence, knowledge, and dedication," was born in Manhattan on June 12, 1915. His mother was the former Abby Aldrich, daughter of Senator Nelson Aldrich of Rhode Island. She had met John D.

YOU MAKE THE CALL

Grepso the Clown Bio

As the public relations director for WAAH-TV, you are assigned to write both a straight bio and narrative bio on the station's ever-popular Grepso the Clown. Here are some key facts.

1. Grepso's real name is Howie Barmad. He is forty-five and a former light-heavyweight boxing contender.
2. Grepso was born in Jersey City, New Jersey.
3. He joined WAAH 10 years ago as a newscaster, later worked as a weatherman, and five years ago became Grepso the Clown.
4. Grepso was educated at Harvard University, where he received a B.A. degree in philosophy and graduated magna cum laude.
5. He has been voted clown of the year for three years in a row and is northeastern chairman of the United Cerebral Palsy Telethon.
6. Grepso lives in Basking Ridge, New Jersey with his beloved nephew, called "Fish," who is training to be a clown. Grepso's hobbies include collecting tropical fish, snorkeling, and fingerpainting.

QUESTION

From the data given, how would you write a straight bio on Grepso? A narrative bio?

Rockefeller, Jr., the shy son of multimillionaire John D. Rockefeller, when he was an undergraduate at Brown University in Providence.

John D. Rockefeller, Jr., was anxious that his children not be spoiled by the fortune his father had created and therefore put them on strict allowances. The household atmosphere was deeply religious, with one of the children reading the scriptures each morning before breakfast. Mrs. Rockefeller was an exceptional woman, with a strong interest in the arts. She and David were very close.

Throughout David's academic career, he attended schools in which the Rockefeller family had an interest—either philanthropic, sentimental, or both. Abby and John D., Jr., had attended traditional private schools, but David and his three brothers were sent to Lincoln School, an experimental venture conducted by the Teachers College of Columbia to try out the progressive techniques of John Dewey.

Because of its personal tone, a good narrative bio is more difficult to write than the standard bio, which allows little room for embellishment.

The Backgrounder

Background pieces, or backgrounders, generally provide additional information about the institution making an announcement (Figure 9–2). Backgrounders are longer and more general in content than the news release. For example, a two-page release announcing the merger of two organizations may not permit much description of the companies involved. A four- or five-page backgrounder provides editors with more depth on the makeup, activities, and history of the merging firms. Backgrounders are usually not used in their entirety by the media but are excerpted.

Subject matter dictates backgrounder style. Some backgrounders are written like a news release, in a snappy and factual manner. Others take a more descriptive and narrative form.

Example One: News Release Style

BACKGROUNDER—SWENSEN'S ICE CREAM COMPANY

The original Swensen's Ice Cream Shoppe was established in 1948 by Earle Swensen at the corner of Union and Hyde in San Francisco.

In 1963 Mr. Swensen licensed the company's predecessor, See Us-Freeze, Inc., later known as United Outlets, Inc., to use Swensen's trade names, trade secrets, recipes, and methods of operation as the basis for Swensen's franchise system. The license agreement was modified in June 1975 and permits the company to use the licensed property and franchise Swensen's shops in all areas of the world except the city and county of San Francisco.

In February 1980 the company became a wholly owned subsidiary of Red River Resources, Inc., and its corporate headquarters was moved to Phoenix, Arizona.

FIGURE 9−2 This issue backgrounder was distributed by Anheuser-Busch to refute a 1987 study that concluded that "American children see something like 100,000 television commercials for beer between the ages of two and eighteen. "False," screamed Anheuser-Busch. The company quickly dispatched letters, news releases, and this backgrounder around the nation. *(Courtesy of Anheuser-Busch Companies)*

Swensen's now has operations in 31 states and the District of Columbia as well as seven foreign countries.

Example Two: Descriptive, Narrative Style

BACKGROUNDER—SICKLE-CELL DISEASE

The man was a West Indian black, a twenty-year-old student in a professional school in Illinois. One day in 1904, he came to James B. Herrick, an eminent Chicago cardiologist, with symptoms Herrick had never seen before and could not find in the literature. The patient had shortness of breath, a disinclination for exercise, palpitation, jaundice, cough, dizziness, headache, leg ulcers, scars from old leg ulcers, many palpable lymph nodes, pale mucous membranes, muscular rheumatism, severe upper abdominal pain, dark urine, and anemia.

> Blood smears showed many odd-shaped cells, but what arrested the eye was the presence of numerous sickle-shaped cells.
>
> Herrick kept the patient under observation for many years. He did not suspect that he was looking at a disease that afflicted millions of people, including thousands of blacks in America.

In devising a backgrounder, a writer enjoys unlimited latitude. As long as the piece catches the interest of the reader/editor, any style is permissible.

The Feature

Closely related to the backgrounder is the feature story. Features in magazines or newspapers are the opposite of news items. They're often light and humorous, although some are serious. One of the foremost sources of feature writing is the *Wall Street Journal*. Each business day the *Journal's* front page is dominated by three "leader" articles, most written in a time-tested feature-writing style. Basically, the *Journal* system separates each story into three distinct parts, sometimes labeled the D-E-E system (description, explanation, evaluation).

Description

The typical *Journal* story begins by describing an existing situation, often with a light or gripping touch, in such a way that readers are drawn directly into the story.

> When General Miguel Maza Marquez boarded a flight to his coastal hometown of Santa Marta not long ago, 17 fellow passengers abandoned the airplane and the pilot refused to take off. On a second flight, the flight engineer balked.
>
> The reason for the skittishness is that General Maza Marquez is the *good* guy, head of Colombia's equivalent of the Federal Bureau of Investigation— and Number One on the Medellin drug cartel's hit list. Few care to be nearby when somebody tries again to collect the cartel's $1.9 million bounty for killing him; too many bystanders already have perished in attempts on his life.[1]

Explanation

The second part of the *Journal* feature explains how a situation, trend, or event came to be. It is often historical in nature, citing dates, places, and people from the past. It often relates how other factors (economic, sociopolitical, or environmental) may have come to bear on the topic.

> More than 500 people have died in Colombia's drug war in the past year. Gen. Maza Marquez, 51, a short, serene, powerfully built but pot-bellied policeman has been lucky to survive. Sixty-five people died and more than 600 were wounded last December when cartel hit men exploded an estimated 1,200 pieces of dynamite just outside the stark, cement high-rise that houses the DAS. 'It was like an atomic bomb,' says the general.[2]

FINE *food & spirits*

May 6, 1985

Ken Fine
(201) 569-8999

TENAFLY "DAIRY QUEEN" SOLD TO OWNERS OF FINE FOOD & SPIRITS

The Tenafly "Dairy Queen", on the verge of being torn down for a retail-office building, has been rescued from the wrecking ball by its next-door neighbors.

The owners of Fine Food & Spirits, 14 Riveredge Road, have agreed to purchase the "Dairy Queen" from Ed and Beatrice Bugash, owners of the Tenafly landmark since 1960.

"We're delighted," said Mr. Bugash, who along with his wife have been fixtures in the ice cream store 12 hours a day, six months a year for the past 25 years.

"This store is a part of Tenafly -- an institution -- and we feel better now knowing the Fines will continue the tradition," said Mr. Bugash.

Ken Fine, co-owner of Fine Food & Spirits, said he and his partners bought the ice cream store as much for the community as they did for themselves. "We've grown up in Tenafly over the past 30 years, and the 'Dairy Queen' has always been a part of this community," said Mr. Fine.

- more -

FINE FOOD & SPIRITS 14 Riveredge Road, Tenafly, New Jersey 07670 (201) 569-8999

FINE FOOD & SPIRITS

- 2 -

"After school, after Little League -- we all had to rush to the 'Dairy Queen.' It was second nature," he added.

Mr. Fine and his associates began negotiating for the property after a proposed sale to Michael Goodman & Associates fell through, when the developers failed to obtain a variance from the Tenafly Planning Board to build a retail-office building on the site.

The new owners began operating the store last month and plan major enhancements in the months ahead. "First, we'll add benches, bike racks and shrubs to create a park-like environment for the family," Mr. Fine said. "Later on, we'll introduce coffee, bagels, rolls and donuts for morning commuters and business people. We'll also sell newspapers."

Mr. Fine said that additional plans call for expanding to a limited menu of light food to go -- hamburgers, hot dogs, chicken nuggets, old-fashioned French fries and the like. "We'll also be adding a cookie and penny candy store," Mr. Fine said.

"Our goal is to ensure that this store which has been a part of Tenafly for 30 years, continues as a community focal point for many years to come," said Mr. Fine.

\# \# \#

A late-inning save for the old Dairy Queen

By John H. Kuhn
Staff Writer

TENAFLY — A tradition is being saved at West Railroad Avenue and Riveredge Road.

While the planning board was considering the now-defunct plan for a two-story commercial building on the Dairy Queen property, youngsters in borough sports programs were asking parents and coaches where they would get their after-game treats if the DQ closed.

But Ken Fine, who owns Fine Foods and Spirits store, has allayed the youngsters' fears. He has bought the half-acre site and plans to continue and expand the business, he said in a recent interview.

The purchase will provide additional parking for Fine's other business, especially if he goes ahead with plans for a cafe restaurant on the second floor of his food-and-liquor store. "That's in the back of my mind," he said, "but not this year."

The Dairy Queen has been a fixture at the corner since it opened in 1954. "It's always been part of the fun of winning," one youngster said between bites from an oversize ice-cream cone."

Remarked a coach: "I'd save some money, but it wouldn't be the same for the kids with the DQ."

Mr. and Mrs. Ed Bugash, who operated the store from 1960 until recently, kept it open from spring until fall and closed the rest of the year. But Fine said he plans to operate it year-round, add a grill and a penny-candy section, and provide cookies and breads.

"There will be a small expansion," said Fine, who also plans to provide breakfast and to clean the area. "The outlook for business is good, and it will benefit the adjacent business."

"We've grown up in Tenafly over the past 30 years," he said, "and the Dairy Queen has always been a part of this community. After school, after Little League, we all had to rush to the DQ."

Said Bugash: "This store is a part of Tenafly — an institution — and we feel better now knowing it will continue the tradition."

Fine would not disclose what he paid for the property and business, but he said it was less than the $550,000 mentioned when the commercial developer was before the planning board. The board rejected the commercial plan because of a lack of off-street parking.

FIGURE 9–3   A news release, written in feature style, may provoke an editor to use material that might not otherwise merit news coverage. This feature release, which resulted in news coverage, is a case in point. *(Newspaper article reprinted by permission from* The Record, *Hackensack, New Jersey)*

Evaluation

The final section of the *Journal* feature evaluates the meaning of what is contained in the first two parts. It often focuses on the future, frequently quoting sociologists, psychologists, or other experts on what is likely to happen to the subject discussed.

> As the general waits for his deadly duel with Mr. Escobar to resume, he draws some comfort from reports that Mr. Rodriguez Gacha, 'the Mexican,' in his last hunted days cursed his name. 'The Mexican died a lonely man,' the general says with satisfaction. As for the future, he is optimistic. 'Come see me when you return to Colombia,' he tells a visitor. 'I should be alive.' Then he disappears behind the heavy, bullet-proof metal doors of his office.[3]

In public relations the D-E-E approach often works in feature writing assignments (Figure 9–3).

The Case History

The case history is frequently used to tell about a customer's favorable use of a company's product or service. Generally, the case-history writer works for the company whose product or service is involved. Magazines, particularly trade journals, often welcome case histories, contending that one person's experience may be instructive to another.

Case-history articles generally follow a five-part formula.

1. They present a problem experienced by one company but applicable to many other firms.
2. They indicate how the dimensions of the problem were defined by the company using the product.
3. They indicate the solution adopted.
4. They explain the advantages of the adopted solution.
5. They detail the user company's experience after adopting the solution.

Incorporating the D-E-E approach into the case-history writing process may interest an editor in a particular product or service. Done skillfully, such a case history is soft sell at its best—beneficial to the company and interesting and informative to the editor and readers.

The By-Liner

The by-lined article, or by-liner, is a story signed and ostensibly authored by an officer of a particular firm. Often, however, the by-liner is ghostwritten by a public relations professional. In addition to carrying considerable prestige in certain publications, by-liners allow corporate spokespeople to express their views without being subject to major reinterpretation by the publication.

Perhaps the major advantage of a by-liner is that it positions executives as experts. The fact that an organization's officer has authored an informed article on a subject means that not only are the officer and the organization credible sources, but also, by inference, that they are perhaps more highly regarded on the issues at hand than their competitors. Indeed, the ultimate audience exposed to a by-liner may greatly exceed the circulation of the periodical in which the article appears. Organizations regularly use by-liner reprints as direct-mail pieces to further their image with key constituent groups. Such use of reprints is further discussed in Chapter 11.

It is often a good idea for a writer to outline the by-liner, noting at the outset the major points the author wishes to get across. Although most by-liners are more formal than case histories and generally contain many facts and figures, they can still lend themselves to the D-E-E writing approach.

The Memorandum

Humorist Art Buchwald tells of the child who visited his father's office. When asked what his dad did, the son replied, "He sends pieces of paper to other people, and other people send pieces of paper to him." Most people who work know a great deal about memoranda. Inside many organizations the memo is the most popular form of communication. Memos are written for a multitude of purposes and adopt numerous forms. Even though almost everyone gets into the memo-writing act, writing memos correctly takes practice and hard work.

The key to writing good memos is clear thinking. Many memos reflect unclear thinking and are plagued by verbosity and fuzzy language. Inverted pyramid style is often a good way to compose a memo. More often, rewriting turns out to be the key.

Public relations people, in particular, must write good memos. Frequently they must prepare long, internal white papers, position papers, or standby statements that are to outline clearly the firm's position. Such documents are used to respond to inquiries on sensitive subjects and can't be vague or subject to misinterpretation.

In general, the more textually taut a memo is, the less chance that it will fall prey to others in the organization who are prone to pounce on it. One rule of thumb for memo writing is to pretend to send the memo to yourself as a straight telegram at your own expense. Chances are, the less your telegram costs, the more effective the memo will be.

The Misleading Memo

To: Public Relations Department
From: Rita Rey, Public Relations Director

It has recently been brought to my attention that many of the press comments our organization has been receiving in the negative may stem from our policy of refusing all press interviews, regardless of the publication making the request.

Obviously, such negative stories do our company no good with its many publics and often present an unfair and misleading presentation as to our philosophy and approach. I wish therefore to inform all concerned—those who have refused interviews in the past and all others as well—that we will immediately change our policy to entertain all requests from the press and judge each on its merits.

If there are any questions about company policy on this matter, please contact me.

QUESTIONS

1. What's wrong with this memo?
2. How would you improve it?

The Pitch Letter

The pitch letter is a sales letter, pure and simple. Its purpose is to interest an editor or reporter in a possible story, interview, or event. Figure 9–4 offers an example of two excellent pitch letters for the same product. Although letter styles run the gamut, the best are direct and to the point, while catchy and evocative.

Some have questioned the utility of the pitch letter, replacing it with a straightforward "media alert" format to grab the attention of editors and news directors. The new format eschews the use of long paragraphs in favor of short, bulleted items highlighting the "5W's" used by journalists: who, what, when, where, and why. The premise of the "media alert" is that it "talks to the media in a language it has been trained to accept."[4]

Such criticism notwithstanding, a good pitch letter—especially one with a provocative lead—can hit a reader right between the eyes. For example, Father Bruce Ritter, the founder of Covenant House, who in 1989 met an ignominious fate due to allegations of financial mismanagement and sexual improprieties, nonetheless was responsible for masterful pitch letters. One of Father Bruce's letters began this way:

> *Please* read what I have to tell you.
> Children are being sold.

IF you EVEr WANT TO SEE the
little NaTioNAL LampooN aLive
Again IN your CRuMMy MailBox,
you KNow whAt you HAVE to Do!!!

you've BEEN WARNed.
DON'T PLAY CuTE.

National Lampoon

This Is Your Last Chance . . .

Say good-bye, sweetheart. This is it! You can kiss the $7.95 one-year subscription to the *National Lampoon* good-bye just as you've said *au revoir* and *harry verderchi* to the fifty-cent gallon of gas, the ten-cent cigar, and the twenty-cent bus ride.

The price is going up and we're giving you fair warning. We're not saying exactly how much we're going to charge for the new one-year subscription but — it's less than the gross national product of Yugoslavia and more than a rubdown in a midget massage parlor.

The reasons for the increase in price are numerous in addition to greed:

1. The cost of paper has skyrocketed. All right, let's examine that. What does it mean to a magazine operation? Well, our editors drink a lot of coffee and this means an increase in the price of coffee cups. They throw paper airplanes around the room while trying to think of funny things to say. Up your cost of paper airplanes by 50 percent.

2. The cost of typewriters has increased. This doesn't affect us since no one on our staff knows how to type.

3. The cost of manufacturing has increased. This means that our editor in chief will be paying more for his Mercedes-Benz this year, and that means more for you to kick in. Would you ask the editor in chief of the world's most widely read adult humor magazine to drive around in last year's Mercedes-Benz?

4. The price of grain is spiraling. (We don't know what that means, but it is an exact quote from the *Wall Street Journal* so it must be important.)

O.K., put this all together and it means — raise the subscription prices. No more $7.95. So, this is it. This is your last chance. From here on in, it's clipsville. You pay more.

If you really want to save, take out a two- or three-year subscription. The savings are so big that we actually lose money every time you or anyone else subscribes for two or three years. We do it only because our subscription manager is insecure and he wants to know that he'll have at least a handful of people around for a long time.

No more message. If you want the latest in yocks, mirth, and lovable satire, subscribe today and subscribe at these pre-inflation prices.

Sincerely,

Herbert Hoover

Herbert Hoover
Subscription Manager

FIGURE 9–4 Pitch letters should be enticing, catchy, and evocative. Even though these examples from the subscription department of the *National Lampoon* magazine may not qualify as garden-variety pitch letters, they certainly are enticing, catchy, and evocative. *(Courtesy of National Lampoon)*

Their bodies and spirits are being corrupted.
They are forced into a life of abuse and degradation.
Where?
India? Uganda? Peru?
No!
Right here in New York, the Big Apple, Fun City.
  Covenant House began as a response to the needs of these children of the streets. Will you join with me in helping to carry out this work?

Such unbridled, heart-tugging language is typical of a good, compassionate pitch letter.

Pitch letters that sell generally contain several key elements. First, they open with a grabber, an interesting statement that impels the reader to read on. Next, they explain why the editor and/or publication should be interested in the pitch, or invitation. Finally, they are personally written to specific people, rather than being addressed to "editor" (which is the journalistic equivalent of "occupant").

Pitch-letter mechanics are similar to those of the release. Writing should be sharp and pointed. Whenever possible, length should be held to one page. Spelling of names, especially the editor's, should be perfect. Facts and statements in the letter should be carefully checked. Practitioners should remember that editors regularly receive many pitch letters. If an editor isn't interested in a pitch, don't badger. The trick is to capture in the letter the essence of a story that the editor can't pass up.

Other Tools

Other public relations tools, such as the round-up article, the fact sheet, and the Q & A, may be helpful in certain infrequent situations.

The Round-Up Article

Although many publications discourage publicity about a single company, they encourage articles that summarize, or round up, the experiences of several companies within an industry. These survey articles may be initiated by the publications themselves or at the suggestions of public relations people. Weaker or smaller companies, in particular, can benefit from being included in a round-up story with stronger, larger adversaries. Thoroughly researching and drafting round-up articles is a good way to secure articles that mention the practitioner's firm in favorable association with top competitors. Wire services, in particular, are regular users of round-ups.

THE C.F. HATHAWAY COMPANY 90 PARK AVENUE NEW YORK, N.Y. 10016   (212) 697-5566

FOR IMMEDIATE RELEASE
AUGUST 13, 1987

FOR MORE INFORMATION CONTACT:
RICK LYKE
ERIC MOWER AND ASSOCIATES INC.
315/472-4703

QUICK FACTS ON THE C.F. HATHAWAY COMPANY

COMPANY: C.F. Hathaway is a division of Warnaco Inc. the $600 million apparel
marketer. Warnaco's Menswear Group includes Hathaway, and lines from
Christian Dior, Chaps by Ralph Lauren, Puritan, Pringle of Scotland
and Thane. Other Warnaco apparel divisions include: Warner's and
Olga intimate apparel, Geoffrey Beene, Hathaway for Women, White Stag
Sportswear for women; and activewear by Speedo, Spalding, Jack
Nicklaus and White Stag Skiwear.

MANAGEMENT: Richard Pressler is president and chief executive officer of
C.F. Hathaway Co.

LOCATION: C.F. Hathaway Co. has corporate offices at 90 Park Avenue in New York
and headquarter manufacturing facilities in Waterville, Maine.
Hathaway apparel is sold worldwide through various licensing
agreements.

SALES: C.F. Hathaway sales increased 22 percent nationwide in 1986, with a 38
percent increase in key brand markets during a year in which the dress
shirt industry reported a flat performance.

PRODUCTS: C.F. Hathaway Company is famous for its dress shirts and is
recognized, as well, for neckwear and sportswear.

LEADERSHIP: C.F. Hathaway Company is America's oldest manufacturer of dress
shirts, with its roots dating back to 1837. The company is
recognized for its many innovations in styling and manufacturing
techniques.

#
A Division of **WARNACO** Inc.

FIGURE 9–5   In this fact sheet, the public relations counsel of C. F. Hathaway
Company describes all that an editor needs to know about the firm—on one
sheet of paper in a rapid-fire, straightforward manner. *(Courtesy of C. F. Hathaway
Company)*

The Fact Sheet

Fact sheets are short documents that compactly profile an organization. They generally support the information in news releases and backgrounders. Editors find fact sheets helpful as a quick supply of resource material for articles.

Fact sheets are designed to provide an editor with a quick thumbnail sketch of an organization, individual, or event. For example, a typical one-page corporate fact sheet includes a brief description of the company and its product lines, the names of its top managers, its location, current sales figures, leading products, and a summary of its history. How is all this possible in a one-page sketch? Figure 9–5 and 9–6 show how.

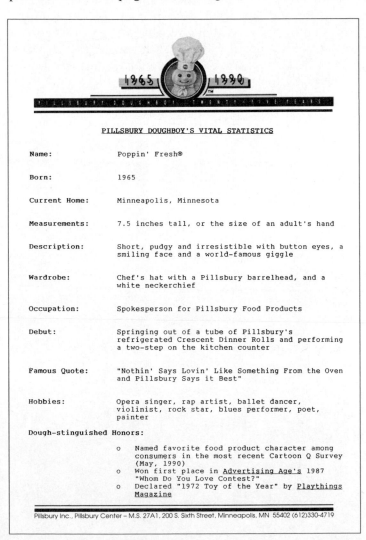

FIGURE 9–6 Another variation on the fact sheet theme is this submission by Pillsbury in recognition of its Dough Boy's 25th birthday. *(Courtesy of Golin Harris Communications)*

The Q & A

The question-and-answer form, or Q & A, often substitutes for or complements a fact sheet in conveying easy-to-follow information. In the Q & A, the writer lists frequently asked questions about the subject and then provides appropriate answers. A skillfully written Q & A can often substitute for a personal interview between an editor and a company official.

Photographic Supports

Photos, when used properly, enhance brochures, annual reports, and even news releases. Any practitioner involved with printed material should know the basics of photography. Although a detailed discussion of photographic terms and techniques falls beyond the scope of this book, public relations practitioners should be relatively conversant with photographic terminology and able to recognize the attributes that characterize good photos.

FIGURE 9–7 Occasionally, a specially conceived photo can attract extensive publicity. In 1959, when Chase Manhattan Bank was in the midst of constructing its downtown One Chase Manhattan Plaza headquarters, photographer Robert Mottar asked the hundreds of workers to freeze for a moment so that this picture could be recorded for posterity. It also was reported in many of New York City's daily newspapers, which acknowledged both the bank and its new location. *(Courtesy of Chase Manhattan Bank)*

BETWEEN THE LINES

Speaking Graphically

Designers have their own language. Public relations professionals, who deal with designers, must understand them. For example, when a designer says, "We spec'd your job based on a magenta and cyan theme for the masthead and Garamond bold for the body copy; we also added clip art. We'll transfer the comp to a mechanical." Here is the translation:

- *Spec*—Short for specifications, the instructions about type style and size, line measure or length, indentations, headlines, etc.
- *Magenta and Cyan*—Magenta is red. Cyan is blue. Together with yellow and black, these constitute the four-process, standard colors used in printing. These four basics can be mixed to yield more than 800 different shades and colors.
- *Masthead*—A design or logo used as identification by a newspaper or other publication.
- *Garamond Bold*—One style and variation of type design. Other common typefaces include Baskerville, Bodoni, Century, and Helvetica.
- *Clip Art*—Reprinted drawings that can be pasted directly on a mechanical. Clip Art is available in books that are arranged by topic.
- *Comp*—Comprehensive design showing type style and colors to help the client envision the final printed product.
- *Mechanical*—The preparation of type, photos, and illustrations to make a design suitable for printing. This is achieved by pasting type and design elements onto a board, often referred to as a mechanical. The mechanical provides the printer with a "source document" with which to begin the printing process.

1. Photos should be "live," in real environments with believable people, instead of studio shots of stilted models (Figure 9–7).
2. They should focus clearly on the issue, product, image, or person that the organization wishes to emphasize, without irrelevant, visually distracting clutter in the foreground or background.
3. They should be eye catching, using angles creatively—overhead, below, to the side—to suggest movement.
4. They must express a viewpoint—an underlying message.

These kinds of shots are often difficult, especially for the novice photographer. It often makes sense, therefore, to hire a professional. Some organizations are fortunate to have photographers on staff. Others must hire freelancers, who may charge upwards of $2,000 to $5,000 per day for annual report work.

Almost as important as the photograph itself is the coordination of photographic assignments. Practitioners should work closely with the photographer and the intended subject, notifying both well in advance of specific needs and dates. Too often, a photographer must wait—and charge for—a day or two just for a setup to be ready. Worse, photos taken in hasty setups may show safety hazards or outdated equipment, necessitating costly retouching or even reshooting. Finally, photographers may not understand the nuances behind a public relations photo without the counsel of the person who scheduled the shot. Consequently, planning for and following through on photographic assignments becomes a critical responsibility for practitioners.

The Standby Statement

Organizations sometimes take actions or make announcements they know will lead to media inquiries or even public protests. In such cases, firms prepare concise statements to clarify their positions, should they be called to explain. Such standby statements generally are defensive. They should be

---

BETWEEN THE LINES

Don't—Repeat—Don't Use "Do Not"

In writing standby statements, public relations practitioners should keep in mind that publications sometimes mistakenly drop words in print. Invariably, the most important words are the ones dropped.

For example, the public relations officer of the labor union who issues the statement "We do not intend to strike," may have his quote appear in the next day's paper as "We do intend to strike"—the *not* having been inadvertently dropped by the paper. A slight, yet significant change.

The remedy: Use contractions. It's pretty hard to drop out a significant word or distort the intended meaning when the statement is "We don't intend to strike."

---

brief and unambiguous, so as not to raise more questions than they answer. Such events as executive firings, layoffs, price increases, and extraordinary losses are all subject to subsequent scrutiny by the media and are therefore proper candidates for standby statements.

Summary

Written methods of communication are often overused. Everyone from editors to corporate presidents complains about getting too much paper. So, before the professional even thinks of putting thoughts on paper, the plan must be assessed and these questions answered:

1. **Will writing serve a practical purpose?** Have a use in mind for the communication before you write it. If you can't come up with a purpose, don't write.

2. **Is writing the most effective way to communicate?** Face-to-face or telephone communication may be better and more direct than writing. Writing occasionally is used as an excuse for not calling or seeing someone in person. In most cases it's better to resolve a situation quickly, and there is no quicker method than going directly to the source.

   Sometimes, too, the written word is lifeless. An audiovisual presentation to a training group, for example, may be more interesting and effective than a training manual. Again, the objective of the message dictates the form.

3. **What is the risk?** Writing is always risky. Just ask a lawyer. Retracting a printed comment is a lot harder than taking back an oral one. Before committing words to paper, carefully weigh the risks. A confidential internal memo from an ITT lobbyist once made its way into the hands of syndicated columnist Jack Anderson, who printed the memo verbatim. The memo concerned sensitive negotiations between ITT and the U.S. Justice Department. Once the secret document was published, ITT's reputation took a severe tumble. Should the memo have been written? No. Could ITT have avoided the scandal? Absolutely.

4. **Are the timing and the person doing the writing right?** Timing is extremely important in writing. A message, like a joke, can fall flat if the timing is off. Timing, of course, depends on the particular subject and the circumstances surrounding it. The question "Would it be better to wait?" should always be asked before writing. The person doing the writing is also important. A writer should always ask whether he or she is the most appropriate person to write. Perhaps the message is right, but someone at a different level or in a different position in the organization may be able to write it better.

The pen—or the typewriter—is a potent weapon. But like any weapon, writing must be used prudently and properly to achieve the desired objective.

1. Through which field have most public relations professionals entered the practice?
2. What are the essential elements of a media kit?
3. What is the difference between a straight biography and a narrative biography?
4. What is a backgrounder?
5. When might one use a feature rather than a news release?
6. What are the essential elements of a case history?
7. What is a by-liner?
8. What is the essence of a good pitch letter?
9. What kind of organization might benefit from a round-up story?
10. When might an organization require a standby statement?

1. Jose de Cordoba, "Marked for Death, Colombia's Top Cop Is a Tough Target," *The Wall Street Journal,* 2 October 1990; A1.
2. Ibid.
3. *Loc. cit.*
4. "Farewell to the Pitch Letter," *Public Relations Journal* (July 1990): 13.

Baird, Russell.   *The Graphics of Communication.* 5th ed. 301 Commerce St. Ft. Worth, TX 76102; New York: Holt, Rinehart & Winston, 1987.

Blythin, Evan, and Larry Samovar.   *Communicating Effectively on Television.* Belmont, CA: Wadsworth, 1985.

The Complete Guide to Creating Successful Brochures. Brentwood, NJ: Asher-Gallent Press, 1988.

Conover, Theodore.   *Graphic Communications Today.* St. Paul, MN: West, 1985.

Crow, Wendell.   *Communication Graphics.* Englewood Cliffs, NJ: Prentice-Hall, 1986.

Crawford, Tad.   *Legal Guide for the Visual Artist.* New York: Allworth Press, 1988.

Degen, Clara.   *Understanding & Using Video.* White Plains, NY: Knowledge Industry, 1985.

Felici, James, and Ted Nace.   *Desktop Publishing Skills.* Reading, MA: Addison-Wesley, 1987.

Gold, Ron.   *The Personal Computer Publicity Book.* Santa Monica, CA: Ron Gold, 1988 (1341 Ocean Ave.).

Harnessing Desktop Publishing. Arlington, VA: National School Public Relations Association, 1987 (1501 Lee Hwy.).

How to Write a Wrong. American Association of Retired Persons (P.O. Box 2400, Long Beach, CA). The objective here is to assist consumers in writing to-the-point complaint letters. Free.

Hudson, Howard Penn.   *Publishing Newsletters.* New York: Scribners, 1988.

The Merriam-Webster Book of Word Histories. Springfield, MA: G & C Merriam Co., 1976. This volume rejects certain accepted theories of meaning but presents

TOP OF THE SHELF

Weiner, Richard. *Dictionary of Media and Communications.* New York: Simon and Schuster, 1990.

How are you fixed for *explosion wipes* and *tombstone heads*? Don't check a heavy-metal magazine for these terms; they can be found only in the *Dictionary of Media and Communications.*

Richard Weiner defines more than 30,000 words and phrases frequently used by professional communicators in public relations, advertising, film, theater, and print and broadcast journalism. When Weiner, a veteran public relations consultant known for his introduction of the Cabbage Patch Kids, tells inaudible communicators they are *out in the alley,* he isn't being rude; he simply means they are beyond the range of the microphone. Similarly, people who enjoy *film noir* aren't necessarily chic or avant-garde; they prefer movies characterized by violence or crime. And those concerned with the *dog watch* don't want a timepiece for their pet; they are interested in the newsroom after the last edition is completed, when a small staff remains on duty.

Publicists, speechwriters, and advertisers must be well versed in the language of their professions. With the *Dictionary of Media and Communications,* you won't have to endure embarrassment the next time someone asks you to find the *spider dolly, trouble box,* or *bleed-face.* (Oh yes, an *explosion wipe,* a term used in television, is the rapid replacement of one scene by another, and *tombstone heads* are headlines of the same structure in terms of typeface, size, and width of line.)

many of interest. Under the G's alone you can learn the origin of genius, gin, goon, gorgeous, gossip, gridiron, and more.

The Merriam-Webster Pocket Dictionary of Synonyms. Springfield, MA: G & C Merriam Co., 1972. This is useful for its careful attention to shades of meaning and for short examples of good usage by established writers.

The Merriam-Webster Thesaurus. Springfield, MA: G & C Merriam Co., 1978. More than 100,000 synonyms, antonyms, idiomatic equivalents, related words, and contrasted terms are included.

Television & Cable Factbook. 2 vols. TV Digest (2115 Ward Court, NW 20037, Washington, DC).

CASE STUDY   The Leather Pitch Letter

In January 1990, Dr. Jane Mellenkamph of the University of Idaho completed experimentation on a novel process through which genuine leather could be made water repellent. With this process, for the first time ever, leather could be washed with ordinary laundry soap and water. Dr. Mellenkamph immediately patented her leather-treating process and spread the word throughout the leather-tanning industry.

In June, Samuel S. Sobelham, president of Associated Leather Tanners of Atlanta, purchased all rights to Dr. Mellenkamph's patent. Sobelham, a veteran in the industry, considered the Mellenkamph formula the most revolutionary breakthrough in history. Sobelham was convinced that glove manufacturers would fall all over each other to purchase his specially treated, water-resistant leather.

But Sobelham misjudged his market. For the next year he tried unsuccessfully to create an interest in the new product. "We've heard all these washable leather stories before," echoed most of the glove manufacturers. "There's no such thing as a washable leather; don't bother us" was the reply he heard most often.

By June 1990, Sobelham concluded it was useless to deal directly with manufacturers. He would have to go around them to the only group who could force glove manufacturers to act—the general public.

He turned to public relations counselor Ed Andrews to come up with a plan to inform the public about the new product. He explained to Andrews that this product was developed at the critical stage of the tanning process and exceeded any federal washability standards. Sobelham said there was no other product like it on the market. He said that the only reason glove manufacturers weren't yet interested in the product was that they frankly couldn't and didn't believe it.

Andrews returned to his small shop and considered his strategy to put the product on the map and convince glove manufacturers that public interest in and potential demand for the product were keen. Three days later he was back to Sobelham with the following plan. He thought that they could hold a press conference in the Grand Ballroom of the Plaza Hotel in New York City at noon on July 1. Rather than bill it as a traditional press conference, it would be a fashion show at which professional models would exhibit all kinds of expensive and nonexpensive gloves made of washable leather. The gloves themselves would run the gamut of textures, styles, and colors.

In addition to the gloves and models, the highlight of the conference would be a long table holding crystal bowls filled with various materials—axle grease, chicken fat, chocolate ice cream, coffee, grape juice, etc. After exhibiting the gloves to the crowd, each model would dip the gloves in a different bowl and would then deposit them in one of two washing machines at the front of the room. The gloves would be washed and the results dramatically revealed to the crowd. This unique fashion show, Andrews reasoned, could provoke important headlines from the nation's influential fashion editors in attendance. With favorable stories from the fashion press, glove manufacturers around the country would be bidding for Associated Leather Tanners' patented process.

Sobelham reacted with one word to Andrews's idea, "Boffo!"

When Andrews returned to his own office, he realized that the fashion editors would have to be drawn to the fashion show through a pitch letter. He knew that, each day, major fashion editors received 10 to 20 letters inviting them to various functions. Sometimes the pitch letter meant the difference between an important attendee and a no-show. Therefore, Andrews figured, his pitch letter had to be tight, catchy, and enticing—in other words, perfect. If the editors failed to show, the Ed Andrews public relations firm would be minus one client.

QUESTIONS

1. What are the essential facts that Andrews must get into his pitch letter?

2. If you were Andrews, would you send every editor the same pitch letter, or would particular editors get different versions?

3. If you were Andrews, what would you say in your pitch letter?

Tips from the Top

LYLE L. ERB

Lyle L. Erb is a columnist for *Public Relations Quarterly.* He was in the newspaper business for 38 years. In addition, he edited *Seminar, A Quarterly Review for Journalists* for nine years, and he published *In Black and White,* the eclectic newsletter for those who write and edit for publication, for three years. Now retired, Erb is a consultant in Pacific Beach, California.

What is public relations?

Public relations—the noble art of pulling the wool over the sheep's eyes so that the wolf appears to be a little lamb (see *Public Relations Counsel*).

Public relations counsel—a wolf in sheep's clothing; sometimes found in Grandma's bed.

—The Devil's Dictionary

Whatever else it may be, public relations is not a profession, except in the narrow sense that a great many people earn their livings from it. Rather, it is an art, a craft, a calling, which, as pursued by the best of practitioners, seeks to communicate a corporate or personal image to the general public with factual accuracy, honest integrity, and incorruptible faith.

How would you assess the state of public relations writing today?

Deplorable. That is a generality, but accurately descriptive of most of the press re-

leases, scripts, pitch letters, etc. that come to me for review.

What are the fundamentals you consider sacrosanct in writing?

Be brief. Use short words. Write short sentences, short paragraphs. Eschew obfuscation. Avoid cliches, slang, fad words. Shun hyperbole and circumlocution. Be direct—active, not passive. Have respect for the tools of our trade, the words we work with. Don't use words like *sacrosanct*.

Do you think anyone can master public relations writing skills?

No. (I assume you mean *everyone.*) Many college graduates today can't write a simple sentence. They are ignorant of basic rules of grammar. They can't spell. Yet some of them are successful public relations practitioners.

As a columnist, what kinds of pitch letters do you especially appreciate?

Those that DO NOT begin with danglers: "As a writer, I want you to know . . ."; "As an investor, there is an opportunity . . . ." For example, in this question, what does the phrase "as a columnist" modify?

What advice would you give a colleague who had to write a public relations feature and couldn't get started?
Do your research thoroughly. Decide what you want to say. Tell them you're going to say it. Say it. Tell them what you said.

What constitutes a good press kit?
A good one presents the facts—"Just the facts, ma'am"—about the product, service, or person. A bad one exaggerates, overemphasizes, intensifies, and is replete with italics, capital letters, and astounders.

How does one become a "good" writer?
By writing. Writing, revising, and rewriting. A good copy editor can improve almost anyone's writing. Good writing is not necessarily fine writing. As one sage put it, "When you think you have written an especially fine line, blot it out. It will do wonders for your style." Remember that facility is not felicity. "You write with ease to show your breeding, but easy writing's curst hard reading" [Thomas Moore's *Life of Sheridan*]. The writing may be easy. It's the revising and rewriting that are hard work.

What constitutes good "public relations writing"?
There is no such thing as good "public relations writing," just as there is no such thing as good "journalistic writing" or say, good "legal writing." Good writing is good writing. Bad writing is what gave rise to such opprobrious terms as *journalese* and *legalese*. Good writing communicates. And that's what public relations is all about. (We are not speaking here of fiction or belles lettres.)

Writing for the Ear

Writing for listening involves the spoken word. A person who hears a speech or a radio or television broadcast generally gets one crack at the message. There is rarely a second chance.

The key to writing for listening is to write as if you are speaking. Use simple, short sentences, active verbs, contractions, and one- and two-syllable words. Let phrases stand alone. Be brief.

This chapter will touch on the most widely used methods of communicating to be heard, including speeches, presentations, video news releases, public service announcements, and film scripts. As people read less and watch and listen more, writing for the ear becomes increasingly important for the public relations professional. Accordingly, where once public relations was dominated by print-oriented professionals, today, more and more practitioners enter the field with strong radio and television orientations.

The Speech

Speech writing has become one of the most coveted public relations skills. Increasingly, speech writers have used their access to management to move up the organizational ladder. The prominence they enjoy is due largely to the importance top executives place on making speeches. Today's executives are called on by government and special-interest groups to defend their policies, justify their prices, and explain their practices to a much greater degree than ever before. In this environment, a good speech writer becomes a valuable asset.

Many public speakers today—from chief executives to presidential candidates to the Pope—rely on public relations professionals to draft their speeches and, in many cases, to contribute ideas for the speech. The work is demanding but rewarding—not only monetarily, but psychically. In many organizations, as scary as it sounds, policies are confirmed or even created through the speechwriting process. In the Reagan White House, according to one speech writer, "Speechwriting was where the administration got invented every day. And so speechwriting was, for some, the center of gravity in that administration. The one point where ideas and principles still counted."[1]

Speechwriters must possess the ability to unite words and ideas in a fast and flawless manner, work under intense deadline pressure, exercise a simultaneous respect and skepticism of those in power, and accept anonymity. The speechwriter, after all, is not the speaker. And speechwriters must accept staying in the background. Indeed, when White House speechwriter Peggy Noonan claimed, in her 1989 book, to have invented for candidate George Bush the rallying phrase "A thousand points of light," one can assume the president was none too pleased that his former speechwriter was stealing the limelight.

A speech possesses five overriding characteristics.

1. **It is designed to be heard, not read.** The mistake of writing for the eye instead of the ear is the most common trap of bad speeches. Speeches needn't be literary gems, but they ought to sound good.
2. **It uses concrete language.** The ear dislikes generalities. It responds to clear images. Ideas must be expressed sharply for the audience to get the point.
3. **It demands a positive response**. Every word, every passage, every phrase should evoke a response from the audience. The speech should possess a special vitality—and so, for that matter, should the speaker.
4. **It must have clear-cut objectives.** The speech and the speaker must have a point—a thesis. If there's no point, then it's not worth the speaker's or the audience's time to be there.
5. **It must be tailored to a specific audience.** An audience needs to feel that it is hearing something special. The most frequent complaint about organizational speeches is that they all seem interchangeable—they lack uniqueness. That's why speeches must be targeted to fit the needs of a specific audience.

Beyond these five principles and before putting words on paper, a speechwriter must have a clear idea of the process—the route—to follow in developing the speech.

The Speechwriting Process

The speechwriting process breaks down into four components: (1) preparing; (2) interviewing; (3) researching; and (4) organizing and writing.

Preparing

One easy way to prepare for a speech is to follow a 4W checklist. In other words, answer the questions who, what, where, and when.

♦ **Who** The who represents two critical elements: the speaker and the audience. A writer should know all about the speaker: manner of speech, use of humor, reaction to an audience, background, and personality. It's almost impossible to write a speech for someone you don't know.

    The writer should also know something about the audience. What does this audience think about this subject? What are its predispositions toward the subject and the speaker? What are the major points with which it might agree? The more familiar the writer is with the who of a speech, the easier the writing will be.

♦ **What** The what is the topic. The assigned subject must be clearly known and well defined by the writer before formal research is begun. If the writer fails to delineate the subject in advance, much of the research will be pointless.

♦ **Where** The where is the setting. A large hall requires a more formal talk than a roundtable forum. Often, the location of the speech—the city, state, or even a particular hall—bears historic or symbolic significance that can enhance a message.

♦ **When** The when is the time of the speech. People are more awake in the morning and get sleepier as the day progresses, so a dinner speech should be kept short. The when also refers to the time of year. A speech can always be linked to an upcoming holiday or special celebration.

Interviewing

Interviewing speakers in advance is essential. Without that chance the results can be dismal. A good interview with a speaker often means the difference between a strong speech and a poor one. Stated another way, the speechwriter is only as good as his access to the speaker.

In the interview the speechwriter gets some time—from as little as 15 minutes to over an hour—to observe the speaker firsthand and probe for the keys to the speech. The interview must accomplish at least three specific goals for the speech writer.

1. **Determine the object of the talk** The object is different from the subject. The subject is the topic, but the object is the purpose of the

speech—that is, what exactly the speaker wants the audience to do after she is finished speaking. Does she want them to storm City Hall? To love big business? To write their congressional representatives? The interviewer's essential question must be "What do you want to leave the audience with at the conclusion of your speech?" Once the speaker answers this question, the rest of the speech should fall into place.

2. **Determine the speaker's main points** Normally, an audience can grasp only a few points during a speech. These points, which should flow directly from the object, become touchstones around which the rest of the speech is woven. Again, the writer must determine the three or four main points during the interview.

3. **Capture the speaker's characteristics** Most of all, during the interview, the writer must observe the speaker. How comfortable is she with humor? How informal or deliberate is she with words? What are her pet phrases and expressions? The writer must file these observations away, recall them during the writing process, and factor them into the speech.

Researching

Like any writer, a speechwriter sometimes develop writer's block: the inability to come up with anything on paper. One way around writer's block is to adopt a formalized research procedure.

1. **Dig into all literature**, books, pamphlets, articles, speeches, and other writings on the speech subject. Prior speeches by the speaker are also important documents to research. A stocked file cabinet is often the speechwriter's best friend.

2. **Think about the subject**. Bring personal thoughts to bear on the topic. Presumably, the speaker has already discussed the topic with the writer, so the writer can amplify the speaker's thoughts with his or her own.

3. **Seek out the opinions** of others on the topic. Perhaps the speaker isn't the most knowledgeable source within an organization about this specific subject. Economists, lawyers, accountants, doctors, and other technical experts may shed additional light on the topic. Outside sources, particularly politicians and business leaders, are often willing to share their ideas when requested.

Organizing and Writing

Once preparation, interviewing, and research have been completed, the fun part begins. Writing a speech becomes easier if, again, the speech is organized into its four essential elements: introduction, thesis, body, and conclusion.

Introduction   A speech introduction is a lot like handling a bar of soap in the shower: the first thing to do is get control. An introduction must grab the audience and hold its interest. An audience is alert at the beginning of a talk and is with the speaker. The writer's job is to make sure the audience stays there.

The speechwriter must take full advantage of the early good nature of the audience by making the introduction snappy. Audience members need time to settle in their seats, and the speaker needs time to get his bearings on the podium. Often, the best way to win early trust and rapport with the audience is to ease into the speech with humor.

> I understand full well that a conference speaker should have one overriding priority: to make it short. Perhaps I'll steal a page from the eight-year-old who was told to write a brief biography of Benjamin Franklin. He wrote, "Benjamin Franklin was born in Boston. At an early age he moved to Philadelphia. As he walked down the street, a lady saw him and started laughing. He married the lady and discovered electricity!"

Thesis   The thesis is the object of the speech—its purpose, or central idea. A good thesis statement lets an audience know in a simple sentence where a speech is going and how it will get there. For example, its purpose can be to persuade:

> The federal government must allow home football games to be televised.

Another thesis statement might be to reinforce or crystallize a belief:

> Sunday football viewing is among the most cherished of winter family home entertainments.

The purpose of yet another thesis statement might merely be to entertain:

> Football viewing in the living room can be a harrowing experience. Let me explain.

In each case, the thesis statement lets the audience know early what the point of the speech will be and leads listeners to the desired conclusion. Many writers prefer to skip the thesis and hit the audience throughout the speech with the central idea in a three-part organization, commonly described as

◆ Tell 'em what you're gonna tell 'em.
◆ Tell 'em.
◆ Tell 'em what you told 'em.

Body   The speech body is just that—the general body of evidence that supports the three or four main points. Although facts, statistics, and figures are important elements, writers should always attempt to use comparisons or contrasts for easier audience understanding. For example, note the comparisons in the following two passages:

> It took 80 years for the telephone to be installed in 34 million American homes. It took 62 years for electrical wiring, 49 years for the automobile, and 47 years for the electric washing machine to arrive in that same number of homes. Television reached that saturation point in a mere 10 years.

> In a single week, 272 million customers passed through the checkout counters of American supermarkets. That's equal to the combined populations of Spain, Mexico, Argentina, France, West Germany, Italy, Sweden, Switzerland, and Belgium.

Such comparisons dramatically hammer points home to a lazy audience.

Conclusion   The best advice on wrapping up a speech is to do it quickly. As the old Texas bromide goes, "If you haven't struck oil in the first 20 minutes, stop boring." Put another way, the conclusion must be blunt, short, and to the point. It may be a good idea to review orally the major points and thesis one last time and then stop. For example, the following quotation makes an excellent conclusion—short, but sweet.

> In closing, it was Malcolm Muggeridge who said, "There is no such thing as darkness; only the failure to see." We in the business community are playing not to lose, instead of playing to win. Let's play to win.

The Spoken Word

Because speeches are meant to be heard, the writer should take advantage of tools that emphasize the special qualities of the spoken word. Such devices can add vitality to a speech, transcending the content of the words themselves. Used skillfully, these devices can elevate a mediocre speech into a memorable one.

1. **Alliteration,** the repetition of initial sounds in words, was used in this famous description of the press in a speech given by former Vice-president Spiro T. Agnew.

   > Nattering nabobs of negativism.

2. **Antithesis** incorporates sharply opposed or contrasting ideas in the same passage. President Kennedy was famous for his savvy use of antithesis.

   > Let us never negotiate out of fear, but let us never fear to negotiate . . . .
   > Ask not what your country can do for you, ask what you can do for your country.

3. **Metonymy** substitutes one term for another closely associated one; it gives a passage more figurative life. For example, the following passage, without metonymy, is flat.

> Ladies and gentlemen, people of Rome, and all of you from the surrounding area, I'd like your attention for the next few moments.

But note the difference when metonymy is used.

> Friends, Romans, countrymen, lend me your ears.

4. **Metaphor and simile** figuratively connect concepts having little literal connection, such as the use of the torch symbol in the following passage from President Kennedy.

> Let the word go forth, from this time and place, to friend and foe alike, that the torch has been passed to a new generation of Americans, born to this century and unwilling to witness or permit the slow undoing of those human rights to which we are committed today at home and around the world.

5. **Personification** gives life to animals, inanimate objects, or ideas, as in the following passage from William Hazlett.

> Prejudice is the child of ignorance.

6. **Repetition** is the use of the same words or phrases over and over again. For example, Churchill's use of the phrase "we shall" in the following:

> We shall fight on the beaches, we shall fight on the landing-grounds, we shall fight in the fields and in the streets, we shall fight in the hills. We shall never surrender . . .

Most of all, in using the spoken word, a writer must always understand fully the spoken words chosen in the speech. And the speaker must also understand the context and definition of the words used. One of the more embarrassing illustrations of this requirement was President John F. Kennedy's use of a German phrase while standing before the Berlin Wall. Agreeing with his speechwriters that it would be appreciated to refer to himself as a symbolic citizen of Berlin, Kennedy proclaimed the immortal line: "Ich bin ein Berliner." What the president and his speechwriters didn't know—but could easily have found out—was that Berlin citizens never refer to themselves as Berliners. They reserve that term for a favorite confection often munched at breakfast. Effectively, then, the president's words meant, "I am a jelly-filled doughnut."

Despite the hidden pitfalls, a public relations professional should not be reluctant to experiment with ear-oriented devices in creating speeches. These devices, after all, are the very essence of writing for listening.

BETWEEN THE LINES

Speechwriting Pays . . . and So Does Speech Giving

Not every practitioner wants to be a speechwriter. Some can't take the deadlines. Others shy away from the responsibility of creating 10 to 15 pages of prose out of a few ideas. But for many who do accept the challenge, speechwriting pays, not only in prestige, but also in remuneration.

In government, experienced writers typically find themselves in the $40,000 to $70,000 pay range. In the corporate ranks the "scarcity of top corporation executive speechwriters has pushed salaries into the $50,000 to $100,000 range." Indeed, large companies will frequently hire top freelance speechwriters, who charge between $1,500 and $4,000 per speech.

One drawback of the executive speechwriter is the frequent feeling of insecurity brought about by disinterested bosses. As one writer put it, "I'd find it easier to write for them if they'd give me 15 god-dammed minutes of their time. I'm amazed at the mentality of so many CEOs . . . who will order up a speech but don't feel any need to communicate with the person writing it. They act as though this is something you hire a trained monkey to do."[*] Nonetheless, speech-writing has become a fine art, practiced by an increasing number of professionals intent on winning greater management respect and earning more money. Even more lucrative today is the practice of speech giving. Every management consultant, out-of-work politician, and fading athlete is out on the hustings delivering 20-minute messages for pay—sometimes magnificent pay. Former President Reagan, for one, commands $50,000 per speech. His wife, Nancy, rates $30,000 for a 20-minute talk. Sound-barrier breaker Chuck Yeager rates a $25,000 fee, $7,000 more than columnist George Will, $9,000 more than Chicago Bears coach Mike Ditka, and a full $10,000 more than former Secretary of State Alexander Haig and race car driver Danny Sullivan.

About the only two who aren't particularly interested in public speaking are golf champs Arnold Palmer and Jack Nicklaus. They ask *$45,000* per speech "because they really don't want to speak"—or "need to," one presumes.

---

*"One Speechwriter's Complaint," The Effective Speechwriters Newsletter (October 6, 1989): 1.

Using Humor

Speech humor can be either a godsend or a curse. It's a tricky business. Humor in a speech should never be too ambitious because the typical executive is not David Letterman. High comedy, rapid-fire jokes, and satire should be avoided at all costs. In general, speech humor must follow three rules.

1. **It must be relevant.** A speaker won't win support by rattling off unrelated jokes. Rather, humor must be an integral part of the talk, used to either underscore a point or introduce one. For example, the following illustration is a good way to introduce a speech about competitiveness and getting ahead.

   > When Woodrow Wilson was governor of New Jersey, a very ambitious young civil servant called him at his home at 3:30 one morning and said urgently, "Mr. Governor, I'm sorry to wake you, but your state auditor has just died and I'd like to know if I can take his place."
   >
   > Mr. Wilson thought that over for a moment and then replied, "Well, I guess it's all right with me, if it's all right with the undertaker!"

2. **It must be in good taste.** Topics such as sex, weight, age, race, and religion should ordinarily be avoided in a speech. People are just too touchy. If there is even the slightest chance that a joke might offend the audience, it should not be used. One safe target is the speaker himself. A speaker willing to poke fun at himself can generally win the admiration of the audience. For example, in assessing his team's chances, Oklahoma basketball coach Billy Tubbs said, "This year we plan to run and shoot. Next year we plan to run and score."

3. **It must be fresh.** Stale humor can sour an audience. A joke that goes over well for millions of people on network television would not be a good candidate for a subsequent speech because too many people have heard it. Speechwriters must carefully select humor for its crispness. Some organizations subscribe to topical humor services to keep speakers current. Other institutions hire freelance joke writers for executive speeches. In each case speechwriters try to avoid the fate of Samuel Johnson's English student, whose paper provoked the professor to respond:

   > I found this report to be good and original. However, the part that was *good* was not original. And the part that was *original* was not good.

Humor is worth experimenting with. It can spark a dull speech. It can give credibility to an unsure speaker. But it's explosive, so handle it with care.

Tightening the Talk

Editing is the final responsibility of the speechwriter. Like any other form of writing, the speech must be tight. After completing the draft, the writer should carefully review each sentence and word. One way to tell if a speech makes sense and moves smoothly is to recite it aloud and have someone listen to it. By obtaining advance audience reaction, a writer can present a final product with more assurance.

How long it takes to write a speech depends on the subject's complexity. Normally, a double-spaced page of speech type takes 2 to 2½ minutes to read. A 20-minute, major address may be 10 to 12 pages in length and take several days to write, exclusive of research and preparation time.

As a general rule, no speech should ever exceed 20 minutes. Most people will just not sit still these days for long addresses. So no audience will be upset at a speaker who gives a 20-minute speech when scheduled to speak for 40 minutes. Indeed, it's much better to leave the audience hungry for more rather than fed up after too much. Some of the most famous speeches in history were the shortest.

- General Douglas MacArthur, on leaving Corregidor, promised, "I shall return."
- Martin Luther King, Jr., leading a civil rights march in the South, proclaimed, "We shall overcome."
- General Dennis McAullife, on being ordered to surrender by the Nazis, defiantly replied, "Nuts!"

Now those are short—but memorable—speeches.

Embellishing the Speech

After a speech is written and approved, the skillful public relations practitioner will embellish it to help stimulate readership or republication. Having endured the arduous process of preparing a speech, the public relations professional has a responsibility to interest others in the talk. Ordinarily, the widest dissemination of an executive speech is through the public media. With many such speeches vying for editorial space, interesting an editor in using a speech is a difficult challenge. One device is to give the speech a provocative title: the title is the first thing an editor sees. Occasionally, a good title may influence an editor's decision to use excerpts from the speech in print.

Another device to disseminate executive speeches is a speakers' bureau. A speakers' bureau, generally established and managed by a firm's public relations group, is an office through which company speakers are recruited, assigned, and equipped with verbal ammunition. In other words, after willing speakers in the organization are located, the public relations department selects appropriate community forums, schedules the speakers, and prepares the speakers with speeches.

The key to speechwriting, just like any other kind of writing, is experience. With speechwriting becoming a more competitive and sought-after pursuit

B E T W E E N   T H E   L I N E S

Every Picture Tells a Story

As executive speechmaking has become more important, a plethora of counseling firms have sprung up to advise executive speakers on how to create and deliver winning speeches. Communispond, Inc. developed one of the most novel concepts. Because most executives are neither comfortable at a podium nor confident in their ability to perform before a large audience, Communispond came up with the concept of drawing pictures to replace formal written speeches. Essentially, after gathering all available evidence and support material and outlining in words what they want to cover, Communispond-trained executives are encouraged to draw pictures, called ideographs, to reflect accurately the subject at hand. For example, a corporate speaker who wants to express the notion that the ship of American capitalism is being fired on by Socialist salvos around the world might sketch an ideograph similar to the one here.

In this way Communispond-trained speakers are taught to use their nervousness to convey natural, human conviction. In other words, not constrained by lifeless written copy, an executive is free, as Communispond puts it, "to speak as well as you think."

Although not right for everyone, Communispond's unique approach, when mastered, allows for a much more extemporaneous and lively discourse than the average prepared text. Fortunately, however (at least as far as corporate speechwriters are concerned), most executives still insist on the security blanket of a full-blown, written text.

among practitioners, it is difficult for an interested novice to break in. However, most political candidates or nonprofit community organizations are more than willing to allow beginners to try their hand at drafting speeches, generally for no compensation. For the budding writer, such voluntarism is a good way to learn the ropes of speechwriting. Few other activities in public relations offer as much fulfillment as does speechwriting.

Making an Effective Presentation

A business presentation is different from a speech. A presentation generally is designed to sell a product, service, or idea. Everyone, somewhere along the line, must deliver a presentation. Like any other speaking device, making an effective presentation depends on following established guidelines. Here are 10 points worth pursuing prior to presenting.

1. **Get organized.** Before considering your presentation, consider the 4*Ws* of speechwriting: Who are you addressing? What are you trying to say? Where and when should something happen?

2. **Get to the point.** Know your thesis. What are you trying to prove? What is the central purpose of your presentation?

3. **Be logical.** Organize the presentation with some logic in mind. Don't skip randomly from one thought to another. Lead from your objective to your strategies to the tactics you will use to achieve your goal.

4. **Write it out.** Don't wing it. If Johnny Carson and David Letterman write out their ad libs, so should you. Always have the words right in front of you.

5. **Anticipate the negatives.** Keep carping critics at bay. Anticipate their objections and defuse them by yourself alluding to vulnerabilities in the presentation.

6. **Speak, don't read.** Sound like you know the information. Practice before the performance. Make the presentation become a part of you. Reading suggests uncertainty. Speaking asserts assurance.

7. **Be understandable.** Speak with clarity and concreteness, so that people understand you. If you want to make the sale, then you must be clear.

8. **Use graphics wisely.** Audiovisual supports should do just that—support the presentation. Graphics should be used more to tease than to provide full-blown information. And graphics shouldn't be crammed with too much information. This will detract from the overall impact of the presentation. Because there are so many audiovisual channels available to a presenter (see Appendix D), it may be wise to seek professional help in devising compelling graphics for a presentation.

9. **Be convincing.** If you aren't enthusiastic about your presentation, no one else will be. Be animated. Be interesting. Be enthusiastic. Sound convinced that what you're presenting is an absolute necessity for the organization.

10. **STOP!** A short, buttoned-up presentation is much more effective than one that goes on and on. At his inaugural, U.S. President William Henry Harrison delivered a two-hour, 6,000-word address into a biting wind on Pennsylvania Avenue. A month later, he died of pneumonia. The lesson: when you've said it all, sit down, and shut up.

One corporate leader who knows how to make an effective presentation is Chrysler chairman Lee Iacocca. So particular is Iacocca as a presenter that he leaves nothing to chance. For example, after many frustrating experiences with lecterns that were too small or too large or that included broken microphones, Iacocca ordered a special $5,000 lectern with special height and width features, a clock, microphones, extra media jacks, and a compressor for a cooling fan.[2] The lectern is covered with leather and prominently displays the Chrysler logo. And everywhere the chairman speaks, his lectern is sure to go.

Radio and Television Writing

As many as two-thirds of the American people get their news from radio and television. Almost every American home has at least one TV set and several radios.

Indeed, there are 97 million U.S. homes with television sets—more than with indoor plumbing. As a nation we have about 1,500 TV stations, 8,000 radio stations, three national TV networks, 25 cable TV networks, and scores of national and regional radio networks.

Unfortunately, TV and radio are the animals public relations people generally understand least. As noted, many professionals were trained in the print medium and feel more comfortable dealing with it. But as more newspapers fade from existence and with 53 percent of all American homes already connected to one of about 7,000 local cable systems, the electronic communications blanket will soon cover virtually the entire United States. And like it or not, public relations professionals will have to direct more of their attention toward the electronic media.

The Broadcast News Release

The principal document in reaching broadcast editors is the basic news release. Most public relations departments don't take the time to prepare special releases for broadcast use, but well they might, because broadcast style differs materially from written style. For example, although the following release might be fine for print use, it would have trouble in a broadcast context.

> GRAND FORKS, ND—The North Dakota National Bank today announced it was lowering its home mortgage lending rate to 12 percent from 12½ percent, effective immediately.
>
> Marcus D. Pickard, III, president and chief executive officer of North Dakota National Bank, said, "We are lowering the home mortgage rate because of increasing competitive pressures in the mortgage market and the trend of declining interest rates generally."
>
> Mr. Pickard added that this was the first reduction in the home mortgage rate in North Dakota in five years.

Fine for print, perhaps. But this translation would be a much better lead for broadcast.

> GRAND FORKS, ND—The home mortgage rate is coming down. North Dakota National Bank today announced it was lowering its home mortgage rate to 12 percent from 12½ percent, effective immediately.
>
> Bank President Marcus Pickard said the move was taken because of "competitive pressures and the trend of declining interest rates."
>
> This marks the first reduction in North Dakota's mortgage rate in five years.

This second release would be an ideal news item on a local TV or radio newscast. Normally, such an item lasts 10, 20, or 30 seconds, no more. Infrequently, an important item may take a minute to cover. Generally, in writing for broadcast, the shorter the better. Material must catch the listener early. The story should be told in the first two or three sentences, allowing the listener to tune out early. In other words, in most broadcast writing, the inverted pyramid must be much more pointed to capture a listener's attention.

The following checklist may be helpful in writing for TV and radio.

1. **Use simple, declarative sentences.** The following sentence is awkward, overly dramatic, and unnatural.

   > Turning the first spade of sod on the site of the new $3 million University Center today, Mayor Grumble hailed the Dexter University building program as a "great step forward for the state's finest university."

   It would be better like this:

   > Construction began today on the $3 million Dexter University Center. Mayor Grumble, on hand for the dedication, called the school's building program "a great step forward for the state's finest university."

2. **Numbers and statistics should be rounded off.** No one will remember this:

   > The Ajax Company today announced year-end earnings of $999,765.

But they may remember this:

> The Ajax Company today announced year-end earnings of slightly under $1 million.

3. Attribution should usually precede the quote.

> Hospital administrator Christie Gardner says, "Winston Hospital will not bow to pressure."

4. Try to avoid direct quotes. Direct quotes often lead to long, clumsy sentence structure. Paraphrase instead.

5. Personalize whenever possible. The following is a good print lead but a poor broadcast one.

> The Bureau of Labor Statistics announced today that the cost of living has gone down another 2 percent in the last quarter.

Personalize it for broadcast.

> If you hadn't noticed, your grocery bill is coming down. That was the good news today from the Bureau of Labor Statistics, which announced that the cost of living has declined 2 percent for the quarter.

6. Avoid extended description. Middle initials, for example, or full corporate titles are unnecessary in the time-constrained environment of broadcast news. For instance, in print, write this:

> Marie M. Daniel, president and chief executive officer of Avorn Products, Inc.

But in broadcast, say this:

> Avorn Products President Marie Daniel

7. Avoid hackneyed expressions and cliches. Trite phrases should be avoided in all writing. But in broadcast such phrases are particularly annoying. Hackneyed jargon changes yearly, but these are typical shopworn expressions: "in the wake of," "passed away," "riot-torn," "scandal-ridden," "flatly denied," and "sharply rebuked."

Public relations people should aim for TV and radio more often and more releases should be written with the needs of broadcasters in mind.

Public Service Announcements

The public service announcement, or PSA, is a TV or radio commercial, usually from 10 to 60 seconds long, that is broadcast at no cost to the sponsor. Nonprofit organizations, such as the Red Cross and United Way, are active users of PSAs (Figure 10–1). Commercial organizations, too, may take advantage of PSAs for their nonprofit activities, such as blood bank collections, voter registration drives, health testing, and the like. The spread

FIGURE 10–1 This is a typical PSA storyboard sent to TV stations. This storyboard enables station personnel to review the content of the Multiple Sclerosis Society PSA before screening. *(Courtesy of National Multiple Sclerosis Society)*

of local cable television stations has expanded the opportunity for placing PSAs on the air. Nevertheless, radio PSAs are still far more widely used.

Unlike news releases, radio PSAs are generally written in advertising-copy style—punchy and pointed. The essential challenge in writing PSAs is to select the small amount of information to be used, discard extraneous information, and persuade the listener to take the desired action. The following is a typical 30-second PSA.

> The challenge of inflation has never been more serious than it is today.
> The need for strong national leadership has never been more pressing than it is today.
> Americans must tell their elected leaders to stop spending and regulating and start listening to the people.
> But they won't until *you* demand it.
> Until you demand that they stop overspending, stop crippling our economy with needless regulation, stop suffocating America with outrageous taxes.
> You can make a difference.
> This message brought to you by Hooter Valley National Bank.

According to survey research, broadcasters use three primary criteria in determining which PSAs make the air: (1) sponsorship, (2) relevance of the message to the community, and (3) message design. In terms of sponsorship, the reputation of the sponsor for honesty and integrity is critical. As to the relevance of the message, urgent social problems, such as health and safety issues, and education and training concerns all rank high with broadcasters. In message design, the more imaginative, original, and exciting the message, the better the chance of its getting free play on the air.[3]

Film Scripts

Film is another important medium for public relations people, especially for those working for national associations and large consumer products companies. Hundreds of firms sponsor films for schools and community groups. Most are professionally written and produced. For example, Modern Talking Picture Service, the nation's largest sponsored film distributor, handles films and collateral services for hundreds of clients.

Writing a film script demands linking audio and video messages. The writer must not overexplain the video but must add just enough dialogue to enhance the visual message. One common film script format is for video directions to be listed on the left side of a page and audio directions and dialogue on the right.

Although practitioners rarely get involved in writing film scripts, some do supervise commercial film companies commissioned to create a sponsored film. Obviously, familiarity with the medium helps greatly.

Video News Releases

One of the most controversial and fastest-growing public relations broadcast tools is the video newsclip—also called video news release, or VNR—in which a practitioner packages a film clip describing a news event involving an organization. VNRs have proliferated as a consequence of the growth in local news programming. Cities around the United States are running three or four half-hour newscasts a day. In the top 125 TV markets alone, there are 275 medical reporters, 155 business reporters, and 184 consumer reporters, all of whom have at least one weekly segment to fill. Much of the time, they need help.[4]

Generally produced by outside production services, VNRs run from 30 to 90 seconds and are designed to be incorporated into local TV newscasts. For example, tobacco and liquor firms have had success placing TV newsclips of auto races—with corporate identification neatly embedded in the passing race cars.

VNR budgets are based on the number of stations serviced. To produce and distribute a VNR, budgets may range from $2,500 to $30,000, depending on complexity and desired reach. The price may be well worth it. In 1990, Star Kist Seafood Co. distributed a VNR in conjunction with its introduction of "Dolphin-safe" tuna. The VNR was viewed by more than 81 million viewers, an audience record. The Star Kist announcement "was a wonderful combination of a hard news story with environmental and consumer angles, and it had the advantage of requiring product identification."[5]

VNRs are not for everyone. In general, an organization should consider producing a video news release when

♦ It is involved in a legitimate medical, scientific, or industrial break-through

♦ The video will clarify or provide a new perspective on issues in the news

♦ Visuals will help a news department provide its viewers with a better story

♦ The video can be used as background footage while a station's reporter discusses pertinent news copy

♦ The organization can provide unusual visuals that stations themselves can't get

♦ The VNR provides an interview segment that stations, again, can't get on their own.[6]

How does one create a VNR? First, the purpose of the video must be considered. Is there a need for it? Second, the time element must be factored in. How much time do we have? Third is the matter of money. How much do we have to spend on it? Fourth, any obstacles must be considered, such as contending with bad weather, unavailability of key people, and so on. After all of these elements are considered, a rough script should be drawn before approaching an outside production company, so that key managers in the organization understand and agree on what the objective of the VNR will be.

Video news releases have triggered heated controversy in recent years. Shortly before Japanese Prime Minister Yasuhiro Nakasone met President Reagan in 1985, U.S. television viewers saw news reports showing American produce on its way to Japan's markets. The reports featured Mike Mansfield, the U.S. ambassador to Japan and a staunch opponent of import quotas, saying, "Japanese markets aren't as closed as we might think." What TV viewers weren't told was that parts or all of the news reports were produced for the government of Japan by a Washington public relations firm, which was later criticized by the Justice Department for failing to "label some of its electronic news releases as political propaganda."[7]

FIGURE 10–2 In 1989, HBO Video reached more than 45 million TV viewers with a VNR announcing its home video of *Sports Illustrated*'s annual swimsuit issue, featuring model Elle McPherson. *(Courtesy of HWH Enterprises, Inc.)*

Many large TV stations will not use sponsored newsclips as a matter of principle, but some smaller stations swear by them. Said one Montana station owner, "We enjoy them. The folks who produce them are nice people, and they're too smart to try and mislead you."[8]

Despite their controversial nature, the fact remains that using VNRs may be a most effective and dramatic way to convey an organization's message to millions of people.

Summary

Writing for the ear—particularly for speeches and the electronic media—has become increasingly important for public relations professionals. As generations weaned on television enter the field, familiarity in writing for broadcast will become more essential.

As cable television stations, in particular, proliferate, the need for additional programming—for more material to fill news and interview holes—also will expand. This phenomenon will open the door for a new breed of public relations professional, comfortable with and proficient in the nuances of writing for broadcast (see the "Guide to Video/Satellite Terms" in Appendix E).

DISCUSSION STARTERS

1. Most executives write their own speeches. True or false?
2. What are the overriding characteristics of a speech?
3. What questions does one ask to begin the speechwriting process?
4. What are the four essential components of a speech?
5. What constitutes "good humor" in an organizational speech?
6. What are the elements that constitute an effective presentation?
7. Why will writing for broadcast become more important for public relations professionals?
8. What are the important elements of a broadcast news release?
9. What are the key facets of a public service announcement?
10. What is a VNR?

NOTES

1. Peggy Noonan, "Confessions of a White House Speechwriter," *The New York Times Magazine* (October 15, 1989): 73.
2. "Create Your Own Comfort," *Decker Communications Report* V, No. 9 (October 1984): 4.
3. R. Irwin Goodman, "Selecting Public Service Announcements for Television," *Public Relations Review* (Fall 1981): 26–28.
4. Richard Green and Denise Shapiro, "A Video News Release Primer," *Public Relations Quarterly* (Winter 1987–88): 10.
5. "Millions Saw News of Dolphin-Safe Star Kist," *Public Relations Reporter* (October 8, 1990): 3.

6. Michael M. Klepper, "Do-It-Yourself Evening News," *IABC Communication World* (July-August 1987): 62–63.
7. "Public Relations Firms Offer 'News' to TV," *The Wall Street Journal*, 2 April 1985, sect. 2, p. 1.
8. Herman M. Rosenthal, "Beware of News Clips Massaging Your Opinions," *TV Guide* (April 21, 1984): 6.

TOP OF THE SHELF

Filson, Brent. *Executive Speeches: 51 CEOs Tell You How To Do Yours.* Williamstown, MA: Williamstown Publishing Company, 1991.

Speechwriters can learn the finer points of their craft from *Executive Speeches,* a book shaped by the advice and experiences of some of the most gifted communicators in business.

Brent Filson, a veteran communications consultant, interviewed 51 CEOs and scores of other executives and speechwriters to assemble the elements that contribute to successful speeches. In this guidebook, he presents dozens of proven tactics for beginning a speech, keeping its middle interesting and concluding it with flair. Filson also teaches how to use humor, control nerves, analyze an audience, and employ visuals to complement the spoken word. His pointers on writing and delivering a speech, as well as strategies to handle the media, round out his instruction. This book's format is a plus: Filson divides his chapters into bite-sized nuggets, so readers can roam freely among the 12 chapters and more than 245 topics.

Executives often ask public relations practitioners to compose speeches. When writing one, authors are well advised to keep *Executive Speeches* close at hand.

SUGGESTED READINGS

Ailes, Roger, and John Kraushar. *You Are the Message.* Homewood, IL: Dow Jones-Irwin, 1988.

Allen, Steve. *How to Make a Speech.* New York: McGraw-Hill, 1986.

Associated Press. *Broadcast News Stylebook.* (Available from the author, 50 Rockefeller Plaza, New York, NY 10020.) A more generalized style is featured than that in the UPI book. Suggestions of methods and treatment for the preparation of news copy and information pertinent to AP broadcast wire operations are given.

Block, Mervin. *Writing Broadcast News—Shorter, Sharper, Stronger.* Chicago: Bonus Books, 1987.

Broadcasting Publications. Broadcasting. (Available from the author, 1735 DeSales St., NW, Washington, DC 20036; published weekly on Monday.) This basic news magazine for radio, television, and cable television industries reports all activities involved in the entire broadcasting field.

A Commonsense Guide to Making Business Videos. (Available from Creative Marketing Corporation, 285 S. 171 St., New Berlin, WI 53151-3511.) Anyone not familiar with business videos will benefit from this booklet, which zeros in on the planning needed to make a successful video.

Daily Variety. (Available from 1400 N. Cahuenga Blvd., Hollywood, CA 90028.) This trade paper for the entertainment industries is centered mainly in Los Angeles, with complete coverage of West Coast production activities; it includes reports from all world entertainment centers.

Detz, Joan. *How to Write and Give a Speech.* New York: St. Martin's Press, 1985.

Executive Speechmaker. New York: Institute for Public Relations Research & Education (310 Madison Ave. 10017) 1980.

Executive Speaker (P.O. Box 292437, Dayton, OH 45429). Newsletter.

Fettig, Art. *How to Hold an Audience in the Hollow of Your Hand.* Battle Creek, MI: Growth Unlimited, Inc., 1988.

Gibbs, Ennis. *The Public Speaker's Emergency Repair Manual and Survival Kit.* Clarement, CA: Alert Publications, 1987.

Green, Richard, and Denise Shapiro. "A Video News Release Primer." *Public Relations Quarterly* (Winter 1987–88): 10–13.

Hannaford, Peter. *Talking Back to the Media.* New York: Facts on File Publications, 1986.

Heinz, J. *Writing Effective Business Speeches.* 1986 (Available from the author, 233 E. Wacker, #3111, Chicago, IL 60601).

Kaplan, Burton. *The Corporate Manager's Guide to Speechwriting.* New York: The Free Press, 1988.

A Layperson's Guide to Satellite Broadcasting. O'Dwyer's *PR Services Report* (December 1987): 4. (271 Madison Ave., New York, NY 10016).

Leech, Thomas. *How to Prepare, Stage, and Deliver Winning, Presentations.* New York: AMACOM, 1985 (135 W. 50th St. 10020).

MacDonald, R. H. *Broadcast News Manual of Style.* White Plains, NY: Longman, 1987.

Public Relations Firms Offer 'News' to TV, Wall Street Journal, 2 April 1985, sect. 2, p. 1.

Rafe, Stephen. *The Executive's Guide to Successful Presentations.* Warrentown, VA: S/RC, 1989 (P.O. Box 3119).

Richardson, Linda. *Winning Group Sales Presentations.* Homewood, IL: Dow Jones-Irwin, 1989.

Radio Interview Guide. New York: Book Promotions, 1988 (26 E. 33rd St.).

Robinson, James W. *Winning Them Over.* Rocklin, CA: Prima Publishing & Communications, 1987.

Roesch, Roberta. *Smart Talk.* New York: AMACOM, 1989 (135 W. 50th St. 10020).

Sarnoff, Dorothy. *Never be Nervous Again.* New York: Crown, 1988.

Speechwriter's Newsletter. (Available from Ragan Communications, 407 S. Dearborn, Chicago, IL 60605).

Stecki, Ed, and Frank Corrado. "How to Make a Video" (Part I). *Public Relations Journal* (February 1988): 33, 34.

United Press International. *Broadcast Stylebook.* (Available from the author, 220 E. 42nd Street, New York 10017). This is not a rule book, but it suggests methods and treatment for properly preparing news copy, with examples of wire copy and brief comments on correct and incorrect methods of news wire copy preparation. It's designed to help people write the kind of copy used by an announcer.

Variety. (Available from 475 Park Ave. South, New York 10016; published weekly on Wednesday.) This paper publishes news, features, and commentary each week on every aspect of show business, with extensive reviews of productions around the world.

CASE STUDY   Illinois Power's Reply

For three decades, no network news program rivaled the incredible impact of CBS-TV's "60 Minutes." Watched each Sunday night by more than 20 million Americans, "60 Minutes" still ranks as one of the most popular programs in the nation and the show most feared by public relations professionals. When "60 Minutes" comes a'calling, scandal, or at least significant problems, can't be far behind.

Such was the thinking at Illinois Power Company (IP) in Decatur in the fall of 1979, when "60 Minutes" sent reporter Harry Reasoner to find out why the company's Clinton nuclear reactor project was behind schedule and over budget.

What followed—the exchange between "60 Minutes" and IP—still ranks as history's most classic confrontation between television and corporate public relations professionals.

Because IP suspected that "60 Minutes" aimed to do a hatchet job, the company agreed to be interviewed only if it, too, videotaped the "60 Minutes" filming on its premises. In other words, IP would video tape the videotapers; it would report on the reporters; it would meet "60 Minutes" on its own terms. Reasoner and his producer reluctantly agreed to the arrangement.

And so in early October, IP's executive vice-president sat for an hour-and-a-half interview before the "60 Minutes"—and the IP—cameras. He answered Reasoner's questions straightforwardly and comprehensively. And he and his company prepared for the worst.

Which is precisely what they received.

On November 25, "60 Minutes" broadcast a 16-minute segment on the Clinton plant, charging IP with mismanagement, missed deadlines, and costly overruns that would be passed on to consumers. Viewers saw three former IP employees accuse the utility of making no effort to control costs, allowing slipshod internal reporting, and fabricating estimates of construction completion timetables. One of the accusers was shown in silhouette with a distorted voice because, as reporter Reasoner intoned, "He fears retribution." To add salt to the IP wound, the 90-minute interview with the company's executive vice-president merited less than two minutes of edited, misleading air time.

Worst of all, 24 million Americans viewed the crucifixion in their living rooms.

The day after the CBS story, IP's stock fell a full point on the New York Stock Exchange in the busiest trading day in the company's history. Rather than responding as most companies do—with bruised feelings, a scorched reputation, and feeble cries of "foul" to its stockholders—IP lashed back with barrels blazing. Within days of the broadcast, IP produced "60 Minutes/Our Reply," a 44-minute film incorporating the entire "60 Minutes" segment, punctuated by insertions and narrative presenting the company's rebuttal.

The rebuttal included videotape of CBS film footage not included in the program, much of which raised serious questions about the integrity of the material CBS used. The rebuttal also documented the backgrounds and possible motives of the three former employees CBS quoted, all of whom had been fired for questionable performance. One of the former employees, in fact, was the leader of the local antinuclear group opposing IP.

Initially, the reply tape was aired to a relatively small audience: the company's employees, customers, shareholders, and investors. But word traveled quickly that Illinois Power had produced a riveting, broadcast-quality production, so true to the "60 Minutes" format—ticking stopwatch and all—that it could easily be mistaken for the original. Within a year, close to 2,500 copies of the devastating rebuttal had been distributed to legislators, corporate executives, journalists, and others. Excerpts were broadcast on television stations throughout the nation, and the IP production became legendary. As the *Wall Street Journal* put it, "The program focuses new attention on news accuracy . . . . Although even a telling, polished, counter-program like Illinois Power's can't reach the masses of a national broadcast, the reply tape has proven effective in reaching a significant 'thinking' audience."

Even CBS was impressed. The producer of the original "60 Minutes" segment called the rebuttal highly sophisticated, especially for a company that had first seemed to him to be a "down-home cracker barrel" outfit. The IP tape soon spawned imitators. Companies such as Chevron, Union Carbide, Common-

wealth Edison, and many others began experimenting with defensive videotaping in dealing with television journalists.

Although "60 Minutes" admitted to some sloppiness in its reporting and to two minor factual inaccuracies, it essentially stood by its account. Complained CBS executive producer Don Hewitt, "We went in as a disinterested party and did a news report. They made a propaganda film for their side, using our reporting for their own purposes."

Perhaps. But one irrefutable result of the dramatic confrontation between the huge national network and the tiny local utility was that the Illinois Power Company—by turning the television tables on the dreaded "60 Minutes"—had earned its place in public relations history.[*]

QUESTIONS

1. Do you agree with Illinois Power's original decision to let "60 Minutes" in despite the suspicion that the program would be a "hatchet job"? What might have happened if IP turned down the "60 Minutes" request?
2. If "60 Minutes" had turned down IP's request to videotape the Reasoner interviews, would you have still allowed the filming?
3. Presume IP didn't tape the "60 Minutes" filming on its premises. What other communications options might the company have pursued to rebut the "60 Minutes" accusations?
4. Do you think IP did better by allowing "60 Minutes" in to film or would they have been better off keeping CBS out?

[*]Sandy Graham, "Illinois Utility Sparks Widespread Interest with Its Videotape," *The Wall Street Journal*, 12 April 1980, 23. For further information on the Illinois Power case, see *Punch, Counterpunch: "60 Minutes" vs. Illinois Power Company*, Washington, D.C.: Media Institute, 1981, and "Turning the Tables on '60 Minutes,' " *Columbia Journalism Review* (May-June 1980): 7–9.

Tips from the Top

RICHARD F. STOCKTON

Richard F. Stockton is the former senior advisor and coordinator of executive presentations for Exxon Corporation. He previously served as a senior speechwriter for Chase Manhattan Bank, Morgan Guaranty Trust Company, and Citibank. Mr. Stockton's two decades of executive speechwriting follow 10 years of dramatic writing for radio, stage, and network television.

How hard is it to write an executive speech?
Like a marriage, it flows along more smoothly when both parties work at it. A speechwriter who has to function in isolation, as a mind reader, is less likely to get the message right the first time. But it can be done. The first draft of a speech is generally the easiest. Then you begin earning your keep.

How does one become a speechwriter?
By infiltration. No one has ever been hired as a speechwriter who wasn't already an employed speechwriter. So a devious strategy is essential. Start with any job that requires writing, then drop hints and samples of your best writing wherever you can. Volunteer. Polish up some earlier speech that flopped. Offer to jot down a few ideas on some future speech—then submit the whole thing. Don't be shy. Don't give up. If

you aren't fired as a nuisance, you may get a shot at it.

How does one approach the speechwriting assignment?
Identify one or two—never more than three—main points about which the speaker has genuinely strong feelings and the listeners have a vested interest. Remember that a captive audience will be wholly dependent on your sense of fair play to spare them a tedious harangue or personal prejudices or a string of shopworn cliches. The audience needn't agree with the points made, so long as each one relates to their interests. If the executive doesn't share any interests with an audience, he shouldn't be there.

Is there a general format to most speeches?
Very general. A lively opening, a genial wrap-up, and no more than the above-mentioned three major points in between. If the framework gets more rigid than that, the audience will become aware of it and start following the format instead of the

text. Public riots have been incited by speakers who announce that they have divided their speech into six themes with four subtopics each from which they will draw nine principles of action.

How liberally should a speechwriter use humor?

Few audiences object to being entertained. In most cases, a bit of humor up front relaxes both the speaker and the audience. But it must amuse the speaker first. If the speaker has any qualms—get it out—quick! Peppering a text with lively anecdotes that the speaker is not comfortable with or not confident of putting across is a disservice to everyone.

How cognizant of the "spoken word" should a speechwriter be?

There is no substitute for a good ear. Any spoken text that can't be grasped on the fly by a reasonably attentive listener is of little use. You can tidy up the grammar for publication, if it gets to that. If an audience once focuses on syntax, it can't focus on anything else. Executives are most effective when speaking in their own, comfortable, everyday vernacular.

Should a speechwriter experiment with rhetorical flourishes?

Like all writers, speechwriters must have a love of language and a passion for the spoken word. But like other passions, it needs restraining. If the second cleverest way of phrasing a point communicates it better, let the first one go—even if it's a line that Oscar Wilde would have envied. Planting a rhetorical landmine in an executive's text, as an experiment, has about the same practical appeal as playing Russian roulette.

How important is it to "know" the speaker?

Both the writer and the speaker will find the end-product more gratifying if it reflects not only the views but the personality of the speaker. Some speakers can inject their personal touch into a text with little studied effort in the final draft. Others can't and end up projecting a different persona from the platform than they display elsewhere. Audiences generally detect the difference and resent it. Most speakers learn from experience that the time spent in working directly with the speechwriter is well invested.

Who are the best speechwriters?

I have a theory, totally unprovable, that speechwriters are people who always think of the perfect retort or the most telling way to drive home an argument after the party's over and everyone has gone home. If this happens to you, you may be a speechwriter. You have only to improve your timing and supply those surefire, verbal dynamics to your speaker before the event.

Public Relations Marketing

Public relations is different from marketing. But elements of public relations—among them product publicity, special events, spokespersons, and similar activities—can enhance a marketing effort. A new discipline—marketing communications—has in fact emerged that uses many of the techniques of public relations. While some may labor over the relative differences and merits of public relations vs. advertising vs. marketing vs. sales promotion, the fact remains that a smart communicator must be knowledgeable about all of them.

Marketing, literally defined, is the selling of a service or product through pricing, distribution, and promotion. Public relations, liberally defined, is the marketing of an organization. Most organizations now realize that public relations can play an expanded role in marketing. In some organizations, particularly service companies, hospitals, and nonprofit institutions, the selling of both individual products and the organization itself are inextricably intertwined.

Stated another way, while the practice of marketing creates and maintains a market for products and services and the practice of public relations creates and maintains a hospitable environment in which the organization may operate, marketing success can be nullified by the social and political forces public relations is designed to confront—thus the interrelationship of the two disciplines.[1]

In the past, marketers treated public relations as an ancillary part of the marketing mix. They were concerned primarily with making sure their products met the needs and desires of customers and were priced competitively, distributed widely, and promoted heavily through advertising and merchandising. Gradually, however, these traditional notions among marketers began to change for several reasons.

◆ Consumer protests about both product value and safety and government scrutiny of product demands began to shake historical views of marketing.

◆ Product recalls—from automobiles to tuna fish—generated recurring headlines.

◆ Ingredient scares began to occur regularly.

◆ Advertisers were asked to justify their messages in terms of social needs and civic responsibilities.

◆ Rumors about particular companies—from fast-food firms to pop rock manufacturers—spread in brushfire manner.

◆ General image problems of certain companies and industries—from oil to banking—were fanned by a continuous blaze of criticism in the media.

The net impact of all this was that, even though a company's products were still important, customers also began to consider a firm's policies and practices on everything from air and water pollution to minority hiring.

Beyond these social concerns, the effectiveness of advertising itself began to be questioned. The increased number of advertisements in newspapers and on the airwaves caused clutter and posed a significant burden on advertisers to make the public aware of their products. In the 1970s, the trend toward shorter TV advertising spots contributed to three times as many products being advertised on TV as there were in the 1960s. In the 1980s, the spread of cable added yet another multichanneled outlet for product advertising. Against this backdrop the potential of public relations as an added ingredient in the marketing mix became increasingly more credible.

Indeed, marketing professor Philip Kotler has suggested that, in addition to the traditional four *Ps* of product, price, place, and promotion, two additional *Ps* be added to define the marketing concept today: (1) political power and (2) public opinion formation through public relations. Said Kotler, "Marketers are always looking at economic factors and rational factors. They should examine the conflicts, the special-interest and pressure groups, the vested interests, the political realities, and create appeals in those arenas."[2]

The Marketing Plan

For public relations to be effective as a tool in marketing, it must be introduced early in the marketing plan rather than as an afterthought. The plan should carefully lay out the organization's objectives, strategies, and tactics for promoting and selling a product. Public relations may be used in the marketing plan to realize a number of objectives:

1. Helping a company and product name become better known
2. Helping introduce new or improved products
3. Helping increase a product's life cycle (i.e., complementing advertising and sales promotion with additional product information)
4. Seeking out new markets and broadening existing ones at reduced costs
5. Establishing an overall favorable image for the product and company

Basically, public relations can play a critical role in positioning a product appropriately in the market. A product's position is the image the product conveys in the public mind. For example, if the public truly believes that Colonel Sanders' chicken is "finger-licking good," then the firm's product-positioning strategy has worked. When the public really believes that the folks at Allstate are "the good hands people" or that the group from Avis really does "try harder," that's effective product positioning. Companies spend millions of dollars trying to position their products in the public mind.

Public relations offers a practical and inexpensive device for conveying product messages and helping position a firm's products. About 8 of 10 new products fail to catch on, and the cost of these annual failures has been estimated in the billions of dollars. Public relations, then, should be involved early and integrated fully into the marketing plan. Whether in helping market a new product or enhancing the staying power of an old one, public relations can make a telling difference in product success.

Product Publicity

In light of the difficulty today in raising advertising awareness above the noise of so many competitive messages, marketers are turning increasingly to product publicity as an important adjunct to advertising. Although the public is generally unaware of it, a great deal of what it knows and believes about a wide variety of products comes through press coverage. Articles in the newspaper's "living" section—describing the attributes of a brand of Burgundy or the advantages of down coats or enriched dog foods—often arise from product-publicity information distributed by the manufacturer.[3]

In certain circumstances, product publicity can be the most effective element in the marketing mix.[4] For example:

◆ *Introducing a revolutionary new product.* Product publicity can start introductory sales at a much higher level of demand by creating more awareness of the product.

FIGURE 11–1 Among companies that chose unique representatives to earn product publicity as an enhanced marketing effort was food manufacturer Pillsbury Inc. When the Pillsbury Dough Boy turned 25 in 1990, the company celebrated with national publicity-inducing events: cookbooks, recipes, and news releases featuring its cuddly and beloved Poppin' Fresh™. *(Courtesy of Golin/Harris Communications)*

◆ *Eliminating distribution problems with retail outlets.* Often, the way to get shelf space is to have consumers demand the product. Product publicity can be extremely effective in creating consumer demand.

◆ *Budgets are small and competition is gigantic.* Advertising is expensive. Product publicity is cheap. Often, publicity is the best way to tell the story.

◆ *The product is great but complicated.* Many products, their use, and their benefits are difficult to explain to mass audiences in a brief ad. Product publicity, through extended news columns, can be invaluable.

◆ *Generating new consumer excitement for an old product.* "Repackaging" an old product to the media can serve as a primary marketing impetus.

◆ *Tying the product to a unique representative.* "Morris the Cat" was one answer to consumer disinterest about cat food. Figure 11–1 illustrates yet another unique and memorable representative.

Third-Party Endorsement

Perhaps more than anything else, the lure of third-party endorsement is the primary reason smart organizations value product publicity as much as they do advertising. Third-party endorsement refers to the tacit support given a product by a newspaper, magazine, or broadcaster who mentions the product as news. Advertising often is perceived as self-serving. People know that the advertiser not only created the message, but also paid for it. Publicity, on the other hand, which appears in news columns, carries no such stigma. When a message is sanctified by third-party editors, it is more persuasive than advertising messages, where the self-serving sponsor of the message is identified.

Editors have become sensitive to mentioning product names in print. Some, in fact, have a policy of deleting brand or company identifications in news columns. Public relations counselors argue that such a policy does a disservice to readers, many of whom are influenced by what they read and may desire the particular products discussed. Counselors further argue that journalists who accept and print public relations material for its intrinsic value and then remove the source of the information give the reader or viewer the false impression that the journalist generated the facts, ideas, or photography.

Equally reprehensible are the public relations practitioners who try to place sponsored features without disclosing promotional origins. In other words, some companies will distribute cartoons or stories—either directly or through mail-order services—without identifying the sponsor of the material. Obviously, such a practice raises ethical questions. Understandably, editors do not soon forgive firms that sponsor such anonymous articles.

BETWEEN THE LINES

The Ultimate Third-Party Endorsers

Third-party endorsement differed dramatically in the decade of the '80s from the decade of the '90s. Consider two of the top endorsers in the two decades.

■ One of the most spectacular third-party endorsements of all time occurred in 1982, when Universal Pictures approached Hershey Foods Corporation for a promotional tie-in between Hershey's candy and the hero of a new Universal movie. Hershey, as it turned out, was Universal's second choice. Reportedly, the movie company's first choice, M&M/Mars, turned down the original offer to tie in its M&M candy. Hershey, however, accepted on behalf on its Reese's Pieces candy and, in a practice unheard of in Hollywood

(Courtesy of Hershey Foods Corp.)

promotional deals, paid no money for the movie plug—so grateful were the filmmakers to land the candy company's endorsement. The rest, as they say, is Hollywood history. The movie was *E.T. The Extra-Terrestial*, one of the biggest box-office draws in the history of moviedom. Early in the movie, a telltale trail of brown, yellow, and orange Reese's Pieces is followed to reveal one of the strangest, most unforgettable, most lovable creatures in the history of film.

■ What a contrast when, a decade later, in 1990 E.T.'s crown as king of third-party endorsers was seized by a fresh-from-the-sewer, pizza-chomping, jive-talking band of Teenage Mutant Ninja Turtles, who endorsed everything from toys to theme parks to breakfast cereals—all eager to be associated with the turtles' magic marketing power.

(Courtesy of Berkheimer, Kline, Golin/Harris Communications)

Most good marketers will use product publicity as an effective complement to advertising. They know that positive publicity adds credibility to advertisements. In rare cases, marketers may forsake advertising entirely and plow all their funds, on a much more limited scale, into public relations.

YOU MAKE THE CALL

The Birth of the Cabbage Patch Doll

They were soft. They were huggable. They were absolutely unique. And in the winter of 1983, they were the hottest thing to hit the toy market since the pet rock. They were the Cabbage Patch Kids, those adorable (or gruesome, depending on your point of view) dolls designed by a Georgia sculptor and adopted by their new owners.

In marketing the Cabbage Patch dolls, the Coleco Company relied on public relations to fan the fires of Cabbage Patch mania. Coleco hired Richard Wiener, Inc., public relations counsel, to promote the Cabbage Patch Kids. Wiener first hired a psychologist to study what made the doll so attractive to children. Among the strongest positive characteristics discovered was that the physical appearance of the dolls inspired a nurturing instinct in children. The adoption idea contributed to that instinct and was therefore good. A position paper on this finding was developed and placed in the Cabbage Patch Kids press kit distributed to the media. Additionally, a "Parenting Guide" was presented to each new Cabbage Patch Kid owner.

The rest of the public relations plan rolled out accordingly.

- In October, a 15-city Cabbage Patch Kids spokesperson tour hit major television and radio news/talk shows in major markets.
- A mass adoption of Cabbage Patch Kids was staged in Boston, with children invited to the affair and promised a free doll.
- Cabbage Patch Kids press kits were mailed to major newspapers around the country. Capitalizing on the media's interest in technology, the public relations material pointed out that the computer-run manufacturing equipment minutely altered the facial features of each doll, so that no two Cabbage Patch Kids were alike.
- Wire services were alerted to shortages in toy stores around the nation.
- Jane Pauley, the pregnant host of the "Today" show, was sent her own Cabbage Patch doll. Shortly thereafter, the Cabbage Patch Kids landed 5½ minutes on "Today." This, according to the Wiener agency, was the turning point. " 'Today' gave our story credibility through third-party endorsement . . . that far outweighs an advertisement."*
- In late November, in light of the tremendous Cabbage Patch crush at toy stores everywhere, Coleco announced it was pulling its advertising from television because it "couldn't get enough dolls into the stores."
- Finally, after donating numerous dolls for promotional giveaways to hospitals and other charities, the Wiener firm arranged to have First

Lady Nancy Reagan present Cabbage Patch Kids to two Korean children who were in the United States for heart operations.

So successful were the Cabbage Patch dolls that in the Christmas season of 1990, the Kids reemerged stronger than ever, under the banner of Hasbro Industries, which bought production and marketing rights from Coleco in 1989.

Toy analysts predicted Cabbage Patch would be the biggest-selling doll of the season. Concluded one amazed analyst, "Kids still feel something for the product."

QUESTIONS

1. What was the risk to Coleco of promoting Cabbage Patch Kids as "available for adoption"?
2. What was the value of first securing and then publicizing the comments of psychologists on the adoption feature of the Cabbage Patch Kids?
3. If you were Coleco's public relations director, how would you answer critics who charged that the only reason the company pulled its Cabbage Patch advertising was to avoid legal liability?
4. Do you think the public relations–oriented marketing approach of the Cabbage Patch Kids would lead to as much as, more, or less recognition than that of other nationally advertised dolls that relied primarily on advertising?

*Jeff Blyskal and Marie Blyskal, *PR: How the Public Relations Industry Writes the News* (New York: William Morrow, 1985), 124.

Public Relations Marketing Activities

In addition to product publicity, a number of other public relations activities are regularly used to help market products. These activities include article reprints, trade show participation, and the use of spokespersons, special events, and consumer-oriented appeals.

Article Reprints

Once an organization has received product publicity in a newspaper or magazine, it should market the publicity further to achieve maximum sales punch. Marketing can be done through article reprints aimed at that part of a target audience—wholesalers, retailers, or consumers—who might not have seen the original article. Reprints also help reinforce the reactions of those who read the original article.

As in any other public relations activity, reprints should be approached systematically, with the following ground rules in mind:

1. **Plan ahead,** especially if an article has major significance to the organization. Ideally, reprints should be ordered before the periodical goes to press, so that customers can receive them shortly after the article hits the newsstands.
2. **Select target publics** and address the recipients by name and title. This strategy will ensure that the reprint reaches the most important audience.
3. **Pinpoint the reprint's significance,** either through underlining pertinent information in the article, making marginal notes, or attaching a cover letter. In this way the target audience will readily understand.
4. **Integrate the reprint** with other similar articles and information on the same or related subjects. Often, several reprints can be combined into a single mailing piece. Also, reprints can be integrated into press kits and displays.

Trade Shows

Trade show participation enables an organization to display its products before important target audiences. The decision to participate should be looked at with the following factors in mind:

1. **Analyze the show carefully.** Make sure the audience is one that can't be reached effectively through other promotional materials, such as article reprints or local publicity. Also be sure the audience is essential to the sale of the product. For example, how responsible are the attendees for the actual purchase?

2. **Select a common theme.** Integrate public relations, publicity, advertising, and sales promotion. Unify all elements for the trade show and avoid, at all costs, any hint of interdepartmental rivalries.

3. **Make sure the products displayed are the right ones.** Decide well in advance exactly which products are the ones to be shown.

4. **Consider the trade books.** Often, trade magazines run special features in conjunction with trade shows, and editors need photos and publicity material. Always know what special editions are coming up, as well as their deadline schedules.

5. **Emphasize what's new.** Talk about the new model that's being displayed. Discuss the additional features, new uses, or recent performance data of the products displayed. Trade show exhibitions should reveal innovation, breakthrough, and newness.

6. **Consider local promotional efforts.** While in town during a trade show, an organization can enhance both the recognition of its product and the traffic at its booth by doing local promotions. This strategy means visiting trade magazine editors and local media people to stir up publicity for the product during the show.

Spokespersons

In recent years, the use of spokespersons to promote products has increased. Spokespersons shouldn't disguise the fact that they are advocates for a particular product. Their purpose is to air their sponsor's viewpoint, which often means going to bat for a controversial product.

One example is the tobacco industry. In the early 1970s, with cigarette and cigar ads banned on television and radio, the Tobacco Institute, funded by the major tobacco companies, launched a far-reaching speakers campaign to get its story to the public. During the first three years of the campaign, tobacco speakers appeared in 350 cities in 48 states and received coverage on 1,300 television and radio shows and in almost 300 newspapers.

Spokespersons must be articulate, fast on their feet, and thoroughly knowledgeable about the subject. When these criteria are met, the use of spokespersons as a marketing tool can be most effective.

Today, spokespersons come in a variety of sizes, shapes, and occupations. The corporate chairmen of firms as diverse as Chrysler cars, Eastern Airlines, and Wendy's hamburgers take the lead in promoting their companies. One local New York chicken supplier, Frank Perdue, single-handedly put his company on the map through advertising and publicity appearances. Celebrities from Bob Hope (Texaco) to Jay Leno (Doritos brand corn chips) to Michael J. Fox (Pepsi-Cola) regularly endorse products for huge sums.

FIGURE 11–2 The king of the 1990s spokespersons was combination football/baseball/you-name-it athlete Bo Jackson. Without breathing hard, the Kansas City Royals outfielder/Los Angeles Raiders halfback walked away with $4 million in 1990 from product endorsements and the licensing of his name on everything from AT&T long distance service to Tiger Electronics computer games to Cramer sports medicine products. Bo's primary endorsement, appropriately enough, was for Nike cross-trainer shoes. Without question, Bo knew bucks. And it was a good thing, too. Because in the spring of 1991, after suffering a career-threatening hip injury in a football playoff game, Bo's future as an athlete—much less his marketability as a spokesperson—stood in jeopardy. *(Courtesy of NIKE, Inc.)*

IF BO JACKSON TAKES UP ANY MORE HOBBIES, WE'RE READY.

Who says Bo has to decide between baseball and football?
We encourage him to take up everything from basketball to cycling. And

to train for them all in the Nike Air Trainer SC.
A cross-training shoe with plenty of cushioning and support for a number of sports. Or should we

say, a number of hobbies?

Air Trainer SC

In the 1990s, the most lucrative field for product spokespersons is sports. In 1990, the 30 highest-paid athletes in the world earned a total of about $230 million—with one-third the income coming from pitching products, not balls.[5] Golfers Jack Nicklaus and Arnold Palmer each made $8 million from endorsements. Basketball superman Michael Jordan and tennis star Boris Becker each made $6 million from endorsements. Hockey great Wayne Gretzky and football legend Joe Montana each pocketed $3 million. But the up-and-coming, undisputed King of the Spokespersons was an all-everything athlete, known simply as Bo (Figure 11–2).

Although celebrity spokesmanship is big business today, it is not without its pitfalls. The two co-stars of the hit TV show, "Moonlighting," both got into hot water with the products they represented. Bruce Willis was spokesman for the liquor manufacturer, The Seagrams Company, when the actor admitted he had a drinking problem. Cybil Shepherd was dropped as spokeswoman for the National Beef Council when she confessed that she shunned the product. Former U.S. Speaker of the House Tip O'Neill was roundly criticized for leaving office and becoming spokesman for every shoe company, beer firm, hotel chain, and airline with whom he could make a connection. Critics thought the Tipster should have been a bit more selective about his endorsements.

Especially picky in marketing their images are rock stars. Indeed, when Prince, the diminutive Minnesota rocker with the risque lyrics, was asked for his photo for use in a certain public relations textbook, the author received the following warning from the decidedly unrocklike law firm of Manatt, Phelps, Rothenberg & Tunney.

> Please be advised that our client does not desire to grant you permission to use any picture or likeness of him in connection with your textbook.[*]

So there.

Special Events

Special public relations events also help to market products. Grand opening celebrations, for example, are a staple in the public relations arsenal. They present publicity opportunities and offer businesses a chance to meet customers face-to-face. With the cost of print and broadcast advertising going up each year, companies increasingly are turning to sponsorship of the arts, education, music, festivals, anniversaries, sports, and charitable causes for promotional and public relations purposes (Figure 11–3).

There are no particular rules for special events. They range from media extravaganzas, such as Coca-Cola's sponsorship of Hands Across America in 1986 with more than six million Americans participating in raising $35 million for the homeless, to simple groundbreaking and open-house ceremonies for businesses, hospitals, schools, and the like. Special events can be risky, however, especially when the party is held and no one from the media attends.

In the 1990s, "cause-related marketing" is popular. Cause-related marketing brings together the fund-raising needs of nonprofit groups with the business objectives of sponsoring companies. Some companies have been called to task for questionable tactics to promote their products by ostensibly "doing good." Perhaps the most blatant example came in the winter of 1990, when Coca-Cola Co. donated 20,000 cases of Coke to American troops in Saudi Arabia. It then promoted the gesture to the national media, which questioned the company's aggressive efforts to seek publicity. Later, Anheuser-Busch donated 22,000 cases of a nonalcoholic beer to the troops in Saudi Arabia and decided, in light of Coke's experience, to soft-pedal the announcement.[6]

[*]Letter from Jody Graham of Manatt, Phelps, Rothenberg & Tunney, Los Angeles, California, May 10, 1985.

FIGURE 11–3   Fleischmann's Margarine sponsored a special national cross-country ski competition, where its name was prominently displayed on all of the competitors at the more than 40 ski touring centers and recreational facilities that hosted the competition. *(Courtesy of Padilla Speer Beardsley, Inc.)*

In planning special events, public relations professionals are well advised to seek outside help, even though it usually doesn't come cheap. Practitioners can find just about any type of assistance by consulting local directories and industry source books, which are periodically updated to include an ever-changing variety of external services that support public relations work—from fund raising to sky writing to blowing up balloons. Done sparingly and conceived thoughtfully, special events can significantly enhance the marketing of a product or institution.

Consumer-Oriented Public Relations

Public relations also helps market products through appeals to consumer demands. Sponsoring nutritional recipes, publishing consumer information advice, and lobbying for consumer-oriented legislation all help market a company's products. If consumers believe a company is sincerely concerned about their welfare, their trust may translate into purchase decisions.

More companies today seek marketing benefits from their goodwill activities. An ideal match raises funds for the nonprofit group, while offering a business visibility among prospects.[7] Figure 11–4 shows how

FIGURE 11–4 The Chase Manhattan Bank in 1990 focused a portion of its charitable contributions on improving literacy in the United States. First Lady Barbara Bush, an ardent literacy advocate, agreed to host a children's story hour on radio, sponsored by Chase, in the best tradition of cause-related marketing. *(Courtesy of J. Walter Thompson)*

Chase Manhattan Bank combined an interest in literacy with a radio show, hosted by the nation's First Lady.

Marketing for the Entrepreneur

For the small entrepreneur starting out in business, public relations sophistication can be a great advantage. A small operation can effectively use public relations techniques to enhance the marketing of its products and itself. The key to using public relations techniques to market a small company is the same as it is in promoting a large company: before any public relations program can be considered, solid results must be achieved. In other words, performance must always precede publicity.

Before deciding on a public relations program, an entrepreneur should consider the following six questions:

1. **What are our long-range goals and objectives?** A clear statement of mission helps an organization target its potential audiences. How many clients does it serve now? Does it want to grow? How fast? Is the mission complementary to the human services, educational, cultural, or arts activities in the community? What problems does the company hope to solve?

2. **What are our short-term goals?** Each short-term objective must be evaluated against the longer-range mission to avoid an appearance of jumping from one short-term goal to another.

3. **Who needs to know about us?** By clearly identifying the individuals or groups that need to know each particular objective, the entrepreneur can determine the appropriate channel of communication to reach that individual or group.

4. **What are we doing now?** The entrepreneur should first carefully audit communication efforts, from updating mailing lists to analyzing how key publics are regularly reached.

5. **What else can we do?** The entrepreneur should look inward to see whether there are programs on which to capitalize by publicly telling the firm's story.

6. **Do we have the money to do what we want?** Many entrepreneurs have limited budgets. Advertising costs money. So does postage. So does telemarketing. Therefore, a pivotal part of the entrepreneur's public relations role is to determine what the proposed program will cost and, if it exceeds available funds, either scale it back appropriately or work to obtain the necessary funds.

If the entrepreneur decides that public relations support will be helpful and can be afforded, the following rules may help secure added recognition for a small firm.

♦ **Work to achieve visibility.** An entrepreneur in a small company can try to publicize the company through free publicity in the media. Local media are generally receptive to the announcement of a new firm, new officers, new products, and new locations of local business operations. An entrepreneur who takes the time to become familiar with local journalists may find a few willing to use the company's announcements.

♦ **Compose a facilities brochure.** No matter how small the firm, a brochure describing its products, prices, and philosophy is a good idea. A facilities brochure can serve as a calling card to potential customers. If done in a quality manner, such a brochure may suggest prestige and credibility, both vital attributes for any business.

◆ **Use direct-mail marketing.** Once a facilities brochure is created, it should be mailed to customers and prospects. In this context it is often wise to use an outside, professional mailing service and mailing list supplier. The facilities brochure should have a return response coupon or a postage-paid response card to facilitate customer inquiries.

◆ **Work at becoming known in the community.** Small-business persons should be joiners. They should join the local Chamber of Commerce, Better Business Bureau, civic clubs such as Rotary and Kiwanis, Junior Achievement, or Big Brother/Big Sister. Achieving recognition in a community isn't difficult for someone willing to put in the work and the hours. For a businessperson in a small company, such active participation in community affairs can mean valuable business contacts.

◆ **Consider advertising.** Advertising for a small business can, of course, be tremendously helpful. However, it is not a necessity. Advertising is expensive and can prove wasteful if it is not used strategically. Advertising in the telephone classified directory is probably a good idea; so, too, is sticking to the local media. Print advertising for a small business should have some built-in mechanism, such as a coupon, to indicate reader response.

Most small entrepreneurs have limited means. Therefore, to increase reach and recognition in the marketplace, a wise entrepreneur will take advantage of public relations techniques to enhance marketing initiatives.

Marketing the Jordache Look

YOU
MAKE
THE
CALL

In the 1980s, few companies could boast as successful a link between public relations and marketing as Jordache, the maker of what used to be called dungarees and today are called blue jeans. Jordache was the creation of Joe Nakash, who began in New York City in the late 1970s with $25 in his pocket, sleeping in the bus terminal by night, and sweeping floors by day.

After beginning several jeans stores in Brooklyn with his brothers, Ralph and Avi, Joe Nakash borrowed $300,000 to begin his own jeans manufacturing company. Using the first names of his brothers and himself and adding a *che* because it sounded French, Joe Nakash invented Jordache and with it the Jordache look. Then the fun started.

The Nakash brothers decided to blow their entire new business loan on promotion.

- They bought time on "60 Minutes" and ran an ad featuring a topless Lady Godiva and a young man wearing Jordache jeans. CBS objected strongly to the commercial, and Jordache achieved significant publicity from its rejection. Orders for Jordache jeans began to pour in.

- The brothers attracted additional publicity when they refused to make jeans larger than size 36 so that only the lean could wear them. Predictably, the Jordache ads provoked cries of "sexism" and "exploitation of women." Equally predictably, the company returned the volley, insisting loudly that their product connoted "vivaciousness and healthy attractiveness." The debate was great media copy.
- When *The New York Times* banned a Jordache ad of a topless couple because "the couple was smiling," the company reshot the ad with the models *not* smiling. Jordache then publicly censured the *Times* for practicing its own brand of morality. More coverage resulted.
- When rival firms began to counterfeit Jordache jeans, the Nakash brothers hired a legal and detective team to track them down and invited reporters to come along for the kill. This, too, got extensive coverage.
- When a Jordache blimp crashed at takeoff, leaving the invited reporters with a nonevent, an ambulance delivered Jordache models to the press conference site and turned a fiasco into a party.

Even though such product publicity techniques may have smacked of the days of P. T. Barnum, the Nakash brothers didn't seem to mind. They seemed quite content with an image that had, in four years, parlayed brother Joe's original $25 into a $350 million, 8,000-employee business.

QUESTIONS

1. Why wouldn't the Jordache public relations/marketing strategy work for other companies?
2. Do you think the word-of-mouth publicity that the Jordache stunts provoked was helpful for the company's image?
3. Was the decision not to market jeans beyond size 36 a good one?
4. How would you rate the Jordache public relations thrust in terms of clearly positioning the company?

Summary

Marketing professor Philip Kotler has said that the days of traditional product marketing may be giving way to a more subtle, social, or public relations marketing. According to Kotler, companies must deal with dwindling resources, inflation that continues to limit buying power, consumers who are becoming more sophisticated, environmental and quality-of-life considerations, and government control. With these worries, companies may be just as concerned about staying in business as they are with maximizing sales.[8] In light of these changing societal characteristics, a new kind of radical marketing may develop.

1. **Quality of life**   Rather than being the "seller science," the purpose of marketing in the future may be to assist sellers in selling better, buyers in buying better, and governments in regulating better. Quality rather than quantity may become the most important variable in marketing goods and services.

2. **Interest orientation**   Rather than being needs-oriented, marketers in the future may be more interest-oriented. That is, they may serve the educational or social interest of consumers more than anything else.

3. **External decision making**   Rather than sellers freely setting prices and controlling marketing factors, external parties may be represented in the marketing decision-making process.

4. **Nonsegmentation**   Rather than varying their product offerings as they choose, marketers may be limited to offering less differentiation in styles, colors, and models.

5. **Restraint**   Rather than catering to all the wants of consumers, future marketers may have to concentrate on conserving resources and counteracting increased and unnecessary costs to customers.

Although Kotler's radical marketing hasn't yet blossomed in the 1990s, his thesis underscores the importance of marketers thinking beyond traditional notions of product, price, distribution, and promotion. More and more, management of both product and service companies, as well as nonprofit institutions, are inviting public relations input in the development of marketing programs. Managers increasingly recognize that, in the 1990s, public relations programs and techniques can add another dimension to a marketing offensive, not only with the same precision that advertising offers, but with better cost efficiency and the potential of even greater impact.

DISCUSSION STARTERS

1. Describe the differences between marketing, advertising, and public relations.
2. What role can public relations play in marketing?
3. What objectives can public relations help realize in the marketing plan?
4. What is meant by third-party endorsement?
5. What factors should be considered in assessing trade-show participation?
6. Discuss the phenomenon of the "spokesperson."
7. Describe the pros and cons of using someone well known as a spokesperson.
8. What is the benefit of staging a special event?
9. What is cause-related marketing?
10. What questions should a small organization ask before employing public relations?

BETWEEN THE LINES

Magic "Like Magic" to Pepsi . . .

Los Angeles Lakers basketball star Earvin "Magic" Johnson is one of the most popular celebrity spokespersons. He's warm. He's smart. And he's articulate. That's why no one could blame Pepsi-Cola Co. when the

(Courtesy of Los Angeles Lakers)

company chose Magic and a group of associates as new owners of Pepsi's lucrative Washington, D.C. franchise. Johnson negotiated a contract with Pepsi that allowed him to buy an equity stake in the franchise in return for appearing in television commercials and as a spokesman for the beverage. Magic was slated to receive an estimated $4.2 million over three years for his Pepsi endorsements. The D.C. franchise itself was estimated to be worth a whopping $60 million.

. . . But Madonna? "Like Aversion"

Pop singer Madonna, on the other hand, was not quite as popular with Pepsi. In 1989, the company decided to dump Madonna as a spokesperson after religious groups complained that a Madonna video was morally objectionable. Threatened with a boycott of Pepsi products because the video looked like Madonna's controversial hit music video, "Like a Prayer," Pepsi decided to ditch Madonna as a

(AP/Wide World Photos)

spokesperson and "eat" her Pepsi contract—reportedly a $5 million dose of indigestion.

NOTES

1. "Colloquium of Marketing and PR Spokespersons Agrees Organizations Suffer When Turf Wars Occur," *Public Relations Reporter* (February 13, 1989): 1.
2. "Kotler: Rethink the Marketing Concept," *Marketing News* (September 14, 1984): 1.
3. Art Stevens, "Brandstanding: Long-Lived Product Promotion," *Harvard Business Review* (May–June 1981): 54.
4. "Marketing PR Can Outperform Advertising, Says Long-Time Counselor Dan Edelman," *Public Relations Reporter* (October 30, 1989): 3.
5. Peter Newcomb and Christopher Palmeri, "Throw a Tantrum, Sign a Contract," *Forbes* (August 20, 1990): 68.
6. Mark Landler and Seth Payne, "Publicity? Why, It Never Even Occurred to Us," *Business Week* (September 24, 1990): 46.
7. Thomas G. Abbott, "Merging Promotion and PR," *Communication Briefings* (November 1988): 5.
8. Philip Kotler, "Marketing Management in an Era of Shortage," speech before the New York/New Jersey chapter of the American Marketing Association, Rutgers University, Newark, NJ, November 10, 1974.

TOP OF THE SHELF

Miller, Peter G. *Media Marketing: How to Get Your Name & Story in Print & on the Air.* New York, NY: Harper & Row, 1987.

You have great ideas and want to sell them to the media—but how do you convince editors to listen? For starters, read *Media Marketing*.

With over 20 years of experience as a writer, broadcaster, and promoter, Peter Miller knows what editors want. In Part One, Miller defines media marketing and the importance of selling news to the press. His "Principles and Protocols" outlines the rules of the craft, including how to tailor efforts to individual reporters and how to avoid promotional excess. Part Two explains the basics of pitching an idea to the media, writing successful news releases, finding the right media outlet for ideas, and contacting reporters in a way that elicits interest and not contempt. Miller addresses the use of specific mediums in Part Three, which teaches students when to use radio, television, and print. Part Four consists of creating media programs for fictitious clients: Bob's Elm Street Gas & Lube, Dr. Gordon's Optometric Practice, and Vanguard City Mortgage Bankers.

Standing out from the competition and getting recognition for products is tough. Reading *Media Marketing* will increase your chances of getting the media placement your story deserves.

Bennet, Peter. *Dictionary of Marketing Terms.* New York: AMACOM, 1989 (135 W. 50th St. 10020).

Benson, Richard. Secrets of Successful Direct Mail. Lincolnwood, IL: National Textbook, 1989.

Communicators' Guide to Marketing. IABC, 1987 (870 Market St., San Francisco, CA 94102).

Cooper, P. *Health Care Marketing Issues/Trends.* Rockville, MD: Aspen, 1986.

Davidson, Jeffrey. *Marketing on a Shoestring.* New York: John Wiley, 1988.

Debelak, Don. *Total Marketing.* Homewood, IL: Dow Jones-Irwin, 1989.

Deran, Elizabeth. *Low-Cost Marketing Strategies: Field-Tested Techniques for Tight Budgets.* New York: Praeger, 1987.

Goldman, Jordan. *Public Relations in the Marketing Mix.* Lincolnwood, IL: Crain Books, 1985.

Gross, Martin. *The Direct Marketer's Idea Book.* New York: AMACOM, 1989 (135 W. 50th St. 10020).

Haley, R. *Developing Effective Communications Strategy: A Benefit Segmentation Approach.* New York: John Wiley, 1985.

Hauman, David. J. *The Capital Campaign Handbook: How to Maximize Your Fund-raising Campaign.* Rockville, MD: Taft Group, 1987 (12300 Twinbrook Parkway, Suite 450, 20852-9830).

Health Care PR Handbook: Success Strategies for PR Pros in Health Care. New York: Madison Avenue Communications, 1987.

Jefkins, Frank. *The Secrets of Successful Direct Response Marketing.* Portsmouth, NH: Heinemann, 1988.

Kotler, Philip, and Gary Armstrong. *Marketing: An Introduction.* Englewood Cliffs, NJ: Prentice-Hall, 1987.

Kotler, Philip, and Karen Fox. *Strategic Marketing for Educational Institutions.* Englewood Cliffs, NJ: Prentice-Hall, 1985.

Lazarus, George, and Bruce Wexler. *Marketing Immunity: Breaking Through Customer Resistance.* Homewood, IL: Dow Jones-Irwin, 1987.

Ljungren, Roy G. *Business to Business Direct Marketing Handbook.* New York: AMACOM, 1988 (135 W. 50th St. 10020).

Marketing Your Hospital: Strategy for Survival. Chicago: AHA (P.O. Box 99376).

McKenna, Regis. *The Regis Touch: New Marketing Strategies for Uncertain Times.* Reading, MA: Addison-Wesley, 1986.

Miller, Peter G. *Media Marketing.* New York: Harper & Row, 1987.

Onkvist, Sak, and John Shaw. *Product Life Cycle and Product Management.* Westport, CT: Greenwood, 1989.

Ostrow, Rona, and Sweetman Smith. *The Dictionary of Marketing.* New York: Adweek Books, 1988.

Quelch, John A. *How to Market to Consumers.* New York: John Wiley, 1988.

Ries, Al, and Jack Trout. *Bottom-up Marketing.* New York: McGraw-Hill, 1989.

Roberts, Mary, and Paul Berger. *Direct Marketing Management.* Englewood Cliffs, NJ: Prentice-Hall, 1989.

Robinson, Larry, and Roy Alder. *Marketing Megaworks: The Top 150 Books and Articles.* New York: Praeger, 1987.

Schwartz, Gerald. "Planning Product Publicity Pays Off." *Nation's Business.* New York: G. S. Schwartz & Co.

SUGGESTED READINGS

Shimp, Terence, and Wayne M. DeLozier. *Promotion Management & Marketing Communications.* Hinsdale, IL: Dryden Press, 1986.

Slutsky, Jeff. *Street Smart Marketing.* New York: John Wiley, 1989.

Smith, W. J. *The Art of Raising Money.* New York: AMACOM, 1985 (135 W. 50th St. 10020).

Special Events Report (213 W. Institute Pl., Chicago, IL 60610). 24 per year.

Sports Marketing News (1771 Post Rd. East, Westport, CT 06880). Biweekly.

Stanley, Thomas J. *Marketing to the Affluent.* Homewood, IL: Dow Jones-Irwin, 1988.

Weinrauch, Donald J., and Nancy Baker. *The Frugal Marketer: Smart Tips for Stretching Your Budget.* New York: AMACOM, 1989 (135 W. 50th St. 10020).

Wiklund, Erik. *International Marketing Strategies: How to Build Market Shares.* New York: McGraw-Hill, 1987.

Domino's Delivers Controversial Pizza Policy*

In the 1990s, Detroiter Thomas Monaghan epitomized the new breed of marketing-oriented chief executive officer. Rising up from poverty, Monaghan acquired a multi-million-dollar classic car collection, bought the Detroit Tigers baseball team, and spoke out in support of conservative causes.

He also founded and served as chairman of Domino's Pizza, the fastest-growing chain in a $13 billion market. From nowhere, Domino's, under Monaghan, became the nation's second fastest-growing franchise operation, with sales leaping from $179 million in 1981 to more than $2 billion at the beginning of 1990.

In a decade, the company grew from 300 outlets to about 5,000 owned and franchised stores, selling about 230 million pizzas per year.

Key to Domino's success, beyond the outspokenness and flamboyance of its owner, was a guarantee that if customers had to wait more than half an hour for their pizza, they'd get a $3 discount or a free pie.

Domino's Pizza's pledge also was the company's Achilles' heel.

Employing between 70,000 and 80,000 drivers, Domino's became the target of critics who claimed that the company's 30-minute policy was causing reckless driving, accidents, and deaths. Through the latter part of 1989, the tension mounted.

- In June, a seventeen-year-old Indiana Domino's driver was killed when his small pickup truck skidded on a rain-slicked road and hit a utility pole. His mother said he was speeding and called Domino's guarantee "an invitation to break the law." In light of the death, Indiana Senator Richard Lugar wrote Domino's president, asking the company to review its 30-minute delivery policy.

- Later that month, after a Domino's delivery car hit a station wagon outside a Pittsburgh store, the driver of the hit car said the Domino's manager rushed to the wreckage and demanded, "Let's get this pizza on the road." The driver subsequently filed a lawsuit against the company.

- In September, the Chicago-based National Safe Workplace Institute issued a report that at least 10 Domino's drivers, many of them students working part-time, were killed in the prior year, and that Domino's drivers were involved in about 100 traffic accidents that resulted in the deaths of 10 other people and many more serious injuries.

By the fourth quarter of 1989, it was clear that Domino's marketing publicity campaign of emphasizing the 30-minute delivery pledge had come back to haunt it.

Officials around the nation pleaded with Domino's to drop its speedy-delivery pledge. Insurance experts argued that the chain should scrap the guarantee because it pres-

"With our team, it only takes 12 minutes to make and bake a great pizza."

"Then I've got plenty of time to deliver safely."

A good system, and good people to run it. That's how we can deliver in 30 minutes or less. Our people are well trained and our kitchens are designed for efficiency. And we only deliver to neighborhoods that are within an average of two miles from the store. Our drivers don't have to hurry. So give us a call. We'll take care to be there.

DOMINO'S PIZZA *Nobody Delivers Better*

©1989 Domino's Pizza, Inc.
Delivery area limited to ensure safe driving.

FIGURE 11–5

sured young drivers to speed. The lawyer in the Pittsburgh case summarized, "People are being injured all over the country. These drivers are trying to deliver pizzas within 30 minutes, and sometimes it's just not physically possible. They may run a stop sign, go over speed limits, or make illegal turns."

Despite the ferocious national pressure, Domino's steadfastly refused to alter its 30-minute policy.

The company's position was that it suffered a "perception problem"—that the "speed" in the delivery process didn't occur on the highway but in the franchise outlet itself. Pizzas, Domino's said, were put together in a few minutes and relayed to drivers speedily enough to allow them adequate time to deliver the product safely. Besides, the company argued, Domino's "gains in customer goodwill what it may lose in income" each time the customer gets a rebate.

Domino's backed up its defense with a massive publicity and advertising effort to dispel the view that its policy endangered motorists. Its nationwide promotional campaign included the following elements:

1. A letter attached to millions of pizza boxes from the company's president, who wrote:

    Yes, a 30-minute delivery is important, but safe delivery is more important. The fact is, our entire delivery system is geared to give our drivers ample time to deliver.

    Since our delivery areas average two miles or less, this leaves our drivers nearly 18 minutes to make it to your home. After millions of safe deliveries, we know that's plenty of time.

2. A toll-free phone number, 1-800-DOMI-NOS for the public to register complaints against reckless delivery drivers.

3. Large posters plastered in Domino's Pizza stores with a photo of a stop sign and a listing of the toll-free number.

4. A publicity offensive, emphasizing safety. Domino's talked about how all drivers must complete an 8-hour, company-designed driving program. It announced the development of a new, more intensive driver-training program in selected locations. And it introduced a new requirement that all corporate-owned outlets—one-third of the chain's 5,000 stores—should terminate or reassign all drivers younger than eighteen.

5. A more candid approach in discussing its safety record. Domino's announced that its employees had been involved in accidents that resulted in 20 fatalities in a one-year period. This, it said, amounted to one fatality for every 11.5 million pizzas sold. It specified that not all of the accidents occurred during deliveries.

   It further specified that drivers were not penalized for failing to meet the 30-minute delivery guarantee . . . that the company, not the driver, paid the $3. It also publicly renounced the practice among some franchises to award "King of Lates" badges to delivery people making the most late deliveries.

   Domino's also announced plans to stop awarding its top driver an all expenses-paid trip to the Indianapolis 500, where the company sponsored a race car. Instead, the firm would reward all drivers with at least 5,000 safe driving hours.

6. A print advertising campaign emphasizing the company's commitment to safety. The ads featured delivery drivers, with the first focusing on a New York driver who administered CPR to a woman while he was delivering a pizza.

By the spring of 1990, the news for Domino's began to get better. For one thing, the steady drumbeat of negative publicity began to subside. Once again, owner Monaghan began to attract coverage—and controversy—but for projects other than the 30-minute guarantee. He announced Domino's intention to expand its one-item menu. He donated money to antiabortion groups. He announced development plans for a 35-story "Leaning Tower of Pizza" on a resort island in Michigan.

In May, a Pittsburgh judge declared a mistrial in the suit over Domino's 30-minute delivery policy, after jurors heard news reports about the trial. Domino's claimed it was "disappointed" that it didn't get its day in court. Said a spokesman, "We've maintained all along that once the facts are on the table, people will find out we are conscientious about safe driving."

QUESTIONS

1. What were Domino's options when faced with the challenge to end its 30-minute delivery policy?
2. Would you have changed the policy? Why didn't Domino's?
3. How would you characterize Domino's publicity posture as part of its promotional program?
4. What additional elements might Domino's have adopted as part of its promotional program?
5. What should Domino's posture be, with respect to its 30-minute delivery pledge?

*For further information on the Domino's Pizza case, see Brian Dumaine, "How Managers Can Succeed Through Speed," *Time* (February 13, 1989): 54; Patrick McMahon, "Publicity Forces Mistrial in Domino's Suit," *United Press International*, 14 May 1990; Bradley A. Stertz, "Domino's Beefs up Menu to Keep Pace with Rivals," *Wall Street Journal*, 21 April 1989, B1-4; "That Quick Pizza Has Safety Costs," *Financial Times*, 5 September 1989, 6; Mark Hofmann, "Domino's Keeps Delivery Policy, Despite Deaths," *Crain's Detroit Business*, 3 July 1989, 29.

Tips from the Top

CHUCK HOLLINSHEAD

Charles Hollinshead is director of the public affairs office at NASA's John F. Kennedy Space Center in Florida. Hollinshead guides the center's educational programs, public information activities, special guest tours and briefings, and the operation of the visitors center, Spaceport USA. Hollinshead has been at the Kennedy Space Center since 1963. He served as news center manager during Apollo missions and provided the countdown commentary for many Apollo, Skylab, Delta, and Centaur launches. In 1986, he received NASA's Outstanding Leadership Medal for his leadership during the difficult and demanding time following the *Challenger* accident.

How can public relations help "market" NASA?
NASA Public Affairs needs to do a better job of relating to the public the complexities and risks involved in the agency's research, development, and exploration mission. It is important that the public understand the long-term benefits of these programs, benefits which are often overshadowed by the excitement and spectacular aspects of space flight.

How do you communicate about NASA activities?
Our primary means of reaching the public is through the media. We hold press briefings and conferences, invite the media to cover our activities, and afford as much access to our operations as possible to help them understand what are sometimes complex and highly technical issues.

We use the excitement of space flight to capture the attention of not just the news media, but of people from all walks of life. We have hosted as many as 80,000 visitors for a space launch. In conjunction with the launch, we conduct briefings, conferences, and workshops to familiarize our guests with the NASA mission.

One of our least-known, but most important outreach programs is aimed at teachers and students. Space is a strong catalyst for learning because it provides real-life mysteries, adventure, and discovery.

How was NASA's image resurrected after the *Challenger* disaster?
As a result of the *Challenger* disaster, NASA made a number of changes in management and in flight hardware. All of these changes and the rationale behind them were thoroughly reviewed with the news media, and thus reported to the public. It

was absolutely critical at that point to be completely open and forthright.

In our Public Affairs Contingency Plan, updated after our *Challenger* experience, we have set up a much better flow of communications between public affairs and the operational elements and have assured timely access to impounded data.

Before the accident, NASA was viewed as a forward-looking, high-tech agency made up of hard-working and exceptionally dedicated people. The agency has not changed. The people have not changed. We will have exciting new programs, perplexing new challenges, and new solutions. We must be open and candid, and do everything we can to help the public understand this exciting and often complex program.

What is entailed in marketing a shuttle launch?

Thirty days before a launch, and sometimes earlier, NASA begins a series of press briefings on the planned mission. By the time a newsman begins coverage of a mission, he or she should be well prepared.

NASA produces press kits, news releases, and other written material relating to each shuttle launch and mission. We invite the media to view the launch and hear briefings and press conferences. Most of these activities are covered by a NASA video system, which is sent via satellite to other NASA centers. In this way, the media can cover the event from any NASA center, or with the proper dish, can receive the TV at their own facility.

What was NASA's response to the problems with the Hubble telescope?

Within hours after NASA's top management was briefed on the problems, Hubble managers and scientists appeared at a press conference where they gave the most complete information known at the time and their best estimate of the telescope's future, and they answered questions from the media.

The Hubble telescope was planned to operate in space over a period of 15 years. Even after the mirror's flaw was discovered, the scientists felt that over that 15-year period they would be able to achieve everything they had set out to accomplish.

How important is public relations to an agency like NASA?

In a democracy, public relations is critical for all government agencies. Taxpayers want to understand how their money is being used.

NASA is in a unique position among government agencies. No matter how hard they try, most agencies will never receive the press attention that NASA does. That is not a credit to our public relations organization but simply is due to the interest generated by the space program. So our task is not in gaining the attention of the media, but directing that attention in a constructive way. Public affairs professionals, working with the media on a daily basis, can do this much more effectively than engineers and managers whose focus of attention needs to be in other areas.

In recent years, I have seen many examples in business and industry where the role of public relations has been a key to an organization's growth, recovery from a calamity, or even its survival.

Public Relations Advertising

12

Advertising—despite what many business managers think—isn't at all the same thing as publicity. The basic difference is that advertising costs money, a lot of it—$250,000 for a single commercial on a top-rated show—because you control what is said, when, where, and to whom. Publicity, which will be discussed further in Chapter 13, is far less costly but also less controllable.

Traditionally, organizations have used advertising to sell products. Only occasionally—for example, the railroads and utilities in the 1920s—have firms used advertisements for purposes other than product promotion. In 1936, Warner & Swasey initiated an ad campaign that stressed the power of America as a nation and the importance of American business in the nation's future. After World War II, Warner & Swasey continued ads promoting the free enterprise system and opposing government regulation of business. This unique type of advertising—the marketing of an image rather than a product—became known variously as institutional advertising, image advertising, public service advertising, and public relations advertising.

Whereas promotional advertising was hard sell, public relations advertising was softer. Whereas promotional advertising talked about the particular virtues of using specific products, public relations advertising focused on the general image the company wanted to convey and the public issues it wanted to confront. Whereas promotional advertising sought purchasing action for its products, public relations advertising sought support for its positions.

Such ads typically were used to announce name changes, management changes, merger plans, or other information that promoted the company in general rather than its particular products. This kind of specialized advertising remained very much the exception rather than the rule until the 1970s.

Advertising Pressures of the 1970s

In 1970, U.S. corporations spent a little more than $150 million to advertise images and issues. By 1974, the amount spent on such advertising increased to $220 million.[1] One reason for this tremendous growth can be summarized in a single word—pressure. By the early 1970s, pressure began to build for a reshaping of traditional advertising approaches. For a variety of reasons, companies had no choice but to strengthen their role in institutional advertising.

The sudden jolt brought about by the Arab oil embargo of the early 1970s changed the rules for a number of advertisers. Oil companies, in particular, no longer had to worry about selling their products, but rather about staying in business. Advertising's most ferocious critics were in the consumer and regulatory areas. Consumer advocates and regulators began to zero in on large corporations and the advertisements they ran. Soon, large companies became once again "everyone's favorite candidate for slaughter."[2]

Counter Advertising

With attacks reminiscent of the earlier muckrakers, consumer advocates of the 1970s went after big business advertising with a vengeance. The weapon they used to attack corporate advertisers was the same tool corporate advertisers used—advertising. Public interest groups sprang up on both coasts to create their own ads in answer to the claims of large corporate advertisers (Figure 12–1). One such concern, Public Media Center (PMC) of San Francisco, adopted this as its creed:

> To represent the unrepresented—in the task of providing media access to those who have important, often vital, information or concerns to share with the public, but who have been denied access to the communications media in this country because of a lack of funds, a lack of professional skills, or because their message was deemed too controversial.[3]

Radio and television stations and newspapers were not obligated to accept such public service advertising, but a few publications and stations did, particularly those on public broadcasting channels. When such counter advertising was accepted, it ran free of charge, falling within the Federal Communications Commission Fairness Doctrine, which allows equal broadcast time for opposing viewpoints on controversial issues.

Corrective Advertising

Increased federal pressure was another major reason for the spread of institutional advertising in the 1970s. The Federal Trade Commission (FTC), for years one of the meeker government agencies, suddenly sprouted teeth in 1970, when it waged a vigorous campaign to deter advertisers from making claims they could not back up with material facts. The cutting edge of the FTC offensive was a corrective advertising campaign, in which advertisers had to correct any advertising claims found to be false and misleading.

One example was Ocean Spray Cranberry Juice Company, which claimed that its product contained "more food energy" than other drinks. Food energy, according to the FTC, meant nothing more than calories. The commission ordered Ocean Spray to run ads stating clearly that previous claims of having more food energy simply meant that the product contained more calories.

Although the FTC succeeded in the Ocean Spray case, it was less successful in an attempt to force ITT Continental Baking to run corrective treatment for its Wonder Bread ads. The commission claimed that Wonder Bread wasn't any different from other breads, even though it boasted it "could build strong bodies 12 ways." The commission claimed that by "implying Wonder Bread is unique," the company's advertising was misleading. ITT appealed the FTC ruling, and a judge ruled, "The record fails, by a wide margin, to show that asserted false aspects of this advertising are presently contributing to Wonder Bread sales or that such aspects have ever had any impact on sales."[4]

In addition to attempts at corrective advertising, government regulators also tried to counter certain advertisements to which they objected. In 1967, for example, the government ordered TV and radio stations to make free time available for messages that said cigarette smoking was dangerous to health. Eventually, cigarette manufacturers removed their ads from the airwaves. Interestingly, in the first year that cigarette advertisements disappeared from TV and radio, cigarette sales rose to record levels.

Emergence of Image Advertising

In the face of such hostile pressure from its critics, advertising in the 1970s took a new turn. Advertisers sought to broaden the use of nonproduct ads to create more responsible images for their firms. Instead of products, they advertised programs, many of which were in the public interest. They talked about social responsibility, equal employment hiring, and minority assistance. Figure 12–2 is a good example of image advertising by Gulf in early 1972.

This oil executive will go to bed hungry tonight.

Diana Church

HIS COMPANY earned almost two billion dollars in profits* last year, but that's not enough for him. Because he knows the world is running out of fossil fuels, and unless he can move in and monopolize a new power source, in the same way he's monopolized oil, he's going to be out of a job before very long.

That's why he says his company's astronomical profits aren't excessive—because he needs those profits to maintain his power. That's why he's asking for huge new handouts and tax incentives from the taxpayers—because he wants the government to pay the bills, and his company to reap the benefits.

If he doesn't get what he wants, he may not be able to go on collecting his $300,000 a year salary. He may not be able to go on manipulating the world energy market to the benefit of his stockholders and to the detriment of everyone else. He may be forced to give way to a system where the public controls the public resources for the public good.

If you think America's energy supply is too important to be left to a few huge multinational conglomerates, write your elected representatives and tell them that. The oil industry is making its voice heard in Washington. Isn't it time the shivering majority was heard from?

*
After-tax oil profits—1973
(millions of dollars)

	First nine months of 1973	Increase over 1972
Exxon	1,656	59.4%
Mobil	571	38.3%
Texaco	839	34.9%
Gulf	570	60.1%
Standard Calif.	560	39.7%
Standard Indiana	390	32.2%
Shell	253	40.6%
Continental	153	23.4%
Atlantic-Richfield	178	36.9%
Total all nine	5,170	**45.2%**
All oil companies	52,500	**30.3%**

Prepared by Public Interest Communications

ENERGY SHOULD BE EVERYBODY'S BUSINESS

FIGURE 12–1 These two ads, both critical of the nation's oil companies, were prepared by Public Interest Communications in the early 1970s and ran free of charge in several newspapers. *(Courtesy of Public Interest Communications)*

The oil companies have us over a barrel

THE NATION'S OIL COMPANIES control the nation's energy supply. And when they want something, they get it. All they have to do is claim that it's not profitable enough for them to produce the energy we need, and the government rushes to make all the concessions the industry wants. The government doesn't even have its own figures on the nation's oil supply—they get all their figures directly from the industry, and make no attempt to have them independently verified.

So if the oil industry wants higher prices, relaxed environmental requirements, the Alaska pipeline, offshore drilling, more tax handouts, and less competition from independent dealers, they simply allow a shortage to occur, and hold our energy supply for ransom.

We think it's time energy policy was based on public need, not corporate greed.

Don't be left out in the cold— write your congressman and insist on public control of the public's resources.

After-tax oil profits—1973
(millions of dollars)

	First nine months of 1973	Increase over 1972
Exxon	1,656	59.4%
Mobil	571	38.3%
Texaco	839	34.9%
Gulf	570	60.1%
Standard Calif.	560	39.7%
Standard Indiana	390	32.2%
Shell	253	40.6%
Continental	153	23.4%
Atlantic-Richfield	178	36.9%
Total all nine	5,170	45.2%
All oil companies	52,500	30.3%

Prepared by Public Interest Communications

ENERGY SHOULD BE EVERYBODY'S BUSINESS

FIGURE 12–1 continued

The trouble with being a big, successful oil company is that nobody believes a word you say.

If you've made up your mind that the guys who run oil companies are bad guys, this isn't your ad.

But if you like to keep an open mind, keep reading. And when you're through, we'd like you to believe one thing: that Gulf is every bit as concerned about preserving and restoring the environment as you are.

One way we can get you to believe this is to tell you what we're doing. So here's what we're doing:

First, we've spent a lot of money fighting pollution for many years—$45 million in 1971 alone, and a projected $196 million during the next five years. And it's bought us some very useful equipment and processes.

It's bought us (and our neighbors) smokeless flare tips at plants and refineries—to insure 100% combustion of hydrocarbons when gases are vented for safety measures.

Closed circuit TV monitoring of flares for combustion

FIGURE 12–2 This Gulf ad, which appeared in *Black Enterprise* magazine in 1972, is a typical image ad. *(Courtesy of Gulf Oil Corporation)*

control. Roofs that float on liquid storage tanks to prevent vapor formation and escape. Gulfining—a process that removes sulfur from home heating oil. And hydrodesulfurization—to produce fuel that reduces sulfur dioxide emissions at industrial and power generating plants.

We're also making progress in abating automotive exhaust emissions. With low-lead gasoline. And a smoke-suppressant additive that helps to minimize emissions from diesel-powered vehicles.

Before you can correct pollution, you have to trace it. So we built three mobile detector vans to use at Gulf plants: one pinpoints emissions into the air; another pinpoints emissions into the water; and the third determines on the spot the best way to treat effluents.

We transport vast amounts of petroleum by transoceanic tankers. So we use special loading devices that keep accidental spills on board or in dock—and out of the water. And we have a major research program on clean-up technology.

We're concerned with wildlife, too. That's one reason we donated the land for the Tinicum Wildlife Preserve in Pennsylvania. It's a major stopping place for migratory birds that travel the Atlantic Flyway. And we've assisted several environmentalists in getting an interstate highway reconstructed so that the natural state of the land can be preserved.

One of the problems with preserving natural resources is that we're simultaneously fighting a national energy shortage. So we're looking for new, ecologically sound fuel sources from coal, tar sands and shale. And we've entered the nuclear energy field. Our choice of nuclear power systems is a High Temperature Gas-cooled Reactor (HTGR) that uses less uranium and discharges only about ⅔ as much waste heat as other nuclear systems now in commercial operation.

We may some day face a water shortage. So we've developed a way to purify brackish water and are working on ways to desalt sea water economically.

This is some of the work Gulf is doing. We know we have a lot more to do. But we're determined to do it. And we'd like you to believe that.

An Equal Opportunity Employer
Gulf Oil Corporation

FIGURE 12–2   continued

This shift from institutional advertising to image advertising was a subtle one. As one ad agency executive put it, "It was a shift from what the company is doing to why it is doing these good things for the public." [5] Advertising headlines of the period underscored the social responsibility theme.

By the mid-1970s people began to distrust image advertising. Issues involved in image advertising were more complex than those involved with selling products. Images by nature are amorphous, whereas products are tangible. People believed the merits of a particular toothpaste or bar of soap because they could taste or feel them, but they were less likely to take on faith the corporate claim of brotherhood, team play, or social responsibility simply by being told that the advertiser practiced it.

Image advertising was suspect even within many of the corporations sponsoring it. In many cases, top management, perhaps because of its lack of understanding about the objectives behind image advertising, apparently didn't trust its own ads. And feedback measurements on image ads were difficult to conceive and implement. Management, which may have grudgingly accepted image advertising on faith, seemed to quickly tire of the idea.

Issues Advertising in the 1980s

The logical extension of image advertising was the birth of issues, or advocacy, advertising in the mid-1970s and its blossoming in the 1980s. Issues advertising, unlike its predecessor, didn't aim to be all things to all people. Its objective was to convey the sponsor's viewpoint on matters of some controversy. Ads were informational, factual, and persuasive. Many tried to be hard-hitting and let the public know exactly where the firm stood on certain issues.

The growth of issues advertising in the 1980s was attributable to several factors.

◆ Many business executives believed that journalists were, in the words of business professor S. Prakash Sethi, "economic illiterates," who limited the extent to which business would be given a fair hearing in the media.

◆ Corporate leaders became more aggressive in responding to their critics, recognizing that past silence generally had been counterproductive.

◆ A Supreme Court decision in 1978 (see the Bellotti case in Chapter 22) held that corporate speech was entitled to First Amendment protection, thereby eliminating many earlier restrictions against such speech. As Chase Manhattan Chairman Bill Butcher put it, "A company not only has rights and privileges like an individual person, but also responsibilities and duties. Any person who claims his rights but shuns his responsibilities fails to contribute to the betterment of mankind and, therefore, has no claim on the respect of mankind. I believe the same holds true for corporations."[6]

◆ The news media, stunned by a proliferation of corporate advertisements criticizing its treatment of business, began to acquiesce to corporate requests for equal time.

◆ The FTC, dubbed the "national nanny" in its salad days, narrowed its approach to deceptive advertising during the Reagan years. Instead of vigorously pursuing national advertisers, the FTC generally relaxed its substantiation program. Advertisers were thus less concerned about their overall image and more interested in publicly pursuing the issues that affected them most.[7]

By 1980, 90 percent of America's independent television stations were accepting advocacy or opinion commercials, compared to about 50 percent five years earlier. By 1984, total spending by the 10 leading U.S. corporate advertisers for what could be classified as public relations advertising had surpassed $300 million.[8] And the issue ads of the 1980s were more pointed than at any previous time. Figure 12–3, for example, shows an ad from W. R. Grace & Co. designed to warn readers of the dangers of a burgeoning federal budget deficit.

By far the leading proponent of issues advertising was the oil industry, barraged by critics who claimed that it profited from the nation's energy miseries. Initially, the oil companies reacted to the energy crisis by sponsoring factual ads explaining the origins of the problem and exhorting the public to conserve energy. But these ads failed miserably. As Texaco's advertising general manager put it,

> We had not done as good a job as we should have in bringing our story to the people and their representatives. We sincerely believe the facts are on our side, but we failed to bring those facts home to the public. We cannot afford to fail again.[9]

Of all the large companies, none was more demonstrative and vocal in issues advertising than Mobil Oil. Each Thursday, Mobil bought space opposite newspaper editorial pages across the country to holler, plead, and proselytize. And Mobil didn't mince words. "Don't read these ads if you've made up your mind about oil profits," began a typical ad. Another urged readers to "fight the two-times-two-equals-five logicians who think the same outfit that brings you the U.S. mail can find oil three miles under the ocean bottom." Strong words. Tough talk. Admonition bound to evoke criticism.

The impact of Mobil's advocacy advertising campaign was difficult to measure. A 1976 Louis Harris survey revealed that Mobil was regarded somewhat more favorably than some other oil companies. Of the people who were familiar with Mobil, 69 percent regarded it as a "progressive,

FIGURE 12–3 W. R. Grace & Co., inspired by its fiery chairman, Peter Grace, launched an issues advertising campaign to highlight the perilous nature of a steadily escalating federal deficit. Grace complemented its print ads with two 60-second commercials, one of which was banned in 1986 by the three major networks because it was seen as "too controversial." The other ad, curiously, was accepted by two of the three networks. *(Courtesy of W. R. Grace & Co.)*

So far it's just a commercial.

A few years ago, the very notion of a $2 trillion national debt seemed a bit farfetched.

Today it's a fact.

And so it's not without good reason that W. R. Grace & Co. peered into the future and produced a commercial called "The Deficit Trials." An admittedly bleak scenario that has children sitting in judgment of an older generation. Ours. A generation charged with the unforgivable crimes of apathy and neglect.

If it all seems overly pessimistic, consider these projections. Consider that today's parents will leave their children a national debt of $13 trillion by the year 2000, just 14 years from now. That debt is as much as 40 times greater than the one you inherited from your parents: a $50,000 debt for every man, woman and child in the year 2000.

What's more, if nothing is done, 94.6% of total Federal personal income tax collections will be used to pay the interest—just the interest—on that staggering $13 trillion debt. The repercussions of that reality are almost unthinkable.

Fortunately, these grim possibilities are just that. Possibilities. After all, no one really knows what another generation of unchecked federal deficits will bring. But we know this much. You can change the future. To find out how you can help, write to: W. R. Grace & Co., Dept. 2017, 1114 Avenue of the Americas, N.Y., N.Y. 10036.

"The Deficit Trials" is still just a commercial. And you can keep it that way.

GRACE
One step ahead
of a changing world.

YOU MAKE THE CALL

Messing with Mr. Rogers

By the mid-1980s, Burger King had become one of the most aggressive national advertisers. The company was particularly aggressive when it came to poking fun at its arch rival, McDonald's. In 1985, Burger King sought to distance itself from its rival by emphasizing that it flame-broiled its hamburgers, whereas McDonald's fried its meat.

To illustrate the difference in the two burgers, in one commercial Burger King decided to parody Fred Rogers, star of the popular children's show "Mr. Rogers' Neighborhood," which appeared nationally each day on the Public Broadcasting System.

Where's the rip-off?

The sharp increase in gasoline prices has sparked thousands of words, most of them accusing the oil industry of reaping undeserved profits. Industry spokesmen have attempted to respond, with little apparent success.

So we decided to let the numbers do the talking.

West Texas Intermediate is a benchmark domestic crude oil. We've translated the price per barrel on the spot market to cents per gallon, and tracked the price movement from early July to last Tuesday. Gasoline also trades on the spot market, and we've shown the average spot price of regular unleaded across the U.S.

Finally, we've shown the average price we charged our dealers in 29 key cities for regular unleaded, along with the price for Mobil distributors. The dealers account for 70 percent and the distributors for about 30 percent of our gasoline business.

CRUDE/PRODUCT PRICES JULY 3, AUGUST 7

(All numbers cents/gallon)	7/3/90	7/17/90	7/31/90*	8/2/90**	8/7/90	Increase 7/3-8/7
West Texas Intermediate Spot Market Crude	40.2	44.4	48.1	55.5	70.5	+30.3
†Regular Unleaded Spot Market Gasoline	60.4	63.7	62.8	68.9	85.1	+24.7
Average Mobil Price To Dealer Regular Unleaded	74.5	73.6	74.7	75.0	81.2	+ 6.7
Average Mobil Price To Distributor Regular Unleaded	67.8	68.0	69.6	69.8	78.3	+10.5

*OPEC Met July 26-27
**Iraq Invaded Kuwait August 2
†Platt's Low Weighted Average

The table shows that market prices for both crude oil and gasoline rose far more sharply than Mobil's.

One final observation: Much crude is now bought on terms specifying that the price is to be set by the spot market at the time of delivery. So the price of the gasoline you buy today was not set in concrete weeks ago.

Mobil®

FIGURE 12—4   In 1990, when gasoline prices rose quickly and the public once again castigated the oil industry, at least one petroleum firm was ready to answer back. *(Copyright © 1990 Mobil Corporation)*

The $150,000 commercial—with an imitator named Mr. Rodney teaching his audience to say the word *McFrying*—ran nationwide for three days before a distressed call came in to Burger King headquarters. The caller was none other than Mr. Rogers himself. And the silver-haired, soft-spoken neighborhood landlord was madder than a dog. Mr. Rogers objected fiercely to the commercial. "To have someone who looks like me doing a commercial is very confusing for children," said the mild-mannered Rogers. He appealed to Burger King's marketing vice-president to pull the popular 30-second spot.

QUESTION

If you were Burger King's marketing vice-president, would you kill the commercial?

forward-thinking company" compared with an average of 66 percent for all the oil companies in the survey. On the question of "helping to improve the quality of life," 60 percent thought well of Mobil, compared with an average of only 53 percent for all the companies. No company came out well on the question of "keeping profits at reasonable levels"; only 34 percent agreed that Mobil did so.[10]

While Mobil's management made no claim that the company had moved public opinion on specific issues, it continued its advertising campaign into the 1990s. In so doing, Mobil reinforced its position as one company that refused to take controversy lying down.

Purposes of Public Relations Advertising

Traditional public relations, or nonproduct, advertising—as opposed to image or issue positioning—is still very much in practice for specific purposes. Such advertising can be appropriate for a number of mutually supportive activities.

1. **Mergers and diversifications**   When a company merges with another, the public needs to be told about the new business lines and divisions. Advertising provides a quick and effective way to convey this message.
2. **Personnel changes**   A firm's greatest asset is usually its managers, its salespeople, and its employees. Presenting staff members in advertising not only impresses a reader with the firm's pride in its workers, but also helps build confidence among employees themselves.
3. **Organizational resources**   A firm's investment in research and development implies that the organization is concerned about meeting the future intelligently, an asset that should be advertised. The scope of a company's services also says something positive about the organization.
4. **Manufacturing and service capabilities**   The ability to deliver quality goods on time is something customers cherish. A firm that can deliver should advertise this capability. Likewise, a firm with a qualified and attentive servicing capability should let clients and potential clients know about it.
5. **Growth history**   A growing firm, one that has developed steadily over time and has taken advantage of its environment, is the kind of company with which people want to deal. It is also the kind of firm for which people will want to work. Growth history, therefore, is a worthwhile subject for nonproduct advertising.

6. **Financial strength and stability** A picture of economic strength and stability is one that all companies like to project. Advertisements that highlight the company's financial position earn confidence, customers, and corporate stockholders.

7. **Company customers** Customers can serve as a marketing tool, too. Well-known personalities who use a certain product may be enough to win additional customers. This strategy may be especially viable in advertising for higher-priced products, such as expensive automobiles or sports equipment.

8. **Organization name change** Occasionally, firms change their names (Jersey Standard to Exxon, American Metal Climax to AMAX, First National City Corporation to Citicorp). To stick in people's minds, a name change must be well promoted and well advertised. Only through constant repetition will people become familiar with the new identity.

9. **Trademark protection** Companies such as Xerox and Coca-Cola,

---

YOU
MAKE
THE
CALL

The Unwanted "Extra" in Corona Beer

Midway through 1987, the importer of Corona Extra, the most successful foreign beer in America, had a problem—a real problem. In a several-week period during the summer, Corona was the victim of an urban myth, apparently started by a jealous competitor, that the beer's unique flavor was the result of its being contaminated with urine at the brewery in Mexico City.

Barton Beers, which imports Corona to the United States, kept getting calls from people who had heard the rumor. The number of calls reached the point that Barton went to court in July, suing Luce and Son, which imports Corona's main competitor, Heineken, on the grounds that Luce representatives were spreading the rumor. In an out-of-court settlement Luce and Son made a public statement that Corona was "free of any contamination."

Nonetheless, the rumor persisted. And U.S. sales, which had grown 170 percent over the previous year, dropped as much as 80 percent in some areas. In Orange County, California, the Corona representative was besieged about the rumor by 35 separate retailers. So the question that faced Barton Beers executives in late summer 1987 was "To advertise or not to advertise?"

QUESTIONS

1. If you were Corona's public relations director, would you advertise?
2. Why or why not?
3. If you did advertise, what would you say?

whose products are household names, are legitimately concerned about the improper generic use of their trademarks in the public domain. Such companies run periodic ads to remind people of the proper status of their marks. In one such ad, a perplexed secretary reminds the boss, "If you had ordered 40 photocopies instead of 40 Xeroxes, we wouldn't have been stuck with all these machines!"

10. **Corporate emergencies** Occasionally, an emergency situation erupts—a labor strike, plant disaster, or service interruption. One quick way to explain the firm's position and procedures without fear of distortion or misinterpretation by editors or reporters is to buy advertising space. This tactic permits a full explanation of the reasons behind the problem and the steps the company plans to take to resolve the dilemma (Figure 12–5).

Public Relations Advertising in the 1990s

The 1990s may signal a reemergence in public relations advertising. In a period of contraction and even recession, profit-making organizations will be called upon to justify their activities. Pressure on nonprofit organizations will intensify to prove why they, rather than others, deserve contributions in a period of scarce resources. Hospitals, faced with declining patient enrollments, increased competition, and rising costs, will have to position themselves in a manner unique enough to stay in business. In every case, public relations advertising will be one way for organizations to differentiate their case before the public.

For such advertising to work in the overcommunicated, skeptical, and sophisticated society of the 1990s, institutions must keep in mind seven cardinal rules of public relations advertising.

1. **Ads must strengthen the bottom line.** The institution must keep in mind its own best long-term interest in its advertising. An organization pays for an ad for selfish reasons. For example, when Dresser Industries warned that "American jobs will be lost if Middle East-dependent firms, like Dresser, are subject to more boycott legislation," the bottom-line impact on Dresser and the country was clear.

2. **Ads must be clear.** One purpose of public relations advertising is to promote understanding. If message and motives are cloudy, people simply won't understand, no matter how well conceived the ad is (Figure 12–6).

3. **Ads must be supported by top management.** The more controversial a public relations ad, the better it is. An ad that is watered down is one that is doomed to failure. Top management must be prepared to take the heat

"Once people called us The Proud Bird. Lately they've been calling us other names."

"Continental is no stranger to success. As 'The Proud Bird,' passengers were calling weeks in advance to be sure of getting a seat with us. But recently, while we combined the operations of four airlines, we grew so fast that we made mistakes. Misplaced baggage. Delays. Reservation errors. You were frustrated and angry. And a lot of hard-working people at Continental were pretty embarrassed.

"It's led us to an intensified commitment to quality. And it's beginning to pay off: Latest reports show Continental's back as one of the top two airlines in on-time arrivals. But we're out to be 'America's Best.' To get there, we're investing more than $1.25 billion this year alone — to upgrade airport facilities and aircraft, and to expand our fleet.

"We're continually evaluating and adjusting our flight schedules for better connections and on-time performance. Working to decrease lost baggage — an area where we've already improved 100% in the last six months. Even adding special trouble-shooters at major airports who can respond instantly if problems occur. But that's just the start.

"We think we'll be the talk of the airline industry. And believe me, it won't sound anything like what you've been hearing lately."

Frank Lorenzo

Frank Lorenzo, Chairman, Continental Airlines

 CONTINENTAL

© 1987 Continental Airlines, Inc.

FIGURE 12–5 In 1987, with Continental Airlines criticized in the wake of rapid mergers and deteriorating service, the company and its gutsy chairman at the time, Frank Lorenzo, decided to go public with this equally gutsy public relations ad. *(Courtesy of Continental Airlines)*

FIGURE 12-6 The graphic photo and copy for this National Multiple Sclerosis Society ad was typical of a campaign that stated its message clearly. *(Courtesy of National Multiple Sclerosis Society)*

EVEN WITH MS, DR. RICHARD RADTKE CONQUERS THE DEEP

Internationally renowned, Dr. Radtke has conducted underwater explorations from Samoa to the Arctic Circle. In 1981 he learned he had multiple sclerosis, but he refused to give up his life's work.

Multiple sclerosis short circuits the central nervous system and impairs balance and coordination. Dr. Radtke decided to compensate for his disabilities by applying his abilities to devise new ways of continuing his work beneath the sea. This included creating special equipment to take him over rough terrain both under sea and over land. He truly believes that one day a cure for MS will be found.

The National Multiple Sclerosis Society is bringing that day closer for over 250,000 Americans who suffer from MS. Through its funding, major hospitals and universities can continue vital research in virology, genetics and immunology, to stop this great crippler of young adults.

Call 1-800-624-8236 today and find out more about multiple sclerosis and how you can help.

Help Us Short Circuit Multiple Sclerosis

NATIONAL MULTIPLE SCLEROSIS SOCIETY
205 EAST 42ND STREET, NEW YORK, NEW YORK 10017.   TEL. (212) 986-3240

and support the advertising. For example, when New York builder Donald Trump took out ads in 1988 to talk about protectionism, they began, "Japan is taking advantage of us." Top management—that is, Trump himself—was fully supportive.

4. Ads must persuade. Again, this is the basis of advertising. Ads shouldn't just inform; they must be persuasive. When public interest groups opposed Judge Robert Bork's nomination to the Supreme Court in 1987, they initiated a public relations advertising campaign that said in part, "We're one vote away from losing our most fundamental rights . . . choosing between sterilization and job loss . . . declaring illegal the use of birth control . . . not being protected from sexual harassment." In other words, they used fear to persuade, and Bork's nomination was defeated.

5. **Ads must sell the persuaded.** All advertising, especially the public relations variety, must appeal to what the public wants—not what the organization wants. This is a subtle distinction that is often lost on public relations advertisers (Figure 12–7).

FIGURE 12–7   The Humane Society's intent through ads like this was to persuade people that the decision *not* to wear fur was an easy one. *(Courtesy of The Humane Society of the United States)*

FIGURE 12—8 The redoubtable boxing promoter Don King celebrated his 1990 exoneration in the courts with this humorous—yet heartfelt—paean to his country. *(Courtesy of Don King Productions, Inc.)*

Only in America...

It may be hard to believe, but it has been said by many that I should stop singing the praises of my country. Some perceive my beliefs in America to be a hollow and shallow facade. Perhaps they do not realize what it really means to be an American. I have experienced the broad spectrum of everything this nation has to offer. I love America!

Throughout my career I have been publicly attacked and falsely accused of corruption, fight fixing, bribery and conflicts of interest. The battles, basically and fundamentally, have been about my rights and whether or not perceptions, accusations, power and influence could arbitrarily take away my precious rights.

The result of these battles by due process: TOTAL VICTORY! Innocent of all charges!

Only in America can a man survive castigation, vilification, accusations, character assassination, indictment and alleged involvement in national and international scandal... not once... but three times! Yet to have that someone not only survive, but succeed, and have his rights fully restored truly is a testament to our judicial system which protects and preserves the rights of each of us. Only in America.

Each and every one of us has so much to be thankful for in this great nation. I am especially thankful and blessed by God to be a proud American and to have the courage, conviction and determination to extol the virtues of my country, decry its inequities and injustices, and to seek better ways to resolve them in the struggle for a better quality of life for all Americans.

Now, at this time of world crisis, it is time for us to unite. It is time for all Americans to stand up for the principles on which these United States were founded and put aside all our differences. Liberty and Freedom are precious and must be preserved. We live in the greatest country in the world. Only in America!

This ad of gratitude is my way of letting my hair down,

Thank you, America.
For the Founding Fathers.
For The Constitution —
the contract by which we exist.

For the Preamble to The Constitution —
the express will of the people.

For the Bill of Rights,
the Declaration of Independence,
and due process.

To the law firm of Sidley & Austin,
who represented me in 1990 —
Mr. Robert W. Hirth, Chief Litigator
Mr. Alan M. Unger
Ms. Merinda D. Wilson
Mr. Charles E. Lomax, General Counsel
and "Legal Traffic Director."

To the witnesses,
who stood up against all odds for truth
which gave us justice.

To the law firm of Williams & Connolly,
who represented me in 1984 —
Mr. Vincent J. Fuller, Brilliant Lead Counsel
Ms. Ellen S. Huvelle
Mr. Steven A. Steinbach
Special thanks to the late, great
Edward Bennett Williams

To the judges and the juries,
the wonderful people
who make our system work.
God bless you.

To my many supporters all over the world.

To my staff,
my supporting cast who stood by me
all the way working countless hours
to keep the wheels of business turning.

Finally, thanks to my lovely wife,
Henrietta, and my family
who have always stood by me.
I love you.

---

6. Ads must be honest. Any advertiser is suspect. All ads begin with a bias. If the organization is to be believed, the ad itself must be scrupulously straightforward and honest. Such was not the case when the head of the United Transportation Union in 1987 ostensibly paid for an ad in the *New York Times* appealing for support to fight a ban on smoking in commuter trains. Several days later, it was revealed that the ad was secretly paid for by the Philip Morris Tobacco Company.

7. **A sense of humor helps.** Organizations, particularly big ones, can't take themselves too seriously, especially in public relations advertising. Humor disarms a skeptical populace, and a light touch can help to influence readers toward a particular viewpoint (Figure 12–8).

Summary

The effectiveness of public relations advertising, particularly with legislators and other opinion leaders, remains an open question. Critics charge that many image and issues ads are examples of organizations "talking to themselves." Indeed, most issues advertisers consider their competitors as important targets for such advertising.

The likelihood of continued nonproduct advertising presents important new challenges for public relations professionals used to dealing with adversarial publics. As advertising moves further into the realm of issues and positions, public relations professionals will be called on to play a greater role.

Already in the 1990s, the climate for public relations advertising seems to be changing. The staunch opposition to issues advertising of the television networks appears to be crumbling amid greater competition for tight ad dollars and demands for extra revenue.[11] In recent years, NBC, ABC, and CBS have quietly dropped their bans against issues advertising. The disappearance of the Fairness Doctrine no longer makes it obligatory to provide free air time for opposing viewpoints, so the issue of "balance" is no longer uppermost in the minds of the networks. On the other hand, many fear that the deceptive advertisements of a bygone day are about to return in the 1990s. Health organizations, like the Center for Science and the Public Interest, for example, decry such practices as touting reduced-calorie products as "lite," because there are no generally accepted standards for making such a claim. There is also much debate over nutritional claims, such as cereal advertising that proclaims to reduce cancer risks.[12] Accordingly, some in Congress are worried about a "letdown in enforcement" of advertising claims.

At the same time, the quantity of advertising is proliferating. Rare is the public space—from matchbook covers to lavatory walls to Zamboni ice-smoothing machines at hockey games—that is free from advertising messages. In 1990, Whittle Communications, a Tennessee-based company part-owned by media giant Time-Warner, began airing Channel One, a controversial TV show for schools that mixes news segments and commercials. One educator responded that, "This kind of intrusion of a commercial venture entering the schools is a Pandora's box."[13]

All this implies that public relations professionals must be sensitive to using advertising in a thoughtful way. As communications professor S. Prakash Sethi once put it:

> Increased access to the marketplace carries with it the obligation to use such access in a responsible manner. Business has most to lose from public misinformation and, therefore, should take every possible step to improve the quality of public information and debate. This would lead to better public understanding of complex issues affecting business and society and would improve the process of public policy formulation.[14]

Clearly, the real advertising giants in the 1990s and beyond may not be those companies that triumph in the marketplace of products, but rather those that are effective in the marketplace of ideas (Figure 12–9).

DISCUSSION STARTERS

1. Traditionally, what did organizations use advertising to sell?
2. What kinds of pressures did advertisers experience in the 1970s?
3. What is counter advertising?
4. What is corrective advertising?
5. Why did image advertising spread in the 1970s?
6. What is the significance of the oil companies in terms of the issues advertising of the 1980s?
7. What are the general purposes of public relations advertising?
8. What rules must organizations keep in mind when attempting public relations advertising?
9. Why did advertising help defeat the nomination of Judge Robert Bork in his 1987 attempt to join the Supreme Court?
10. What is the significance of Channel One?

NOTES

1. Mead & Bender Communications, *Advertising in the National Interest*, Boston: Mead & Bender Communications, January 1979.
2. "Problems of the Credibility of Big Business," *National Observer*, 26 January 1975, 14.
3. Public Media Center Annual Report, 1974/1975. (Available from the Public Media Center, 2751 Hyde St., San Francisco, CA 94109.)
4. "ITT Continental Baking Unit Is Backed by Examiner on Wonder Bread Ads," *Wall Street Journal*, 29 December 1972, 4.
5. Audrey Allen, "Corporate Advertising: Its New Look," *Public Relations Journal* (November 1971): 6.
6. Willard C. Butcher, "Total Corporate Responsibility in the 80s," address at the University of North Carolina, Charlotte, NC, October 16, 1981.
7. Christine Dugas, "Deceptive Ads: The FTC's Laissez-Faire Approach Is Backfiring," *Business Week* (December 2, 1985): 136.
8. Josephine Curran, "Corporate Advertising Expenditures," *Public Relations Journal* (December 1985): 28.
9. "Oil's New Sell," *Time* (November 11, 1974): 30.

In fact, we've made it a tradition. The reason is simple: we've got the best on our side.

In health, education and municipalities, Clark Burrus, Craig Bouchard and their people have made us the #1 bank for the hospital industry. The #1 U.S. Government bank in the Midwest. The #1 bank for Illinois municipalities. The leader in innovative college and university finance. By far.

In communications finance, no one can touch us. Led by Jackie Hurlbutt, we offer more expertise in cable, broadcasting, newspapers and telecommunications than anyone. Anywhere. That's a commitment backed by nearly $2 billion in loans outstanding.

In real estate finance, we're a lead bank to the country's leading real estate and mortgage companies. With Dan Lupiani and his experienced team, our clients get a combination of market knowledge and financial expertise that's hard to beat.

For more than a dozen specialized industries, First Chicago has the players, the speed, the depth, the drive.

All we need is you.

SPECTACULAR PERFORMANCE IS NOTHING NEW TO CHICAGO.

Performance has always been a Chicago tradition.

FIRST CHICAGO

FIGURE 12–9 First Chicago's advertising campaign combined the best of marketing promotion and public relations techniques in an ad series that at once appealed to societal values and civic pride, in addition to highlighting the institution's premier standing in certain markets. *(Courtesy of First Chicago)*

10. Irwin Ross, "Public Relations Isn't Kid Glove Stuff at Mobil," *Fortune* (September 1976): 202.
11. Joann S. Lublin, "TV Networks Gingerly Lift Prohibition on 'Issue Ads,' " *The Wall Street Journal*, 15 October 1990, B1.
12. Paul Farhi, "'Misleading' Ads Seen on Rise as Federal Policing Efforts Diminish," *The Washington Post*, 23 May 1989, C1, C5.
13. Paul Farhi, "Channel One Takes Ads to School," *The Washington Post*, 6 March 1990, D1.
14. S. Prakash Sethi, "Battling Antibusiness Bias: Is There a Chance of Overkill?" *Public Relations Journal* (November 1981): 64.

TOP OF THE SHELF

Ogilvy, David. *Confessions of an Advertising Man.* New York: Macmillan, 1963.

If lively copy and eye-catching graphics are the ingredients of great advertising, then the consummate chef is David Ogilvy, who reveals his blue-ribbon recipe in *Confessions of an Advertising Man.*

Ogilvy, one of advertising's most formidable minds, sets forth the principles and tactics that created potent campaigns for clients like Hathaway, Helena Rubinstein, Maxwell House, and Rolls-Royce. When writing ad headlines, Ogilvy insists, always include facts and shun "puns, literary allusions, and other obscurities." As for body copy, he stresses: "Don't be a bore. Tell the truth, but make the truth fascinating." To make advertising stand out, Ogilvy emphasizes, among other things, bold photographs, simple layouts, and a variety of type sizes. He also offers guidance to the aspiring professional: "you must be ambitious," Ogilvy advises, "but you must not be so nakedly aggressive that your fellow workers rise up and destroy you."

Confessions of an Advertising Man is a classic. Public relations practitioners who want to learn advertising fundamentals from a legend should heed Ogilvy's instruction.

SUGGESTED READINGS

Advertising Handbook for Health Care Services. Binghamton, NY: Haworth Press, 1986 (10 Alice St. 13904).

Anderson, Walter. *Handbook of Business Communications*. (Available from Box 243, Lenox Hill Station, New York, NY 10021.)

The Complete Guide to Creating Successful Brochures. Brentwood, NJ: Asher-Gallent Press, 1988 (131 Heartland Blvd. 11717).

Corbett, William. "The Bottom Line in International Communications: The Human Factor." *Tips & Tactics* (May 30, 1988) (Supplement of *Public Relations Reporter*). The writer stresses how important informed, motivated staffers are to their firms. He goes on to detail various channels of company communications.

Curran, Josephine. "Corporate Advertising Expenditures." *Public Relations Journal* (December 1985): 28–40.

Current Company Practices in the Use of Corporate Advertising. New York: Association of National Advertisers, 1988 (155 East 44th St. 10017).

Degan, Clara. *Understanding & Using Video.* White Plains, NY: Knowledge Industry, 1985 (701 Westchester Ave. 10604).

Denbow, Carl J., and Hugh M. Culbertson. "Linkage Beliefs and Diagnosing an Image." *Public Relations Review* (Spring 1985): 29–37. The authors diagnose the public image of an osteopathic medical clinic to develop a national public relations program.

Dugas, Christine. "Deceptive Ads: The FTC's Laissez-Faire Approach Is Backfiring." *Business Week* (December 2, 1985): 136–140.

Employee Annual Report and Update. Chicago: Ragan Communications, 1986 (407 S. Dearborn 60605).

Haller, Robert T. *Creative Power! Grow Faster with New Proactive Tactics in Advertising & Public Relations.* New York: Leister & Sons, 1988.

How to Prepare and Write Your Employee Handbook. 2nd ed. New York: AMACOM, 1988 (135 W. 50th St. 10020).

Kaatz, Ron. *Advertising and Marketing Checklists.* Skokie, IL: NTC Business Books, 1988 (P.O. Box 554 60076).

Kern, Monague. *30-Second Politics: Political Advertising in the Eighties.* New York: Praeger, 1989.

Kiechel, Walter, III. "No Word from on High." *Fortune* (January 6, 1986): 125–126.

Lyons, John. *Guts: Advertising from the Inside Out.* New York: AMACOM, 1989 (135 W. 50th St. 10020).

McGann, Anthony, and Thomas J. Russell. *Advertising Media.* Homewood, IL: Richard Irwin, 1987.

McNamara, Jay. *Advertising Agency Management.* Homewood, IL: Dow Jones-Irwin, 1990.

Sethi, S. Prakash. *Handbook of Advocacy Advertising Concepts, Strategies, and Applications.* Cambridge, MA: Ballinger, 1987.

CASE STUDY   The Bank That Cried "Wolf!"

In the fall of 1975, Chase Manhattan Bank told the world, through a series of advertisements in major national media, that it was very worried. The object of Chase's concern was an impending shortage of capital, which the bank thought threatened the nation. Chase said in its ads that the United States was "underinvesting $400 million each day," and that if that trend continued, there would be a shortfall of $1.5 trillion in 10 years.

Translated into common terms, that shortfall would mean a decline in growth and prosperity in the United States. To underscore its concern, Chase announced that it had decided to cry "Wolf!" and said it would debate the capital-formation argument anywhere and any time (Figure 12–10).

One person who wanted to take the bank up on its offer was a twenty-eight-year-old data-processing executive in Helena, Arkan-

"Wolf!"

The Chase is crying "Wolf!" Again. And we mean it. Again.

America is faced with a shortage of capital. Capital vital to the healthy growth this nation must have if it is to maintain and improve the living standards of all Americans.

In 1952, we published a study warning against government disincentives to the continuing search for natural gas. We raised more caution flags in 1956, 1957, and 1961 about industry's ability to continue "to deliver low-cost petroleum energy."

We were accused of crying "Wolf!" at that time. And indeed we were. But it was no pretense.

Our warnings were based on hard facts which became even harder with every disappearing drop of cheap imported oil.

Today we face an equally hard set of facts regarding the level of capital formation and mounting capital needs:

Fact 1: The next ten years will require twice as much capital as the past ten.

Fact 2: It will take a tremendous effort of husbanding sources and resources — far more than it took to win World War II or to put a man on the moon.

Fact 3: We will be lucky if there is as much as $2.6 trillion for building and rebuilding our industrial capacity.

Fact 4: Set against the needs of $4.1 trillion, there'll be a shortfall of $1.5 trillion.

Which means we will be under-investing $400 million a day every day for the next ten years.

The highest priority of our economy right now should lie in the nurture and stimulation of capital formation. Because everything the American people need and want grows out of that.

How do we deal with the problem? Chase proposes a six-part action program:

• Provide sufficient inducements for an ever-growing base of personal savings.

• Establish more realistic guidelines for depreciation allowances.

• Give preferential tax treatment for retained corporate earnings used for investment purposes.

• Ameliorate our relatively harsh treatment of capital gains compared with that of most other countries.

• Stabilize our monetary and fiscal policies to prevent violent swings in the economy.

• Eliminate unnecessary controls. And do away with outmoded government regulations and agencies that restrict our free market economy.

Capital formation must be government's business, businesses' business, labor's business, banking's business — everybody's business.

Your business.

CHASE

FIGURE 12–10 *(Courtesy of Chase Manhattan Bank)*

sas, Robert Sitarzewski. Seeing the Chase ads in a national magazine in September, Sitarzewski wrote Chase's chairman, David Rockefeller, saying, "You don't know what you're talking about." Sitarzewski then challenged the New York banker to a public debate.

After several weeks Mr. Sitarzewski received a response from Chase's corporate communications director advising him that although Mr. Rockefeller would not be able to debate, the bank's chief domestic economist would accept the challenge. And so the Great Debate was planned.

In the spring of 1976, Chase sent Richard Everett, vice-president and head of Chase's domestic economic policy unit, to Helena, via the bank's private jet. Everett was accompanied by several bank employees. The event attracted print and electronic media representatives from across the country. Network television covered. Wire services were represented. The *Washington Post* sent its reporter. So did the *New York Times*. As the wife of Helena's mayor put it, "This is the first time since the Civil War we've had this many Yankees in town."

During the debate, which took place in a local community college auditorium, Sitarzewski told the audience of about 600 that the free functioning of the market would allocate the nation's resources adequately. He said the bank's proposals to stimulate capital investment would "destroy the American capitalistic system." Everett parried that the federal government would have to provide more tax incentives for industry, encourage personal savings, and attract foreign investments "or the economy would suffer major setbacks."

And who won the Great Debate? Most of the hundreds of follow-up media accounts called the contest a draw. The Associated Press, however, quoted one member of the audience as saying, "Sitarzewski clearly won because he made the bank come to Helena, Arkansas."

QUESTIONS

1. Do you think the bank handled the challenge correctly?
2. How would you have modified Chase's response?
3. Do you agree with the audience member that Sitarzewski won the debate?
4. What do you think Chase got out of the debate?
5. From a public relations standpoint, was Chase correct in participating?

Tips from the Top

STEVE RIVKIN

Steve Rivkin is president of his own communications counseling firm in New York City. Before forming Rivkin & Associates, he was executive vice-president of Trout & Ries, Inc., the prestigious marketing strategy firm known for its pioneering work in "positioning." Before joining Trout & Ries in 1974, Rivkin worked in public affairs, advertising, and corporate identity for IU International Corp., a Philadelphia-based conglomerate. He was previously associate editor of *Iron Age Magazine,* a weekly business publication. Rivkin speaks and lectures frequently on communications topics.

What do you mean by "positioning" a company?
Positioning a company means getting into the mind of your prospect with a single, memorable concept or set of ideas about that company. The basic approach of positioning is not to create something new and different, but rather to manipulate what's already there, to retie the connections that already exist.

How do you go about positioning an individual company or product?
Positioning a company is actually thinking in reverse. Instead of starting with you or your company, you start with the prospect.

Step 1 is to research how your company is perceived in the minds of whatever marketplace is important to you. (Perception is more important than reality.) Don't rely on what management says the company's perceived image is. Your audience's answer may be 180 degrees away.

Step 2 is to get some internal consensus on what position you ideally want to occupy. (If everybody wants to face a different direction, it's going to be a very difficult march.)

Wishing alone won't make it so. So Step 3 is to find out who's in the way of obtaining your desired position. (Maybe you'd like to be known as the world's largest maker of digital widgets. Unfortunately, your competitor is the Global Widget Corp., with five times your revenues and three times your awareness.

Step 4 is money. Do you have enough money to make it happen? Communications is incredibly expensive today. It takes money to establish a position; it takes money to hold a position once you've established it.

Positioning is also a process that's cumulative. Step 5 is a willingness to hang in there with the same basic idea, year after year. Most successful companies rarely change a winning formula. (How many years have you seen those Marlboro men riding into the sunset? Crest has been fighting cavities for so long, they're into their third generation of kids.)

Finally, you should be sure that your carefully honed positioning strategy doesn't vanish in a cloud of confusion. Step 6 demands that everything you communicate match your position. (There's nothing more counterproductive than a speech before a securities analysts group that contradicts the message in the same day's *Wall Street Journal* advertisement.)

As long as an organization's products are good, why should it worry about its corporate image?

It shouldn't have to. (But whoever said life was fair?) In a multinational, multiproduct, multimedia world, getting noticed is getting tougher. Companies are buying and selling companies at a dizzying rate. Does the reputation of a product or brand automatically transfer along with stock ownership? For most companies, a corporate audience is different from a product audience. (Your banker may not buy your motor oil, but your garage owner isn't going to lend you $10 million, either.)

So, despite all the good things your product may do and may say about you, your corporate image may ultimately have to stand on its own two feet.

What about the role of names in the communications process?

What to name a company, product, or service may be the single most important communications decision you ever make. In the past, when the volume of communications was lower, a name wasn't nearly as significant. But today, there are 700,000 active trademarks in the United States, and more than twice that number actually registered. A lazy name won't be sharp enough to cut into the mind.

The best names set up a communications premise. They connect to some reality about the company, or they suggest some benefit of the product.

Good names should be distinct and unique, to differentiate you from the competition. They should be crisp and concise. They should be easy to use and understand. They should be pleasing to the eye and ear. They should have no negative connotations, either in slang, regional usage, or translation. And they should be available for ownership and legal registration.

Publicity is but one weapon in the arsenal of public relations professionals. The variety of promotional vehicles available to public relations people is limited only by the imagination of the practitioner.

Organizational periodicals can be as simple as a one-page, typewritten sheet or as visually uplifting as Washington University School of Medicine's *Outlook*.

♦ Comic books, such as The First Children's Bank's *The Buck Stops Here*, can be a friendly and memorable way to introduce children to products and services they will grow up with.

♦ A bit more revolutionary is the way Watt/Peterson color printers work to differentiate organizations in their printed materials. Watt/Peterson says it will "move mountains, if we have to," and the annual reports and brochures the firm produces reflect its innovative approach.

The next several pages illustrate the diversity of colorful promotional vehicles available to public relations professionals.

At New Retail Concepts, Inc., advertising was clearly an afterthought for "No Excuses" jeans. Publicity and promotion, however, took center stage.

No Excuses capitalized on the notoriety of women in the news—first, talk show host Joan Rivers; then, rumored Gary Hart paramour Donna Rice; and finally, Donald Trump's "used-to-be other woman," Marla Maples. Each became the focal point of No Excuses' tremendously successful publicity campaigns.

In 1990, No Excuses signed Ms. Maples to a one-year contract, reportedly for $600,000. The publicity value alone was worth the cost. But just to make sure, No Excuses bolstered its spokesperson with a $1 million advertising campaign. Said the firm's president, "We're hoping to attract the attention of our customers through the humor of these ads."

excuses. I just wear them."

—Donna Rice

no excuses.

Contact: Rena Franklin
Jeaneane Judelson
Roberta Greene
& Associates
(212) 753-4170

**NEW RETAIL CONCEPTS, INC. SIGNS MARLA MAPLES
TO APPEAR IN "NO EXCUSES" JEANS ADS**

New York, NY, May 24 -- New Retail Concepts, Inc. announced today that Marla Maples is the new spokesperson for No Excuses Jeans.

"The selection of Marla Maples is in keeping with the style and theme of our No Excuses campaign," said Neil Cole, president and founder of New Retail Concepts, Inc. "She projects the young, independent, intelligent image we want to project."

Integral to the Marla Maples No Excuses campaign will be an ongoing commitment to the Better World Society, a non-profit organization dedicated to making people aware of global problems that threaten our planet. New Retail Concepts and Marla Mapl will each donate $25,000 to this worthy cause. As the company looking to develop an environmental program, and as Ms. Maples looking for a company to support her interest in the environm was a natural.

In the 1990s, innovation and creativity are key to getting across organizational themes. The publications pictured here illustrate the lengths to which organizations must go to rise above the "clutter" of an overcommunicated society.

♦ Goldome Bank, in 1988, created a colorful, provocative, and eminently readable annual report that capitalized on the growing popularity of USA Today. The report was written in USA Today style—designed to be read. It stood head and shoulders above an otherwise uninspiring crop of annual reports.

♦ Atlantic Richfield, a pioneer in producing provocative publications, outdid itself with an employee update that looked suspiciously like a supermarket tabloid. Just as supermarket tabloids are snapped up weekly, so, too, was ARCO's Spark.

♦ In the same spirit, Union Carbide chimed in with a People magazine look-alike, entitled Pride. The "people" that Pride championed were the people of Union Carbide.

♦ Finally, in the blockbuster tradition of Indiana Jones, Levi Strauss employees, through this swashbuckling vehicle, became "Crusaders of the Golden Needle."

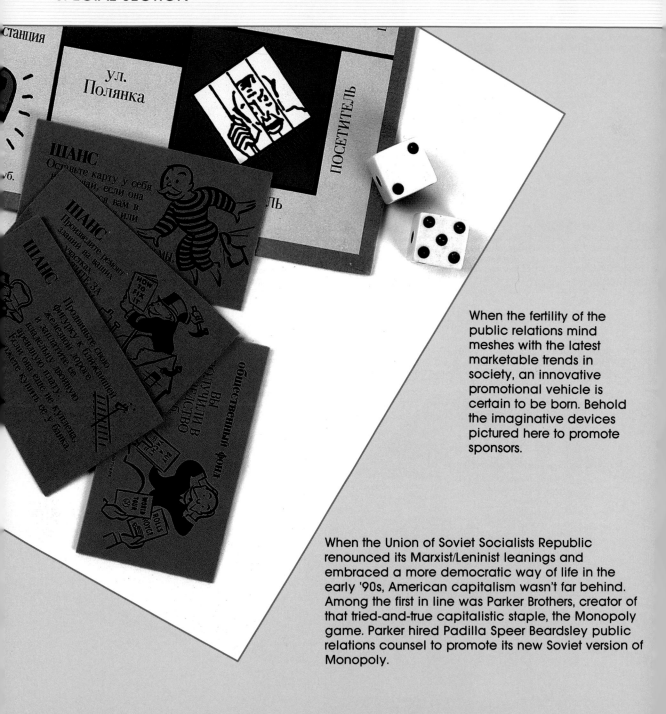

When the fertility of the public relations mind meshes with the latest marketable trends in society, an innovative promotional vehicle is certain to be born. Behold the imaginative devices pictured here to promote sponsors.

When the Union of Soviet Socialists Republic renounced its Marxist/Leninist leanings and embraced a more democratic way of life in the early '90s, American capitalism wasn't far behind. Among the first in line was Parker Brothers, creator of that tried-and-true capitalistic staple, the Monopoly game. Parker hired Padilla Speer Beardsley public relations counsel to promote its new Soviet version of Monopoly.

◆ In Seattle, entrepreneur Jeff Scott Cook seized the trend of increased organizational speech making by creating the CANNED SPEECH, which was just that: a pop-top tin can with ceremonial speech scripts, speaking tips for a compelling delivery, and, at no extra charge, an applause sign.

◆ Sports stars in the 1990s have used their extraordinary celebrity appeal to promote products from toilet tissue to toothpaste. Among the most popular pitchmen were football legend Joe Montana, who *doubled* his $4 million annual salary with promotional endorsements, and basketball great Magic Johnson, who *tripled* his $3 million annual salary with a string of lucrative promotional sponsorships.

THE FUTURE ACCORDING TO ALLEN

FOCUS □ FEBRUARY 1990 23

know, and
tell us first.
and such
but not until
ative technolo-
researchers in
ions that will jus-
ment.

at would you hope
Il Street Journal say
come 1990?
would hope they'd
us as a company
for its knowledge of
rs, and its technology,
's bringing leading-edge
tions to consumers and
ess people all over the
. I'd like to read that 10 of
best people had been stolen
some of the best companies,
cause we're that respected, and
at the stock price has contin-
ed to increase.

I hope people will look back
and say this was a company that
was a sleeping giant in the mid-
'80s, that demonstrated it could
change from a monopolist to a
fast-moving player in the global
marketplace.

—Kevin Compton

be
that
got
want.

FOCUS □ FEBRUARY 1990 25

SPECIAL SECTION

Mobil World

A worldwide newspaper for Mobil people
Vol. 25, No. 3
March 1989

Let's talk
Second annual employee dialogue with the chairman—Page

Without question, management in the 1990s must speak with "candor."
Employees today seek frankness and honesty from their supervisors. They
simply want the facts—the good as well as the bad.

The realization of this has spawned a new generation of more candid—
and colorful—employee newsletters.

◆ AT&T's *Focus* is the best of the lot. Featuring frank discussion about job-re-
lated issues, *Focus* contains a brutally honest Letters to the Editor section,
as well as frequent and frank messages from management.
◆ *Mobil World* is an equally candid and refreshing oil company newsletter
that downplays "puff" and emphasizes corporate reality.

A key reason for the straightforwardness and success of both *Focus* and
Mobil World is the wholehearted support each receives from its senior
management.

13

Publicity Techniques

No matter whether you work for the largest manufacturing company, the poorest politician, or the tiniest nonprofit organization, chances are good that if you are engaged in public relations work, attracting positive publicity will be among your primary responsibilities. Securing publicity is perhaps the best-known aspect of public relations work. Certainly, it is the function most associated with public relations. In fact, in most people's minds, publicity *is* public relations.

Publicity, through news releases and other methods, is designed to broaden knowledge and positive recognition of an organization, its personnel, and its activities. Publicity is most often gained by dealing directly with the media, either initiating the communication or reacting to inquiries. Publicity differs dramatically from advertising, despite the fact that most people confuse the two.

Advertising possesses the following characteristics:

1. You pay for it.
2. You control what is said.
3. You control how it is said.
4. You control to whom it is said.
5. To a degree, you control where it is put in a publication or on the air.
6. You control the frequency of its use.

Publicity, on the other hand, offers no such controls. Typically, publicity is subject to review by news editors, who may decide to use all of a story, some of it, or none of it. When it will run, who will see it, how often it will be used—all such factors are subject, to a large degree, to the whims of a news editor. However, even though publicity is by no means a sure thing, it does offer two overriding benefits that enhance its appeal, even beyond that of advertising.

♦ First, although not free, publicity costs only the time and effort expended by public relations personnel and management in attempting to place it in the media. Therefore, relatively speaking, its cost is minimal, especially when compared with the costs of advertising and assessed against potential returns.

♦ Second and most important, publicity, which appears in news rather than in advertising columns, carries the implicit endorsement of the publication in which it appears. In other words, publicity is perceived as objective news rather than self-serving promotion, which translates into the most sought-after of commodities for an organization: credibility. And this is the true value of publicity over advertising.

Securing Publicity

Gaining access to the media is a common problem among organizations wishing to attract positive publicity. People often complain that the media are more interested in bad news than in anything positive. To a degree, this complaint is valid. Although no two reporters or editors can agree on what constitutes news, more often than not, news is the sensational, the unusual, or the unexpected. And oftentimes for an organization, this equals bad news. Indeed, in recent years, large multinationals like Mobil Oil and Kaiser Aluminum have taken the unprecedented step of purchasing media air time to tell their side of a story.

Obviously, most organizations lack the resources to do this. But clearly, every organization yearns to earn positive mentions in the media. And this objective is indeed attainable. Overall, what's required is a basic, common sense knowledge of the media people with whom you're dealing and a sense of courtesy, responsiveness, and respect in dealing with them. It bears repeating: journalists—or at least most of them—are people, too. Treat them that way, and the goal of penetrating the print or broadcast barriers lies within reach. The next several pages offer specific suggestions for developing a positive relationship with the media.

Variety of Forms

Occasionally, events trigger an immediate need to disseminate company news. A sudden change in management, a fire or explosion at a plant, a labor strike or settlement—all engender the need for news publicity. In a more controlled sense, news publicity is used to announce plant openings, executive speeches, groundbreakings, charitable donations, major appointments, and product changes.

♦ **Feature** Less news-oriented material provides the media with features: personality profiles on management and company personnel, helpful hints from company experts, case studies of ongoing and successful company programs, innovative ways of opening up production bottle-necks, or unusual applications of new products. Practitioners also often help freelance writers in this task.

♦ **Financial** Generally, this material concerns earnings releases, dividend announcements, and other financial affairs. The Securities and Exchange Commission requires that all publicly held companies announce important financial information promptly, through the media and news wires.

♦ **Product** Publicizing new or improved products has enormous potential to aid bottom-line profits. However, such publicity should be used judiciously, so that the media do not feel that the organization is going overboard in attempting to boost sales.

♦ **Picture** The old maxim "A picture is worth a thousand words" is particularly true in public relations. Good photos can frequently tell a story about a new product or company announcement without the necessity of a lengthy news release. If an accompanying photo caption of three or four lines is pointed and provocative, the photo has an even greater chance of being used (Figure 13–1).

Avenues of Publicity

Many vehicles can be used for publicity purposes—from skywriting to pennysavers to the bullhorn at a political rally. The four most important avenues for publicity remain newspapers, magazines, radio, and television.

Newspapers

Even though television has become a major news disseminator, newspapers continue to hold their own as a news source. A survey by Audits & Surveys showed that television and newspapers were on a par in terms of cumulative daily exposure. Any day of the week, in fact, almost 70 percent of the adult population watches some television news and reads at least one newspaper.[1]

Newspapers provide more diversity and depth of coverage than television or radio. It may be for this reason that approximately 63 million copies of daily newspapers are sold each day. Newspapers range from giant dailies with circulations approaching two million to small weekly papers, written, edited, and produced by a single individual. There are approximately 1,626 daily newspapers in the United States, most of which are afternoon papers (Tables 13–1 and 13–2).

FIGURE 13—1 The more interesting the photo, the better chance it has of being used in the media. Once a photo appears in print, the reader often presumes that the publication (not the sponsoring agency) took the picture and therefore considers it news. These Kodak photos, which portray the company's exhibition at Florida's Epcot Center, are examples of excellent publicity photos. *(Photos courtesy of Eastman Kodak)*

In recent years, as operating costs have skyrocketed and many Americans have left central cities for the suburbs, some urban papers have folded. In such cities, traditional competition between the morning and evening newspapers has diminished. Occasionally, the same publishing firm owns both papers. The huge Rochester-based Gannett chain, for example, owns 97 daily newspapers reaching 6 million readers as well as 8 TV stations and 15 radio stations.

In 1982, Gannett launched its most ambitious project to date with the publication of *USA Today,* a truly national newspaper, transmitted from Rosslyn, Virginia, to major American cities via satellite. The paper costs Gannett upwards of $50 million per year. The full-color newspaper lists daily news from all 50 states; offers national weather, sports, and business; and downplays international news. Gannett's hope is that *USA Today* will become "America's hometown newspaper." Critics charge that *USA Today*'s abbreviated articles are fast-food journalism and derisively label the publication "McPaper." Nevertheless, its circulation has reached 1.3 million, second only to the *The Wall Street Journal.*

Despite the loss of journalistic competition in many cities, the newspaper is still a primary target for media relations activities. To practitioners and their managements, penetrating the daily with positive publicity is a critical challenge. To many corporate managements, favorable publicity in *The New York Times* is a special achievement. To politicians, a complimentary story in the *Washington Post* is equally cherished. In other communities, a positive piece in the local daily is just as rewarding.

One newspaper that is a frequent target for public relations professionals, particularly those who work for publicly held firms, is *The Wall Street Journal.* The *Journal,* commonly called the business bible, prints several daily editions for different geographic regions. Although its circulation is nearly two million, more than four million people a day read the paper because of high pass-along readership. The paper is put together by 500 reporters, 500 editors, and bureau chiefs worldwide. The average annual income of a *Journal* subscriber is close to $62,200. More than one-half of its readers are employed in professional or managerial occupations; 262,000 are company presidents. Thus, *The Wall Street Journal* is a prime target for public relations publicity initiatives, including all four U.S. editions and the Asian and European editions, as well.

Not to be overlooked in media relations are the suburban newspapers, the small-city dailies, and the nearly 7,500 weekly newspapers. All are targets for news releases and story ideas. When an organization has a branch or plant in an area, these local media contacts can be of critical importance, particularly for consumer product publicity.

Successful Placement   How does a practitioner place a story in a newspaper? After getting the release written, the following hints may help achieve placement.

Table 13–1

This table lists the 50 largest daily newspapers (according to 1990 daily circulation) in the United States. By September 30, 1990, the nation's largest daily circulation newspaper remained *The Wall Street Journal,* with slightly under two million readers daily. *USA Today,* published by Gannett Company, showed a strong circulation gain. *(Courtesy of American Newspaper Publishers Association)*

U.S. Newspapers with Highest Circulation

Newspaper	Average Daily Circulation
1. The Wall Street Journal	1,857,131
2. USA Today	1,347,450
3. Los Angeles Times	1,177,679
4. The New York Times	1,074,881
5. (New York) Daily News	1,057,361
6. The Washington Post	773,326
7. Chicago Tribune	703,015
8. Newsday	698,983
9. Detroit Free Press	636,182
10. San Francisco Chronicle	555,172
11. The Boston Globe	515,393
12. The Atlanta Journal/Constitution	512,396
13. The Philadelphia Inquirer	507,203
14. The Detroit News	500,980
15. Chicago Sun-Times	499,823
16. New York Post	484,768
17. The (Newark) Star-Ledger	468,376
18. Houston Chronicle	442,044
19. The (Cleveland) Plain Dealer	428,012
20. The Miami Herald	414,646
21. (Minneapolis) Star Tribune	407,441
22. The Dallas Morning News	397,555
23. St. Louis Post-Dispatch	377,827
24. The Orange County Register	352,165
25. (Denver) Rocky Mountain News	351,996

1. **Know deadlines.** Time governs every newspaper. *The New York Times* has different deadlines for different sections of the paper, with its business section essentially closing down between 6:00 and 7:00 P.M. News events should be scheduled, whenever possible, to accommodate deadlines. An old and despised practice (at least by journalists) is to announce bad news right around deadline time on Friday afternoon, the premise being that newspaper journalists won't have time to follow up on the story and that few people will read Saturday's paper anyway. Although this technique may work on occasion, it leaves reporters and editors hostile.

Table 13–1   continued

U.S. Newspapers with Highest Circulation

Newspaper	Average Daily Circulation
26. Boston Herald	346,912
27. The (Phoenix) Arizona Republic	330,706
28. The Houston Post	328,671
29. St. Petersburg Times	324,982
30. The (Portland) Oregonian	323,068
31. The Buffalo News	304,699
32. The Kansas City Star	287,345
33. San Jose Mercury News	275,839
34. The (New Orleans) Times-Picayune	275,811
35. The Orlando Sentinel	273,761
36. Tampa Tribune	270,360
37. The (Baltimore) Sun	265,672
38. The Milwaukee Journal	265,461
39. The San Diego Union	265,246
40. The Sacramento Bee	264,462
41. Fort Worth Star-Telegram	260,438
42. The Columbus (Ohio) Dispatch	250,572
43. The Denver Post	243,292
44. The Charlotte (N.C.) Observer	236,802
45. The Seattle Times	233,995
46. The (Louisville) Courier-Journal	233,714
47. (Norfolk) Virginian-Pilot/Star Ledger	232,318
48. The Indianapolis Star	228,582
49. The Hartford Courant	228,075
50. Dallas Times-Herald	227,758

SOURCE: Audit Bureau of Circulations, New York (September, 30 1990).

2. **Generally write, don't call.** Reporters are barraged with deadlines. They are busiest right around deadline time, late afternoon for morning newspapers and morning for afternoon papers. Thus, it's preferable to mail or send news releases by messenger rather than try to explain them over the telephone. Also, follow-up calls to reporters to "make sure you got our release" should be avoided. If reporters are unclear on a certain point, they'll call to check.

Table 13–2

This table lists the 20 largest newspaper companies (according to 1989 daily circulation) in the United States. The 82 dailies put out by Gannett reached more than six million readers every day. *(Courtesy of American Newspaper Publishers Association)*

20 Largest Newspaper Companies

Company	Daily Circulation	Number of Dailies
Gannett Co. Inc.	6,022,929	82
Knight-Ridder Inc.	3,794,809	28
Newhouse Newspapers	2,997,699	26
Times Mirror Co.	2,626,259	8
Tribune Co.	2,608,222	9
Dow Jones & Co. Inc.	2,409,955	23
Thomson Newspapers Inc.	2,127,123	122
The New York Times Co.	1,919,094	27
Scripps Howard	1,570,957	21
Cox Enterprises Inc.	1,280,040	18
Hearst Newspapers	1,207,089	13
Media News	1,123,552	19
Freedom Newspapers Inc.	938,862	27
Capital Cities/ABC Inc.	898,927	9
The Washington Post Co.	826,871	2
Central Newspapers Inc.	824,782	7
Donrey Media Group	790,982	57
Copley Newspapers	767,955	12
McClatchy Newspapers	753,558	11
The Chronicle Publishing Co.	742,410	6

SOURCE: Morton Research: Lynch, Jones & Ryan; Audit Bureau of Circulations. Average for six months ended September 30, 1989.

3. **Direct the release to a specific person or editor.** Newspapers are divided into departments: business, sports, style, entertainment, and the like. The release directed to a specific person or editor has a greater chance of being read than one addressed simply to "editor." In smaller papers, for example, one person may handle all financial news. At larger papers, the financial news section may have different editors for banking, chemicals, oil, electronics, and many other specialties. Public relations people should know who covers their beat and target releases accordingly.

Public relations professionals should also know the differences in the functions of newspaper personnel. For example, the publisher is the person responsible for overall newspaper policy. The editorial editor is generally responsible for editorial page content, including the opinion-editorial (oped) section. The managing editor is responsible for overall news content. These three should rarely, if ever, be called to secure publicity. That leaves the various section editors and reporters as key contacts for public relations practitioners.

4. **Make personal contact.** Knowing a reporter may not result in an immediate story, but it can pay residual dividends. Those who know the local weekly editor or the daily city editor have an advantage over colleagues who don't. Also, when a reporter uses your story idea, follow up with a note of commendation—particularly on the story's accuracy.

5. **Don't badger.** Newspapers are generally fiercely independent about the copy they use. Even a major advertiser will usually fail to get a piece of puffery published. Badgering an editor about a certain story is bad form, as is complaining excessively about the treatment given a certain story. Worst of all, it achieves little to act outraged when a newspaper chooses not to run a story. Editors are human beings, too. For every release they use, dozens get discarded. If a public relations person protests too much, editors will remember.

6. **Use exclusives sparingly.** Sometimes public relations people promise exclusive stories to particular newspapers. The exclusive promises one newspaper a scoop over its competitors. For example, practitioners frequently arrange to have a visiting executive interviewed by only one local newspaper. Although the chances of securing a story are heightened by the promise of an exclusive, there is a risk of alienating the other papers. Thus, the exclusive should be used sparingly.

7. **When you call, do your own calling.** Reporters and editors generally don't have assistants. Most do not like to be kept waiting by a secretary calling for the boss. Public relations professionals should make their own initial and follow-up calls. Letting a secretary handle a journalist can alienate a good news contact. And above all, be pleasant and courteous.

Magazines

Although magazine publishing experienced a renaissance in the 1980s, the decade of the 90s confronts publishers with a number of vexing problems. Profit margins are being squeezed as advertisers bargain harder for special rates. After years of selling cut-rate subscriptions and bargain cover prices, many magazines don't have the circulation revenue to fall back on. Meanwhile the U.S. Postal Service continues to increase rates. Add to this a downturn in economic activity, and it all spells trouble for the magazine business in the 1990s.[2]

Nonetheless, there are approximately 11,000 magazines published in the United States. They range from gossip-oriented publications, such as *People* and *Us*, to publications a bit farther afield, such as *Wet*, "the magazine of

Table 13–3

This table lists the leading magazines in terms of circulation, compiled by the Magazine Publishers of America. *Modern Maturity* and *NRTA/AARP Bulletin* are both beamed at the growing senior citizens market. *(Courtesy of Magazine Publishers of America)*

50 Leading A.B.C. Magazines

Rank	Magazine	Subscription Circulation	% Change From Jan–Jun '89
1	MODERN MATURITY	22,443,464	10.4
2	NRTA/AARP NEWS BULLETIN	22,105,308	10.5
3	READER'S DIGEST	15,488,919	−0.1
4	NATIONAL GEOGRAPHIC MAGAZINE	10,102,385	−6.1
5	TV GUIDE	8,861,412	−1.6
6	BETTER HOMES AND GARDENS	7,477,561	0.4
7	MCCALL'S	4,620,529	0.7
8	GUIDEPOSTS	4,131,548	−2.5
9	LADIES' HOME JOURNAL	4,113,036	0.1
10	TIME-THE WEEKLY NEWSMAGAZINE	4,061,606	−2.7
11	GOOD HOUSEKEEPING	3,720,004	1.2
12	SPORTS ILLUSTRATED	3,339,364	−6.6
13	REDBOOK	3,212,140	3.2
14	NEWSWEEK	3,050,064	−2.2
15	THE AMERICAN LEGION MAGAZINE	2,858,405	−0.5
16	PREVENTION	2,694,772	−3.5
17	PLAYBOY	2,603,895	1.4
18	SMITHSONIAN	2,280,350	−1.4
19	U.S. NEWS & WORLD REPORT	2,251,807	0.4
20	SOUTHERN LIVING	2,127,420	1.2
21	FIELD & STREAM	1,920,298	−0.6
22	NEA TODAY	1,915,891	9.0
23	FAMILY CIRCLE	1,912,308	26.3
24	MOTORLAND	1,902,234	3.6
25	HOME & AWAY	1,882,064	6.0

gourmet bathing;" *Chocolate News*, a bimonthly featuring every imaginable form of chocolate; and perhaps the strangest of all, the *Quayle Quarterly*, dedicated exclusively to tracking the exploits and malapropisms of America's favorite vice-president, Dan Quayle.

Most magazines can be classified into general interest, news, quality, business-oriented, trade, men's/women's interest, and special interest.

♦ **General interest**   These magazines are aimed at the entire population and are designed to appeal to all groups. The two largest are *Reader's Digest* and *TV Guide*. Although different in format and treatment, they both appeal to millions of readers.

Table 13-3   continued

50 Leading A.B.C. Magazines

Rank	Magazine	Subscription Circulation	% Change From Jan–Jun '89
26	V.F.W. MAGAZINE	1,861,182	1.8
27	MONEY	1,659,948	8.1
28	DISCOVERY	1,621,268	1.5
29	POPULAR SCIENCE	1,603,638	−0.4
30	PARENTS MAGAZINE	1,603,464	−0.6
31	1,001 HOME IDEAS	1,596,204	5.3
32	EBONY	1,593,341	3.2
33	PEOPLE WEEKLY	1,485,624	−3.9
34	THE ELKS MAGAZINE	1,459,251	−2.8
35	BOYS' LIFE	1,434,486	−0.4
36	OUTDOOR LIFE	1,412,761	1.7
37	THE AMERICAN RIFLEMAN	1,398,666	−1.5
38	POPULAR MECHANICS	1,360,710	−2.9
39	SEVENTEEN	1,319,588	0.0
40	SUNSET, THE MAGAZINE OF WESTERN LIVING	1,311,389	−0.4
41	THE AMERICAN HUNTER	1,284,762	−9.0
42	SESAME STREET MAGAZINE	1,271,403	4.6
43	THE FAMILY HANDYMAN	1,267,775	−10.9
44	BON APPETIT	1,266,859	1.4
45	THE WORKBASKET	1,232,506	−4.5
46	LIFE	1,220,306	4.6
47	GOLF DIGEST	1,211,461	0.9
48	COUNTRY LIVING	1,182,021	2.3
49	HOME MECHANIX	1,159,103	0.5
50	CHANGING TIMES	1,147,372	11.2

♦ **News** These weeklies summarize news events, provide background, and add depth to evolving stories. *Time, Newsweek,* and *U.S. News and World Report* dominate this group. *Time,* the first news magazine, made its debut in 1923 and now has a circulation in excess of four million.

♦ **Quality** These publications are targeted to a more selective readership. *Smithsonian, National Geographic, Harper's, Saturday Review,* and *The New Yorker* are examples. Often these magazines offer more scholarly writing than news magazines do. Some, such as *The Nation* and *The New Republic,* have more limited circulations but command national respect as journals of political insight.

◆ **Business-oriented** *Forbes, Business Week, Money, Working Woman, Fortune,* and *Barron's* are among the fastest-growing of all periodicals. All influence the attitudes of the nation's business leadership and are the objects of considerable public relations activity. One area of rapid growth is that of regional business journals. Indeed, the Association of Area Business Publications, organized in late 1978 with 14 members, soon had 50 publishers with a combined circulation in 60 tabloids and magazines of more than 900,000. And there were perhaps another 30 to 40 similar publications across the nation ready to join the group. As the association's executive director explained the boom, "It's very simple. There's a tremendous hunger for local and regional business news. The national business publications can't possibly begin to touch it. And the local dailies, for the most part, do a very poor job."[3]

◆ **Trade** Magazines such as *Advertising Age, Supermarket Age, Iron Age, Convenience Store News, Metalworking News,* and many others are trade-oriented and are important publicity targets for practitioners serving in specific fields. Most of these are avidly read in the industry.

◆ **Men's/women's interest** These magazines cater specifically to either the men's or women's market. For example, *Playboy* and *Penthouse* are clearly designed for men, whereas *Cosmopolitan, Vogue, Glamour,* and *Playgirl* are aimed at women. Teenage girls have *Seventeen, Teen, Model,* and *Sassy,* which sport headlines like "Losing Your Virginity—Read This Before You Decide." One recent trend in these magazines has been toward body toning. A clutch of new titles—*Shape, Fit, Pretty Body,* and

---

B E T W E E N   T H E   L I N E S

Handling the Media

How well would you do if asked to go toe-to-toe with a reporter? Take this yes-or-no quiz, borrowed from *Public Relations Reporter,* and find out. Answers are found below.

1. When addressing a print reporter or electronic moderator, should you use his or her first name?
2. Should you ever challenge a reporter in a verbal duel the way President Bush did with Dan Rather? (See this chapter's case study.)
3. Are reporters correct in thinking they can ask embarrassing questions of anyone in public office?
4. Should you answer a hypothetical question?
5. Should you ever say, "No comment"?

6. When a reporter calls on the telephone, should you assume the conversation is being taped?
7. Do audiences remember most of the content of a TV interview 30 minutes after it is broadcast?
8. Should you ever admit you had professional training to handle the media?
9. If you don't know the correct answer to a reporter's question, should you try to answer it anyway?

Bonus Question:
What did Henry Kissinger say at the start of his press briefings as secretary of state?

Answers

1. Yes. In most cases, using first names is the best strategy. It makes the discussion much more conversational and less formal than using Mr. or Ms.
2. No. Bush had one objective—to get votes. He gained votes by "de-wimping" himself and by attacking Rather. Most people, though, try to gain goodwill in an interview. This is rarely achieved by getting into an acrimonious debate.
3. Yes. Journalists must be suspicious of any claim by a public person that he or she is telling not only the truth, but the whole truth. Anyone in public office must be prepared to respond to such questions.
4. No. Avoid hypothetical questions. Rarely can you win by dealing with them.
5. No. It is tantamount to taking the Fifth Amendment against self-incrimination. You appear to be hiding something.
6. Yes. Many state laws no longer require the "beep" that signals a taped call. Always assume everything you say is being recorded and will be used.
7. No. Studies have found audiences remember only 60 percent of the content after 30 minutes. They remember 40 percent at the end of the day and 10 percent by the end of the week.
8. Yes. By all means. You should point out that good communications with the public is a hallmark of your organization, and that you're proud it has such a high priority.
9. No. Don't be afraid to say, "I don't know." Offer to find the answer and get back to the interviewer. Don't dig yourself into a hole you can't get out of.

Bonus Answer:
"Does anyone have any questions . . . for my answers?"

Slimmer—have taken their place next to the more traditional *Better Homes and Gardens, Ladies' Home Journal, Ms.,* and *Mademoiselle.* All, once again, are excellent outlets for potential public relations placements.

♦ **Special interest** These periodicals target virtually every special interest group: black life-style—*Ebony* and *Jet;* science—*Popular Mechanics* and *Scientific American;* farming—*Farm Journal;* journalism—*The Quill* and *Editor & Publisher;* sports—*Sports Illustrated, Sport,* and *Runner;* success—*Vanity Fair, GQ,* and *Smart;* aviation—*Flying, Air Cargo,* and *Aviation Week;* and on and on. And this doesn't include magazines for airline passengers, homosexuals, classic car owners, apartment dwellers, divorced persons, and marijuana smokers. Even *Wet* has 45,000 regular readers.

Successful Placement How does one take advantage of the magazine boom? Magazine placement differs from newspaper placement in a number of ways. For one thing, magazines have longer lead times than newspapers: stories take longer to get printed, so articles must be less time-oriented than daily press material and must be written more in a feature style. They must also be scheduled further in advance. Here are five general suggestions for attempting to place publicity in magazines.

1. **Choose target publications carefully.** Know what the magazine uses. Read and study back issues for at least six months to determine whether your subject fits.

2. **Innovate.** Magazines like creative ideas and shun run-of-the-mill material. Suggest new approaches and break new ground. Retreaded news releases seldom have a chance.

3. **Take care with the cover letter.** A short cover letter can help sell a story idea. The letter should state simply why it's in the magazine's best interest to publish the suggested story. The letter should be just thorough enough to interest the editor and make the sale without supplying the finished article.

4. **Use exclusives.** With public relations material, many magazines insist on exclusives. For example, *Time* may not accept a feature idea or a by-lined guest column from an executive if *Newsweek* has already run such an article from the same executive. As a matter of courtesy and prudence, practitioners should seek only one placement per story idea in a particular magazine category. If the idea is rejected by the first choice, the practitioner should then approach the next choice.

5. **Use freelancers.** Magazines frequently buy articles from freelance writers. Some freelancers know magazine editors well enough to have a feel for what the editors like. A practitioner should stay in contact with freelancers, who are willing recipients of story ideas that can then be marketed by the writers to magazine editors.

Radio and Television

For more than two decades, radio was the nation's dominant electronic news source. Then came television, and radio slipped into a subordinate position. Although the golden years of radio may have passed, the medium is still important as a news source. Here are the facts according to the Radio Advertising Bureau.

♦ There are more than 527 million radios in the United States.
♦ There are 5.6 radios per household.
♦ Ninety-nine percent of all homes and 97 percent of all cars have radios.
♦ Nearly half of all American adults turn to radio as their first source of news in the morning.[4]

As TV has taken on the entertainment characteristics of radio, radio has moved more strongly into news dissemination. At least one all-news radio station is available in major cities, broadcasting a constant stream of news around the clock. Several radio networks—including ABC, NBC, CBS, and Mutual—compete to service the approximately 6,000 stations in the United States. Radio journalists are often receptive to the story ideas of public relations people.

Television also offers a variety of opportunities, particularly on the local level, for groups to tell their stories through film, videotape, and on-the-air interviews. As noted, there are about 1,500 television stations in the United States. Each week night about 44 million Americans get their news from one of the three major television network shows.

Additionally, the networks, local stations, and public broadcasting all feature interview programs to complement nightly news shows. Also, with cable television introducing a host of business and economics-oriented programs, the networks, too, have begun to increase their quantity of business and economic news. Unfortunately, many Americans think that by watching TV, they are getting all the news. TV news personnel are the first to admit that their coverage is, of necessity, capsulized and condensed. The typical 30-minute show provides fewer than 20 minutes of news coverage. In terms of words, a TV news show would fill only about one-half page of the average daily newspaper. When Edward R. Murrow was reminded of this fact by a listener, he changed his opening from "This is the news" to "This is *some* of the news." People who rely solely on television for their news are missing much of what's happening in the world, the nation, and their own community.

Film and videotape are the special appeals of television and are used liberally to heighten the impact of stories. Practitioners should be aware that occasionally an important story that lacks film may be limited in its air time, whereas a less important one with film may receive greater play. This, of course, helps influence people's judgments about the relative importance of specific news. Indeed, broadcasters are often faulted by their critics for using faulty judgment in visually biasing viewers with only one side of a story.

Nonetheless, TV's growth is indisputable. The growth of cable television in the 1990s promises to be formidable. Without question, the most stunning development in cable television is the way the Cable News Network (CNN) has become the world's real-time, 24-hour-a-day primary news source. Entrepreneur Ted Turner's brainchild—which competitors mocked as "Chicken Noodle Network" when it began a decade ago—today boasts a domestic U.S. audience of 56 million homes, an international viewership in more than seven million homes and 250,000 hotel rooms outside the U.S., news bureaus in 25 world cities, and availability in 105 countries. When Americans were trapped in Kuwait in the fall of 1990, they watched CNN to determine their next move. So did President Bush. And so, too, did Iraqi President Saddam Hussein, who crafted statements especially for CNN to satellite back to American officials.[5] The growth of cable television in general and CNN in particular has created enormous new possibilities for publicity placement for public relations professionals.

Successful Placement   The public relations professional can approach radio and television similarly for publicity placement, using these guidelines:

1. **Generally call, don't write.** Radio and television are more telephone-oriented than newspapers are. To begin each day, radio news directors and television assignment editors plot their staff assignments. A phone call to these people—and generally not to reporters or correspondents themselves—during their early scheduling periods may evoke some interest. However, most news directors appreciate advance warning, so an early letter about an upcoming event may be a good idea.

2. **Keep the story simple.** Radio and TV don't have the editorial space that newspapers and magazines offer. Rarely does a radio story last one minute—the equivalent of perhaps a page and a half of triple-spaced copy. Television stories may be a bit longer, but not much. Therefore, the more succinct a story is, the better.

3. **Know deadlines.** Deadlines in radio and TV may be even stricter than in newspaper work. Unless a TV story can be filmed or taped in time to return for the six o'clock news (ideally, mid-morning), it will be useless. Radio offers greater flexibility because interviews can be taped on-the-scene or on the telephone and aired immediately. Frequently, short interview snatches or "actualities" from longer interviews are aired. In any event, it's a good idea to schedule radio and TV publicity early enough in the day to avoid running up against competition from unexpected breaking news.

4. **For TV, be visual.** TV assignment editors are rarely interested in nonvisual stories. Talking heads (shots of people moving their mouths

FIGURE 13—2 Television is always looking for a visual angle. And that's just what Guinness World of Records and its public relations counselor, Dorf & Stanton, came up with in the spring of 1988 to publicize the opening of the renovated Guinness World of Records in New York City. Specifically, they had Bruce Block, holder of the record for cigar box balancing, demonstrate his talent. And the cameras rolled to the tune of 15,470,000 viewers reached through television coverage. *(Courtesy of Guinness World of Records/Dorf & Stanton Communications)*

and nothing else) are anathema to TV producers. On the other hand, stories that offer dramatic, interesting visuals may have a good chance of being used (Figure 13–3).

5. **Get to know the talent coordinator/producer.** In placing clients on radio and television talk shows, it helps to know the people who book the talent. Talk shows are excellent vehicles through which to discuss products, books, or ideas. Earning the trust of the talent coordinator or producer will help ensure that invitations continue to appear (Figure 13–3).

Wire Services

Traditionally, two news-gathering organizations formed the backbone of the nation's news delivery system, supplying up-to-the-minute dispatches from around the world to both the print and electronic media. The Associated Press (AP) and United Press International (UPI) wire services compete to deliver the most accurate news first. The AP serves more than

FIGURE 13–3 In the 1990s, TV talk shows dominated the airwaves. From Oprah Winfrey to Geraldo Rivera, from Morton Downey to Larry King—talk shows were eager to air the clients of public relations professionals. Among the most popular of talk shows was "Donahue." Host Phil Donahue interviewed people like public relations client Gary Hirmer of Group Health, Inc., who taught men how to deal with women experiencing premenstrual syndrome. *(Courtesy of Padilla Speer Beardsley)*

15,000 worldwide clients—newspapers, magazines, TV, and radio stations—through 220 bureaus around the country and the world. UPI, which experienced financial problems in 1986, has far fewer subscribers. Both wire services report in a simple, readable, understandable style.

Staging as intense a rivalry on the financial side are two business wires—Dow Jones and Reuters. These wires specialize in business-oriented news. Reuters, based in London, is a worldwide business service plus a general news service. Dow Jones, whose flagship publication is *The Wall Street Journal,* also has an international affiliate in AP-Dow Jones.

When a company releases news that may influence the decision of an investor to hold, sell, or buy the company's stock, it is required to release the information promptly to the broadest group of investors. In such an instance, Dow Jones, Reuters, and the local press are notified simultaneously. Dow Jones and Reuters news wires, like those of AP and UPI, are found in newspaper offices, brokerage firms, banks, investment houses, and many corporate offices throughout the country.

Additionally, commercial wire services, such as PR News Wire and Business Wire, distribute public relations material to news outlets nationwide. Unlike AP and UPI, these commercial wires charge organizations a fee for running news release stories verbatim on their wires. Such commercial wires serve as an effective backup, ensuring that announcements at least reach news outlets.

Feature syndicates, such as North American Newspaper Alliance and King Features, are another source of editorial material for newspapers and magazines. They provide subscribing newspapers with a broad spectrum of material, ranging from business commentaries to comic strips to gossip columns. Some of their writers—such as Art Buchwald, Jack Anderson, and Jane Bryant Quinn— have built national reputations. Many such columnists depend heavily on source material provided by public relations personnel.

Media Directories

Another publicity support is the media directory, which describes in detail the various media.

1. *Gale's Directory of Publications* lists about 20,000 publications, including daily and weekly newspapers as well as general circulation, trade, and special interest magazines. *Gale's* also includes the names, addresses, and phone numbers of publication editors.

2. *Bacon's Publicity Checker* provides data on almost 5,000 U.S. and Canadian trade and business publications, organized in some 100 categories—from accounting and advertising to woolens and yachting. *Bacon's* includes editors, addresses, and phone numbers.

3. *Broadcasting Yearbook* contains information on radio and TV stations in the United States, Canada, and Latin America. It also lists key personnel, addresses, and telephones.

4. *Editor & Publisher Yearbook* lists newspapers across the United States (daily, weekly, national, black, college and university, foreign language) and their personnel.

5. *Working Press of the Nation* is a five-volume effort. It lists locations and editorial staff for the following media: newspapers, magazines, radio, television, feature writers, syndicates, and house magazines.

6. Specialized directories—from *Hudson's Washington News Media Directory* and *Congressional Staff Guide* to the *Anglo-Jewish Media List*—and various state media directories, published by state press or broadcasters' associations, are also excellent resources for publicity purposes. Appendix C offers a comprehensive list of leading media directories, compiled from *O'Dwyer's PR Services Report*.

Measurement Assistance

After an organization has distributed its press materials, it needs an effective way to measure the results of its publicity. A variety of outside services can help.

Press Clipping Bureaus

Some agencies will monitor company mentions in the press. These press clipping bureaus can supply newspaper and magazine clippings on any subject and about any company. The two largest, Burrelle's and Luce, each receive hundreds of newspapers and magazines daily. Both services dispatch nearly 50,000 clippings to their clients each day. Burrelle's, for example, employs about 800 people and subscribes to about 1,700 daily newspapers, 8,300 weeklies, 6,300 consumer and trade magazines, and various other publications.

These bureaus may also be hired in certain regions to monitor local news or for certain projects that require special scrutiny. Most charge $200 monthly fees plus $1.00 per clipping. For a practitioner who must keep management informed of press reports on the firm, the expense is generally worthwhile.

Broadcast Transcription Services

Specialized transcription services have arisen to monitor broadcast stories. A handful of such broadcast transcription services exist in the country, the largest being Radio-TV Reports, with offices in several cities.

This firm monitors all major radio and TV stations around the clock, checking for messages concerning client companies. After a client orders a particular segment of a broadcast program, Radio-TV Reports either prepares a typed transcript or secures an audiotape. Costs for transcripts are relatively high.

Content Analysis Services

A more sophisticated analysis of results in the media is supplied by firms that evaluate the content of media mentions concerning clients. Firms such as Ketchum Public Relations and PR Data use computer analysis to discern positive and negative mentions about organizations. Although this measurement technique is rough and somewhat subjective, it nevertheless enables an organization to get a clearer idea about how it is being portrayed in the media. However, such press-clipping computer analysis stops short of being a true test of audience attitudes.

Handling Interviews

Public relations people coordinate interviews for both print and broadcast media. Most executives are neither familiar with nor comfortable in such interview situations. For one thing, reporters ask a lot of searching questions, some of which may seem impertinent. Executives aren't used to being put on the spot. Instinctively, they may resent it. So the counseling of executives for interviews has become an important and strategic task of the in-house practitioner, as well as a lucrative profession for media consultants.

Print Interviews

The following 10 do's and don'ts are important in newspaper, magazine, or other print interviews.

1. **Do your homework in advance.** An interviewee must be thoroughly briefed—either verbally or in writing—before the interview. Know what the interviewer writes, for whom she writes, and what her opinions are. Also determine what the audience wants to know.

2. **Relax.** Remember that the interviewer is a person, too, and is just trying to do a good job. Building rapport will help the interview.

3. **Speak in personal terms.** People distrust large organizations. References to "the company" and "we believe" sound ominous. Use "I" instead. Speak as an individual, as a member of the public, rather than as a mouthpiece for an impersonal bureaucracy.

4. **Welcome the naive question.** If the question sounds simple, it should be answered anyway. It may be helpful to those who don't possess much knowledge of the organization or industry.

5. **Answer questions briefly and directly.** Avoid rambling. Be brief, concise, and to the point. An interviewee shouldn't get into subject areas about which he knows nothing. This situation can be dangerous and counterproductive when words are transcribed in print.

6. **Don't bluff.** If a reporter asks a question that you can't answer, admit it. If there are others in the organization more knowledgeable about a particular issue, the interviewee or the practitioner should point that out and get the answer.

7. **State facts and back up generalities.** Facts and examples always bolster an interview. An interviewee should come armed with specific data that support general statements. Again, the practitioner should furnish all the specifics.

8. **If the reporter is promised further information, get it to her quickly.** Remember, reporters work under time pressures and need information quickly to meet deadlines. Anything promised in an interview should be granted soon. Conveniently forgetting to answer a request may return to haunt the organization when the interview is printed.

9. **There is no such thing as off-the-record.** A person who doesn't want to see something in print shouldn't say it. It's that simple. Reporters may get confused as to what was off-the-record during the interview. And although most journalists will honor an off-the-record statement, some may not. Usually, it's not worth taking the risk. Occasionally, reporters will agree not to attribute a statement to the interviewee but to use it as background. Mostly, though, interviewees should be willing to have whatever they say in the interview appear in print.

10. **Tell the truth.** Telling the truth is the cardinal rule. Journalists are generally perceptive; they can detect a fraud. So don't be evasive, don't cover up, and, most of all, don't lie. Be positive, but be truthful. Occasionally, an interviewee must decline to answer specific questions but should candidly explain why. This approach always wins in the long run.[6]

YOU MAKE THE CALL

"Over The Top" with Donald

Sometimes reporters get the story wrong.

When they do, what does a public relations professional do? Ignore the mistake? Call the reporter on it? Or go over the reporter's head—"over the top" if you will?

To wit, this real-life case-in-point involves a certain friendly lending institution and one Donald Trump, a most public builder who fell on turbulent times in the summer of 1990.

- On Monday morning, Dan Dorfman, a popular gossip-mongering financial journalist, wrote in *USA Today*, "Chase Manhattan Bank, I am told, has called in a loan of roughly $100 million to Donald Trump on an undeveloped 78-acre Manhattan property."

  Monday afternoon, a *USA Today* reporter called for the bank's response. Chase, like most firms, has an inviolate policy that forbids revealing confidential information about customers. So even though the printed story on Trump was flat wrong, the bank held to its policy and responded with a firm, "No comment."
- On Tuesday, *USA Today* reported again that "Chase Manhattan Bank had no comment" on the report that it called in the $100 million loan to Trump. The story went on to talk about the "scoop" its columnist had reported the day before.
- On Wednesday, Trump was scheduled to appear on an ABC-TV network interview program. His interviewer—an erstwhile White House press corps pain-in-the-butt named Sam Donaldson—called Chase for comment. Donaldson was told "off the record" that the story was false. That night's broadcast made no mention of the so-called "called" Chase loan.
- On Thursday, *USA Today* called again. This time Chase told the reporter "off the record" that the report in the Monday column was false. Chase suggested that the paper report the denial from "informed sources."

  The bank should have saved its breath.
- On Friday, *USA Today* ran a front-page story on Trump, repeating the original story that Chase had called in the $100 million Trump loan. The story went on to say that even though Trump himself had "denied the report, Chase Manhattan won't comment."

So at the end of the week—despite the bank's off-the-record attempts to put the matter to rest—Chase and Trump still looked guilty.

In the words of Bart Simpson, "Ay caramba!"

The choice for Chase, as it sifted through the wreckage of the week, was whether to shelve its proprietary policy, forget reasoning with the reporters who got it into this mess, and go "over the top" to the paper's editor.

QUESTIONS

1. Would you go "over the top?"
2. What are the risks if you do?
3. Would you keep your conversation with the editor "off the record"?
4. If you speak "on the record," what are the implications for the customer-confidentiality policy?

Broadcast Interviews

As the broadcast media, particularly television, have become more potent channels of news to the public, executives are being called on to appear on news and interview shows to air their viewpoints. For the uninitiated and the unprepared, a TV interview can be a harrowing experience.

To be effective on TV takes practice. Executives and public relations people must accept guidance on acting appropriately before the camera. In recent years, elaborate programs have been constructed by counseling firms to teach executives how to act on TV. The following 11 do's and don'ts may help.

1. **Do prepare.** Preparation is the key to successful broadcast appearances. Executives should know the main points they wish to make before the interview begins. They should know the audience. They should know who the reporter is and something about the reporter's beliefs. They should also rehearse answering tough hypothetical questions before entering the studio.

2. **Do be yourself.** Interviewees should appear relaxed. Smiles are appropriate. Nonverbal signs of tension (clenched fists, gripping the arms of a chair, or tightly holding one hand with the other) should be avoided. Gesturing with palms open, on the other hand, suggests relaxation and an eagerness to discuss issues. Giggling, smoking, or chewing gum should be avoided during the interview. Proper posture is also important.

3. **Do be open and honest.** Television magnifies everything, especially phoniness. If facts are twisted, it will show. On TV a half-truth becomes a half-lie. Credibility should be established early.

4. **Do be brief.** TV and radio have no time for beating around the bush. Main points must be summarized at the beginning of sentences. English must be understandable; neither the reporter nor the public can be expected to be familiar with technical jargon.

5. **Do play it straight; be careful with humor.** An interviewee can't be giddy, vacuous, or irreverent. Attempts to be a comic may be interpreted as being foolish. However, the natural and relaxed use of appropriate humor may be a big plus for getting a point across. If humor does not come naturally, interviewees should play it straight. That way, they won't look stupid.

6. **Do dress for the occasion.** Bold patterns, checks, or pinstripes should be avoided; so should jewelry that shines or glitters. Skirts should fall easily below a woman's knees. Men's socks should be high enough to prevent a gap between socks and pants. Colors on shirts, socks, suits, and accessories should generally be muted.

7. **Don't assume the interviewer is out to get you.** Arguments or hostilities come through clearly on TV. In a discussion on a controver-

sial subject with a professional interviewer, the guest usually comes out looking like the bad guy. All questions, even naive ones, should be treated with respect and deference. If an interviewee becomes defensive, it will show.

8. **Don't think everything you say will be aired.** TV is a quick and imperfect medium. When Equitable Life Assurance fired several hundred managers, a reporter spent hours chatting with top Equitable executives. That evening 30 seconds' worth of interviews was aired. In other words, to make a point on TV, one needs to be brief and direct in responses.

9. **Don't let the interviewer dominate.** Interviewees can control the interview by varying the length and content of their responses. If a question requires a complicated answer, the interviewee should clarify that before getting trapped in an incomplete and misleading response. If interviewees make mistakes, they should correct them and go on. If they don't understand a question, they should ask for clarification.

10. **Don't say, "No comment."** "No comment" sounds evasive (Figure 13–4). If interviewees can't answer certain questions, they should clearly explain why. Begging off for competitive or proprietary reasons is perfectly allowable as long as some explanation is offered.

11. **Do stop.** One regularly practiced broadcast technique is to leave cameras running and mikes on even after an interviewee has responded to a question. Often the most revealing, misleading, and damaging statements are made by interviewees embarrassed by the silence. They should not fall for the bait; silence can always be edited out later. The interviewer knows that, and the interviewee should, too, before getting trapped.

These are just a few hints about dealing with what often turns out to be a difficult situation for the uninitiated. In general, the best advice for an interviewee is to be natural, straight, and prepared.

Press Conferences

Press conferences, the convening of the media for a specific purpose, are generally not a good idea. Unless an organization has real news to communicate, press conferences can flop. Reporters don't have the time for meetings offering little news. Therefore, before attempting a conference, ask this question: Can this information be disseminated just as easily in a news release? If the answer is yes, the conference should be scratched.

Eventually, though, every organization must face the media in a conference—in connection with an annual meeting or a major announcement or a presentation to securities analysts. The same rules and guidelines hold true for dealing with the press in conference as in a one-on-one

FIGURE 13—4 Typical of an enlightened media relations attitude is this ad by Adolph Coors Co., a firm that once had been criticized in the media as espousing a particularly silent posture. *(Courtesy of Adolph Coors Co.)*

We used to say no comment.

Now we're asking for your questions.

For years at Adolph Coors Company we were quiet about our business. We paid our people to tell the media, "No comment."

Not that we had anything to hide. Just the opposite. Since that first barrel of Coors beer was brewed in 1873 we've taken great pride in the quality of our product, in our concern for the community, the environment, the world around us. We've always had a good story to tell. We were just a little shy in telling it.

But that's all changed. Now we're asking for your questions. We realize that as competition in the brewing industry gets stiffer, a company who is bent on surviving must be willing to talk to the media. Openly and frankly. About anything. Coors' responsibility for the environment, brewing processes, contributions, relations with minority groups.

So call us toll free. Give us a chance to answer your questions. We'll give you the facts.

Coors

interview. Be honest, candid, forthright, and fair. Follow these additional guidelines in a press conference.

1. **Don't play favorites; invite representatives from all major news outlets.** Normally, it makes sense to alert wire services, which in turn may have the resources to advise their print and broadcast subscribers. For example, both the AP and UPI carry daily listings, called day books, of news events in major cities.

2. **Notify the media by mail well in advance of the conference and follow up by phone.** Ordinarily, the memo announcing the event should be straightforward and to the point, listing the subject, date, time, and place, as well as the speaker and the public relations contact's name, title, and phone number. If possible, the memo should reach the editor's desk at least 7 to 10 days before the event. Also, the day before the event, a follow-up phone call reminder is wise.

3. **Schedule the conference early in the day.** Again, the earlier in the business day, the better, particularly for TV consumption.

FIGURE 13–5 Press conferences are often dangerous enough to merit a "battle plan." *(By permission of Johnny Hart and NAS, Inc.)*

4. **Hold the conference in a meeting room, not someone's office.** Office auditoriums and hotel meeting rooms are good places for news conferences. Chairs should be provided for all reporters, and space should be allowed for TV crews to set up cameras. The speaker at the conference should preside from either a table or a lectern, so that microphones and tape recorders can be placed nearby.

5. **The time allotted for the conference should be stated in advance.** Reporters should be told at the beginning of the conference how much time they will have. Then no one can complain later.

6. **Keep the speaker away from the reporters before the conference.** Mingling prior to the conference will only give someone an edge. Keep all reporters on equal footing in their contact with the speaker.

7. **Prepare materials to complement the speaker's presentation.** The news conference is an apt place for a press kit, which should include all the pertinent information about the speaker, the subject, and the organization.

8. **Let the reporters know the end has come.** Just before the stated time has elapsed, the practitioner should announce to the reporters that the next question will be the last one. After the final question, the speaker should thank the reporters for coming and should take no more questions. After the conference, some reporters (particularly broadcast journalists) may want to ask follow-up questions on an individual basis. Do so only if all reporters have an opportunity to share in the one-on-one format.

Press Junkets

A junket is a kind of press conference on wheels. It is usually billed as an information visit by journalists to a particular site, paid for by a sponsoring organization. The purpose of the trip—for example, film critics to Hollywood to screen a new film or travel writers to a far-away island to sample its hospitality—is to secure positive publicity. In 1986, in the largest press junket ever, Walt Disney World flew 10,000 journalists to Florida to celebrate its fifteenth anniversary.

Some news organizations flat-out reject junkets. *Harper's Magazine,* for instance, has a policy "not to solicit or accept contributions or subsidies from interested parties on matters on which the magazine plans to write." Others are less doctrinaire. Indeed, less prosperous publications find junkets a good way to report on out-of-the-way places and events that they couldn't afford to cover otherwise. As the *New Republic's* editor put it, "If you have honest people going, they will not be persuaded by the purchase of an airplane ticket for them."

Nonetheless, journalistic junkets should be arranged with extreme care. Occasionally, in fact, a sponsoring organization has been sandbagged by a cynical journalist who accepted the firm's generosity only to write sarcastically of the excesses viewed or received. The bottom line on junkets is for public relations professionals to approach them with extreme caution.

Summary

As is true with any other specialty in public relations work, the key to securing publicity is professionalism. Because management relies on the practitioners for expertise in handling the media effectively, practitioners must not only know their own organization and management, but must also be conversant in and respectful of the role and practice of journalists. In Chapter 14, the proper relationship between journalists and public relations people is further examined.

Publicists, who charge clients for getting their names in print or on the air, are the latest innovation in the relationship between journalists and public relations people. One Mill Valley, California, practitioner received extensive publicity when he announced his publicity price list in 1987— $24,075 for a placement on "20/20," $21,560 for a placement on "NBC Nightly News," $21,400 for a placement in *The Wall Street Journal,* and $21,135 for a placement in *People* magazine. Such schemes, however, are in the minority.

The role of public relations professionals in the news-gathering process has become more respected by journalists. As Fred Andrews, the business/finance editor of *The New York Times,* has said, "PR has gotten more professional. PR people can be a critical element for us. It makes a difference how efficiently they handle things, how complete the information is that they have at hand. We value that and understand all the work that goes into it."[6] Indeed, the best public relations/journalist relationship today—the only successful one over the long term—must be based on mutual understanding, trust, and respect.

DISCUSSION STARTERS

1. What is the difference between advertising and publicity?
2. What is the current state of the newspaper industry?
3. Why should public relations professionals be familiar with newspaper deadlines?
4. Is magazine publishing likely to experience a renaissance in the 1990s?
5. What is the key to securing publicity on television?
6. What are the general interest, financial, and commercial wire services?
7. How can public relations professionals keep track of the publicity they receive for their organizations?
8. What are the several do's and don'ts of print interviews?
9. Are press conferences advisable in most cases?
10. What is a press junket?

NOTES

1. Leo Bogart, "The Public's Use and Perception of Newspapers," *Public Opinion Quarterly* 48 (Winter 1984): 709.
2. Patrick M. Reilly, "As Magazine Industry Faces a Shakeout, Some Publishers Start to Close the Books," *The Wall Street Journal,* 31 January 1990; B3.
3. Bill Hogan, "The Boom in Regional Business Journals," *Washington Journalism Review* (July-August 1982): 35.
4. Bill Patterson, "Using Radio News Today," *Public Relations Journal* (November 1989): 22.
5. Roxanne Roberts, "CNN, on Top of the World," *The Washington Post,* 21 August 1990, C1, C10.
6. "Getting into the *Times:* How Andrews Views PR," *Across the Board* (August 1989): 21.

SUGGESTED READINGS

American Society of Journalists & Authors Directory (1501 Broadway, New York, NY 10036). Freelance writers.
Barhydt, James D. *The Complete Book of Product Publicity.* New York: AMACOM, 1987 (135 W. 50th St. 10020).
Boyden, Donald P. *Gale Directory of Publications* (Formerly *Ayer's Directory of Publications*). Detroit, MI 48226 (Gale Research Inc., 1989).
Brough, Bruce. *Publicity and Public Relations Guide for Business.* Sunnyvale, CA: Oasis Press, 1986.
Chambers, Wicke, and Spring Asher. *TV PR: How to Promote Yourself, Your Product/Service or Your Organization on TV.* Rocklin, CA: Prima, 1987.
Danzig, Fred, and Ted Klein. *Publicity: How to Make the Media Work for You.* New York: Scribner's, 1985.

TOP OF THE SHELF

Gannett Center Journal: Publicity. New York: Gannett Center for Media Studies and the Gannett Foundation, 1990 (Columbia University, 2950 Broadway).

Experts in academia, journalism, and public relations examine the power of publicity in the Spring 1990 Gannett Center Journal.

Several penetrating essays in this journal explore a variety of publicity-related issues. In "Journalism, Publicity and the Lost Art of Argument," Christopher Lasch, a professor at the University of Rochester, suggests that publicists, not reporters, determine the majority of what people read in newspapers. In "God Understands When the Cause Is Noble," University of Wisconsin professor Charles Salmons argues that special-interest groups manipulate the media. In "We Don't Do Coups," Hill & Knowlton CEO Bob Dilen-

schneider embraces the use of publicity in corporate and government relations. David Hoffman, a *Washington Post* reporter, says in "The Frictionless Presidency" that George Bush's mastery of presidential communications is reflected in everyday media reports. *The New York Times'* Randall Rothenberg looks at the explosive growth of video news releases in "The Journalist as Maytag Repairman." Related issues are dissected in other articles.

Read the Spring 1990 *Gannett Center Journal* to cull the pros and cons of publicity as seen by people who study this field and its effects on public opinion.

Feinman, Jeffrey, and Robert Blashek. *Sweepstakes, Prizes, Promotions, Games and Contests.* New York: Sales and Marketing Management (633 Third Ave. 10017).

Getting Your Public Relations Story on TV/Radio. Babylon, NY: Pilot Books, 1986.

Govoni, Norman. *Promotional Management.* Englewood Cliffs, NJ: Prentice-Hall, 1986.

Hart, Norman. *Practical Advertising and Publicity.* New York: McGraw-Hill, 1989.

International Directory of Special Events & Festivals. Chicago: Special Events Reports (213 W. Institute Place 60610).

Jefkins, Frank. *Planned Press and Public Relations.* Philadelphia: Trans-Atlantic, 1986.

National Research Bureau. *Working Press of the Nation.* (Available from the author, 242 N. 3rd St, Burlington, IA 52601.) Each of multiple volumes covers a different medium—newspapers, magazines, radio-TV, feature writers, syndicates, and house organs.

Network Futures (Television Index, 40–29 27th St., Long Island City, New York 11101). Monthly.

O'Dwyer, Jack, ed. *O'Dwyer's Directory of Corporation Communications.* New York: J. R. O'Dwyer, 1991. This guide provides a full listing of the public relations departments of nearly 3,000 companies and shows how the largest companies define public relations and staff and budget for it.

O'Dwyer, Jack, ed. *O'Dwyer's Directory of PR Firms.* New York: J. R. O'Dwyer, 1991. This directory has listings of 1,200 public relations firms. In addition to information on executives, accounts, type of agency, and branch office locations, the guide offers a geographical index to firms and cross-indexes more than 8,000 clients.

Pollack, Martin. *Publicity: How To.* Ft. Lauderdale, FL: Alliance Pub., 1989.

Power-Packed PR: Ideas That Work. Pitman, NJ: Communication Publications & Resources, 1988 (140 South Broadway 08071).

PR Aids' Party Line. (Available from 221 Park Ave., South, New York, NY 10003.) This information service weekly, published on Monday, lists editorial placement opportunities in all media, including network and local radio and TV.

The Publicity Process. 3rd ed. Ames: Iowa State University Press, 1989.

Public Relations Aids, Inc. (221 Park Ave., South, New York, NY 10003). A computerized media system lets a client select local broadcast media by market, type of programming, power of radio stations, network for TV, department (news, program, women's interest, public service, etc.).

Rein, Irving, Philip Kotler, and Martin Stoller. *High Visibility.* New York: Dodd Mead, 1987.

Ruffner, R. *Handbook of Publicity and PR for the Nonprofit Organization.* Englewood Cliffs, NJ: Prentice-Hall, 1985.

Schmertz, Herb. *Good-bye to the Low Profile: The Art of Creative Confrontation.* Boston: Little Brown, 1986.

St. John, Tracy. *Getting Your Public Relations Story on TV and Radio.* Babylon, NY: Pilot Books, 1986.

Tharpe, Louis. *The Complete Manager's Guide to Promotional Merchandise.* Homewood, IL: Dow Jones-Irwin, 1989.

What to Do When the Media Contact You (New York State Bar Association, Dept. of Communications & Public Affairs, One Elk St., Albany, NY 12207).

CASE STUDY   Dashing Dan Gets Bushwhacked

It was the first great debate of 1988, or at least nine minutes of great TV. What happened on the "CBS Evening News" on January 26, 1988, will probably have implications for years to come for presidential campaigns, media coverage, and preparation prior to publicity.

A feisty Vice-president George Bush, appearing live from the White House, attacked CBS anchorman Dan Rather for impugning his character during Bush's run for the Republican nomination. Bush also accused Rather and CBS of misrepresenting themselves in obtaining the interview. He said that CBS had promised his appearance would be for a political profile, not a rehash of the arms-for-hostages issues that had set off the Iran-Contra affair and had clouded Bush's candidacy.

At one point during the interview, Bush seemed to stun Rather by referring to the anchorman's much-noted walkout from the set of the "CBS Evening News" a few months earlier, when a broadcast tennis match ran too long. Rather's walkout had caused CBS to transmit a blank signal for nearly seven minutes, and the anchorman was roundly criticized by others in the profession, including his predecessor, Walter Cronkite.

"I want to talk about why I want to be president," Mr. Bush said in the interview. "It's not fair to judge my whole career by a rehash on Iran. How would you like it if I judged *your* career by those seven minutes when you walked off the set in New York?" When Rather did not immediately answer, Bush asked again, "How would you like that?"

Bush was initially angered when his interview was preceded by a taped report that suggested that he had played a greater role in the Iran-Contra affair than had been previously acknowledged. After the airing of the report, Bush threatened to cancel the interview. But he didn't. Instead, Bush went on and immediately got feisty. "You've impugned my integrity by suggesting here that I didn't tell the truth. I'm asking for fair play," the vice-president said.

What followed was nine minutes of shouting and cross-talk, broadcast mayhem, and great theater, all at the same time. CBS News was understandably stunned by the vice-president's combativeness. After the broadcast, it issued a statement saying that it had negotiated for the interview for three weeks and had told Bush campaign aides "that the interview would be 'issue-oriented and tough.'"

Bush, after the interview, was unrelenting. "I'm very upset about it," he told CBS staff members afterward. "Tell your goddamned network that if they want to talk to me again to raise their hands at a press conference. No more Mr. Insider stuff after that!"

The winner around the country—10 million households watched the mugging—was not even close. CBS switchboards were flooded with phone calls, overwhelmingly critical of Rather and supportive of Bush. So spirited was the backlash against Rather's badgering of Bush that CBS affiliates debated whether to protest formally the anchorman's performance. Bush, who up to that point in the campaign had been derisively called a wimp by his opponents, was clearly reinvigorated.

But there was more than met the eye. The confrontation that appeared on the screen to millions of viewers at home was just a part of the story. It had all begun about a month before the interview. When the vice-president saw the CBS letter inviting him to participate with the anchorman, he wrote on his copy, "I feel confident with Rather. Make sure this guy gets a reply soon." Immediately, the Bush people began negotiating with CBS over the ground rules. For one thing, the Bush people insisted that the interview be live or not at all. Early on, they suspected that the interview would be highly confrontational, and they didn't want CBS to be able to edit anything.

CBS, for its part, was uncomfortable. Live interviews, particularly on nightly news shows, are unpredictable. Whereas a taped interview allows for network editing and shaping, a live interview gives the subject a chance to manipulate the conversation. He can filibuster, evade a probing question, or generally be too elusive to pin down. Nonetheless, CBS finally agreed to do the interview live, and Rather's associates warned Bush's staff that the anchorman's questions were going to be "tough and pointed."

On the weekend before the broadcast, CBS began airing promotions for the Bush-Rather interview and calling political writers to let them know CBS would be airing the "first interview on Iran-Contra that Bush has done with any network." The day of the interview, Rather had three one-hour rehearsals with the people involved in the broadcast. He was coached as if he were a candidate preparing for a debate or a boxer preparing for a fight, rather than a journalist going into an interview.

The Bush camp reportedly knew full well that they were heading into an ambush, and they prepared the vice-president accordingly. Before the interview, one of Bush's advisers predicted that "the vice-president would be prepared to answer the questions and may indeed have something of his own he wants to go into." That "something of his own" was apparently the reference to Rather's walking off the set. If so, then the vice-president was well prepared for the Iran-Contra segment. And his initial barrage, which left Rather stunned and reeling, might well have been rehearsed.

Whatever. What is indisputable is that the bout with Rather turned the tide for George Bush's campaign. The publicity submerged once and for all the wimp image, and George Bush walked away with his party's presidential nomination.*

QUESTIONS

1. Had you been George Bush's public relations counselor, how would you have prepared him for the Rather debate?
2. Had you been Dan Rather's public relations counselor, how would you have prepared him for the Bush debate?
3. From your knowledge of this case, which one of the combatants do you think was perceived as the bully. Why?
4. Do you think George Bush planned the whole thing? Why or why not?

*For additional information on this case, see Peter J. Boyer, "Rather's Questioning of Bush Sets Off Shouting on Live Broadcast," *The New York Times*, 26 January 1988, A1, 9; David Colton and Matt Roush, "On-Air Bash: Who Got Mugged?" *USA Today*, 26 January 1988, 1–2A; E. J. Dionne, Jr., "Bush Camp Feels Galvanized After Showdown with Rather," *The New York Times*, 27 January 1988, A1, 9; Ned Schurman, "Bush vs. Rather: A Tonic for TV News," *The New York Times*, 27 January 1988, A27; Gerald F. Seib and Monica Langley, "Bush Wins a Clear Victory in TV-Interview Spat but Doesn't Dispel His Iran-Contra Problems . . ." *The Wall Street Journal*, 27 January 1988, 52; Richard Stengel, "Bushwhacked!" *Time*, (February 8, 1988), 16–20.

Tips from the Top

ANDREW S. EDSON

Andrew S. Edson is senior vice-president and managing director of the New York office of Padilla Speer Beardsley, Inc., a leading Minneapolis-based public relations agency. Edson's extensive background in public relations includes periods as an account executive for Hatshe-Rotman & Druck and for Ruder & Finn. He was also assistant director of corporate public relations for the Anaconda Company and public affairs manager for Citicorp. Edson has taught public relations at Pratt Institute and New York University and lectures frequently on public relations subjects.

How would you define public relations?
Advertising is what you pay for. Public relations is what you pray for.

How does one deal effectively with the media?
You must know the media you plan to deal with. Read the pertinent publications, listen to or watch the actual news program. In short, do your homework beforehand. This will show when you write that first pitch letter or make the introductory call. Honesty also counts. Don't hide under a hundred platitudes once you've established a contact. If you cannot effectively answer a question or aid a journalist, be truthful and let that person know. It'll pay off in the long run.

How important are contacts in media relations?
Very. If you develop a good working relationship with members of the fourth estate, you, too, can engage in a game of "give and go." It's not imprudent to ask a favor or question a journalist. Basically, it's a two-way street. The newsperson wants your help when he or she needs it. Conversely, there will come a day when you will need a favor in return. Good media contacts are invaluable in practicing public relations.

What is the proper relationship between a journalist and a public relations practitioner?
Some say at "arm's distance," while others make it a habit of getting to know a journalist on an almost personal and social basis. There really isn't any concrete formula for setting the tone of a practitioner/

journalist relationship. Common sense and an adherence to a professional code of ethics, such as that of the Public Relations Society of America, more than anything else, constitute what is proper and improper.

What steps do you follow in publicizing a client?

I first try to put together a publicity plan that will help the client achieve his or her objectives through proven strategies and action programs. Sure, everyone would love to be in *The New York Times* or *Wall Street Journal* or on ABC's "Good Morning America" program, but it doesn't always happen. While your client may push for his or her appearance in a national book, the company and its products may be more appropriate for a series of by-lined articles in trade publications (not at all unlike hitting a few singles in baseball) before pitching a major book or program. Those singles will help you get a home run and build a better case for pitching your client before other target media.

Are clients understanding when they don't attract publicity?

Some are. Some aren't. If you make the client aware from the outset of the success/ failure ratio and don't make any unnecessary promises, then you won't get harmed. All too often, public relations practitioners get overzealous and almost guarantee that certain things will happen when they may not. Unlike advertising, we don't control what gets into print, or heard on the airwaves, or seen on the tube.

What special tips can you offer in dealing with the media?

Be honest, forthright, and cooperate with the media person in a professional manner. Don't forget to send a proper thank you note when the occasion calls for it. Think of your relationship as continuing, not a one-shot deal. Stay in touch, even if you have nothing in particular to sell.

How can you stay current with an ever-expanding media universe?

While it may appear to be a difficult task, it requires good time management. Peruse new publications. Scan new television programs. This gives you a leg up on the competition and will enable you to counsel your organization or client from a stronger position. Not every publication or program will withstand the test of time, advertising, or ratings. Still, in order to be adept at your job, you must read, listen, and watch.

14

Media

The mass media comprise the public that is most associated with public relations. As noted, many people believe that the term *public relations* is synonymous with *publicity*. It isn't. However, few are able to distinguish between securing favorable publicity for an organization and winning positive public relations.

As also noted, despite the fact that most public relations professionals use the mass media more than any other communications vehicle, recent research has indicated that with public relations becoming a more sophisticated profession, it should rely less on the mass media than in the past.[1] The mass media, according to this line of thought, are less pivotal in influencing public opinion in the 1990s.

Perhaps.

But the fact remains that securing positive publicity through the mass media, as discussed in Chapter 13, is still a critical activity for most public relations professionals. Moreover, public relations professionals still regard the mass media as an institution of awesome power—and approach it with considerable caution. Consider the following:

♦ When Iran's Ayatollah Khomeini called for the death of author Salman Rushdie for his controversial book *The Satanic Verses*, the word to employees from Walden Books' headquarters was, "If anyone asks about the book, ask them if they're with the media. Do not answer any media inquiries and do not give your name. Just say, 'No comment.' This is our corporate statement."[2]

♦ After a New York public relations professional agreed to appear on NBC's "Today" show, she sued the program and its former co-host Jane Pauley for $2 million, charging the show falsely depicted her as a "financial illiterate."[3]

◆ Corporate public relations people in 1989 were reported to be "minimizing" face-to-face contact with the media because, according to one reporter, "No one knows or trusts anyone anymore."[4]

The focus of this chapter, picking up from Chapter 13, is how to coexist with the mass media. It is still axiomatic in public relations that a good working relationship with the media is essential for a successful communications program. Dealing with the media has traditionally been a primary responsibility for public relations professionals, and media relations has developed into a career specialty for many in the field.

It is indisputable that when the media take aim at a particular individual or institution, the results can be devastating. Recent U.S. history is studded with examples of people and organizations whose power and influence have been cut short as a result of their having attracted extensive, critical media attention.

President Bush, perhaps cognizant of this reality, has made presidential appointments with great care. Nonetheless, when Bush chose former Senator John Tower to be secretary of defense, the hard-living Texan went down in the flames of a media onslaught. Learning from the experience, Bush, in 1990, selected a virtual unknown, David Souter, as his first appointment to the U.S. Supreme Court. Souter's nomination sailed through. Bush's presidential predecessors were not as fortunate in dealing with the media.

◆ President Reagan's Supreme Court nominations in 1987 were treated especially harshly by the media. First Judge Robert Bork and then Judge Douglas Ginsburg was attacked by an unrelenting press corps, and both nominations were withdrawn. Bork, unquestionably one of the brightest jurists to come before the Senate for confirmation, was portrayed as being anti-women, anti-Black, and anti-just-about-everything-else. Ginsburg, a Yale law professor, was pummeled when he admitted smoking marijuana in his youth.

◆ Later in the Reagan administration, the president's trusted aide, Edwin Meese, nearly failed in his bid to become U.S. attorney general when the media dug up questionable loans with which he was involved. Then, when Meese got the job, the media continued to hound him. Things got so bad that, in 1988, Meese canned his Justice Department press secretary for not representing him forcefully enough with the media. Several months later Meese himself resigned.

◆ Nor was President Carter's administration immune from media attack. After newspaper reports revealed questionable personal financial dealings by Bert Lance, prior to his being selected by President Carter as the nation's director of the Office of Management and Budget, the Georgia banker went before the Congress and a national television audience to deny the various allegations. Shortly after his testimony, he resigned from the administration.

◆ President Carter's chief drug advisor, Dr. Peter Bourne, also resigned after newspaper stories revealed first that Bourne had written a false prescription for an employee and later that he had occasionally smoked marijuana.

◆ During President Ford's administration, Secretary of Agriculture Earl Butz resigned when a magazine revealed a tasteless joke that Butz had recounted in confidence to a reporter aboard an airplane.

The vigilance of the media in exposing fraud, deception, and questionable practices in society is a tradition (Figure 14–1). The media's crowning achievement in this regard was the exposure of the Watergate break-in, which eventually led to the resignation of President Nixon (see the case study in Chapter 2). The success of *The Washington Post* in getting to the bottom of Watergate encouraged journalists to focus on abuses of power in all areas of society. Over the years since Watergate, investigative reporting has gained a solid foothold, particularly on television, where one picture is worth a thousand words. The cream of the TV investigative crop, of course, is "60 Minutes," among the nation's most widely watched shows for the better part of three decades. But even "60 Minutes" is not without its faults. According to CBS anchorman Dan Rather, "We make mistakes so often, violating the basics of accuracy, clarity, or fairness, that sometimes it shatters me. If with our budget and our staff and time, we make so many mistakes in exposé material, what's it like under less luxurious circumstances?"[5]

What indeed? With the spate of gossip columnists and commentators in the 1990s—from Geraldo Rivera to Oprah Winfrey, from "A Current Affair" to "Entertainment Tonight," from Liz Smith to the *National Enquirer*—the spread of tattletale journalism in the 1990s has put an added burden on public relations professionals who, as the primary voice of management, seek fair and unbiased treatment of their organizations in the media.

What Research Tells Us About the Media

The relationship between journalists and public relations people has never been an easy one. The former often accuse the latter of withholding information. The latter often accuse the former of liberal, one-sided reporting. Recent research corroborates an uneasy relationship between those who interview and those who are being interviewed. In one 1987 telephone survey of 100 top-level executives, 59 percent of those polled

FIGURE 14–1 The oil companies have had their share of problems with investigative reporting. However, as this Mobil ad demonstrates, when the oil giants believe the media have learned from past mistakes, they occasionally duly acknowledge it. *(Courtesy of Mobil Oil Corporation)*

claimed that they "invariably get misquoted" by the press. "Journalistic
ignorance" was cited by 39 percent, with 25 percent saying that journalists
were guilty of an "overemphasis on the negative." Another 22 percent cited

---

BETWEEN THE LINES

Turning the Cameras on "Open Mike"

No investigative journalist has gained as fearsome a reputation for
catching subjects off guard as television reporter Mike Wallace of
CBS-TV's "60 Minutes." Indeed public relations professionals live in
dread of the day that Mike Wallace appears at their door. That's why,
in January 1982, many public relations practitioners may have felt a
bit more chipper than usual when they read that Mike Wallace had
been caught at his own game.

The story started when Wallace took his "60 Minutes" crew to the
San Diego Federal Savings and Loan Company to interview a
vice-president on the plight of low-income Californians—most of
them either Black or Hispanic, with minimal reading skills—who
faced foreclosures after signing contracts for expensive air condition-
ers without realizing that their houses served as collateral. As a
precondition of the interview, San Diego Federal insisted on filming
the proceedings for its own use.

During a break in the filming, with the CBS camera off but the San
Diego Federal camera still rolling, Wallace commented on the complex
lien-sale bank contracts. "You bet your ***** they are hard to read," he
said, "if you're reading them over the watermelon or over the tacos!"
Thereupon, according to observers, Mike began to laugh uproari-
ously—but not for long.

A few weeks later Wallace learned that the San Diego Federal crew
had videotaped his offhand remark, and he and CBS tried desperately
to retrieve the offensive tape from the bank. They failed, and the story
received nationwide coverage. Later, Wallace called the retrieval idea
a "lame one," and he and CBS apologized for the racially disparaging
remark.

Ironically, during a prior "60 Minutes" show about the behind-the-
scenes workings of the broadcast, Wallace was asked how he would
feel if a hidden camera one day captured some embarrassing material
about him. "I wouldn't like it," he replied. Boy, was he right!

"sensationalist tendencies," and 12 percent cited clear-cut "bias" among members of the press.[6]

As to a liberal bias among journalists, a 1986 study of so-called elite journalists working for major news organs in Washington, D.C., and New York found evidence to support such a view. The authors concluded that evidence "does not imply a conspiracy to exclude conservative voices, but merely reflects the human tendency to turn more often to those you trust, and to trust most those who think most like you do." They suggest that when it comes time to find expert commentary on policy issues, it is the liberal left that most often provides that commentary. As proof, they cited investigations of articles on welfare reform, consumer protection, nuclear energy, and other issues for which liberal sources were quoted significantly more than conservative ones.[7]

Recent studies show that neither journalists nor public relations people hold the strong negative views that may once have been common. According to several studies, there seems to be a fairly high level of mutual respect within the two camps: journalists tend to think that most public relations people do a good job and vice versa.

As for the general public, one 1985 study revealed that the public has a high level of confidence in the media.[8] This confidence is affected from time to time by controversial events, such as the Bush-Rather debate discussed in Chapter 13. After his bout with Bush, Rather's favorability rating fell a monumental 18 points. His fall coincided with a general weakening of support for news organizations in the late 1980s, particularly network news. Early in 1988, only 44 percent of the public believed that "news organizations get the facts straight," an 11-point drop in 2½ years.[9] Despite the decline, twice as many people still "trusted" Rather more than Bush to tell the truth.

Objectivity in the Media

Total objectivity in reporting is unattainable: it would require complete neutrality and near-total detachment in reporting a story. Most people start with biases and preconceived notions about almost any subject. Reporting, then, is subjective. Nevertheless, scholars of journalism believe that reporters and editors should strive for maximum objectivity.

American journalism has evolved through several stages. After the turn of the century, journalism was dominated by reporters seeking to learn the answers to six key questions: who, what, where, when, why, and how. After World War I, led by the examples of the *New York Herald Tribune* newspaper and *The New Yorker* magazine, reporters became more interpretive. After

World War II, advocacy journalism—in which reporters and columnists tended to take sides and support causes—became the order of the day.

In the 1970s, the so-called new journalism took over, in which reporters emphasized details, facial expressions, gestures, the setting, behavioral patterns, and the like. Advocates of this form of journalism included Jimmy Breslin, Gay Talese, *New York Magazine,* and *Rolling Stone.* New journalism was upended in the 1980s, when *Washington Post* reporter Janet Cooke was awarded journalism's highest honor, the Pulitzer Prize, for a front-page story about an eight-year-old heroin addict. Cooke's story, as was later revealed, lacked only one ingredient—truth. It was, in fact, all a lie, created in the fertile imagination of the reporter and slipped by red-faced *Washington Post* editors. Cooke was summarily stripped of her Pulitzer and fired from the *Post,* but the damage to new journalism was done.

By the 1990s, the "who, what, why, where, when, and how" approach to reporting had returned to American journalism. This more factual style is complemented by a healthy dollop of skepticism for the establishment and an aggressiveness in seeking the truth. Occasionally reporters are rewarded with revealing "scoops," such as the one described in the case study in Chapter 5.

The point remains that if an organization in the 1990s expects fair and positive treatment in print or on the air, its statements must always hold up to a test of truth. Journalists, by the same token, are expected to uphold certain standards of their own, outlined in Figure 14–2.

Media's View of Officialdom

By virtue of their role, the media view officials, particularly business and government spokespersons, with a degree of skepticism. Reporters shouldn't be expected to accept on faith the party line. By the same token, once a business or government official effectively substantiates the official view and demonstrates its merit, the media should be willing to report this accurately, without editorial distortion.

Stated another way, the relationship between the media and the establishment should be one of healthy adversaries rather than bitter enemies. Unfortunately, this is not always the case. According to one network anchorman, the fault lies at the foot of the First Amendment, which discourages critical analysis of the press by the press. Says NBC's Tom Brokaw, "In American journalism, we generally are inclined to call attention to almost everyone's failings but our own. When criticism is directed at us, we are very likely to develop a glass jaw."[10] Author Janet Malcolm takes an even dimmer view: "Every journalist who is not too stupid or too full of himself to notice what is going on knows that what he does is morally

THE JOURNALIST'S Creed

I believe IN THE PROFESSION OF JOURNALISM.

I BELIEVE THAT THE PUBLIC JOURNAL IS A PUBLIC TRUST; THAT ALL CONNECTED WITH IT ARE, TO THE FULL MEASURE OF THEIR RESPONSIBILITY, TRUSTEES FOR THE PUBLIC; THAT ACCEPTANCE OF A LESSER SERVICE THAN THE PUBLIC SERVICE IS BETRAYAL OF THIS TRUST.

I BELIEVE THAT CLEAR THINKING AND CLEAR STATEMENT, ACCURACY, AND FAIRNESS ARE FUNDAMENTAL TO GOOD JOURNALISM.

I BELIEVE THAT A JOURNALIST SHOULD WRITE ONLY WHAT HE HOLDS IN HIS HEART TO BE TRUE.

I BELIEVE THAT SUPPRESSION OF THE NEWS, FOR ANY CONSIDERATION OTHER THAN THE WELFARE OF SOCIETY, IS INDEFENSIBLE.

I BELIEVE THAT NO ONE SHOULD WRITE AS A JOURNALIST WHAT HE WOULD NOT SAY AS A GENTLEMAN; THAT BRIBERY BY ONE'S OWN POCKETBOOK IS AS MUCH TO BE AVOIDED AS BRIBERY BY THE POCKETBOOK OF ANOTHER; THAT INDIVIDUAL RESPONSIBILITY MAY NOT BE ESCAPED BY PLEADING ANOTHER'S INSTRUCTIONS OR ANOTHER'S DIVIDENDS.

I BELIEVE THAT ADVERTISING, NEWS AND EDITORIAL COLUMNS SHOULD ALIKE SERVE THE BEST INTERESTS OF READERS; THAT A SINGLE STANDARD OF HELPFUL TRUTH AND CLEANNESS SHOULD PREVAIL FOR ALL; THAT THE SUPREME TEST OF GOOD JOURNALISM IS THE MEASURE OF ITS PUBLIC SERVICE.

I BELIEVE THAT THE JOURNALISM WHICH SUCCEEDS BEST—AND BEST DESERVES SUCCESS—FEARS GOD AND HONORS MAN; IS STOUTLY INDEPENDENT, UNMOVED BY PRIDE OF OPINION OR GREED OF POWER, CONSTRUCTIVE, TOLERANT BUT NEVER CARELESS, SELF-CONTROLLED, PATIENT, ALWAYS RESPECTFUL OF ITS READERS BUT ALWAYS UNAFRAID, IS QUICKLY INDIGNANT AT INJUSTICE; IS UNSWAYED BY THE APPEAL OF PRIVILEGE OR THE CLAMOR OF THE MOB; SEEKS TO GIVE EVERY MAN A CHANCE, AND, AS FAR AS LAW AND HONEST WAGE AND RECOGNITION OF HUMAN BROTHERHOOD CAN MAKE IT SO, AN EQUAL CHANCE; IS PROFOUNDLY PATRIOTIC WHILE SINCERELY PROMOTING INTERNATIONAL GOOD WILL AND CEMENTING WORLD-COMRADESHIP; IS A JOURNALISM OF HUMANITY, OF AND FOR TODAY'S WORLD.

Walter Williams

DEAN SCHOOL OF JOURNALISM, UNIVERSITY OF MISSOURI, 1908-1935

FIGURE 14—2 "The Journalist's Creed" was coined after World War I by Dr. Walter Williams, dean of the School of Journalism at the University of Missouri. *(Courtesy of the University of Missouri School of Journalism)*

The Media Relations Ruckus at Goliath Industries

Compared to that of most organizations, the media relations policy at Detroit's huge Goliath Industries was exemplary. The company, the nation's largest manufacturer, was generally forthright in its public statements and frequently led industry on such issues as corporate disclosure and South African business policy.

Goliath was such a business leader, in fact, that most observers were puzzled on May 18, when C. A. Wheat, Goliath's vice-chairman and likely successor to the firm's president, unexpectedly resigned. In response to Wheat's departure, Goliath Industries issued a terse news release indicating that Wheat was leaving "to pursue personal business opportunities." Goliath refused to amplify the brief announcement, despite constant prodding by the media. The company cited as its primary reason for secrecy the concept of privacy with respect to personnel records.

The announcement that Wheat was leaving the $325,000-a-year job started rumor mills humming, not only in Detroit but throughout the nation. The media, predictably, refused to drop the story. Eventually, one enterprising reporter turned up the fact that Wheat had been asked to leave by Goliath's president, as a result of an internal audit that reportedly revealed conflicts in Wheat's handling of a customer with whom Wheat shared business interests.

After this revelation, the Goliath story became fair game for business journalists everywhere. The firm quickly acknowledged the existence of the internal audit but refused to discuss its content, claiming that such a confidential matter was exempt from its internal disclosure code. Details of the report were subsequently made public by the *Detroit Free Press.* Indeed, even Wheat acknowledged the accuracy of the transactions described, maintaining that there was nothing improper about them.

In the months that followed *l'Affaire Wheat,* as the Detroit newspapers called it, it was revealed that the Federal Bureau of Investigation had launched a probe of the matter, and a federal grand jury had also been impaneled to investigate. Eventually, Wheat was cleared of all possible violations of law. Nevertheless, the positive public image of Goliath Industries had suffered a tremendous blow. *Forbes* magazine labeled it "the industry's biggest public relations blunder in years." One source close to Goliath's board of directors summed it up by saying, "It could not have been handled any worse."

QUESTIONS

1. Had you been Goliath's public relations director, what strategy would you have recommended on May 18?
2. What would you have suggested the firm do after the revelation of the internal audit?
3. How would you suggest that Goliath's management handle the Wheat affair at the company's next annual meeting? Should they bring it up at all? What should they say?

indefensible. He is a kind of confidence man, preying on people's vanity, ignorance, or loneliness, gaining their trust and betraying them without remorse."[11] Whew!

Fortunately, such journalists are in the minority. Most want to get the facts from all sides, and they acknowledge and respect the public relations practitioner's role in the process. If they are dealt with fairly, they will reciprocate in kind. However, some executives fail to understand the essential difference between the media and their own organizations. The reporter wants to get all the information he or she can and interpret it as he or she sees fit, while the people in the organizations being covered want things to be presented in the best light. Because of this difference, some executives consider journalists to be feared adversaries, and they fear and distrust the media.

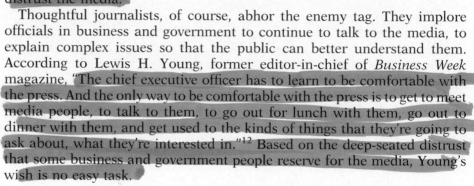

Thoughtful journalists, of course, abhor the enemy tag. They implore officials in business and government to continue to talk to the media, to explain complex issues so that the public can better understand them. According to Lewis H. Young, former editor-in-chief of *Business Week* magazine, "The chief executive officer has to learn to be comfortable with the press. And the only way to be comfortable with the press is to get to meet media people, to talk to them, to go out for lunch with them, go out to dinner with them, and get used to the kinds of things that they're going to ask about, what they're interested in."[12] Based on the deep-seated distrust that some business and government people reserve for the media, Young's wish is no easy task.

Officialdom's View of the Media

In the 1980s, the pervasive fear and distrust of the news media among executives, particularly among those in business, seemed to diminish. To be sure, there were still those who charged that the media were liberally biased.

♦ Senator Jesse Helms formed a Fairness in Media group and attempted to take over CBS. The attempt failed.

♦ President Reagan's science adviser, George Keyworth, charged that the national press was drawn predominantly from a narrow fringe element on the far left and was "intent on trying to tear down America."[13]

♦ President Reagan himself, in an unusual slip of the lip after posing for White House photographers, muttered an ever-so-audible "sons of bitches" when besieged by reporters to respond to the 1986 overthrow of Philippine President Ferdinand Marcos.

Nonetheless, as the 1980s wore on and the 1990s beckoned, the trust between people in power and people who report the activities of the powerful increased a bit. In one 1981 study, some 71 percent of executives considered themselves "usually accessible to the media." However, 73

BETWEEN　THE　LINES

Confessions of a Media Maven

Dealing with the media for fun and profit, even for an experienced public relations hand, is a constant learning experience. Often, such learning is achieved the hard way.

By the spring of 1984, many of the nation's largest banks were a bit jittery about negative publicity about their loans to lesser developed countries. One of the most vociferous bank bashers was Patrick J. Buchanan, a syndicated columnist who later became President Reagan's communications director.

After one particularly venomous syndicated attack on the banks, a certain bank public affairs director wrote directly to Buchanan's editor asking whether he couldn't "muzzle at least for a little while" his wild-eyed columnist. The letter's language, in retrospect, was perhaps a bit harsh.

Some weeks later, in a six-column article that ran throughout the nation, Mr. Buchanan wrote in part:

> Another sign that the banks are awaking to the reality of the nightmare is a screed that lately arrived at this writer's syndicate from one Fraser P. Seitel, vice-president of Chase Manhattan.
>
> Terming this writer's comments "wrong," "stupid," "inflammatory," and "the nonsensical ravings of a lunatic," Seitel nevertheless suggested that the syndicate "tone down" future writings, "at least 'til the frenetic financial markets get over the current hysteria."*

The columnist went on to describe the fallacy in bankers' arguments and ended by suggesting that banks begin immediately to cut unnecessary frills—such as directors of public affairs.

Moral: Never get into a shouting match with somebody who buys ink by the barrel.

Secondary moral: Just because you write a textbook doesn't mean you know everything!

*Patrick J. Buchanan, "The Banks Must Face Up to Losses on Third World Loans," *New York Post*, 12 July 1984, 35.

percent of those polled believed that "fewer than half the reporters understand the subject they are writing about."[14] In another study of top communications officers in 1,300 large corporations, the broad majority said that senior executives were actively participating in news interviews and that, in general, corporate spokespersons were treated fairly in most interviews.[15]

Most attitude studies about the media have been inconclusive. One by the America Society of Newspaper Editors concluded that 75 percent of U.S. adults "have some problem with media credibility." However, a later study commissioned for Times Mirror Co., the publisher of the *Los Angeles Times*, found "there is no credibility crisis for the nation's news media." Among the findings from the 5,000 interviews were that 79 percent believe the media care about the quality of their work; 72 percent rated the media "highly professional"; and 55 percent said the media report accurately.[16]

In the 1990s though, the media continued to present an inconsistent display of honesty. In one celebrated 1989 episode, ABC News faked footage depicting an American diplomat handing a briefcase to a Soviet agent. Peter Jennings, the network anchorman, later apologized because viewers were advised too late that the footage was a "simulation." The simulation technique, which became a staple of the expanding roster of gossipy, news-oriented shows, was branded bluntly by the former president of NBC News as "marvelous for drama, but for news, it's lies."[17]

So even in the '90s, with the media and the public still on different philosophical wavelengths, the challenge for public relations professionals remains one of fostering a closer relationship between their organizations and those who present the news.

Handling the Media

It falls on public relations professionals to orchestrate the relationship between their organizations and the media. To be sure, the media can't ordinarily be "manipulated" in our society. They can, however, be confronted in an honest and interactive way to convey the organization's point of view in a manner that may merit being reported. First, an organization must establish a formal media relations policy (Figure 14–3). Second, an organization must establish a philosophy for dealing with the media, keeping in mind the following 10 principles:

1. *Flexibility is key.*

Having a plan to deal with the media is fine. But an organization must remain flexible, dealing with media inquiries on a case-by-case basis and not being locked into an overly restrictive policy.

CHASE

Organization and Policy Guide

**Unit with Primary
Responsibility for Review** Corporate Communications

It is frequently in Chase's best interest to take advantage of interest from the media to further the reputation and services of the bank. In dealing with the media, Chase officers must be careful to protect the best interests of the bank, particularly with regard to the area of customer confidence.

The following policies will serve as a guideline for media relationships. Specific questions regarding the media should be addressed to the Public Relations Division.

Inquiries from the Media

Most journalists call the Public Relations Division when they need information about the bank or wish to arrange an interview with a bank officer. Many times, public relations officers are able to handle inquiries directly. Occasionally, however, more complex questions require input from appropriate bank officers. In these cases, inasmuch as journalists are often under deadline pressures, it is important that bank officers cooperate as fully and respond as promptly as possible. Such cooperation enhances Chase's reputation for integrity with the news media.

Less frequently, reporter inquiries will go directly to line officers. In this case, either one of two responses may be appropriate:

1. If a journalist seeks simple, factual information such as Chase's current rate on a particular savings instrument or the factual details of a new bank service, officers may provide it directly.

2. If a reporter seeks Chase policy or official opinion on such subjects as trends in interest rates, legislation, etc., responses should be reviewed with the Public Relations Division. If an officer is unfamiliar with a particular policy or requires clarification of it, he or she should always check first with the Public Relations Division before committing the bank in print.

In talking with a reporter, it is normally assumed that whatever a bank officer says may be quoted and attributed directly to him or her by name as a spokesperson for the bank. An officer not wishing to be quoted must specify that desire to the journalist.

Most reporters with whom the bank deals will respect an officer's wishes to maintain anonymity. Most journalists recognize that it is as important for them to honor the wishes of their sources at the bank as it is for the bank to disseminate its comments and information to the public through the news media. Chase's policy toward the media should be one of mutual trust, understanding and benefit.

Interviews With the Media

In order to monitor the bank's relationships with journalists, all requests for interviews with bank officers by journalists must be routed through the Public Relations Division.

As a rule, public relations officers check the credentials of the journalist and determine the specific areas of inquiry to be examined. The public relations officer will then decide whether the interview is appropriate for the bank. When the decision is affirmative, the public relations officer will discuss subject matter with the recommended interviewee and together they will decide on a course of action and Chase objectives for the interview.

A member of the public relations staff is normally present during any face-to-face interview with an officer of the bank. The purpose of the public relations staffer's attendance is to provide assistance in handling the interview situation as well as to aid the reporter with follow-up material.

When a reporter calls an officer directly to request an interview, the officer should check with the Public Relations Division before making a commitment.

Authorized Spokespersons

Vice presidents and above are normally authorized to speak for the bank on matters in their own area of responsibility.

Normally, officers below the level of vice president are not authorized to speak for attribution on behalf of the bank except where they are specialists in a particular field, such as technical directors, economists, etc.

Exceptions may be made in special situations and in concert with the Public Relations Division.

Written Material for the Media

Chase articles bylined by officers may either be written by the officer approached or by a member of the public relations staff. If an officer decided to author his or her own article, the public relations division must be consulted for editing, photographic support and policy proofing.

Occasionally, customers or suppliers may wish to include Chase in an article or advertisement they are preparing. This material too must be routed through the Public Relations Division for review.

FIGURE 14–3 This press relations policy of Chase Manhattan Bank is typical of that found in many large organizations. Relationships with the media are generally encouraged, with the public relations division taking overall responsibility for all of the bank's relationships with journalists. *(Courtesy of Chase Manhattan Bank)*

2. *Provide the media with only one voice.*

The media prefer many spokespeople, but an organization should stick to just one. He or she should be available to one and all in the press, and everyone in the organization should understand that it is that person's job alone to convey information to the outside world.

3. *Don't volunteer the chief as spokesman.*

The media insist on speaking to the "top man." Sometimes this makes sense. Normally, though, exposing the chief executive to the media is the worst thing one can do. It is much better to offer a trained spokesperson, knowledgeable and experienced in dealing with the idiosyncracies of reporters and the media.

4. *Don't always take the lawyers' advice.*

A lawyer's job is to protect the organization from challenge in a court of law. However, a lawyer's advice often may not be responsive to the likely perception of the institution in another critical court—the "court of public opinion." The smart manager always weighs legal advice against public relations advice.

5. *Don't wait until you've got all the facts.*

If you sit there waiting for all the data, you may still be sitting after the public has branded you "guilty as charged." Often, it makes sense to launch a preemptory rebuttal to media charges. It shows the public you're not going to accept unfounded accusations lying down.

6. *Don't answer every question.*

Just because the media ask doesn't mean you have to answer. You have no obligation to answer every question. And you should only answer questions you are prepared to handle.

7. *Squawk if you're wronged.*

If the media print inaccuracies, blast them. Call the reporter and demand a correction. Correct the public record. If you don't, the inaccuracy will go uncorrected for so long that eventually it will become a "media fact."

8. *Don't keep journalists at arm's length.*

As noted, a journalist's job is to get a story, whatever that entails. The public relations professional's role is to be an advocate for the institution. As long as both understand and respect each other's position, cooperating with a journalist can often be in an organization's best interest.

9. *Share information with allies.*

Limiting information only to those who "need to know" can be counterproductive. Employees, customers, and even stockholders can serve as valuable allies with the public and the media. They should be kept aware of the organization's position on issues of media interest.

10. *You can lose the media battle but still win the longer-term credibility war.*

Sometimes, especially if you're wrong, the most sensible thing to do is admit it. Had Richard Nixon done this over Watergate, he might still be president! There is nothing as refreshing as hearing an official admit, "We made a mistake. We'll make restitution. It won't happen again." That's how an organization retains its credibility.[18]

BETWEEN THE LINES

Aw Shaddup!

Nothing was sweeter in the 1990s than hearing about experienced journalists, who ought to know better, putting their proverbial feet in their proverbial mouths.

- In the winter of 1990, network interviewer and Miss America judge Larry King answered another interviewer's question by denouncing Miss Pennsylvania as the "ugliest contestant in the pageant." A devastated Miss Pennsylvania demanded an apology, which was quickly volunteered.

  Poor Larry was at it again some weeks later when he asked, on a national broadcast, if a certain pro football holdout had "a drug problem." The player didn't. But that didn't prevent him and his agent from blasting King for raising the question before 15 million viewers.

- Another cable commentator joined King in the "foot-in-mouth" derby for making what sounded suspiciously like anti-Semitic remarks about Israel's views on a possible war in the Middle East. The commentator, who was denounced by friend and foe alike, had earlier defended a Nazi gas chamber operator being prosecuted for war crimes. The bombastic broadcaster's name? Patrick J. Buchanan (see Between the Lines, p. 375).

Moral: What goes around, comes around.

Summary

A good public relations person can be a great help to a journalist. Generally, practitioners are the first people reporters call inside an organization.

Frequently, the reporter's questions can be handled directly or channeled to a more knowledgeable source within the organization. Often, the intermediation of a practitioner can help journalists reach company sources. In addition, public relations professionals can arrange interviews between journalists and executives. Frequently, practitioners sit in on such interviews to assist interviewees and reporters. The role of the practitioner in these situations should not be to obstruct the interview but to facilitate it.

At the heart of the journalist-practitioner relationship is credibility and trust. True, the two professions march to the beat of different drummers, but they should respect each other's views and responsibilities. Only through mutual respect can adversarial relationships be avoided. Lasting respect can neither be bribed nor bullied. It must be earned through the consistent practice of fair, open, and honest dealings and, again, through the highest degree of professionalism.

DISCUSSION STARTERS

1. What is the difference between public relations and publicity?
2. Do all scholars believe the mass media are as potent a persuasive force today as they were in the past?
3. Describe the difference between 5W's, advocacy, and new journalism.
4. What is the point of view of most journalists toward the establishment?
5. How does the general public view the news media?
6. What is "simulation" in a television news story?
7. Why is the chief executive sometimes *not* the best spokesperson for an organization?
8. Why shouldn't an organization always take its lawyers' advice in dealing with the media?
9. Why should an organization not keep the media at arm's length?
10. What is the best philosophy in dealing with journalists?

NOTES

1. James E. Grunig, "Theory and Practice of Interactive Media Relations," *Public Relations Quarterly* (Fall 1990): 18.
2. "Overheard," *Newsweek* (February 27, 1989): 13.
3. Linda Stevens, " 'Today' Guest Sues—Says Tube Treated Her Like Boob," *New York Post,* 16 March 1990, 6.
4. Jack O'Dwyer, "Corp. PR People Minimize Face-to-Face Press Contact," *O'Dwyer's PR Services Report* (July 1989): 1–2.
5. Kevin Goldman, "TV Network News Is Making Re-Creation a Form of Recreation," *The Wall Street Journal,* 30 October 1989, A4.
6. Judith A. Mapes, "Top Management and the Press—The Uneasy Relationship Revisited," *Corporate Issues Monitor,* Egon Zehnder International, vol. 11, no. 1 (1987): 2.
7. S. Robert Lichter, Stanley Rothman, and Linda S. Lichter, *The Media Elite: America's New Powerbrokers* (Bethesda, MD: Adler & Adler, 1986).
8. John V. Pavlik, *Public Relations: What Research Tells Us* (Newbury Park, CA: Sage Publications, 1987), 59.

9. Bush-Rather Debate Adds to Eroding Public Attitudes Toward News Media," *PR Reporter Purview* (May 9, 1988): 1.

10. "What's News?" *New York University Magazine* (Fall 1989): 16–17.

11. Janet Malcolm, "The Journalist and the Murderer," *The New Yorker* (March 13, 1989): 38.

12. Lewis H. Young, "The Media's View of Corporate Communications in the '80s," *Public Relations Quarterly* (Fall 1981): 10.

13. Albert R. Hunt, "Media Bias Is in Eye of the Beholder," *The Wall Street Journal*, 23 July 1985, 32.

14. Roger Ricklefs, "Business Relations with the Press: Three Versions of the Way It Is," *The Wall Street Journal*, 6 July 1981, 15.

15. "Antagonism: Myth or Reality?" *Public Relations Journal* (November 1981): 62.

16. Jack Kelley, "An Absence of Malice," *USA Today*, 16 January 1986, 6A.

17. Goldman, op. cit., A1.

18. Fraser P. Seitel, "Confronting the Media," *United States Banker* (January 1989): 53.

TOP OF THE SHELF

Irvine, Robert B. *When You Are the Headline: Managing a Major News Story*. Homewood, IL: Dow Jones-Irwin, 1987.

You're NASA's spokesperson when the *Challenger* space shuttle explodes. How do you prepare for the media scrutiny that in moments will descend upon your organization? The answer to this and other media dilemmas is given in *When You Are the Headline*, a guide to dealing with journalists when major news breaks.

Bob Irvine, former chief spokesperson for the first heart transplant patients at Humana Hospital, employs contemporary news stories to show the do's and don'ts of managing situations that attract intense media interest: Do be candid and forthright with the press, as Delta Air Lines was after a plane crash in Dallas; don't let hours elapse before providing critical information, as NASA did following the *Challenger* disaster. Irvine suggests enacting a "60-Minute Game Plan" after important news erupts. In it, he advises specific action for handling everything from responding to initial media calls to gathering information to securing management approval. He details these and other steps, providing students with a complete lesson in press relations.

When You Are the Headline offers useful advice that enables practitioners to deal confidently with the press and protect their organization's reputation. This book is recommended for anyone intrigued by the challenging and unpredictable world of media relations.

Bacon's Media Alerts. Chicago, IL: Bacon Publishing Co. (332 S. Michigan 60604). Bimonthly.

Biagi, Shirley. *Media/Impact*. Belmont, CA: Wadsworth, 1988.

Blohowiak, Donald W. *No Comment! An Executive's Essential Guide to the News Media*. New York: Praeger, 1987.

Blyskal, Jeff, and Marie Blyskal. *PR: How the Public Relations Industry Writes the News*. New York: Morrow, 1985.

Blythin, Evan, and Larry Samovar. *Communicating Effectively on Television*. Belmont, CA: Wadsworth, 1985.

Boot, William. "Capital Letter: The New Tattlers." *Columbia Journalism Review* (January–February 1988): 14–18. New York: Columbia University. This article discusses distinguishing between news and gossip.

Cook, Timothy E. *Making Laws & Making News*. Washington, DC: The Brookings Institution, 1989 (1775 Massachusetts Avenue, NW 20036).

Danzig, Fred, and Ted Klein. *Publicity: How to Make the Media Work for You*. New York: Scribner's, 1985.

Electronic News Releases. Washington, DC: U.S. Newswire, 1988. (1272 National Press Building 20045).

Evans, Fred J. *Managing the Media: Proactive Strategy for Better Business-Press Relations.* Westport, CT: Quorum Books, 1987.

"Funding the News. Nonprofits and the Media Elite." *Organization Trends*. Washington, DC: Capital Research Center (December 1987) (1612 K Street, NW, Suite 605 20006).

Goulden, Joseph C. *Fit to Print: A. M. Rosenthal and His Times*. Secaucus, NJ: Lyle Stuart, 1988.

Hannaford, Peter. *Talking Back to the Media*. New York: Facts on File, 1986.

Hiebert, Ray E., and Carol Ruess. *Impact of Mass Media*. 2nd ed. White Plains, NY: Longman, 1988.

Hiebert, Ray E., Donald F. Ungurait, and Thomas W. Bohn. *Mass Media V*. White Plains, NY: Longman, 1987.

Hilton, Jack. *How to Meet the Press: A Survival Guide*. New York: Dodd, Mead, 1987.

Howard, Carol, and Wilma Mathews. *On Deadline: Managing Media Relations*. Prospect Heights, IL: Waveland, 1988.

Hunt, Albert R. "Media Bias Is in Eye of the Beholder," *The Wall Street Journal*, 23 July 1985, 32.

Jefkins, Frank. *Planned Press & Public Relations*. Philadelphia: Trans-Atlantic, 1986.

Lavine, John, and Daniel Wackerman. *Managing Media Organizations*. White Plains, NY: Longman, 1987.

Martel, Myles, Ph.D. *Mastering the Art of Q&A*. Homewood, IL: Dow Jones-Irwin, 1989.

Martin, Dick. *Executive's Guide to Handling a Press Interview*. Babylon, NY: Pilot Books, 1985.

Media News Keys (40-29 27th St., Long Island City, NY 11101). Weekly.

Miller, Peter G. *Media Marketing*. New York: Harper & Row, 1987.

Newletter on Newsletters (P.O. Box 311, Rhinebeck, NY 12572). Weekly.

"The People and the Press." New York: Times Mirror Co. (January 1986). An investigation of public attitudes toward the news media was conducted by the Gallup organization.

Radio Interview Guide. New York: Book Promotions, 1988.

Robinson, James W. *Winning Them Over.* Rocklin, CA: Prima Publishing & Communications, 1987.

Sellers, Jim. *The Only Press Guide You'll Ever Need.* Eugene, OR: Capital Ideas Press, 1988.

Speakes, Larry. *Speaking Out.* New York: Macmillan, 1988.

St. John, Tracy. *Getting Your Public Relations Story on TV and Radio.* Babylon, NY: Pilot Books, 1986.

Ungurait, Donald F., Thomas W. Bohn, and Ray Eldon Hiebert. *Media Now.* White Plains, NY: Longman, 1986.

Weiner, Richard. *Dictionary of Media and Communications.* New York: Simon & Schuster, 1990.

CASE STUDY   They're Heeere!

Suppose you gave a party and "60 Minutes" showed up at the door. Would you let them in? Would you evict them? Would you commit hara-kiri?

Those were the choices that confronted The Chase Manhattan Bank at the American Bankers Association convention in 1988, when "60 Minutes" came to Honolulu to "get the bankers."

The banking industry at the time was taking its lumps. Profits were lagging. Loans to foreign governments weren't being repaid. And it was getting difficult for poor people to open bank accounts.

Understandably, few bankers at the Honolulu convention cared to share their thoughts on camera with "60 Minutes." Some headed for cover when the cameras approached. Others barred the unwanted visitors from their receptions. In at least one case, a "60 Minutes" cameraman was physically removed from the hall. By the convention's third day, the "60 Minutes" team was decrying its treatment at the hands of the

bankers as the "most vicious" it had ever been accorded.

By the third night, correspondent Morley Safer and his "60 Minutes" crew were steaming and itching for a confrontation.

And that's when "60 Minutes" showed up at our party.

For 10 years, Chase Manhattan had sponsored a private convention reception for the media. It combined an informal cocktail party, where journalists and bankers could chat and munch hors d'oeuvres, with a more formal, 30-minute press conference with the bank's president. The press conference was on-the-record, no-holds-barred, and frequently generated news coverage by the wire services, newspapers, and magazines that regularly sent representatives. No TV cameras were permitted.

But when we arrived at Honolulu's scenic Pacific Club, there to greet us—unannounced and uninvited—were Morley and the men from "60 Minutes"—ready to do battle.

The ball was in our court. We faced five questions that demanded immediate answers.

■ *First, should we let them in?*

What they wanted, said Safer, was to interview our president about "critical banking issues." He said they had been "hassled" all week and were "entitled" to attend our media reception.

But we hadn't invited them. And they hadn't had the courtesy to let us know they were coming. But it was true that they were members of the working press. And it was also true that our reception was intended to generate news.

So we had a dilemma.

■ *Second, should we let them film the press conference?*

Chase's annual convention press conference had never before been filmed. TV cameras are bulky, noisy, and intrusive. They threatened to sabotage the normally convivial atmosphere of our party. Equally disconcerting would be the glaring TV lights that would have to be set up. The "60 Minutes" boys countered that their coverage was worthless without film. Theirs, after all, was a medium of pictures, and without the pictures, there could be no story. As appetizing as this proposition sounded to us, we were worried that if we refused their cameras, what they might film instead would be us blocking the door at an otherwise open news conference.

So we had another problem.

■ *Third, should we let them film the cocktail party?*

Like labor leader Samuel Gompers, television people are interested in only thing: "More!" In the case of our reception, we weren't eager to have CBS film the cocktails

and hors d'oeuvres part of our party. We were certain the journalists on hand would agree with us. After all, who wants to see themselves getting sloshed on national television when they're supposed to be working?

■ *Fourth, should we let them film a separate interview with our president?*

Because few top people at the convention were willing to speak to CBS, "60 Minutes" was eager to question our president in as extensive and uninterrupted a format as possible. Safer wanted a separate interview before the formal press conference started.

So we also had to deal with the question of whether to expose our president to a lengthy, one-on-one, side-room interview with the most powerful—and potentially negative—television news program in the land.

■ *Fifth, should we change our format?*

The annual media reception/press conference had always been an informal affair. Our executives joked with the journalists, shared self-deprecating asides, and generally relaxed. Thus, in light of the possible presence of "60 Minutes," we wondered if we should alter this laid-back approach and adopt a more on-guard stance.

We had 10 minutes to make our decisions. And we also had a splitting headache.

QUESTIONS

1. Would you let "60 Minutes" in?
2. Would you let them film the press conference?
3. Would you let them film the cocktail party?
4. Would you let them film a separate interview with the president?
5. Would you change the format of the party?

Tips from the Top

MYRON KANDEL

Myron Kandel is one of the country's best-known financial writers and broadcasters. After serving as financial editor of three major newspapers, he switched to television in 1980 and helped start Cable News Network. He continues to serve as deputy managing editor of CNN Business News and on-air economics commentator. Kandel lectures frequently and has taught journalism at Columbia University Graduate School of Journalism and City College of New York. He is the author of *How to Cash In on the Coming Stock Market Boom*, published in 1982.

What is the quality of business news coverage on television?

Business news, once the wasteland of television news coverage, has made great strides over a relatively short period of time. It was as recently as June 1980 that Cable News Network began broadcasting the first nightly half-hour business news program in the history of network television. Now, many other news organizations—on cable and public television, in syndication, and to a lesser extent on the broadcast networks—are offering a wide assortment of business news programming. Up to now, however, local television stations have not devoted any real resources or time to such coverage.

What do journalists think of public relations people?

It once was the conventional wisdom that journalists and public relations people were adversaries. I like to think of them, instead, as fellow communicators with different agendas. As long as each understands the other's goals, the relationship can be productive both ways. Some news people—a declining percentage, I think—still dismiss PR people as mere flacks, trying to foist untrue, misleading, or inappropriate facts or stories on the media. Although there may be some of those types still around, that's an antiquated image. As PR people get more and more professional, that image will continue to diminish.

What kind of public relations person do you appreciate?

The PR person I like best is the one who knows what my news organization does, understands our needs, and is responsive to them. Conversely, those I like least don't know enough, or don't care enough, to relate to us specifically. This doesn't mean

385

that a good PR person must necessarily grant our every request. But, first, he or she should know what we do, what kind of programming we're presenting, and who the relevant contacts are. They should understand our time constraints and deadlines and should get back to us accordingly, even if they can't provide a definitive answer. It's always a pleasure to find a PR person who anticipates a need and offers a way to meet it.

A spokesperson who is knowledgeable about his or her organization and has the necessary access to the top to get queries answered impresses me the most. The least impressive are those who obviously don't have the confidence of management to speak for the organization. I'm surprised at how often supposedly professional people are in that situation.

What problems have you encountered with public relations people?

I can't remember an occasion where a PR person lied to me deliberately, but there have been instances where they passed on incorrect information because they themselves were misinformed or were kept in the dark. That kind of situation undermines their credibility and sours any relationship that previously existed. Credibility and integrity are two attributes that any professional PR person must safeguard jealously.

Are most reporters hostile to organizations?

They often give that impression because they must be probing in their questioning and unwilling to accept statements they're given at face value. Rather than hostile or antiestablishment, they are nonestablishment, and that approach may seem hostile. Some news people do have biases that creep into their reports. As an editor, it's my responsibility to see that this does not happen. If a persistent pattern exists, I would welcome being informed about it. The principal goal of any news organization is to present the news fairly and objectively.

What is the status of the relationship between journalists and public relations people?

I like to refer to the state of the journalist-public relations relationship as an uneasy alliance, meaning that although they work together, each side may on occasion have a different objective. Nearly all the time, but not always, they share the goal of truth. They always share a desire for accuracy. The trend in recent years has been toward greater professionalism on both sides, and that means more respect and cooperation.

15

Employees

The first step in promoting positive external public relations is achieving good internal public relations. If management speaks out of one side of its mouth to its external constituencies and out of the other to its internal groups, it will lose credibility. And employees must be solidly on management's side; without their support, a company is unlikely to communicate convincingly with the outside world. In effect, every employee is a public relations spokesperson for the organization. Consequently, practitioners are finding more and more that sound public relations begins at home (Figure 15–1).

Internal communications has become a "hot ticket" in public relations, particularly as organizations face the harsh realities of the 1990s. With fewer employees expected to do more work, staff members are calling for "empowerment"—for more of a voice in decision making. Although some managements are willing, others evidently are not. Resultant relations between employer and employee these days are not particularly good. Just about every researcher who keeps tabs on employee opinion finds evidence of a "trust gap" between management and rank-and-file workers.[1]

Evidence of this trust gap was among the findings of a 1990 opinion study of employees in nearly 300 organizations, conducted by the International Association of Business Communicators in conjunction with employee benefits consultant Towers, Perrin, Forster and Crosby. Among other findings, the study concluded:

- The majority of employees want face-to-face information from first-line supervisors as the preferred source of communication.
- First-line supervisors aren't communicating at satisfactory levels. Senior management remains invisible and out-of-touch.

Pardon our pride.

For generations GE and RCA have touched the lives of millions of people. We have embodied the creative spirit of America. Its technological greatness, scientific advances, dynamism and movement.

We have entertained America and defended it. Illuminated its homes and made its airwaves dance.

Above all, we have been a pulse of progress and free enterprise.

The planned merger of our two great companies is an event that makes us very proud. And equally optimistic.

We will be a company whose strengths will have profound and beneficial effects. A company that will compete with anyone. Anywhere. In every market we serve.

We are proud of the people who over the years have built our two companies into great organizations achieving modern-day miracles. And of the people who've worked so diligently to keep our companies great—through periods of economic difficulties and technological change.

We are two companies with proud pasts. We will become one company with an important future. For the people of this country and countless millions of others around the world.

All will benefit from our products, our services, and our capabilities.

That makes us especially proud. And very enthusiastic.

FIGURE 15–1 Late in 1985, the merger of two huge companies, General Electric and RCA, was heralded by this full-page ad that appeared in the nation's leading newspapers. The ad was designed as much to reinforce employee morale as to win public support. *(Courtesy of General Electric Co.)*

◆ The companywide publication scores high marks from employees in many respects, yet it rates low as a preferred source of information. Although employees are more satisfied with the information they're getting, communications efforts are still not meeting their needs.

◆ Employees are intensely critical of management's unwillingness to listen to them or to act on their ideas.[2]

The employee public itself is composed of numerous subpublics: hourly workers, salaried workers, supervisory staff, union members, official staff, craftsmen, and white-collar workers. With such a diverse mix of subpublics, mass communications aimed at no group in particular may not succeed. Internal communications, like external messages, must be targeted to reach specific subgroups, and communications must be continuous to reinforce consistently management's interest in its employees.

In recent years, several trends have affected employee communications.[3]

◆ **Externalization of communications** With a greater emphasis on relations with the media, government officials, opinion leaders, and external constituencies of all stripes, the need has intensified for employee communication not only to be in sync with the external program, but also to play a larger role in the overall corporate communications function.

◆ **Targeting of the organization** As interest groups swipe at corporations, in particular, employees become much more important to their firms as voters, advocates, and concerned citizens in the political process.

◆ **Changing nature of the internal audience** Employees no longer accept organizational pronouncements at face value. The staff today is generally younger, less well-educated increasingly female, ambitious, and career-oriented at all levels. Today's more hard-nosed employee demands candor in communication.

◆ **Businesslike approach to employee communication** Larger budgets and staffs in internal communications functions have allowed a greater emphasis on research-oriented services, such as climate studies, effectiveness audits, economic education programs, and the like.

◆ **Nonprint emphasis** Face-to-face communication has been emphasized. More emphasis has been placed on small-group meetings, visibility of top executives, and use of audiovisual—particularly video—communications.

One goal of all employee communications must be credibility. The task for management is to convince employees that it not only wants to communicate with them, but also wishes to do so in a truthful, frank, and direct manner.

Credibility: The Key

The employee public is a savvy one. Employees can't be conned because they live with the organization every day. They generally know what's going on and whether management is being honest with them. That's why management must be truthful.

Evidently "being truthful" isn't so easy for many managements. Recent studies indicate that "the days management could say 'Trust us, this is for your own good' are over."[4] Other research indicates that if organizations would (1) communicate earlier and more frequently, (2) demonstrate trust in employees by sharing bad news as well as good, and (3) involve employees in the process by asking for their ideas and opinions, they could substantially increase trust in management.[5] The fact is, employees desperately want to know in what direction an organization is headed and what their own role is in getting it there.

In the '90s, smart companies have begun to realize that well-informed employees are the organization's best goodwill ambassadors. These managements have become more candid in their communications with the staff. One example is AT&T, which introduced, in 1990, a frank and hard-hitting employee magazine, *Focus*. It regularly makes sure that employees hear the news before the outside world does. *Focus* editors invite the staff to challenge management through *signed* Letters to the Editor. One employee wrote, "Although AT&T denies that it discriminates against people with many years of service, . . . believe me it does." Another declared, "I succumb to the prevalent wave of poor morale and general contempt for the company." Explained the editor of *Focus*, "Faith in the company has been shaken," and an honest, straightforward magazine was designed to help restore that faith.[6]

In any organization, employees must feel that they are appreciated. They want to be treated as important parts of an organization; they should not be taken for granted, nor should they be shielded from the truth. Thus, the most important ingredient of any internal communications program must be its credibility.

Employee Communications Strategies for the '90s

Enhancing credibility, being candid, and winning trust must be the primary employee communications objectives in the decade of the '90s. Earning employee trust may result in more committed and productive employees. But scraping away the scar tissue of distrust that exists in many organizations requires a strategic approach to employee communications. Five elements are key in any strategic program.

When something terrible happens

Mourning is a process. When people go through it in the workplace, managers need to understand how to help themselves and others deal with grief.

by Don Vandegrift

The man was struggling with the reality of the untimely death of Jim Olson. "To be honest with you, I don't like going through the process right now of assessing the loss of this man to this company. It's just too difficult to move from the feeling level to the intellectual level so soon.

"My sense of personal loss is much too acute. I haven't allowed myself to think about the full meaning of his death since I got the news."

The employee was in one of the stages of mourning—what the experts call denial. If this sense of loss follows the usual pattern, he will move from denial to anger, guilt, anxiety, disorganization, despair, and powerlessness—not necessarily in that order and not necessarily including every one of these emotions.

As with all processes, mourning can be managed. That may sound cold, but it *must* be managed, or the results of not facing the loss can be disastrous to morale, production, teamwork—

is a process—a necessary process not understood by most. This is particularly true of death in the workplace, a topic sadly current in this corporation. It includes not only the loss of a leader but also the death of a colleague—the person who sits at the desk next to you —a member of your staff, or your boss.

nearly everything that makes an organization effective.

So every supervisor needs to learn how to deal with the individual emotions of his or her staff following a death in the group or in the larger organization. At the same time, the supervisor has to handle his or her own emotions.

Where do you go to get guidance on this subject?

It's not easy. There are countless books and articles on living through the deaths of spouses, parents, children, and friends, and other books on dealing with sudden losses, such as those resulting from accidents and suicides. But it's hard to find books or articles on death in the workplace.

What's left is to extrapolate what is common to all personal loss and grieving into the work situation. And one message above all comes through clearly in material on the subject: we must accept the fact that grief and mourning are normal, and supervisors should be prepared to provide a channel for everyone involved to mourn in their own way and their own time.

This is particularly difficult in the business world, where emotion of the depth that grief produces has not been traditionally acceptable and might even be thought to be frivolous in some quarters. So, in effect, the supervisor must almost give permission to grieve.

Experts on this aspect of human behavior agree that conciously grieving over a loss is necessary if people expect to get on with business. One way the supervisor can facilitate the process is to call a special meeting to talk about the deceased or to make such a talk part of a regular staff meeting. Unlike regular business discussions, which help staffs examine complex issues or reach consensus, this type of discussion will allow people to examine their own feelings about the deceased.

Discovering that there are no good or bad feelings—only feelings— may help wipe away guilt stemming,

for example, from selfish reactions to a death: "What does it mean to me? to the business?"

Discussion also helps to actualize the loss of a fellow worker. There is a

The results of not facing a loss can be disastrous to morale, production, teamwork—nearly everything that makes an organization effective.

certain unreality to death, and a frank talk about the details of a person's death and the circumstances surrounding it can bring some people out of the initial shock and numbness resulting from a tragedy to the realization that someone who was part of your day-to-day life is not coming back.

Facing reality in this fashion can

For more information

Much of this article is based on discussions with Alan Youngblood, of the health affairs organization; Joan Tracey, New York/New Jersey regional manager of the employee assistance program (EAP) and her staff of consultants; and AT&T psychologist Dr. Joel Moses. The EAP coordinator in your region is a good source for guidance on managing the mourning process. Books of interest include the following:

On Death and Dying, by Dr. Elisabeth Kübler-Ross.

Death, Grief, and Mourning, by John S. Stephenson.

The Courage to Grieve, by Judy Tatelbaum.

Grief Counseling and Grief Therapy, by J. William Worden, Ph.D.

help a corporate team deal with the practical aspects of the job ahead within the person who died. The process forces introspection and turns energies back toward life. Far from seeming insensitive to the loss suffered by the members of the work group, the entire process can be helpful to them. Death is a crisis—another form of change.

But a warning is necessary here: don't rush the grieving process. Allow for individual differences and continue to provide support, with an understanding that grief and mourning are normal.

Another way of helping people reach restoration and recovery—what counselors on grief call reorganized behavior—is public acknowledgment of the deceased's contributions to the company. This acknowledgment could range from the personal remembrances of individuals in a group to full-scale memorials, possibly involving the entire company.

All of this applies equally in the case of people who had only a superficial relationship with the one who died. The determining factor is not necessarily the closeness or the social significance of the relationship, but the importance that the griever assigns to the lost person. For example, the death of a leader who symbolized important values can be seen as a personal loss by a great many people, and the mourning period should be handled in a fashion similar to those already mentioned.

It is important to demonstrate that the company is interested in people. These efforts to guide people through grief reinforce the company's interest in people by revealing the humanness of an honest display of emotion.

In general, being an understanding, sensitive human being seems to be the key to managing through mourning. When those whom you supervise—and you—can recall the deceased person and the circumstances of the death without pain, you know you've done your job. ∎

FIGURE 15–2   After the shock brought on by phone company divestiture in the 1980s, AT&T has gained a reputation for its candor in employee publications. Typical of its straightforward approach is this article to help employees cope with their grief over the sudden death of beloved AT&T chairman James Olson in 1988. *(Reprinted by permission of AT&T)*

YOU MAKE THE CALL

Buffalo Bank Bashed Over Botched Layoffs

The banking crisis of the late '80s and early '90s spared few institutions. Faced with a more competitive industry and declining profits, banks were forced to lay off substantial numbers of employees. Such was the case for 150 workers at Goldome Bank in Buffalo, NY in 1989. But Goldome's handling of the layoffs created an employee relations nightmare.

- First, employees weren't given advance warning about the layoffs. "Everyone is sitting on pins and needles thinking it's only a matter of time for them, too," said one anonymous employee in press coverage that followed the firings. "They're putting the screws a little tighter all the time. Everyone is very nervous."
- Second, the bank announced nothing to the press. Said Goldome's president, "It is our policy not to comment on staffing levels because there is nothing positive to be gained. We never comment on any specific employee matters." Not unexpectedly, once word seeped out of the Goldome firings, the media were all over the story.
- Finally, and most serious of all, Goldome asked all terminated employees to sign a "Release and Confidentiality Agreement," preventing them from suing Goldome or discussing the layoffs with anyone except "counsel, personal tax adviser, immediate family, or as required by law." The bank threatened to cut a worker's severance pay if he or she refused to sign the confidentiality agreement.

What happened next could have been predicted by any student of public relations. The story was picked up not only in Buffalo, but by the national wires. Goldome employees were labeled "Victims of the Press." Civil liberties advocates and lawyers joined in support of the employees.

So embarrassing did the employee relations furor become that Goldome's president hastily announced that the bank would rescind the confidentiality agreement because its intent "has been submerged by misconceptions . . . . This makes its continued use counterproductive."

In retrospect, Goldome's public relations manager admitted, the negative feelings evoked by the policy "made the whole thing counterproductive. People are fallible. We realized a mistake was made and that our policy was unacceptable to employees and the public-at-large."

QUESTIONS

1. What would you have advised Goldome's president in terms of communications policy at the time of the layoffs?
2. Where did Goldome go wrong in its approach to the layoffs?
3. How would you assess Goldome's remedial actions in the wake of the controversy generated by its layoff policy?

1. *Survey employees' attitudes regularly.*

Ironically, it is organizations that audit their financial resources on a daily basis that regularly fail to take the temperature of their own employees. They "fly blind." Attitude surveys can identify problems before they become crises. Employees who are surveyed about their attitudes, consulted on what the surveys reveal, and then shown action as a result of the survey findings will be much more willing to accept management policies.

2. *Be consistent.*

Management that promises "open and honest communications" must practice them. An open door must *remain* open—not just be partly open, part of the time. Communications must be consistent to be believed. That means conveying the good and the bad on a regular basis.

3. *Personalize communications.*

One study found that 80 percent of corporate chief executives believed "personally communicating with employees benefits the bottom line." Only 22 percent of them did it on any regular basis, however. Workers want personal attention from those for whom they work, particularly their immediate supervisor. In light of this, companies like Union Carbide conduct "town meetings," at which senior managers barnstorm around the nation to answer employee questions.

4. *Be candid.*

Employees in the 1990s are younger, less well-educated, less loyal, and represent more women, minorities, and immigrants than workers of the past. These new, more skeptical, less trusting employees demand honesty, truth, and candor in everything management says.

5. *Be innovative.*

New employees in the work force and increased skepticism in the workplace demand new communications solutions. This means resorting to the new technology—voice, video, data transmission on PCs, and all the rest—to reach workers. Today's work force, weaned as it's been on a daily diet of high-resolution, mind-numbing television, demands innovative solutions to counteract the "trust gap."[7]

Employee Communications Tactics

Once objectives are set, a variety of techniques can be adopted to reach the staff. The initial tool again is research. Before any communications program can be implemented, communicators must have a good sense of staff attitudes. Perhaps the most beneficial form of research to lay the groundwork for effective employee communications is the internal communications audit. This consists essentially of old-fashioned personal, in-depth interviews to determine staff attitudes about their jobs, the organization, and its management, coupled with an analysis of existing communications techniques. The findings of such audits are often startling, always informative, and never easily ignored.[8]

Once internal communications research is completed, the public relations practitioner has a clearer idea of the kinds of communications vehicles that make sense for the organization. Several of the more popular vehicles are discussed here.

Newsletters

By far the medium most heavily used to communicate with employees is print. The long-heralded revolution of pictures and electronics may be the wave of the future, but isn't yet a serious challenger to letters, bulletins, brochures, manuals, and, particularly, the oldest staple in the employee communications arsenal—the employee newsletter.[9]

The format and content of the employee newsletter varies from organization to organization. However, the broad concept of informing the staff through one major organizational publication has stood the test of time.

A traditional "first job" for an entry public relations professional is working on the employee newsletter. In approaching the writing or editing of an employee newsletter, the professional should ponder the following questions.

1. Who is this paper designed to reach?
2. What kind of articles should be featured?
3. What is the budget for the newsletter?
4. What is the appropriate format for the newsletter?
5. How frequently should the newsletter be published?
6. What is the desired approval process for the newsletter?

The answers to these questions, of course, vary from one organization to another, but all should be tackled before approaching the assignment. Employee newsletters should appear regularly, on time, and with a consistent format. Employees should expect them and even look forward to them.

The employee newsletter serves as a first-line communications vehicle from management to explain philosophy and policies. In the 1990s, it becomes increasingly important that such newsletters serve as two-way communications, expressing not only management wishes, but staff concerns as well.

A typical employee newsletter editor must consider the following steps in approaching the task.

1. *Assigning stories.*

   Article assignments must revolve around organizational strategies and management objectives. Job information—organizational changes, mergers, reasons behind decisions, etc.—should be stressed (Figure 15–3). Articles must reflect the diversity of the organization: different locations and departments, as well as the different kinds of people the organization employs. The editor must review with each writer the desired "thesis" conveyed by the article.

2. *Enforcing deadlines.*

   Employees respect a newsletter that comes out at a specific time— whether weekly, bimonthly, or monthly. An editor therefore must assign and enforce rigid copy deadlines. Deadline slippage can't be tolerated if the newsletter is to be respected.

3. *Assigning photos.*

   Many newsletters include photographs. Because internal publications compete with glossy, high-tech newspapers and magazines, organizational photos can't be dull. Editors must take pains to "think visually" by assigning visually arresting photos. The more provocative, the better (Figure 15–4).

4. *Editing copy.*

   An editor must be just that: a critic of sloppy writing, a student of forceful prose, a motivator to improve copy style. Employees must "want" to read what's going on in the organization. Riveting writing must be the goal of a good newsletter.

5. *Formatting copy.*

   An editor must also make the final decisions on the format of the newsletter: how long articles should run, where to put photos, how to crop artwork, what headlines should say, etc. As desktop publishing becomes more pervasive among organizational newsletters, the task of formatting becomes more important for an editor.

6. *Ensuring on-time publication.*

   An editor's job doesn't stop when the newsletter is sent to the printer. It is the editor's responsibility to ensure that no last-minute glitches interfere with the on-time publication of the finished product.

7. *Critiquing.*

   After the publication hits the stands, the editor's job must continue. He or she must scrupulously review copy, photos, placement, content, philosophy,

WEDDING OF THE CENTURY

INNISBROOK, Florida — Lender's Bagels and Kraft Inc. tied the knot in a spectacular wedding celebration held here on Saturday, September 15.

The joining of the two dynamic food companies was symbolized in a colorful ceremony which included eight-foot-high replicas of Kraft and Lender's products marching down the aisle.

"This is the proudest moment of our lives," said Murray and Marvin Lender as they escorted Len, the groom.

The bride, Phyl, was given away by the president of Kraft's Retail Food Group, Keith Ridgway. Len and Phyl had been dating for 20 years.

The weekend was filled with much eating, drinking and merriment as a crowd of more than 250 people including brokers, wives and associates enjoyed the luxurious accommodations at Innisbrook, the world-famous resort hotel in Tampa.

Most guests gained at least five pounds.

FIGURE 15–3 One of the most unusual employee publications in recent years was this issue of the *Bagel Bugle*, published by Lender's Bagel Bakery of West Haven, CT. Lender's commemorated its merger with Kraft, maker of Philadelphia cream cheese, with this special "wedding" edition. *(Courtesy of Lender's Bagel Bakery)*

ALLSTATE INSURANCE COMPANY
ALLSTATE PLAZA CO6
NORTHBROOK, IL 60062

BULK RATE
U.S. POSTAGE
PAID
PERMIT # 170
MELROSE PARK, IL

Agent Andy Wood *was standing in his office, when he looked up and saw a car coming straight for him. He jumped onto his desk, and then onto the car hood to avoid getting hit. With his office in shambles, and while the debris was being hauled away, he's seen here taking a call from a customer. Talk about service!*

FIGURE 15—4   Provocative photos must be one of a newsletter editor's prime considerations. This 1989 example from Allstate's *Team*, its personal property and casualty magazine, set a new standard. *(Courtesy of Allstate Insurance Company)*

and all the other elements that constitute the current product. The goal in critiquing, stated simply, is to make certain that the next edition will be even better. It is this challenge, in particular, that makes the task of a newsletter editor among the most rewarding in public relations work.

One organization devoted originally to internal communications, the International Association of Business Communicators (IABC), has, in a relatively short time, come to rival the much older Public Relations Society of America. With more than 120 chapters throughout the United States, Canada, and the United Kingdom and affiliates in 15 countries, the IABC helps set journalistic standards for communicators.[10]

Management Publications

Managerial employees must know what's going on in the organization, also. The company needs their support. Continual, reliable communication is one way to ensure it. Many firms publish frequent bulletins for management with updates on personnel changes, office relocations, new telephone numbers, and revised company policies. Occasionally, special bulletins concerning new-product developments, breaking company news, or other matters of urgent interest are circulated.

More formal publications, such as management magazines, are often more technical and more confidential than related employee newspapers. For example, a firm may release its corporate mission to all employees through the employee newspaper but may reveal its business profitability objectives only in the management magazine. This element of confidentiality is always a sensitive one. Employees occasionally object that internal publications don't reveal enough pertinent details about corporate decisions and policy. One common complaint is that outside newspaper reporters "know more than we do about our own firm's activities." Although limitations may be necessary for certain issues, those who run the organization must try to be as candid as possible, and in particular with fellow managers.

Because of the very personal, vested interest of a manager in an organization, management publications are generally among the best read of any internal communication. They shouldn't be underestimated as a way to build confidence, enhance credibility, and promote a team spirit.

Employee Annual Reports

It often makes sense to print a separate annual report just for employees. Frequently, the lure of this report—published in addition to the regular corporate shareholder annual report—is that it is written for, about, and by the employees.

Most employees do care about how their organization functions and what its management is thinking. The annual report to the staff is a good place to discuss such issues informally, yet candidly. The report can be both factual, explaining the performance of the organization during the year, and informational, reviewing organizational changes and significant milestones during the year. It can also be motivational in its implicit appeal to team spirit and pride.

Staff reports observe few hard-and-fast rules about concept and format. Staff annuals can be as complex as the shareholder annual report itself or as simple as a brief outline of the highlights of the year for the company. Typical features in the employee annual report include the following:

1. **Chief executive's letter** A special report to the staff reviewing the performance and highlights of the year and thanking employees for their help (Figure 15–5)
2. **Use-of-funds statement** Often a graphic chart describing how the organization used each dollar it took in

3. **Financial condition** Frequently a chart describing the assets and liabilities of the corporation and the stockholders' equity

4. **Description of the company** Simple, graphic explanation of what the organization is and where its facilities are located

5. **Social responsibility highlights** Discussion of the organization's role in aiding society through monetary assistance and employee participation during the year

6. **Staff financial highlights** General description, usually in chart form, of salaries, benefits, and other staff-related expense items

7. **Organizational policy** Discussion of current issues about which management feels strongly and for which it seeks employee support

8. **Emphasis on people** One general theme throughout the report is the importance of the people who make up the organization: in-depth profiles of people on the job, comments from people about their jobs, and/or pictorial essays on people at work

Employees appreciate recognition. The special annual report is a measure of recognition that does not go unnoticed—or unread—by a firm's workers.

Dear fellow employee:

A look at 1988 shows a year of growth, transition and a new momentum that will build on Dow Corning's competitive strengths.

Performance in 1988 was mixed, however new records were set: the sixth consecutive year for sales and the fifth for profits. Considering the global competitive environment, Dow Corning's record of continuously improving performance is a testimonial to the outstanding and sustained efforts of all of you—individually and together.

Sales revenue increased 13% over 1987 with over 55% of our total sales coming from operations outside the United States. Business in Europe slowed from the high growth rates of the past three years. The negative impact of currency translation affected European results in the second half of the year. U. S. results were disappointing. In the U.S. sales volume was up 7.5% over 1987, but margins slipped due to sharp cost increases for our raw materials that were not offset by necessary price increases. Growth was exceptionally strong throughout the Pacific Basin—from Japan all the way down to Australia. Physical volume and favorable currency exchange were major contributors. Inter-America also had an excellent year.

This year's report highlights some exciting new ways Dow Corning people are working together. It also reflects our growing attention to our customers. New facilities in 1988—the Woluwe Personal and Household Care facility, the Automotive Development Center, the Greensboro Technical Service Center—all were conceived with a singular purpose: to better serve our customers.

Today Dow Corning is a growing company with an excellent performance history and competitive advantages where they count the most—technology, product line, production, sales and distribution and finance. We are well positioned for the future. This enviable position largely came about during the 1970s and '80s under the leadership and direction of Jack Ludington. I am pleased that he is continuing in an active role as Chairman.

In less than five years - in 1993 - Dow Corning will celebrate its 50th anniversary. What kind of a company will we be then? What will we *need* to be? It's not too early for all of us to start asking these questions and working together on the solutions. Some things such as improved quality and service are obvious and we have good momentum. On the other hand, we have further to go in customer responsiveness and developing teamwork in all parts of our organization. Your management is committed to make the changes that we need, but *we* need help from each of you. It will take the brainpower and energy of everyone to get the results we need. I am confident we *can* and *will do* what is needed, and we can't wait.

Thank you for your efforts in making as much progress as we did last year. Now, together, let's use '89 as the springboard towards our 50th anniversary. Let's make some real steps in making happen the things we need to do for the Corporation and our own departments and personal activities.

Let's make '89 another year that we can really be proud of.

Lawrence A. Reed
President and Chief Executive Officer

FIGURE 15—5 Typical of the chief executive's letter section in an employee annual report is this 1989 missive from the chairman of Dow Corning to his colleagues around the world. *(Courtesy of Dow Corning)*

BETWEEN THE LINES

Desktop Publishing Emerges

In the 1990s, the advent of desktop publishing, in which a professional can produce a newsletter at his or her own desk, promises to revolutionize employee communications.

Introduced in 1985, desktop publishing allows an editor to write, lay out, and typeset a piece of copy. Indeed, the term *desktop publishing* itself is a misnomer. Desktop layout or desktop page layout is more accurate. Desktop publishing requires a personal computer, a laser printer, and software for word processing, charts, and drawings, if desired, and publishing applications such as layout. Experts say that anything less than a $10,000 investment for a desktop publishing workstation and software might not be worth the aggravation.

Desktop publishing allows a user to control the typesetting process in-house, provides faster turnaround for clients, and saves money on outside design.

The near-term future for desktop publishing will include scanning photos and drawings, incorporating those images into page layouts, using the computer to assign color in design elements, and, instead of printing camera-ready pages, producing entire color-separated pages of film from which a printer can create plates for printing.

To be sure, desktop publishing is still in its infancy for internal communicators. Most who have switched to desktop publishing to gain control and curb costs of their printed materials combine the new high technology with more conventional editing methods. Some who have tried desktop publishing complain that it takes the human part of writing and editing out of newsletter production.

Nonetheless, with desktop video already being hailed as the next generation of desktop publishing, the continued perfection of the new technology will surely change the way that public relations writers and editors approach employee communications in the 1990s.

Bulletin Boards

Bulletin boards are making a comeback in corporations, hospitals, and other organizations. For years they were considered second-string information channels, generally relegated to the display of federally required information and policy data for such activities as fire drills and emergency procedures. Most employees rarely consulted them. But the bulletin board has experienced a renaissance and is now being used to improve productivity, cut waste, and reduce accidents on the job. Best of all, employees are taking notice.

How come? For one thing, yesterday's bulletin board has become today's news center. It has been repackaged into a more lively visual and graphically arresting medium. Using enlarged news pictures and texts, motivational messages, and other company announcements—all illustrated with a flair—the bulletin board has become a primary source of employee communications. Hospitals in particular have found that a strategically situated bulletin board outside a cafeteria is a good way to promote employee understanding and cooperation.

One key to stimulating readership is to keep boards current. One person in the public relations unit should be assigned to this weekly task.

Internal Video

Just as increasing numbers today are receiving their external news from television, so, too, is television—more specifically, videotape—becoming an internal medium of preference for many organizations. Faced with the fact that upward of 80 percent of the public gets much of its news from television, major companies have headed to the tube to compete for their employees' attention.

Internal television can be demonstrably effective. A 10-minute videotape of an executive announcing a new corporate policy imparts hundreds of times more information than an audiotape of that same message, which, in turn, contains hundreds of times more information than a printed text of the same message.[11]

In the 1990s, internal video, like desktop publishing, appears ready to take off.

♦ Burger King in Miami produces video in an in-house studio and sound stage to train workers in its 5,000 restaurants. All Burger King restaurants have playback equipment. Key messages and philosophies are distributed to run 20 minutes or less.

♦ Miller Brewing Company produces a 20-minute video magazine, distributed every three months to all company locations. It features new company commercials, brand promotions, happenings at Miller plants, and employee human interest stories. Miller's reasoning is that it's top executives can more easily talk on a five-minute video than in person to its far-flung locations.[12]

♦ The Ford Motor Company takes the unprecedented step of stopping work on assembly lines to show videotapes to workers. In one celebrated 1988 incident, Ford showed a quality-improvement videotape at 35 plants employing 100,000 workers. By doing so, Ford underscored the importance of the message conveyed in its tapes and also the new prominence of internal video.[13]

◆ General Electric Company in 1989 announced the creation of an international telecommunications network to permit employees to communicate worldwide, using voice, video, and computer data. The network will allow face-to-face meetings of GE employees around the globe, reducing the need for overseas travel.[14]

Notwithstanding its power, internal video also is a medium that must be approached with caution. Specifically, a public relations professional must raise at least a dozen questions before embarking on an internal video excursion.

1. Why are we doing this video?
2. Whom are we trying to reach with this video?
3. What's the point of the video?
4. What do we want viewers to do after seeing the video?
5. How good is our video script?
6. How sophisticated is the quality of our broadcast?
7. How innovative and creative is the broadcast? Does it measure up to regular television?
8. How competent is our talent?
9. How proficient is our crew?
10. Where will our viewers screen the video?
11. With what communications vehicles will we supplement the video?
12. How much money can we spend?[15]

The key to any internal video production is first to examine internal needs, then to plan thoughtfully before using the medium, and finally to reach target publics through the highest-quality programming possible. Broadcast quality is a tough standard to meet. If an organization can't afford high-quality video, it shouldn't get involved.

Supervisory Communications

First and foremost, employees want information from their supervisors. Supervisors, in fact, are the preferred means for 90 percent of employees, making them the top choice by far. In 1980, about two-thirds of employees surveyed said that their supervisors discussed job performance at least once a year. Today that percentage has jumped to close to 90 percent.[16]

That's the good news.

The bad news is that while 55 percent of employees in 1980 said their supervisor was a good source of information, that percentage hasn't

The Bilgewater Breakthrough

For 20 years the *Bilgewater Bugle* has served the faculty of Bilgewater College. The *Bugle* reports regular employee newspaper fare, including research grants, personnel changes, and employee features. Bilgewater's public information office has not surveyed faculty opinions about the *Bugle* for some time, but director Chico Chesterton feels it's time for a change. "Television," according to Chesterton, "is the name of the game these days. What we really need is a video house organ to complement the *Bugle,* for faculty and students."

In setting out to convince the college president, Chesterton posits the following:

1. Because students spend more time watching television than they do reading, TV is an excellent way to inform them about the school's policies and programs.
2. TV monitors can be situated throughout student and faculty lounges so that in-house television can be continuously broadcast during the lunch hour. In this way, normal class time need not be disturbed.
3. Students and faculty might be quite willing to watch the lunchtime TV shows as they relax before or after they have eaten or after their normal shopping and browsing time at the numerous stores in the area.
4. People will like seeing their fellow students and teachers in the roles of television personalities.
5. Students will appreciate having a choice between the daily feature films shown in the student union and the in-house TV shows shown in the lounge.
6. The constant broadcast of in-house television may help motivate those who normally sleep in the lounge during their lunch period.
7. By seeing faculty and administration in interviews on the screen at lunchtime, students and teachers will feel closer to and more a part of the college team.

QUESTION

What do you think of Chico's reasoning?

changed in a decade. While employees today are somewhat more likely to think that their supervisors are being kept informed by higher management, they are not reaping the benefits any more today than they did in the 1980s. Thus, while most employees vastly prefer information from their supervisor over what they learn through rumors, many still rely on the grapevine as a primary source of information.

What can public relations departments do to combat this?

Some departments formalize the meeting process by mixing management and staff in a variety of formats, from gripe sessions to marketing/planning meetings. Many organizations embrace the concept of skip-level meetings, in which top-level managers meet periodically with employees at levels several notches below them in the organizational hierarchy. Just as with any other form of communication, the value of meetings lies in their substance, regularity, and the candor managers bring to face-to-face sessions.

Dealing with the Grapevine

In many organizations, the company grapevine is one of the most powerful means of communications. But the rumor mill can be devastating. As one employee publication described the grapevine:

> It's faster than a public address announcement and more powerful than a general instruction. It's able to leap from L.A. to San Francisco in a single bound. And its credibility is almost beyond Walter Cronkite's.

Rumors, once they pick up steam, are difficult to stop. Consequently, an organization must work to correct rumors as soon as possible, because employees tend to distort future events to conform to a rumor.

Identifying the source of a rumor is often difficult, if not impossible—and it's usually not worth the time. However, dispelling the rumor quickly and frankly is another story. Often a bad news rumor—about layoffs, closings, and so on—can be most effectively dealt with through forthright communication. Generally, an organization makes a difficult decision after a thorough review of many alternatives. The final decision is often a compromise, reflecting the needs of the firm and its various publics, including, importantly, the work force. However, in presenting a final decision to employees, management often overlooks the value of explaining how it reached its decision. By comparing alternative solutions so that employees can more clearly understand the rationale behind management decisions, an organization may make bad news more palatable.

As demonic as the grapevine can become, it shouldn't necessarily be treated as the enemy in effective communications with employees. A company grapevine can be as much a communications vehicle as internal publications or employee meetings. It may even be more valuable because it is believed, and everyone seems to tap into it.

Summary

The best defense against damaging grapevine rumors is a strong and candid communications system. Employee communications may just be the most neglected strategic opportunity in corporate America. Organizations build massive marketing plans to sell products but often fail to apply that same knowledge and energy to communicating with their own employees.

In the 1990s, organizations have no choice but to build rapport with and morale among employees. Public relations professionals must seize this initiative to foster the open climate that employees want and the two-way communications that organizations need. If public relations people don't rise to this challenge, the employee communications function is likely to fall to the management of human resources professionals.

It is up to public relations professionals to suggest appropriate vehicles, tone, and content, to ensure meaningful and effective communication with employees.

DISCUSSION STARTERS

1. According to recent research, are employees satisfied with the level and content of the communications they receive from management?
2. What one element is the key to organizational communication?
3. What are five strategic keys to effective employee communications in the 1990s?
4. What method of employee communications is making a "comeback" in many organizations?
5. What are the primary tasks of an employee newsletter editor?
6. What are typical features in an employee annual report?
7. What questions should be raised before communicating through internal video?
8. What is the preferred channel of communications among most employees?
9. What is the best way to combat the grapevine?
10. What function has challenged public relations in the management of employee communications?

NOTES

1. Alan Farnham, "Bridging the Trust Gap," *Fortune* (December 4, 1989).
2. Julie Foehrenbach and Steve Goldfarb, "Employee Communications in the 90s: Greater Expectations," *IABC Communication World* (May–June 1990): 101.
3. Roy G. Foltz, "Learning to Speak with One Voice," *Public Relations Journal* 1982): 30–31.
4. Farnham, loc. cit.
5. Foehrenbach and Goldfarb, loc. cit.
6. "'Focus' Strives for Credibility Through Candor," *Ragan Report* (October 1, 1990): 3.
7. Fraser P. Seitel, "Leaping the 'Trust Gap'," *United States Banker* (November 1990): 61.
8. Ronald Goodman and Richard S. Ruch, "The Role of Research in Internal Communication," *Public Relations Journal* (July 1982): 19.
9. "The Winner and Champeen Is: Print," *Ragan Report* (January 16, 1989): 1.
10. For further information about the International Association of Business Communicators, write IABC, 807 Market Street, Suite 940, San Francisco, CA 94101.
11. Douglas P. Brush, "Internal Communications and the New Technology," *Public Relations Journal* (February 1981): 10–11.
12. "Trends in Non-Print Employee Communications," *Ragan Report* (May 8, 1989): 3.

13. John Holusha, "Live, From Detroit, The Big Three on TV," *The New York Times*, 14 November 1988, D3.

14. Calvin Sims, "Global Communications Net Planned by GE for Its Staff," *The New York Times*, 31 May 1989, D1.

15. Fraser P. Seitel, "In-House Video: Think Before You Tape," *United States Banker* (December 1989): 60–61.

16. Foehrenbach and Goldfarb, op. cit., 104.

TOP OF THE SHELF

Smith, Alvie L. *Innovative Employee Communication.* Englewood Cliffs, NJ: Prentice-Hall, 1991.

Alvie Smith says an informed employee is a more productive and satisfied employee. This belief is the heart of *Innovative Employee Communication,* Smith's complete guide to internal communications.

A former director of corporate communications for General Motors, Alvie Smith provides the essentials for planning, organizing, and conducting employee communications programs that help generate enthusiasm, commitment, teamwork, and better performance. He counsels communicators to engage a variety of media—publications, video, face-to-face meetings—to provide workers with meaningful information consistent with management's objectives. Smith also promotes research, which he says should be used not only to help plot future communications programs, but to gauge the success of current ones. He accentuates his instruction with meaty case studies featuring corporate titans like AT&T, General Electric, and Union Carbide.

Smith says that "winning back the loyalty and commitment of employees" will be the paramount challenge facing communicators in the 1990s. If that's true, then reading *Innovative Employee Communication* is the first step toward victory.

SUGGESTED READINGS

Anderson, Walter. *Handbook of Business Communications.* (Available from Box 243, Lenox Hill Station, New York, NY 10021.)

Corbett, William. "The Bottom Line in Intern Communications: The Human Factor." *Tips & Tactics* (May 30, 1988). (Supplement of *PR Reporter*). The writer stresses how important informed, motivated staffers are to their firms. He goes on to detail various channels of company communications.

Employee Annual Report and Update. Chicago: Ragan Communications, 1986 (407 S. Dearborn 60605).

How to Prepare and Write Your Employee Handbook, 2nd ed. New York: AMACOM, 1988 (135 W. 50th St. 10020).

Kiechel, Walter, III. "No Word from on High." *Fortune* (January 6, 1986): 125–126.

CASE STUDY   Hill & Knowlton's Employee Relations Snafu

As the nation's largest public relations counseling firm, Hill & Knowlton is used to helping its customers deal with crises. But in the spring of 1990, H&K created a knotty public relations problem for itself, particularly with its own employees, by agreeing to promote the antiabortion views of the Bishop's Pro-Life Committee of the U.S. Catholic Conference. The new account, which reportedly would generate $5 million over five years, drew intense criticism both within and outside the firm.

The issue actually began in 1989, when the Supreme Court agreed to address once again the issue of legalized abortion, originally addressed in the landmark case *Roe v. Wade*. The National Conference of Catholic Bishops and the U.S. Catholic Conference decided at a conference in Washington, D.C. that "the rights of the unborn child is the fundamental human rights issue of our time." They decided that they had lost ground to "pro-choice" advocates and needed to reframe the debate—thus the decision to hire a public relations firm to help them.

In early 1990, the bishops reportedly approached Burson-Marsteller, the second largest public relations firm, and were turned down. Then they turned to H&K.

H&K president Bob Dilenschneider didn't hesitate. "Ever since John W. Hill founded the firm, Hill & Knowlton has recognized that every legitimate organization or cause has the constitutional right to self-expression," Dilenschneider said. "When considering an offer from the Catholic bishops, we were clearly aware that our acceptance would subject us to criticism and possible villification."

Including, most stingingly, from the H&K staff.

An estimated 65 percent of H&K employees were women. When word of the new account spread, more than a third of the headquarters staff signed a petition of protest. Dozens of employees in Washington and New York refused to work on the project. Many were outraged, especially at the way management made known its acceptance of the account.

Indeed, the first many staffers knew about it was when syndicated columnists Rowland Evans and Robert Novak reported that H&K had been retained by the U.S. Catholic Conference to represent the group in its fight against abortion rights. Said one H&K executive, "Everyone was wandering around in a daze, asking, 'Do you know anything about this? What is going on here?'" Incredibly, H&K had been blindsided by the press—the very consequence it makes a living counseling others to avoid.

Ultimately, a memo, citing the First Amendment rights of free speech, was sent to employees. The memo noted that anyone who didn't want to work on the account would not be compelled to do so. But because the memo was given to department heads, with no explicit instructions to circulate it, most employees reportedly never saw it. Those who did took the memo for what it seemed to be: a news release, rather than a sincere attempt at personal communication.

Some employees felt betrayed. Said one, "I don't want to know that the person I work with 10 hours a day doesn't believe a woman has a right to do what she wants with her body."

Eventually, a month after the Evans and Novak column, a meeting was called in the New York office and an attempt made to put the controversy to rest.

Said Dilenschneider, "An important part of our business is helping clients deal with controversial issues. In this sense, we are advocates. But whenever a cause we agree to represent goes against the grain of an employee or employees, they are automatically exempted from working on it. We have had people, for instance, who refused to work on cigarette accounts and alcoholic beverages. We have always respected their scruples. We always will."

Nonetheless, according to reports, H&K women staffers remained "apoplectic" about the firm's new client. Reports circulated about "regular meetings in the ladies' room." Some suspected that the source of negative media accounts about the bishops' account was Hill & Knowlton employees themselves.

Many in the field rose to Hill & Knowlton's defense. Said one public relations scholar, "H&K's representation of pro-life does not automatically mean that all H&K employees support this position. A PR firm that takes a controversial account is showing that it believes the account has the right to be heard in a meaningful way. The true PR professional at H&K, for instance, could disagree with the pro-life position but still feel pro-life is entitled to a full and fair public hearing. If the PR person does not believe that all legitimate positions are entitled to such a hearing, he or she should get out of the practice."

The real problem for many H&K staffers seemed to lie in the belief that the firm was implicitly attempting to change the law on abortion. Said one 23-year H&K veteran about her company's participation in the issue, "It will ultimately lead to legislation that will interfere with a woman's right to choose what she does with her body . . . legislation that will be, in effect, a form of coercion. And I don't think Hill & Knowlton should be in the business of coercion."

Throughout his most grueling employee communications crisis, Dilenschneider stood his ground. "Our agreement with the Catholic Conference specifies that we will not engage in lobbying. But as an agency that helps the Church voice and project its opinion on the subject, we are doing work that is unquestionably legitimate and, in fact, that millions of Americans agree with.

"To those who criticize us for accepting this assignment, there is no other answer."

QUESTIONS

1. When should H&K have informed employees about the bishops' account?
2. What do you think of the memorandum H&K sent to employees about the account? How might the memo have been refined?
3. What would you have advised H&K management upon receiving the petition of protest from employees?
4. Should H&K have accepted the U.S. Catholic Conference account?

For further information, see James N. Baker with Eleanor Clift, "The Bishops Under Fire," *Newsweek* (April 23, 1990), 24; Jeffrey Goodell, "What Hill & Knowlton Can Do for You," *The New York Times Magazine*, 9 September 1990, 44, 74–75, 102–104; Kevin McCauley, "H&K Keeps Pro-Life Account Despite Heavy Opposition," *O'Dwyer's PR Services Report* (June 1990), 1, 8, 31–35; Barbara W. Selvin, "Abortion Battle at Hill & Knowlton, *Newsday* (April 5, 1990), 51, 54; Peter M. Stevenson, "Hill & Knowlton's Big PR Problem," *Manhattan, Inc.* (July 1990), 61–68; and Harold W. Suckenik, "H&K's Pro-Life Account Is Example of Professionalism," *O'Dwyer's Services Report* (July 1990), 43.

Tips from the Top

ROBERT S. COLE

Robert S. Cole is vice-president and director of public relations for the New York State Bankers Association. He has also served as manager of Bank of America's public relations activities in the Eastern United States and Canada, director of development for the Deafness Research Foundation, and assistant director of public relations at Queens College. A former reporter for the *New York Daily News*, he teaches public relations at St. John's University in New York City and is the author of *The Practical Handbook of Public Relations*. Cole also chairs the financial services section of the Public Relations Society of America.

What are the fundamental principles in dealing with employees?

Management must be honest with employees, maintain a two-way flow of communications, and be willing to share bad, as well as good, news. Most of all, management has to demonstrate through verbal, print, and electronic communications that it genuinely cares about getting information to and from its staff.

How can employee communications influence morale?

Very simply, informed workers are better workers—hence, happier and more productive. They know how their work fits into the overall operations of an organization, and they are better able to shape career goals. A well-managed internal communications program can convince employees they'll be told what they need to know to maximize their value to the organization and that they are welcome to contribute ideas and opinions.

Should certain information (e.g., layoffs, losses, lawsuits, etc.) be kept from employees?

Never and yes. Never on layoffs, losses, lawsuits, or the like because these are important stories that must be shared with employees who have a right and a need to know about them. Moreover, these stories will be covered in the media and through the grapevine, anyway. If employees, on learning of such incidents, don't believe they'll get the real facts through internal communications, the company has a credibility problem—probably a morale problem, too. Yes, however, on the small number of details that violate employee or customer confidentiality. But employees should then be told why they can't have all the facts.

What are the most effective ways to communicate to employees?

It's hard to generalize. Some people prefer to get their information in print; others like video; others remember it better if they are told verbally by their boss, or their boss's boss. With apologies for the mom-and-apple-pie message, I believe honesty, timeliness, thoroughness, and a willingness to receive as well as dispense information have to be parts of the process, regardless of how the message is conveyed. It is also important to recognize that a certain degree of targeting is in order. We can't expect one internal vehicle to meet the needs of all employee groups.

Is the employee newsletter an outmoded concept?

I hope not. Some of the nicer people I know are newsletter editors. More important, people are used to (and receptive to) receiving information in printed form at regular intervals. Additionally, the permanence of words on paper provides a valuable historic perspective. I think, however, that the concept of a newsletter serving as the beginning and the end of employee communications is outdated. There are too many other written, electronic, and verbal vehicles at our disposal. And speaking of "electronic," it would be wise for *all* internal communicators to learn, and master,

desktop publishing. Additionally, they should prepare themselves for video house organs—a medium that didn't live up to its early 1970s promise, but one that seems ready to advance in the '90s.

What are the characteristics that distinguish good employee communicators from mediocre ones?

The ability to (1) educate in an entertaining manner, (2) show how jobs and processes fit into the overall operation, (3) explain how what happens outside the organization can affect the bottom line, and (4) find interesting, work-related ways to get the clerical staff (as opposed to officers only) into company publications. Creativity, flexibility, and empathy help a lot, too. Finally, smart employee communicators recognize that employees and their families are potential goodwill ambassadors. They act accordingly.

How important is top management involvement in employee communications?

Very. Top management must recognize (via budget and staff allocations) the importance of employee communications. They must also participate in the process as spokespeople and listeners, and they must encourage middle management to do the same.

16

Government

The growth of public relations work both *with* the government and *in* the government has exploded in recent years. Although it is difficult to categorize exactly how many public relations professionals are employed at the federal level, it's safe to assume that thousands of public relations-related jobs exist in the federal government and countless others in government at state and local levels. Thus, the field of government relations is a fertile one for public relations graduates.

Since 1970 some 20 new federal regulatory agencies have sprung up, from the Environmental Protection Agency to the Consumer Product Safety Commission to the Department of Energy to the Department of Education to the Drug Enforcement Agency. Moreover, according to the Government Accounting Office GAO, some 116 government agencies and programs now regulate business.

Little wonder that in the 1990s, American business will spend more time calling on, talking with, and lobbying government representatives on such generic issues as trade, interest rates, taxes, budget deficits, and all the other specific issues that concern individual industries and companies. Accordingly, organizations in the 1990s will continue to emphasize and expand their own government relations functions.

Beyond this, the nation's defense establishment offers some 3,000 public relations jobs in military and civilian positions. Indeed, with military service in the 1990s purely "voluntary," the nation's defense machine must emphasize its public information, education, and recruiting efforts in order to maintain a sufficient military force. Thus, public relations opportunities in this realm of government work should expand, as well.

Ironically, the public relations function has traditionally been something of a stepchild in the government. In 1913, Congress enacted the Gillett

amendment, which almost barred the practice of public relations in government. The amendment stemmed from efforts by President Theodore Roosevelt to win public support for his programs through the use of a network of publicity experts. Congress, worried about the potential of this unlimited presidential persuasive power, passed an amendment stating: "Appropriated funds may not be used to pay a publicity expert unless specifically appropriated for that purpose."

Several years later, still leery of the president's power to influence legislation through communication, Congress passed the gag law, which prohibited "using any part of an appropriation for services, messages, or publications designed to influence any member of Congress in his attitude toward legislation or appropriations." Even today, no government worker may be employed in the practice of public relations. However, the government is flooded with public affairs experts, information officers, press secretaries, and communications specialists.

Public Relations in Government

Unfortunately, when people think about the practice of public relations as it applies to government, they tend to envision a blond bombshell bursting onto the Capitol scene, a piggish congressman stuffing cash in his pockets as a secret videotape camera records the scene, or some senator or another checking into a hospital for treatment of some kind of antisocial behavior. Such predilections are indeed unfortunate and unfair.

Most practitioners in government communicate the activities of the various agencies, commissions, and bureaus to the public. As consumer activist Ralph Nader has said, "In this nation, where the ultimate power is said to rest with the people, it is clear that a free and prompt flow of information from government to the people is essential."

It wasn't always as essential to form informational links between government officials and the public. In 1888, when there were 39 states in the Union and 330 members in the House of Representatives, the entire official Washington press corps consisted of 127 reporters. Today there are close to 4,000 full-time journalists covering the capital.

In 1990, the U.S. Office of Personnel Management reported nearly 15,000 public relations-related jobs in government. These consisted of nearly 4,000 in public affairs; 2,000 in writing and editing; 1,700 in technical writing and editing; 2,000 in visual information; 3,300 in foreign information; and 2,000 in editorial assistance.[1]

In 1986, the GAO responded to an inquiry by Senator William Proxmire requesting "how much federal executive agencies spend on public relations." The GAO reported that the 13 cabinet departments and 18 independent agencies spent about $337 million for public affairs activities during fiscal 1985, with almost 5,600 full-time employees assigned to public affairs duties. In addition, about $100 million was spent for congressional affairs activities, with almost 2,000 full-time employees assigned. Also, about $1.9 billion—that's $1.9 *billion*—was spent, primarily in the Department of Defense, "for certain public affairs-related activities not classified as public affairs." These included more than $65 million for military bands, $13 million for aerial teams, $11 million for military museums, and more than $1 billion for advertising and printing regarding recruitment.[2]

United States Information Agency (USIA)

The most far-reaching of the federal government's public relations arms is the United States Information Agency (USIA), an independent foreign affairs agency within the executive branch. USIA maintains 205 posts in 128 countries, where it is known as USIS, the U.S. Information Service. The agency employs 9,000, most of whom are Americans working in Washington, D.C., and overseas and almost 4,000 foreign nationals hired locally in countries abroad.

Under law, the purpose of USIA is to disseminate information abroad about the United States, its people, culture, and policies (Smith-Mundt Act of 1948) and to conduct educational and cultural exchanges between the United States and other countries (Fulbright-Hays Act of 1961). The director of USIA reports to the president and receives policy guidance from the secretary of state.

USIA's 1991 budget estimate totaled nearly $987 million, up about $60 million from 1990, and more than $100 million from 1989. Although this might seem rather hefty as public relations budgets go, USIA officials claim that the USSR has 77,000 people and a budget of billions of dollars to perform this same function.

In the 1990s, with democracy spreading throughout the globe, USIA's mission "to support the national interest by conveying an understanding abroad of what the United States stands for" has been modified to include five new challenges:

1. Build the intellectual and institutional foundations of democracies in societies throughout the world.
2. Support the "war on drugs" in producer and consumer countries.
3. Develop worldwide information programs to address environmental challenges.
4. Bring the truth to any society that fails to exercise free and open communication.
5. Advise the president on foreign public opinion considerations.[3]

Under the direction of such well-known media personalities as Edward R. Murrow, Carl Rowan, and Frank Shakespeare, the agency prospered. However, under the Reagan administration's director, Charles Z. Wick, USIA became an unsurpassed force in communicating America's message. One of Wick's innovations was WORLDNET, a 30-country satellite television network, dubbed the "jewel in the crown" of USIA communications techniques. Other USIA vehicles include the following:

1. **Radio**   Voice of America has 111 transmitters, broadcasts in 42 languages, and reaches 120 million people in an average week. In addition to Voice of America, the USIA in 1985 began Radio Marti, in honor of José Marti, father of Cuban independence. Radio Marti's purpose is to broadcast to Cuba in Spanish and "tell the truth to the Cuban people."

2. **Film and television**   USIA annually produces and acquires an extensive number of films and videocassettes for distribution in 125 countries.

3. **Media**   About 25,000 words a day are radio-teletyped to 214 overseas posts for placement in the media.

4. **Publications**   Overseas regional service centers publish 16 magazines in 18 languages and distribute pamphlets, leaflets, and posters to more than 100 countries.

5. **Exhibitions**   USIA designs and manages about 35 major exhibits each year throughout the world, including Eastern European countries and the Soviet Union.

6. **Libraries and books**   USIA maintains or supports libraries in over 200 information centers and binational centers in more than 90 countries and assists publishers in distributing books overseas.

7. **Education**   USIA is also active overseas in sponsoring educational programs through 111 binational centers where English is taught and in 11 language centers. Classes draw about 350,000 students annually.

Government Bureaus

Nowhere has government public relations activity become more aggressive than in federal departments and regulatory agencies (Figure 16–1). Many agencies, in fact, have found that the quickest way to gain recognition is to increase public relations aggressiveness.

The Federal Trade Commission (FTC), which columnist Jack Anderson once called a "sepulcher of official secrets," opened up in the late 1970s to become one of the most active of government communicators. As a former FTC director of public information described the agency's attitude, "The basic premise underlying the commission's public information program is the public's inherent right to know what the FTC is doing."[4] When the FTC

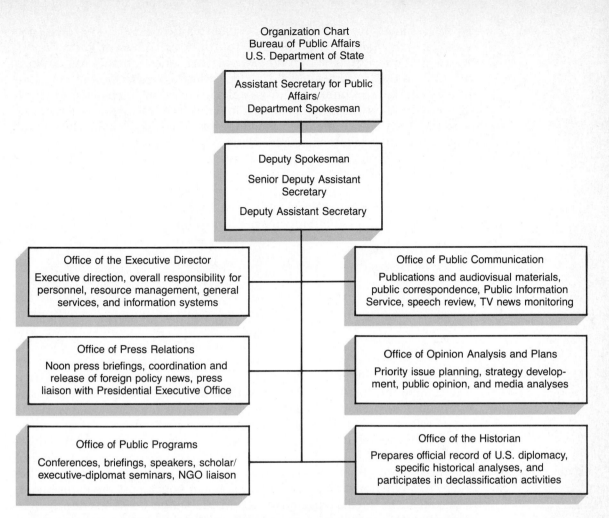

FIGURE 16–1 The Bureau of Public Affairs in the U.S. Department of State is typical of the public information mechanism in a federal department. The assistant secretary for public affairs in the State Department and in most other federal agencies reports directly to the secretary. *(Courtesy of United States Department of State)*

found a company's products wanting in standards of safety or quality, it often announced its complaint through a press conference. Although corporate critics branded this process "trial by press release," it helped transform the agency from a meek, mild-mannered bureau into an office with real teeth.

As noted, other government departments also have stepped up their public relations efforts. The Department of Defense has more than 1,000 people assigned to public relations-related work. In 1986, the Air Force alone answered about 35,000 letters from schoolchildren inquiring about this military branch.[5] The Department of Health and Human Services has a public affairs staff of 700 people. The departments of Agriculture, State, and Treasury each have communications staffs in excess of 400 people, and each spends more than $20 million per year in public relations-related activities.[6] Even the U.S. Central Intelligence Agency has three spokesmen. Out of how many CIA public relations people? Sorry, that's classified.

The most proficient government agencies in public relations must nonetheless work constantly at improving relationships with taxpayers. As the case study at the end of this chapter illustrates, with the *Challenger* disaster of the National Aeronautics and Space Administration in 1986, a government agency's credibility takes years to build up but just a few tragic seconds to lose.

The President

Despite early congressional efforts to limit the persuasive power of the nation's chief executive, the president today wields unprecedented public relations clout. Almost anything the president does or says makes news. The broadcast networks, daily newspapers, and national magazines follow his every move. His press secretary provides the White House press corps (a group of national reporters assigned to cover the president) with a constant flow of announcements supplemented by daily press briefings. Unlike many organizational press releases that seldom make it into print, many White House releases achieve national exposure.

Although most journalists resent administration attempts at news management (some call it news manipulation), most succumb to it. Typical of such news management was President Jimmy Carter's administration in the late 1970s. When his image as a forceful leader began to wane in late 1978, he brought in media specialist Gerald Rafshoon to help improve it. Thereafter, the president began announcing federal grants in local communities, holding town meetings around the country, and even taking adventurous vacations, such as a raft trip down the Idaho rapids. Some believed that even the historic Camp David summit, which brought together traditional enemies Israel and Egypt, was (at least below the surface) a Rafshoon production.

Ronald Reagan was perhaps the most masterful presidential communicator in history. Reagan gained experience in the movies and on television, and even his most ardent critics agreed that he possessed a compelling stage presence. As America's president, he was truly "The Great Communicator." Reagan and his communications advisers followed seven principles in helping "manage the news."

1. Plan ahead.
2. Stay on the offensive.

3. Control the flow of information.

4. Limit reporters' access to the president.

5. Talk about the issues *you* want to talk about.

6. Speak in one voice.

7. Repeat the same message many times.[7]

So coordinated was Reagan's effort to "get the right story out" that even in his greatest public relations test—the accusation at the end of his presidency that he and his aides shipped arms to Iran and funneled the payments to support Contra rebels in Nicaragua, in defiance of the Congress—the president's "Teflon" image remained largely intact. The smears simply washed away.

George Bush was not as masterful as his predecessor in communicating with the American public. But neither was he a slouch at communicating. Bush's primary communications tactic was to hold informal, impromptu news conferences in non-primetime hours. This allowed the president to be more freewheeling and less stiff than in the more formal evening sessions that other presidents favored. While Bush's speech patterns may have sounded like a cross between John Wayne and Jack Nicholson, he earned generally high marks for his accessibility to the public.[8]

While critics in the 1990s complained that American presidents no longer moved without first checking with their media advisers, one of Mr. Bush's key strategists, Roger Ailes, put it thusly:

> The reality is that every successful politician in the history of the world had people around to make them look good. Who do you think told Caesar to wear the purple cape? Who do you think told him he needed six horses pulling a chariot instead of just four? Why do you think he rode through Rome denying he wanted to be king? Who do you think thought that up, him? C'mon![9]

The President's Press Secretary

Some have called the job of presidential press secretary the second most difficult position in any administration. The press secretary is the chief public relations spokesperson for the administration. Like practitioners in private industry, the press secretary must communicate the policies and practices of the management (the president) to the public. Often, it is an impossible job.

In 1974, Gerald terHorst, President Ford's press secretary, quit after disagreeing with the pardon of former President Richard Nixon. Said terHorst, "A spokesman should feel in his heart and mind that the chief's decision is the right one, so that he can speak with a persuasiveness that stems from conviction."[10] A contrasting view of the press secretary's role was expressed by terHorst's replacement in the job, former NBC reporter Ron Nessen. Said Nessen, "A press secretary does not always have to agree with the president. His first loyalty is to the public, and he should not knowingly lie or mislead the press."[11] Still a third view of the proper role of the press secretary was offered by a former public relations professional and Nixon speechwriter who became a *New York Times* political columnist, William Safire.

> A good press secretary speaks up for the press to the president and speaks out for the president to the press. He makes his home in the pitted no-man's-land of an adversary relationship and is primarily an advocate, interpreter, and amplifier. He must be more the president's man than the press's. But he can be his own man as well.[12]

In recent years, the position of press secretary to the president has taken on increased responsibility and has attained a higher public profile. Jimmy Carter's press secretary, Jody Powell, for example, was among Carter's closest confidants and frequently advised the president on policy matters. Powell's successor as press secretary, James Brady, was seriously wounded in 1981 by a bullet aimed at President Reagan as they both departed from a Washington, D.C., hotel. Although Brady was permanently paralyzed, he retained his title as presidential press secretary and returned for limited work at the White House.

Brady was then replaced by Larry Speakes, a former Hill & Knowlton executive, who was universally hailed by the media for his professionalism. During Reagan's second term, Speakes apparently was purposely kept in the dark by Reagan's military advisors planning an invasion of the island of Grenada. An upset Speakes later apologized to reporters for misleading them on the Grenada invasion.

Unfortunately for Speakes, when he resigned in 1988 and published a controversial book about his White House experience, passages involving fabricated presidential quotes (See Chapter 5) made him an easy target for retrospective criticism from former adversaries in the media. Speakes was replaced by a low-key, trusted, and respected lifetime government public relations professional, Marlin Fitzwater (See Chapter 1). Fitzwater distinguished himself in the last two years of the Reagan presidency and in the subsequent administration as President Bush's White House press secretary.

Over the years the number of reporters hounding the presidential press secretary—dubbed by some an imperial press corps—has grown from fewer than 300 reporters during President Kennedy's term to around 3,000 today. Salaries of $40,000 to $70,000, relatively rare in most newspaper offices in prior years, are today commonplace in Washington bureaus. And TV network White House correspondents command six-figure incomes, with each major network assigning two or three correspondents to cover the White House simultaneously. Dealing with such a host of characters is no easy task. Perhaps Lyndon Johnson, the first chief executive to be labeled an imperial president by the Washington press corps, said it best when asked

BETWEEN THE LINES

A Close Call for the Great Communicator

Every iota of Ronald Reagan's communications skill was tested in the spring of 1985, when the president agreed to visit a West German cemetery that turned out to be a burial place for former Nazi SS troops. Jewish and veterans groups implored the president to boycott the cemetery. Indeed, Reagan's advisers were apparently split on whether he should go through with the visit. In the end, the potential embarrassment of West German government officials made the trip to the cemetery at Bitburg an imperative stop.

Right up until the visit, the Washington press corps wrote of little else. Bitburg dominated the daily headlines and evening news broadcasts. And Reagan was the villain. On the day of the fateful visit, ABC and NBC covered it live, and CBS dispatched its anchor, Dan Rather, to London to interview news correspondents who had covered World War II.

The president, like a Christian thrown to the lions, was painted inescapably into a corner. The world waited to see whether "The Great Communicator" could once again wriggle out of his predicament. He did.

Reagan's trip to the Bitburg cemetery was brisk and uneventful. He immediately left the cemetery to visit a nearby concentration camp at Bergen-Belsen. Referring to the 5,000 victims of the Nazi holocaust buried at the Bergen-Belsen site, Reagan said, "Here they lie—never to hope, never to pray, never to love, never to heal, never to laugh, never to cry." So moving and memorable was Reagan's stirring speech at the former Nazi death camp that days later most Americans remembered little else—including the controversy that had preceded the West German trip.

Chalk up another one for The Great Communicator.

by a TV reporter what force or influence he thought had done the most to shape the nature of Washington policy. "You bastards," Johnson snapped.[13]

Dealing with Government

The business community, foundations, and philanthropic and quasi-public organizations have a common problem: dealing with government, particularly the mammoth federal bureaucracy. Because government has become so pervasive in organizational and individual life, the number of corporations and trade associations with government relations units has grown steadily in recent years.

Government relations people are primarily concerned with weighing the impact of impending legislation on the company, industry group, or client organization. Generally, a head office government relations staff complements staff members who represent the organization in Washington, D.C., and state capitals. These representatives have several objectives.

1. To improve communications with government personnel and agencies
2. To monitor legislators and regulatory agencies in areas affecting constituent operations
3. To encourage constituent participation at all levels of government
4. To influence legislation affecting the economy of the constituent's area, as well as its operations
5. To advance awareness and understanding among lawmakers of the activities and operations of constituent organizations

Carrying out these objectives requires knowing your way around the federal government and acquiring connections. A full-time Washington representative is often employed for these tasks.

To the uninitiated, Washington (or almost any state capital) can seem an incomprehensible maze. Consequently, organizations with an interest in government relations usually employ a professional representative, who may or may not be a registered lobbyist, whose responsibility, among other things, is to influence legislation. Lobbyists are required to comply with the federal Lobbying Act of 1947, which imposes certain reporting requirements on individuals or organizations that spend a significant portion of time or money attempting to influence members of Congress on legislation.

In point of fact, one need not register as a lobbyist in order to speak to a senator, congressional representative, or staff member about legislation. But a good lobbyist can earn the respect and trust of a legislator. Because of the need to analyze legislative proposals and deal with members of Congress, many lobbyists are lawyers with a heavy Washington background. Lobbying ranks are filled with former administration officials and congressional members, who often turn immediately to lobbying when they move out of office.

Although lobbyists, at times, have been labeled everything from influence peddlers to fixers, such epithets are generally inaccurate and unfair. Today's lobbyist is more likely to be well informed in his or her field, furnishing Congress with facts and information." Indeed, the lobbyist's function is rooted in the First Amendment right of all citizens to petition government.

What Do Lobbyists Do?

Lobbyists registered with the U.S. Senate have increased from just over 3,000 in 1976 to well over 33,000 in 1990.[14] With the cost of lobbying efforts in the neighborhood of $100 million per year, lobbying has become big business.

But what exactly do lobbyists do?

Lobbyists inform and persuade. Their contacts are important, but they must also have the right information available for the right legislator. The time to plant ideas with legislators is well before a bill is drawn up, and skillful lobbyists recognize that timing is critical in influencing legislation. The specific activities performed by individual lobbyists vary with the nature of the industry or group represented. Most take part in these activities:

1. **Fact finding** The government is an incredible storehouse of facts, statistics, economic data, opinions, and decisions that generally are available for the asking.

2. **Interpretation of government actions** A key function of the lobbyist is to interpret for management the significance of government events and the potential implications of pending legislation. Often, a lobbyist predicts what can be expected to happen legislatively and recommends actions to deal with the expected outcome.

3. **Interpretation of company actions** Through almost daily contact with congressional members and staff assistants, a lobbyist conveys how a specific group feels about legislation. The lobbyist must be completely versed in the business of the client and the attitude of the organization toward governmental actions.

4. **Advocacy of a position** Beyond the presentation of facts, a lobbyist also advocates positions on behalf of clients, both pro and con. Often, hitting a congressional representative early with a stand on pending legislation can mean getting a fair hearing for the client's position. Indeed, few congressional representatives have the time to study—or even read—every piece of legislation on which they are asked to vote. Therefore, they depend on lobbyists for information, especially for information on how the proposed legislation may affect their constituents.

5. **Publicity springboard** More news comes out of Washington than any other city in the world. It is the base for thousands of press, TV, radio, and magazine correspondents. This multiplicity of media makes it the ideal springboard for launching organizational publicity. The same holds true, to a lesser degree, in state capitals.

6. **Support of company sales** The government is one of the nation's largest purchasers of products. Lobbyists often serve as conduits through

YOU
MAKE
THE
CALL

Defusing the Dioxin Controversy

In early 1987, the nation's paper manufacturers faced an impending disaster. Dioxin, the cancer-causing chemical, was believed to be bubbling up in the bleaching process of paper mills, contaminating discharges and pulp in tiny quantities. It seemed unavoidable that the substance would turn up in everyday products. As one official at the American Paper Institute (API) warned colleagues, "The industry could be responding to claims of skin rashes, upset stomachs, aches and pains, animal ills, bad-tasting water, etc., all blamed on our products or processes."

So, rather than wait for the dioxin shoe to drop, the industry took immediate action. Fueled by a $300,000 industry war chest, the paper industry set out to manage public and official views of the controversy.

- It independently tested its products.
- It worked hand in hand with the Environmental Protection Agency, surveying the pollution of paper mills around the country.
- It hired outside experts, who challenged the EPA's view of dioxin risks.
- It trained industry spokespersons to take to the airwaves for interviews about dioxin.
- It launched a consumer survey to assess the public's knowledge of the product.
- It met with journalists of influential media to discuss dioxin.

The industry's objective, according to an API executive, was "that accurate information get out." The industry agreed to have a quick response plan and team in place for the day the dioxin issue would become public news.

One way the industry succeeded in getting the news out objectively was to encourage the EPA itself to discuss dioxin with the media in a balanced, nonhysterical manner. API representatives met regularly with the EPA to discuss the hazards of dioxin and the way the industry was containing them. According to industry memoranda, the paper manufacturers sought to "avoid confrontations with government agencies that might trigger concerns about health risks or raise the visibility of the issue generally."

In September, when the EPA finally held a news conference disclosing dioxin in the pulp and discharges of paper mills, the effect on the public was muted. The EPA's announcement was reasoned and reasonable, helping avert public alarm. Basically, the EPA acknowledged that it and the industry had the potential dangers of dioxin well in hand. Environmentalists, who later criticized the public relations offensive of the paper industry, could only shake their heads at having been caught so off-guard.[*]

QUESTIONS

1. What do you think was key to the paper industry's public relations strategy?
2. Why did the industry enlist the support of the Environmental Protection Agency?

which sales are made. A lobbyist who is friendly with government personnel can serve as a valuable link for leads to company business.

As noted in Chapter 5, the advent of ethics committees in the U.S. Congress has focused increased attention on the role of Washington lobbyists. The 1990 spotlight on the activities of five U.S. senators to win regulatory concessions on behalf of Charles Keating and his Lincoln Savings and Loan empire portrayed in sorry detail how campaign contributors can wield enormous power in influencing legislators. In the main, however, the activities of Washington and statehouse lobbyists, while aggressive and activist, are nonetheless generally above reproach.

Grass-Roots Lobbying

Particularly effective recently has been the use of indirect, or grass roots, lobbying (as opposed to conventional lobbying by paid agents). The main thrust of such lobbying is to mobilize local constituents of congressional members, together with the general public, to write, telephone, fax, or buttonhole members of Congress on legislation.

Grass-roots lobbying is a tactic that has been used most effectively by everyone from so-called consumer advocates, such as the Ralph Nader organization and Common Cause, to President George Bush. In the early 1980s, a resurgence of citizens' activism, not seen since the 1960s, began to appear. Coalitions formed on both national and local levels on issues from arms to economics. Locally, tenants' organizations, neighborhood associations, and various other groups won significant concessions from government and corporate bodies.

The success of such grass-roots campaigns was not lost on big business. Business learned that grass-roots lobbying—applying pressure from the 50 states and the 435 congressional constituencies, from corporate headquarters to plant communities—was at the heart of moving the powers in Washington. In one of the most successful grass-roots campaigns in history, the upstart money-market fund industry in 1981 soundly trounced the more entrenched banking establishment by organizing a massive grass-roots letter-writing campaign. Constituents from all over the country wrote their congressional representatives and state legislators, telling them to keep their hands off the money funds. One outgrowth was that threatened legislation to limit the funds never was instituted.

Effective grass-roots coalitions literally are grown blade by blade. Coalition experts suggest that because public policy agendas are so crowded, only coalitions with a broad-based constituency will succeed.[15] Grass-roots lobbying may include the following steps: (1) persuading community leaders to meet directly with congressional representatives, (2) mobilizing telephone banks and individualized letters to congressional members, (3) instigating mass mailings of postcards or coupons, (4) exhorting shareholders, members, employees, and customers to pressure Congress, and (5) getting the grass-roots organization noticed, through credible and outspoken spokespeople, or even through provocative causes and names, such as Mothers Against Drunk Drivers (MADD).

Whatever the objectives, grass-roots lobbying and lobbying in general are very much in vogue in the 1990s. Rare is the group not represented in Washington. The popcorn industry has its Popcorn Institute. The International Llama Association has its own lobbyists. Hunters have Safari Club International. Those against hunting have the Fund for Animals. Those opposed to increased packaging requirements have United We Resist Additional Packaging (UNWRAP). And all believe their lobbying efforts are most worthwhile.

Political Action Committees

The rise of political action committees (PACs) has been among the most controversial political developments in the last two decades. From about 600 PACs in 1974, the number today stands at just under 4,200, sponsored by corporations, trade associations, labor unions, and ideological groups. Their contributions to House and Senate campaigns have skyrocketed from $8.5 million in 1972 to almost $150 million in 1988.[16] In the 1988 congressional elections, PACs contributed almost one-third of the total funds raised by House and Senate candidates, including almost half the funds raised by House incumbents.

The increased influence of such groups on candidates is one reason why many people—including some legislators themselves—would like to see PACs severely curtailed or even banned.

For many years, the law prohibited corporations from making direct political contributions. In recent years, however, the Federal Election Campaign Act of 1971, with subsequent amendments, has generally allowed incorporated bodies to "solicit funds, maintain them in a segregated fund, pay all expenses of the fund, and disperse the funds at the discretion of the organization's management."[17]

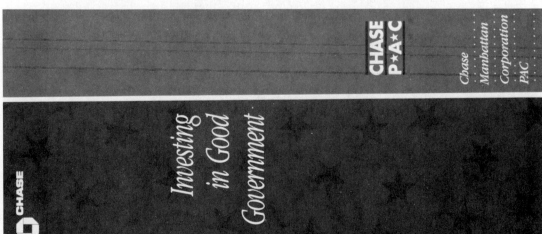

ChasePAC Board Approves New Contribution Guidelines

(Note: ChasePAC's Board passed the following "PAC Contribution Guidelines" at its meeting on January 24, 1990. After vigorous debate, the Board concluded that these guidelines best reflect the Corporation's interests in the political arena.)

Chase Manhattan Corporation's PAC Contribution Guidelines

The Chase Manhattan Corporation Political Action Committee (ChasePAC) makes contributions to create a better business climate and a favorable environment for Chase. ChasePAC funds candidates who demonstrate a philosophical outlook similar to the Corporation's, be they incumbents, challengers or open seat candidates.

ChasePAC has set the following guidelines to help determine which candidates and political committees best forward corporate public policy goals. Extenuating circumstances may necessitate exceptions to this contribution policy.

ChasePAC Guidelines

1. ChasePAC should fund candidates whose philosophical outlook is compatible with that of the Corporation.

2. ChasePAC should avoid giving to competing candidates in any primary, general or special election.

3. ChasePAC should consider a candidate's leadership ability and political effectiveness.

4. The amount of contribution to each meritorious candidate should reflect the candidate's need for funding.

5. ChasePAC should avoid giving to "leadership PACs." These funds may ultimately be funneled to candidates antithetical to ChasePAC goals.

6. ChasePAC should consider a candidate's likelihood of election. Although it shouldn't contribute exclusively to "sure bets," ChasePAC should avoid funding candidates without a logical hope of winning.

7. ChasePAC should concentrate its state and local contributions in areas where Chase Manhattan Corporation has significant resources, facilities and employees.

Above all, ChasePAC funds candidates whose philosophical outlook is compatible with that of the Corporation.

Why Is ChasePAC Important?

A. Wright Elliott:
"Through such programs as ChasePAC, Chase employees have developed a proud record of civic and political activity. ChasePAC remains a valuable asset in corporate efforts to construct a strong bridge between business and government."

Marshall N. Carter:
"Having worked in Washington during the Ford Administration, I can assure you that the PACs are effective—both houses of Congress listen to concerned, informed industry and business spokespersons. Your ChasePAC is one of Chase's most direct ways of making our voice heard."

Elaine Dinn:
"Assuring an even playing field in the 1990s for all institutions competing in the financial services arena is the most important regulatory challenge we face. Your PAC dollars will help us make significant progress toward this goal."

Robert K. Fredrickson:
"Operating in a small state such as Delaware provides great visibility for Chase. ChasePAC contributions at the local level certainly enhance our ability to influence state lawmakers."

Joseph M. Giglio:
"Through ChasePAC, the corporation is able to play a bipartisan role in supporting those candidates at the federal, state and local level who believe in fostering an open and competitive business environment."

CHASE

Investing in Good Government

CHASE P★A★C

Chase Manhattan Corporation PAC

FIGURE 16–2 Organizations sponsor political action committees (PACs) essentially to fund candidates who they think will support their organizational goals. The "guidelines" enumerated here by The Chase Manhattan Corporation are typical of PAC philosophy. *(Courtesy of The Chase Manhattan Corporation)*

With just under 2,000 corporations, 750 associations, and 346 labor organizations sponsoring PACs, concern continues about the influence wielded by these committees. The evidence thus far is inconclusive. Although the number and size of PACs have increased, evidence of PAC-inspired indiscretions or illegalities has been minimal. Nonetheless, the furor over the heightened role of PACs in funding elections is bound to continue until campaign reform becomes reality.

Dealing with Congress

The name of the game in government relations is influencing legislation, and the key to such influence is good information. Legislators work on information. Hence, it is the timely presentation of accurate information that counts. A key vote may be affected by other considerations from time to time, but usually members of Congress are most sensitive to what will affect the voting in their area.

Testify

One way to reach Congress, of course, is by giving testimony in connection with legislation, a special investigation, or a nonlegislative study designed to examine a particular issue. Cleverly staged hearings on shocking topics are quite the rage in Washington today. By feeding the media's appetite for dramatic news, oversight hearings provide members of Congress with valuable publicity that sidesteps the frustrating and often thankless legislative process. One senator's agenda for a legislative session included hearings on child abuse, rape, spouse beating, alcoholism, and drugs—just for starters.

Congressional witnesses must do their homework. They must write out their testimony and know it well enough to explain it confidently and articulately. They also prepare for sharp interrogation by members of Congress. Even if testifying on legislation with general backing, there are always at least two points of view that invariably emerge in every hearing: Republicans versus Democrats, conservatives versus liberals, business versus labor, one-worlders versus protectionists—the gamut of ideological, philosophical, ethnic, and religious viewpoints.

Write

Another effective means of getting through to a busy legislator is by writing. Members of Congress and state government receive scores of letters. Part of their job is to read them.

A letter should be brief and to the point. It should identify the subject clearly, giving the bill number, if that is what is at issue. The best time to write is when a bill is in committee; legislators are more responsive when a bill is being discussed in the committee forum.

Letters should also be original. Often, lobbying groups direct thousands of form letters to government officials. Typically, these form appeals are tossed, so it's much better to tailor each letter. Keep in mind that the purpose is to convince, not intimidate.

Finally, it is important to learn the names of the people behind the official. More than 14,000 staff members work on Capitol Hill in Washington, supporting members of Congress. Often, a letter directed to one of those staff associates, who may wield significant influence, may be more valuable than a letter to the actual legislator.

B E T W E E N   T H E   L I N E S

The "Be" List of Getting Through to Legislators

Pat Choate, a veteran government relations professional at TRW Corporation, offered the following "be" list for anyone wishing to get through to legislators.

- **Be independent.** Policymakers value an independent view.
- **Be informed.** Government thrives on information. Timely facts, a deep knowledge of the subject, and specific examples are invaluable.
- **Be bipartisan.** Matters are more likely to be addressed on merit if approached in a bipartisan manner. Although it is necessary to be sensitive to political nuances, politics is best left to the politicians.
- **Be published.** Clear and cogent thinking, in articles and op-ed pieces, is noticed in Washington and at the statehouse.
- **Be broad-minded.** Don't peddle petty self-interest. Address the broader interests, and your counsel will be sought.
- **Be persistent.** A long-term, persistent commitment of time is mandatory in dealing with legislators.
- **Be practical.** Politicians value practical recommendations they can defend to their constituents.
- **Be honest.** Politicians and the press are skilled at spotting phonies. Honesty is the best policy. It works.[*]

[*]Cindy Skrzycki, "Possible Leaders Abound in Business Community," *The Washington Post*, 24 January 1988.

Visiting the Capitol

Perhaps the most effective way of reaching legislators is to visit them. First, arrange to meet your representative or senator early in a congressional session, not to press for consideration of particular legislation, but rather to introduce yourself. If there is particular legislation in which you are interested, also see your legislator early in the process. You must track the subcommittee calendars closely; decisions in subcommittees are critical and their impact grossly underestimated.

When you get inside the door, realize that your representative's time is short. Usually, you've got 15 minutes to make your case. What the representative wants to know is this:

1. What's the problem?
2. What does it mean to my state or district in terms of the economy, jobs, or general welfare?
3. How can I help?

Tell your representative of your concern as simply and succinctly as possible.

After the visit, follow up with a short letter to the legislator or legislative aide and keep track of legislative developments. An occasional reminder nudge may be helpful, but too much pressure will be counterproductive. Just as in dealing with the media, the best relationships between you and your legislator or all-important aides are developed over time and are based on mutual trust.[18]

Dealing with Local Government

In 1980, Ronald Reagan rode to power on a platform of New Federalism, calling for a shift of political debate and public policy decisions to state and local levels. Thus, it became more important for public relations people to deal with local, state, and regional governments.

Dealing with such local entities, of course, differs considerably from dealing with the federal government. For example, opinion leaders in communities (those constituents with whom an organization might want to affiliate to influence public policy decisions) might include such sectors as local labor unions, teachers, civil service workers, and the like. Building consensus among such diverse constituents is pure grass-roots public relations.

The very nature of state and local issues makes it impossible to give one, all-encompassing blueprint for successful government relations strategies.

Public relations advertising may be appropriate in some cases; area philanthropic contributions may be called for; and, certainly, closer contact with local legislators, to impress them with the investment, facilities, and jobs created by the organization, will become increasingly important.

In local government offices themselves, the need for public relations assistance is equally important. Local agencies deal directly—much more so than their counterparts in Washington—with individuals. State, county, and local officials must make themselves available for local media interviews, community forums and debates, and even door-to-door campaigning. In recent years, local and state officials have found that direct contact with constituents—often through call-in radio programs—is invaluable not only in projecting an "image," but in keeping in touch with the voters.

Such officials, assigned to ensure the quality of local schools, the efficiency of local agencies, and the reliability of local fire and police departments, increasingly require smart and experienced public relations counsel. State and local information officer positions therefore have become valued and important posts for public relations graduates.

Summary

The pervasive growth of government at all levels of society may not be welcome news for many people. However, government's growth has stimulated the need for increased public relations support and counsel.

The massive federal government bureaucracy, organized through individual agencies that each seek to communicate with the public, is a vast repository for public relations jobs. The most powerful position in the land—the president of the United States—has come to rely on public relations counsel to help maintain a positive public opinion of the office and the incumbent's handling of it.

On state and local levels, public relations expertise also has become a valued commodity. Local officials, too, attempt to describe their programs in the most effective manner.

In profit-making and non-profit-making organizations alike, the need to communicate with the layers of government also is imperative. Government relations positions in industry, associations, labor unions, and nonprofit organizations have multiplied.

Like it or not, the growth of government in our society appears unstoppable. As a result, the need for public relations support in government relations will clearly continue to be a growth area throughout the 1990s.

1. Why is the public relations function regarded as something of a "stepchild" in government?
2. What is the primary function of the United States Information Agency?
3. What is meant by "trial by press release"?
4. Why was Ronald Reagan called The Great Communicator?
5. What is the function of the White House press secretary?
6. What are the objectives of government relations officers?
7. What are the primary functions of lobbyists?
8. What is meant by grass-roots lobbying?
9. What are the pros and cons of political action committees?
10. What are the key rules in getting through to legislators?

NOTES

1. Interview with Office of Communications, U.S. Office of Personnel Management, December 10, 1990.
2. "Public Affairs and Congressional Affairs Activities of Federal Agencies," U.S. General Accounting Office Report to the Honorable William Proxmire United States Senate, February 1986.
3. "A Critical Article About Bruce Gelb," *Public Relations News* (June 25, 1990): 1.
4. David H. Buswell, "Trial by Press Release?" *NAM Reports* (January 17, 1972): 9–11.
5. "How the U.S. Air Force Communicates," *IABC Communication World* (May 1987): 14.
6. "Public Affairs and Congressional Affairs Activities of Federal Agencies," loc. cit.
7. Mark Hertsgaard, "Journalists Played Dead for Reagan—Will They Roll Over Again for Bush?" *Washington Journalism Review* (January-February 1989): 31.
8. Tom Shales, "The Bush Blackout," *The Washington Post,* 28 June 1989, C2.
9. Maureen Dowd, "George Bush's Communication Breakdown on the Budget," *The New York Times,* 21 October 1990, D5.
10. Robert U. Brown, "Role of Press Secretary," *Editor & Publisher* (October 19, 1974): 40.
11. I. William Hill, "Nessen Lists Ways He Has Improved Press Relations," *Editor & Publisher* (April 10, 1975): 40.
12. William Safire, "One of Our Own," *The New York Times,* 19 September 1974, 43.
13. Michael J. Bennett, "The 'Imperial' Press Corps," *Public Relations Journal* (June 1982): 13.
14. "Number of Lobbyists Is on the Rise," *Jack O'Dwyer's Newsletter* (October 31, 1990): 7.
15. "Grass Roots—'Blade by Blade,' " *Corporate Public Issues* (December 1, 1989): 136.
16. Alan I. Abramowitz, "Finance House Campaigns," *The New York Times,* 27 June 1989, A23.
17. William L. Dupuy, "The Political Action Committee and the Public Relations Practitioner," *Public Relations Quarterly* (Spring 1981): 14.
18. E. Bruce Peters, "You Can Be Wise in the Ways of Washington," *Enterprise* (December 1981–January 1982): 8–9.

TOP OF THE SHELF

Cook, Timothy E. *Making Laws and Making News: Media Strategies in the U.S. House of Representatives.* Washington, DC: The Brookings Institution, 1989 (1775 Massachusetts Avenue, NW 20036)

Making Laws and Making News takes a penetrating look at how congressional media strategies are used to achieve policy goals and further political careers.

A political science teacher at Williams College in Massachusetts, Professor Cook dissects the sophisticated press operations of House members and how they use journalists to address particular issues, move a proposal along, and help them get re-elected. Cook also looks at the roles of those who cover the Capitol—local reporters interested in interpreting legislators to small-town constituencies and journalists on the national beat. The press, he argues, wields influence by ultimately deciding what is newsworthy. If both press and politicians hold power, who manipulates whom? Cook sees the tug-of-war as a draw: "Each side holds important power—members of the House by controlling whether, when, where, and how to grant access; journalists by deciding whether, when, where, and how to pay attention."

Read *Making Laws and Making News* to understand why lawmakers seek publicity and how that need for exposure impacts legislation. Cook adeptly shows how two formidable institutions—the media and Congress—interact to shape the legislative agenda and define political thought.

Armstrong, Richard. *The Next Hurrah: The Changing Face of the American Political Process.* New York: Morrow, 1988.

How to Find Business Intelligence in Washington. Washington, DC: Washington Researchers Publishing Co., 1988.

Hudson, Howard Penn, and Mary Elizabeth Judson, eds. *Hudson's Washington News Media Contact Directory.* (Available from 2626 Pennsylvania Ave., NW, Washington, DC 20037.) This directory lists the Washington correspondents for major newspapers (by state or origin), news bureaus, foreign newspapers and news services, radio and TV networks (both domestic and foreign), magazines, specialized newsletters and periodicals, freelance writers, and photographic services.

Kern, Monague. *30-Second Politics: Political Advertising in the Eighties.* New York: Praeger, 1989.

Manthorne, Joseph P. *Public Relations Tips in Small Business, the Arts, Education and Service Organizations.* Natick, MA: Manthorne Co., 1987 (48 Charles St.).

Morrison, Catherine. *Managing Corporate Political Action Committees.* New York: The Conference Board, 1986 (845 Third Ave. 10022).

SUGGESTED READINGS

Napolitan, Joseph. "100 Things I Have Learned in 30 Years as a Political Consultant." (Available from Public Affairs Analysts, 342 Madison Ave., New York, NY 10173.) Paper for the 19th annual conference of the International Association of Political Consultants, November 1986.

National Directory of State Agencies 1987. (5161 River Rd., Bethesda, MD 20816).

Remmes, Harold. *Lobbying for Your Cause.* Babylon, NY: Pilot Books, 1986.

Social Science Writer (10606 Mantz Rd., Silver Spring, MD 20903). Monthly.

Timberg, Robert. "The Hill Handlers." *Washington Journalism Review* (June 1985): 39–43.

CASE STUDY   NASA's *Challenger* Disaster

The National Aeronautics and Space Administration (NASA) had one of the largest public affairs budgets in government—almost $20 million. That included not only $5 million for public information, but also $3.5 million for public services, such as handling more than two million visitors annually at nine space centers. Traditionally, NASA was regarded as one of the smartest, most buttoned-up public information efforts in government.

NASA's spotless information reputation lasted until January 28, 1986, when, in just 73 seconds, the agency—and the nation—suffered an unprecedented tragedy: the space shuttle *Challenger* exploded before a national television audience. Its crew of seven—which included America's first citizen-astronaut, New Hampshire high school teacher Christa McAuliffe—was killed.

Not only was the *Challenger* explosion a national tragedy, but NASA's public relations handling of the aftermath was also viewed as a disaster in its own right. For one thing, when TV screens clearly showed a fireball fewer than two minutes into the launch, NASA's mission control commentator coolly spoke of a "major malfunction" and "apparent explosion." In addition, al-

though NASA's public relations emergency plan emphasized the importance of issuing a public statement within 20 minutes of an accident, noting that "rumors and speculation creating further problems will result if release is delayed," the agency waited almost five full hours to hold a news conference to explain what had happened. Even then, NASA's shuttle chief, who presided at the news conference, offered little in the way of new information to the hundreds of reporters who attended. What made the information vacuum even worse was the fact that millions of schoolchildren around the nation, intrigued by the presence in space of the first teacher-astronaut, were tuned in to the shuttle's flight.

In the days immediately following the disaster, NASA impounded all documents pertaining to the launch. Even the weather report and temperature readings in the hours before lift-off became classified information. The unwillingness of the space agency to release substantive information on the explosion forced reporters to rely on unofficial, unnamed sources. Some sources speculated that sabotage was involved. Others, who had been covering the space agency for some 20 years, speculated that a flame

FIGURE 16—3

from the solid-fuel booster rocket was the likely trigger of the explosion. As a subsequent presidential commission revealed, this theory wasn't far from wrong.

NASA officials stuck to their position that no information would be released until the facts were known. As one NASA employee put it, their first reaction was to draw the wagons in a circle to fight off attacks on the shuttle program and the agency's opera-

tions. Predictably, the media objected violently to NASA's withholding of information, claiming that NASA had turned a significant loss of human life and technology into a public relations fiasco that would undermine the agency's credibility and prestige for years to come.

How prophetic that claim was. The next 2½ years for NASA were nightmarish. NASA's public relations performance in the *Challenger* disaster was picked apart from numerous perspectives. The media bridled at NASA's directive that ships returning *Challenger* debris wait offshore until dark so that video crews and photographers could not shoot them without special equipment. The media were also incensed when NASA sent empty ambulances to a nearby Air Force base hospital as a diversion when astronaut remains were returned.

Nor was the manufacturer of the solid-fuel rocket, Morton Thiokol, spared the media's wrath. Morton Thiokol scarcely mentioned its role in the tragedy in its 1986 annual report, and the media took note. Specifically cited in media reviews was Thiokol's failure to mention that its rockets were blamed for the accident or that the presidential commission investigating the tragedy concluded that Thiokol managers had overruled lower-ranking engineers who argued against the launching. Little wonder that it was front page news in June 1988, when Thiokol announced that it would not bid to build the next generation of rocket motors for U.S. manned space shuttles.

In the winter of 1988, a damning article in *Public Relations Review*, "Rockwell Fails in Response to Shuttle Disaster," accused the prime contractor of the space shuttle program, Rockwell International, of following NASA's lead in ignoring the press. The author, John A. Kaufman, suggested that

Rockwell's no-comment policy, coupled with that of NASA's, led to a "frustrating information vacuum" that reporters were forced to fill by seeking out their own inside—often hostile—sources.

All in all, the *Challenger* disaster was as much a public relations tragedy as it was a human one. The public relations mishandling by those associated with the *Challenger* clearly resulted in long-term damage to America's space program.[*]

[*]For further information on the *Challenger* disaster, see William J. Broad, "Thiokol Is Ending Booster Output on Space Shuttle," *The New York Times*, 7 June 1988, 1; Matt Moffett and Laurie McGinley, "NASA, Once a Master of Publicity, Fumbles in Handling Shuttle Crisis," *The Wall Street Journal*, 14 February 1986, 23; John Noble Wilford, "*Challenger*, Disclosure and an 8th Casualty for NASA," *The New York Times*, 14 February 1986, B5; and "The Space Shuttle Tragedy," *Public Relations News*, 10 February 1986, 1.

QUESTIONS

1. How soon after the *Challenger* disaster should NASA have held its news conference?
2. Assuming few of the facts were known at the time, what key messages should NASA officials have tried to convey at the news conference?
3. How would you assess NASA's policy of impounding all documents in the days following the disaster and not reporting information until all the facts were known?
4. Would the agency have been justified in stating probable causes of the disaster?

Tips from the Top

ROGER E. AILES

Roger Ailes is chairman and chief executive officer of Ailes Communications, Inc., and has been a leading communications consultant since 1968. He is one of television's most respected producers, communications adviser to political leaders, consultant to corporate executives, and award-winning theatrical producer. Mr. Ailes served as senior media adviser to the George Bush for President campaign and several other 1988 races. He has advised and helped elect many candidates for state and national office, including 14 United States senators. Mr. Ailes is co-author of *You Are the Message: Secrets of the Master Communicators.*

What are the key elements in an effective communications strategy?
Any communications strategy, whether it is for a candidate or corporation, needs first to take its audiences into account. Different audiences will view a candidate through their individual filters, so you must design messages that will reach the audience. You must set your own message agenda and not let it be established by outsiders.

What are the key elements in effective political advertising?
Anticipating the communications challenges, analyzing the dangers and opportunities, and developing the appropriate mes-

sages. Basically, you must creatively build bridges to your target audiences.

How do you answer critics of "negative political advertising?"
Before producing a comparative ad, we answer two questions: *one,* is it true? and *two,* is it fair? We check all our facts through researchers and stay completely away from personal attacks. We also never underestimate the audience's ability to distinguish a fair criticism. Campaigns or corporations that hit below the belt pay dearly.

Every year the press loves to say, "This was the most negative campaign ever." The 1988 campaign looked like Pee Wee Herman's Playhouse, if you compare it to what Johnson did to Goldwater with his nuclear war ad.

What were the strategies behind the successful Bush presidential advertising campaign?
We had a living strategy. Early in the campaign, I wrote a general message strategy for the election, but it was basically how to

435

remind the public of George Bush's accomplishments.

We always knew that we would have to define Dukakis, as well. Whichever of us defined the other and ourselves most effectively would win. The strategy was that simple. Coordinating the free media with the paid was another thing.

How do you defend the well-publicized Willie Horton ads in the Bush presidential campaign that focused on a Massachusetts killer freed from jail?
I don't. Neither our company nor the Bush campaign ever produced or aired a Willie Horton ad; groups independent of the Bush campaign produced and aired it.

Interestingly enough, the news media promoted that issue. Hardly anyone saw that commercial on television; most people saw it replayed in the news.

How important is "image" vs. "substance" for a politician?
A good politician must have both.

How can government improve its image in the eyes of the public?
Politicians should spend as much time spending the public's money effectively as they do trying to get reelected.

The Community

President Calvin Coolidge once said, "The business of America is business." Today, some argue, "The business of business is America." In the early 1960s, any business executive worth his salt would have stated immediately that a company's job is to make money for its owners—period. Indeed, Nobel Price-winning economist Milton Friedman argued just that: that the corporation's responsibility is to produce profits and that the cost of corporate social goals amounts to a hidden tax on workers, customers, and shareholders.

Professor Friedman is in the minority. More and more, companies and other organizations acknowledge their responsibilities to the community: helping to maintain clean air and water, providing jobs for minorities, and, in general, enhancing everyone's quality of life. This concept of social responsibility has become widely accepted among enlightened organizations. For example, most companies today donate a percentage of their profits to nonprofit organizations—schools, hospitals, social welfare institutions, and the like. Employee volunteer programs, to assist local charitable groups, are also commonplace. In the 1990s, social responsibility is no longer the exception but the rule among organizations.

This enlightened self-interest among executives has taken time to develop. The social and political upheavals of the 1960s forced organizations to confront the real or perceived injustices inflicted on certain social groups. The 1970s brought a partial resolution of those problems, as government and the courts moved together to compensate for past inequities, outlaw current abuses, and prevent future injustice.

In the 1980s, the conflict between organizations and society became one of setting priorities—of deciding which community group deserved to be the beneficiary of corporate involvement. Today, most organizations accept their role as an agent for social change in the community. For an organization to coexist peacefully in its community in the 1990s requires three skills in particular: (1) determining what the community knows and thinks about the organization, (2) informing the community of the organization's point of view, and (3) negotiating or mediating between the organization and the community, should there be a significant discrepancy.

Basically, every organization wants to foster positive reactions in its community. This becomes increasingly difficult in the face of protests from and disagreements with community activists. Community relations, therefore—to analyze the community, help understand its makeup and expectations, and communicate the organization's story in an understandable and uninterrupted way—is critical in the 1990s.

Community Components and Expectations

The community of an organization can vary widely, depending on the size and the nature of the business. The mom-and-pop grocery store may have a community of only a few city blocks; the community of a Buick assembly plant may be the city where the plant is located; and the community of a multinational corporation may embrace much of the world.

Who are the principal members of a firm's community? At the local level, there are several discrete types of community members.

Community leaders These are the shapers of opinion in the community: public officials, major employers, old-guard families, vocal advocates, and, occasionally, informal thought leaders. They can generally be reached through regular contact with influential local groups, face-to-face meetings, and special mailings.

Local press It is important to get to know the local news media for effective community relations. However, attempting to coerce the media by purchasing or canceling advertising should not be contemplated. More practical is getting to know local journalists in an informal, low-pressure way.

Civic groups There are many ways to reach local civic groups: regularly donating to local charities, using radio programs, forming a speakers' bureau to meet local organizations, filling emergency needs, or providing free movies for use by nonprofit groups.

Students, faculty, school officials Educating young people and informing their mentors about the benefits of the firm is time well spent. Eventually, students will become customers and employees.

◆ **Municipal employees and local officials** Organizations should encourage employees to take active roles on the city council and the police or fire commission and in civil defense and other municipal agencies.

Concerned citizenship on the individual level translates directly into corporate community concern.

◆ **Local merchants, industrialists** A brief congratulatory letter to a businessperson recently honored or promoted is always welcomed. So, too, are visits to new merchants, industry officials, and new residents, to acquaint them with the local community.

◆ **Women, homemakers** Increasingly, women are becoming as important a public as any in a community. Their rise in the labor force gives them greater knowledge and resources for family decisions. At the same time, the role of women in the work force has caused employers to reach out with child care, pregnancy leaves, flexible hours, and so on. Retailers and service providers pay maximum attention to what women want because they are responsible for a steadily expanding percentage of buying decisions.

Again, key constituencies vary from community to community, but everyone today seems organized. So much so, in fact, that when Phil Donahue devoted his 1988 network talk show to the problems of a New York City homeless woman named Joyce Brown, the woman arrived on the set with a vocal cadre of fellow homeless citizens. Every organization must learn which publics in its community are organized and capable of influencing others. Knowing which civic group is more influential with the alderman and which alderman is more influential with the mayor, for example, may be of crucial importance to the management of a local organization. Identifying and being able to tap influence networks is a valuable skill of the community relations specialist.

What the Community Expects

Communities expect from resident organizations such tangible commodities as wages, employment, and taxes. But communities have come to expect intangible contributions, too.

◆ **Appearance** The community hopes that the firm will contribute positively to life in the area. It expects facilities to be attractive, with care spent on the grounds and the plant (Figure 17–1). Increasingly, community neighbors object to plants that belch smoke and pollute water and air. Occasionally, neighbors organize to oppose the entrance of factories, coal mines, oil wells, drug treatment centers, and other facilities suspected of being harmful into the community environment. Government, too, is acting more vigorously to punish offenders and to make sure that organizations comply with zoning, environmental, and safety regulations.

◆ **Participation** As a citizen of the community, an organization is expected to participate responsibly in community affairs, such as civic

functions, park and recreational activities, education, welfare, and support of religious institutions. Organizations generally cannot shirk such participation by blaming headquarters' policy.

◆ **Stability** A business that fluctuates sharply in volume of business, number of employees, and taxes paid can adversely affect the community through its impact on municipal services, school loads, public facilities, and tax revenues. Communities prefer stable organizations that will grow with the area. Conversely, they want to keep out short-term operations that could create temporary boom conditions and leave ghost towns in their wake.

◆ **Pride** Any organization that can help put the community on the map simply by being there is usually a valuable addition. Communities want firms that are proud to be residents. For instance, to most Americans, Battle Creek, Michigan, means cereal; Hershey, Pennsylvania, means chocolate; and Armonk, New York, means IBM. Organizations that help make the town usually become symbols of pride.

What the Organization Expects

Organizations expect to be provided with adequate municipal services, fair taxation, good living conditions for employees, a good labor supply, and a reasonable degree of support for the business and its products. When some of these requirements are missing, organizations may pick up and move to communities where such benefits are more readily available.

New York City, for example, experienced a substantial exodus of corporations during the 1970s, when firms fled to neighboring Connecticut and New Jersey, as well as to the Sun Belt states of the Southeast and Southwest. These became commercial centers because of tax moratoriums, lower labor costs, and business incentives. New York state and city legislators responded to the challenge by working more closely with business residents in such areas as corporate taxation. By the 1980s, not only had the corporate flight to the Sun Belt been arrested, but some firms decided that they agreed with the "I Love New York" ad campaign and returned to the state.

The issue for most urban areas, faced with steadily eroding tax bases, is to find a formula that meets the concerns of business corporations while accommodating the needs of other members of the community.

FIGURE 17—1 Every community wants its corporate citizens to care about its appearance. In this case, Chase Manhattan Bank let its customers know that it, too, cared about cleaning up its headquarters city. *(Courtesy of Chase Manhattan Bank)*

Community Relations Objectives

Research into community relations indicates that winning community support for an organization is no easy task. One study suggested that the goal of compatibility between organization and community "is quite unrealistic in many situations." Researchers found that conflict often exists between a community and an agency or corporation that is controlled elsewhere.[1] Additional community relations research has shown that a high level of public communication does not always lead to increased support for a newly introduced community relations program.

Such studies indicate something of the difficulty in achieving rapport with community neighbors. One device that is helpful is a written community relations policy. A community relations policy must clearly define the philosophy of management as it views its obligation to the community. Employees, in particular, must understand and exemplify their firm's community relations policy; to many in the community, the workers *are* the company.

An organization's community relations policy may be "played out" in what has been described as either *expressive* or *instrumental* ways. Expressive community relations activities are used by organizations to promote themselves and to show their goodwill to the community. Instrumental activities are used by organizations to improve the community itself or to make the community a better place in which to reside.[2] Often, community relations objectives are a hybrid between the two. Typical community relations objectives might include the following:

1. To tell the community about the operations of the firm: its products, number of employees, size of payroll, tax payments, employee benefits, growth, and support of community projects

2. To correct misunderstanding, reply to criticism, and remove any disaffection that may exist among community neighbors

3. To gain the favorable opinion of the community, particularly during strikes and periods of labor unrest, by stating the company's position on issues involved

4. To inform employees and their families about company activities and developments, so that they can tell their friends and neighbors about the company and favorably influence opinions of the organization

5. To inform people in local government about the firm's contributions to community welfare and to obtain support for legislation that will favorably affect the business climate in the community

6. To find out what residents think about the company, why they like or dislike its policies and practices and how much they know of its policy, operations, and problems

7. To establish a personal relationship between management and community leaders by inviting leaders to visit the plant and offices, meet management, and see employees at work

8. To support health programs through contributions of both funds and employee services to local campaigns

9. To contribute to culture by providing funds for art exhibits, concerts, and drama festivals and by promoting attendance at such affairs (Figure 17–2)

10. To aid youth and adult education by cooperating with administrators and teachers in providing student vocational guidance, plant tours, speakers, films, and teaching aids and by giving financial support to higher education

11. To encourage sports and recreational activities by providing athletic fields, swimming pools, golf courses, and/or tennis courts for use by community residents and by sponsoring teams and sports events

FIGURE 17–2 Typical of programs to win community approval by supporting local cultural enrichment was this elephantine check from The Chase Manhattan Bank to support the Northeast Tour of New York's Big Apple Circus. *(Courtesy of The Chase Manhattan Bank)*

12. To promote better local and county government by encouraging employees to run for public office or volunteer to serve on administrative boards; lending company executives to community agencies or to local government to give specialized advice and assistance on municipal problems; and making company facilities and equipment available to the community in times of emergency

13. To assist the economy of the community by purchasing operating supplies and equipment from local merchants and manufacturers whenever possible

14. To operate a profitable business to provide jobs and to pay competitive wages that increase the community's purchasing power and strengthen its economy

15. To cooperate with other local businesses in advancing economic and social welfare through joint community relations programs, financed and directed by the participating organizations

Emergence of Public Affairs

In recent years, community relations has evolved into the more all-encompassing activity of public affairs. Although a precise definition of *public affairs* is elusive, this Conference Board definition is a good one.

> A significant and substantial concern and involvement by individuals, business, labor, foundations, private institutions, and government with the social, economic, and political forces that singly or through interaction shape the environment within which the free enterprise system exists.

The emergence and expansion of public affairs activities is a response to public demands that organizations act responsibly in employee hiring and promotion, product safety and pricing, advertising, merchandising, and labeling.

Distinctions between public relations and public affairs are often blurry, and in some organizations the functions may overlap. Certain differences, however, are clear. The public affairs function usually operates through either the political or the social service process; practitioners tend to be knowledgeable about liberal arts or political science. In contrast, public relations usually operates through the communications process, with practitioners oriented toward journalism. As public relations counselor John W. Hill once said, "The difference between the two functions is marked by an exceedingly fine line. Actually, the two activities are brothers under the skin."

Even though no clear-cut distinction between the two functions has yet been established, the team concept of many large organizations helps guard against duplication of efforts. In smaller operations these two functions are often combined.

Nonprofit Public Relations

Among the most important organizations in any community are those represented in the not-for-profit sector. Nonprofit organizations serve the social, educational, religious, and cultural needs of the community around them. So important is the role of public relations in nonprofit organizations, this sector is a primary source of employment for public relations graduates.

The nonprofit sector is characterized by a panoply of institutions: hospitals, schools, social welfare agencies, religious institutions, cultural organizations, and the like. The general goals of nonprofit agencies are not dissimilar to those of corporations. Nonprofits seek to win public support of their mission and programs through active and open communications. Unlike corporations though, nonprofits also seek to broaden volunteer participation in their efforts. This spirit of "voluntarism" lies at the heart of President Bush's "Thousand Points of Light Program," a hallmark of his administration.

Because America is a nation of joiners and belongers, nonprofit organizations in our society are encouraged to proliferate. As the number of nonprofit agencies has grown, it has become increasingly difficult to find funding sources. Most nonprofits depend on a combination of government funding and private support. In 1989, total corporate giving to all causes rose to an estimated $6.5 billion, a little over 2 percent of pretax corporate profits. The largest portion of that money—about $2.8 billion—went toward educational institutions.[3] In the '90s, as resources become more scarce, the competition among nonprofits to attract funding promises to become more intense. One 1987 Conference Board study showed a 2.5 percent decline in charitable giving among leading corporate donors, with half of the major contributors—those donating more than $10 million annually—cutting back to 78 percent.[4]

All of this suggests that public relations professionals at nonprofits—in addition to writing speeches, dealing with the media, communicating with employees, and counseling managements—must also be prepared to devote increased efforts to one activity that corporate communicators ordinarily aren't involved in—fund raising.

Fund Raising

Fund raising—the need to raise money to support operations—lies at the heart of every nonprofit institution (Figure 17–3). Schools, hospitals,

FIGURE 17—3   The granddaddy of all fund raisers is the United Way, which uses provocative advertising like this to raise the enormous sums necessary to fund thousands of community nonprofits. *(Courtesy of United Way)*

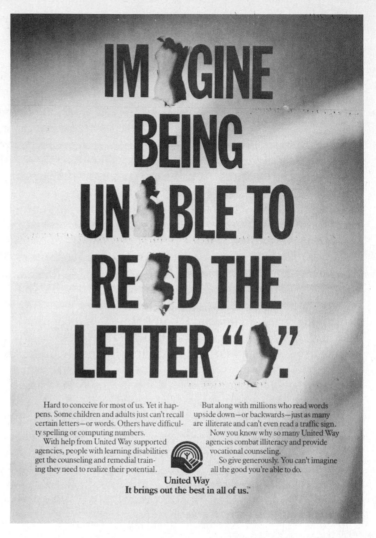

churches, and organizations—from the mighty United Way to the smallest block association—can't exist without a constant source of private funds. Frequently, the fund-raising assignment becomes the province of public relations professionals. Just as in other aspects of public relations work, fund raising must be accomplished in a planned and programmatic way.

A successful fund-raising campaign should include several basic steps.

1. *Identify campaign plans and objectives.*

Broad financial targets should be set. A goal should be announced. Specific sectors of the community, from which funds might be extracted, should be targeted in advance.

2. *Organize fact finding.*

Relevant trends that might affect giving should be noted. Relations with various elements of the community should be defined. The national and local economy should be considered, as should current attitudes toward charitable contributions.

3. *Recruit leaders.*

The best fund-raising campaigns are ones with strong leadership. A hallmark of local United Way campaigns, for example, is the recruitment of strong business leaders to spearhead contribution efforts. Leaders should be designated to coordinate the various targets of opportunity defined in the fund-raising program. United Way designates leaders in each industry group to tap potential funding sources.

4. *Plan and implement strong communications activities.*

The best fund-raising campaigns are also the most visible. Publicity and promotion must be stressed. Special events should be organized, particularly featuring national and local celebrities to support the drive. Updates on fund-raising progress should be communicated, particularly to volunteers and contributors. Unique communications vehicles—from direct mail to raffles to bazaars to the sale of stamps and seals—should be considered. All help "get out the word" and increase campaign coffers.

5. *Periodically review and evaluate.*

Review the fund-raising program as it progresses. Make mid-course corrections when activities succeed or fail beyond expectations. Evaluate program achievements against program targets. Revise strategies constantly as the goal becomes nearer.

Because many public relations graduates enter the nonprofit realm, a knowledge of fund-raising strategies and techniques is especially important. Beginning practitioners, once hired in the public relations office of a college, hospital, charitable organization, or other nonprofit, are soon confronted with questions about how public relations can help raise money for the organization.

Health and Hospitals

Perhaps no industry in the nonprofit world has been more affected by the growth of public affairs in general and community relations in particular than the health and hospital field. The health and hospital industry is among the nation's largest employers: it is a nearly $400 billion enterprise consisting of about 7,000 institutions that serve hundreds of millions of people annually.

Hospitals today are in a state of unprecedented flux.

◆ Doctors are moving out on their own, creating competition for hospitals.

◆ New survival organizations with not-for-profit holding companies and profit-center units are proliferating.

◆ Huge chains, such as the Hospital Corporation of America and Humana, are causing great concern among hospital boards and administrators regarding takeovers, mergers, and competition.

◆ A highly competitive environment exists among once-coexisting hospitals.

◆ There has been an enormous decline in the number of beds filled and an increase in home health care.

◆ Emergency-care centers—so-called doc-in-the-box facilities—have sprung up to compete head-to-head with hospital emergency rooms.

◆ Costs for hospital services have skyrocketed, and hospitals have become centers of scientific progress.

One outgrowth of this dynamic environment has been an increasing concern among doctors, administrators, and trustees about positioning the hospital through public relations efforts.

A reality for hospital public relations practitioners today is the need to market the health services that people require rather than create an artificial demand. Community needs must be considered along with institutional needs to determine what hospital services will be offered, who will be served, and what effect this will have on pricing, referral, and access to health care.

Marketing also means educating hospital publics through such vehicles as open houses that demonstrate and explain services, sponsorship of health and medical events and seminars, and distribution of health-related information through newspaper columns, radio spot announcements, television interviews, and telephone hotlines. Indeed, the increase of medical-care costs has enhanced the importance of health education as a primary source of hospital-community interaction.

Community relations is a key aspect of hospital public relations. Practitioners must keep neighborhoods informed about such controversial programs as alcohol and drug treatment and must involve area residents as much as possible in hospital affairs. One critical function of hospital public relations practitioners is to seek out human interest stories for the media to demonstrate the hospital's concern for its community.

Competing with hospitals and also depending largely on public relations to communicate its role is the health maintenance organization (HMO), an association of physicians that emphasizes early detection of potential health concerns. The public relations challenge of HMOs includes persuading the public that regular health maintenance can detect and help prevent illness and that the HMO approach warrants their participation.

With hospital costs continuing to rise, medical practice is being placed under increased scrutiny, and corporations are taking over an increasing number of hospitals and health care facilities. The importance of hospital public relations promises to increase in the future, and health care public relations will be a growing arena for public relations professionals.

Serving Minorities

Among the most important communities with which public relations professionals must be concerned are so-called minorities. Because one-third of the American population will be composed of "minorities" by the year 2000, public relations professionals must know how to communicate with minority groups. Minorities will become increasingly important as employees, consumers, and constituents in the years ahead. While a detailed analysis of African-Americans, Hispanics, the elderly, ethnic minorities, disabled people, and the like transcends the scope of this text, some understanding of the most influential minorities is important.

For many years, women were considered a minority by public relations professionals. This is no longer the case, especially, as already noted, with women now dominating not only the public relations field but many service industries. Women have become a staple of the labor force and an important source of discretionary income. Public relations professionals must be sensitive to the demands of women for equal pay, promotional opportunities, and equal rights in the workplace. Sensitivity must also be shown in avoiding sexist language in communications messages.

African-Americans

The socioeconomic status of Blacks has improved markedly in the last decade. Today, 25 of the nation's largest cities—including Chicago, Detroit, and Los Angeles—have a majority population of Blacks, Hispanics, and Asians. Blacks—or as they have become known recently, African-Americans—represent almost 12 percent of the U.S. population and had a disposable income of $214 billion in 1984, compared to $42 billion a decade earlier.[5] The number of African-American families with incomes in excess of $15,000 is seven times as great as it was in 1970. Indeed, as the 1984 *Black Book* summarized:

> A new breed of Black American has emerged who is impacting upon decisions and implementing policies at every level of American life. They are more willing to contribute economically to our future in America, more apt to reject

the status quo, more assertive and aggressive, ready to seize every opportunity available, and willing to create opportunities where none exist.[6]

Despite their continuing evolution in the white-dominated workplace, African-Americans can still be reached effectively through special media. Magazines such as *Ebony, Jet, Black Enterprise,* and *Essence* are natural vehicles. *Ebony,* the largest African-American-oriented publication in the world, has a circulation of 1.3 million. Newspapers such as the *Amsterdam News* in New York City and the *Daily Defender* in Chicago also are targeted to African-Americans. Such newspapers are controlled by active owners whose personal viewpoints dominate editorial policy. All should be included in the normal media relations functions of any organization.

Companies in recent years have made a concerted push to reach African-Americans. Occasionally, these attempts have been controversial. In 1990, for example, R. J. Reynolds Tobacco Company announced a promotional campaign to target its "Uptown" cigarette toward African-Americans. Reminiscent of the protests against Aunt Jemima in an earlier era, African-Americans outspokenly opposed the campaign. Reynolds was forced to drop its product after spending $10 million to develop it.[7] African-American leaders, including U.S. Secretary of Health and Human Services Louis Sullivan, condemned the proliferation of advertisements for cigarettes and alcohol in Black neighborhoods. Other leaders, like civil rights activist Benjamin Hooks, condemned the condemnation as a form of paternalism. "Buried in this line of thinking," he said, "is the rationale that Blacks are not capable of making their own free choices."[8] At the root of Hooks' comments was the realization that tobacco companies donated huge sums to support African-American causes, ranging from jazz festivals to the United Negro College Fund.

The practice of public relations also has come in for criticism with respect to African-American practitioners. In recent years, the field has been frustrated in its efforts to recruit African-Americans. In 1990, the Public Relations Society of America introduced a two-year management-training program designed to help rectify this situation. The program included on-the-job training, mentoring by experienced public relations professionals, management seminars, and evaluation.

Hispanics

Hispanics, like African-Americans, make up a growing portion of the labor and consumer markets in major American cities. There are 20 million Hispanics in the United States, with a median family income of more than $16,000. More than 70 percent of all U.S. Hispanics reside in California, Texas, New York, and Florida. The majority of U.S. Hispanics—62 percent—are of Mexican origin. About 13 percent are of Puerto Rican origin, and 5 percent are of Cuban origin.

Mucho
depende
de usted.

FIGURE 17–4 Hispanics
have become an increasingly
important constituent public,
not only as consumers of
goods but also as donors of
funds. As this United Way ad
suggests, "much depends" on
the Hispanic community. *(Courtesy of United Way)*

Because 75 percent of Hispanics communicate primarily in Spanish, smart organizations can readily identify and target this public—and increase their retail sales simply by communicating in the Spanish language (Figure 17–4). In an attempt to reach Hispanics, advertisers spent $550 million in 1988, with the overwhelming percentage going to television.[9] In addition, radio stations and newspapers that communicate in Spanish, such as New York City's *El Diario* and *La Prensa,* are prominent voices in reaching this increasingly important community.

Other Minorities

Other ethnic groups—particularly Asians—also have increased their importance in the American marketplace. Japanese, Chinese, Koreans, Vietnamese, and others have gained new prominence as consumers and constituents.

Beyond these ethnic minorities, so-called senior citizens also have become an important community for public relations professionals and the organizations they represent. People over fifty years of age control more than 50 percent of America's discretionary income. By the year 2000, 13 percent of the population will be older than 65.[10] As the American population grows older, the importance of senior citizens will increase. Public relations professionals must be sensitive to that reality, as well as the fact that other special communities in the society demand specialized treatment and targeted communications.

Summary

In the 1990s, community relations promises to become even more important, as community activists—from animal rights proponents to antiabortion advocates to citizens concerned about preserving the environment—reappear to pressure organizations to deal responsibly with societal issues. Spearheading this charge are activist organizations, which flourished in the late 1960s during the Vietnam War and are beginning again to "spread their wings." Among them are the National Council of Churches, which has lobbied aggressively against corporate and university support of the apartheid policies in South Africa, and Nader's Raiders, the several organizations led by consumer crusader Ralph Nader, which is involved in everything from banking and insurance to automobile and nursing home regulations.

Intelligent organizations in our society must be responsive to the needs and desires of their communities. Positive community relations in the '90s must begin with a clear understanding of community concerns, an open door for community leaders, an open and honest flow of information from the organization, and an ongoing sense of continuous involvement and interaction with community publics.

Boiled down, community relations is only as effective as the support it receives from top management. Once that support is clear, it becomes the responsibility of the public relations professional to ensure that the relationship between the organization and the community is one of mutual trust, understanding, and support.

DISCUSSION STARTERS

1. How is the atmosphere for "community relations" different in the 1990s than it was in the 1960s?
2. What are the several discrete types of community members?
3. In general terms, what does a community expect from a resident organization?
4. What are typical community relations objectives for an organization?
5. What is meant by the term *public affairs?*
6. What are the key steps in mounting a sound fund-raising program?
7. What does the term *marketing* signify in the area of hospitals and health care?

8. What was the conflict with respect to African-Americans in the introduction of "Uptown" cigarettes?
9. What communications vehicles should be used in appealing to Hispanics?
10. Why might there be a resurgence in community relations during the 1990s?

NOTES

1. John V. Pavlik, *Public Relations: What Research Tells Us* (Newbury Park, CA: Sage Publications, 1987), 109.
2. James E. Grunig and Todd Hunt, *Managing Public Relations* (New York: Holt, Rinehart and Winston, 1984), 265.
3. "Corporate Giving to Rise 5% in 1990, Survey Says," *The Wall Street Journal*, 8 August 1990, A2.
4. Fraser P. Seitel, "Giving Wisely," *United States Banker* (April 1989): 64.
5. Marilyn Kern-Foxworth, "Status and Roles of Minority Public Relations Practitioners," *Public Relations Review* (Fall 1989): 39.
6. "As Minorities Grow in Number and Influence, They Will Become Vital Publics," *Public Relations Reporter* (February 11, 1985): 1.
7. Marilyn Kern-Foxworth, "Plantation Kitchen to American Icon: Aunt Jemima," *Public Relations Review* (Fall 1990): 64.
8. Michael Quinn, "Don't Aim That Pack at Us," *Time* (January 29, 1990): 60.
9. Anna Veciana-Suarez, "Hispanic Media: Impact and Influence," (Washington, D.C.: The Media Institute, 1990): 15.
10. Peter Kreysa, "You Can Improve Your Bank's Service to Older Customers," *Hoosier Banker* (November 1990): 48.

TOP OF THE SHELF

Alinsky, Saul D. *Rules for Radicals.* New York: Vintage Books, 1971.

Alinsky's *Rules for Radicals* is a classic handbook for those bent on organizing communities, rattling the status quo, and effecting social and political change, as well as for those who wish to learn from a legendary master.

Alinsky, a veteran community activist who fought on behalf of the poor from New York to California, provides strategies for building coalitions and for using communication, conflict, and confrontation advantageously. In "Of Means and Ends," Alinsky lists 11 rules of ethics that define the uses of radical power. His discussion of tactics suggests 13 ways to help organizers defeat their foes.

Rule Three, for instance, tells activists to go outside the experience of their enemy to "cause confusion, fear, and retreat."

Alinsky supports his principles with numerous examples, the most colorful of which is when he wanted to draw attention to a particular cause in Rochester, NY. To do so, Alinsky and his group attended a Rochester Symphony performance—after a meal of nothing but beans. The results were hilarious.

Alinsky died in 1972, but his lessons endure in this offbeat guide to seizing power. Whether your goal is to fluster the establishment or defend it, *Rules for Radicals* is must reading.

SUGGESTED
READINGS

Basic Guide to Hospital Public Relations. Chicago: AHA, 1984 (P.O. Box 99376 60693).

Blake, Rich. "Reaching the Ninth Largest Market." *Public Relations Journal* (June 1985): 30–31. This article discusses the need for companies to market more actively to minorities.

Bonus, T. *Improving Internal Communications* (college). Washington, DC: Case 1984 (11 Dupont Circle 20036).

Brown, Peter C. *The Complete Guide to Money Making Ventures for Nonprofit Organizations.* Washington, DC: Taft Group, 1987 (5130 MacArthur Blvd., NW 20016).

Community Relations Report (P.O. Box X, Bartlesville, OK 74005).

Corporate 500 Directory of Corporate Philanthropy. Detroit: Gale Research, 1988 (835 Penobscot Bldg. 48226).

Corporate Giving Watch. Washington DC: Taft Group (5130 MacArthur Blvd., NW 20016).

Dannelley, Paul. *Fund Raising and Public Relations: A Critical Guide to Literature and Resources.* Norman, OK: University of Oklahoma Press, 1986.

Effective Public Relations for Colleges. Washington, DC: Case (11 Dupont Circle 20036).

Foster, Lawrence G. *A Company That Cares: Johnson & Johnson.* New Brunswick, NJ: Johnson & Johnson, 1989.

Harris, April. *Special Events: Planning for Success.* Washington, DC: Case, 1988 (11 Dupont Circle 20036).

Hospital and the News Media: Guide to Media Relations. Chicago: AHA, 1985 (P.O. Box 99376 60643).

Kruckeberg, Dean, and Kenneth Stark. *Public Relations & Community: A Reconstructed Theory.* New York: Praeger, 1988.

Making Community Relations Pay Off. Washington, DC: Public Affairs Counsel, 1987.

Religious Public Relations Handbook for Local Congregations. Gladwyne, PA: RPRC, 1988 (P.O. Box 315 19035).

CASE STUDY   Nike Won't Be PUSH-ed

The summer of 1990 was a combative one for Nike. That was the summer the nation's leading athletic shoe manufacturer went toe-to-toe with Operation PUSH.

It all began "semi-harmlessly" enough in July, when Nike announced that its president, Richard K. Donahue, would meet with Reverend Jesse Jackson to discuss "information about Nike's minority hiring, philanthropy, and business development pro-grams." In the weeks prior to that meeting, Nike and its fellow footwear makers had been criticized for selling products so prized in the ghetto that poor kids literally killed to acquire them. Nike and its colleagues argued that sneakers didn't cause the violence, bullets did. Nike looked forward to discussing this controversy with Reverend Jackson.

Shortly after the meeting, Operation PUSH, the Chicago-based civil rights organization begun by Jackson, called for a national boycott of Nike, saying the company was guilty of hiring too few minority workers. The boycott call was reminiscent of the '80s, when PUSH regularly stormed corporate bastions such as Ford and Coca-Cola with a list of demands.

While most firms in the '80s decided to compromise with PUSH, Nike took a decidedly different tack. It fought back with both barrels.

- When PUSH asked for detailed business and market information from Nike, the company refused, claiming the information was proprietary. Then Nike counterattacked, asking for sensitive financial data from PUSH.
- Nike then accused PUSH of being prodded in its action by the company's foremost competitor, Reebok. Reebok, it seemed, had suspiciously advertised in an Operation PUSH magazine. The ad cost about $6,000.
- PUSH responded by having its receptionist at Chicago headquarters answer the phones, "Say no to Nike."

The battle, as they say, was joined.

Nike president Donahue said he was "surprised" by the boycott, because his company was still negotiating with Reverend Jackson. "I understood that we were in an educational phase," said Donahue. Responded Reverend Tyrone Crider, national executive director of PUSH, "It is Nike who chose confrontation over negotiation. It's the Nike Corporation that lied to us all around the world and all around the nation. If they think Nike can slam-dunk, we can slam-dunk."

Among its charges, PUSH said that Nike had no Black members on its board of directors or any Black vice-presidents. It also accused the company of not using a Black ad agency. It said that of Nike's $2.2 billion in annual revenue, Blacks accounted for $200 million.

For its part, Nike refused to divulge details PUSH requested about its banking, purchasing, credit limits, and investment plans until it received information on PUSH finances and practices. Furthermore, said the company, "Nike is proud of our association with such great Black role models as Michael Jordan, David Robinson, Bo Jackson, Spike Lee, and John Thompson, all of whom have been featured in our advertising." This, said Nike, was an "outward indication of our inner commitment to the minority community."

Basketball god Jordan called the PUSH boycott "unfair for singling out Nike." Basketball coach Thompson, with a $200,000 per year contract with Nike, said the company was sensitive to minority issues in hiring and in the community. "I don't think that Nike has ever claimed it is a perfect company. I've been reasonably visible as a Black man. If I'm expected to support the boycott, somebody should at least tell me why I should support it," argued Thompson.

Nike still wasn't through. It increased its counterattack by focusing on the "cozy" relationship between PUSH and Reebok. In mid-August, an industry newsletter, *Sporting Goods Intelligence*, coincidentally reported that officials from Reebok and PUSH held "quiet breakfast meetings" before PUSH announced its Nike boycott. When challenged on the meeting, PUSH founder Jackson admitted he had met with Reebok officials in June but only to look at the entire athletic shoe industry. "There is something wrong with them having a series of meetings and then having PUSH turn and target Reebok's biggest competitor," said a Nike spokeswoman.

PUSH was stunned.

Air Jordan from Nike.

NEWS RELEASE

NIKE, Inc.
One Bowerman Drive
Beaverton, Oregon 97005-6453
Telephone 503/671-6453

THE NIKE COMMITMENT

A letter from Philip Knight and Richard Donahue to Nike employees

Each year for the past four years, every manager has received a memorandum from us outlining our affirmative action programs and reminding them of our corporate commitment to cultural diversity.

For the first two years (1987, 1988), we made slow but steady progress toward our goals. Slow because we were laying off employees during that time, not hiring. Steady because we know that our employees share the goal of sustaining Nike's open, diverse and untraditional environment.

In the past two years, we have been in ascendancy and our progress towards our affirmative action goals has been significant. We are hiring aggressively now and it has given us the opportunity to act on many of our plans.

Since January of this year, Nike has hired more than 1039 new employees. Twenty-one percent of those have been minorities. Keep up the good work. In total, our domestic workforce is 14.4% minority. In Portland, where most of our employees are, we have a 7% available minority workforce and we employ 10% minority.

In order for Nike to be competitive around the world, we must seek out the best talent. Talent comes in every size, shape, race and sex. All should be represented at Nike.

Our business in the African-American community is important. We have increased the number of African-American executives we have and need to keep increasing it - in finance, in production, in sales, in marketing, in every department at Nike. The same can be said of each minority group in this country. Hispanics, Asians, Native Americans: all should be represented at Nike and we have a commitment to that. Frankly, our biggest disagreement with PUSH is that they are focused exclusively on African-Americans and we have a broader vision of equal opportunity than they do. They have also specifically excluded women from their goals. We cannot do that. Our workforce is 51% female and we are as committed to helping women work their way into every part of this company as we are to minorities.

Cultural diversity is the key. We do not believe in quotas but we do believe in setting aggressive goals for every facet of our business, so let us share our own goals with you.

1) Within the next 12 months, we will name a minority to Nike's Board of Directors.

2) Within the next 24 months, we will name a minority Vice President.

3) Within the next 12 months, we will increase our minority representation at the department head level by 10%.

In order to monitor these goals, we will turn to two sources. The first will be internal. All employees should share these goals and help us meet them.

The second source will be an outside community board we are naming today to monitor our progress. We have asked minority community leaders to help us assemble that board. We plan to include representatives of minority organizations in the communities in which we work. This board will review our progress each six months.

Those are our goals.

As we review each department's business plans for our current year, we see that you have already set your own internal goals. Those include:

-- The establishment of 10 minority internships to begin this winter in conjunction with the United Negro College Fund.

-- An increase of 20% in minority participation in our NIKE STEP management training program.

-- An increase in the national recruiting of minority candidates for professional, technical and managerial positions by naming a full-time Director of Minority Recruiting and doubling representation at minority job fairs, conventions and colleges.

-- The creation of an internal committee of minority employees to advise on recruiting and training.

These are practical, achievable goals set out for our fiscal year which began June 1, 1990. On December 1, 1990 we will review our six month progress internally with every department head and externally with our new Community Board. We are certain that we will see progress at that time.

We cannot close this memorandum without mentioning the current scrutiny we are under. We can only say this: Nike believes in the aggressive pursuit of affirmative action and economic development programs. We have many partners in the minority community who have helped us make great progress already. We are gaining momentum. Don't let anyone tell you otherwise. Don't let anyone divert you from our shared goal of cultural diversity.

Philip H. Knight, Chairman   Richard K. Donahue, President

FIGURE 17–5

"We're in a war now until Nike agrees to reinvest in our community," said Crider. Echoed Jackson, "Our mission is to confront the company and show just how nasty Nike has been." Jackson promised to expand the nationwide boycott—a boycott Nike argued was falling flat on its face.

"We are responding to inquiries, and we plan to make people aware of the things we've done," said Donahue. To back up his claim, Donahue released a Nike statement on its "Goals on Minority Practices." Among other things, Nike promised:

- To name a minority to the board of directors within 12 months.
- To name a minority to the vice-presidential ranks within 24 months.
- To form an outside minority advisory board to monitor progress.

Donahue insisted that these announced goals had been planned well before the PUSH challenge.

After Donahue's statement, he, along with basketball coach Thompson, sat down again with Reverend Jackson. Thereafter, the crisis faded from the public spotlight.

In November, Nike quietly announced it had hired a Los Angeles minority advertising agency, Muse Cordero Chen Inc., to work with its primary corporate agency. Acknowledged Nike's advertising director,

"To be fair, this move is partially in response to Operation PUSH, because they made it clear that Nike does have a deficiency, albeit slight."

In December, despite the nationwide PUSH boycott of Nike products, the company announced quarterly earnings up 58 percent from the corresponding period a year earlier. The strong earnings, according to Nike, were fueled by robust sales of basketball shoes.

Thus ended with a whimper the in-your-face public relations battle between Nike and Operation PUSH.

QUESTIONS

1. What options did Nike have in responding to the Operation PUSH challenge?
2. How do you feel about the way Nike responded?
3. What do you surmise will be the impact of Nike's response to PUSH in terms of the company's long-term credibility?

For further information on the Nike-PUSH controversy, see Todd Barrett and Daniel Glick, "When Games Turn Nasty," *Newsweek* (August 27, 1990); 44–45; James Cox, "PUSH Pushes for Boycott of Nike," *USA Today*, 13 August 1990, 2B; Carol Herwig, "PUSH, Nike Finally Sit Down to Talk," *USA Today*, 24 August 1990, B2; and Chip Johnson, "Rights Group to Kick Harder at Sneaker Firm's Policies," *The Wall Street Journal*, 17 August 1990, B1.

Tips from the Top

BILL MC PHATTER

Bill McPhatter, veteran practitioner and teacher, has managed both large and small public relations functions for profit and nonprofit organizations, including R. J. Reynolds Industries, Amtrak, the NAACP Legal Defense and Educational Fund, and the U.S. Postal Service. He also has served as senior counselor for Ketchum Communications, a leading public relations firm. As a teacher, Mr. McPhatter has headed the public relations sequence at Howard University and the business journalism fellowship program at the University of Missouri.

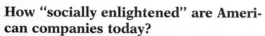

How "socially enlightened" are American companies today?
One can see appreciable progress. A continually increasing number of companies are acting on the realization that making a profit and being socially enlightened constitute an ineluctable part of the formula for sustained success in our world today. Many companies have not only accepted the reality that their work force is rapidly becoming more and more a multicultural array of men and women, they have recognized that they must take steps to ensure respectful management of this onrushing phenomenon.

What constitutes an organization's "social responsibilities?"
Operating from the bedrock of the nation's great social precepts. Organizational leadership that strives to accept nothing to the contrary from both its internal and external environments. Leaders of profit and nonprofit organizations, through the public relations process, should inspire their people to internalize and practice the "good news" that they would want to report to those beyond its walls. This kind of sustained effort plays a powerful role in creating an external environment favorable to an organization and all of its publics.

What should be the proper relationship between an organization and its community?
An organization should take pains to integrate its policies and practices with the most enlightened policies and practices of its community. If an organization finds need for enlightenment in a community (and its public relations people should take a look around), the organization should, as

a responsible citizen, search for ways to help institute wiser policies and practices, thereby improving the environment for everyone, including the organization itself.

What is the state of minority hiring in public relations today?
It is noticeably better than it has ever been, but there is still much yet undone. How many minority citizens head public relations departments of major organizations? How many have even made it to middle management? Most public relations firms have embarrassingly few. In fact, the latest data show that there are significantly fewer minorities in public relations than in any of the other, more traditional professions. An organization's public relations and social responsibility are reflected in a very telling way by the makeup of its own public relations staff and leadership. And if that's the case, we're not practicing the most exemplary public relations these days—not by a long shot.

What role can public relations play in combating racial polarization in society?
I don't know how we can combat racial polarization *without* effective public relations. We, as public relations practitioners, are supposed to know how to solve tough human problems, and taking on the damnable affliction of racism should be no exception. We need to work at this problem far more than we do. We ought to counsel against racist and polarizing practices by clearly demonstrating the severe damage done to everyone. Public relations practitioners are obligated to be well enlightened about the racial and ethnic makeup of our nation; we should feel obligated to have a genuine respect and appreciation for the role every group has played in building our nation; we must understand that it takes all of us to keep our country moving in the direction of its most noble ideals. Public relations professionals need to do a better job of letting this reality shine through in their work.

What are the prospects for minorities in the practice of public relations in the 1990s?
I think the prospects for African-Americans, Hispanics, Oriental Americans, and other minorities in public relations will be better in the 1990s than they have ever been, especially for entry level people. Many more who are minorities in our population are studying public relations and will enter the marketplace well prepared to assume responsible positions in the profession. But if these entry level people are to be persuaded that public relations has a future for them, they must be able to identify members of their group at the higher rungs in the profession. Unrelenting diversity in the workplace necessitates greater progress.

Consumers

Consumer relations

The watchword for American consumers in the 1990s is *quality*. Everyone, it seems, is shouting the Q word.

Even the U.S. Congress has jumped on the bandwagon. In 1987, Congress created the Malcolm Baldrige National Quality Award, after President Reagan's late secretary of commerce. Patterned after Japan's coveted Deming Prize for business excellence, Baldrige awards are presented to organizations that exhibit the very best qualities in terms of leadership, information and analysis, strategic quality planning, human resources, quality assurance of products and services, quality results, and customer satisfaction. The fact that 175,000 U.S. companies requested Baldrige applications in 1990 indicates that "quality" is catching on.[1]

In the 1990s, consumers simply won't tolerate defective merchandise, misleading advertising, packaging and labeling abuses, quality and safety failures, inadequate service and repair, diffident corporate complaint handlers, incomprehensible or inadequate guarantees and warranties, or slow settlements when products don't live up to advance claims.

Whether or not today's consumer is "king," he or she *demands* quality. Organizations, locked in an increasingly competitive battle for consumer loyalty, must be responsive to consumer demands. Thus, the practice of consumer relations has increased in importance among business organizations.

Growth of the Consumer Movement

Although consumerism is considered to be a relatively recent concept, legislation to protect consumers first emerged in the United States in 1872, when Congress enacted the Criminal Fraud Statute to protect consumers against corporate abuses. In 1887, Congress established the Interstate Commerce Commission to curb freewheeling railroad tycoons.

However, the first real consumer movement came right after the turn of the century when journalistic muckrakers encouraged legislation to protect the consumer. Upton Sinclair's novel *The Jungle* revealed scandalous conditions in the meat-packing industry and helped establish federal meat inspection standards as Congress passed the Food and Drug Act and the Trade Commission Act. In the second wave of the movement, 1927 to 1938, consumers were safeguarded from the abuses of manufacturers, advertisers, and retailers of well-known brands of commercial products. During this time, Congress passed the Food, Drug, and Cosmetic Act.

By the early 1960s, the movement had become stronger and more unified. President John F. Kennedy, in fact, proposed that consumers have their own Bill of Rights, containing four basic principles.

1. **The right to safety**—to be protected against the marketing of goods hazardous to health or life
2. **The right to be informed**—to be protected against fraudulent, deceitful, or grossly misleading information, advertising, labeling, or other practices and to be given the facts needed to make an informed choice
3. **The right to choose**—to be assured access, whenever possible, to a variety of products and services at competitive prices
4. **The right to be heard**—to be assured that consumer interests will receive full and sympathetic consideration in the formulation of government policy

In 1962, the first National Consumer Advisory Panel was established to "bring to the president's attention matters relating to the consumer." Two years later, President Lyndon Johnson appointed the first special assistant to the president for consumer affairs. In 1971, President Richard Nixon expanded the concept still further, with the creation of the Office of Consumer Affairs, which was given broad responsibility to analyze and coordinate all federal activities in the field of consumer protection.

Subsequent American presidents have continued to emphasize consumer rights and protection. Labeling, packaging, product safety, and a variety of other issues continue to concern government overseers of consumer interests.

Federal Consumer Agencies

Today, a massive government bureaucracy attempts to protect the consumer against abuse: upward of 900 different programs, administered by more than 400 federal entities. Key agencies include the Justice Department, Federal Trade Commission, Food and Drug Administration, Consumer Product Safety Commission, and Office of Consumer Affairs.

◆ **Justice Department** The Justice Department has had a consumer affairs section in the antitrust division since 1970. Its responsibilities include the enforcement of such consumer protection measures as the Truth in Lending Act and the Product Safety Act.

◆ **Federal Trade Commission** The FTC, perhaps more than any other agency, has vigorously enforced consumer protection. Its national advertising division covers television and radio advertising, with special emphasis on foods, drugs, and cosmetics. Its general litigation division covers areas not included by national advertising, such as magazine subscription agencies, door-to-door sales, and income tax services. Its consumer credit and special programs division deals with such areas as fair credit reporting and truth in packaging.

◆ **Food and Drug Administration** The FDA is responsible for protecting consumers from hazardous items: foods, drugs, cosmetics, therapeutic and radiological devices, food additives, and serums and vaccines.

◆ **Consumer Product Safety Commission** This bureau is responsible for overseeing product safety and standards.

◆ **Office of Consumer Affairs** This agency, the central point of consumer activities in the government, publishes literature to inform the public of recent developments in consumer affairs.

By the 1980s, the public had become increasingly disenchanted with nonstop government growth. Presidents Carter, Reagan, and Bush all espoused reducing the size of government bureaucracy and deregulating industries to assist the consumer. Trucking, airlines, telephones, banking, and a variety of other industry groups all have been deregulated during the past decade. While some assail the problems of deregulation—service quality deficiencies, increased costs of doing business, some loss of jobs, etc.—others applaud the removal of government intervention in the market process.

Regardless of whether more or less government protection is needed, corporations in the 1990s will continue to have to deal with those who regulate them. Companies—from banks to public utilities to consumer product firms—must communicate directly and frequently with the regulators in Washington. Often, the best policy is to keep regulators advised of corporate developments and to work at winning their understanding, if not their support.

Consumer Activists

The consumerist movement has attracted a host of activists in recent years. Private testing organizations, which evaluate products and inform consumers about potential dangers, have proliferated. Perhaps the best known, Consumers Union, was formed in 1936 to test products across a wide spectrum of industries. It publishes the results in a monthly magazine, *Consumer Reports*, which reaches about 3.5 million readers. Often, an evaluation in *Consumer Reports*, either pro or con, greatly affects how customers view particular products (see this chapter's case study). Consumers Union also produces books, a travel newsletter, a column for 450 newspapers, and monthly features for network television. It has an annual budget of $70 million.

Consumers have also begun taking a more active role in their own affairs. The Consumer Federation of America was formed in 1967 to unify lobbying efforts for proconsumer legislation. Today, the federation consists of 200 national, state, and local consumer groups, labor unions, electric cooperatives, and other organizations with consumer interests.

Although companies often find activists' criticism annoying, the emergence of the consumer watchdog movement has generally been a positive development for consumers. Ralph Nader and others have forced organizations to consider, even more than usual, the downside of the products and services they offer. Smart companies have come to take seriously the pronouncements of consumer activists.

Business Gets the Message

Obviously, few organizations can afford to shirk their responsibilities to consumers. Consumer relations divisions have sprung up, either as separate entities or as part of public relations departments. The title of vice-president for consumer relations is showing up with more frequency on corporate organization charts.

In many companies, consumer relations began strictly as a way to handle complaints, an area to which all unanswerable complaints were sent. Such units have frequently provided an alert to management. In recent years, some companies have broadened the consumer relations function to encompass such activities as developing guidelines to evaluate services and products for management, developing consumer programs that meet consumer needs and increase sales, developing field-training programs, evaluating service approaches, and evaluating company effectiveness in demonstrating concern for customers.

The investment in consumer service apparently pays off. Marketers of consumer products say most customer criticism can be mollified with a prompt, personalized reply—and a couple of coupons. Failing to answer a question, satisfy a complaint, or solve a problem, however, can result in a blitz of bad word-of-mouth advertising.[2] More typical of the increased concern shown today by most business organizations are the following:

▲ When Alamo Rent-A-Car experienced a shortage of vehicles in a busy vacation season at certain locations, it eagerly reimbursed customers for

COMMAND//AIRWAYSINC.
DUTCHESS COUNTY AIRPORT
WAPPINGERS FALLS, NEW YORK 12590   (914) 462-6100   TELEX: 289371 COMD UR

January 21, 1985

Mr. David Kemp
176 West 87th Street
New York, NY 10024

Dear Mr. Kemp:

Clearly we screwed up. Please accept our apologies.

Attached is a check for $168.00, which represents a full
refund.

Again, please accept our apologies.

Sincerely,

Kingsley G. Morse,
President

KGM:nj
Encl.

FIGURE 18–1   Here's a refreshing straightforward response, from the chief executive officer no less, that is guaranteed to restore consumer confidence in Command Airways. *(Courtesy of Command Airways)*

the difference between their reserved Alamo rate and that which they were forced to pay.

◆ When the Swingline Company received numerous complaints about its Tot stapler, it reconstituted the product and sent new models, free of charge, to people who complained.

◆ When Newman's Own Microwave Popcorn received complaints that its bags were leaking, it hired a technical consulting organization to reevaluate the bag sealing system. It also refunded the cost of the purchase.

In adopting a more activist consumerist philosophy, firms like these have found that consumer relations need not take a defensive posture. Rather, consumer questions can be a valuable source of information for marketers. In 1990, for instance, when consumers objected to the bland seasonings in a new potato chip product called "Krunchers!," the Borden Company discovered a manufacturing error. When Campbell decided to roll out its low-sodium Special Request soups, its consumer relations division assembled a list of every customer who had inquired about the salt content of its other soups. Each one received information about Special Request soups, as well as a few coupons.

Accordingly, the consumer affairs function has grown in stature. In 1987, the Society of Consumer Affairs Professionals had 600 companies among its members. By 1990, the association boasted 1,400 members.

Consumerist Philosophy

Most companies begin with the premise that customers, if they are to remain customers, deserve to be treated fairly and honestly. Historically, the companies that initiated their own activist consumer affairs units have been those to escape the wrath of outside activists.

The Grand Union Company, second oldest food chain in the nation, began a consumer affairs department two decades ago and drew up its own Consumer Bill of Rights. Its example has been followed by numerous companies in a variety of industries. Typical is Chrysler Motors "Car Buyer's Bill of Rights."

1. Every American has the right to quality.
2. Every American has the right to long-term protection.
3. Every American has the right to friendly treatment, honest service, and competent repairs.
4. Every American has the right to a safe vehicle.
5. Every American has the right to address grievances.
6. Every American has the right to satisfaction.

Chrysler, like other companies, backed up its Bill of Rights with a customer arbitration board to deal with warranty-related problems and commissioned a research organization to survey car owners periodically on customer satisfaction.

Such an enlightened approach to customer relations was typical of businesses in the 1990s (Figure 18–2).

A Customer's Bill Of Rights

1. A customer has the right to courteous, considerate treatment at all times by all members of the seller organization.

2. A customer has the right to receive accurate information about features, applications, prices and availability of products or services which are offered for sale.

3. A customer has the right to have his or her expectations met that quality, price and delivery of the product or service will be as represented prior to having made the purchase.

4. A customer has the right to be served by skilled, knowledgeable personnel dedicated to representing his or her best interests with other departments in the seller organization.

5. A customer has the right to be promptly and fully informed when the seller's commitment cannot be met as originally stated.

6. A customer has the right to complain—and to receive prompt, fair handling and resolution of the complaint on its merits.

7. A customer has the right to expect extra effort by the seller's personnel in genuine emergencies, regardless of their cause.

8. A customer has the right to expect honesty and integrity at all levels in the seller organization, and assurance that all legal requirements have been met and rights observed.

9. A customer has the right to expect teamwork from the seller—and never to hear the expression: "That's not my department!"

10. A customer has the right to expect appreciation from everybody in the seller organization with which he or she does business, appreciation for business already given as well as for business to be given in the future . . . provided this Customer's Bill of Rights continues to be observed by the seller organization.

FIGURE 18−2 The Customer Service Institute lived up to its name with the publication of this manifesto, which summarizes what a customer ought to be entitled to. *(Courtesy of the Customer Service Institute)*

Glass in the Baby Food

For Gerber Products, a company that keeps a stash of teddy bears and cookies to welcome children to the lobby of its Michigan headquarters, the events of February 1986 were unsettling. Specifically, a jar of Gerber's baby food in Schenectady, NY, was reported to have glass in it. Tests at a Gerber laboratory showed that there was no glass in the jar turned in, and the supermarket reporting the incident said it had lost the fragment the customer had turned in and therefore couldn't prove the existence of the glass.

Nonetheless, the action triggered a wave of similar complaints about glass in Gerber baby food across the nation. Gerber, rejecting the conciliatory posture adopted by other companies in crisis situations, decided to shed its cuddly image and get tough. "We feel strongly we're being had," the company's chief executive officer said. He noted that the Food and Drug Administration tested 40,000 unopened jars of Gerber baby food and concluded there was no public health problem.

The company refused to knuckle under to nationwide consumer groups that urged a recall. It denounced the Brooklyn, NY, district attorney's announcement that she was opening a criminal investigation of the matter. When the governor of Maryland ordered Gerber's strained peaches off his state's supermarket shelves, the company filed a $150 million lawsuit against Maryland officials, asserting that the action had injured its 58-year reputation for integrity and quality.

Gerber officials argued that it was virtually impossible that the chunks of glass consumers were reporting could have come from its jars. They said each year Gerber produces about a billion jars of baby food under tight technical controls, using advanced glass-washing equipment and screens designed to filter out any particle larger than four-thousandths of an inch. The company added that it kept X-ray machines in factories to check for breakage along the fast-moving production line.

Gerber officials further noted that in special tests, where chunks of glass were crammed into its jars, special jar washers successfully flushed out every last fragment. Said Gerber's director of corporate communications, "We feel this is a lynch mob," and added that the company's objective was "not to get panicked." So, in the face of 227 complaints to the Food and Drug Administration about Gerber baby food jars, the nation's largest manufacturer of baby food continued to hang tough.[*]

QUESTIONS

1. What do you think of Gerber's public relations strategy?
2. What other public relations options could the company consider?
3. If you were Gerber's public relations director, would you have assumed a higher profile?
4. Would you appear on television to defend the company?
5. Would you run 30-second commercials on television to talk about the problem? If so, would you mention the glass problem in the spots?

[*]For further information on the Gerber case, see James Barron, "Gerber Deals Gingerly with Tales of Tainting," *The New York Times,* 8 March 1986, 8; and John Bussey, "Gerber Takes Risky Stance as Fears Spread About Glass in Baby Food," *The Wall Street Journal,* 6 March 1986, 27.

Consumerist Objectives

Building sales is the primary consumer relations objective. A satisfied customer may return; an unhappy customer may not. Here are some typical goals.

◆ **Keeping old customers** Most sales are made to established customers. Consumer relations efforts should be expended to keep these customers happy. Pains should be taken to respond to customer concerns. For example, when the San Francisco earthquake struck on October 17, 1989, AT&T suspended normal practice and asked operators to make three and even four attempts to complete calls. AT&T operators worked throughout the night handling 253,000 calls—double the normal volume.

◆ **Attracting new customers** Every business must work constantly to develop new customers. In many industries, the prices and quality of competing products are similar. Customers may base decisions among brands on how they have been treated.

◆ **Marketing new items or services** Customer relations techniques can influence the sale of new products. Thousands of new products flood the market each year, and the vast array of information about these products can confuse the consumer. When General Electric's research revealed that consumers want personalized service and more information on new products, it established the GE Answer Center, a national toll-free, 24-hour service that informed consumers about new GE products and services. Building such company and product loyalty lies at the heart of a solid consumer relations effort.

◆ **Expediting complaint handling** Few companies are free of complaints. Customers protest when appliances don't work, errors are made in billing, or deliveries aren't made on time. Many large firms have established response procedures. Often, a company ombudsman can salvage a customer relationship with a speedy and satisfactory answer to a complaint.

◆ **Reducing costs** To most companies, an educated consumer is the best consumer. Uninformed buyers cost a company time and money—when goods are returned, service calls are made, and instructions are misunderstood. Many firms have adopted programs to educate customers about many topics: what to look for in choosing fruits and vegetables, how to shop for durable goods, how to use credit wisely, and how to conserve electricity (Figure 18–3).

Consumer Programs

Some of the nation's most marketing-oriented firms are leaders in creating innovative consumer relations programs. Most apparently believe

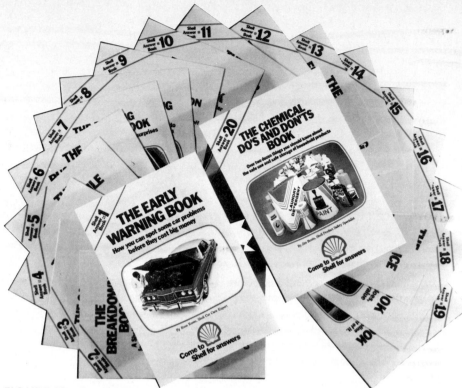

FIGURE 18—3   Typical of the desire of the nation's oil companies to present a proconsumer image, Shell Oil published a complete set of easy-to-read, illustrated manuals teaching people how to care for their cars, their homes, and themselves. The free "answer books" were available in Shell stations around the country. *(Courtesy of Shell Oil Co.)*

that, by investing in consumer relations activities, they are safeguarding and ensuring future sales. Here are some of the more novel approaches to consumer relations.

1. The major automobile companies are all engaged actively in consumer relations, although each takes a different tack. The Ford Motor Company established a Consumer Affairs Board to meet periodically and mediate unresolved product complaints, rendering binding judgments on the company and its dealers. Ford's initial board consisted of educators, dealers, and motor vehicle officials. At General Motors, each car division offered specific consumer relations programs for dealers, introducing them to techniques for handling complaints and getting to the root of customer dissatisfaction. Chrysler Corporation held seminars for its dealers on handling customer complaints and conducted Women on

Wheels workshops dealing with basic car repair and maintenance. Chrysler also introduced free, long-term warranties, suggesting confidence in the reliability of its product.

2. Food and pharmaceutical firms have taken the lead in listing product ingredients and nutritional information on their packages. Del Monte was one of the first food processors to list ingredients and nutritional information on its labels and to offer customers further product information on request. Eli Lilly offered a similar product-labeling service for its drug items and went one step further by providing label information for immediate antidotal analysis in case of emergencies.

3. Other companies, from appliance sellers (Sears, General Electric, and Whirlpool) to banks (Citibank, Chemical Bank), have translated jargon into easily understandable English on their warranties and loan agreements. Gulf went so far as to publish a booklet called "The Art of Complaining," so its customers would know how and to whom to voice complaints and what to expect in response. All of these companies and many more like them have recognized that, in consumer relations, as in many other activities in the public relations field, the best defense is a good offense.

B E T W E E N   T H E   L I N E S

Yo Dudes! Can the Sexist Suds Special!

Occasionally, in their zeal to "relate" to consumers, companies go a tad too far.

Such was the case during spring break of 1989, when Miller Brewing Company had to destroy 700,000 copies of a special college advertising supplement that was, like, totally offensive to "hot babes" and other students.

The 16-page, full-color *Beachin' Times* featured stories on such questionable topics as "Four Sure Ways to Scam Babes" and "How to Find the Ultimate Babe." Many of the items, written in college slang, included sexual references and illustrations, while other articles glorified excessive consumption of alcohol.

When students at one university threatened a boycott of Miller products if the ads weren't stopped, Miller officials immediately apologized and destroyed the remaining supplements.

Said Miller's public relations manager, "Sometimes when you try to create ads that rise above the clutter, you make mistakes. Clearly, that's what happened in this case."

Office of the Ombuds Officer

One classic research project for the White House Office on Consumer Affairs revealed the following:

♦ Only four of 100 dissatisfied customers will complain.
♦ For every complainer there are 24 with the same complaint who never say anything.
♦ About 13 percent of dissatisfied customers will tell 20 people about it.
♦ Almost 90 percent of dissatisfied customers don't repurchase from the offending company, compared to 54 to 70 percent who remain loyal when complaints are satisfactorily handled.[3]

At many companies the most immediate response to complaints has been the establishment of ombudsman offices. The term *ombudsman* originally described a government official—in Sweden and New Zealand, for example—appointed to investigate complaints against abuses of public officials. In most firms, the office of the ombuds officer investigates complaints made against the company and its managers. Such an office generally provides a central location that customers can call to seek redress of grievances.

A five-year study of consumer complaint handling commissioned by the U.S. Office of Consumer Affairs suggested two important caveats for suppliers of consumer goods and services.

1. Consumers who do not complain when they are dissatisfied are often unhappy enough to switch product brands, companies, or both.
2. Because marketing costs are extremely high, it may be less expensive to resolve the complaints of existing customers than to win new ones.[4]

Typically, the ombuds officer monitors the difficulties customers are having with products. Often, he or she can anticipate product or performance deficiencies. Ombuds officers are in business to inspire customer confidence and to influence an organization's behavior toward improved service. They accomplish this by responding, more often than not, in the following manner:

♦ "We'll take care of that for you."
♦ "We'll take full responsibility for that defect."
♦ "We want your business."
♦ "Thank you for thinking of us."
♦ "Consider it done."[5]

Such "magic words" should be heard more often in many organizations. Courteous, knowledgeable, and skilled complaint-handling ombuds officers—cheerful, positive, and genuinely concerned with solving a customer's problems—can keep clients happy—and loyal—for many years.

A Day in the Life of the Ombuds Officer

So you want to handle consumer complaints? Here is a random selection of complaints received by the consumer affairs division of Chase Manhattan Bank. How would you have handled them?

1. A businessman, carrying an attaché case, made a deposit at a midtown branch before going to his office. Inadvertently, he left his case on the main banking floor. By the time he discovered that it was missing, the police bomb squad had smashed the innocent case and cordoned off the area. The owner asked the bank for a replacement. Would you have given it to him?

2. After making a deposit and leaving the bank, a woman reported that a huge icicle fell from the bank's roof and nearly hit her. She complained bitterly to consumer affairs. How would you appease her?

3. A young installment-loan customer claimed that his car had been removed for reclamation because of delinquent loan payments. He claimed that he had paid the loan on time and objected to the illegal seizure. On checking, it was determined that several loan payments were, in fact, delinquent. Nevertheless, the car was returned, in a very damaged condition. The young man sought reimbursement for repairs. What would you recommend?

4. A customer complained that she had received no response to her numerous letters and memos concerning the hostile treatment accorded her at the local branch. After investigation, it was learned that the woman was a nuisance to branch officers, yet kept a very healthy balance in her savings account. Furthermore, all the correspondence to which she referred was written on the backs of checks she submitted in loan payments. How would you handle this problem?

5. The executor of an estate complained that his deceased client, who had been a bank customer, had received a card reading, "Best wishes in your new residence." What remedial action would you recommend?

Summary

Despite periodic legislative setbacks and shifting consumerist leadership, the cause of consumerism seems destined to remain strong. Although critics may argue that nobody uses unit pricing and nobody wears seat belts, the push for product safety and quality will likely increase in the years ahead. The granddaddy of the consumer movement, Ralph Nader, has suggested that the movement is heading toward more "citizens' groups set up

The Chase Manhattan Bank, N.A.
1 Chase Manhattan Plaza
New York, New York 10081

Fraser P. Seitel
Senior Vice President
Director-Public Affairs

 CHASE

October 26, 1989

Mr. Barry F. Sullivan
Chairman
First Chicago Corporation
1 First National Plaza
Chicago, IL 60670

Dear Barry:

Greetings from the home of the 1990 NBA champion New York Knicks.
I do hope things are well with you.

The reason I'm writing is that I wanted you to know about the
magnificent, above-and-beyond-the-call-of-duty service accorded
me by your Rose Svendsen in credit control at the First Card unit
in Elgin.

I told Ms. Svendsen that rather than using several bank cards, I
wished to increase my First Card line to a level that would more
adequately accommodate my family's well-developed spending
habits. I promised, in return, to destroy my other cards.
Ms. Svendsen immediately cut through any bureaucracy that may
exist in your fine institution and got me the line increase.

What a woman! What a bank! And because of her efforts -- I
promise to pay my bills!

Best regards,

Yours in customer satisfaction,

FIRST CHICAGO
FCC National Bank

Mail Suite 0340
Chicago, Illinois 60670-0340
Telephone: (312) 732-2014

Scott P. Marks, Jr.
Chairman
FCC National Bank

October 31, 1989

Mr. Fraser P. Seitel
Senior Vice President -
  Director of Public Affairs
The Chase Manhattan Bank, N. A.
One Chase Manhattan Plaza
New York, New York 10081

Dear Mr. Seitel:

Barry Sullivan has passed on to me your kind letter of
October 26.

As you can imagine, people usually send letters to
Barry when they are not pleased with the services they
have obtained from our Bankcard Group. What a
pleasure to hear from someone who feels they have
received proper treatment! I will pass on your kind
words to Ms. Svendsen, who I know will appreciate your
words of praise.

Thank you again for your letter.

Sincerely,

SPM:mry

cc: Barry F. Sullivan
    Rosemary Svendsen
    Ronald H. Bohnsak

FIGURE 18—4 Most companies receive their
fair share of complaint letters. Rare, however, is
the customer letter that actually praises a firm's
good works. When it happens—as these examples demonstrate—everybody, up to and including the chairman of the board, can't wait to respond.

FIRST CHICAGO
The First National Bank of Chicago

Barry F. Sullivan
Chairman of the Board

November 1, 1989

Dear Fraser:

Thanks for your letter.

Thanks for the kind words about Rosemary Svendsen.

Thanks for the hillarious opening prediction. The
Great Omarr need not fear any competition from
you. (Now if you had sent greetings to the home of
the 1990 NBA champs....!)

Warm regards,

Mr. Fraser P. Seitel
Senior Vice President
Director - Public Affairs
The Chase Manhattan Bank, N.A.
1 Chase Manhattan Plaza
New York, New York 10081

specifically to deal with new, complicated issues, such as computers, genetic engineering, toxic wastes, and multinational corporations."[6]

Congress and federal agencies today subject companies to more scrutiny in their consumer policies. The phrase *caveat emptor* ("Let the buyer beware") has been replaced by *caveat venditor* ("Let the seller beware"). For example, in 1960, there were fewer than 50,000 product liability cases, dealing with faulty merchandise, warranties, or performance. By 1970, that number had mushroomed to 500,000 cases. In the 1990s, such cases will continue to increase.

Public interest groups see an opportunity to set the agenda for the nation in the 1990s. However, according to one current activist and former Federal Trade Commission member, the goals for the 1990s don't relate especially to product quality and consumer rights. Among key goals are to "restore excellence and universal opportunity in education and housing, defend the environment, redeem civil rights and liberty, reverse the increase in poverty with a secure net for children and the elderly, and defuse nuclear terror."[7]

The likely reemergence of activism in the '90s means businesses must respond with an even greater sense of consumerism. In 1990, when Star Kist Tuna received thousands of letters from schoolchildren protesting the killing of dolphins in the hunt for tuna, the company changed its tuna-fishing policy. As a result of Star Kist's action to refit boats and retrain fishermen, fewer dolphin died, and the company was hailed as a hero.[8]

That same year, the Walt Disney Company pulled a controversial "Steve the Tramp" doll off the market, after homeless rights groups complained. Although "Steve the Tramp" was one of 14 Disney action figures of criminals and gangsters inspired by the hit *Dick Tracy* movie, Disney didn't hesitate to yank the doll and lose thousands of dollars, in the face of a nationwide firestorm.[9]

Similarly, any organization in the 1990s interested in muffling activist protests and ensuring a reputation of integrity must meet the consumerist challenge by practicing safety, performance, and service standards that demonstrate good faith and public interest. In the long run, the firm that lives by a proconsumer philosophy will prosper. The firm that ignores the irresistible push of consumerism risks not only growth, but survival.

1. What did President Kennedy contribute to the consumerist movement?
2. What are the key federal agencies involved in consumerism?
3. What is Consumers Union?
4. How do companies typically handle the challenge of consumerism?
5. What is a consumer bill of rights?
6. What are typical consumerist objectives?
7. What is the Office of the Ombuds Officer?
8. Why must firms fear too many dissatisfied customers?

DISCUSSION STARTERS

9. What is meant by the term *caveat emptor*? *Caveat venditor*?
10. What can be learned from the Star Kist and Disney experiences in confronting increased consumer activism?

NOTES

1. Paul Burnham Finney, "Everyone Is Shouting the Q Word." Special Digest Advertising Section, *Newsweek* (December 10, 1990): 12.
2. Kathleen Deveny, "For Marketers, No Peeve Is Too Petty," *The Wall Street Journal,* 14 November 1990, B1.
3. "How Much More Does It Cost to Create a New Customer Compared to Keeping an Existing One," *Public Relations Reporter* (May 30, 1988): 1.
4. Robert M. Cosenza and Jerry W. Wilson, "Managing Consumer Dissatisfaction: The Effective Use of the Corporate Written Response to Complaints," *Public Relations Quarterly* (Spring 1982): 17.
5. John R. Graham, "Words to Inspire Confidence," *Communication Briefings* (November 1988): 8.
6. "Whither Consumerism?" *The New York Times,* 23 November 1985, 17.
7. Michael Pertschuk, "The Role of Public Interest Groups in Setting the Public Agenda for the '90s," *Journal of Consumer Affairs* 21 (Winter 1987): 171.
8. "Star Kist Explains How Consumer Advocacy Inspired Its Decision for Policy Change," *Public Relations Reporter* (May 14, 1990): 4.
9. "Disney Pulls Doll Offensive to Homeless." *The Record,* 15 December 1990, A-5.

TOP OF THE SHELF

Ries, Al, and Jack Trout. *Bottom-Up Marketing.*
New York: McGraw-Hill, 1989.

Practitioners looking for new ways to reach consumers ought to consider *Bottom-Up Marketing,* which turns conventional marketing wisdom on its head.

Al Ries and Jack Trout, savvy marketers who have counseled leading corporations, tell you to ignore traditional "top-down" marketing—deciding what to do and then how to do it—and instead adopt a single competitive tactic *before* devising a strategy. The authors outline the bottom-up process: conduct research, monitor trends, narrow your focus to find a tactic, turn your tactic into a strategy, sell the strategy to senior management, then launch your pro-

gram. They offer two ways to introduce your plan: "the big bang" and "slow roll out," each of which has advantages depending on the company behind the launch. Should the plan flounder, Ries and Trout say revive it by "shifting the battlefield." The authors pepper their instruction with numerous examples of companies that do and don't practice bottom-up marketing.

Marketing public relations pros need fresh thinking to break through product clutter and influence consumers. They could gain several innovative approaches by reading *Bottom-Up Marketing.*

Communications Counselors. *Capital Contacts in Consumerism.* (Available from the author, 1701 K Street, NW, Washington, DC 20006.)

Davidow, William H., and Bro Uttal. *Total Customer Service.* New York: Harper & Row, 1989.

DeCourcy Hinds, Michael. "Seeking Profits in Consumer Complaints." *The New York Times,* 26 March 1988. The author points out that competition necessitates keeping customers happy.

Francese, Peter. *Capturing Consumers.* Ithaca, NY: American Demographics, 1989 (P.O. Box 68).

Hanan, Mack, and Peter Karp. *Customer Satisfaction.* New York: AMACOM, 1989 (135 W. 50th St. 10020).

Pertschuk, Michael. "The Role of Public Interest Groups in Setting the Public Agenda for the '90s." *Journal of Consumer Affairs* (Winter 1987): 171–182.

Rudd, Joel, and Vicki L. Buttolph. "Consumer Curriculum Materials: The First Content Analysis." *Journal of Consumer Affairs* (Summer 1987): 108–121. The researchers conclude that business-sponsored curriculum publications have more commercial and advertising content than do nonbusiness materials.

"Spending to Keep Customers Makes Sense Right on the Bottom Line . . ." *Public Relations Reporter* (May 30, 1988).

CASE STUDY   A Tough Turn for the Suzuki Samurai

For the Suzuki Motor Company, it was the public relations equivalent of a head-on collision. In June 1988, Consumers Union, publisher of *Consumer Reports,* announced that it had found the Samurai, Suzuki's fast-selling cross between a Jeep and an economy car, "not acceptable" (Figure 18–5). Even more extraordinary, *Consumer Reports* said the vehicle was so unsafe that Suzuki should buy back every one of the 150,000 Samurais sold in the United States since their introduction in 1985.

The watchdog organization said that the Samurai repeatedly toppled after making sharp turns at about 40 miles per hour. Even though the tests involved slightly tighter turns than *Consumer Reports* used with other cars, Consumers Union's technical director said, "The car shouldn't roll over. It's as simple as that. The problem is inher-

ent in its design. The only way to fix it is to make the vehicle longer, wider, and heavier." Consumers Union went on to say that owners should be given refunds.

The *Consumer Reports* announcement, made at an unusual New York City news conference that happened to coincide with the first day of congressional hearings on sport utility vehicles, drew immediate cries of "foul" from Suzuki officials. The company pointed out that, for years, so-called consumer advocate groups had been petitioning the National Highway Traffic Safety Administration (NHTSA) for rollover standards for sport utility vehicles. The government had resisted such a move.

Suzuki cited government statistics that the Samurai had a lower propensity to turn over than most other similar vehicles (Figure 18–6). The company said *Consumer*

FIGURE 18—5
The Suzuki Samurai is classified as a sport utility vehicle. *(Courtesy of Suzuki)*

Reports had put the Samurai through a second, more difficult maneuvering test after it had passed the test that *Consumer Reports* used with hundreds of other vehicles. In the revised test the course was changed by bringing obstacles closer together, which required sharper turns to avoid them. On the revised test course, the Samurai flunked. Three rival utility vehicles passed both tests.

"Suzuki will not allow *Consumer Reports'* statements that result from distorted testing and irresponsible reporting to go unchallenged," said an American Suzuki vice-president. "*Consumer Reports* has led the media and consumer to believe that the Samurai was subjected to the same tests done on all of the vehicles it has reviewed in the past 10 years. This is not true. The magazine changed its test for the first time in its history. It appears as though the magazine wants the Samurai to fail," the vice-president added.

What made Suzuki's problems even worse was that the NHTSA said the Samurai had been involved in 44 reported rollover incidents, resulting in 16 deaths and 53 injuries. Earlier in the year, the Center for Auto Safety, a consumer advocacy group in Washington, had petitioned the NHTSA to recall the Samurai. That petition was being reviewed at the time of the *Consumer Reports* announcement.

Despite all this bad news, Suzuki refused to roll over and play dead. On the contrary, the company responded aggressively, announcing that it would launch its own investigation into Consumers Union and its testing procedure. Suzuki threatened legal action against consumer organizations making "erroneous and inaccurate claims." American Suzuki also announced that it had increased its annual advertising budget by $1.5 million, to counter the negative publicity. In its ads it said, "Testing on the Samurai before and since its introduction, combined

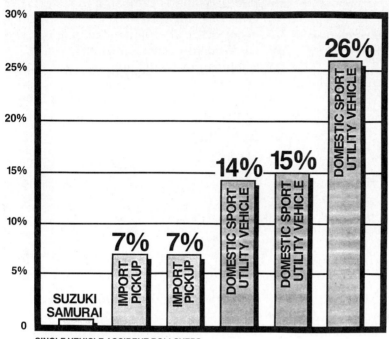

COMPARATIVE INCIDENCE OF ROLLOVER

SINGLE VEHICLE ACCIDENT ROLLOVERS
1987 FARS Data (through 11/1/87)
Compiled by National Highway Traffic Safety Administration

FIGURE 18—6 Despite *Consumer Reports'* allegations, the Suzuki Samurai fared better than most other sport utility vehicles and small trucks in terms of the incidence of rollovers, according to the government's 1987 Fatal Accident Reporting System data compiled by the National Highway Traffic Safety Administration.

with federal government statistics, provides substantial proof that the Samurai is a safe vehicle."

Other automobile observers tended to agree with Suzuki's rebuttal. Said the executive editor of *Car and Driver* magazine, "We thought it was an okay vehicle for what it was. We don't expect off-road vehicles to act like sports cars." To punctuate its argument, Suzuki released an earlier company video of several imported and domestic cars and trucks being rolled over by test drivers as "proof that any vehicle can be rolled over under certain conditions." The tests shown on the video were similar to those done by Consumers Union.

Indeed, it seemed curious that Consumers Union would take off after Suzuki, a relatively new company with just one product in the United States. Although Samurai dominated the sport utility vehicle market and the car sported a high profile on television and in movies, nonetheless Suzuki was the smallest Japanese car company operating in the United States.

The results of the charges and countercharges were inconclusive. Caught in the middle were 150,000 Samurai owners, destined to have difficulty selling or insuring their vehicles, not to mention driving them with confidence. They, beyond all others, could clearly see the gallows humor of the tag line of American Suzuki's advertising campaign: "Never a dull moment."*

*For further information, see Michael deCourcy Hinds, "How Consumers Union Puts Teeth into 'Let the Seller Beware,'" *The New York Times*, 11 June 1988, 37; Doron P. Levin, "Test Change Draws Fire from Suzuki," *The New York Times*, 10 June 1988, D14; Doron P. Levin, "Consumer Group Asks Recall of Suzuki Samurai as Unsafe," *The New York Times*, 3 June 1988, Al; and Stewart Troy, "Will Samurai Marketing Work for Suzuki?" *Business Week* (June 27, 1988): 33–34.

QUESTIONS

1. What do you think of Suzuki's aggressive public relations campaign in response to *Consumer Reports?*
2. What other alternative campaigns could the company have launched?
3. Should the company sue Consumers Union?
4. Why did *Consumer Reports* attack Suzuki rather than a competitor like Ford or General Motors?

Tips from the Top

STEPHEN BROBECK

Stephen Brobeck has served as executive director of the Consumer Federation of America (CFA) since 1980. A federation of 220 groups with more than 30 million members, CFA is the nation's largest consumer advocacy organization. Brobeck frequently testifies before congressional committees and is often interviewed by the national news media. He has co-authored two books, *The Bank Book* and *The Product Safety Book*.

Are consumers today more enlightened?
It is unclear whether consumers are smarter shoppers than they were 20 years ago. There is no question, however, that they're more aware of their interests as consumers and of the obligations of sellers.

Are companies today more enlightened?
Most companies not only are aware that consumers expect more from them, but also have taken steps—ranging from improved product quality to effective complaint resolution—to meet these higher expectations.

What is the general state of consumer relations in America?
Although consumer relations can vary widely from company to company and even from industry to industry, it is far more advanced than 20 years ago. Just one indication is that the Society of Consumer Affairs Professionals in Business, founded only in 1973, has 1,500 members.

How important today is the consumer movement?
Over the past decade, the consumer movement has had successes and disappointments. But organizations such as Consumers Union, Center for Science in the Public Interest, CFA, and state public utility advocates are far stronger institutionally than they've ever been. And they continue to enjoy strong public support.

What are the responsibilities of an organization to the consumers of its products?
Most importantly, to provide good value in products—quality that is never less than satisfactory at a reasonable price. In addition, sellers must supply accurate, useful prepurchase information and respond adequately to postpurchase requests for information or redress.

481

What is the worst situation you've ever run into as a consumer advocate?
While working with a self-help complaint resolution group in the 1970s, I encountered several dozen sellers who stole from their customers. Typically, these were home repair contractors, appliance repairmen, or mail order firms that received payments from customers yet supplied no product value, sometimes no product at all.

How should a company react to criticism of its products by consumers, advocates, or the media?
If the criticism is totally baseless, correct it with an objective, documented response. However, if the complaint is valid, acknowledge the problem and explain how it will be corrected. Research shows that resolving an individual complaint, or generic problem, can build company credibility and customer satisfaction.

Investors

Financial relations—or investor relations, or just IR—has been a growth area in public relations since the 1960s. Financial relations generally blends the skills of finance and writing with knowledge of the media, marketing, and, more recently, government, because of its increased role in the capital markets.

Financial relations was born in the mid-1930s, shortly after the passage of the Securities Act of 1933 and the Securities Exchange Act of 1934, which attempted to protect the public from abuses in the issuance and sale of securities. Financial relations remained in relative obscurity, however, until the 1960s, when investors rushed to the stock market to strike their fortunes. Stock prices escalated, and IR enjoyed a heyday.

After a brief interruption in the 1970s, the investing public returned with a roar to the stock market in the 1980s. Then, in October 1987, a funny thing happened to the "bull market"—it "crashed" 500 points, sending stocks and investors tumbling back to reality.

The markets were resilient, though, and by the end of the 1980s, investors again were buying securities. The Wall Street scandals of the late '80s—punctuated by the fines and jail terms levied against Ivan Boesky and Michael Milken—heightened the public's wariness of "Wall Street." (Which was also the title of a blockbuster Michael Douglas film that didn't help matters any.)

Against this backdrop, the investor relations function has emerged as a senior-level position that helps plan, position, and market the perception of a company and justify the performance of its stock to the financial community and investors.[1]

Investor relations combines the disciplines of finance and communications, as it portrays to current and future investors a company's financial performance and prospects. What distinguishes investor relations people from others in public relations are the specialized financial skills and experience required to communicate effectively with numbers-oriented audiences, like individual and institutional investors and "buy side" and "sell side" stock-market analysts.

It is little wonder that chief executives pay good money for IR professionals. Salary surveys indicate that IR practitioners are generally paid in the upper range of all public relations salaries, with the better IR pros earning up to $150,000 a year.[2] Not surprisingly, the financial relations field has become a specialized one in which the inexperienced are at a definite disadvantage.

Essence of Investor Relations

The end of the 1980s was marked by a bustling period of mergers, leveraged buy outs, and other competition for investor capital, all of which stimulated a growing need among companies for people skilled at investor relations. What exactly is investor relations? Basically, IR is the effort to narrow the gap between the perception of a company and the reality; in other words, helping the firm's securities reach their "appropriate" market price. To do this, investor relations professionals must encourage stockholders to hold company shares and persuade Wall Street financial analysts, banks, and mutual funds to take an interest.

A company's stock price is its currency. Premium stock prices allow an organization to acquire others, whereas a low stock price encourages raids from competitors. If shares are fairly priced in relation to current or future expectations, the company has a better chance of raising money for future expansion. In any event, a strong shareholder base is necessary to support management's objectives.

A public company must communicate promptly and candidly any information, both good and bad, that may have an effect on its securities. Practitioners must see that shareholders receive such information fully, fairly, and quickly so that they can decide whether to buy, hold, or sell the company's securities. Chapter 22 expands on this concept.

The institutions and individuals who own the common stock of a company are, in effect, its owners. The shareholders, in person or by proxy, elect the board of directors, which in turn selects the officers who run the company. So, in theory at least, shareholders (who own the company) influence the operations of that company. In practice, corporate officers manage companies with relative independence. Nevertheless, shareholders constitute a critical public for any firm.

Why do investors buy a company's shares? The first requisite must be performance. A company that fails to perform can't expect good communications to sell its stock. On the other hand, a thoughtfully planned and executed financial communications program may materially enhance the reputation and therefore the market popularity of a company that performs well.

Organizing the Program

The most effective way to reach the investing public—individuals as well as institutions—is through a systematic program of financial relations, ordinarily managed by an IR director. Frequently, programs are bolstered by the involvement of a financial relations counseling firm.

Because most public companies perpetually compete for equity capital, an organized IR program is essential. IR has many audiences, including

FIGURE 19–1 The increased clout of institutional investors in the 1990s has caused concern about the diminished role of individual investors in the securities markets. This New York Stock Exchange ad illustrates what the world's largest stock exchange is doing to confront the issue. *(Courtesy of New York Stock Exchange)*

HOW IMPORTANT IS THE INDIVIDUAL INVESTOR?

Individual investors are a very important part of the New York Stock Exchange.

They are important because they provide capital for the growth of business and the economy. That means new jobs and a better quality of life in the communities in which we live.

They are important because they bring a diversity of investment goals and preferences. Their active participation adds significantly to the liquidity of the market—the ability to buy and sell shares at stable prices.

The NYSE demonstrates its commitment to the individual investor in many ways.

At the NYSE—and only at the NYSE—individual investors always get preferential treatment. Through an exclusive **NYSE Individual Investor Express Delivery Service,** individual investor orders get priority status over all other orders at all times. Even in periods of unusual activity, those orders go to the head of the line, in front of all others, including institutional and program trading orders.

America has a long history of individual investor involvement in business. In fact, one in five Americans directly owns stocks or shares of stock mutual funds. And the market they most often choose, and their funds most often choose, is the New York Stock Exchange.

The NYSE is dedicated to continuing that tradition and to making this market work for all investors.

When investors hold stock in NYSE-listed companies, they are sharing in a history of growth that outshines most other major investment vehicles. In the decade of the '80s, the compound rate of return on the Standard & Poor's 500 was 17.4%, compared with 10.6% for commercial real estate and 9.6% for money market funds.

When investors purchase NYSE-listed stock, they choose from 1,800 of the best U.S. and foreign businesses, companies with proven track records. They benefit from NYSE rules that ensure shareholder participation in corporate governance and full disclosure of corporate developments.

By placing orders on the NYSE, investors are assured of the best available price in a market that sets the standard for the world in terms of fairness, openness and liquidity. They are participating in a market that combines the most sophisticated technology and communications systems with the best professional judgment.

The NYSE provides the most meaningful market regulation in the world. Surveillance and enforcement activities include a close watch on industry sales practices. And NYSE arbitration procedures offer investors an efficient and inexpensive way to resolve any disputes with brokerage firms.

The NYSE's board of directors has approved a series of measures to address the problem of excess volatility in the market on both a short-term and a long-term basis.

Short-term measures include slowing the market down during hectic periods so that all investors can obtain information and participate equally in trading.

For the long term, the board created a blue-ribbon Panel on Market Volatility and Investor Confidence. Headed by General Motors Chairman Roger B. Smith, the panel has recommended added initiatives to maintain a strong market for all participants.

These are compelling reasons for individuals to invest in NYSE-listed stocks. And it is why they should be looking to invest for the long term, for their future and the future of their families.

The best way to begin is by sitting down and discussing investment goals with a broker who is registered and part of an NYSE-member organization. That means the investor is assured of dealing with a trained individual, qualified to provide advice and to serve the investor's needs with all the resources of a reputable firm.

At the New York Stock Exchange, concern for the individual investor will always be a priority.

NYSE

© 1990 New York Stock Exchange, Inc.

FOR THE BEST POSSIBLE PRICE, ASK YOUR BROKER TO TRADE NYSE-LISTED STOCKS ONLY ON THE NYSE.

analysts who recommend the purchase and sale of securities, brokers, market makers who specialize in a stock, institutional and individual investors, the media, and even employees. All must receive direct communications but each has different needs.

The IR professional must be a good communicator and a good salesperson, knowledgeable in finance and accounting, conversant in the language of Wall Street, and outgoing. The rapidly changing practice of financial relations also means that the IR director must be up-to-date on recent SEC rulings (See appendix E).

Sources of Investor Information

Investors receive corporate information from securities analysts, public media, and corporate communications vehicles, such as annual and quarterly reports, fact books, and annual meetings.

Securities Analysts

Securities analysts greatly influence the buying habits of institutional investors and others. Today, analysts are asked to follow an increasing number of companies, with the average analyst keeping tabs on as many as 40 firms. Frequently, analysts aren't able to evaluate a company that does not meet rigid criteria in terms of market value, capitalization, and trading volume. Additionally, many analysts today are young and inexperienced, further complicating the role of the practitioner. Nevertheless, in financial relations analysts are a key public and must be reached.

To reach analysts effectively, credible communications must play a major role. In that effort, a firm's management should be accessible; otherwise, a corporate message will likely fall on deaf ears, no matter how good a company's earnings record is. Good practitioners make sure that key analysts are heavily exposed to corporate management. In addition, analyst meetings, presentations, and field trips are most important. A luncheon appearance before the New York Society of Security Analysts, for example, can be a significant platform for reaching Wall Street. Company-sponsored meetings in secondary cities can also serve to broaden interest in a company. Finally, inviting analysts to tour plants, visit headquarters, and meet corporate management on the firm's own turf is another way to introduce and educate analysts about a company and its leadership.

In recent years, analysts have been questioned on their objectivity in evaluating companies. The use of analysts to explain corporate decisions has become standard newspaper practice. But many times—particularly in securities underwritings and takeover situations—an analyst's firm also may serve as an advisor to a company. The use of analysts by the media to

B E T W E E N   T H E   L I N E S

The Donald Snuffs the Pest

In the spring of 1990, when the financial empire of Donald Trump stood on shaky ground, the worst chapter in the history of investor relations was written.

When a little-known Philadelphia securities analyst named Marvin Roffman was quoted in *The Wall Street Journal* as questioning whether Trump's gaudy Atlantic City Taj Mahal casino would generate enough revenue to meet its $95 million debt service, The Donald, in effect, had Roffman fired.

Specifically, the morning after the article ran, Trump faxed a letter to the brokerage firm president threatening a lawsuit unless the firm agreed either to fire Roffman or issue a letter of apology for his "outrageous" analysis. The firm caved in immediately and made Roffman sign a letter of apology. Muttered the firm's president, "We thought that in view of the fact that Trump was an influential person he was due an apology."

A few days later, Roffman had second thoughts and retracted his apology. When he did, he was fired.

In the wake of the Trump-Roffman affair, investors correctly wondered how much they could "trust" other securities analysts if their firms were similarly chilled by threatened lawsuits. It's a good question.

P.S. Several months later, Mr. Roffman sued his former employer for improper dismissal. A few weeks after that, Mr. Trump renegotiated his Taj Mahal debt because he couldn't meet the interest payments.

P.P.S. In spring 1991, Mr. Roffman was awarded $750,000 by a three-member arbitration panel of the New York Stock Exchange. The award was paid by Mr. Roffman's former employer.

explain corporate decisions in such situations—especially when those comments may influence stockholders—is suspect.[3] Nonetheless, dealing with analysts on a regular basis is a hallmark of a solid IR program.

Financial Press

The stock exchanges insist that material corporate announcements must be released by the fastest available means. Ordinarily, this means that such information as top-management changes and dividend or earnings announcements must be disseminated by telephone, telegraph, or hand delivery to media outlets. Basically, companies are expected to release material information through the following channels:

1. **Major wire services**—Dow Jones & Company, Reuters Economic Service, Associated Press, or United Press International
2. **Major New York City newspapers**—one or more of the New York City newspapers of general circulation that publish financial news (*The New York Times* and *The Wall Street Journal*)

FIGURE 19–2 Perhaps no financial medium is as powerful as the daily *Wall Street Journal*. When a company is subject to a scathing first-page *Journal* article, it often fights back to reassure investors. Such was the case with this Dun & Bradstreet ad. *(Courtesy of Dun & Bradstreet Corporation)*

IN ALL FAIRNESS, WE SAY FOUL.

Recently The Wall Street Journal devoted a good bit of space to an "exposé" of Dun & Bradstreet Business Credit Services.

In a nutshell, it was stated that D&B's data are inaccurate, outdated and skimpy, and that our methods for collection are suspect. In addition, it was alleged that we encourage our people to produce too many reports too quickly, that we rarely question data provided by the companies we report on, and that when problems do come to our attention, we're unresponsive.

Now, we'll be first to admit we're not perfect. Like every large database, ours contains errors. But to say that we ignore them, much less condone them, is irresponsible.

Over 60,000 customers rely on D&B business information for making millions of credit decisions every year. If things were even a tiny fraction as grim as The Journal suggests, the American economy would be in serious disarray.

The fact is, today's D&B information is far and away the best it has ever been and getting even better; it is the best available anywhere. Our investment in both human and technological resources is tremendous. We spend over $200,000,000 a year gathering and verifying fresh information, updating our files with more than 100,000,000 new data elements annually. We hire the best college graduates we possibly can, and we reward them with bonuses, not for quantity but for quality. Our quality-control standards are more exacting than ever, and our automated verifications are state-of-the-art.

We also ask the businesses we report on to review the reports for accuracy. Of the millions of reports we send out for review every year, fewer than 2% are returned for significant correction. And, of course, we correct them.

Even a casual reading of The Journal article reveals glaring inconsistencies and self-contradictions, but the biggest one is truly ironic: Dow Jones News Retrieval, a blood relative of The Wall Street Journal, sells large amounts of Dun & Bradstreet business information to its own customers.

If Dow Jones thinks our quality is so questionable, why do they accept money for it?

Which leads us to believe that the real issue raised by The Wall Street Journal isn't *caveat emptor*, but rather *caveat lector*.

"Let the reader beware."

Dun & Bradstreet
Business Credit Services

a company of:
The Dun & Bradstreet Corporation

3. **Statistical services**—particularly Standard & Poor's Corporation and Moody's Investor Service, which keep complete records on all publicly held companies
4. **Private wire services**—services such as PR News Wire and Business Wire, which guarantee, for a fee, that corporate news is carried promptly and reaches newspaper newsrooms and brokerage offices

Achieving broad disclosure for a small company is not easy. A major corporation automatically attracts the attention of the financial community, but the smaller firm, in order to satisfy disclosure requirements, may have to use paid wire services and direct mailings to shareholders. For example, to make the Dow Jones wire, a firm's stock must be listed in the national or supplemental list of *The Wall Street Journal*. The burden of proof in conforming to disclosure requirements, however, rests squarely with the issuer, so a company must take appropriate measures to assure that SEC requirements for prompt disclosure are met.

Positive media stories about a company offer substantial benefits. Investment community professionals read the trade press avidly. Consequently, strategically placed articles discussing technological innovations or effective strategies may boost a company in the eyes of security analysts, stockbrokers, and institutional portfolio managers.

In the 1990s, television is an important source for financial information. The nation's top financial show, "Wall Street Week," has become an investor staple, reaching millions of viewers each week on the Public Broadcasting System (PBS). PBS also presents "The Nightly Business Report" each evening, to review the day's financial news. CNN has its own half-hour program, "Money Line." The Financial News Network provides cable viewers an around-the-clock look at everything from commodity prices to leading economic indicators to international news events with potential market impact. The Consumer News and Business Channel (CNBC), which purchased FNN in 1991, also provides round-the-clock financial news. CNBC, backed by the vast resources of the National Broadcasting Company, seemed willing to absorb early losses to establish a longer-term future in reporting financial news.

Corporate Communications Tools

A company has numerous vehicles for financial communications at its disposal, including an annual report, quarterly reports, an annual meeting, and fact books.

The Annual Report

The annual report is a company's key financial communications tool. Many investor relations professionals swear by it. Others argue that the annual report is exaggerated in importance, contending that the ideal annual report might simply read:

> Dear Shareholder,
> We did well in 1991. Earnings and sales were up. Customers were happy and buying. Your dividend was increased. Thanks for purchasing our stock and not selling it.

Clearly, such brevity is not the trend. In fact, in the 1990s, annual reports have been pilloried as expensive, overblown, out-of-touch diatribes. One study found that annual reports failed to serve the information needs of stockholders. Eight of 10 shareholders said the annual report was "an important source of information, but that management often glosses over what problems the company is having." Many didn't believe management's statements, and 20 percent didn't even think annual reports made clear the nature of the company's business.[4]

All of this is too bad, because corporate America spends $5 billion each year on the annual report. The average annual report costs a company about $3.52 per copy, is 44 pages in length, and entails an average printing of 129,000 copies.[5]

In recent years, in an attempt to make annual reports more responsive to investors' needs, the government has modified its annual report standards.

In 1987, as a result of lengthy correspondence between the General Motors Corporation and the SEC, it was ruled that companies may reduce their traditional annual report to shareholders, so long as they include all the required disclosure information in an appendix to the proxy statement or in another formal investor document, the 10-K. In making its ruling, the SEC tacitly acknowledged that annual reports were becoming too complex, legalistic, and expensive. Immediately after the SEC's pronouncement, the McKesson Corporation of San Francisco introduced a summary annual report along the lines the SEC had suggested. Said McKesson's vice-president for corporate relations, "We think we have a tighter, better written, good-looking report that's going to be a more effective communications device and provide users of the information with all, if not more, information than we have in the past."[6] Nonetheless, the summary annual report form was slow to catch on, particularly in the wake of the stock market plunge in October 1987. Most companies produced traditional, lengthy reports as a way to reassure investors that all was well.

Although the individual elements and the general tone of annual reports change gradually over the years and among firms, most reports include a company description, letter to shareholders, financial review, explanation and analysis, management/marketing/issues discussion, and graphics.

Company description This should include the company name, its headquarters address, a description of its overall business, and a summary of its operations in both narrative and numerical form. Many firms begin their annual reports with a one-page, easily readable summary of financial highlights.

◆ **Letter to shareholders** This letter ordinarily incorporates a photo of the firm's chairperson and president. It covers these key areas: (1) an accounting of last year's achievements; (2) discussion of both the general and the industry environment in which the company operated over the past year and will operate in the future; (3) a discussion of strategies for growth, the general operating philosophy for the future, and new product and capital spending plans; and (4) general targets for increased earnings and returns.

◆ **Financial review** In light of the SEC's increasing demands for corporate disclosure, many companies have expanded financial reviews to encompass the data historically included in other reports, such as the 10-K. Financial reviews generally include 5- or 10-year summaries of such items as sales, cost of goods, operating costs, operating margin, expenses, capital expenditures, income taxes, and net earnings and such salient shareholder information as price/earnings ratios, debt ratios, return on assets, and return on equity.

◆ **Explanation and analysis** This complement to the financial review is a general discussion of the factors influencing the numbers in terms of earnings performance, operating income and expenses, asset growth, and other key financial indicators.

◆ **Management/marketing/issues discussion** The annual report's narrative section may be devoted to a general profile of key managers, an explanation of the company's markets or products, or essays detailing the company's view on emerging public issues.

◆ **Graphics** Photographs and charts are critical to the annual report. So, too, is an annual's cover, which should be warm and inviting[7] (Figure 19–3). Most people have limited time to read a report, so a dynamic chart or striking photo may serve to draw readers into the annual's body copy. In recent years, criticism of the blandness, dullness, and sameness of annual reports has intensified. In 1990, Time Warner responded with a multicolored, oddly designed annual, which asked the question "Why?" on its cover. Many readers, confused by the weirdness, asked the same question.

Surveys indicate that about half of all shareholders spend fewer than 10 minutes flipping through an annual report, and 35 percent of financial professionals spend only 15 minutes reading one. Another 15 percent don't read them at all.[8] In response, firms like International Paper and Emhart Corporation have pioneered the transfer of the annual report from paper to videotape (Figure 19–4). Both firms advised stockholders in advance that the televised reports would be cablecast at a particular time on a particular

FIGURE 19—3   Experts say that annual report covers should be "warm." But this one from Lind & Associates communications/public relations firm is positively "hot." *(Courtesy of Lind & Associates)*

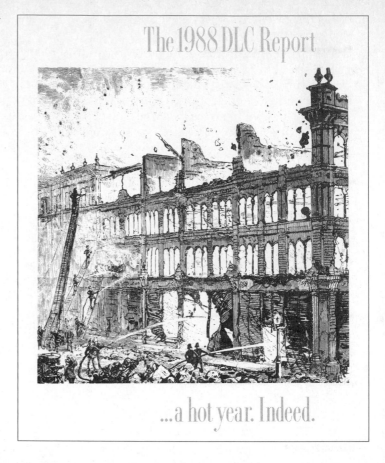

channel. Summarized William F. May, former dean of the New York University Graduate School of Business, "Moving from the hard, cold printed page into the warmth of television serves a tremendous purpose in educating the shareholder on the nature of the company. It gives it flesh and blood."[9]

Quarterly Reports

Quarterly reports or interim reports keep shareholders abreast of corporate developments between annual reports. In general, the SEC recommends that the quarterly report include comparative financial data for the most recent quarter and year-to-date for the current and preceding year. Such items as net sales, costs and expenses, gross and net income, assets, liabilities, net worth, and earnings per share should always be included. So, too, should a letter to the shareholders that analyzes the

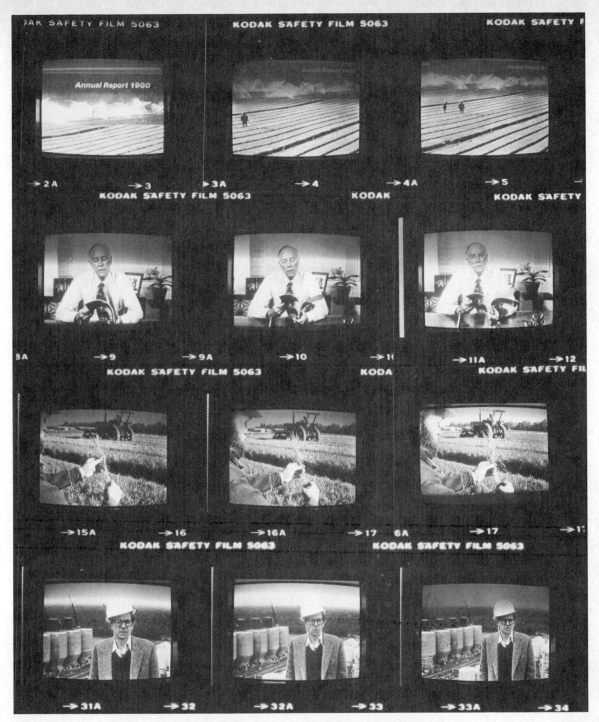

FIGURE 19–4 The International Paper videotape annual report included scenes from IP's seedling nursery, its chairman at his desk, and a report on construction progress at the company's containerboard complex. *(Courtesy of International Paper Co.)*

YOU MAKE THE CALL

The Adelstein Letter

The following is the letter to shareholders in the current annual report of Adelstein, Inc., a national manufacturer of ball bearings.

Dear Friends:

All things considered, 1991 wasn't a bad year for your company.

Although earnings declined by 10 percent, sales nevertheless reached the $300 million mark last year. We experienced strong demand in most of our domestic markets. However, unexpected environmental difficulties in both our Brazilian and Argentine operations caused a downturn in earnings. Our cut in the dividend for the last quarter was a direct outgrowth of the problems in Brazil and Argentina.

We had great concern once again this year about the rate of domestic inflation in the United States. In order to continue to ensure that our shareholders will receive growth in earnings and dividends, inflation must be kept to a minimum. This is why we feel strongly that it is Adelstein's responsibility to speak out both at the federal and local levels about the evils of inflation. One way Adelstein acts to circumvent the dangers of inflation is through diversification around the world.

Our ball bearing operations in Central America and Canada experienced strong growth last year. Central American operations grew by 6 percent, and Canadian operations, although not growing in percentage terms, nevertheless continued to achieve good operating performance.

Our South American performance, on the other hand, was limited by the problems in Argentina and Brazil. In the year to come, we are confident about the near-term future of Adelstein, Inc. The uncertainty in the economy must be counteracted by strong management controls and rigorous enforcement of expense monitoring. Last year, in an increasingly expansionary inflationary period, Adelstein's expenses increased by 14 percent year to year. This year we plan to do even better.

Clearly, with our plans and strategies firmly in place, we expect Adelstein's operating and financial condition to continue to improve in the coming year.

Todd O. Adelstein
Chairperson of the Board

QUESTIONS

1. As an Adelstein stockholder, would you be pleased with this letter?
2. Did the letter leave out any areas?
3. Did it leave any questions unanswered?
4. From what you read in the letter, how would you assess Adelstein's prospects for improvement next year?

important developments during the quarter. In recent years, the SEC has been less rigorous in its quarterly report requirements, and some firms have cut back on expenses in producing such reports. McKesson Corporation, following publication of its summary annual report in 1987, went one step further by combining its quarterly report to shareholders with its employee magazine. The company reasoned that because many employees were also shareholders, combining the two publications could save money and be more all-encompassing.

Annual Meeting

Once a year the management of public companies is required to meet with the shareholders in a forum. Occasionally, this annual "mating dance" inspires fear and trepidation among managers unused to the glare of public questioning and skepticism. Indeed, several annual meeting gadflies travel from annual meeting to annual meeting, probing management on unpleasant, difficult, and, occasionally, embarrassing subjects. The existence of these gadflies has led some managers to view the meeting with a degree of loathing.

In one celebrated instance, former General Motors chairman Roger Smith proposed having two annual meetings on the same day. The first meeting, said Smith, would be a short business meeting at which all of GM's top managers would be present, but no shareholder questions would be entertained. The second meeting would be held miles away from the first and would feature a designated GM executive to answer shareholder questions. So great was the opposition to Smith's proposition that GM, several days before its meetings, announced that it would hold only one annual meeting after all.

A well-planned and well-executed annual meeting enables corporate managers to communicate effectively with investors (see Appendix G for an annual meeting checklist). Here are a few hints for organizing a successful meeting.

♦ **Management speeches** Beginning with short, punchy speeches from the chairman or president, or both, can establish the tone for the meeting. These speeches set an upbeat tempo for the rest of the meeting, emphasizing current developments and perhaps even announcing quarterly earnings or management changes.

♦ **Stockholder voting** Voting includes choosing directors and auditors and deciding on proposals presented by shareholders. Management's viewpoint on these proposals is spelled out in previously mailed proxy statements.

♦ **Question-and-answer sessions** The Q&A portion of the meeting is the reason that many stockholders attend. They like to see management in action, answering pertinent questions from the floor. How managers handle questions is thought to reflect their competence in running the company.

Management must be thoroughly briefed about potential questions. Indeed, managers should plan answers before the meeting. Preparing for Q&A sessions may require monitoring other corporate annual meetings, preparing briefing books on potential questions, and even meeting in advance with potential questioners. Some managements, for example, find it worthwhile to lunch with selected gadflies to find out in advance what's on their minds.

Questions should be handled candidly, succinctly, and, whenever possible, in a light, nonthreatening manner. Most stockholders agree that the best meetings are those conducted in a friendly atmosphere. After all, stockholders own the business. A manager's light touch at an annual meeting may win over even the most skeptical stockholders.

The necessity of holding annual meetings has come under question in recent years. Many meetings are dominated by gadflies who care little about the company and lots about generating personal publicity. Attempts have even been made by some managements to propose rule changes that would require shareholder meetings only when a matter of substance is discussed. (Ironically, most of these proposals have been defeated because not enough shareholders return their proxies.) The Investment Company Act of 1940, which calls for regular annual meetings, probably should be reconsidered.

Nonetheless, for now the annual meeting is still a corporate custom. Like any other communications tool, it should be actively managed to promote goodwill and further the positive perception of the company among its shareholders.

Other Specialized Communications

Periodically, companies complement the traditional array of financial communications with specialized vehicles.

- **Fact books** Corporate fact books and fact sheets are statistical publications distributed primarily to securities analysts and institutional investors as supplements to the annual report. Their main value lies in giving a busy analyst a quick snapshot of a company's position and prospects (Figure 19–5).

- **Investors' guides** These mini fact books give a general corporate description and list leading products, office locations, and financial highlights. Such guides introduce a company and frequently contain tear-out cards for acquiring additional corporate information.

- **Private television packages** In addition to video annual reports and meetings, videocassette packages showing presentations by corporate

FIGURE 19—5   Fact books and fact sheets come in a variety of sizes and shapes. All, however, have the same objective: to give as clear and as accurate an organizational snapshot in as brief a time as possible.

officers can be shipped directly to portfolio managers and analysts around the country at a comparatively low cost. Video can extend and expand an executive's time and deliver the corporate story to a larger, more targeted financial public over a wider geographic area.

◆ **Dividend stuffers**   Frequently, practitioners include management messages in dividend mailings. Shareholders tend to take seriously mailings that include checks; thus, these mailings help greatly in delivering the firm's ideas.

◆ **Paid advertising space**   Periodically, a company can reprint its income statement or balance sheet to encourage a broad audience to find out more about its securities.

◆ **Special meetings**   Some companies have taken the unusual step of organizing special meetings of interested publics, largely to reinspire investors to own the company's stock. The most famous recent gathering of this type was General Motors' extravagant and extraordinary exhibition in New York City in 1988 at a cost of $20 million. GM attracted 14,000 guests to the Waldorf-Astoria Hotel to show off present and future products. Although the event attracted its share of criticism, many believed that it was a sensible step to restabilize the company's declining image.

Takeover Contests

The hysteria on Wall Street in the late 1980s, caused by an unprecedented wave of outsider attempts to take over bedrock American companies, greatly influenced investor relations. General Electric, DuPont, and American Express were among the acquirers. RCA, Getty Oil, McGraw-Hill, Disney, and Conoco were among the targeted. One venerable company, Texaco, found itself on both sides of the fence, first as acquirer and later as "acquiree," sought by arch raider Carl Icahn. Such takeovers couldn't help leaving bad feelings among the affected. When the Bank of New York attempted to purchase the Irving Trust Company in 1988, Irving spent $40 million of stockholders' money defending itself before caving in. When the Campeau Corporation of Canada took over Federated Department Stores of Cincinnati in 1988, extensive bloodletting was the result. And when the aggressive British company, Beazer PLC, successfully completed its hostile takeover of Koppers Company of Pittsburgh, Beazer's advisor, Shearson Lehman Hutton, was lambasted for its questionable takeover tactics.

Normally, a substantial undervaluation of a company's stock price may precipitate an outsider's attempt to win control of the company in one of two ways.

♦ A tender offer for shares of stock, in which the raiding party offers shareholders cash, securities, or both
♦ A proxy contest, in which certain shareholders attempt to oust present management by obtaining sufficient shareholder votes to seize control of the board of directors

While some think that the 1990s will see a lessening of the corporate raiding hysteria of the late '80s, the ugliness and rough-and-tumble nature of such actions won't soon subside. One runaway bestseller in 1990, *Barbarians at the Gate,* traced the greed and duplicity surrounding the leveraged buyout of RJR Nabisco by Kolberg Kravis Roberts. The public was stunned to learn that RJR's chairman, according to leaked documents, had dealt himself in for more than $1 billion from the spoils of his company.[10] In 1991, another acrimonious takeover attempt made the front page when giant telephone company AT&T went after and eventually acquired giant computer company NCR.

Indeed, the transgressions of raiders like Boesky, Milken, and a host of lesser lights and the firms they represented have cast an ethical cloud over the whole business of corporate takeovers and the possible insider trading that may result.

Just Call Him "Mike"*

After making financial history for most of the booming '80s, Drexel Burnham superstar Michael Milken made a different kind of history in the spring of 1989. Never before had a billionaire been mug-shot, finger-printed, urine-tested for drugs, and arraigned on 98 counts of securities-related racketeering.

In the year between the time Milken was charged and then convicted in 1990 after a plea bargain, a public relations offensive to reveal the true "Michael Milken" was launched. Through the efforts of the public relations firm Robinson, Lake, Lerer & Montgomery, the Milken truth offensive included the following elements:

- Full-page ads in national newspapers, in which supporters trumpeted the headline, "Mike Milken, We believe in you."
- Tee-shirts and caps, distributed to children, proclaiming the same message.
- Appearances on national television programs such as "Nightline."
- A raft of public speeches before a diverse roster of groups from the Philadelphia Treasurers Club on the Main Line to the Four River Service Club at the Sons of Italy Hall in Rockland, Mass.
- Children's charity events, such as escorting 1,700 underprivileged youngsters to a New York Mets game at Shea Stadium, where Milken bounced kids on his knee and roamed the aisles passing out pretzels.
- Frequent tête-à-têtes with reporters, at which he urged everyone to "Call me Mike . . . . When I hear you call me Mr. Milken, it sounds strange."

The transformation to a blatantly public citizen by a man whom some called "a recluse," struck some public relations professionals as "transparent." Said one, "It seems obvious that there is a campaign being staged, which may be counterproductive in the long run."

Mr. Milken's public relations firm bristled at the suggestion: "No one is trying to sell Michael Milken in any way, shape, or form," huffed the financier's chief spokesman.

Despite the campaign to humanize Milken, events kept getting in the way. While the junk-bond maven debated with the government, it was revealed that he earned an unheard of $550 million from Drexel in 1987. The Guinness Book of World Records quickly announced that Milken's earnings would be mentioned in upcoming listings.

Milken's supporters stuck with him to the bitter end. Late in 1990, a grieving Milken was sentenced to a huge fine and an extended jail term. Summarized one communications executive, "No public relations in the world can deal with something so big, so late."*

QUESTIONS

1. What do you think of Michael Milken's public relations strategy?
2. What would you have done differently?

*For further information, see Bryan Burrough, "Just Call Me Mike: Drexel's Mr. Milken Works on His Image," The Wall Street Journal, 12 October 1988, A-1; and John Riley, "Pro-Milken Propaganda," New York Newsday, 15 May 1989, III-6, 7.

Often, it is the job of the IR professional to establish the preparatory steps to be taken prior to a takeover attempt, including an outline of the moves to resist the actual takeover. Overall strategy must be based on the maintenance of an excellent relationship with stockholders, particularly with those who hold a large amount of stock. Specific IR activities might include the following:

♦ Appoint a defense committee
♦ Prepare and update a large-stockholders list
♦ Maintain a watch to determine whether company shares are being accumulated rapidly
♦ Step up personal contacts with important stockholders in order to secure their loyalty
♦ Increase contacts with top-flight securities analysts and investors to improve chances of obtaining intelligence from them
♦ Prepare envelopes for emergency stockholder mailings
♦ Retain professional proxy solicitors
♦ Prepare basic letters and news release forms to be sent immediately to stockholders within hours of learning about the takeover attempt
♦ Prepare lists of major newspapers in which takeover defense advertisements might appear and prepare the ads themselves
♦ Organize a public relations campaign to enhance the image of the company both internally and externally

These are but a few of the actions that must be taken in anticipating and warding off a takeover attempt. The key, which many companies under attack fail to recognize until it's too late, is to focus communications strategy on the real worth of the company.[11] A value-oriented emphasis could help wake up the market to the company's true value, force the bidder to up the ante, generate a higher bid from another group, or even price all bidders out of the market. The no-holds-barred takeover phenomenon of the later 1980s put an increased premium on the ability of firms to practice open and honest communications with their shareholders.

Summary

The real bottom line in financial communications is improving corporate credibility. Investors show support only when they believe in a firm and its management. Double-talk, fudging, and gobbledygook have no place in communicating with investors, who want to know all the news, the bad as well as the good, quickly and accurately. Because corporate candor is the only path to credibility and respect, these general guidelines should be followed in communicating with the investment community.

1. **Be aggressive.** Aggressive companies don't necessarily acquire the reputation of being stock promoters. Companies today must compete vigorously for visibility. Analysts and investors want to stay informed. Therefore, aggressive communications, truthfully delivered, are the best kind.

2. **Promote success.** The record ordinarily does not speak for itself. Companies must communicate to investors an intelligent evaluation of their securities, competitive position, and market outlook.

3. **Meet despite bad news.** Companies should meet with investors in bad and good times; investors need constant communication. If there are problems within a firm, investors want to know what management is doing to solve them. Most of all, investors hate surprises.

4. **Go to investors; don't make them come to you.** Investors expect to be courted. Firms need to broaden investment ownership. Therefore, a company should volunteer information rather than make investors pry it loose.

5. **Enlist investors in the public policy area.** There are millions of stockholders in the United States today. The implications of even partially mobilizing this vast constituency are awesome. Historically, corporations have not sought out stockholder support for public policy viewpoints, which seems a tragic mistake. To accomplish meaningful legislative and regulatory reforms that favor free enterprise, all concerned parties—shareholders and management alike—must join the fight.

In the 1990s, as corporate America continues to be restructured, financial markets become more global, and the trading of securities becomes a 24-hour process—largely due to the explosion in computer technology—investor relations will increase in importance. The best investor relations policy will continue to be one based on preserving and enhancing corporate credibility *all* the time (Figure 19–6).

DISCUSSION STARTERS

1. What was the significance to investor relations of the securities acts of 1933 and 1934?
2. What are the primary responsibilities in communicating to shareholders?
3. Why are securities analysts significant to a corporation?
4. What is required of companies in disseminating "material" news announcements?
5. How important is the annual report today?
6. What are the essential elements in the annual report's Letter to Shareholders?
7. What happens at an annual meeting?
8. What are some of the specialized communications that firms use to reach shareholders?

WHAT JUDGE CASSEB REALLY SAID

Judge Solomon Casseb, who presided over the Texaco-Pennzoil case, spoke April 2 before the trial lawyers section of the Los Angeles Bar.

There is no official transcript of his remarks. But Texaco's PR people have tried to peddle a Texaco tape and Texaco transcript to selected media. Several major papers turned it down. Others swallowed the bait whole.

What did the Judge actually say? Judith Bloom, vice chair of the trial lawyers section of the Los Angeles County Bar Association, who introduced him, said of the news reports: "The words are probably accurate but the sense was different...the sense was that Judge Casseb didn't feel he was wrong."

Robert Forgnone of Gibson, Dunn and Crutcher, the attorney who chaired the program, wrote us: "I can state that I had no doubts after hearing Judge Casseb's remarks that the Judge believed he would not be reversed on appeal." Judge Casseb himself has repeatedly said he expects to be affirmed on appeal.

So far, the information available on this story is solely what Texaco chose to furnish to selected media. In some cases, they tried to furnish it anonymously. Why? Texaco's management seems to approve of that tactic, judging by the following article.

SATURDAY
APRIL 12, 1986
FINAL
☆☆

San Antonio Light

How Texaco told of Casseb speech
Public relations firm wanted to be silent source on story

By STEVEN H. LEE
Staff Writer

"I don't exist," said the public relations man late Thursday, requesting anonymity as a caveat to what he was about to present to reporters of The Light.

He held in his hands a tape and transcript of a week-old speech delivered by retired District Judge Solomon Casseb Jr., the San Antonio jurist who upheld an $11.1 billion judgment against Texaco Inc. for illegally breaking a merger agreement between Pennzoil and Getty Oil Co.

It was the largest court damage award in history.

Throughout the transcript of the speech, made before the trial lawyers section of the Los Angeles County Bar Association, were excerpts that the public relations executive had highlighted in yellow—statements that he felt either were in error or indicated Casseb had been in Pennzoil's corner.

It was Pennzoil, after all, which had won the suit, having claimed tortuous interference by Texaco in its tentative merger with Getty, after which Texaco snatched Getty for itself. And the public relations man now was working for Texaco—searching for any information that might work to aid Texaco as it appeals that judgment.

"I think this is a story," he said, pointing out a particular passage on page 30 of the transcript.

It had not been part of Casseb's speech, but was taken from an informal question-answer session that followed. The judge had been asked what he thought would happen to the case during appeal.

Although the case was tried in Texas, the issue of whether Pennzoil actually had a binding agreement with Getty was a matter of New York Law—since that was where the alleged agreement took place.

Based on the cases cited as precedent by attorneys in the trial, Casseb made clear that he was confident of his interpretation. But he also held out the possibility that he could have been in error, in the following passage the public relations executive deemed to be particularly damning:

"I feel that there is a good chance that perhaps I may have read the cases wrong, and not have applied it correctly. And as I've said, you know, this is my first experience in trying to analyze New York law after I did 46 years with Texas. So you can see, that can happen to any judge. I mean, none of us are infallible, and that can happen. But if they (the appellate courts) don't (believe I was in error), then I feel that they are going to uphold that verdict and that judgment."

An admission of possible error or a philosophical statement on the fallibility of judges? The public relations executive, as he reviewed the transcript with reporters, pressed the view that Casseb's statement was a significant admission.

However, editors of The Light came to a different conclusion, and decided that the judge's statements were more in the nature of self-deprecating musings.

The editors felt a more significant story was the public relations

executive's attempt to use the confidentiality agreement, which is a vital part of the news-gathering relationship, simply to cloak Texaco's attempt to get negative stories about Casseb into print.

Consequently, when the Friday editions of the Houston Chronicle ran the story of Casseb's comments last week, and the wire services distributed the Chronicle piece, The Light chose not to print it.

The Los Angeles Times, which has provided significant coverage of the Texaco-Pennzoil dispute, likewise chose not to print a story about Casseb's comments.

A Times reporter Friday said the paper had sent a reporter to cover Casseb's speech last week, but that a story was not written. Also, she said the Times declined to run Friday's wire story, saying the paper had determined the Casseb quotes to be incidental.

On Friday, Texaco Vice Chairman James W. Kinnear, in a telephone interview, confirmed New York-based Hill & Knowlton Inc. as Texaco's public relations firm of more than 30 years. And he said he assumed that providing information anonymously was "general practice" for the firm.

However, Dr. Frank Walsh, an associate professor of journalism at the University of Texas at Austin, and an authority on public relations issues, disagreed that information of that nature should be presented anonymously. He said the source of the information in this case almost was as significant as what Casseb had to say.

"I think the reader deserves to know that he (the reporter) got the information from Texaco," Walsh said.

Ever since the landmark court decision last November, Texaco has been taking its case to the media. That effort apparently continued Thursday when the public relations executive met with reporters.

When asked why the information provided to The Light Thursday was done so under a cloak of secrecy, Kinnear replied, "I really don't know. As far as I was aware, that meeting (in Los Angeles) was public. And we have made no secret of the fact that Hill & Knowlton has represented us for the past 30 years."

Also, when asked to reply to Casseb's statements, Kinnear said, "I don't think I want to characterize what the man said. He said what he said."

Casseb could not be reached for comment Friday.

Anthony Franco, president of the 13,200-member Public Relations Society of America, refused to speak specifically about Hill & Knowlton, or about Texaco. But, when asked, he offered his views on how he would handle a similar situation.

"I wouldn't feel comfortable doing that (anonymously)," Franco said. "I would feel more comfortable saying (to the media), 'I came across this information and thought you'd be interested.'

"Public relations people don't want necessarily to be quoted in front of their client. However, it's usually an either/or situation. A member of the (public relations) society should be prepared to identify himself publicly if he's called upon to do so."

—Reprinted in its entirety with permission of the San Antonio Light.

PENNZOIL COMPANY

FIGURE 19–6   Ooops. Sometimes even the best investor relations counselors make mistakes. *(Courtesy of Pennzoil Co.)*

9. What are the duties of an investor relations officer in the face of a takeover attempt?
10. What is the key element in preserving an organization's credibility?

1. Robert E. Brown, "How Investor Relations Has Evolved," *Social Science Monitor* (August 1990): 1.
2. "Higher Pay, Greater Angst Disclosed by Compensation Survey," *Corporate Communications Report* 16, no. 3 (August 1985): 1.
3. Paul Bernish, "Fighting a Takeover Battle in the Press," *Across the Board* (July-August 1989): 28.
4. "Annual Reports Are Failing," *Public Relations News* (December 4, 1989): 1.
5. *Annual Report Production Cost Survey.* (New York: Padilla Speer Beardsley Inc., 1989).
6. Fraser P. Seitel, "Rethinking the Annual Report," *United States Banker* (October 1989): 89.
7. Bev Freeman, "Special Report: Annual Reports," *IABC Focus* (March 1990): 1.
8. "Annual Reports—It's a Multi-Billion Business, But Is Anyone Paying Attention?" *Business and Economic Communication Letter* (February 1989): 1.
9. John F. Budd, Jr., and Bruce Pennington, "Financial Reporting by Television," *Public Relations Journal* (April 1982): 40.

TOP OF THE SHELF

Hill & Knowlton. *The SEC, The Securities Markets and Your Financial Communications.* New York: Hill & Knowlton, Inc., scheduled for 1991.

Investor relations practitioners should have a firm grasp of financial disclosure rules. The authoritative source for this is *The SEC, The Securities Markets and Your Financial Communications.*

Scheduled to be published by Hill & Knowlton, this handbook summarizes disclosure guidelines for public companies, which are regulated by government, and stock exchange rules pertaining to dividends, annual reports, stockholders' meetings, public offerings, proxy solicitations, and tender offers, among other financial areas. Hill & Knowlton clarifies these issues by explaining when and how such "material" news must be released. This handbook has two case studies: one illustrates disclosure rules; the other highlights obligations of firms offering stock to the public.

Students interested in the interplay among public companies, securities markets, and government regulators should consult *The SEC, The Securities Markets and Your Financial Communications.* It is a most knowledgeable resource.

10. Connie Bruck, "Undoing the 80s," *The New Yorker* (July 23, 1990): 68.
11. Marvin A. Chatinover, "Communications During a Contested Takeover," *Sorg Says Newsletter* 1, no. 1 (Fall 1985): 1. (Available from Sorg Printing Company, 111 Eighth Avenue, New York, NY 10011)
12. Kevin McCauley, "'Roger & Me' Film Mocks GM and Chairman Roger Smith," *O'Dwyer's PR Services Report,* March 1990: 1, 8–11, 44.

SUGGESTED READINGS

A.R.3: The Complete Annual Report & Corporate Image Planning Book. New York: Macmillan, 1988.

Casper, P. *The Corporate Annual Report and Corporate Identity Planning Book.* Chicago: Alexander, Communications, 1987 (212 W. Superior 60610).

Corporate Annual Report Newsletter (407 S. Dearborn, Chicago, IL 60605).

Fowler, Elizabeth. "The Lure of Investor Relations," *The New York Times,* 18 November 1986. The writer sees IR as a growing career path. People are needed to help their employers by encouraging stockholders to hold on to shares and by persuading the financial industry and general public to take an interest in their firms.

Graves, Joseph. *Investor Relations Today.* Glen Ellyn, IL: Investor Relations Association, 1985 (364 Lorraine Ave. 60137).

Hogan, Bill. "The Asset Test." *Washington Journalism Review* (July 1985): 38–43.

Idea Bank for Annual Reports. New York: Corporate Shareholder Press, 1987 (271 Madison Ave., NY 10016).

Investment Newsletters (Larimi Communications Associates, 5 W. 37th St., New York, NY 10018).

Investor Relations Almanac/Resource Directory. New York: Corporate Shareholder Press (271 Madison Ave., NY 10016).

Lewis, Richard A. *The Annual Report: A Tool to Achieve the CEO's Objectives.* New York: Corporate Annual Reports, 1987 (112 E. 31st Street 10016).

Nicholas, Donald. *The Handbook of Investor Relations.* Homewood, IL: Dow Jones-Irwin, 1988.

Powell, Joanna. "Institutional Investor." *Washington Journalism Review* (July 1985): 44–46.

Watt, Roop & Co. *Street Talk.* Cleveland, OH: Watt, Roop & Co. Watt, a public relations and marketing counseling firm, prepared this IR planning guide for companies that go public.

What Non-U.S. Companies Need to Know About Financial Disclosure in the United States. New York: Hill & Knowlton, 1989 (420 Lexington Ave. 10017).

Winter, Elmer L. *A Complete Guide to Preparing a Corporate Annual Report.* New York: Van Nostrand Reinhold, 1987.

CASE STUDY   Roger and Him

For any major corporation, dealing with investors also means being sensitive to the "big picture"—particularly the way a company and its leaders are portrayed in public.

The chief executive officer is the organization's most pivotal spokesperson. How a CEO's strength, courage, and character are characterized may significantly influence an investor's decision to buy, hold, or sell a stock.

And so it was in the spring of 1990 that the nation's premier automobile company, General Motors, and its chairman, Roger Smith, became a source of national derision as they fumbled and bumbled in the face of an unabashedly biased, shoestring-budgeted movie entitled *Roger & Me*.

The $200,000 film was the brainchild of one Michael Moore, a chubby, left-leaning, independent producer born in Flint, Michigan—the town that was the subject of the film.

In his work, Moore portrayed GM and its officials as callous, remote, and unfair toward those who live in Flint—the city in which GM itself also was born.

The film's tone was revealed early when Moore began:

> Maybe I got this wrong, but I thought companies lay off people when they hit hard times. GM was the richest company in the world and was closing factories when it was making profits in the billions. GM chairman Roger Smith appeared to have a brilliant plan: First close 11 factories in the United States, then open 11 in Mexico where you pay the workers 70 cents an hour. Then use the money you save by building cars in Mexico to take over other companies, preferably high-tech firms and weapons manufacturers. Next, tell the union you're broke and they happily agree to give back a couple billion dollars in wage cuts. Take that money from the workers and eliminate their jobs by building more foreign factories.

The film got more vicious.

Complicating matters was GM's response to Moore. The company avoided the producer at every turn. The premise of the film, in fact, was Moore's futile attempt to track Smith down, to question him about GM plant closings in Flint.

Along the way, moviegoers witnessed the following:

- Flint's civic leaders pictured as buffoons, unhatching one harebrained scheme after another, in an attempt to spur economic development.

  In one scene, Flint's upper crust threw a "Great Gatsby" party, hiring unemployed GM workers as human statues to brighten the festivities.

- Flint portrayed as a city of abandoned buildings, boarded-up businesses, and impoverished people. One woman said she raised rabbits "for pets or meat" to supplement her Social Security check. In one charming scene, she obligingly clubs a rabbit into submission and then skins the cuddly creature on camera.

■ Interviews with laid-off GM workers revealed desperation. One declared, "GM should get rid of Smith and all the other SOBs. I am sick and tired of the fat cats. Smith can't look an auto worker in the eye."

And neither, so it seemed, could the GM chairman.

The producer sought the chairman at the swank Grosse Point Yacht Club, the Detroit Athletic Club, and New York's Waldorf-Astoria. Moore was booted from each location.

He then attended GM's annual meeting, waiting patiently until all the stockholders had their say at mikes placed around the room. Then, just as he was about to fire a question at Smith, the GM chairman cut Moore off and declared the meeting closed. The last laugh, however, was on Roger. Moore's camera crew zeroed in on Smith and the other executives on the rostrum, who were heard congratulating themselves on how they dispensed with Moore.

Finally, the film producer and the chairman came face-to-face—at the annual GM Christmas party that Moore invaded. After Moore told Smith of the mass evictions of the poor people in Flint, Smith responded, "GM did not evict them." He then refused Moore's coaxing to go to Flint. While the chairman partied, the scene was interrupted by yet another Flint family being thrown out of its home, Christmas tree and all, the day before Christmas Eve.

By the beginning of 1991, millions of film buffs had seen *Roger & Me.* The film—biased as it surely was—nonetheless was

critically acclaimed and won numerous awards. Warner Brothers spent millions promoting the movie, and it became a box-office and video-store smash. Even Michael Moore became rich as a result, although he insisted on continuing to dress shabbily and wear a baseball cap.

In a written statement after the film's release, GM Chairman Smith said,

> I haven't seen the film, but from what I have read it does a great disservice to the community of Flint and the thousands of GM employees who are making a positive contribution to the city and to GM. How I personally feel is unimportant. It is unfortunate that people who have pride in their community and the products they build are subjected to public embarrassment at a time when they are producing some of the finest products in America.[12]

GM's public relations executives defended their decision not to meet with Moore. They insisted that Moore would "have taken advantage of Smith" if they had agreed to a meeting. Even if Smith had agreed to give an interview, Moore would have found a way to make him look silly, the executives said.

Not only did GM refuse to meet with Moore, but even after the film's success, the company wouldn't budge. When Moore appeared on not one, but two live Phil Donahue broadcasts from Flint, GM still refused to send a representative. Even worse, reports circulated that GM had asked its advertising agencies not to place commercials on television programs that featured Michael Moore.

At the end of 1990, Roger Smith, regarded by many as a fine executive and decent man, retired from GM. In his final interview as chairman, Smith told *The Wall Street Journal* that, while he regretted the movie and found it completely unfair and prejudiced, had he been faced with the same situation again, he wouldn't have altered GM's posture one bit.

QUESTIONS

1. How do you think *Roger & Me* portrayed the chairman of General Motors?
2. How do you think *Roger & Me* portrayed GM's public relations people?
3. Do you agree with GM's handling of Michael Moore?
4. Had you been the public relations director of General Motors, what would you have advised Chairman Smith to do?
5. Do you think *Roger & Me* will hurt GM's long-term image?

Tips from the Top

CAROL SANGER

Carol Sanger is vice-president of corporate communications for Federated Department Stores, Inc., and Allied Stores Corporation. Previously she served in a similar capacity for the Campeau Corporation in both the United States and Canada. Prior to joining Federated in 1984, Ms. Sanger was business editor of *The Cincinnati Enquirer.* She also served as press secretary to U.S. Senator Birch Bayh of Indiana and has received numerous honors in the fields of communications and journalism.

What is the essence of effective investor relations?
An open two-way communications pipeline between the company and its key markets is essential to an effective IR program. Beyond the ability to channel the right information into the right external hands, an effective IR function needs to act as a filter and gauge for incoming data about the company and how it is being perceived in the financial marketplace. Because perception often is a more salient measure of reality than fact, the key is knowing and responding to what actually is out there in the markets. Yet, this often is the most difficult aspect of the job because what you must respond to is not necessarily what a company's management may want to acknowledge, much less address.

Can IR impact the price of a company's stock?
Perhaps minimally and in the short term it can. It certainly can be useful in helping to prevent surprises, which—good or bad—the market never likes. Over the long haul, however, unless you have financial and operating performance to back you up, nothing an IR program can do will make a meaningful difference.

How important was public relations in the takeover of Federated?
Public relations, however, can influence perceptions among key internal and external audiences, and that factor can be of vital importance both during and in the aftermath of a corporate takeover. In the 1988 takeover of Federated Department Stores, for instance, an aggressive grassroots public relations effort waged in the media, as well as at the community and state legislative levels, forced Campeau to commit to maintaining Federated's corporate headquarters operations in Cincinnati. That decision clearly had a major impact on the local and state economy and on

hundreds of lives that otherwise might have been uprooted.

How important is the annual report?
I'd like to say it is an important—or at least an effective—communications tool. That would help justify the innumerable hours, not to mention the cost, that goes into producing it. But I honestly don't think it's either. Many companies began using the annual report as a marketing vehicle in the late '60s, and this approach continued to evolve, so that each year's book was glossier, glitzier, and, not incidentally, costlier than the one before. Meanwhile, the editorial content has come to be viewed as less and less credible. There's an axiom that holds that more people read an annual report *before* it is published than after, and this is probably all too true.

How important is the small shareholder?
It depends on your objective. If you want to broaden your shareholder base, putting more stock in more hands, then you'll pay attention to the small investor. You'll encourage stock dividend reinvestment programs, and you'll be responsive through your IR program in any number of other ways. But if this is not your objective—if the majority of your stock is in the hands of institutional investors, and that's the way you like it—then the small share-holder obviously doesn't merit as high a priority.

What distinguishes successful IR programs from unsuccessful ones?
Knowing your objective. If you don't know where you're going, you'll never get there. You'll just be wasting a lot of time and effort in the process and have nothing measurable to show for it in the end.

How do you view the emergence of women as a majority in public relations?
This question raises the specter of the "velvet ghetto," which suggests that once women are a majority in a field, its median level of compensation necessarily declines, along with its professional status. This, unfortunately, has been all too true in some fields in the past. Whether it will be as true in the future is debatable, but it definitely is a concern for today's public relations professional. A larger issue is the status assigned to the public relations profession overall. This has less to do with gender than it does with the expertise and legitimate professional credentials of individuals in the field. So long as public relations is an unregulated profession, in which all comers are free to enter and assign themselves professional standing at will, public relations will never attain the recognition or status of the licensed and regulated professions.

The International Community

People used to use the term *internationalization* to signify how U.S. products and services were being exported around the world. Today, however, because of such factors as computer technology, resource transfers, wealth shifts, satellite communications, democratic upheavals, and all the rest, the United States is no longer the "center of the universe."

"Internationalization," in fact, has been replaced by the term *globalization,* to signify that the world truly has become a much more interrelated place. In no field is this truer than in the practice of public relations.

Major political shifts throughout the world have focused new attention on public relations in the 1990s. The fall of the Berlin Wall and the Iron Curtain, the emergence of Mikhail Gorbachev and the collapse of Soviet socialism, the coming together of European economies, and the Iraqi invasion of Kuwait and the resulting war in the Persian Gulf brought the global role of public relations into a new spotlight.[1]

Historically, U.S. business firms were not overly interested in sales abroad. Today, with the incursion into the United States of the Toyotas, Sonys, Lufthansas, and BMWs of the world, U.S. companies look to expand their reach into overseas markets.

In many countries, public relations is exceedingly important. International trade is more complicated than domestic commerce. Conditions of competition abroad often seem unfair and unfamiliar to American businesspeople. Local laws and customs and protocol may be alien to the U.S. businessperson abroad. Professional public relations becomes critical.

The revolution in communications that has burst upon the world in recent years has been a boon to the public relations profession. In Europe, Asia, Africa, and even Eastern Europe and Russia, public relations has taken on revitalized import.

The International Professional

In addition to possessing the more traditional public relations skills, the overseas practitioner must be a combination marketing tactician, diplomat, troubleshooter, and government relations expert. A skillful professional can help prevent a foreign government from legislating against a company, nationalizing its property, or ordering its removal.

To win acceptance of an idea, product, or person in any community abroad, it is essential to be thoroughly familiar with the customs, beliefs, and history of the area, current economic and political realities, newest fashions, and, of course, the language. At the same time, the effective international representative must have a thorough and current knowledge of what is going on back home. A misinformed representative can communicate the wrong message locally because he or she hasn't been adequately briefed.

In effect, international public relations representatives are the communications link between the host country and the home office. It is essential, therefore, that they convey to the local constituency a fair and accurate portrayal of the organization's positions and, to the home office, a candid climate analysis of the local area. It is equally important for public relations professionals operating in foreign markets and communicating with foreign citizens to speak the native tongue of their clients and employees (Figure 20–1).

Organizing International Public Relations

In the typical multinational company the international public relations manager usually reports to both the headquarters public relations director and the international department. This latter relationship is extremely important because the international practitioner must be intimately involved with line activities and decisions.

Practitioners are situated in strategic overseas locations. Some U.S. multinationals, for example, position representatives in the Caribbean to cover Latin America, in Hong Kong or Tokyo to cover Asia and the Far East, and in London or Paris to cover Great Britain and Western Europe. In recent years, companies have expanded public relations coverage to the Mideast and Africa.

Counseling firms have also expanded their international capabilities. Large agencies (e.g., Hill & Knowlton, Burson-Marsteller, and Shandwick) represent three kinds of clients on the international level.

1. American firms doing business internationally
2. Foreign companies competing for business in the United States

大通銀行
The Chase Manhattan Bank, N.A.
Chinatown Branch 華埠分行
185 Canal Street
New York, New York 10013

NEWS RELEASE

紐約市，堅尼路街，一百八十五號，紐約區號一〇〇一三

DEC. 7, 1984

中美旅游社提供大通銀行客戶之特別旅遊優待

為使大通銀行華埠分行客戶享有旅遊之特別優待，現在大通銀行華埠分行與中美旅游社已協議一項合作計劃。

凡是大通銀行華埠分行之客戶無論支票帳戶，儲蓄存欵帳戶，貨幣市場存欵帳戶或六個月以上之優利定期存欵帳戶等保持有二千元之存欵額一年以上者便可享有中美旅游社之各種旅遊折扣。

合乎上項條件之大通銀行客戶向中美旅遊社訂購機票時可享有百分之五之折扣優待，另外，中美旅游社舉辦之特別旅遊節目大通銀行的客戶還可享有百分之五至百分之十五之折扣優待。

凡在大通銀行申請貸欵三千元以上業經批准並在廿四個月以上分期攤還者亦可享有中美旅游社同樣之折扣優待。大通銀行貸欵手續方便，快捷，四十八小時內便可知曉。

大通銀行華埠分行曾經理說，"大通銀行華埠分行與中美旅游社這次的合作也可增進華埠整個社區之繁榮，大通銀行之客戶不但可以得到高利率之存欵收入，又可購到廉價旅遊之機票，真是一舉兩得。"

FIGURE 20–1 American companies with foreign-born customers now living in the United States occasionally attempt to win their hearts, minds, and business by speaking to them in their native tongues, as illustrated by this Chase Manhattan Bank Chinatown branch news release. *(Courtesy of Chase Manhattan Bank)*

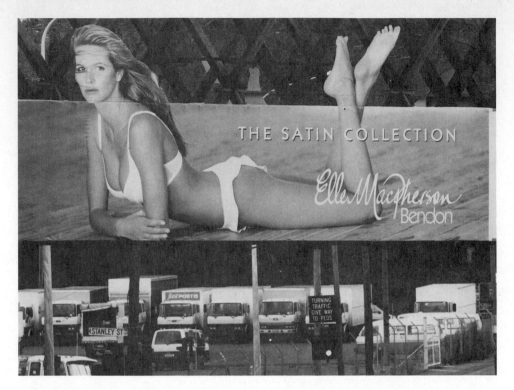

FIGURE 20—2   When New Zealand's largest manufacturer of women's underwear hired WORLDCOM partner David Lawson Consultants to secure publicity, little did the firm anticipate it would literally stop traffic in downtown Auckland by hiring supermodel Elle MacPherson to billboard the product. *(Courtesy of David Lawson Consultants Limited)*

3. Foreign governments seeking to advance the interests of their nations in the United States

Additionally, several public relations networks have developed over the years, linking U.S. counterparts with counselors in other parts of the world to establish quality international standards and take the guesswork out of such relationships.[2]

One such network, which connects the world and public relations activities, is WORLDCOM, uniting nearly 80 public relations firms from Africa, Asia/Pacific, Canada, Europe, Latin America, and the United States in an integrated communications approach to serve local clients operating elsewhere in the world.

International public relations continues to experience healthy growth. The International Public Relations Association (IPRA), established in 1955 "to contribute to the growth and professionalism of public relations practice on a worldwide basis," has more than 1,000 members in 60 countries (Figure 20–3). Particularly remarkable was IPRA's 11th PR World Congress in Melbourne, Australia, in 1988. Public relations representatives from China, Hungary, and the Soviet Union were among the more than 700 delegates from 45 countries. During the conference, Soviet journalism professor Yassen Zassoursky conceded that the greatest failure of the Chernobyl nuclear accident that claimed hundreds of Soviet lives "was the communications failure." He went on to suggest that "truth is the best way to solve problems." The IPRA Australian conference underscored the growth of public relations practice around the world.

Although the quality of such practice varies from country to country, in

FIGURE 20–3 This Code of Ethics governs the 1,000 individual members of the International Public Relations Association in more than 60 countries. *(Courtesy of International Public Relations Association)*

INTERNATIONAL CODE OF ETHICS

CODE OF ATHENS

English Version

**adopted by IPRA General Assembly at Athens on 12 May 1965
and modified at Tehran on 17 April 1968**

CONSIDERING that all Member countries of the United Nations Organisation have agreed to abide by its Charter which reaffirms "its faith in fundamental human rights, in the dignity and worth of the human person" and that having regard to the very nature of their profession, Public Relations practitioners in these countries should undertake to ascertain and observe the principles set out in this Charter;

CONSIDERING that, apart from "rights", human beings have not only physical or material needs but also intellectual, moral and social needs, and that their rights are of real benefit to them only in so far as these needs are essentially met;

CONSIDERING that, in the course of their professional duties and depending on how these duties are performed, Public Relations practitioners can substantially help to meet these intellectual, moral and social needs;

And lastly, CONSIDERING that the use of techniques enabling them to come simultaneously into contact with millions of people gives Public Relations practitioners a power that has to be restrained by the observance of a strict moral code.

On all these grounds, the undersigned Public Relations Associations hereby declare that they accept as their moral charter the principles of the following Code of Ethics, and that if, in the light of evidence submitted to the Council, a member of these associations should be found to have infringed this Code in the course of his professional duties, he will be deemed to be guilty of serious misconduct calling for an appropriate penalty.

Accordingly, each Member of these Associations:

SHALL ENDEAVOUR

1 To contribute to the achievement of the moral and cultural conditions enabling human beings to reach their full stature and enjoy the indefeasible rights to which they are entitled under the "Universal Declaration of Human Rights";

2 To establish communication patterns and channels which, by fostering the free flow of essential information, will make each member of the society in which he lives feel that he is being kept informed, and also give him an awareness of his own personal involvement and responsibility, and of his solidarity with other members;

3 To bear in mind that, because of the relationship between his profession and the public, his conduct – even in private – will have an impact on the way in which the profession as a whole is appraised;

4 To respect, in the course of his professional duties, the moral principles and rules of the "Universal Declaration of Human Rights";

5 To pay due regard to, and uphold, human dignity, and to recognise the right of each individual to judge for himself;

6 To encourage the moral, psychological and intellectual conditions for dialogue in its true sense, and to recognise the right of the parties involved to state their case and express their views;

SHALL UNDERTAKE

7 To conduct himself always and in all circumstances in such a manner as to deserve and secure the confidence of those with whom he comes into contact;

8 To act, in all circumstances, in such a manner as to take account of the respective interests of the parties involved: both the interests of the organisation which he serves and the interests of the publics concerned;

9 To carry out his duties with integrity, avoiding language likely to lead to ambiguity or misunderstanding, and to maintain loyalty to his clients or employers, whether past or present;

SHALL REFRAIN FROM

10 Subordinating the truth to other requirements;

11 Circulating information which is not based on established and ascertainable facts;

12 Taking part in any venture or undertaking which is unethical or dishonest or capable of impairing human dignity and integrity;

13 Using any "manipulative" methods or techniques designed to create subconscious motivations which the individual cannot control of his own free will and so cannot be held accountable for the action taken on them.

virtually every nation the practice of public relations has improved markedly in recent years.

Canada

Canadian public relations is the rival of American practice in terms of its level of acceptance, respect for the function, and maturity. The Canadian Public Relations Society, formed in 1948, is extremely active. Canada does differ from the United States in the "aggressiveness" of public relations practice there. While most communications programs, activities, and theories appear, on the surface, to be the same as in the United States, Canadian communications—particularly internal communications—is still some years behind its southern neighbor.[3]

Latin America

In Latin America the scene is more chaotic. The field is most highly developed in Mexico, where public relations practice began in the 1930s. Mexican schools of higher learning also teach public relations. The practice is less highly developed farther south, but the use of public relations counsel, often affiliated with advertising agencies, is not unusual. One problem in certain South American countries is the repressive control of the media by the government. In Puerto Rico, by contrast, the public relations industry earns well over $25 million a year in revenues. The first public relations firms were established in Puerto Rico during the 1950s, and the function has grown in competence and status ever since.[4]

Great Britain

Public relations has experienced tremendous growth in Great Britain. The largest United Kingdom-based public relations operation—and the world's largest independent agency—is the Shandwick Group. No public relations firm in the world has been more aggressive than Shandwick in acquiring other counselors in other countries. A 1987 survey of 400 CEOs in the United States and the United Kingdom found that British companies are more active and sophisticated users of public relations than their American counterparts.[5] More than half of the companies in Great Britain formally integrate public relations into their corporate planning systems, compared with one-third of American companies.

Public relations managers in half the British companies report directly to the board of directors, compared with one-third in U.S. companies. Although there is only one university, Sterling, teaching public relations to a degree level in the United Kingdom, public relations education in the

1990s in Great Britain—and the practice of public relations—is certain to expand.

The Continent

As for the rest of Europe, the integration of 12 European economies to form one Common Market in Europe 1992 is of immense importance for public relations. This coming together of the nations of the European Economic Community means not only the crumbling of economic borders, but the furthering of communications frontiers. Companies, governments, financial institutions, and other organizations will need to reach a single, more unified European audience.

Communications vehicles must be found to link 360 million people, speaking 12 different languages. This "macro challenge" will be compounded by other equally imposing challenges on a "micro" basis, such as the public issues inherent in reunifying the two Germanies. Little wonder that Peter Gummer (See Tips from the Top at the end of this chapter), executive chairman of Shandwick, predicts a period of "explosive public relations growth in Europe" in the years ahead.[6]

Eastern Europe

In the six countries of Eastern Europe—the USSR, Poland, Czechoslovakia, Hungary, Romania, and Bulgaria—there are 370 million consumers. True consumerism, however, may be some years away in certain countries. Nonetheless, the craving for Western brands, coupled with the availability of media, and the thirst for communications will make Eastern Europe a flashpoint for public relations practice.[7] Consider the following:

♦ More than 80 percent of all Eastern Europeans watch television daily. Nearly 100 percent watch at least several times a week.

♦ In Hungary, about 20 percent of the population have TV sets connected to satellite dishes.

♦ In Poland, 13 percent of the population report owning VCR machines.

♦ In Hungary and Czechoslovakia, about two-thirds of the population read newspapers daily.

Little wonder that the dramatic upheaval in Eastern Europe in recent years has spurred a communications revolution. Less wonder that firms like Burson-Marsteller, which opened offices in Berlin and Bonn in 1990, are flocking to the area to provide public relations resources.

Nowhere is this change more dramatic than in Russia, where Mikhail Gorbachev's efforts to "open up" the Soviet Union—at least prior to the 1991 repression in Latvia and Lithuania—took *glastnost* and *perestroika* to extraordinary levels.

Australia

The 1988 IPRA conference in Melbourne was indicative of the rapid advance of the public relations practice "down under." The Public Relations Institute of Australia is an extremely active organization, and the practice is widespread, particularly in Sydney and Melbourne, Australia's two commercial centers.

Asia

In much of Asia, public relations has evolved slowly. Japan has the most highly developed practice, with more than 100 full-time firms. In Japan, the field runs the gamut from press relations to employee communications to management consulting. The special problems of tradition-bound, bureaucratic Japanese companies have hindered the development of public relations. However, the media in Japan—six major national newspapers and four national networks—are extremely important. As Japan's role in the world increases in stature, so too will the importance of the practice of public relations increase in the country.

Elsewhere in Asia, the practice is less active, although countries such as India, China, and even Bangladesh have progressed in the public relations area. In China, notwithstanding the tragic events suffered in Tiananmen Square in 1989, the practice also is spreading. In 1986, Hill & Knowlton opened the first People's Republic public relations office in Beijing. A year later, the China Public Relations Society was launched with about 400 practitioners.

Africa

Even in Africa, the practice of public relations is growing. In 1990, the largest public relations meeting in the history of the continent was held in Abuja, Nigeria, with 1,000 attendees from 25 countries. It was announced at the meeting that Nigeria had given legal recognition to the public relations profession, instituting educational and certification requirements to be administered by the Nigerian Institute of Public Relations.[9]

Middle East

Finally, while the public relations profession is not particularly active in the Middle East, the power of public relations is well known and understood. Saddam Hussein was quick to harness communications media when he invaded Kuwait in 1990. The Kuwaitis responded by commissioning Hill & Knowlton public relations representation to appeal to Americans for support. All-in-all, the globalization of public relations in the 1990s will know no bounds.

Toshiba Faces a Trade Ban

In 1987, the huge Toshiba Company of Japan faced the threat of a total ban of its $2.6 billion exports to the United States. The ban was in retaliation for the illegal sale by one of its subsidiaries, Toshiba Machine Company, of sophisticated equipment to the Soviets, which enabled them to make ultraquiet submarine propellers that are difficult for the United States to detect. The sale violated the international agreement of the Coordinating Committee on Export Controls and was condemned in the United States. A significant number of U.S. congressional representatives vowed to single out Toshiba for retribution in the U.S. trade bill being debated.

In the first few months after the sale, Toshiba ignored the situation, going about its business as usual. But when momentum started to build against the company, it adopted an aggressive public relations campaign.

- First, it retained a Washington law firm under the Foreign Registration Act.
- Second, it undertook a full-scale independent investigation of its own policies and practices, with the help of the international accounting firm of Price Waterhouse.
- Third, it formulated a compliance program to make sure that no illegal sales would ever occur in the future.
- Fourth, it agreed to the resignation of both the chairman and the president of the parent Toshiba Corporation.
- Fifth, it sent a letter to U.S. congressional representatives, signed by the new Toshiba president, expressing regret and apologizing for the incident.
- Sixth, it published an ad in U.S. newspapers and magazines bearing the headline "Toshiba Corporation Extends Its Deepest Regrets to the American People."
- Seventh, it enlisted grass roots support from Toshiba's U.S. employees, suppliers, distributors, customers, and others, such as the governors of two states where Toshiba plants already existed or were expected to be located.

The end result of all of this was that the only restrictions in the trade bill a year later were a three-year suspension of the offending subsidiary's products and a three-year ban on government contracts with Toshiba. Toshiba's tardy, yet targeted, public relations campaign had salvaged the bulk of its export business in its most important foreign market.*

QUESTIONS

1. What is your reaction to Toshiba's public relations strategy?
2. Why do you think Toshiba waited before launching its public relations offensive?
3. Why were Toshiba employees and suppliers enlisted in the campaign?
4. If you were the company's public relations counsel, what would your approach be in the United States from here on?

*For further information, see Damon Darlin, "The Toshiba Case: Japanese Firm's Push to Sell to Soviets Led to Securities Breaches," *The Wall Street Journal,* 4 August 1987, 1; and Thane Peterson, "No Tears for Toshiba," *Business Week* (June 6, 1988), 52.

The Media Overseas

In many foreign countries, the term *public relations* is a euphemism for *press relations*. Working with the press abroad is not easy; there is often a language barrier, and in many countries the government controls the media. In some foreign nations, company developments (sales, earnings, and management changes) are not considered news. In Canada, for example, most management change announcements would have to be paid for to make the newspapers. Here are some other idiosyncrasies in dealing with the media in other nations.

♦ The time-honored U.S. press lunch to introduce products, management changes, or financial information is much less common overseas, where the company frequently meets the press at the close of the business day.

♦ Press conferences in countries such as West Germany, Switzerland, the Netherlands, Norway, and Sweden begin promptly on the appointed hour. Elsewhere, it is customary to wait 15 to 30 minutes.

♦ Press conference attendees in some countries must include government officials, local bankers, and other dignitaries. In other nations, local custom dictates that the company's customers and representatives be included.

♦ Press kits should usually be composed in both English and the main language of the host country. The press kit should contain (in addition to immediate news and a background on the company) statements on the benefits the company offers the host country.

Dealing with Foreign Clients Abroad

There is nothing magical about providing public relations services in overseas markets. As noted earlier, the key element in dealing effectively overseas lies in the development of a good working knowledge of the language, customs, climate, and people of the particular host area. Other suggestions for dealing effectively in a public relations context overseas include the following:

♦ Be innovative, flexible, and prepared to take risks. Stated another way: Don't believe that what works at home will work worldwide.

♦ Develop a continuing dialogue with consumer, business, and government leaders in the host country.

♦ Use the expertise of other local public relations practitioners or agencies.

♦ Foster contacts with foreign government and trade offices in the United States, foreign service people, commercial attachés of foreign consulates, and visiting representatives.

BETWEEN THE LINES

When in Rome . . .

Communicating overseas can be a tricky business. Words, mannerisms, figures of speech, customs—all are different in other countries.

- In Latin America, *no* is almost a dirty word in polite society. Not wanting to give a flatly negative answer to a friend or colleague, Latin Americans customarily say "Yes" or "Of course."
- *Yes* in Japanese means "Yes, I hear what you say," but it doesn't necessarily mean "Yes, I agree."
- In Bulgaria, a nod means no and a shake of the head means yes.
- In Italy, if you don't use your hands in an animated fashion in conversation, you are perceived as a big fat bore.
- Arabs point or beckon in summoning dogs, so they don't appreciate that gesture for people.
- The Japanese are overt with their humor. Slapstick humor is popular in Japan. A subtle approach in communications, such as Australia's tourism campaign using the dry-witted Paul Hogan, just doesn't work.

And then there is the minefield of fast-food communications and routines in other countries.

- When Burger King opened its first restaurant in London, employees found the floor littered with pickles. The English, you see, don't care for pickles on their burgers.
- Pizza Hut found that one of the best-selling items in its Far Eastern restaurants was seaweed pizza.
- Employees of the 515 Kentucky Fried Chicken restaurants in Japan take time off to pray for the souls of dead chickens.
- Wendy's International removed the "hot stuffed" baked potato description from its British menu when it found the expression had a most improper connotation in the United Kingdom.

- ◆ Introduce philanthropic programs locally.
- ◆ Dismiss the myth that overseas media will never report events unless it is paid for. If activities are newsworthy, chances are good that local media won't ignore them.[10]

Public relations practitioners operating abroad shouldn't think they have to out-native the natives. No one will expect the local practitioner to be a linguistic expert or to have full knowledge of the country's customs. However, convincing a host of one's willingness to learn about the local country will help immeasurably in ingratiating the public relations practitioner abroad.

Foreign Press in the United States

Many foreign publications have bureaus in New York City and Washington, D.C. The foreign press represents the single most important source of information about America for hundreds of millions of people throughout the world. There are more than 1,000 active representatives of foreign media in the United States, representing more than 500 news organizations. About 80 percent of the U.S. foreign press corps represents European media; Japan is also broadly represented.

Most foreign correspondents are interested mainly in American politics. Normally, about one-half of a correspondent's time is spent on politics and the other half on such subjects as science, art, business, crime, civil rights, and finance. Foreign bureaus are often one-person operations, and an active international public relations representative can keep foreign journalists constantly serviced with topical and timely information for use in overseas markets.

Representing Foreign Clients in the United States

One growth area for U.S. public relations firms has been with foreign companies and governments seeking to expand their influence in America. Just as U.S. multinational companies need public relations assistance abroad, foreign multinationals need help in doing business in the United States—whether in introducing a product, setting up a subsidiary, opening a new plant, or expanding existing operations. A U.S. consultant can be of tremendous value in working with state and federal legislatures and agencies, as well as with the press.

Foreign countries retain the services of public relations counselors to fill a variety of needs.

♦ Advancing political objectives
♦ Counseling on the probable U.S. reaction to a government's projected action
♦ Advancing a country's commercial interests (e.g., sales in the United States, increased private U.S. investment, tourism, etc.)
♦ Assisting in communications in English

Brushing Away a Dark Blot

Colgate-Palmolive is one of the most savvy international conglomerates. Colgate's toothpaste, shampoo, detergent, and other household and hygiene products account for more than $6 billion in worldwide sales.

However, when Colgate purchased 50 percent of the Hawley & Hazel Company in Hong Kong in 1985, it had no idea of the international controversy the union would spark. Hawley & Hazel marketed "Darkie," the best-selling toothpaste brand in several Asian countries. Darkie toothpaste was identifiable in Asia by the picture of a minstrel in black face on the package. The minstrel became part of the product's package design in the 1920s, after the then CEO of Hawley & Hazel saw American singer Al Jolson and thought his wide, white, toothy smile would make an excellent logo.

And for many years, it did—until the union with Colgate-Palmolive brought intense criticism from religious groups and others, not only for the depiction of the minstrel, but also for using the name Darkie.

In 1986, three Roman Catholic groups filed a shareholder petition demanding that Colgate-Palmolive change the Darkie name and logotype.

Michigan Congressman John Conyers joined the fracas when he learned about Darkie while traveling in Taiwan in 1988.

Colgate responded by conducting extensive consumer studies and considering hundreds of alternatives. Because Darkie accounted for nearly all of Hawley & Hazel's business, with a market share ranging from 20 to 70 percent in Hong Kong, Malaysia, Singapore, Taiwan, and Thailand, the company feared a false step.

Finally, in 1989, Colgate Chairman Ruben Mark announced the toothpaste would be renamed Darlie, and the logotype would become a portrait of a man of ambiguous race wearing a silk top hat, tuxedo, and bow tie. Said Mr. Mark, "It's just plain wrong. It's just offensive. The morally right thing dictated that we must change. What we have to do is find a way to change that is least damaging to the economic interests of our partners."

Under the agreement, Colgate-Palmolive agreed to pay for all redesign and repackaging costs and for the added advertising costs involved in the changeover. It also said it would reimburse Hawley & Hazel for any loss in profits caused by customer confusion over the change to Darlie.

QUESTIONS

1. How do you think Colgate-Palmolive handled this controversy?
2. What would you expect to be the impact of the name and logotype change in the United States? In Asia?

◆ Counseling and help in winning understanding and support on a specific issue that might undermine the client's standing in the United States and the world community

◆ Helping modify laws and regulations inhibiting the client's activities in the United States[11]

A foreign government that seeks to hire an American public relations firm often begins by having its embassy in Washington solicit competitive bids. The winner is expected to provide expertise in disseminating positive news to the media and other public opinion channels. Often it may be necessary to explain to foreign clients—some of whom may totally control the flow of news in their own countries—how an independent press works. Typically, a consultant begins the assignment by identifying potential sources of public opinion and surveying news coverage about the client country. Then, the consultant may suggest activities, such as the following:

1. Selectively contacting influential writers and editors and providing them with background information about the country.
2. Inviting media to visit the client country. Such expense-paid trips (junkets) are often frowned on by responsible media.
3. Checking with foreign policy experts, educators, business leaders, and government officials about current American attitudes toward the country. The results of these surveys, as well as more formal research, are turned over to the client.

Counselors who work for foreign governments must register with the U.S. Department of Justice and list all their activities on behalf of a foreign principal, including compensation received and expenses incurred. Occasionally, representing a foreign nation, particularly one whose policies differ from those of the United States, is an unpopular task for public relations agencies.

Summary

The spread of the practice of public relations around the world is consistent with the global spread of democracy.

Little wonder that public relations networks, including Shandwick in Britain, Hill & Knowlton and Burson-Marsteller in the United States, WORLDCOM, and a host of others have arisen.

In the '90s, corporate mergers and joint ventures have crossed national borders: Pillsbury was acquired by Britain's Grand Metropolitan, Whirlpool merged with the Netherlands' Philips N.V., Hill & Knowlton was even taken over by Britain's WPP Group. Such marriages require press, government, and IR work across many borders.

Technology meanwhile has made international communications easier. Satellites and computer networks, fax machines and electronic mail, and all the rest have helped public relations professionals feed information around the globe.[12]

FIGURE 20—4 If you're still not convinced that public relations is taken seriously overseas, here's unequivocal proof. In the winter of 1989, when the tumultuous events in East Germany caused the country to change leaders as often as Arsenio Hall changed hairstyles, the interim acting head of state, Manfred Gerlach, refused to be denied his "moment in the sun." Can you guess which one is Manfred? *(Courtesy Reuters/Bettmann)*

On the other hand, culture, customs, regulations, media practices, and government relations all differ from country to country. This necessitates that public relations activities be tailored to fit national requirements.

Therefore, it is likely that the "golden age" of international public relations will occur in the 1990s, as communication and the practice that depends on it become increasingly more global.

1. What has changed the way the world looks at public relations in the 1990s?
2. Describe the general task of the international public relations professional.
3. What is the IPRA?
4. What is the status of public relations in Europe?
5. What is the status of public relations in Asia?
6. What is the potential for public relations work in Eastern Europe?
7. How does dealing with the overseas media differ from dealing with the media in the United States?
8. What duties are generally assigned U.S. public relations firms working for overseas clients?
9. What interest group was Colgate-Palmolive most concerned about when it changed the name of its Darkie toothpaste?
10. How important is the foreign press in the United States?

DISCUSSION STARTERS

NOTES

1. Ray E. Hiebert, "Globalizing Public Relations," *Social Science Monitor* (September 1990): 1.
2. Ernest Wittenberg, "Getting It Done Overseas," *Public Relations Journal* (June 1982): 14.
3. Roger Feather, "Internal Communications in Canada," *IABC Communications World* (December 1990): 37.

4. Emilia Abislaiman, "Public Relations," *Caribbean Business,* 9 August 1990, S4.

5. Jean L. Farinelli, "The Globalization of PR," speech to the Public Relations Society of America Northeast District Conference, Newport, Rhode Island, May 22, 1990.

6. "Europe's PR Industry Is Booming," *Public Relations Reporter,* 10 December 1990, 3.

7. Ray Hiebert, "Special Report: Communication in Eastern Europe," *Social Science Monitor* (November 1990): 1.

8. Richard Edelman, "Japanese Executives Still Have Much to Learn About PR American-Style," *Business Journalism Review* (Fall 1989): 50.

9. "The Largest Meeting in Africa," *Public Relations News,* 22 October 1990, 1.

10. *Public Relations News* 38, no. 47 (November 29, 1982): 1.

11. Carl Levin, "Representing Foreign Interests," *Public Relations Journal* (June 1982): 22.

12. Claudia H. Deutsch, "The Image Polishers Go Global," *The New York Times,* 25 June 1989, p. 2.

TOP OF THE SHELF

Ruch, William V. *International Handbook of Corporate Communication.* Jefferson, NC: McFarland & Company, Inc., 1989.

Appropriate business behavior in more than 130 countries is described in *International Handbook of Corporate Communication,* a text that prepares organizations for communicating abroad.

Bill Ruch has observed organizational communication in Asia, Europe, Latin America, and Africa. Choose a region or country, and he describes, in depth, how its land, people, history, economy, and culture have shaped the area's corporate communication. Ruch also highlights cultural preferences for the written word, eye contact, speech, and touch. For example, when having a conversation in Saudi Arabia, remember that "Arabs maintain eye contact . . . . The American approach is to maintain eye contact intermittently, looking away frequently." When in Zimbabwe, keep in mind that "Zimbabweans dislike sarcasm and loud, showy behavior." Ruch punctuates his global communication survey with 46 case studies of well-known firms, including Japan's Mazda Motors, Switzerland's Nestle Group, and Jordan's Royal Jordanian Airline.

As the world becomes increasingly interdependent, a knowledge of how to act in overseas markets will become more important. *International Handbook of Corporate Communication* provides information to help public relations people get their message across wherever they are.

Carvounis, Chris, and Brinda Carvounis. *U.S. Commercial Opportunities in the Soviet Union.* Westport, CT: Greenwood, 1989.

Hibbert, Edgar P. *Marketing Strategies in International Business.* New York: McGraw-Hill, 1988.

IEG Directory of Sponsorship Marketing (Available from Special Events Reports, 213 W. Institute Place, Chicago, IL 60610.)

International Literary Market Place. New York: R. R. Bowker Co, 1990.

IPRA Review (Longman, Westgate House, The High, Essex, England CM20 INE). Quarterly.

Japan Marketing Handbook. Detroit: Gale Research, 1988 (835 Penobscot Bldg. 48226).

Nadel, Jack. *Cracking the Global Market: How to Do Business Around the World.* New York: AMACOM, 1987 (135 W. 50th St. 10020).

Rautenberg, Steven. "Crisis Public Relations in the Age of Apology: From Chernobyl to Monongahela." Address to the American Bankers Association Security and Planning Conference, Orlando, FL, January 28, 1988.

Singer, Joseph. "How to Work with Foreign Clients." *Public Relations Journal* (October 1987): 35–37.

"Special Report: PR in the UK." *PR Week* (May 30–June 5, 1988): 8–11.

Weber, Robert. *The Marketer's Guide to Selling Products Abroad.* Westport, CT: Greenwood, 1989.

Wiklund, Erik. *International Marketing Strategies: How to Build International Market Share.* New York: McGraw-Hill, 1987.

CASE STUDY   Bhopal

The worst industrial accident in the history of the world occurred on December 3, 1984, when a poison gas leak at a Union Carbide factory in Bhopal, India, killed more than 2,500 people and injured another 200,000. Thereafter, Union Carbide Chairman Warren Anderson and his colleagues confronted perhaps the worst crisis ever faced by an American corporation. Their immediate corporate mission was to strike a difficult balance among the instincts of human compassion, the demands of public relations, and the dictates of corporate survival.

In the days following the Bhopal incident, Carbide executives faced a series of immediate management problems: how best to aid the victims; how to be sure whatever happened at Bhopal wouldn't happen again somewhere else; how to help employees keep up morale; how to assure investors of the corporation's financial stability; and how to begin protecting the company from excessive legal liabilities. Each question had to be faced—and answered—at once. And each issue had a public relations side to it.

To complicate matters, Carbide headquarters in Danbury, Connecticut, was besieged by hundreds of reporters who wanted immediate answers. Getting information out of India proved practically impossible, partly because there were only two open phone lines between Bhopal and Bombay, where Union Carbide of India was headquartered. In addition, the Indian government arrested the top company officials in Bhopal and refused to make them available to Carbide

JANUARY/FEBRUARY 1985

To Carbiders:

I'm greatly encouraged by recent reports from India that there appears to be virtually no lasting damage to the people injured by the incident at Bhopal. Just before the Christmas holiday, The New York Times reported, and eminent doctors (whom we asked to go to Bhopal and give their independent appraisal of the situation there) confirmed, that almost none of the dire consequences predicted following the catastrophy — permanent blindness, paralysis, severe damage — are, in fact, occuring.

Of course, this in no way diminishes the shock and sadness experienced by Carbiders everywhere.

(continued on page 3)

FIGURE 20—5

(continued from cover)

On one day, we were working for a company that had one of the best safety records in the industry, which has one of the best records of any in the nation. On the next, every one of us couldn't believe what happened. Why it did is still a mystery; one that we intend to unravel.

One of the reasons I went to India was to help provide immediate relief for the people in Bhopal. Humanitarian efforts are being made by Union Carbide Corporation and Union Carbide India Limited. And I'm particularly gratified by the personal efforts of Carbide employees to establish the relief fund for Bhopal.

We're showing the world that Union Carbide is, indeed, a family, one with a heart and soul in all the countries where we do business. Some observers have also raised questions about our future. Let me put those questions to rest.

The many people who depend on Carbide — employees, investors, customers, and suppliers — may rest assured that we continue to be a strong company, and we resolve to maintain leadership in our various businesses. We are confident that compensation for the Bhopal victims can be arranged in a fair and equitable manner that will not have a material effect on the financial condition of the corporation. Nothing has changed our determination to go forward with the plans and strategies intended to help us reach higher levels of performance.

In December, the corporation faced a crisis, one that will affect us for a long time to come. However, throughout most of our businesses, we're ready to return to the tasks that were in front of us when we entered the month.

Necessary business steps taken in '84 have substantially improved our prospects for 1985. We have important work to do. As difficult as December was for all of us, that work goes forward.

Union Carbide and the chemical industry have been major contributors to the changes that have made this a better century. Our products have improved life for many millions, and chemicals have an enormous contribution yet to make. I'm confident that all of us will be proud to participate in our future efforts.

Warren M. Anderson

FIGURE 20–5 (cont'd)

executives in the United States. Nonetheless, Carbide officials agreed that, however unreliable, the news from India warranted swift, sweeping, and immediate decisions.

The first decision was to send help to India—medical supplies, respirators, and a doctor with extensive knowledge of methyl isocyanate, the poisonous chemical released from the Carbide plant. Carbide also sent a team of technical experts to examine the plant.

Next, Chairman Anderson, admitting that Bhopal had left him "shattered," decided to hop the company jet and follow the technical team to India to view the situation. As a practical matter, Anderson's journey accomplished nothing. He was arrested on arrival, held briefly, released on $2,500 bail, and told to leave the country. Indian officials refused Anderson's offer of $1 million in immediate aid and use of the company's guest house above Bhopal to house orphans of the victims. Some ridiculed Anderson's trip. Others praised it.

In Connecticut, meanwhile, the company set up a media center at the Danbury Hilton across from Carbide's front gate and refused journalists admission to the headquarters building. The firm chose as its chief spokesman a cautious lawyer and engineer, Carbide's director of safety and environmental affairs. In light of the complexity of the lawsuits it faced, Carbide was circumspect in releasing information. Indeed, it took several months for the company to release its own report about what happened at Bhopal.

Predictably, reporters filled the vacuum by investigating on their own, concluding that many safety rules were routinely ignored in India, that both the staff and nearby residents were largely unaware of how dangerous the chemicals were, that monitoring equipment was often inadequate or poorly understood, and that there was no special siren to warn residents of imminent danger. Until a tour of Carbide's West Virginia pesticide plant was given some weeks after the tragedy, company spokespersons had declined to provide any technical data on the manufacturing and storage of methyl isocyanate. On the other hand, Carbide regularly held press briefings in order to, as one executive put it, "express our sympathy and share with everyone all the information we didn't know."

Internally, to buck up sagging morale, Carbide executives taped video messages for employees around the world and kept a steady stream of encouragement flowing through internal publications (see Figure 20–5). Externally, the plunge in Carbide's stock caused the company to begin emphasizing its financial soundness in news releases and briefings. This action tended to give the impression that Carbide was more bottom-line oriented than compassionate. Not helping the situation were the ballyhooed flights to India of publicity-seeking lawyers intent on cashing in on the Bhopal tragedy.

In the months following the crisis, a *Business Week*/Harris poll revealed that fewer than 4 out of 10 Americans who had heard about the Bhopal disaster believed Carbide had done an "excellent" or "good" job. Almost half of those surveyed were able to name Carbide, without prompting, as the company involved in the Bhopal disaster. A year after Bhopal, Carbide faced mounting problems.

- It set up a reserve of nearly $200 million to handle Bhopal-related lawsuits.
- A toxic chemical leak at its West Virginia plant injured more than 100 people, and Carbide was fined $1.37 million for "willful disregard for health and safety."
- The GAF Corporation tried to take it over.
- The company shook up its top management and announced plans to cut more than 5,000 jobs, close several plants, and sell off more than $1 billion in assets, including its Danbury headquarters.

The legacy of Bhopal continues to dog Union Carbide. In 1989, the company reached a $470 million settlement to compensate victims of the catastrophe. The company declared that the settlement closed all civil and criminal charges against it. Wall Street analysts hailed the news. At last Carbide could put Bhopal behind it.

Or could it?

In 1990, the Indian government demanded that the $470 million settlement be overturned. It claimed that the former government, led by Prime Minister Rajiv Gandhi, never consulted victims' groups at the time, and that the $470 million sum was grossly inadequate.

Bhopal, it seemed, simply wouldn't die.

Chairman Anderson, having retired from Union Carbide, reflected on the experience that will be linked forever to the company he ran: "I don't look back. If you get mired down, you can't make things happen. If we come out feeling we did the right thing, and the world agrees, then that's the best that could be done."*

QUESTIONS

1. Do you think Warren Anderson made the right decision in flying immediately to Bhopal?
2. How would you assess Union Carbide's public relations posture in the wake of Bhopal?
3. What do you think of the company's reluctance in the first months immediately following the tragedy to announce what specifically had happened?
4. What do you think of the strategy to emphasize the company's financial strength at Bhopal press briefings?

5. Had you been Carbide's public relations director, would you have allowed reporters access to Danbury headquarters and Carbide employees?

*For further information on Bhopal, see Robert Garfield, "Union Carbide Team: Managing a Crisis," *USA Today*, 7 December 1984, 1B; Michael Isikoff, "Crisis Management: Has Carbide Met the Test?" *The Washington Post*, 24 February 1985, G1–20; Stuart Jackson, "Union Carbide's Good Name Takes a Beating," *Business Week* (December 31, 1984): 40; Richard I. Kirkland, Jr., "Union Carbide Coping with Catastrophe," *Fortune* (January 7, 1985): 50–53; Thomas J. Lueck, "Crisis Management at Carbide," *The New York Times*, 14 December 1984, D1–2; and Barry Meier and James B. Stewart, "A Year After Bhopal, Union Carbide Faces a Slew of Problems," *The Wall Street Journal*, 26 November 1985, 1, 56.

Tips from the Top

PETER GUMMER

Peter Gummer is chairman of Shandwick PLC, the largest public relations agency group in the world. Shandwick employs more than 2,400 people in 80 offices around the globe, and serves 5,000 clients with net fees in excess of $175 million annually. After a period of working on local newspapers and in a number of public relations posts, both in consultancy and in-house, Mr. Gummer founded Shandwick in 1974.

What is the state of international public relations today?
It has changed enormously in recent years. It used to be that the majority of international public relations was structured through two U.S. agencies who followed their American clients overseas. That is no longer the case, primarily because of two factors. First, important media are no longer limited by geography. The *Financial Times* is as readily available in New York as it is in Tokyo as it is in London. The Cable News Network and its derivatives are increasingly making satellite television into a worldwide activity. Second, the breakdown in international trade barriers—between Canada and the United States, in Western Europe, in the Eastern Bloc, and so on—has had an extraordinary impact on the world.

What has this meant to the international public relations client?
What already has happened and what will happen increasingly is that companies will demand multinational public relations service—that is, an international public relations strategy, implemented with a very high degree of local, cultural feel. That's what's behind the growth of Shandwick.

What is the state of public relations practice today in Europe?
It's terribly confused. The United Kingdom is very well serviced, but it's much more patchy on the Continent. In Italy and Germany, public relations practice is fairly sophisticated and mature. In Switzerland, you will find public relations companies interested in investor relations. In France, you'll find much smaller, less sophisticated players. So it is mixed.

What about Asia?
By the year 2000, Asia Pacific will dominate the world, not only in public relations but in everything else. It will be led by Ja-

pan, with the emerging economies of Thailand, Korea, probably Singapore, and Australia. It is clearly the most exciting part of the world.

How will the Japanese approach public relations practice?

Japan doesn't think about public relations in a consumer sense. It thinks about its role in the world internationally, and that's how it treats public relations. It also is responsible for the most highly sophisticated investor and government relations programs of any that I've seen.

What about China?

Public relations practice in China is underdeveloped today. But wait. In 10 years, people will say that the events of 1989 in Tiananmen Square were but a "blip" in the inevitable march of the People's Republic becoming the most powerful economic force in the world. But it will take a decade.

What about other areas of the world?

Public relations in the United States and Canada, of course, is highly sophisticated and well developed. We have regarded places like Africa and even South America as second-phase development activities at Shandwick. There is little public relations in Russia at the moment, but we're engaged in a major program for the development of the Russian shipping industry and helped launch McDonald's hamburgers in Moscow.

How important is public relations to a Mikhail Gorbachev?

Gorbachev, until 1991, was the best advertisement in the world both for public relations and for Russian tailoring. Governments that succeed are governments that communicate and manage communications well. That's the lesson of the 1990s.

What about the Eastern Bloc as a whole?

The opening up of countries like East Germany, Hungary, Romania, and Poland is extraordinary. Their industries and governments will want to tell the outside world, in as favorable a way as possible, what has happened as a result of the tremendous change that has taken place. There will be a demand for tourism, for investment, for industry, and, quite soon, urban infrastructure. Therefore, there will be a demand for public relations at the sharp cutting edge of all of these activities.

What is the outlook for public relations in the 1990s?

The healthiest communications market that one can imagine. But one of great change. In-house departments will get substantially smaller over the next several years, with highly paid generalists working for corporations. Counseling firms will split between huge worldwide players and smaller-niche players. The market for public relations counsel will double as companies become even more global and the need for specialty skills increases.

What about the prospects for public relations in a recession?
The field will thrive. Recession means change. Recession means problems. And the more problems and difficulties one encounters, the more public relations assistance is needed. I think public relations—good public relations—is recession-proof.

Managing Crisis and Opportunity

When public relations professionals are asked what subject they want covered in mid-career seminars, "Crisis Communications" invariably heads the list. Some scholars suggest that any self-respecting introductory public relations text should contain an *entire chapter* devoted to Crisis Management. (Sorry, scholars!) Indeed, many of the case studies in this book—from the Exxon Valdez tanker spill to the Watergate political scandal to the Tylenol murders at the end of this chapter—concern public relations crises.

Helping to manage both crisis and opportunity is the ultimate assignment for a public relations professional. Smart managements value public relations advice in developing an organization's response not only to crises, but to public issues in general. Hundreds of American companies, in fact, have created executive posts for "issues managers," whose task is to help the organization define and deal with the political, economic, and social issues that affect it.

The list of such issues—and of the crises they often evoke—is unending. Consider the following rash of crises that confronted American companies in the space of just a few months during 1990:

♦ The General Electric Company agreed to pay a $16 million fine to settle charges that it overcharged the Defense Department.

♦ The Northrop Corporation paid a $17 million fine after pleading guilty to charges of faking tests on weapons.

♦ The Nynex Corporation admitted that several of its purchasing managers had attended lewd parties with suppliers, creating the appearance of conflict of interest.[1]

Add to these special problems, societal issues resulting from abortion, asbestos, and AIDS; discrimination, downsizing, and drugs; takeovers, transplants, and terrorism, and one can readily see why the domain of issues management has become increasingly important for public relations professionals.

Defining Issues Management

Public relations pioneer W. Howard Chase, who helped coin the term *issues management,* defined it this way:

> Issues management is the capacity to understand, mobilize, coordinate, and direct all strategic and policy planning functions, and all public affairs/public relations skills, toward achievement of one objective: meaningful participation in creation of public policy that affects personal and institutional destiny.
>
> Issues management is dynamic and proactive. It rejects the hypothesis that any institution must be the pawn of the public policy determined solely by others.
>
> The noblest aspect of freedom is that human beings and their institutions have the right to help determine their own destinies. Issues management is the systems process that maximizes self-expression and action programming for most effective participation in public policy formation.
>
> Thus, issues management is the highest form of sound management applied to institutional survival.[2]

As the Chase/Jones management process model in Figure 21–1 illustrates, issues management is a five-step process that (1) *identifies* issues with which the organization must be concerned, (2) *analyzes* and delimits each issue with respect to its impact on constituent publics, (3) *displays* the various strategic options available to the organization, (4) *implements* an action program to communicate the organization's views and influence perception on the issue, and (5) *evaluates* its program in terms of reaching organizational goals.

Many suggest that the term *issues management* is another way of saying that the most important public relations skill is counseling management. This skill, in fact, was at the heart of the reputation enjoyed by public relations pioneers such as Ivy Lee, Edward Bernays, Carl Byoir, and John Hill. Today, issues management as a specialized discipline has developed to the point where the Issues Management Association, founded in the 1980s, has hundreds of active members.

In specific terms, organizations can manage their own response to issues and, therefore, influence issues development in the ways identified here.

Anticipate emerging issues   Normally, the issues management process anticipates issues 18 months to 3 years away. Therefore, it is neither crisis planning nor postcrisis planning, but rather precrisis planning. In other words, issues management deals with an issue that will hit the

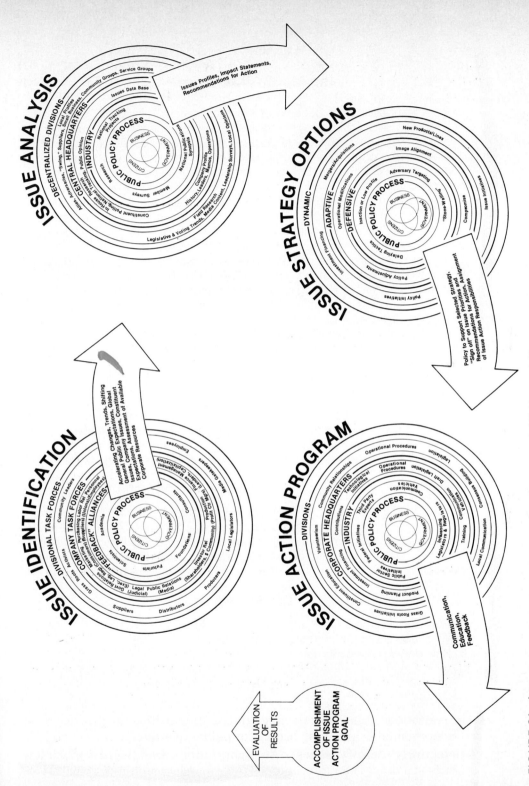

FIGURE 21–1 A pioneer in the field of issues management, W. Howard Chase, along with Barrie L. Jones, developed this tool for predicting the effect of internal and external environmental changes on the performance of the overall corporate system. The model itself assigns decision-making authority and evaluation of issues manager performance. (Courtesy of Issue Action Publications)

The Mouse That Poured

Product tampering can be among the most serious crises with which an organization is faced. The key in any crisis is to act decisively and quickly.

In July 1988, an unemployed Jacksonville, Florida, construction worker, James Harvey, angry over a traffic accident involving a Coors beer truck, called the Coors Consumer Hotline to complain that he had found a mouse in his beer can.

When Coors got the hotline call, it sent two headquarters consumer affairs people the next day to placate Harvey with $1,500, in exchange for the canned mouse. Harvey refused the offer and tried to raise the ante first to $35,000, and then $50,000, for the mouse and the can. Coors refused.

Several days later, after shopping the story around to local TV stations, Harvey struck pay dirt. Gannett-owned WTLV-TV aired a 6 o'clock piece on the local man who felt "something against my mouth while drinking beer." Harvey and a camera crew took the can to the local Board of Health, where the mouse was exposed—on camera.

Reports of the mouse being poured out of a 16-ounce Coors can reached Coors public relations officials in Colorado, who then reported the dilemma to top management.

Coors wasted no time. It insisted that lab tests be conducted immediately on the mouse. The subsequent tests revealed two crucial facts:

- First, the mouse had died about a week before the tests, but the can had been sealed at the Coors brewery a full three months earlier.
- Second, the mouse hadn't drowned, but rather had wounds that indicated it had been stuffed through the can's pop-top opening.

Despite the clear implication of tampering, Coors couldn't keep the film footage off the airwaves. Mouse-in-the-can film aired 72 times in Jacksonville alone, where the local Coors distributor lost more than $250,000 in sales and probably much more in public image.

It was little consolation to Coors that four months to the day the original story aired, Harvey was exposed as a fraud, arrested, and jailed for attempted extortion.

QUESTIONS

1. How do you assess Coors' response to this crisis?
2. What else could the company have done?
3. How do you assess the performance of WTLV-TV?

organization a year down the road, thus distinguishing the practice from the normal crisis planning aspects of public relations.

Selectively identify issues   An organization can influence only a few issues at a time. Therefore, a good issues management process will select several—perhaps 5 to 10—specific priority issues with which to deal. In this way, issues management can focus on the most important issues affecting the organization.

◆ **Deal with opportunities and vulnerabilities** Most issues, anticipated well in advance, offer both opportunities and vulnerabilities for organizations. For example, in assessing promised federal budget cuts, an insurance company might anticipate that less money will mean fewer people driving and therefore fewer accident claims. This would mark an opportunity. On the other hand, those cuts might mean that more people are unable to pay their premiums. This, clearly, is a vulnerability that a sharp company should anticipate well in advance.

◆ **Plan from the outside-in** The external environment—not internal strategies—dictates the selection of priority issues. This differs from the normal strategic planning approach, which, to a large degree, is driven by internal strengths and objectives. Issues management is very much driven by external factors.

◆ **Profit-line orientation** Although many people tend to look at issues management as anticipating crises, its real purpose should be to defend the organization in the light of external factors, as well as to enhance the firm's business by seizing imminent opportunities.

◆ **Action timetable** Even as the issues management process must identify emerging issues and selectively set them in priority order, it must also propose policy, programs, and an implementation timetable to deal with those issues. Action is the key to an effective issues management process.

◆ **Dealing from the top** Just as a public relations department is powerless without the confidence and respect of top management, so, too, must the issues management process operate with the support of the chief executive. The chief executive's personal sanction is critical to the acceptance and conduct of issues management within a firm.

Implementing Issues Management

In a typical organization, the tactical implementation of issues management has tended to fall into four specific job tasks.

1. **Identifying issues and trends** Issue identification can be accomplished through traditional research techniques, as well as through more informal methods. Organizations are most concerned about issues that affect their own residential area. For example, in 1990, when Southern California's sunny skies were steadily threatened by increasingly significant doses of smog, the Unocal Corporation, a Los Angeles-based oil company, seized the initiative. Unocal announced an innovative pro-

gram, called SCRAP, in which it promised to spend more than $5 million to eliminate six million pounds of air pollution by paying for and scrapping 7,000 old cars. Thanks to SCRAP, in four months California rid its highways of 8,376 gas-guzzling pollution machines. And Unocal won millions in positive goodwill[3] (Figure 21–2).

One way to keep informed about what is being said about a company, industry, or issue is to subscribe to issues-oriented publications of every political persuasion—from *Mother Jones* and *The Village Voice* on the far left to the Liberty Lobby's *Spotlight* on the far right and everything else in between.

2. Evaluating issue impact and setting priorities   Evaluation and analysis may be handled by issues committees within an organization. Committees can set priorities for issues management action. At the Upjohn Company, for example, a senior policy committee—composed

Unocal Corporation
1201 West 5th Street, P.O. Box 7600
Los Angeles, California 90051

UNOCAL 76

News Release

Contact: Barry Lane   213/977-7601
          Jim Bray   213/977-5390
          Jeff Callender 213/977-7208

FOR IMMEDIATE RELEASE

Los Angeles, May 10 -- The end of the road is already in sight for more than 2,500 of the 7,000 model year 1970 or older cars Unocal has promised to junk through its SCRAP project.

As part of its South Coast Recycled Auto Program announced last month to fight air pollution in the Los Angeles basin, Unocal has pledged to remove 7,000 1970 or older cars from Southern California freeways. Beginning June 1, the company will pay $700 for each vehicle.

Since the program was announced April 26, Unocal has made appointments to accept autos from more than 2,500 prospective sellers. The cars, which pollute 15 to 30 times more than new models, will be crushed and shredded, and the metal recycled.

The response by sellers to a toll-free telephone number (800-866-2251) was so heavy it prompted telephone company intervention and required the installation of numerous additional lines, according to Richard J. Stegemeier, chairman, president and chief executive officer.

MORE...

-2-

"We were swamped with calls," Stegemeier said. "We couldn't answer the phones fast enough. We're well on our way to reaching the 7,000-car mark and taking millions of pounds of pollutants out of our air permanently."

The 7,000 vehicles Unocal will scrap are estimated to emit 6 million pounds of carbon monoxide, reactive organic gases and nitrogen oxides annually, according to Stegemeier. Among automobiles, 1970 or older cars are the worst polluters on the road.

Other companies also think the program is a good idea. T. J. Rodgers, president and chief executive officer of Cypress Semiconductor, San Jose, Calif., sent Stegemeier a note and a check for $700.

"What a great idea!" Rodgers wrote. "The employees of Cypress Semiconductor and I would like you to buy and bury one for us, too."

The program is part of a three-point Unocal offensive against vehicle emissions. They cause at least 60 percent of the basin's smog, according to the California Air Resources Board.

Besides SCRAP, the other programs are Smog-Fighter, which offers free smog checks and low-emission tune-ups to owners of 1974 and older vehicles, and Protech Patrol, in which emergency vehicles will offer free service to motorists stranded on freeways.

-30-

May 10, 1990

FIGURE 21–2 Unocal's campaign in the spring of 1990, to rid the Los Angeles Basin of millions of pounds of air pollution, was an outstanding example of managing a public relations opportunity. *(Courtesy of Unocal Corporation)*

of managers in each of the firm's major divisions, as well as public affairs and legal staff members—meets quarterly to set issues priorities.

3. **Establishing a company position**   Establishing a position can be a formal process. After the Upjohn senior policy committee has met and decided on issues, Upjohn's public affairs staff prepares policy statements on each topic. At PPG Industries, individual issues managers prepare position papers for executive review on topics of direct concern.

4. **Designing company action and response to achieve results**   The best-organized companies for issues management orchestrate integrated responses to achieve results. Typically, companies may coordinate their Washington offices, state lobbying operations, management speeches, advertising messages, and employee communications to forward the firm's point of view (Figure 21–3).

Managing in a Crisis

The most significant test for any organization comes when it is hit by a major accident or disaster. How it handles itself in the midst of a crisis may influence how it is perceived for years to come. Poor handling of events with the magnitude of NASA's shuttle disaster, Tylenol's capsule poisoning, or Union Carbide's Bhopal tragedy not only can cripple an organization's reputation, but also can cause it enormous monetary loss. It is essential, therefore, that such emergencies be managed intelligently and forthrightly, with the news media, employees, and the community at large.

One key to mitigating a disaster lies in crisis planning. Surprisingly, a study commissioned by Western Union Corporation found that out of 390 of the largest industrial and service companies, only 207—slightly more than half—had plans for informing the public in a crisis.[4] Years ago, in the airline industry, crisis planning meant that "one of the PR man's first responsibilities when a crash occurred was to paint over the company's name" on the wreckage before news photographers arrived.[5] Fortunately, times have changed.

Today, organizations—from airlines to banks, from amusement parks to hospitals—prepare for potential crises in a more thoughtful and deliberate way. Having an agreed-upon crisis plan can be invaluable when the dreaded day occurs. As any organization unfortunate enough to experience a crisis recognizes, when the crisis strikes, seven instant warning signs invariably appear:

1. *Surprise*

When a crisis breaks out, it's usually unexpected. Often, it's a natural disaster—a tornado or hurricane. Sometimes, it's a man-made disaster— robbery, embezzlement, or large loss. Frequently, the first a public relations

Has America become shortsighted?

America once had a vision of its future.

And that vision led us to become the most productive nation on earth, with our citizens enjoying the highest standard of living of any nation in the world.

Today, inflation erodes our economic growth. Inadequate capital investment limits opportunity and undermines our international competitive position. Our companies are hard pressed to keep up with accelerating technological developments. Productivity has been growing much faster in other major industrial nations than it has in the United States.

Why has American economic performance slipped?

Essentially, we seem to have lost sight of what truly drives our economy and what is required to keep our products and ser-vices competitive in world markets. Worse, our vision of the future appears to have narrowed to include only that which is politically fashionable and expedient for the short-term.

It is politically fashionable, for example, to charge that company profits are too high...are a "windfall" ...or are even "obscene." Yet profits constitute the key support for expanding company facilities, financing new research and development, replacing outmoded and inefficient equipment and, ultimately, ensuring greater productivity, higher wages and more jobs.

It's also politically fashionable to demand greater governmental "safeguards," i.e. regulations on the activities of companies. Yet, each year, government regulations cost our society —both companies and individuals—about $100 billion. Much of which could be used instead for new plants, for new products, for new research, for new technology to create new jobs. All of which would make us more competitive in world markets.

It's politically expedient for government—in the interest of "protecting the general welfare"—to spend billions of taxpayer dollars on overregulation without fully weighing costs against benefits. Government overspending ,and the resulting federal budget deficit , remains a primary cause of our nation's most serious problem, inflation.

Clearly, we must, as a nation, restore our vision and, with it, our productive capacity.

In the months ahead, we at Chase intend to speak out on the "productive capacity" question: on inflation, on profits, on government regulation, on business investment, on research and development.

Our reason for doing so is quite straightforward. If, as a nation, we are unable to revitalize our productive capacity, Chase's shareholders, customers and employees—together with millions of other Americans —will pay the price. It's a price we need not, and should not, have to pay.

So, we will speak out— as loudly and clearly as we can. We'll do it in our own self interest. And, we believe, in yours.

CHASE

FIGURE 21–3 Companies such as Chase Manhattan Bank are not reluctant to exercise their First Amendment rights on public issues of national and international concern. *(Courtesy of Chase Manhattan Bank)*

Watering Down the Apple Juice

When a company is accused of selling fraudulent products, it is a serious issue. When the fraudulent products are sold to babies, it is even more serious. But that's exactly the issue with which Beech-Nut Nutrition Corporation was faced in late 1986, when the federal government charged that Beech-Nut and other defendants had intentionally shipped adulterated and misbranded apple juice for babies to 20 states, Puerto Rico, the Virgin Islands, and five foreign countries, with the intent to defraud and mislead.

The government's indictment said that the product that Beech-Nut marketed as 100 percent apple juice was really made from beet sugar, cane sugar syrup, corn syrup, and other ingredients, with little if any apple juice in the mixture. The bogus apple juice cost about 20 percent less to make than real apple juice.

After a year of consultation with the Food and Drug Administration, Beech-Nut agreed to pay a $2 million fine, the largest penalty ever paid under the Food, Drug and Cosmetic Act since its enactment in 1938. The corporation also agreed, as part of a plea arrangement with the government, to pay $140,000 in investigative costs to the FDA. The company pleaded guilty to 215 counts charging that it had shipped mislabeled products purporting to be apple juice. Another 145 counts, including charges of conspiracy and mail fraud, were dismissed as part of the plea agreement. Beech-Nut settled the issue a few days before two of its former top officials, including its former president, were to go on trial for conspiracy to distribute adulterated apple juice.

At its announcement, Beech-Nut's new president, Dr. Richard Theuer, said that the company had taken measures to improve quality control and prevent similar situations from occurring again. He said that the misrepresented juice, although not pure apple juice, contained only "safe food ingredients" and had presented no danger to health. "Under the law Beech-Nut as a corporation is assumed to have the knowledge of the employees about its operation. Rather than engage in a long trial which would not serve the interest of Beech-Nut or its customers, the company chose to plead guilty and put the past behind it," Dr. Theuer said.

In response, the U.S. Attorney assigned to the case said, "It is refreshing to see a corporation come to grips with their wrongdoing and agree to an early resolution by the acceptance of today's fine and plea."

In the winter of 1989, in a small room in the Federal District Court in Brooklyn, NY, the former president of Beech-Nut pleaded guilty to 10 felony counts of violating the Food, Drug and Cosmetic Act. The executive, fifty-six-year-old Niels L. Hoyvald, was fined $100,000 and sentenced to five years' probation and six consecutive months of full-time community service. In the intervening years between the time Beech-Nut was charged and the sentencing, the company's share of the overall baby food market had fallen about 4 percent. Summarized the assistant U.S. Attorney, "This case is a story of corporate greed and irresponsibility."

QUESTIONS

1. How would you assess Beech-Nut's handling of this issue?
2. What was the public relations strategy Beech-Nut employed relative to the public? Relative to its two former employees?
3. If you were Beech-Nut's public relations counsel, what would you do now, in terms of Beech-Nut's credibility?

professional learns of such an event is when the media call and demand to know what immediate action will be taken.

2. *Insufficient information*

Lots of things happen at once. Rumors fly. Wire services want to know why the company's stock is falling. It's difficult to get a grip on everything that's happening.

3. *Escalating events*

The crisis expands. The Stock Exchange wants to know what's going on. Will the organization issue a statement? Are the rumors true? While rumors run rampant, truthful information is difficult to obtain. You want to respond in an orderly manner, but events are unfolding too quickly. This is what Johnson & Johnson experienced, as the reports of deaths from Tylenol kept rising.

4. *Loss of control*

The unfortunate natural outgrowth of escalating events is that too many things are happening simultaneously. Erroneous stories hit the wires and then the newsstands and then the airwaves. As in the case of the Coors' mouse in the can, rampant rumors can't easily be lassoed.

5. *Increased outside scrutiny*

The media, stockbrokers, talk-show hosts, and the public in general feed on rumors. "Helpful" politicians and observers of all stripes volunteer their two cents on what's going on. The media want responses. Investors demand answers. Customers must know what's going on.

6. *Siege mentality*

The organization, understandably, feels surrounded. Lawyers counsel, "Anything we say will be held against us." The easiest thing to do is to say nothing. But does that make sense?

7. *Panic*

With the walls caving in and with leaks too numerous to plug, a sense of panic pervades. In such an environment, it is difficult to convince management to "pull the trigger," to take immediate action, to communicate what's going on.[6]

Communicating in a Crisis

The key communications principle in dealing with a crisis is not to clam up when disaster strikes. The most effective crisis communicators are those who provide prompt, frank, and full information to the media in the eye of the storm. Invariably, the first inclination of executives is to say, "Let's wait until all the facts are in." But as President Carter's press secretary, Jody Powell, used to say, "Bad news is a lot like fish. It doesn't get better with age." In saying nothing, an organization is perceived as already having made a decision. That angers the media and compounds the problem. On the other hand, inexperienced spokespersons, speculating nervously or using emotionally charged language, are even worse.

Most public relations professionals consider the cardinal rule for communications during a crisis to be:

TELL IT ALL AND TELL IT FAST!

As a general rule, when information gets out quickly, rumors are stopped and nerves are calmed. A continuous flow of information indicates that people are working on the problem.[7] Messages should be consistent, using a limited number of spokespersons—preferably only one. Comparisons should be avoided: Don't give people the opportunity to link your accident with a worse one. Statements should be limited to facts, not speculation or guesswork. But as a senior communications manager for Dow Chemical put it:

> The public must be fully informed frequently and accurately through the media from the outset . . . by credible senior spokesmen accustomed to dealing with the media in a responsible, respectful manner, who understand and can explain clearly, in lay language, complex information.[8]

Another key in intelligently communicating in a crisis is to evaluate each media request separately, on the basis of several questions:

1. *What do we gain by participating?* If you have absolutely nothing to gain from an interview, then don't give one. Period.
2. *What are the risks?* This is based on your level of comfort with the medium, who the interviewer is, the amount of preparation time available to you, legal liability, and how much the organization loses if the story is told without the interview.

YOU MAKE THE CALL

The Alar Scare

The "Alar scare" of 1989 is a classic example of how a crisis—even one based on spurious information—can spread like wildfire unless it is immediately challenged.

One cold Sunday night, the agricultural chemical Alar was introduced to 40 million Americans via the CBS-TV show, "60 Minutes." Citing a "study" by the Natural Resources Defense Council (NRDC), "60 Minutes" said that Alar, used as it was on a small portion of America's red apple production, posed an intolerable threat to preschool children, who could develop cancer from it later in life.

Once the dreaded "C" word was aired, all hell broke loose.

- Grocers pulled apples from their shelves.
- School officials in New York City and elsewhere removed apples and apple products from school lunch menus.
- Parents by the thousands swamped Washington, D.C. with protests.
- The government didn't know what to do. The Environmental Protection Agency ordered an emergency temporary ban on the rarely used chemical. However, other government-related experts, like the American Council on Science and Health, weren't so sure and publicly wondered whether the threat was being overstated.
- The media, on the other hand, jumped into the crisis with both feet. NRDC held a Monday morning news conference after the "60 Minutes" show, and 70 journalists and 12 camera crews attended. Actress Meryl Streep and the casts of the popular television shows "L.A. Law" and "Thirty-something" joined the anti-Alar bandwagon. NRDC received coverage in virtually every newspaper and magazine in the land, as well as featured appearances on "The Today Show," "Entertainment Tonight," and the "Phil Donahue Show."

By the time the apple-growing industry got its act together and hired a public relations firm to combat the misinformation, the damage already was done. The Reuters news agency reported that the Alar scare caused an estimated $100 to $140 million in losses to Washington State apple growers alone during 1989.

Ironically, the NRDC "study" proved scientifically questionable. The chairman of the biochemistry department at the University of California at Berkeley claimed that "none of the experts" in the fields of epidemiology or toxicology agreed with the NRDC conclusion that humans were threatened by the tiny trace amounts of carcinogens found in Alar.

No scientific case, in fact, was ever made against Alar. Even worse, the vast majority of apples and apple derivatives were never even touched by the chemical. The public, however, was already convinced.

Somewhere in the middle of the Alar scare, a spokesman for one of the supermarket chains, stampeded into taking a brand of supposedly contaminated apple juice off its shelves, put the matter into irrefutable perspective: "We're dealing with perceptions here. We're not dealing with reality."

QUESTIONS

1. What was wrong with the apple-growing industry's approach in the face of the Alar scare?
2. What else could the industry have done?
3. What does this case suggest about the media's reaction in a crisis?
4. How important are "perceptions" in a crisis like the Alar scare?

3. *Can we get our message across?* Will this particular medium allow us clearly to deliver our message to the public?
4. *Is this audience worth it?* Often, a particular television program or newspaper may not be germane to the specific audience the organization needs to reach.
5. *How will management react?* An important variable in assessing whether to appear is the potential reaction of top management. In the final analysis, you have to explain your recommendation or action to them.
6. *Does your legal liability outweigh the public interest?* This is seldom the case, although company lawyers often disagree.
7. *Is there a better way?* Key question. If an uncontrolled media interview can be avoided, avoid it. However, reaching pertinent publics through the press is often, the best way to communicate in a crisis.[9]

In the final analysis, communicating in a crisis depends on a rigorous analysis of the risks versus the benefits of going public. Communicating effectively also depends on the judgment and experience of the public relations professional. Every call is a close one, and there is no guarantee that the organization will benefit, no matter what course is chosen. One thing is clear: helping navigate the organization through the shoals of a crisis is the ultimate test of a public relations professional.

Summary

Crisis management has become one of the most revered skills in the practice of public relations. Organizations of every variety are faced, sooner or later, with crisis. Nor are crises limited by geographical boundaries. Japan, in recent years, has suffered a rash of major crises and handled them in uniquely Japanese fashion. (When a Japan Air Lines jet crashed in 1985, killing more than 500 people, the airline's president retired after traveling

THE STORY OF A GOVERNMENT THAT ALMOST DIDN'T HAPPEN.

In 1787 a group of concerned citizens wanted to see the proposed Constitution go down to defeat. They viewed it as a plot to install a tyrannical government, not unlike that of the despised British colonial system.

The alarm was triggered not by what they saw, but by what they didn't see.

After the injustices the colonies suffered under the Crown, how could they be expected to ratify a document that contained no explicit guarantee for the protection of individual freedoms?

Indeed, our Minister to France, Thomas Jefferson, wrote James Madison from Paris expressing his concern about "the omission of a bill of rights...providing clearly...for freedom of religion, freedom of the press, protection against standing armies, and restriction against monopolies."

Ultimately, the proposed Constitution was ratified, but not before reassurances were given that it would be amended to correct its shortcomings. That process took 2½ years, but in the end we had something very special— the Bill of Rights.

We had what President Franklin D. Roosevelt described as "the great American charter of personal liberty and human dignity."

Not just a piece of parchment, we had a living, breathing testament to the individual freedoms of men and women.

For 200 years we've been enjoying these rights and exercising them in our everyday lives. Little wonder that we sometimes fall into the trap of taking them for granted.

The government that almost didn't happen could still unravel unless we all remain vigilant and work to make the Bill of Rights work better for everyone.

Philip Morris Companies Inc.

KRAFT GENERAL FOODS · MILLER BREWING COMPANY · PHILIP MORRIS U.S.A.

Join Philip Morris and the National Archives in celebrating the 200th anniversary of the Bill of Rights. For a free copy of this historic document, call 1-800-552-2222, or write Bill of Rights · Philip Morris Companies Inc. · 2020 Pennsylvania Ave. N.W. · Suite 533 · Washington D.C. 20006

FIGURE 21–4   Sometimes, organizations don't even realize they've got a crisis on their hands until someone calls them on it. Such was the case in 1989, when Philip Morris ran national ads in support of the National Archives' celebration of the 200th anniversary of the Bill of Rights. Charging that the agreement between the company and the Archives "smears the Bill of Rights with the blood of all Americans killed as a result of smoking," the Public Citizen Health Research Group called on Congress to nullify the deal. Answered the vice-president of corporate affairs for Philip Morris, "What you see is what you get . . . There's no subliminal message at all." *(Courtesy of Philip Morris Companies Inc.)*

across the country personally to express his apologies to the families of the victims.)

The issues that confront society—from consumerism to energy and the environment, from health and nutrition to corporate social responsibility and minority rights, from peace and disarmament to private enterprise—will not soon abate. Indeed, issues such as Acquired Immune Deficiency Syndrome (AIDS) have gripped society to such a dramatic degree that no organization can be silent on the topic.

FIGURE 21−5 The issue of health and nutrition is of vital importance in the 1990s. The American Cancer Society used *Star Trek* favorite Mr. Spock to offer this gesture of salutation common to the inhabitants of his home planet, Vulcan. *(Courtesy of American Cancer Society)*

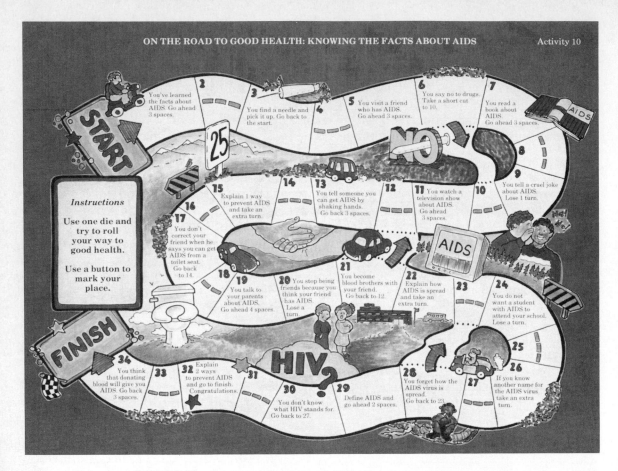

FIGURE 21–6 Canadian Life and Health Insurance companies teamed up with the Canadian Public Health Association to produce Canada's first AIDS teaching resource for fifth- and sixth-grade students. The package included a student book-let, teacher's guide, word games, and quizzes about the deadly disease. *(Courtesy of Canadian Life and Health Insurance Inc.)*

All of this suggests that experienced and knowledgeable crisis managers, who can skillfully navigate and effectively communicate, turning crisis into opportunity, will be valuable resources for organizations in the 1990s. In the years ahead, few challenges will be more significant for public relations professionals than helping to manage crisis.

DISCUSSION STARTERS

1. What is meant by the term *issues management*?
2. How can an organization influence the development of an issue in society?
3. What are the general steps in implementing an issues management program?
4. What are the usual stages that an organization experiences in a crisis?

5. What is the cardinal rule for communicating in a crisis?
6. What are the keys to successful crisis communication?
7. Contrast the way Beech-Nut handled its apple juice crisis with the way that Coors handled its mouse crisis.
8. What was the primary lesson to be learned in industry's handling of the Alar scare?
9. What was the crisis that Philip Morris confronted when it sponsored the anniversary of the Bill of Rights?
10. What are likely to be the flashpoint issues in the 1990s?

NOTES

1. Andrew Pollack, "Accepting the Blame," *The New York Times,* 30 July 1990, D1.
2. "Issues Management Conference—A Special Report," *Corporate Public Issues* 7, no. 23 (December 1, 1982): 1–2.
3. Michael Lev, "Give Me Your Tired, Your Rusty . . ." *The New York Times,* 6 October 1990, D1.
4. "Crisis: Not All Firms Prepared," *USA Today,* 16 August 1984.
5. Thomas Petzinger, Jr., "When Disaster Comes, Public-Relations Men Won't Be Far Behind," *The Wall Street Journal,* 23 August 1979, 1.
6. Fraser P. Seitel, "Communicating in Crisis," *United States Banker* (December 1990): 49.
7. Frank M. Corrado, *Media for Managers* (Englewood Cliffs, NJ: Prentice-Hall, 1984).

TOP OF THE SHELF

Sauerhaft, Stan, and Chris Atkins. *Image Wars.*
New York: John Wiley, 1989.

The success or failure of a firm may have less to do with its goods and services than with its public image. At least that's the premise of *Image Wars.*

Stan Sauerhaft and Chris Atkins, two Burson-Marsteller executives, write that corporate image is one of a company's most valuable assets, influencing everything from staff recruitment to profits. The key, then, is to enhance the corporate identity in good times and protect and preserve it during difficult periods. *Image Wars* provides the tools for such image maintenance, emphasizing event sponsorship, philanthropy, and speaking out on public issues as ways to foster and alter public perceptions. Sauerhaft and Atkins say these activities should be publicized through press releases, media events, and political action committees. The authors, who reinforce their theory with timely examples, also devote chapters to financial issues and crisis situations.

Firms that can't shake an unfavorable image won't remain in business for long. Practitioners need to learn how to nurture and defend their companies' reputations, and *Image Wars* is a highly qualified teacher.

8. Michael Cooper, "Crisis Public Relations," *Public Relations Journal* (November 1981): 53.

9. Martin Arnold, "Crisis Communication," *IABC Communication World* (June 1989): 44.

SUGGESTED READINGS

Banta, William. *AIDS in the Workplace: Legal and Practical Answers*. Lexington, MA: Lexington Books, 1987.

Bergner, Douglas J., ed. *Public Interest Profiles*. 5th ed. Washington, DC: Foundation for Public Affairs, 1987 (1019 19th St., NW, 20036).

Bernstein, Alan. *Emergency Public Relations Manual*. 3rd ed. Highland Park, NJ: Pase, 1988 (P.O. Box 1299 08904).

Blakey, H. Allen. *Environmental Communications and Public Relations Handbook*. Rockville, MD: Government Institute Inc., 1989 (966 Hungerford Dr. 20850).

Bogue, Donald. *The Population of the U.S.: Historical Trends & Future Projections*. Ithaca, NY: American Demographics, 1988 (P.O. Box 68 14851).

Brown, Kathleen, and Joan Turner. *AIDS: Policies and Programs for the Workplace*. New York: Van Nostrand Reinhold, 1989.

Buchholz, Rogene. *Business Environment and Public Policy: Implications for Management*. Englewood Cliffs, NJ: Prentice-Hall, 1989.

Ciabattari, Jane. *Winning Moves: How to Survive (& Manage) a Corporate Shakeup*. New York: Rawson Associates, 1988 (866 Third Ave. 10022).

Cook, Timothy E. *Making Laws & Making News*. Washington, DC: The Brookings Institution, 1989 (1775 Massachusetts Avenue, NW 20036).

Cost Effective Management for Today's Public Affairs. Washington, DC: Public Affairs Council, 1987.

"Crisis Can Occur at Anytime, Anywhere, to Any Organization." *Public Relations Reporter* (November 24, 1986): 3.

Crisis Management: A Workbook for Survival. Belleville, NJ: The Lempert Co., 1987.

Ewing, Raymond, P. *Managing the New Bottom Line: Issues Management for Top Executives*. Homewood, IL: Dow Jones-Irwin, 1987.

Federal Register. (Available from Superintendent of Documents, Government Printing Office, Washington DC, 20402.) The *Federal Register* provides a method of tracking rules and regulations from government agencies and keeping abreast of changes.

Fink, Steven. *Crisis Management: Planning for the Inevitable*. New York: AMACOM, 1986 (135 W. 50th St. 10020).

The Fundamentals of Issue Management. Monograph. (Available from Public Affairs Council, 1220 16th St., NW, Washington, DC 20036.)

Griswold, Denny, ed. *PR News*. (Available from PR News, 127 E. 80th St., New York, NY 10021.) This weekly newsletter carries industry news and case studies illustrating public relations problems and solutions.

Health, Robert. *Strategic Issues Management*. San Francisco: Jossey-Bass, 1988.

Health, Robert, and Richard Nelson. *Issues Management*. San Mateo, CA: Sage, 1986.

"It Can Happen to Anyone in a Few Short Seconds." *PR Week* (April 18–24, 1988): 10, 11.

Irvine, Robert, B. *When You Are the Headline: Managing a News Story*. Homewood, IL: Dow Jones-Irwin, 1987.

Janis, Irving L. *Crucial Decisions: Leadership in Policy Making and Crisis Management.* New York: Free Press, 1988.

Lerbinger, Otto. *Managing Corporate Crises: Strategies for Executives.* Boston, MA: Barrington Press, 1986 (P.O. Box 291, Boston University Station 02215).

Marcus, Alfred. *Business Strategy & Public Policy.* Westport, CT: Quorum Books, 1987.

Merriam, John, and Joel Makower. *Trend Watching.* New York: AMACOM, 1988 (135 W. 50th St.).

Meyers, Gerald. *When It Hits the Fan.* Scarborough, Ontario: The New American Library of Canada Limited, 1987.

Morrison, Catherine. *Managing Corporate Political Action Committees.* New York: Conference Board, 1986 (845 Third Ave. 10022).

————. *Forecasting Public Affairs Priorities.* New York: Conference Board, 1987 (845 Third Ave. 10022).

Murphy, Priscilla. "Using Games as a Model for Crisis Communications," *Public Relations Review,* vol. 13, no. 4: 19–28.

O'Dwyer, Jack, ed. *Jack O'Dwyer's Newsletter.* Weekly newsletter. (Available from 271 Madison Ave., New York, NY 10016.)

Pinsdorf, Marion. *Communicating When Your Company Is Under Siege.* Lexington, MA: Lexington Books, 1986.

PR Reporter. Weekly Newsletter. (Available from Box 600, Exeter, NH 03833.)

Public Relations Review. Quarterly. (Available from the Foundation for Public Relations Research and Education, University of Maryland College of Journalism, College Park, MD 20742.)

Rautenberg, Steven. "Crisis Public Relations in the Age of Apology: From Chernobyl to Monongahela." Address to the American Bankers Association Security and Planning Conference, Orlando, FL, January 28, 1988.

Remmes, Harold. *Lobbying for Your Cause.* Babylon, NY: Pilot Books, 1986 (103 Cooper St. 11702.)

Sauerhaft, Stan, and Chris Atkins. *Image Wars.* New York: John Wiley, 1989.

CASE STUDY   The Tylenol Murders

For close to 100 years, Johnson & Johnson Company of New Brunswick, NJ, was the epitome of a well-managed, highly profitable, and tight-lipped consumer products manufacturer.

Round I

All that changed on the morning of September 30, 1982, when Johnson & Johnson (J&J) faced as devastating a public relations problem as had confronted any company in history. It was on that morning that Johnson & Johnson management learned that its premier product, extra-strength Tylenol, had been used as a murder weapon to kill three people. In the days that followed, another three people died from swallowing Tylenol capsules loaded with cyanide. And although all the cyanide deaths occurred in Chicago, reports from other parts of the country also implicated extra-strength Tylenol capsules in illnesses of various sorts. These latter reports were later proved to be unfounded, but Johnson & Johnson and its

Tylenol-producing subsidiary, McNeil Consumer Products Company, found themselves at the center of a public relations trauma, the likes of which few companies had ever experienced.

Tylenol had been an astoundingly profitable product for Johnson & Johnson. At the time of the Tylenol murders, the product held 35 percent of the $1 billion analgesic market. It contributed an estimated 7 percent to J&J's worldwide sales and almost 20 percent to its profits. Throughout the years, Johnson & Johnson had not been—and hadn't needed to be—a particularly high-profile company. Its chairman, James E. Burke, who had been with the company almost 30 years, had never appeared on television and had rarely participated in print interviews.

Johnson & Johnson management, understandably, was caught totally by surprise when the news hit. Initially, Johnson & Johnson had no facts and, indeed, learned much of its information from the media calls that inundated the firm from the beginning. The company recognized that it needed the media to get out as much information to the public as quickly as possible to prevent a panic. Therefore, almost immediately, Johnson & Johnson made a key decision: to open its doors to the media.

On the second day of the crisis, Johnson & Johnson discovered that an earlier statement, that no cyanide was used on its premises, was wrong. The company didn't hesitate. Its public relations department quickly announced that the earlier information had been false. Even though the reversal embarrassed the company briefly, Johnson & Johnson's openness was hailed and made up for any damage to its credibility.

Early on in the crisis, the company was largely convinced that the poisonings had not occurred at any of its plants. Nonethe-less, Johnson & Johnson recalled an entire lot of 93,000 bottles of extra-strength Tylenol associated with the reported murders. In the process, it telegrammed warnings to doctors, hospitals, and distributors, at a cost of half a million dollars. McNeil also suspended all Tylenol advertising to reduce attention to the product.

By the second day, the company was convinced that the tampering had taken place during Chicago distribution and not in the manufacturing process. Therefore, a total Tylenol recall did not seem obligatory. Chairman Burke himself leaned toward immediately recalling all extra-strength Tylenol capsules, but after consulting with the Federal Bureau of Investigation, the J&J chairman decided not to recall all capsules. The FBI was worried that a precipitous recall would encourage copycat poisoning attempts. Nonetheless, five days later, when a copycat strychnine poisoning occurred in California, Johnson & Johnson did recall all extra-strength Tylenol capsules—31 million bottles—at a cost of over $100 million.

Although the company knew it had done nothing wrong, J&J resisted the temptation to disclaim any possible connection between its product and the murders. Rather, even as it moved quickly to trace the lot numbers of the poisoned packages, it also posted a $100,000 reward for the killer. Through advertisements promising to exchange capsules for tablets, through thousands of letters to the trade, and through statements to the media, the company hoped to put the incident into proper perspective.

At the same time, Johnson & Johnson commissioned a nationwide opinion survey to assess the consumer implications of the Tylenol poisonings. The good news was that 87 percent of Tylenol users surveyed said they realized the maker of Tylenol was not responsible for the deaths. The bad news

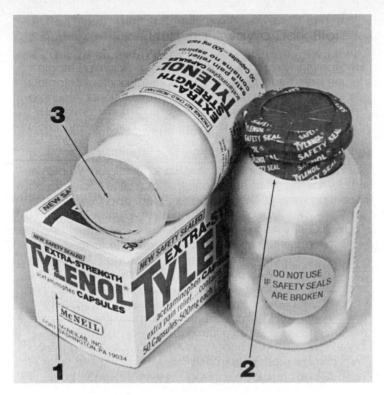

FIGURE 21–7   The triple-safety-sealed, tamper-resistant package for Tylenol capsules had (1) glued flaps on the outer box, (2) a tight plastic neck seal, and (3) a strong inner foil seal over the mouth of the bottle. A bright yellow label on the bottle was imprinted with a red warning, "Do not use if safety seals are broken." As it turned out, all these precautions didn't work. *(Courtesy of Johnson & Johnson)*

was that, although a high percentage didn't blame Tylenol, 61 percent still said they were not likely to buy extra-strength Tylenol capsules in the future. In other words, even though most consumers knew the deaths weren't Tylenol's fault, they still feared using the product.

But Chairman Burke and Johnson & Johnson weren't about to knuckle under to the deranged saboteur or saboteurs who poisoned their product. Despite predictions of the imminent demise of extra-strength Tylenol, Johnson & Johnson decided to relaunch the product in a new triple-safety-sealed, tamper-resistant package (Figure 21–7). Many on Wall Street and in the marketing community were stunned by Johnson & Johnson's bold decision.

But so confident was Johnson & Johnson management, it launched an all-out media blitz to make sure that people understood its commitment. Chairman Burke appeared on the widely watched Phil Donahue network television program and skillfully handled 60 minutes of intense public questioning. The investigative news program "60 Minutes"— the scourge of corporate America—was invited by Johnson & Johnson to film its executive strategy sessions to prepare for the new launch. When the program was aired, reporter Mike Wallace concluded that although Wall Street had been ready at first to write off the company, it was now "hedging its bets because of J&J's stunning campaign of facts, money, the media, and truth."

Finally, on November 11, 1982, less than two months after the murders, Tylenol management held an elaborate video press conference in New York City, beamed to additional locations around the country, to introduce the new extra-strength Tylenol package. Said Tylenol's chairman to the media,

> It is our job at Johnson & Johnson to ensure the survival of Tylenol, and we are pledged to do this. While we consider this crime an assault on society, we are nevertheless ready to fulfill our responsibility, which includes paying the price of this heinous crime. But I urge you not to make Tylenol the scapegoat.

In the days and months that followed Burke's news conference, it became clear that Tylenol would not become a scapegoat. In fact, by the beginning of 1983, Tylenol had recaptured an astounding 95 percent of its prior market share. Morale at the company, according to its chairman, was "higher than in years" (Figure 21–8). The euphoria lasted until February 1986, when, unbelievably, tragedy struck again.

Round II

Late in the evening of February 10, 1986, news reports began to circulate that a woman had died in Yonkers, NY, after taking poisoned capsules of extra-strength Tylenol. The nightmare for Johnson & Johnson began anew.

Once again, the company sprang into action. Chairman Burke addressed reporters at a news conference a day after the incident. A phone survey found that the public didn't blame the company. With discovery of other poisoned Tylenol capsules two days later, the nightmare intensified. The company recorded 15,000 toll-free calls to its Tylenol hotline. And, once again, production of Tylenol capsules was halted. "I'm heartsick," Burke told the press. "We didn't believe it could happen again, and nobody else did either."

This time, although Tylenol earned Johnson & Johnson some 13 percent of the company's net profits, the firm decided once and for all to cease production of its over-the-counter medications in capsule form. It offered to replace all unused Tylenol capsules with new Tylenol caplets, a solid form of medication that was less tamper-prone (Figure 21–9). This time the withdrawal of its capsules cost Johnson & Johnson upward of $150 million after taxes.

And, once again, in the face of tragedy, the company and its chairman received high marks. As President Reagan said at a White House reception two weeks after the crisis hit, "Jim Burke of Johnson & Johnson, you have our deepest appreciation for living up to the highest ideals of corporate responsibility and grace under pressure."*

---

*For further information on the first round of Tylenol murders, see Jerry Knight, "Tylenol's Maker Shows How to Respond to Crisis," *The Washington Post*, 11 October 1982, 1; Thomas Moore, "The Fight to Save Tylenol," *Fortune* (November 29, 1982): 48; Michael Waldholz, "Tylenol Regains Most of No. 1 Market Share, Amazing Doomsayers," *The Wall Street Journal*, 24 December 1982, 1, 19; and "60 Minutes," CBS-TV, December 19, 1982.

For further information on the second round of Tylenol murders, see Irvin Molotsky, "Tylenol Maker Hopeful on Solving Poisoning Case," *The New York Times*, 20 February 1986; Steven Prokesch, "A Leader in a Crisis," *The New York Times*, 19 February 1986, B4; Michael Waldholz, "For Tylenol's Manufacturer, The Dilemma Is to Be Aggressive—But Not Appear Pushy," *The Wall Street Journal*, 20 February 1986, 27; and "Tylenol II: How a Company Responds to a Calamity," *U.S. News & World Report* (February 24, 1986): 49.

Our Credo

We believe our first responsibility is to the doctors, nurses and patients,
to mothers and all others who use our products and services.
In meeting their needs everything we do must be of high quality.
We must constantly strive to reduce our costs
in order to maintain reasonable prices.
Customers' orders must be serviced promptly and accurately.
Our suppliers and distributors must have an opportunity
to make a fair profit.

We are responsible to our employees,
the men and women who work with us throughout the world.
Everyone must be considered as an individual.
We must respect their dignity and recognize their merit.
They must have a sense of security in their jobs.
Compensation must be fair and adequate,
and working conditions clean, orderly and safe.
Employees must feel free to make suggestions and complaints.
There must be equal opportunity for employment, development
and advancement for those qualified.
We must provide competent management,
and their actions must be just and ethical.

We are responsible to the communities in which we live and work
and to the world community as well.
We must be good citizens — support good works and charities
and bear our fair share of taxes.
We must encourage civic improvements and better health and education.
We must maintain in good order
the property we are privileged to use,
protecting the environment and natural resources.

Our final responsibility is to our stockholders.
Business must make a sound profit.
We must experiment with new ideas.
Research must be carried on, innovative programs developed
and mistakes paid for.
New equipment must be purchased, new facilities provided
and new products launched.
Reserves must be created to provide for adverse times.
When we operate according to these principles,
the stockholders should realize a fair return.

Johnson & Johnson

FIGURE 21–8   *(Courtesy of Johnson & Johnson)*

QUESTIONS

1. What might have been the consequences if J&J had decided to "tough out" the first reports of Tylenol-related deaths and not recall the product?

2. What other public relations options did J&J have in responding to the first round of Tylenol murders?

3. Do you think the company made a wise decision by reintroducing extra-strength Tylenol?

If you have TYLENOL capsules, we'll replace them with TYLENOL caplets.

And we'll do it at our expense.

As you know, there has been a tragic event. A small number of Extra-Strength TYLENOL Capsules in one isolated area in New York have been criminally tampered with.

This was an outrageous act which damages all of us.

Both federal and local authorities have established that it was only capsules that were tampered with.

In order to prevent any further capsule tampering, we have removed all our capsules from your retailers' shelves. This includes Regular and Extra-Strength TYLENOL capsules, CO-TYLENOL capsules, Maximum-Strength TYLENOL Sinus Medication capsules, Extra-Strength SINE-AID capsules, and DIMENSYN Menstrual Relief capsules.

And Johnson & Johnson's McNeil Consumer Products Company has decided to cease the manufacture, sale, and distribution of **all** capsule forms of over-the-counter medicines.

If you're a regular capsule user, you may be wondering what to use instead. That's why we'd like you to try TYLENOL caplets.

The caplet is a solid form of TYLENOL pain reliever, which research has proven is the form most preferred by consumers. Unlike tablets, it is specially shaped and coated for easy, comfortable swallowing.

And the caplet delivers a full extra-strength dose quickly and effectively.

So, if you have any TYLENOL Capsules in your home, do one of the following:

1. Return the bottles with the unused portion to us, together with your name and address on the form below. And we'll replace your TYLENOL capsules with TYLENOL Caplets (or tablets, if you prefer). We'll also refund your postage. Or...

2. If you prefer, you can receive a cash refund for the unused capsules by sending the bottle to us along with a letter requesting the refund.

We are taking this step because, for the past 25 years, over 100 million Americans have made TYLENOL products a trusted part of their health care.

We're continuing to do everything we can to keep your trust.

Send to:

TYLENOL Capsule Exchange
P.O. Box 2000
Maple Plain, MN 55348

Please send my coupon for free replacement caplets or tablets to:

Please print

Name _____

Address _____

City _____

State _____ Zip _____

Offer expires May 1, 1986   Necessary

FIGURE 21–9   *(Courtesy of Johnson & Johnson)*

4. In light of the response of other companies not to move precipitously when faced with a crisis, do you think J&J should have acted so quickly to remove the Tylenol product when the second round of Tylenol murders occurred in 1986?

5. What specific lessons can be derived from the way in which J&J handled the public relations aspects of these tragedies?

Tips from the Top

JOHN SCANLON

John Scanlon has pioneered the field of litigation public relations, first as senior executive vice-president of Daniel J. Edelman, Inc. and today at Sawyer/Miller. Among his clients Scanlon represented CBS in its suit by General Westmoreland and the *Boston Globe* in its suit by politician John Lakian. In a long and varied career, Scanlon has specialized in entertainment public relations, issues management, and politics. He served as deputy commissioner for economic development under New York City Mayor John V. Lindsay and also as press secretary for the city's Municipal Assistance Corporation during New York's fiscal crisis in 1975.

What is issues management?
Issues management anticipates and prepares organizations, through strategic planning, to predict problems, anticipate threats, minimize surprises, and develop coalitions to effect defined goals and implant solutions.

How important is issues management?
Issues management is essential to contemporary business organizations. To remain passive to emerging public disputes and to fail to plan for them ensures that someone else will frame the issue.

Can an organization like CBS really manage issues like the ones involved in the Westmoreland case?
Yes. In the Westmoreland/CBS case the network could have chosen simply to respond to the media. By developing a strategy, CBS recaptured the ability to frame the dispute on its terms.

Do the media today recognize the value of issues management?
It is ironic that the media are remarkably inexperienced when they are the focus of a story. We have counseled several media clients, and they have indicated a new respect for the PR business as a result of the experiences.

How can an organization keep in front of an emerging issue?
Organizations can keep in front of issues by scanning the "nonprice" [i.e., intangible] environments of the culture. A company futurist, if you will, should follow changing values and political and general trends, and thereby anticipate issues. These issues should then be ranked by im-

pact, probability, and timing. Finally, policies and strategies should be devised prior to implementing programs.

How important are media relationships in managing public issues?

Media relations are extremely important. News unreported is of no impact. Issues tend to be more abstract and less dramatic than breaking news. They are, in short, not "mediagenic." Long-term and credible relationships with media can go far in selling such stories.

What are the basics in helping manage an issue for a client?

The total confidence of the client is important. Full and total access to all the appropriate information is paramount. But accurate and thorough research is and will always be the essential key to proper issues management. In short, a thorough understanding of the issue is critical.

Public Relations and the Law

The legal and public relations professions have always had an uneasy alliance. Public relations practitioners must always understand the legal implications of any issue with which they become involved, and a firm's legal position must always be the first consideration. Lawyers, correctly, must uphold an organization's standing in a court of law. However, public relations professionals are concerned with an organization's standing in another court: the court of public opinion. Whereas a lawyer's job is to tell an organization what it must do, a public relations professional's job is to tell the organization what it should do. And there's a big difference.

From a legal point of view, normally the less an organization says prior to its day in court, the better. In that way, the opposition can't gain any new ammunition that will become part of the public record. From a public relations standpoint, though, it may often make sense to go public early on, especially if the organization's integrity or credibility is being called into public question. Such different views often manifest themselves in different advice. A smart general manager carefully weighs both legal and public relations counsel before making a decision.

It also should be noted that law and ethics are interrelated. The PRSA Code of Professional Standards (Appendix A) notes that many activities that are unethical are also illegal. However, there are instances where something is perfectly legal but unethical, and other instances where things might be illegal but otherwise ethical. Thus, when a public relations professional reflects on what course to take in a particular situation, he or she must not only consider the legal ramifications, but also the ethical considerations.[1]

This chapter will examine the relationship between the law and public relations, and the more prominent role the law plays in public relations practice. This discussion will not be all-encompassing. Rather, it will introduce the legal concerns of public relations professionals today—First Amendment considerations, insider trading, disclosure law, ethics law, privacy law, and copyright law—concerns that have become primary for public relations in the 1990s.

Public Relations and the First Amendment

Any discussion of law and public relations should start with the First Amendment, which states: "Congress shall make no law . . . abridging the freedom of speech or the press." The First Amendment is the cornerstone of free speech in our society: what distinguishes America from many other nations.

Although the decade has barely begun, the 1990s already have witnessed a fusillade of attacks on the First Amendment.

◆ In the latter part of 1989, the Supreme Court gave state and federal officials broader leeway under the First Amendment to restrict the free speech rights of corporations. Commercial messages had been entitled to First Amendment protection since 1976. In a landmark 1978 case, *First National Bank of Boston v. Bellotti*, the Supreme Court struck down a Massachusetts law that permitted a business corporation to speak only on those issues "that materially affect its business, property, or assets."

But in the 1989 decision, the court continued cutting back corporate free speech, particularly if it was found to be "misleading."[2]

◆ In the summer of 1990, the rap group 2 Live Crew was arrested in Hollywood, FL, when they sang tunes from their album, "As Nasty as They Want to Be," whose sexual explicitness a federal judge ruled was obscene.

◆ That same summer, North Carolina Senator Jesse Helms introduced an amendment to restrict the National Endowment for the Arts from funding "obscene or indecent materials," defined as a whole host of antisocial acts (Figure 22–1).

◆ In November 1990, after a trial judge forbade the Cable News Network from playing a tape of a conversation between imprisoned former Panamanian leader General Manuel Noriega and his lawyers, CNN defied the judge and played the tape on the air. Thus, broadcasters found themselves fighting a battle they thought they had won long ago: their right, under the First Amendment, not to be stopped in advance from printing or televising the news.[3]

◆ That same month, the Burger King Corporation, without explanation, took out large newspaper advertisements all over the country to say that the fast-food company "wishes to go on record as supporting traditional American values on television." Although Burger King denied it, the ads

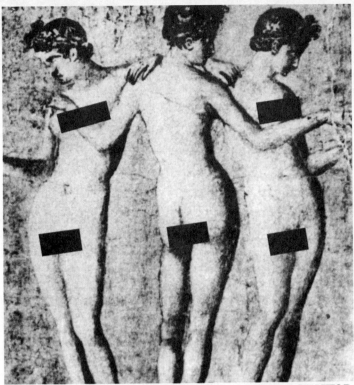

IMAGINE IF JESSE HELMS HAD BEEN A ROMAN SENATOR.

While one can only imagine the impact Mr. Helms might have had on the arts 2,000 years ago, it's tragically clear that he poses a serious threat to artistic freedom today.

The Senator—and a small, yet highly vocal minority—want to restrict the National Endowment for the Arts (which for the past 25 years has provided support for over 80,000 cultural projects nationwide) from funding anything they consider "indecent or obscene."

And though this type of censorship seems implausible in our society, this well-funded group of extremists has organized a massive campaign to pressure Congress to vote their way.

That's why it's imperative that your opinion be heard, too.

To show that you strongly endorse freedom of the arts, please call the toll-free number.

When you do, two pre-written Western Union messages will be sent to Congress in your name.

And perhaps in another 2,000 years, people will still be appreciating your concern.

People For The American Way
ACTION FUND

SEND A MESSAGE TO CONGRESS.
1-800-257-4900
OPERATOR 9681

$6.75 will be charged to your phone bill for two messages. $1.00 of this amount will help defray the cost of this ad.

FIGURE 22—1 The arts community was chilled in 1990 by attempts by Senator Jesse Helms to restrict federal funding from anything considered "indecent or obscene." *(Courtesy of People for the American Way)*

apparently were provoked by a religious group's threat of boycotting the chain because the company sponsored TV shows that were "against family values."[4] Burger King, evidently embarrassed about the First Amendment controversy, refused to have its "Open Letter to the American People" ad reprinted in this book.

As these recent skirmishes suggest, interpreting the First Amendment is no simple matter. One person's definition of "obscenity" may be another's definition of "art." Interestingly, in 1990, the case against 2 Live Crew was dismissed, as was a celebrated case against the Cincinnati Contemporary Arts Center that had exhibited a graphic retrospective on the effects of AIDS. Despite continuing challenges to the First Amendment, Americans continue to enjoy broad freedom of speech and expression. Because the First Amendment lies at the heart of the communications business, defending it is a front-line responsibility of the public relations profession.

Public Relations and Insider Trading

Every public relations professional should know the laws that govern an organization. A practitioner in a hospital should have a general understanding of health care law. A practitioner working for a nonprofit organization should understand the laws that govern donors and recipients. A practitioner who works in a particular industry—chemicals, computers, sports—should understand the laws germane to that particular area.

Nowhere in public relations practice is an understanding of the law more important than in the area of financial disclosure. Every public company has an obligation to deal frankly, comprehensively, and immediately with any information that is considered material in a decision to buy, sell, or even hold the organization's securities. The Securities and Exchange Commission (SEC)—through a series of court cases, consent decrees, complaints, and comments over the years—has painted a general portrait of disclosure requirements for practitioners (see Appendix E), with which all practitioners in public companies should be familiar.

As mentioned in Chapter 19, the SEC's overriding concern is that all investors have an opportunity to learn about material information as promptly as possible. Through its general antifraud statute, Rule 10b-5 of the Securities and Exchange Act, the SEC strictly prohibits the dissemination of false or misleading information to investors. It also prohibits insider trading of securities on the basis of material information not disclosed to the public.

In recent years, the public has been shocked by a series of celebrated cases involving the use of insider information to amass illegal securities gains. The two most celebrated insider trading cases were those of Ivan Boesky and Michael Milken, Wall Street legends who were both slapped with nine-figure fines and jail terms. A host of their associates, equally guilty of insider trading violations, also were dispatched to the slammer.

Nor have journalists escaped the ignominy of insider trading convictions. The most famous case involved a *Wall Street Journal* reporter, R. Foster Winans, Jr., who was convicted in the summer of 1985 of illegally using his newspaper column in a get-rich-quick stock-trading scheme. Basically, Winans gave favorable opinions about companies in which a couple of his stockbroker friends had already invested heavily. The stocks then generally went up, the brokers and their clients profited handsomely, and Winans was sentenced to prison.

The Supreme Court, in 1987, upheld Winans' conviction for securities fraud by the narrowest of votes. In so doing, the court reasoned that by "misappropriating information belonging to the *Journal,*" Winans had violated the newspaper's intangible property rights. According to legal experts, this ruling has widespread implications for anyone with access to business information, including public relations professionals.

What the Supreme Court ruling means, in effect, is that an employer can adopt work rules or a code of ethics that can carry a criminal penalty. This may create problems for those, like public relations people, who share information with journalists; for whistle-blowers, who could be threatened with prosecution for unauthorized disclosure of confidential information; or for anyone involved in the dissemination of sensitive company data.

The court acted forcefully on the question of property rights in the Winans case and, in so doing, left the way open for Congress and the courts to define insider trading as theft. As one victim in the case, *The Wall Street Journal,* summarized it, "Clearly Mr. Winans did wrong, but the law will develop more soundly in the future if everyone understands the nature of the crime: not buying and selling stocks but stealing property."[5]

Public Relations and Disclosure Law

Besides cracking down on insider trading, the SEC has also challenged public relations firms on the accuracy of information they disseminate for clients. In 1982 the SEC issued a 95-page release, "Adoption of Integrated Disclosure System," which attempted to bring some order to the chaotic SEC requirements. Essentially, the new document tried to make more uniform the instructions governing corporate disclosure of information. Today, in an environment of mergers, takeovers, leveraged buyouts, and the incessant rumors that circulate around them, a knowledge of disclosure law, a sensitivity to disclosure requirements, and a bias toward disclosing rather than withholding material information are important attributes of public relations officials.

Public Relations and Ethics Law

The laws regarding ethical misconduct in society have gotten quite a workout in recent years. Regrettably, public relations practitioners have, in several well-known cases, been at the center of the storm. In 1988, Lyn Nofziger, former White House political director and communications counselor, was sentenced to 90 days in prison and fined $30,000 for violating the Federal Ethics in Government Act, which forbids lobbying former contacts within one year of leaving the government. The clients with which Nofziger was associated included Wedtech Corporation, a New York City–based minority contractor that later became the central focus in another ethics investigation surrounding Attorney General Edwin Meese.

Also in 1988, former White House Deputy Chief of Staff Michael K. Deaver, another well-known public relations professional, was found guilty of perjury—lying to a grand jury—about his lobbying activities. He also faced a lengthy jail sentence and a serious fine. In response, Deaver railed against the "outrageousness of congressmen saying that I violated the public trust, when they go out and make all the money they want on speaking fees" paid for by special-interest groups.[6]

Deaver had a point. Some of the most powerful representatives in Congress—from former House Speaker Jim Wright to former Banking Committee chairman Ferdnand St. Germain to the 1990 "Keating Five" senators—were also called on the carpet and accused of violating government ethics laws.

The problems of Nofziger and Deaver called into question the role of lobbyists in government. As explained in Chapter 16, the activities of lobbyists have been closely watched by Congress since the imposition of the Lobbying Act of 1947. In recent years, however, the practice of lobbying has expanded greatly.

Complicating the lobbyist issue still further, foreign governments are particularly eager to retain savvy Washington insiders to guide them through the bureaucratic and congressional maze and polish their images in the United States. Public relations counselors are strictly mandated by law to register the foreign entities they represent. However, in recent years a number of representatives of foreign clients have been the subject of scandals and legal investigations. By 1988, there were signs that the public had had enough of international ethics violations. In one jury trial in Kentucky, two former Ashland Oil vice-presidents—who had lost their jobs in 1983 because they refused, first, to pay bribes to foreign officials and, then, to lie about the bribes—were awarded $69 million for lost pay and punitive damages against the company. Ashland Oil immediately appealed the landmark verdict.

The increasing number of government officials who resign to become play-for-pay lobbyists may indicate that those who govern and those who attempt to influence them will in the future be scrutinized more closely for how ethically they do business and how scrupulously they follow the law. The lingering legal problems of prominent public relations people like Nofziger and Deaver and the increasing concern in all sectors of society for more ethical behavior may ensure this.

Public Relations and Privacy Law

The laws that govern a person's privacy also have implications for the public relations profession. Privacy laws, particularly those that touch on libel and slander by the media, are curious indeed. When such alleged defamation involves a public figure, the laws get even more curious. Generally, the privacy of an ordinary citizen is protected under the law. A citizen in the limelight, however, has a more difficult problem, especially in proving defamation of character.

To prove such a charge, a public figure must show that the media acted with actual malice in its reporting. "Actual malice" in a public figure slander case means that statements have been published with the knowledge that they were false or with reckless disregard for whether the statements were false. In a landmark case in 1964, *New York Times v. Sullivan*, the Supreme Court nullified a libel award of $500,000 to an Alabama police official, holding that no damages could be awarded "in actions brought by public officials against critics of their official conduct" unless there was proof of "actual malice." And proving actual malice is difficult.

What has happened in practice is that journalists have often triumphed when sued by public figures. Several libel cases during the 1980s were particularly noteworthy.

♦ In 1982, the Philadelphia CBS affiliate was hit with a $5.1 million libel suit brought by Mayor William Green when the station aired an erroneous report that Green was the target of a federal grand jury investigation of an alleged $50,000 kickback in return for millions of dollars in sludge-removal contracts.

♦ CBS-TV itself was hit by a $120 million libel suit, filed by Army General William C. Westmoreland, over a 1982 documentary that accused the general of falsifying enemy troop strengths in Vietnam. After the suit was filed, CBS launched its own internal investigation of its program on Westmoreland and found numerous improprieties and biases in the TV production process. But a libel law showdown was not to be. Early in 1985, after 2½ years of litigation, nearly half a million pages of documents, extensive media coverage, and 65 grueling days in court, General Westmoreland settled out of court with CBS, "winning" an eight-sentence joint statement that said the network did not "believe that General Westmoreland was unpatriotic or disloyal in performing his duties as he saw them."

♦ Also in 1982, *The Washington Post* initially lost a $2 million suit after a federal jury decided that the newspaper had libeled William P. Tavou-lareas when it alleged that he had used his position as president of Mobil Oil to further his son's career in a shipping business (Figure 22–2). The next year a federal judge overturned the verdict against the *Post* because

"It's a great commentary on our times when a jury finds for an oil company against a newspaper."

Frederick Taylor
Executive Editor, The Wall Street Journal,
quoted in Newsweek, October 25, 1982

To avoid any misquotation we wrote Mr. Taylor and asked him if the quote were accurate. His entire reply was the following: "I said it. And you can use it."

For several reasons we think the statement reflects an astonishing degree of irresponsibility—particularly since Mr. Taylor is the Executive Editor of such a prestigious publication. Specifically—

ONE. The statement was made in reference to a unanimous verdict by a jury which found that *The Washington Post* and two reporters had libeled the President of Mobil. This was a personal suit brought by him as an individual which he totally paid for himself, to which Mobil was not a party. The jury did not "find for" Mobil. We seriously doubt that Mr. Taylor was unaware of this distinction. After all, his paper provided coverage of the case and clearly reported its private nature. It was an attempt to substitute a giant oil company as the Goliath attacking the "David-like" *Washington Post.* (Some David!) It was an attempt to erase the fact that the issue in the case involved damage to an individual's reputation. No oil company was involved.

TWO. Even worse, the statement seems to betray a shocking bias. It appears to us that Mr. Taylor thinks oil companies are so venal, so inherently evil that no matter what injustices a newspaper might heap upon them, they should not prevail in a court of law before a jury.

Is Mr. Taylor suggesting that oil companies and their executives be stripped of their civil rights? Or that newspapers should be free to knowingly print false information about them? And, finally, should such behavior be immune from liability?

Mobil

FIGURE 22–2 The initial 1982 libel verdict against *The Washington Post* and in favor of the president of Mobil Oil and his son was chilling to journalists. In a three-column story, *The Wall Street Journal's* executive editor, Frederick Taylor, blamed the verdict on growing public disenchantment with the press. Mobil, almost immediately, responded to Taylor's charge with this ad. *(Courtesy of Mobil Oil Corporation)*

B E T W E E N   T H E   L I N E S

Privacy For Nonpublic Figures

Historically, courts have ruled differently in First Amendment cases regarding public and private officials who have been subject to libel, or written defamation, and slander, or spoken defamation.

Ordinarily, it is much harder to prove "actual malice" in the case of a so-called "public figure" than it is for a nonpublic figure. But even in the case of as nonpublic a figure as a public relations professional, the law remains murky.

In 1988, a Minneapolis jury ordered the city's two leading newspapers to pay a public relations consultant $700,000 for using his name in a news article after reporters had agreed to keep his identity confidential. The consultant, an advisor to the Republican candidate for governor, furnished the newspapers with documents showing that a Democratic candidate had admitted shoplifting $6 in merchandise. Although reporters at the two papers had promised not to divulge the consultant's identity, their editors overruled them. The article appeared. The consultant's name was used, and the same day he was fired from his $35,000-a-year job.

The jury agreed that the newspapers' pledge to protect the man's privacy had been breached, and his ability to earn a living as a result was damaged.

On appeal, however, the Minnesota Supreme Court, ruling that a "reporter's promise of anonymity is given as a moral commitment and not as a contractual promise," vacated the $700,000 verdict, corroborating yet again the immortal words of Justice Yogi Berra, "It ain't over 'til it's over."

the article in question didn't contain "knowing lies or statements made in reckless disregard of the truth."

In 1985, a federal appeals court reinstated the $2 million libel verdict against the *Post*. But later that year, the U.S. Court of Appeals of the District of Columbia agreed to reconsider the reinstatement. Finally, in 1988, the Supreme Court ruled in favor of the *Post* by throwing out the Tavoulareas suit for lack of merit. A contrary ruling would have restricted the limits of investigative journalism and broadened the interpretation of defamation of character. Reporters breathed a sigh of relief at the decision.

◆ In another celebrated case in 1985, Israeli General Ariel Sharon brought a $50 million libel suit against *Time* magazine. It, too, ended without a libel verdict. However, once again, the jury criticized *Time* for negligent journalism in reporting Sharon's role in a massacre in a Palestinian refugee camp.

◆ In 1988, the Supreme Court threw out a suit brought by conservative televangelist/preacher Jerry Falwell against *Hustler* magazine, accusing the sex-oriented periodical with defaming his character in a fictitious liquor advertisement about his mother. Despite the grossness of the ad, the Supreme Court ruled that what was written was clearly a spoof of a public figure and that Falwell, therefore, didn't have a case.

What all these cases illustrate is a growing trend in society to challenge the media over their invasion of personal privacy. Although cases like these tend to confirm the rights of the media to report on public figures, in other cases—particularly those involving gossip-oriented tabloids—the courts have awarded settlements to celebrities who have been wronged.

Public Relations and Copyright Law

One body of law that is particularly relevant to public relations professionals is copyright law and the protections it offers writers. Copyright law provides basic, automatic protection for writers, whether a manuscript is registered with the Copyright Office or even published. Under the Copyright Act of 1976, an "original work of authorship" has copyright protection from the moment the work is in fixed form. As soon as an article, short story, or book is put on paper or a computer disk or is spoken into a tape recorder, it is protected by copyright law. You created it, and you own it. What you sell to an editor isn't the article itself, but the right to use the material.

Copyright protection exists for broad categories of works: literary works; musical works, including any accompanying words; dramatic works, including any accompanying music; pantomimes and choreographic works; pictorial, graphic, and sculptural works; motion pictures and other audio-visual works; and sound recordings. Copyright law gives the owner of the copyright the exclusive right to reproduce and authorize others to reproduce the work, prepare derivative works based on the copyrighted material, and perform and/or display the work publicly.[7] That's why Michael Jackson had to pay $47.5 million in 1987 for the rights to the Beatles' compositions to the duly sworn representatives and heirs of John, Paul, George, and Ringo.

In 1989, the Supreme Court strengthened the copyright status of freelance artists and writers when it ruled that such professionals retain the right to copyright what they create "as long as they were not in a conventional employment relationship with the organization that commissioned their work."[8] The Court's revision of the copyright law set the stage for a wholesale reassessment of the ownership of billions of dollars in reproduction rights for computer programs, fiction and nonfiction writing, advertising copy, drawings, photographs, etc.[9] As a result of the modification, public relations professionals must carefully document the authorization that has been secured for using freelance material. In other words, when engaging a freelance professional, public relations people must know the law.

Several categories of material are not eligible for copyright protection, such as titles and short slogans; works consisting entirely of information from common sources and public documents, such as calendars, lists, and tables; and speeches and performances that have not been fixed on paper or recorded. Work in the public domain—material that was never covered by copyright or for which the copyright has lapsed, material that lacks sufficient originality, and basic themes and plots—can't be protected by copyright.

BETWEEN THE LINES

Suing Vanna the Robot

When glamorous game-show letter turner, Vanna White, saw a videocassette recorder ad that showed a robot dressed up just like her, blond wig and all, on a game show set that looked suspiciously like her "Wheel of Fortune," she sued.

Ms. White was in glittering company, as a host of celebrities in the 1990s invaded the courts to sue advertising agencies with misappropriating their look, their voice, even their mannerisms in ads.

The floodgates opened when singer Bette Midler won a $400,000 jury verdict, in 1989, against Young & Rubicam ad agency, which had created a Ford car ad using a Midler sound-alike. After Ms. Midler declined appearing in the ad, the agency hired the star's former backup singer, who belted out a sound-alike version of Ms. Midler's 1973 hit song, "Do You Wanna Dance?"

In awarding Ms. Midler the verdict, the Federal Appeals Court ruled, "When a distinctive voice of a professional singer is widely known and deliberately imitated in order to sell a product, the sellers have appropriated what is not theirs." From that moment on, it was open season on all those advertising spokespersons who looked and sounded a little too much like "the real thing."

Ideas cannot be protected either. This means that an old idea, newly packaged, is absolutely permissible, legal, and even recommended. Indeed, there are few truly new ideas in the world, only old ideas put together in new and different ways. So a public relations practitioner shouldn't be overly concerned with violating copyright laws when devising a campaign, program, or manuscript in support of a client's activity.

Public Relations and the Legal Profession

What has always been an uneasy alliance between lawyers and public relations professionals has today evolved into a relationship of grudging mutual respect. Lawyers, in fact, are making more use of public relations strategies than ever before. In one 1987 poll, 17 percent of lawyers surveyed reported using public relations, up from 14 percent in 1985. Twenty-three percent said they had used public relations at some point.[10]

By 1990, it was estimated that 75 percent of all major law firms used public relations consultants.[11] Lawyers and legal consultants attributed the increased use of public relations firms to heightened competition within the top tier of the legal profession. Many law firms have grown rapidly in the last decade and have to fight harder for clients and for top law school graduates. As a result, public relations has emerged as an important tool to get these firms' names circulated among clients, potential clients, and possible hires.

In 1984, the Supreme Court eased the ban on self-advertisement by lawyers. And while some lawyers are still reluctant to trumpet their capabilities, others are much less so. The leader of this ilk is Jacoby & Meyers, which, because of its pervasive national advertising, was derided by some as a "fast-food law firm."[12] But there was nothing funny about Jacoby & Meyers client roster of 175,000 people and its $42 million business in 1989. For Jacoby & Meyers, advertising and publicity have paid very well, indeed.

For their part, public relations counselors have become more open to lawyers and have relaxed the tensions that have existed between the two professions. One public relations practitioner offers these insights in working with lawyers.

1. **Become an equal partner with legal counsel.** At all times, maintain an overview of the legal cases before your organization or industry. Take the initiative with legal counsel to discuss those that you believe may have major public relations implications.

2. **Combat the legal no-comment syndrome.** Research cases in which an organization has publicly discussed issues without damage.

3. **Take the initiative in making announcements.** This will help manage public perception of the issue. If an indictment is pending, consult the

BETWEEN THE LINES

What's in a Squiggle?

People are curious about the tiny squiggles that appear above the names of certain company products or slogans.

They're trademarks.

Trademark is a kind of copyright that protects intellectual property. It gives one exclusive use of a particular word, name, symbol, or slogan—Kleenex®, Xerox®, and Coke®, for example. The squiggle ® indicates the mark you have registered with the U.S. Office of Patents and Trademarks.

A similar squiggle is called a service mark. This applies to an organization selling a service rather than a product—American Airlines' slogan, "Something Special in the Air,"[SM] or, the U.S. Army Reserve's slogan we used to chant, "Be All That You Can Be."[SM]

A similar squiggle,[TM], is the trademark symbol. (TM also stands for "transcendental meditation," but that's another story completely.)

legal staff on the advisability of making statements—before you become a target.

4. **Research the background of the jury.** Past lists of jurors in a particular jurisdiction indicate occupations and other important demographic information.

5. **Winning may not be everything.** Outside law firms, trained in an adversarial mode and charging fees that depend on the size of the award, always want to "win." For legal counsel the stakes may also include a winning reputation, which helps to secure future cases. Public relations must bring a long-term perspective to strategic decisions.

6. **Beware of leaving a paper trail.** Any piece of paper that you create may end up in court. That includes desk calendars and notes to yourself. So be careful.[13]

Summary

As our society becomes more contentious, fractious, and litigious, public relations must become more concerned with the law. Indeed, public relations has already become involved with the law in many areas of communications beyond those already cited in this chapter.

◆ The Federal Communications Commission (FCC), in 1987, ruled that the Fairness Doctrine, the subject of years of debate among broadcasters and others, unconstitutionally restricted the First Amendment rights of broadcasters. The FCC said that broadcasters were no longer obligated to provide equal time for dissenting views. Congressional efforts to turn the doctrine into law were vetoed by President Reagan, but the debate may not be finished.

◆ Malpractice suits have proliferated against celebrity spokespersons, who endorse merchandise that ultimately proves faulty, as in the case of legendary quarterback Johnny Unitas and a bankrupt financial services firm that he mistakenly endorsed in 1985.

◆ The right of publicity has been challenged by the estates of deceased celebrities like Charlie Chaplin, W. C. Fields, Mae West, and the Marx brothers, whose likenesses have been portrayed in product advertisements without the permission of their heirs.

◆ The 1988 Supreme Court decision that public school officials have broad power to censor school newspapers, plays, and other school-sponsored expressive activities also is sure to be challenged in the years ahead.

◆ Also in 1988, a federal jury found a cigarette manufacturer liable in the lung-cancer death of a New Jersey woman because the company failed to warn of smoking's health risks before such warnings were required on cigarette packs in 1966. The verdict, which was upheld by the New Jersey Supreme Court in 1990, was hailed by antismoking advocates as the most important breakthrough since cigarette company advertising was forced off of television in 1971. With many similar antitobacco cases pending in the United States, it seems quite likely that advertised and publicized corporate claims will come under increased legal scrutiny, not only for cigarette manufacturers, but for all those who promote product and service claims.

In addition to all these legal areas, the public relations business itself increasingly is based on legal contracts: between agencies and clients, between employers and employees, between purchasers and vendors.[14] All contracts—both written and oral—must be binding and enforceable.

In recent years, controversy in the field has erupted over noncompete clauses, in which former employees are prohibited, within certain time parameters, from working for a competitor or pitching a former account. Legal issues also have arisen over the postal laws that govern public relations people who disseminate materials through the mails. Add to these the blurring of the lines between public relations advice on the one hand and legal advice on the other, and it becomes clear that the connection between public relations and the law will intensify dramatically through the remainder of this decade.

1. What is the difference between a public relations professional's responsibility and a lawyer's responsibility?
2. What have been recent challenges to the First Amendment?
3. What is meant by the term *insider trading*?
4. What was the essence of the Foster Winans, *Wall Street Journal* case?
5. What kinds of information *must* public companies disclose immediately?
6. What is meant by the legal term *actual malice,* with respect to privacy law?
7. Whom does copyright law protect?
8. What group is protected by the most recent revisions in copyright law?
9. What is the attitude of law firms toward public relations counsel?
10. What general advice should a public relations professional consider in working with lawyers?

1. Gerhart L. Klein, *Public Relations Law—The Basics* (Mt. Laurel, NJ: Anne Klein and Associates, Inc., 1990), 1–2.
2. Stephen Wermiel, "U.S., State Officials Win Wider Leeway to Restrict Free Speech of Corporations," *The Wall Street Journal,* 30 June 1989, B6.
3. Randall Rothenberg, "Noriega Tape Case Reviving Clash Over First Amendment," *The New York Times,* 14 November 1990, B1.

TOP OF THE SHELF

Klein, Gerhart L. *Public Relations Law: The Basics.* Mt. Laurel, NJ: Anne Klein & Associates, Inc., 1990.

Can public relations people tape their phone conversations? It depends. What constitutes defamation? Lots of things. To get some straight answers, consult *Public Relations Law,* which addresses the legal implications of public relations activities.

Gerhart Klein, a lawyer and seasoned public relations counselor, presents the legal issues practitioners need to check before performing their duties. In readable fashion, he covers the First Amendment, restrictions on free speech, copyright and trademark law, and financial disclosure. Of exceptional interest are his explanations of

disclosure and "materiality," always murky areas for communicators. Klein also points out the pitfalls of contracts and employing freelancers. If something's legal, It's also ethical, right? Not really. Klein cautions communicators to consider both issues when deciding what to do in certain situations.

Practitioners must be aware of the legal matters that affect their profession. While Klein's primer is no substitute for a lawyer's advice, *Public Relations Law* capably introduces practitioners to the legal ramifications of their actions.

4. Anthony Ramirez, "Burger King Ads Help End Boycott by Religious Groups," *The New York Times*, 7 November 1990, D1.
5. "We Were Robbed," *The Wall Street Journal*, 17 November 1987, 38.
6. Evan Thomas and Thomas M. DeFrank, "Mike Deaver's Rise and Fall," *Newsweek* (March 23, 1987): 23.
7. Jay Stuller, "Your Guide to Copyright," *Writer's Digest* (June 1988): 29.
8. Linda Greenhouse, "Court Strengthens Copyright Status of Free-Lance Artists on Commission," *The New York Times*, 6 June 1989, A24.
9. Albert Scardino, "Copyright Ruling Opens a Costly Can of Worms," *The New York Times*, 12 June 1989, D12.
10. "How Lawyers Use Public Relations," *Public Relations Journal* (January 1988): 30.
11. Ellen Joan Pollock, "Lawyers Are Cautiously Embracing PR Firms," *The Wall Street Journal*, 14 March 1990, B1.
12. Robyn Kelley, "Legal Beagles," *Spy* (August 1990): 74.
13. Lloyd Newman, "Litigation Public Relations: How to Work with Lawyers," *PR Reporter Tips & Tactics* (November 23, 1987): 2.
14. Klein, op. cit., 35.

SUGGESTED READINGS

Banta, William. *AIDS in the Workplace: Legal and Practical Answers.* Lexington, MA: Lexington Books, 1987.

Brown, Kathleen, and Joan Turner. *AIDS: Policies and Programs for the Workplace.* New York: Van Nostrand Reinhold, 1989.

Crisis Management: A Workbook for Survival. Belleville, NJ: The Lempert Co., 1987.

Fink, Steven. *Crisis Management: Planning for the Inevitable.* New York: AMA-COM, 1986 (135 W. 50th St. 10020).

Lerbinger, Otto. *Managing Corporate Crises: Strategies for Executives.* Boston: Barrington Press, 1986 (P.O. Box 291, Boston University Station 02215).

Meyers, Gerald. *When It Hits the Fan.* Scarborough, Ontario: The New American Library Of Canada Limited, 1987.

New Principles for Public Companies After the Supreme Court Decision. Englewood Cliffs, NJ: Prentice-Hall, 1988.

Pinsdorf, Marion. *Communicating When Your Company Is Under Siege.* Lexington, MA: Lexington Books, 1986.

Posner, Ari. "The Culture of Plagiarism." *New Republic* vol. 198, no. 16, p. 19. (1988).

The SEC, the Securities Market and Your Financial Communications. New York: Hill & Knowlton 1991 (420 Lexington Ave. 10017).

Walsh, Frank. *Public Relations and the Law.* New York: Institute for PR Research & Education, 1988 (310 Madison Ave.).

What Non-U.S. Companies Need to Know About Financial Disclosure in the United States. New York: Hill & Knowlton, 1990 (420 Lexington Ave. 10017).

CASE STUDY   The Screwed-Up Odometers

Listen to the lawyers sometimes? Yes. But always? No. Public relations advice must be weighed against legal advice when faced with an organizational crisis. The Chrysler Corporation was tested in this regard in 1987, when it and two of its executives were indicted on criminal charges for selling cars as new that had in fact been driven with their odometers disconnected.

Although the indictment covered only an 18-month period, the Justice Department asserted that Chrysler odometers had been disconnected for decades and that millions of cars had been sold with inaccurate mileage readings. According to the indictment, executives at Chrysler assembly plants routinely took new cars off the assembly line and drove them as many as 400 miles with the odometers disconnected. In addition, the indictment charged that some cars were damaged in the testing and were only superficially repaired before being shipped to dealers for sale.

Initially, the company, on the advice of its lawyers, responded by arguing that it had done nothing illegal. But its tune quickly changed when it saw that public opinion was running decidedly against it. That's when Chrysler Chairman Lee Iacocca, known for his blunt speech, called a news conference at the company's Michigan headquarters and termed the action "dumb" and "unforgivable." "Did we screw up?" Iacocca asked rhetorically. "You bet we did," he answered.

Iacocca said that he had been personally unaware of the disconnecting of odometers until a few months before the indictment. He said that even though disconnecting odometers was standard industry practice, it was still "dumb." Beyond this, however, he

said that Chrysler employees had driven 40 cars that had been seriously damaged in accidents, repaired, and then sold as new. "Simply stated," the chairman said, "that's unforgivable, and we've got nobody but ourselves to blame."

At the news conference, Chrysler announced that it would give new cars to the 40 owners of the affected models. Other owners, the company said, would be offered longer warranties with broader coverage. "Our big concern is for our customers, the people who had enough faith in Chrysler to buy a vehicle from us," Iacocca said. "These charges and the press reports about them are causing some of those customers to question that faith, and we simply cannot tolerate that."

Apparently, the unvarnished, straightforward Iacocca approach, devoid of legalistic posturing, worked splendidly. Four days after the charges had been announced, 55 percent of adult Americans polled in a public opinion survey thought that Chrysler faced a serious problem. In a follow-up survey four days after the news conference, 67 percent of those contacted believed Chrysler had adequately dealt with the issue. Chrysler officials added that the company experienced no ill effect on vehicle sales or stock prices.

A few days after the Chrysler news conference, the company was socked with a fine of $1.5 million for alleged health and safety violations at a Newark, DE, plant. Ordinarily, this fine, on top of Chrysler's $300,000 fine in the odometer case, would have been more than enough to send public opinion plummeting. But in Chrysler's case, top management had been willing to adopt a practical public relations approach rather

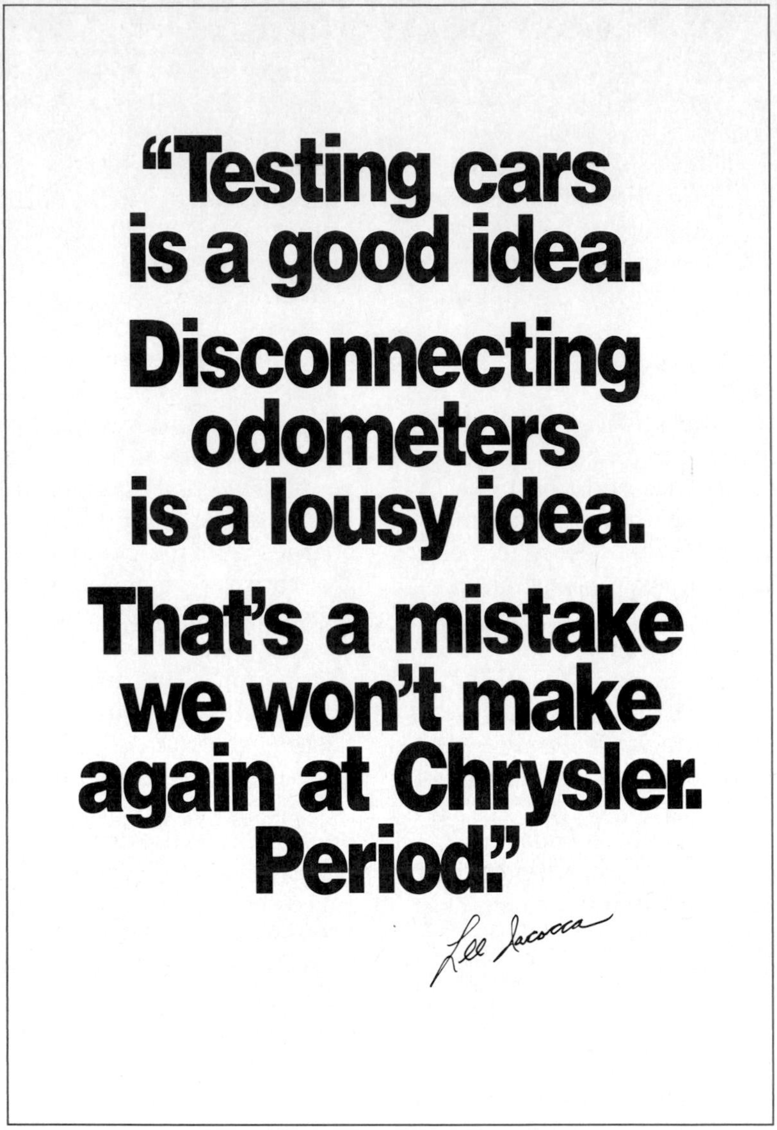

"Testing cars is a good idea.

Disconnecting odometers is a lousy idea.

That's a mistake we won't make again at Chrysler. Period."

Lee Iacocca

FIGURE 22–3   *(Courtesy of Chrysler Corporation)*

than an overly legalistic one. As a *Boston Globe* reporter put it, "Iacocca seemed to have patched up the company's image when he did something a corporate chairman rarely does: He apologized for his company, called the odometer tampering 'dumb' and termed the selling of damaged cars 'stupid.'" All of which demonstrates once again that management candor is often preferable to legal pussyfooting in confronting a major public opinion crisis.

LET ME SET THE RECORD STRAIGHT.

1. For years, spot checking and road testing new cars and trucks that come off the assembly line with the odometers disengaged was standard industry practice. In our case, the average test mileage was 40 miles.

2. Even though the practice wasn't illegal, some companies began connecting their odometers. We didn't. In retrospect, that was dumb. Since October 1986, however, the odometer of every car and truck we've built has been connected, including those in the test program.

3. A few cars—and I mean a few—were damaged in testing badly enough that they should not have been fixed and sold as new. That was a mistake in an otherwise valid quality assurance program. And now we have to make it right.

WHAT WE'RE DOING TO MAKE THINGS RIGHT.

1. In all instances where our records show a vehicle was damaged in the test program and repaired and sold, *we will offer to replace that vehicle* with a brand new 1987 Chrysler Corporation model of comparable value. No ifs ands or buts.

2. We are sending letters to everyone our records show bought a vehicle that was in the test program and offering a free inspection. If anything is wrong because of a product deficiency, we will make it right.

3. Along with the free inspection, we are extending their present 5-year or 50,000-mile protection plan on engine and powertrain to 7 years or 70,000 miles.

4. And to put their minds completely at ease, we are extending the 7-year or 70,000-mile protection to *all major systems:* brakes, suspension, air conditioning, electrical and steering.

The quality testing program is a good program. But there were mistakes and we were too slow in stopping them. Now they're stopped. Done. Finished. Over.

Personally, I'm proud of our products. Proud of the quality improvements we've made. So we're going to keep right on testing. Because without it we couldn't have given America 5-year 50,000-mile protection five years ahead of everyone else. Or maintained our warranty leadership with 7-year 70,000-mile protection. I'm proud, too, of our leadership in safety-related recalls.

But I'm not proud of this episode. Not at all.

As Harry Truman once said, "The buck stops here." It just stopped. Period.

CHRYSLER MOTORS 770 *LIMITED WARRANTY*
CHRYSLER · PLYMOUTH · DODGE CARS · DODGE TRUCKS

We just want to be the best.

QUESTIONS

1. Why do you think Chrysler originally refused to take the heat on the odometer tampering issue?

2. How would you describe Chairman Iacocca's approach to dealing with bad news?

3. What might have happened if Chrysler had followed its lawyers' advice and remained silent?

4. What else would you suggest that Chrysler consider, in addition to the news conference and the national advertising?

Tips from the Top

MARJORIE M. SCARDINO

Marjorie M. Scardino is the president of The Economist Newspaper Group, Inc. In addition to the North American operations of *The Economist* magazine, which has a U.S. circulation of more than 190,000, The Economist Newspaper Group also oversees a growing range of business information publications and services and The Economist diaries. Before taking this position in 1985, Scardino was the managing partner of the Savannah, GA, law firm of Brannen, Wessels & Searcy and founder and publisher, with her husband, of the Pulitzer Prize-winning newspaper *The Georgia Gazette*.

How important is the law in communications work today?

Our society continues to favor the courts rather than personal negotiations to settle disputes. As long as that is the case, the law will be a spectre in most of the things we do. But from the journalist's point of view, the law should be only an after-the-fact player. A reporter researches and writes a story, governing her- or himself by the rules of fairness and the public's need for an open discussion of all issues that are of public interest. The law should be merely a framework and process for judging whether the reporter has done his or her job when there is a dispute.

What are the principal legal obligations of public relations people?

I think it is not productive to describe obligations in terms of the law, unless you are a lawyer or a policeman. The public relations person's obligation is fairly to represent his or her client's story to the public (or, conversely, to try to explain to the client his or her public impact or impression). In doing this the public relations practitioner must take care to present all the truth, without obfuscation. As a practical matter, he or she must make the story credible, and that means it must include the warts and the beauty marks. Against the truth the practitioner must balance a client's privacy, some of which the client must necessarily be prepared to give up to avoid seeing his or her name in the papers. In the course of this truth telling, the public relations person might be both providing the disclosure that satisfies the law and making someone (such as the client's competitor) look pretty bad. To fear that result is to find oneself shying away from the truth.

In recent years, has press freedom gotten more or less liberalized?
From my perspective, press freedom has contracted seriously over the last several years. This is illustrated by events such as the invasion of Grenada (which the press was not allowed to cover firsthand); the Iran-contra scandal (which involved not only misinforming the public through the press, but also misinforming the Congress); restrictions on the Freedom of Information Act (where new rules may be adopted that will both add to the cost of pursuing an information request and require that—in spite of the fact that your right to such material is established in the act—you must justify why you should have the information). Add to this the public's feeling that the press is manipulating, rather than reporting, public opinion and is unduly intrusive and arrogant in the exercise of its power, and you have all the ingredients for a free-speech disaster.

Should there ever be censorship in a democracy?
Not censorship defined and monitored by the government. There is always a place for censorship within a relationship—that of parent to child or corporation to employee, for instance—but those relationships are private. I don't believe there is any social purpose susceptible to enough refinement that government could regulate its attainment by stemming the flow of information.

What is the relationship between ethics and the law?
I think the law should be looked upon as a set of principles that articulates what our society judges to be the citizens' behavior needed to keep order. Ethics often turn out to be more personal, whether to an individual or to a company or institution. What is ethical for you because of your particular professional position or interests may not be ethical for me because I am in a different position. Therefore, the law may not help you when you must decide whether you have a conflict of interest or whether you have fairly dealt with a competitor or a customer.

In my view, it is best if the tenets of ethical behavior—fairness, honesty, and integrity—are part of the corporate culture. That way, ethics will run not only to fair treatment of your client's needs and resources, but also to fair treatment of your own company's. It will make ethics affirmative, not negative.

The Future

The two essential rules in textbook writing—in any kind of writing for that matter—are (1) never introduce new ideas in the conclusion and (2) when you're through, quit! In that spirit, we will conclude by repeating what by now should be obvious: the practice of public relations is an accepted, respected, and necessary management discipline in the 1990s.

Consider some of the facts already cited:

♦ Public relations is a multi-billion-dollar business in the United States, practiced by upward of 159,000 professionals.

♦ Two hundred universities offer concentrated study in public relations with many more offering at least one course dealing with the profession.[1] Public relations is far and away the most popular major in the journalism programs in which it is offered.

♦ The Public Relations Society of America boasts a national membership of 15,000 professionals. The Public Relations Student Society of America is composed of 171 chapters with 5,700 students. Two decades ago there were only six chapters and 56 students.

♦ The International Association of Business Communicators has 11,500 members.

♦ The International Public Relations Association lists 1,000 members from 60 countries, reflecting the globalization of the field.

♦ The net fee income of the three largest public relations agencies exceeds half a billion dollars a year.

♦ Probably most important, chief executives today not only "understand the value of communication to their organizations," but rate public relations highly.[2]

Clearly, the practice of public relations has found its place in society. But what of the future?

Public relations is faced with all the challenges associated with an increasingly popular field. The practice is "hot," and many want to enter it. However, with the mergers and takeovers of the 1980s and recession and cutbacks of the early 1990s, fewer public relations positions are available. This is particularly true at large American companies—like General Motors, Ford, Kodak—once the staple of the public relations industry.[3]

In addition, as management becomes more aware of the role of public relations, its performance expectations of the practice become higher. Thus, the standards to which public relations professionals are held will also increase. Finally, because access to top management is a coveted role and public relations is generally granted that access, key public relations positions will be sought eagerly by managers outside the public relations discipline. This is yet another key challenge that confronts public relations professionals in this decade of the '90s.

A Society in Flux

Undeniably, the people who practice public relations today must be better than those who came before them. Institutions today operate in a pressure-cooker environment and must keep several steps ahead of the rapid pace of social, economic, and political change. The environment is being shaped by many factors.

♦ **Economic globalization** This is affecting all organizations, even non-multinational companies. Competition will intensify, and so will communications, making it easier to communicate around the world but much more difficult to be heard.

♦ **Shifting public opinion** Sudden shifts in public opinion are being ignited by instantaneous communications, challenging the ability of communicators to respond to fast-moving events.

♦ **Aging of society** Households headed by people over fifty-five are the fastest-growing segment of the consumer market in America, and these "oldsters" control about 30 percent of all personal income.

♦ **Tenders, mergers, leveraged buyouts** The stock market plunge of October 19, 1987, still reverberates, making American companies more vulnerable to tender offers, mergers, and leveraged buyouts. Increasingly, foreign interests will take over U.S. firms, revising the concept of a domestic marketplace.

♦ **Downsizing** With downsizing, a euphemism for firing people, companies are continuing to pare overhead and trim staff to become more competitive. The effect on business and employee morale is profound, and the need for good internal communications is critical.

♦ **Corporate responsibility** This buzzword of the 1960s and 1970s, which all but disappeared in the 1980s, has resurfaced in the 1990s. This is especially true as organizations eliminate jobs and as legal and ethical questions arise on issues from AIDS to corporate democracy to proper treatment of the environment (Figure 23–1).[4]

♦ **Feminization of the workplace** As noted, the feminization not only in public relations, but in all industries, is a fact of life in the 1990s, as greater numbers of women join the work force. Women already comprise the majority of public relations professionals. Their numbers and status will continue to increase as the decade continues.

Coupled with these factors is a society that seems incapable of leashing its voracious appetite for costly litigation. No product or service area is immune from potential suit. And bigness is back in vogue, with mergers not only among huge industrial corporations, but also among hospitals, banks, media companies, and others. Yet, at the same time, a growing body of

FIGURE 23–1 In 1990, according to a Louis Harris poll, many Americans rate a "clean environment more important than a satisfactory sex life." Society's renewed concern with the environment, symbolized by this original poster for the first Earth Day two decades ago, will be a front-burner public relations issue in the '90s. *(Photographed by Don Brewster of Lieber Brewster Corporate Design, New York City. The designer-photographer team of Robert Leydenfrost and Don Brewster created the poster as a public service for the Port Authority of New York and New Jersey.)*

opinion sees big business as a threat, especially because it has become more active politically. Product stewardship, an idea that holds a manufacturer responsible for products in perpetuity, is gaining advocacy.[5] Additionally, consumers are demanding greater accountability from all institutions, as well as higher standards of ethical conduct.

In the face of all these changes, it is understandable that management today is giving greater attention than ever before to the public's opinions of its organization and to public relations professionals who can help deal with those opinions.

Public Relations Challenges for the 1990s

As the significance of the practice of public relations intensifies, so, too, will the challenges confronting the public relations profession. The challenges will be worldwide, just as the field itself has become worldwide. The power of communication, especially global communication, will no longer be an American domain. Among the major challenges confronting public relations professionals will be these:

Need for tailored approaches Demographic changes will affect the way professionals communicate. Public relations practitioners will have to target messages across cultural lines to special groups within the population. This will involve narrowcasting, as opposed to broadcasting. With the mass media, as noted, playing a less important role in the '90s, more emphasis will be required on personalized, tailored approaches.

Development of new media As technology continues to advance, new and exotic forms of information dissemination will evolve. These media will capture public attention in the most creative ways—talking billboards, blimps, in-flight headsets, and a myriad of others. Public relations will have to be equally creative to keep up with the new media and harness it for persuasive purposes.

Increased specialization Public relations professionals will have to be much more than a conduit between an organization and the public. They will have to be much more fully informed about company policy and activities. They will have to be specialists—experts in dealing with, for example, the media, consumers, and investors—possessing the sophisticated writing ability that management demands.[6] One Hill & Knowlton survey of senior managers showed "great promise" for public relations but found that many practitioners were inexperienced and lacked training in business. Such a shortcoming won't be tolerated in the 1990s.

Results orientation The growth of research to measure and evaluate public relations results will continue. Public relations professionals must find ways to improve their measurement capability and justify their performance—that is, the results of their actions—to management.

Brave, New Computerized World of Public Relations
by Bradley L. Pick

With the deadline rapidly approaching for an important news release, a public relations executive is mired in traffic, miles from her office—and her word processor. No problem. She switches on a briefcase-sized computer and begins writing the announcement. Needing more information, she pulls out a portable phone and makes a couple of calls. Good news: although a colleague is away from his desk, he left the details she needed on voice mail. She finishes the release just as the cab reaches her office. Once upstairs, she transmits her document to a facsimile machine, which routes the release to dozens of news organizations across the country, just in time to make the next day's papers.

If this scenario seems a bit of a stretch, think again. Technology—from laptop computers to facsimile machines, from voice mail systems to cellular phones—is dramatically changing the way public relations people do their jobs.

Gone are the days of typewriters and liquid "white out." Today, word processors let users manipulate and store data in complex ways. Research, too, has been simplified, as online data bases supply a wealth of information on almost any subject (see Appendix H). Need to organize publicity efforts? Software is available to manage media lists and news clippings and to analyze publicity results.

All this technology enables communicators to do their jobs faster and more efficiently. Consider this: It used to take weeks to research and complete a project. Now, with the assistance of computer technology, that same assignment can be completed in hours.

Here are some of the more useful technologies available to public relations professionals:

Have Computer, Will Travel. The portable office has arrived. Laptop terminals provide everything communicators need to write and edit at home or on the road. Modems, which let two computers exchange information over telephone lines, allow laptops to transfer and retrieve data; to access electronic mail, databases, and news monitoring services; and to send documents to a facsimile machine. To support laptops, there are now portable printers, copiers, and fax machines.

Do It Yourself. Electronic publishing, or desktop publishing, enables public relations people to create documents—from simple news releases to flashy brochures—with vivid charts, drawings, and tables. Producing material in-house can save a great deal of money. Internal production means more time spent working on a project and not on routing material between the office and outside design firms, typesetters, etc.

Just Fax It. The facsimile machine, which uses telephone lines to transmit documents, has become as common as the office copier. Whereas mail delivery can take days, a fax unit can transmit information in less than a minute. Instead of mass mailings, users can program a machine to distribute a document to many recipients simultaneously. In fact, there are companies, like PR Newswire, that will provide bulk fax distribution for public relations divisions and firms.

Leave a Message at the Beep. Computer-based voice mail systems can answer phone calls and dispense information 24 hours a day. Unlike regular answering machines, voice mail systems can take a message even when the phone is in use, eliminating the frustration of busy signals and "telephone tag." Messages can be transferred from one person to another or circulated like memos. Users also can send copies of the same message to many people at once by pressing a button or two on the phone. In this fashion, important messages can be distributed quickly. Voice mail, always on duty, is particularly useful for people communicating across time zones.

In a related context, 900 pay-per-call services allow callers to access information by simply keying in a 900-number on a touchtone phone. Public relations people use these numbers as part of promotions and to provide information in times of crisis, like Johnson & Johnson did during the Tylenol crisis in the mid-'80s.

Through Rain, Sleet, . . . or Power Outage? Electronic mail, or "e-mail," lets subscribers transmit information—from short memos to long reports—to other people's computers. All a user has to do is type a document and press a button and off goes the message. Company e-mail networks are usually internal, although some have been linked to public e-mail systems, letting communicators exchange information with people outside their firms. Soon, professionals will use e-mail to send news releases directly to reporters' terminals.

Wireless Wonders. Cellular phones have become indispensable to many public relations professionals, who use these battery-powered devices to keep in touch with colleagues and clients at virtually all times. Increasingly, practitioners do business on cellular phones in cars, restaurants, shopping malls—you name it. The phones, which can fit into a coat pocket, can run for upward of four hours. Sometimes, however, the transmission signals are weak and the voice on the other end is barely audible. Just the same, many professionals won't do without hand-held phones and the mobility and convenience they provide.

◆ **Creativity** Innovation in the 1990s will be at a premium. Management will expect public relations people to demonstrate bright approaches to organizational problems, thoughtful programs for overcoming or avoiding trouble, and novel ideas for getting attention. This will be particularly true in the increased need for marketing support by public relations professionals. The public relations department must be the storehouse of creativity in the organization.[7]

◆ **Decreased sexism** Women are becoming more dominant in public relations. Their numbers are increasing, and the salary gap is decreasing. While women have not yet achieved parity in salary, power, or recognition, the gap may be eliminated by the year 2000.

◆ **Increased globalization** The globalization of public relations will accelerate for three reasons in the 1990s. First, U.S. and international companies will increasingly recognize the potential of overseas expansion. Second, media globalization will mandate that stories be told worldwide and not kept within national borders. Third, more countries will realize the benefits of professional public relations assistance.

◆ **Technology** Public relations professionals will be blessed with an expanding array of technological tools to cope with the speed and impact of rapid, more global communications. Professionals must be aware of and master the technology described in the next section, if the field is to continue to develop.[8]

Counseling Top Management

No challenge for public relations professionals in the 1990s is more important than counseling senior management. Top managers in companies, hospitals, associations, governments, educational institutions, and most other organizations need counsel because, as they say, "It's lonely at the top." Top managers require:

> Advisers not flunkies, not cronies, not yes-men or sycophants, not merely assistants and associates and aides and attaches—but advisers: men and women who are willing to correct the leader's views when they are unwise, to reject his instructions when they are unworthy, and to convey information to him even when it is unwelcome.[9]

Public relations people in the '90s should be willing and eager to provide such a counseling role to management. Accomplishing such a task will depend on the following nine qualities:

1. **Intimate knowledge of the institution** A public relations professional may be an excellent communicator, but without knowledge of the industry or institution represented, ultimate value will be limited.

2. **Access to and respect for management**   The public relations professional who acquires the respect of top management is a powerful force in an organization. Respect comes only from exposure. Thus, it is essential that the public relations professional have ready access to the most senior managers in an organization.

3. **Access to an intelligence network**   Public relations professionals need their own intelligence network to give them the unvarnished truth about programs and projects. If the executive vice-president is an idiot . . . if the employee incentive program isn't working . . . if the chairman's speech was terrible . . . the public relations professional must be able to tap a team of candid employees who will tell the truth, so that the practitioner can "tell it like it is" to top management—unexpurgated, uncensored, between the eyes.

4. **Familiarity with the reporter on the beat**   A public relations professional—no matter how high up in an organization—should keep in touch with the reporters and analysts who follow the organization. Valuable information can be gleaned from such observers and can be most helpful to top management.

5. **Solid skills base**   The most competent public relations counselors don't just give orders, they demonstrate skills. They are generally good writers, who don't mind "getting their hands dirty" to complete a job competently. In public relations, communications competence is a prerequisite for counseling competence.

6. **Propensity toward action**   In working for top management, results and performance are all that count. Certainly, planning and setting strategies are critical aspects of public relations. But practitioners, especially those who counsel management, must be inclined toward action. They must be doers. That's what management demands.

7. **Knowledge of the law**   Public relations work today confronts legal issues: privacy, copyright, lobbying, and securities laws, broadcasting regulations, and on and on. Although public relations professionals need not be trained lawyers, they must at least be a conversant in the general concepts of the law in order to counsel management effectively and also to deal with legal counselors.

8. **Strong sense of integrity and confidence**   As noted in Chapter 5, public relations professionals must be the ethical conscience of organizations. Their motives and methods must be above reproach. It's also important that public relations counselors demonstrate a confidence in their own positions and abilities. They must surround themselves with the highest caliber performers to enhance the status of the public relations function within the organization.

9. **Contentment with anonymity**   Public relations counselors must understand that they are exactly that: counselors to top management. It is

the chief who delivers the speeches, charts the strategies, and makes the decisions. And it is the chief, too, who derives the credit. Public relations counselors must remain in the background and should try to stay anonymous. Today, with newspapers demanding the names of spokespersons, with some public relations practitioners attaining national celebrity status, and with the field itself becoming more and more prominent, the challenge of anonymity becomes increasingly more difficult.[10]

Emerging Issues in Public Relations

The issues that concern public relations professionals vary from organization to organization and from industry to industry. Nonetheless, several issues concern all practitioners, especially as the field continues to grow in respect and improve its credibility.

Public Relations Education

For public relations to continue to prosper, a solid educational foundation for public relations students must be in place. Today's practitioner has two key stakes in public relations education: future employees and the profession itself.

Over the last few years the Public Relations Society of America and others have focused efforts on the formal education of public relations students. In 1987, a design for undergraduate public relations education was authored by the Public Relations Division of the Association for Education in Journalism and Mass Communication, the Educator's Section of PRSA, and PRSA itself.[11] Among the highlights of the report were these findings and recommendations:

♦ Two subjects tied for the highest ratings by practitioners and educators: English (within general education) and an internship/practicum/work-study program (within public relations education).

♦ It is recommended that public relations students, especially those planning to enter the corporate or agency world, give strong consideration to business as their secondary area of concentrated study.

♦ The traditional arts and sciences remain the solid basis for the undergraduate education of public relations students, essential to their functioning professionally in a complex society.

The report indicated strong agreement between practitioners and educators on what the content of undergraduate public relations education should be. Basically, strong emphasis was placed on communications studies, public relations principles and practices, and ethics. The report further concluded that the growing cooperation and relationships among professionals in the practice of public relations and in education should be nurtured and strengthened, to benefit today's students of the field.

Women in Public Relations

Another issue of concern in the field is the aforementioned impact of the increasing percentage of women in public relations and business communications. In 1980, women accounted for only 10 percent of the public relations population. Today, that number is well over 50 percent.[12] Many practitioners express concern that public relations could become a "velvet ghetto," populated almost entirely by women. The expansion of women in public relations is not surprising. Women account for up to 65 percent of all journalism graduates in the United States. According to a study at the University of Maryland, female students are attracted to public relations and advertising because they think these areas are more open to women.[13]

One of the most comprehensive studies of this issue was launched in 1986 by the International Association of Business Communicators. Its results indicated that women are increasingly filling the role of communications technicians rather than managers. As a result, women are being paid less than men, with gender being the strongest predictor of salary. Among its conclusions, the report found that the situation does not appear to be improving. Instead, men are turning to other professions or are positioning themselves in the most highly paid areas within the field, such as communications management.

All of this should change shortly—perhaps by the end of this decade. Clearly, more women will enter top management jobs, not only in public relations but in many other fields. Some predict the 1990s will be the "Decade of Women in Leadership Positions." Two who do are John Naisbitt and Patricia Aburdene, co-authors of *Megatrends 2000*, who point to the following:

◆ Women already hold 39 percent of the 14 million U.S. executive, administrative, and management jobs, according to the Bureau of Labor Statistics—nearly double the figure of two decades ago.

◆ More than half of all officers, managers, and professionals in the nation's 50 largest commercial banks are women.

◆ More than one-third of Procter & Gamble's marketing executives are women. At the Gannett Company, almost 40 percent of the company's managers, professionals, technicians, and sales force are women. At Apple Computer, the numbers are similar.

◆ Of today's MBA degree recipients, 33 percent are women. Women now earn 13 times more engineering degrees than they did 15 years ago.

♦ In 1966, fewer than 7 percent of M.D. degrees were granted to women. Today, the number is 33 percent. In 1966, women were awarded 3 percent of all law degrees. Today, 40 percent of all law degrees are granted to women.

♦ Women are starting their own businesses at twice the rate of men.[14]

In light of these data, the emergence of women as leaders in the public relations field is inevitable during the 1990s.

Licensing

For many years, practitioners have argued over the merits of licensing public relations professionals. Among the most outspoken advocates of public relations licensure has been public relations patriarch Edward Bernays. He and others have argued that by licensing public relations people, the quality of those who practice public relations could be protected.

Others, like counselor Philip Lesly, have argued that for public relations people to seek government control "is ludicrously out of step with either logic or the times."[15] Lesly and others have argued that licensing would have a number of damaging effects.

♦ Government control by licensure would create real or implied threats to public relations people, who might be called on to further a viewpoint that politicians oppose.

♦ State licensing would stifle out-of-state competition, as it does with lawyers, banks, and others.

♦ State licensing would lead to a parochial, state-centered view of what public relations is and would create artificial boundaries that would unnecessarily inhibit the practice of public relations across state and even national lines.

♦ In a day when professionals can't agree on the benefits of being an accredited member of the Public Relations Society of America, licensing would segment the public relations field even more and cause more public confusion.

♦ The ability to have a license denied or revoked could encourage extremists to demand "delicensing" of anyone who supports an opposing viewpoint.

With no easy answer available on either accreditation or licensing, the debate is likely to continue in the 1990s.

External Challenges

Inevitably, as public relations has enhanced its role in society and increased its respect within organizations, the field itself has attracted

A Glossary for the '90s

Like it or not, getting along as a public relations professional in the 1990s demands a working knowledge of the vocabulary common to the age group that dominates our society: ugh, teenagers. Here's a taste of teen terminology in the '90s.

Abusak: Elevator music, a blend of "abuse" and "Muzak."
Airmail: Garbage thrown out the window.
Arbuckle: Dingbat.
Bad: Good. (A term that keeps hanging on.)
Bail: Either to cut a class or to put something down, as in "bail that."
Biscuit: Easy.
Bogus: Phoney. Bad (as in "bad," not good.)
Brainiac: Intelligent student.
Buff: Muscular, tough.
Bust a move: Try it. Go for it.
Cheesehead: A jerk. Also known as cheese meister.
Clydesdale: A stud, a good-lookin' guy.
Daddylac: An expensive car that has been given to a young driver by his or her parents.
Death: To be very appealing, to die for.
Def: Outstanding, terrific.
Dexter: Nerd.
Homeboy/Homegirl: Friendly term of address for someone of the same neighborhood or school.
Lame: State of boredom, nerdy.
Sick: Good, awesome.
Tamale time: Embarrassment.
Waldo: Out of it.
Woof: To brag.

Even with this cursory introduction to 1990s terminology, a professional should be able to avoid tamale time when asked, "Who's that def Clydesdale in the Daddylac?" Just don't woof about knowing the answer.

others—lawyers, accountants, personnel managers, and general managers of varying backgrounds. Because the public relations executive of an organization is usually close to top management and because access is power in an organization, the role occupied by public relations has become a coveted one. In the 1990s, incursions into public relations by others in an organization are apt to intensify, thereby increasing the pressure on practitioners to use their special expertise and unique experience to reinforce their prominent positions in the organizational hierarchy.

Implications for Beginners

The reality of a more respected and, therefore, more competitive public relations profession has numerous implications for people just starting out in the field. Although competition for public relations positions is stiff,

---

B E T W E E N   T H E   L I N E S

All Is Not Won . . .

Legendary columnists like James "Scotty" Reston of *The New York Times* and Meg Greenfield of *The Washington Post* complain that the practice of public relations confirms George Orwell's darkest prognostication that a "consummate manipulator of information controls people's thoughts in a systematic and sustained way." Horsefeathers! Much closer to the truth is the wisdom of one Ivan Kershner, administrative assistant for the North Platte, Nebraska, public schools, who offers eight guiding principles for public relations.[*]

1. No matter what you do, it isn't enough.
2. No matter what you do, it will be misinterpreted by somebody.
3. No matter how many copies you distribute, you will have forgotten somebody.
4. Media importance is awarded to an issue in direct opposition to that given the issue by your boss.
5. Never fall prey to the thought that your organization's side of an issue is understood.
6. Assume a total vacuum of comprehension on the part of all parties, and you shall not be disappointed.
7. No matter whom you know, somebody else knows somebody more important.
8. No matter how many people proofread, something is always *mispelled.*

So there, Scotty and Meg!

[*]"8 Rules for Public Relations," *Communication Briefings* 5, no. 6 (April 1986).

experience is the great equalizer, and smart beginners can optimize their potential for employment by getting a jump on the competition through early experience. How?

◆ By becoming involved with and active in student public relations organizations

◆ By securing—through faculty or others—part-time employment that uses the skills important in public relations work

◆ By attending professional meetings in the community, learning about public relations activities, and meeting public relations practitioners who might prove to be valuable contacts later on

◆ By seizing every opportunity, from informal internships to voluntary work for nonprofit associations or political candidates to service on the school newspaper to merchandising in-class projects to local merchants

The key to finding and securing a job in public relations is experience. So, rather than bemoan the "Catch 22" reality of a field in which you must have worked first in order to land a job, full-time students should use their college days to begin to acquire working knowledge in public relations. That way when they look for that first job, they already have experience.

Summary

Most professions undergo constant change, but few experience more critical or frequent change than public relations. In the 1970s, practitioners were introduced to a tidal wave of primary concerns: consumerism, environmentalism, government relations, and public policy forecasting. Areas of public relations opportunity shifted quickly from marketing publicity to financial relations to employee communications to public issues management. Steadily, the field has expanded its horizons and increased its influence.

In the 1990s, the U.S. Department of Labor's Bureau of Labor Statistics expects the number of managerial jobs at public relations, marketing, and advertising firms to expand more than 32 percent annually, whereas public relations employment for all industries will grow at a rate of about 39 percent. By the year 2000, say the department's experts, managers with public relations, marketing, and advertising companies will number 427,400.[16] Thus, despite the many challenges it faces, public relations work appears to be on the threshold of its most significant period in history. Never before has society been so vocal in its acknowledgment of and need for the practice of public relations.

As Chrysler Chairman Lee Iacocca put it in describing how his company made it back from the brink of bankruptcy:

Effective public relations was our life support system for a while. And believe me, I'm not overstating the case. We weren't running on fumes anymore, we were running on faith. The faith of the public that we could make it allowed us to stay in business. And we kept that faith only through our ability to communicate.[17]

The future of the practice of public relations appears very bright indeed. At the same time, the challenges to the field are numerous and significant.

BETWEEN THE LINES

. . . But All Is Not Lost

"The Edsel is the car of the future!" "Dewey elected President!" "There is no market for personal computers!" "Madonna is a flash in the pan."

Rumors, hearsay, bad guesses—they are all around us. Hardly a week goes by without someone, somewhere emerging with a profound pronouncement that is pithy, novel, and wrong. That's why when a well-known California public relations counselor (who later claimed he was misquoted) announced to one and all that "PR is dead as a concept," his statement was quickly rebutted by this offering from McGrath/Power West public relations agency.

I rest my case.

MAR/COM MURPHY

The Lighter Side of Marketing Communications, *courtesy of McGrath/Power Public Relations, Santa Clara, CA/New York, NY. © 1988 McGrath/Power.*

In the 1990s, if those who practice public relations stand up for what they believe in and have learned . . . if they counsel their clients always to "do the right thing" . . . and if they have the courage to innovate and the desire to lead not only their organizations and their profession, but society as well . . . then the 1990s will be the most influential and rewarding decade ever for the practice of public relations.

DISCUSSION STARTERS

1. What evidence can you point to to indicate the increased stature of public relations practice?
2. What factors are shaping the environment of the '90s?
3. What are the primary challenges for public relations in the '90s?
4. What are the skills requisite for counseling management in the '90s?
5. How should a public relations professional regard "anonymity"?
6. What are the pressing issues in public relations education in the '90s?
7. What is the outlook for women in public relations in the '90s?
8. What are the issues involved with public relations licensing in the '90s?
9. What is the key challenge for entry-level public relations professionals in the '90s?
10. What is the outlook for public relations practice in the '90s?

NOTES

1. James E. Grunig, "Teaching Public Relations in the Future," *Public Relations Review* (Spring 1989): 12.
2. James E. Grunig, "IABC Study Shows CEOs Value PR," *IABC Communication World* (August 1990): 5.
3. "Sales Boom but PR Staffs Are Down," *O'Dwyer's PR Services Report* (July 1989): 12.
4. Bill Cantor, "A Wild Plunge into the Future," *Cantor Commentary* (October 1987): 2.
5. Joseph Nolan, "To Gain a Good Reputation," *Across the Board* (October 1985): 36.
6. "Cantor's Cycle of Corporate Public Relations Staffing," *Cantor Concern* (January 1986): 1.
7. Robert L. Dilenschneider, "What's Ahead for Public Relations: Problems or Progress?" *Public Relations Quarterly* (Fall 1987): 8.
8. Dirk C. Gibson, "Future Trends in Public Relations," *Social Science Monitor* (February 1990): 1–3.
9. "Leadership in Transition," address by Theodore Sorenson to the Future Focus Conference, Ontario Liberal Party, Geneva Park, Ontario, January 24, 1987.
10. Fraser Seitel, "Staying There," *United States Banker* (May 1989): 67, 69.
11. "The Design for Undergraduate Public Relations Education," study co-sponsored by the Public Relations Division of the Association for Education in Journalism and Mass Communications, The Public Relations Society of America, and the Educators Section of PRSA (1987): 1.
12. *The Velvet Ghetto: The Impact of the Increasing Percentage of Women in Public Relations and Business Communications* (San Francisco: IABC Foundation, 1986): 1.

13. "Women: The New Majority in Journalism School," *Glamour* (July 1986): 208.

14. John Naisbitt and Patricia Aburdene, *Megatrends 2000* (New York: William Morrow, 1990), 224–225.

15. Philip Lesly, "Analysis of Proposals for Licensing Public Relations," speech delivered before a Symposium on Professionalism, Itasca, IL, September 5, 1986.

16. Bill Cantor, "Sixth Annual Review and Forecast of Public Relations Trends," *Cantor Commentary* (January 1988): 5.

17. Lee A. Iacocca, remarks delivered to the PR News Awards Banquet, New York City, June 20, 1985.

TOP OF THE SHELF

Naisbitt, John, and Patricia Aburdene. *Megatrends 2000*. New York: William Morrow, 1990.

Prepare for a voyage into the future, as *Megatrends 2000* explores 10 themes that will define the 1990s.

John Naisbitt and Patricia Aburdene gained publicity several years ago for *Megatrends,* which forecast the dominant trends of the '80s. Their sequel provides a glimpse at the social, political, economic, and technological changes that will shape the 1990s. For example, Trend Two, "A Renaissance in the Arts," predicts that museums, theaters, and galleries will replace sports as the primary leisure activity. Trend Five, "The Privatization of the Welfare State," presages the the end of "the liberal way of social welfare," resulting in a shift from public housing to home ownership and from welfare to workfare. The remaining eight trends, which include, "The Rise of the Pacific Rim" and "The Age of Biology," are equally thought provoking.

Turn to *Megatrends 2000* to understand the momentous changes that may influence life and the practice of public relations as the twentieth century winds down.

SUGGESTED READINGS

Bogue, Donald. *The Population of the U.S.: Historical Trends & Future Projections.* Ithaca, NY: American Demographics, 1988.

Careers in Public Relations. (Available from the Public Relations Society of America, 845 Third Ave., New York, NY 10022.)

Design for Public Relations Education. (Available from the Public Relations Society of America, 845 Third Ave., New York, NY 10022.)

Didsbury, Howard. *Communications and the Future,* 1986. (Available from World Future Society, 4916 St. Elmo Ave., Washington, DC 20014.)

Dilenschneider, Robert L. "What's Ahead for Public Relations: Problems or Progress?" *Public Relations Quarterly* (Fall 1987): 5–8.

Drucker, Peter F. *The New Realities.* New York: Harper & Row, 1989.

Futurist. (Available from World Future Society, 4916 St. Elmo Ave., Washington, DC 20014.) This bimonthly journal includes forecasts, trends, and ideas about the future on all topics.

Jackson, Patrick. "Tomorrow's Public Relations." *Public Relations Journal* (March 1985): 24–25.

Joseph, Ted. "The Women Are Coming, The Women Are Coming." *Public Relations Quarterly* (Winter 1985): 21, 22.

Naisbitt, John, and Patricia Aburdene. *Megatrends 2000.* New York: William Morrow, 1990.

Nolan, Joseph. "To Gain a Good Reputation." *Across the Board* (October 1985): 35–40.

"Sixth Annual Review and Forecast of Public Relations Trends." *Cantor Commentary* (January 1988) (171 Madison Ave., New York, NY 10016).

"A Wild Plunge into the Future." *Cantor Commentary* (October 1987) (171 Madison Ave., New York, NY 10016).

CASE STUDY   Raymond

This is the greatest public relations story ever told.

It is at once sad, yet hopeful. It is a simple tale that involves the generosity of a group of workers and their company and the refusal of a mother to accept "no" for an answer.

Raymond Dunn, Jr., was a teenage boy in upstate New York who weighed only 31 pounds, was severely physically and mentally retarded, and could not speak or see.

Raymond was born with an abnormally small head and brain. His parents soon discovered that he was also asthmatic and allergic to almost everything. The only nutritious food Raymond could digest was a special meat-based formula, MBF, produced at the Gerber Products Company research center in Fremont, MI.

And that's what Raymond's daily diet consisted of for the first 11 years of his life.

Midway through 1985, Raymond's parents received disastrous news. The formula that kept their son alive did not conform with new standards set by the Infant Formula Act of 1980. Even worse, because there was so little demand for the formula, Gerber could no longer produce it.

With a year-and-a-half supply of the formula in the Dunn's basement, and with Raymond consuming one can a day, it was just a matter of time before Raymond would run out of food and die.

Upon learning of the company's decision, the Dunns began to scour warehouses throughout the United States, looking for the discontinued MBF formula. They shipped the few cans they found to their upstate New York home to keep Raymond alive. "People told me that my son would 'be better off dead,' " Mrs. Dunn recalled. "But we didn't see it that way."

Mrs. Dunn contacted leaders everywhere—from President Bush to the Princess of Wales—to get them to intercede in Raymond's behalf. While some offered words of encouragement, little action was taken. For its part, Gerber agreed to share its MBF formula and process with any manufacturer who would supply Raymond. There were no takers.

By the spring of 1989, the fifteen-year-

FIGURE 23—2   Carol Dunn and her 16-year-old son, Raymond. *(Courtesy of Carol Dunn)*

old's supply of MBF was running perilously low. His doctors said he would die without it.

Mrs. Dunn wouldn't hear of it. She pleaded with Gerber management, until finally the company came up with a miraculous solution.

The Dunns were advised that Gerber employees—on their own time using company resources—had decided voluntarily to resume production of MBF for a clientele of one, Raymond Dunn.

Using the facilities at the Fremont research center, the Gerber employees assembled the equipment and special ingredients necessary to keep Raymond alive.

Gerber sought no recognition for its kind-spirited action. The company, in fact, attempted to avoid the spotlight of publicity about its volunteer project. Said the Gerber research director, "I don't want to talk too much about it. It's just something we can do, so we're doing it. The Dunns have nowhere else to turn."

But Mrs. Dunn, ever the fighter, insisted on recognizing Gerber for the decency of its action. Gerber's kindness and Mrs. Dunn's courage to save Raymond became the subject of national television and newspaper coverage.

Said Mrs. Dunn about Gerber and its employees, "I believed they wouldn't let me down because there are human beings in that corporation. I felt that, somehow, Gerber would not let Raymond die."

QUESTION

What principle of proper public relations does this case underscore?

Tips from the Top

JOSEPH T. NOLAN

Joseph T. Nolan, associate professor of communications at the University of North Florida, was vice-president of public affairs for Monsanto Company. He had overall responsibility for public and government relations, advertising, community affairs, and social responsibility. Before joining Monsanto in 1976, Nolan had been a newspaper editor and correspondent with *The New York Times* and United Press International, a professor of journalism and public affairs at the University of South Carolina, and a senior communications manager at Chase Manhattan Bank and RCA Corporation. *Business Week* magazine cited him as one of the "top 10 executives in corporate public relations."

What are the most significant challenges that confront the public relations profession?
Gaining management's confidence by providing high-quality advice and mature judgment, by focusing on results rather than on activities, and by being able to measure the results with greater precision than is now being done.

What do you see as the future of public relations education?
More emphasis on business management and on the social sciences, such as eco-nomics, social psychology, and sociology, and less on developing techniques and understanding gadgetry.

In order to get that first job, a student must be familiar with the carpentry of communications. But to advance on the job, he or she must demonstrate an ability to analyze, reason, and make judgments.

What do you see as the prospects for growth in employment in the public relations profession?
I think that employment will expand steadily, but not explosively, over the next decade or two, as more and more enterprises understand what public relations can do to help them.

What parts of the field do you see as growth areas in the 1990s?
Fund raising and investor and international relations are likely to increase, but I think that one of the biggest areas of growth will be in dealing with television in all of its aspects. Surveys show that perhaps 80 percent of the public gets its news through television, and yet most public re-

lations departments suffer from a serious print bias.

What parts of the profession do you see as becoming more limited in available opportunities?
I suspect we've reached the saturation point in the placement area and in press agentry.

What are the greatest threats to the future of public relations?
Inept practitioners—men and women who don't understand thoroughly the enterprise they're trying to represent, or the most effective ways of carrying out that representation.

Do you envision that public relations practitioners will be called on to manage organizations in the future?
The best of the public relations practitioners will move up to top management roles, just as marketing and financial specialists, engineers, and lawyers have done in the past.

Will public relations ever attain the same stature as the professions of law and accounting?
If public relations keeps working at its accreditation procedure, improving it as it goes along, and does a better job of policing its ranks, it could very well eventually achieve a place alongside accounting, law, and the other professions. This would be an important development, but its importance should not be exaggerated. The only way to get this kind of stature is to merit it, and that must be done day by day.

What are the emerging trends you foresee in public relations over the next 20 years?
The most formidable challenge is likely to be managing the new business environment, both at home and abroad. The decisive issues will be external rather than internal, social and political rather than economic. The challenge will come primarily from the impact of laws and public opinion. Practitioners must understand how they are shaped, and how they can be changed.

By the year 2000, what do you predict will be the general state of the practice of public relations?
I predict that major organizations will have a public relations practitioner very near the top, and that they will weigh every major decision in light of its public relations impact, just as they do now with respect to its business and financial impact.

APPENDICES

APPENDIX A
Code of Professional Standards

APPENDIX B
Advertising Effectiveness Tracking Study

APPENDIX C
Leading Media Directories

APPENDIX D
Audiovisual Supports

APPENDIX E
Guide to Video/Satellite Terms

APPENDIX F
Corporate Reporting Requirements

APPENDIX G
Annual Meeting Checklist

APPENDIX H
On-line Databases

PRSA

CODE OF PROFESSIONAL STANDARDS FOR THE PRACTICE OF PUBLIC RELATIONS

Public Relations Society of America

This Code was adopted by the PRSA Assembly in 1988. It replaces a Code of Ethics in force since 1950 and revised in 1954, 1959, 1963, 1977, and 1983.

> On November 12, 1988, PRSA's Assembly approved a revision of the Society's Code for the following reasons:
>
> 1. To make the language clearer and more understandable—hence easier to apply and to follow.
>
> As Elias "Buck" Buchwald, APR, chairman of the Board of Ethics and Professional Standards, explained to the Assembly, the revision introduced no substantive changes to the code; it merely clarified and strengthened the language.
>
> 2. To help advance the unification of the public relations profession—part of PRSA's mission.
>
> The PRSA Code revision was based on the Code of the North American Public Relations Council, an organization of 13-member groups, including PRSA. Eight of the 13 have now revised their own codes in accordance with the NAPRC Code—an important step toward unification.
>
> Code interpretations, as published on pages 17–20 of the 1988–1989 Register, remain in effect. However, the Board of Ethics and Professional Standards is in the process of revising and updating them.

Declaration of Principles

Members of the Public Relations Society of America base their professional principles on the fundamental value and dignity of the individual, holding that the free exercise of human rights, especially freedom of speech, freedom of assembly, and freedom of the press, is essential to the practice of public relations.

In serving the interests of clients and employers, we dedicate ourselves to the goals of better communication, understanding, and cooperation among the diverse individuals, groups, and institutions of society, and of equal opportunity of employment in the public relations profession.

We pledge:

To conduct ourselves professionally, with truth, accuracy, fairness, and responsibility to the public;

To improve our individual competence and

advance the knowledge and proficiency of the profession through continuing research and education;

And to adhere to the articles of the Code of Professional Standards for the Practice of Public Relations as adopted by the governing Assembly of the Society.

Code of Professional Standards for the Practice of Public Relations

These articles have been adopted by the Public Relations Society of America to promote and maintain high standards of public service and ethical conduct among its members.

1. A member shall conduct his or her professional life in accord with the **public interest.**

2. A member shall exemplify high standards of **honesty and integrity** while carrying out dual obligations to a client or employer and to the democratic process.

3. A member shall **deal fairly** with the public, with past or present clients or employers, and with fellow practitioners, giving due respect to the ideal of free inquiry and to the opinions of others.

4. A member shall adhere to the highest standards of **accuracy and truth,** avoiding extravagant claims or unfair comparisons and giving credit for ideas and words borrowed from others.

5. A member shall not knowingly disseminate **false or misleading information** and shall act promptly to correct erroneous communications for which he or she is responsible.

6. A member shall not engage in any practice which has the purpose of **corrupting** the integrity of channels of communications or the processes of government.

7. A member shall be prepared to **identify publicly** the name of the client or employer on whose behalf any public communication is made.

8. A member shall not use any individual or organization professing to serve or represent an announced cause, or professing to be independent or unbiased, but actually serving another or **undisclosed interest.**

9. A member shall not **guarantee the achievement** of specified results beyond the member's direct control.

10. A member shall **not represent conflicting** or competing interests without the express consent of those concerned, given after a full disclosure of the facts.

11. A member shall not place himself or herself in a position where the member's **personal interest is or may be in conflict** with an obligation to an employer or client, or others, without full disclosure of such interests to all involved.

12. A member shall **not accept fees, commissions, gifts, or any other consideration** from anyone except clients or employers for whom services are performed without their express consent, given after full disclosure of the facts.

13. A member shall scrupulously safeguard the **confidences and privacy rights** of present, former, and prospective clients or employers.

14. A member shall not intentionally **damage the professional reputation** or practice of another practitioner.

15. If a member has evidence that another member has been guilty of unethical, illegal, or unfair practices, including those in violation of this Code, the member is obligated to present the information promptly to the proper authorities of the Society for action in accordance with the procedure set forth in Article XII of the By-laws.

16. A member called as a witness in a proceeding for enforcement of this Code is obligated to appear, unless excused for sufficient reason by the judicial panel.

17. A member shall, as soon as possible, sever relations with any organization or individual if such relationship requires conduct contrary to the articles of this Code.

Advertising Effectiveness Tracking Study

APPENDIX
B

CONTEMPORARY MARKETING RESEARCH INC.
1270 Broadway
New York, NY 10001

#6-1-107
February, 1986

<u>ADVERTISING EFFECTIVENESS TRACKING STUDY</u>
<u>MAIN QUESTIONNAIRE</u>

<u>Card 1</u>
(11-17Ƶ)

RESPONDENT'S NAME: _____

1a. Today, I am interested in obtaining your opinions of financial institutions. To begin with, I'd like you to tell me the names of all the financial institutions you have heard of. (DO <u>NOT</u> READ LIST. RECORD FIRST INSTITUTION MENTIONED SEPARATELY FROM ALL OTHERS UNDER "FIRST MENTION.") (PROBE:) Any others? (RECORD BELOW UNDER "OTHERS.")

1b. Now, thinking only of <u>banks</u> in the New York area, what (other) banks have you heard of (RECORD BELOW UNDER "OTHERS.")

2. And what financial institutions, including banks, have you seen or heard advertised within the past 3 months? (DO <u>NOT</u> READ LIST. RECORD BELOW UNDER Q.2.)

3. <u>FOR EACH ASTERISKED INSTITUTION LISTED BELOW AND NOT MENTIONED IN Q.1a/1b OR Q.2, ASK:</u>

Have you ever heard of (<u>NAME</u>)? (RECORD BELOW UNDER Q.3.)

4. <u>FOR EACH ASTERISKED INSTITUTION CIRCLED IN Q.1a/1b OR Q.3 AND NOT CIRCLED IN Q.2, ASK:</u>

Have you seen or heard advertising for (<u>NAME</u>) within the past 3 months? (RECORD BELOW UNDER Q.4.)

	Q. 1a/1b		Q.2	Q.3	Q.4
	AWARE OF		AWARE ADVTG.	AWARE OF (AIDED)	AWARE ADVTG. (AIDED)
	FIRST MENTION	OTHERS			
	(18)	(21)	(24)		
Anchor Savings Bank	1	1	1		
Apple Savings Bank	2	2	2		
Astoria Federal Savings	3	3	3		
Bank Of Commerce	4	4	4		
Bank Of New York	5	5	5		
Bankers Trust	6	6	6		

Card 1

	Q. 1a/1b		Q.2	Q.3	Q.4
	AWARE OF		AWARE ADVTG.	AWARE OF (AIDED)	AWARE ADVTG. (AIDED)
	FIRST MENTION	OTHERS			
	(18)	(21)	(24)		
Barclays Bank	7	7	7		
Bowery Savings Bank	8	8	8		
*Chase Manhattan Bank	9	9	9	9 (27)	9 (29)
*Chemical Bank	0	0	0	0	0
*Citibank	X	X	X	X	X
Crossland Savings Bank	Y	Y	Y		
*Dean Witter	1 (19)	1 (22)	1 (25)	1 (28)	1 (30)
Dime Savings Bank	2	2	2		
Dollar Dry Dock Savings Bank	3	3	3		
*Dreyfus	4	4	4	4	4
Emigrant Savings Bank	5	5	5		
European American Bank	6	6	6		
Fidelity	7	7	7		
Goldome Savings Bank	8	8	8		
*Manufacturer's Hanover Trust	9	9	9	9	9
*Marine Midland Bank	0	0	0	0	0
*Merrill Lynch	X	X	X	X	X
*National Westminster Bank	Y	Y	Y	Y	Y
Prudential Bache	1 (20)	1 (23)	1 (26)		
Shearson-Lehman	2	2	2		
Other (SPECIFY):					
_____	X	X	X		
_____					
_____					

REFER BACK TO Q.2 AND 4. IF RESPONDENT IS AWARE OF ADVERTISING FOR CHASE
MANHATTAN BANK IN Q.2 OR Q.4, ASK Q.5a. OTHERWISE, SKIP TO Q.6.

5a. Today we are asking different people about different banks. In your case, we'd like to talk about Chase Manhattan Bank. You just mentioned that you remember seeing or hearing advertising for Chase Manhattan Bank. Please tell me everything you remember seeing or hearing in the advertising. (PROBE FOR SPECIFICS) What else?

_____ (31) _____

_____ (32) _____

_____ (33) _____

_____ (34) _____

_____ (35) _____

5b. And where did you see or hear advertising for Chase Manhattan Bank? (Do NOT READ LIST) (MORE THAN ONE ANSWER MAY BE GIVEN).

(36)

Television. 1
Radio 2
Newspaper 3
Magazine. 4
Billboard. 5
Other (SPECIFY):_____ X

6. Different banks use different slogans. (START WITH THE X'D QUESTION BELOW AND CONTINUE UNTIL ALL FOUR QUESTIONS (Q.6a-6d) HAVE BEEN ASKED.)

START:

(√) 6a. What slogan or statement do you associate with Chase Manhattan Bank? (DO NOT READ LIST)

(37)

Chase. The Experience Shows. 1
You Have A Friend At Chase 2
Ideas You Can Bank On. 3
The Chase Is On 4
Other (SPECIFY)_____ X

_____
_____

( ) 6b. What slogan does Chemical Bank use? (DO NOT READ LIST)

(38)

The Chemistry's Just Right At Chemical . . 1
Other (SPECIFY) X

( ) 6c. What slogan or statement do you associate with Citibank? (DO NOT READ LIST)

(39)

It's Your Citi. 1
The Citi Never Sleeps 2
Other (SPECIFY)_____ X

_____
_____

( ) 6d. What slogan does Manufacturer's Hanover Trust use? (DO NOT READ LIST)

(40)

The Financial Source. Worldwide 1
We Realize Your Potential. 2
Other (SPECIFY)_____ X

_____
_____

7. Now, I'd like to know how likely you, yourself, are to consider banking at several different banks in the future. For each bank I read, please tell me whether you would definitely consider banking there, probably consider banking there, might or might not consider banking there, probably not consider banking there or definitely not consider banking there in the future. Now, how likely are you to consider banking at (READ X'D BANK) in the future? (REPEAT SCALE IF NECESSARY. OBTAIN A RATING FOR EACH BANK.)

	START: ( )	( )	( )	(√)
	CHASE MANHATTAN BANK	CHEMICAL BANK	CITIBANK	MANU-FACTURER'S HANOVER TRUST
Definitely Consider Banking There	5 (41)	5 (42)	5 (43)	5 (44)
Probably Consider Banking There	4	4	4	4
Might Or Might Not Consider Banking There	3	3	3	3
Probably Not Consider Banking There	2	2	2	2
Definitely Not Consider Banking There	1	1	1	1
(DO NOT READ)→(Currently Bank There)	X	X	X	X

(45-1)

8a. Now, I'd like you to rate one bank on a series of statements—Chase Manhattan Bank. If you have never banked there, please base your answers on what you know about this bank and your perceptions of it. After I read each statement, please tell me whether you agree completely, agree somewhat, neither agree nor disagree, disagree somewhat or disagree completely that this statement describes Chase Manhattan Bank. (START WITH X'D STATEMENT AND CONTINUE UNTIL ALL ARE RATED.)

START HERE:	AGREE COM-PLETELY	AGREE SOME-WHAT	NEITHER AGREE NOR DISAGREE	DISAGREE SOME-WHAT	DISAGREE COM-PLETELY
[ ] Is Responsive To Your Needs	5	4	3	2	1 (46)
[ ] Offers High Quality Accounts And Services	5	4	3	2	1 (47)
[ ] Deals With Its Customers On A Personalized Level	5	4	3	2	1 (48)
[ ] Helps Make Banking Easier	5	4	3	2	1 (49)
[ ] Has Bank Personnel That Are Concerned About You	5	4	3	2	1 (50)
[ ] Designs Accounts To Meet Your Special Needs	5	4	3	2	1 (51)
[ ] Is Responsive To Community Needs	5	4	3	2	1 (52)
[ ] Makes It Easy To Open An IRA Account	5	4	3	2	1 (53)
[ ] Has A Full Range Of Banking And Investment Services	5	4	3	2	1 (54)
[ ] Is A Bank Where You Want To Have Most Of Your Accounts	5	4	3	2	1 (55)

START HERE:	AGREE COM-PLETELY	AGREE SOME-WHAT	NEITHER AGREE NOR DISAGREE	DISAGREE SOME-WHAT	DISAGREE COM-PLETELY	
[ ] Has Bank Personnel That Are Experienced	5	4	3	2	1	(56)
[ ] Has Innovative Accounts And Services . .	5	4	3	2	1	(57)
[ ] Understands Your Banking Needs	5	4	3	2	1	(58)
[ ] Has Branches That Are Pleasant To Bank In.	5	4	3	2	1	(59)
[ ] Has Accounts To Help People Just Starting Out	5	4	3	2	1	(60)
[ ] Continuously Develops Services To Meet Your Needs.	5	4	3	2	1	(61)
[ ] Has Bank Personnel That Are Friendly And Courteous	5	4	3	2	1	(62)
[ ] Has Accounts And Services That Are Right For You	5	4	3	2	1	(63)
[√] Puts Customers' Needs First	5	4	3	2	1	(64)
[ ] Is A Modern, Up-To-Date Bank	5	4	3	2	1	(65)

END CARD 1

Leading Media Directories

When PR professionals are asked which media directories they use most often, their answers are as varied as the tasks their firms perform. Publishers have carved such precise market niches for their wares that direct comparison of one directory to another is usually inappropriate. A comprehensive list of media directories begins on this page. Directories are listed by category, and then alphabetically. Another list provides complete names and addresses of the publishers cited.

Newspapers

E&P International Yearbook. Annual list of U.S. and Canadian daily newspaper personnel and other data. $60. **Editor & Publisher.**

Family Page Directory. $60 for two editions printed at six-month intervals. Contains information about home, cooking, and family interest sections of newspapers. **Public Relations Plus.**

Media Alerts. Data on 200 major dailies as well as 1,900 magazines. $155. **Bacon's.**

National Directory of Community Newspapers. Listings on newspapers serving smaller communities. $35. **American Newspaper Representatives.**

Publicity Checker, Volume 2: Newspapers. $155 when purchased with Volume 1 on magazines. Two volumes list over 7,500 publications. **Bacon's.**

Working Press of the Nation, Volume I: Newspapers. Part of a $260 five-volume set with 25,000 publicity outlets. **National Research Bureau.**

1988 News Bureaus in the U.S. $133. **Larimi.**

Magazines

Media Alerts. Data on 1,900 magazines and 200 major daily newspapers. $155. **Bacon's.**

National Directory of Magazines. Lists basic information on 1,300 magazines in the U.S. and Canada. $125. **Oxbridge.**

Publicity Checker, Vol. 1. Part of a two-volume set (for magazines and newspapers) with over 7,500 listings. $155 for both volumes. **Bacon's.**

Standard Periodical Directory. Has 60,000 titles with 50 fields of data per title, divided into 250 subject areas. $295. **Oxbridge.**

Working Press of the Nation, Volume 2: Magazines. Part of a five-volume set with data on 25,000 publicity outlets. $260 for set. **National Research Bureau.**

Television

Cable Contacts Yearbook. Lists all cable systems. $184. **Larimi.**

Radio-TV Directory. Over 1,300 TV stations and 9,000 radio stations. $155. **Bacon's.**

Talk Show Selects. Identifies talk show contacts nationwide for both TV and radio. Emphasizes network and syndication programs. $185. **Broadcast Interview.**

Television Contacts. Updated extensive listings. $233. **Larimi.**

TV News. Guide to news directors and assignment editors. $172. **Larimi.**

TV Publicity Outlets. Two editions are printed at six-month intervals. $159.50. **Public Relations Plus.**

Working Press of the Nation, Volume 3: TV and Radio. Part of a $260 five-volume set with

25,000 publicity outlets. **National Research Bureau.**

Radio

National Radio Publicity Outlets. Two editions are printed at six-month intervals. $159.50 for both. **Public Relations Plus.**

Radio Contacts. Extensive, updated listings. $239. **Larimi.**

Radio-TV Directory. Over 9,000 radio and 1,300 TV stations. $155. **Bacon's.**

Talk Show Selects. Identifies both radio and TV talk show contacts nationwide. Emphasis is on syndicated and network programs. $185. **Broadcast Interview.**

Working Press of the Nation, Volume 3. Includes both radio and TV. Part of a five-volume set that sells for $260 and contains data on 25,000 publicity outlets. **National Research Bureau.**

Newsletters

Directory of Newsletters. Has 13,500 newsletters in U.S. and Canada. Publications are divided into 168 categories. $125. **Oxbridge.**

The Newsletter Yearbook Directory. Lists worldwide newsletters available by subscription. $60. **Newsletter Clearinghouse.**

Newsletters Directory. Guide to more than 8,000 subscription, membership and free newsletters. $140. **Gale Research.**

1988 Investment Newsletters. Lists over 1,000 newsletters. $160. **Larimi.**

Regional

Burrelle's Media Directories. Regional directories for New York State ($85), New Jersey ($70), Pennsylvania ($38), New England ($95), Connecticut ($32), Maine ($25), New Hampshire ($25), Massachusetts ($44), Rhode Island ($25), Vermont ($25), and Greater Boston ($29). **Burrelle's.**

Metro California Media. Detailed listing of California media. $89.50 includes semi-annual revised edition. **Public Relations Plus.**

Minnesota Non-Metro Media Directory. Guide to the media in the Twin Cities region. $90. **Publicity Central.**

New York Publicity Outlets. Media in a 50-mile radius of New York City. $89.50 includes the semiannual revised edition. **Public Relations Plus.**

New York TV Directory. Lists producers, directors, and others active in the New York market. Published annually. $15. **National Academy.**

Vermont Media Directory. TV, radio, newspaper, and magazine listings. $99. **Kelliher.**

Washington News Media. Detailed listings of wire services, newspapers, magazines, radio-TV, and foreign correspondents. $99. **Hudson's.**

1988 Media Guide and Membership Directory. Chicago media outlets. $75. **Publicity Club of Chicago.**

International

International Literary Market Place. $85. **R.R. Bowker.**

International Media Guide. Publishers of Newspapers Worldwide and Consumer Magazines Worldwide. A four-volume set covers business and professional publications for Asia/Pacific; Middle East and Africa; Latin America, and Europe. Each volume sells for $100. **International Media Guide.**

International Publicity Checker. Lists 10,000 western European business, trade, and technical magazines, and 1,000 national and regional newspapers. $165. **Bacon's.**

Ulrich's International Periodicals Directory. Lists 70,730 periodicals in 542 subject areas, in two volumes. Over 40,000 entries from the previous edition have been updated. $159.95. **Ulrich's.**

United Kingdom

Benn's Media Directory. Available in two books, one for the U.K. and the other for international listings. Each is $95; both are $160. Published by Benn Business Information Services. **Nichols.**

Bowdens Media Directory. Updated three times annually with complete media listings. **Bowdens.**

Editors Media Directories. Series of directories covering journalists, features, profiles. **Editors.**

Hollis Press and Public Relations Annual. Over 18,000 organizations in the PR industry, with a full range of media. $36. **Hollis.**

PIMS United Kingdom Media Directory. Provides detailed access to the total range of U.K. media. $390 annually, $220 quarterly, or $90 for a single issue. **PIMS U.S.A.**

PIMS United Kingdom Financial Directory. Detailed listings. $300 annually or $90 for a single copy. **PIMS U.S.A.**

Willing's Press Guide. Extensive U.K. media listings. $105 plus $5 shipping. Published by Thomas Skinner Directories. **Business Press International.**

Canada

Matthews List. Has 3,600 media throughout Canada. Updated three times annually. $130 per year. **Publicorp.**

Australia

Margaret Gee's Media Guide. Lists 2,400 Australian media, updated three times annually. $100. **Margaret Gee.**

Japan

Publishers in English in Japan. Media selection for English-speaking readers. Published by Japan Publications Guide Service. **Pacific Subscription Service.**

Africa

African Book World and Press. Lists over 4,000 publishers. The latest edition is 1983. $78. **K.G. Saur.**

Specialists

Business and Financial News Media. Print, electronic, syndicated columns, and individual writers. $85. **Larriston.**

Business and Technical Media. Available on paper and floppy disk, at $200 total for both. **Ron Gold.**

Computer Industry Almanac. Extensive industry data as well as a publications directory. $49.50 hardcover; $29.95 softcover. **Computer Industry Almanac.**

Directory of the College Student Press in America. Has 5,000 student newspapers and magazines on 3,600 campuses. $75. **Oxbridge.**

Encyclopedia of Association Periodicals. Three-volume directory sells for $150, but individual ones sell for $60. Vol. I: business and finance. Vol. II: science and medicine. Vol. III: social sciences and education. **Gale Research.**

Medical and Science News Media. Specialized listings with major news contacts. $85. **Larriston.**

Medical Press List. Available on paper and floppy disk, at a combination price of $125. **Ron Gold.**

Nelson's Directory of Investment Research. Contact information and areas of specialization for over 3,000 security analysts. $259. **W.R. Nelson.**

TIA International Travel News Directory. Comprehensive travel media listings. $35. **Travel Industry Association.**

Travel, Leisure and Entertainment News Media. Major nationwide contacts. $85. **Larriston.**

1988 College/Alumni/Military Publications. Over 1,150 publications in these three fields. $87. **Larimi.**

Working Press of the Nation, Volume 5. Internal Publications Directory. Describes house organs published primarily for distribution inside companies. Part of a five-volume library selling for $250. **National Research Bureau.**

Ethnic

Black Media in America. $50. **Hall Co.**

Burrelle's Special Directories. Directories of Black, Hispanic, and women's media are covered in three volumes at $50 each. **Burrelle's.**

Hispanic Media, U.S.A. Provides a narrative description of Spanish-language media. Includes newspapers, radio, and TV stations. $75 plus $1.50 handling. **The Media Institute.**

General

Business Publications Rates and Data. Monthly directory of magazines and newspapers categorized by field. $398 for 12 monthly issues, or $194 for one copy. **Standard Rate and Data Service.**

Directory of Directories. More than 10,000 entries in two volumes. $195. **Gale Research.**

Gale Directory of Publications. Annual directory to newspapers, magazines, journals, and related publications. $135. **Gale.**

Gebbie All-In-One Directory. Comprehensive listings of all media. $79.25. **Gebbie Press.**

Market Guide. Has data on population, income, households, and retail sales for markets around the nation. $70. **E&P.**

Print Media Editorial Calendars. Lists 12-month editorial calendars for 4,200 trades, 1,700 newspapers, 1,500 consumer magazines, and 400 farm publications. $195. **Standard Rate and Data Service.**

Experts and Writers

Directory of Experts, Authorities and Spokespersons. Access to over 3,569 experts. $19.95 plus $3.50 shipping. Can be ordered on Rolodex cards for $165. **Broadcast Interview.**

1988 Syndicated Columnists. Over 1,400 columnists listed. $157. **Larimi.**

Syndicate Directory. Lists syndicated features by classification, by-lines, as well as how material is furnished. $6. **E&P.**

Working Press of the Nation, Volume 4: Feature Writer & Photographer Directory. Part of a five-volume set selling for $260. **National Research Bureau.**

Directory Publishers

Publishers of media directories can be found in alphabetical order in the list that follows.

American Newspaper Representatives
12 South Sixth St., Ste. 520
Minneapolis, MN 55402
612/332-8686
 National Directory of Community Newspapers

Bacon's PR and Media Information Systems
332 S. Michigan Ave.
Chicago, IL 60604
800/621-0561
 Publicity Checker
 Radio-TV Directory
 Media Alerts
 International Publicity Checker

Bowden's Information Services
624 King Street West
Toronto ON M5V 2X9, Canada
416/860-0794
 Bowden's Media Directory

Broadcast Interview Source
2500 Wisconsin Ave., NW
Suite 930
Washington, DC 20007
202/333-4904
 Directory of Experts
 Talk Show Selects

Burrelle's Press Clipping Service
75 East Northfield Ave.
Livingston, NJ 07039
201/992-6600
 Regional Media Directories

Computer Industry Almanac
8111 LBJ Freeway, 13th floor
Dallas, TX 75251-1313
214/231-8735
 Computer Industry Almanac

Editor and Publisher
11 West 19th St.
New York, NY 10011
212/675-4380
 E&P International Yearbook
 Market Guide
 Syndicate Directory

Directory Publishers

Editors Media Directories
9/10 Great Sutton St.
London EC1 VOBX England
 Editors Media Directories

Gale Research
Book Tower
Detroit, MI 48226
313/961-2242
  Directory of Directories
  Directory of Publications
  Encyclopedia of Association Periodicals
  Newsletters Directory

Gebbie Press
Box 1000
New Paltz, NY 12561
914/255-7560
  Gebbie All-In-One Directory

Hollis Directories
Contact House
Sunbury-On-Thames
Middlesex TW16 5HG, England
  Hollis Press and Public Relations Annual

International Media Guide Enterprises
22 Elizabeth St.
South Norwalk, CT 06856
203/853-7880
  International Media Guide

Kelliher/Samets
130 South Willard St.
Burlington, VT 05401
802/862-8261
  Vermont Media Directory

Larimi Communications Associates
5 West 37th St.
New York, NY 10018
800/634-4020
212/819-9310
  Cable Contacts Yearbook
  Radio Contacts
  Television Contacts
  TV News
  1988 News Bureaus in the U.S.

Larriston Communicatons
P.O. Box 20229
New York, NY 10025
212/864-0150
  Business and Financial News Media
  Medical and Science News Media
  Travel, Leisure and Entertainment News
    Media

Margaret Gee Media Group
384 Flinders Lane
Melbourne, Victoria 3000 Australia
  Margaret Gee's Media Guide
  Information Australia

The Media Institute
3017 M Street
Washington, DC 20007
202/298-7512
  Hispanic Media, U.S.A.

National Academy of Television
Arts and Sciences
New York Chapter
110 West 57th St.
New York, NY 10019
212/765-2450
  New York TV Directory

National Research Bureau
310 S. Michigan Ave.
Chicago, IL 60604
312/663-5580
  Working Press of the Nation

W.R. Nelson Co.
1 Gateway Plaza
Port Chester, NY 10573
914/937-8400
  Nelson's Directory of Investment Research

Newsletter Clearinghouse
44 W. Market St.
P.O. Box 311
Rhinebeck, NY 12572
914/876-2081
  Hudson's Washington News Media
  Newsletter Yearbook Directory

Nichols Publishing
Box 96
New York, NY 10024
212/580-8079
　Benn's Media Directory

Oxbridge Communications
150 Fifth Ave.
New York, NY 10011
212/741-0231
　National Directory of Magazines
　Standard Periodical Directory

Pacific Subscription Service
Box 811
FDR Station
New York, NY 10150
212/929-1629
　Publishers in English in Japan

PIMS U.S.A.
1133 Broadway
New York, NY 10010
212/645-5112
　United Kingdom Financial Directory
　United Kingdom Media Directory

Public Relations Plus
P.O. Drawer 1197
New Milford, CT 06776
203/354-9361
　All TV Publicity Outlets
　The Family Page Directory
　Metro California Media
　National Radio Publicity Outlets
　New York Publicity Outlets

Publicorp Communications
Box 1029
Pointe Claire PQ
W9S 4H9 Canada
　Matthews List

Publicity Club of Chicago
1441 Shermer Rd. (#110)
Northbrook, IL 60062
　1988 Media Guide
　Publicity Club of Chicago Membership
　　Directory

Reed Business Publishing
205 E. 42nd St., Ste. 1705
New York, NY 10017
212/867-2080
　Willing's Press Guide

Ron Gold, N.A.
1341 Ocean Ave. (#366)
Santa Monica, CA 90401
213/399-7938
　Business and Technical Media
　Medical Press List

R.R. Bowker
245 West 17th St.
New York, NY 10011
212/645-9700
　Ulrich's International Periodicals Directory

Audiovisual Supports

Material	Advantages	Limitations
Slide series A form of projected audiovisual materials easy to prepare with any 35mm camera	1. Prepared with any 35mm camera for most uses 2. Requires only filming, with processing and mounting by film laboratory 3. Colorful, realistic reproductions of original subjects 4. Easily revised, updated, handled, stored, and rearranged 5. Can be combined with taped narration for greater effectiveness 6. May be played through remote control presentation	1. Requires some skill in photography 2. Requires special equipment for close-up photography and copying 3. Prone to get out of sequence and be projected incorrectly
Filmstrips Closely related to slides, but instead of being mounted as separate pictures, remains uncut as a continuous strip	1. Compact, easily handled, and always in proper sequence 2. Can be supplemented with captions or recordings 3. Inexpensive when quantity reproduction is required 4. Projected with simple, lightweight equipment 5. Projection rate controlled by presenter	1. Relatively difficult to prepare locally 2. Requires film laboratory service to convert slides to filmstrip form 3. In permanent sequence and therefore cannot be rearranged or revised
Overhead transparencies A popular form of locally prepared materials, requiring an overhead projector for presentation	1. Can present information in systematic, developmental sequences 2. Simple-to-operate projector with presentation rate controlled by presenter 3. Requires limited planning 4. Can be prepared by a variety of simple, inexpensive methods	1. Requires special equipment, facilities, and skills for more advanced preparation methods 2. May be cumbersome and lack finesse of more remote processes

Guide to Video/Satellite Terms

People in the video field use a number of terms that may be unfamiliar to PR professionals. *O'Dwyer's PR Services Report* presents a glossary of key terms as a service to its readers.

Actuality: The voices of people involved in a news story. Also called a sound cut or sound bite.

ADI: Area of Dominant Influence is Arbitron Rating Co.'s geographic market designation that defines each TV market based on measurable viewing patterns.

Assignment Editor: Newsperson who is responsible for assigning stories to reporters and camera crews.

Audience Reach: The estimated number of viewers for a specific station or show, based on the number of TV households.

Background Package: The hard copy or background materials which are often sent to journalists prior to an interview via satellite. May include press releases, videocassette, etc.

Betacam: Form of videotape with a higher resolution quality than its forerunner, 3/4 inch U-Matic. More commonly used worldwide because of its high picture quality.

Bridge: Words that connect one piece of narration or sound bite to another.

B-roll: This is usually an unedited version of the same visuals without narration, which permits stations to edit and air the footage using their own announcers to create the feeling that the material was gathered and is being presented by their own news bureau.

C-Band: A term identifying satellite services, literally the 6/4 GHz portion of the spectrum. Like AM and FM on radio band.

Character Generator: Electronic equipment used to produce supers (lettering) over video.

Chromakey: The electronic placement of pictures behind the talent on camera.

Conversion: Process of changing video footage from one format to another.

Cover Footage: Video shot used to cover or replace the picture of the interviewer and interviewee while their voices are being heard.

Cue Card: A large hand-lettered card that contains copy usually held next to the camera lens by floor personnel.

Cutaway: A shot used to avoid a jump cut.

Degauss: To wipe or clean audio or videotape electronically before reusing.

Depth of Field: The range in which objects will appear in focus.

Digital Video Effects: Also called DVE, visual effects produced by devices that change normal video signals into digitial (numerical) information.

Digital Still Store: Also called electronic still store system or ESS, device that grabs a single video frame from any video source and stores it in digital form on a disk.

Dissolve: Special video effect that slowly replaces one image on the screen with another.

DMA: Designated Market Area, a viewing region defined by Nielsen Media Research.

Downlink: Retransmission of a signal from a satellite down to earth for reception by ground stations.

Dub: To copy or record audio or video material.

Dub Master: First generation copy of the original tape master.

Eng Crew: Electronic news-gathering crew, usually one camera person and one audio technician with portable, self-contained, and largely automated video equipment.

Establishing Shot: A wide shot of a scene, usually used at the beginning of a story to orient viewers with the location of the story.

Evergreens: TV stories with a "shelf-life," updated material that can be used at any time. Also known as a feature.

Gain: Volume of an audio or video signal.

Ground Station: The originators and receivers of satellite transmissons. Also known as Earth Stations.

Hard-copy: A cassette copy of video material.

Hard Lead: A lead that includes the most important information in the first sentence.

IFB: Interrupted Feedback System, a small earpiece worn by the talent that carries program sound or instructions from the director or producer.

Indie: Independent, as in independent producer or independent TV station, the first not affiliated with a major studio, the latter not affiliated or owned by a network.

Insert Studio: Small studio used for interviews or shoots.

Jump-cut: An erratic movement of a head that results when video is edited internally to eliminate some of the speaker's words.

Keeper: Usable tape.

Ku-band: A term identifying satellite services in the 11–24 GHz portion of the spectrum.

Live Shot: A live, or videotaped as live, interactive interview with video signal transmitted via satellite and audio carried on telephone lines.

Live-on-tape: A satellite interview taped for playback in a later broadcast. Also: Taped-as-live.

Medium Shot: Camera shot that shows about half of a person's body. Also called a waist shot.

Mix Minus: Prevents the interview subject from hearing his own voice echoing back to him on the IFB line from the station conducting the interview.

Montage: A series of audio or video segments edited together. Used frequently in reaction or "man on the street" interviews.

Moray: Video disturbance caused by object being videotaped. Jewelry and clothing colors are two common causes.

Multi-Screen Presentations: Video, slide, or film presentations where TV screens are "stacked" and used to present the entire image that would normally appear on one screen.

Natsot: Abbreviation for "natural sound," background sound recorded on tape during a shoot. Also called "ambience."

O/C: Abbreviation of "on camera."

Off-Line Editing: Editing process for producing videotape workprints, not intended for broadcast. The workprint information is then fed into the "on-line" (system for production of the release master tape).

On-Line Editing: A master editing system, using high quality videotape recorders for high-band release master tapes.

On-Location Shot: Represents a production where the camera is brought to the scene. Also known as "field shoot."

Origination Site: Term indicating where satellite transmission will originate.

Package: A news story that includes an interview, narration, and cover footage.

Pan: Camera moving in a horizontal position.

Post-production: Any production activity that occurs after production, including announcer recording, editing, sound mixing.

Pre-production: Any production activity that takes place before a production, including scripting and location survey.

Pre-roll: To start a videotape and let it roll for a few seconds before it is put in the playback or record mode in order to give the electronic system time to stabilize.

Production Line: Line between the director of the live shot and the producer at the TV station receiving the satellite transmission.

Receive Site: Term indicating where satellite transmission is being fed.

Reversal: A shot of the interviewer looking at the person being interviewed, used as a cutaway.

Satellite Coordinates: Designation for fixing the location of a satellite, for uplinking and downlinking satellite signals. Like latitude and longitude.

Satellite Media Tour: A series of interviews, via satellite, by journalists, with representatives of business or organizations. The spokesperson, in a fixed location, is interviewed by journalists, anywhere in the world, who have access to satellite downlink facilities. Also: Satellite Tour and Satellite Press Tour.

Scroll: Horizontal or vertical movement of word supers either up or across the TV screen.

Segue: Flow smoothly from one topic to another.

Slate: Names on billboard.

Soft Lead: A lead in which the most important information is not given immediately.

Soft-out: A satellite or studio booking with an option to go past the scheduled end time.

Sot: Abbreviation for "sound on tape" used to indicate the use of videotape with sound, usually a sound bite.

Sound Bite or Cut: Portion of statement or inteview that is included in a packaged news story.

Space Segment: The actual time-slot booked on a satellite. Also a "window."

Squeeze Frame: Reducing a picture on camera until it takes up only part of the screen. Also known as squeeze zoom.

Super: Short for superimposing lettering over graphics or video. Most commonly used to give the names and titles of interview subjects while on screen. Also known as "font."

Tag: Sentence or two used to end a story or introduce a second part in a multi-part series.

Tight Shot: Close-up camera shot of individual or object.

Time-coding: The recording of the time of day on the edge of the videotape as it is being shot to assist the editing process.

Time-in: The specific time when a window begins.

Time-out: The specific time when a window ends—usually very firm as another window or interview is scheduled to immediately follow.

Transponder: Equipment on a satellite, including a receiver, transmitter, and antennae, forming a channel or link between two Earth Stations.

Two-shot: Camera shot of two people.

Two-way audio: Audio signals between the interviewer and the spokesperson being interviewed, so the interviewer and spokesperson can hear each other.

Upcut: The loss of words at the beginning of the videotape.

VNR: Stands for video news release, which may be transmitted to stations by satellite or sent via videocassette. Usually used for soft news and runs about 90 seconds.

V/O: Abbreviation for "voice-over," the term used to indicate that the announcer's voice is being heard over the video for cover footage.

VTR: Videotape recorder.

Corporate Reporting Requirements

APPENDIX
F

Periodically, the Hill & Knowlton public relations firm updates its compilation of "Disclosure and Filing Requirements for Public Companies."

Because Hill & Knowlton planned an update of its compilation coincident with the publication of this book, Senior Vice-President Edward O. Raynolds was kind enough to permit excerpts from this guide to corporate reporting requirements, in advance of the full Hill & Knowlton report.

Disclosure Requirements

Reporting Required for:	Securities and Exchange Commission	New York Stock Exchange	American Stock Exchange	National Association of Securities Dealers	Generally Recommended Publicity Practice, All Companies
Accounting: Change in Auditors	Form 8-K; if principal accountant (or accountant for a subsidiary) resigns, declines to be re-elected, or is dismissed or if another is engaged. Disclose date of resignation, details of disagreement (any adverse opinions, disclaimers of opinion, or qualifications of opinion occurring during the audits of the two most recent fiscal years), comment letters to SEC by former accountant on whether he agrees with the Company's statements in the 8-K. See also Regulations S-K, Item 304.	Prompt notice to Exchange, 8-K when filed.	Prompt notification of Listing Representative, prior to filing of 8-K, *and* must state reason for change (Listing Form SD-1, Item 1a).	Prompt notification concurrently with press disclosure (company must file 8-K with SEC and information may be material enough to warrant trading halt. See NASD Schedule D). Contact NASD's Market Surveillance Section at (202)728-8187, preferably before public release and when in doubt about "material information." (NASD Schedule D.) Promptly confirm in writing all oral communication to NASD. If public release made after 5:30 p.m. Eastern Time, notify NASD by 9:30 a.m. the following trading day. (NASD Schedule D).	Press release desirable at time of filing 8-K if differences are major. Consider clear statement in annual report or elsewhere on independence of auditors including their reporting relationship to Board's audit committee; state company policy on rotation/nonrotation of auditors periodically.

continued

Reporting Required for:	Securities and Exchange Commission	New York Stock Exchange	American Stock Exchange	National Association of Securities Dealers	Generally Recommended Publicity Practice, All Companies
Annual (or Special) Meeting of Stock-holders	10-Q following meeting including date of meeting, name of each director elected, summary of other matters voted on.	Five copies of all proxy material sent to shareholders filed with Exchange not later than date material sent to any shareholder. Ten days advance notice of record date or closing transfer books to Exchange. The notice should state the purpose(s) for which the record date has been fixed. Preferably, notice should be given by TWX (TWX No. 710-581-2801); or, if by telephone, promptly confirmed by TWX, telegram, or letter.	Six copies of all material sent to shareholders should be sent to the Securities Division as soon as mailed to shareholders (Listing Form SD-1, Item 13). Other requirements same as NYSE (Listing Form SD-1, Item 1H for notice regarding record date)	File 10-Q concurrently with SEC filing.	Press release at time of meeting. Competition for news space minimizes public coverage except on actively contested issues. Check NYSE schedules for competing meetings. Recommended wide distribution of post-meeting report to shareholders.
Annual Report to Share-holders: Contents	Requirements listed under Rule 14a-3 of the 1934 Act. They include: audited balance sheets for 2 most recent fiscal years; audited income statements and changes in financial position for each of 3 most recent fiscal years; management's discussion and analysis of financial condition and results of financial operations; brief description of general nature and scope of the business; industry segment information; company directors and officers; stock price and dividends. SEC encourages "freedom of management expression."	Include in annual report: principal office's address; directors and officers names; audit committee and other committee members; trustees, transfer agents, and registrars; numbers of employees and shareholders (NYSE Company Manual Section 203.01). Also include: the number of shares of stock issuable under outstanding options at the beginning of the year; separate totals of changes in the number of shares of its stock under option resulting from issuance, exercise, expiration, or cancellation of options; and the number of shares issuable under outstanding options at the close of the year, the number of	Annual report must contain: balance sheets, income statements, and statements of changes in financial position. Financial statements should be prepared in accordance with generally accepted accounting principles, and SEC Regulation S-X.	No specific requirements, but NASD receives 10-K.	Check printed annual report and appropriate news release to ensure they conform to information reported on Form 10-K. News releases necessary if annual report contains previously undisclosed material information. Trend is to consider report a marketing tool.

continued

Disclosure Requirements

Reporting Required for:	Securities and Exchange Commission	New York Stock Exchange	American Stock Exchange	National Association of Securities Dealers	Generally Recommended Publicity Practice, All Companies
		unoptioned shares available at the beginning and at the close of the year for the granting of options under an option plan, and any changes in the price of outstanding options, through cancellation and reissuance or otherwise, except price changes resulting from the normal operation of antidilution provisions of the options (NYSE Listing Agreement, Section 901.01).			
Annual Report to Shareholders: Time and Distribution	Annual report to shareholders must precede or accompany delivery of proxy material. State law notice requirements govern the timing of proxy material mailing prior to annual meeting. Form 10-K must be filed within 90 days of close of year.	Published and submitted to shareholders at least 15 days before annual meeting but no later than three months after close of fiscal year. Four copies to Exchange together with advice as to the date of mailing to shareholders. PROMPTEST POSSIBLE ISSUANCE URGED. Recommend release of audited figures as soon as available.	Published and submitted to shareholders at least 15 days before annual meeting but no later than four months after close of fiscal year. PROMPTEST POSSIBLE ISSUANCE URGED. Recommend release of audited figures as soon as available. Six copies of the report to be filed with the Securities division of the Exchange (Listing Form SD-1, Item 17).	File 10-K concurrently with SEC filing.	Financial information should be released as soon as available; second release at time printed report is issued if report contains other material information. NYSE and AMEX urge broad distribution of report—including distribution to statistical services—so company information is available for "ready public reference."
Annual Report: Form 10-K	Required by Section 13 or 15(d) of Securities Exchange Act of 1934 on Form 10-K. To be filed with SEC no later than 90 days after close of fiscal year. (Some schedules may be filed 120 days thereafter.) Extensive incorporation by reference from annual report to sharehold-	Four copies must be filed with Exchange concurrently with SEC filing; also provide notice to Exchange as to date mailed to shareholders. (NYSE Company Manual Sections 203.01 and 204.04).	Three copies must be filed with Exchange concurrently with SEC filing. (See Company Guide, pp. 12-2.)	File 10-K concurrently with SEC filing.	Publicity usually not necessary unless 10-K contains previously unreported material information.

continued

Reporting Required for:	Securities and Exchange Commission	New York Stock Exchange	American Stock Exchange	National Association of Securities Dealers	Generally Recommended Publicity Practice, All Companies
	ers and from proxy statement now make integration of Form 10-K and report to shareholders more practical (see general instructions G and H of Form 10-K).				
Cash Dividends (See Stock Split)	All issuers of publicly traded securities are required to give notice of dividend declarations pursuant to Rule 10B-17. Over-the-counter companies must provide the NASD with advance notice of record date for subsequent dissemination to investors, extending comparable stock exchange requirements to OTC market. Failure to comply places issuer in violation of Section 10(b) of the Securities Exchange Act of 1934.	Prompt notice to Exchange and immediate publicity required for *any* action related to a dividend including omission or postponement of dividend at customary time. The NYSE prefers that it be given notice by TWX (TWX No. 710-581-2801) or by telephone promptly confirmed by TWX, telegram, or letter. Ten days advance notice of record date. NYSE manual implies announcement of management intention prior to formal board action may be required in case of a "leak" or rumor. *Notice regarding declaration of a cash dividend should include:* declaration date; record date(s) for closing or re-opening transfer books (or any other meaningful dates); per share amount of tax to be withheld with respect to the dividend, description of tax, net after-tax fee share dividend; any conditions upon which payment of dividend hinges.	Same as NYSE. Notification to Exchange by telephone or telegram with confirmation by letter (Listing Form SD-1, Item 1g).	Prompt notification 10 days before record date. File one copy of 10b-17 Report (included in "Reporting Requirements for NASDAQ Companies") with officer's signature.	Prepare publicity in advance and release immediately by a designated officer on word of declaration. Publicity especially important when dividend rate changes. Statement of dividend policy now common In annual reports. Statements of "intention" to take dividend policy now common in annual reports. Statements of "intention" to take dividend action also becoming common.

continued

Disclosure Requirements

Reporting Required for:	Securities and Exchange Commission	New York Stock Exchange	American Stock Exchange	National Association of Securities Dealers	Generally Recommended Publicity Practice, All Companies
Earnings	Form 10-Q required within 45 days of close of each of first three fiscal quarters. Include information outlined in 10-Q plus a narrative management analysis in form outlined in Form S-K, Item 303. Summary of quarterly results for two years in "unaudited" annual report footnote. Form 10-K required to report full year's earnings.	Quarterly. Publicity required. No fourth quarter statement is required, though items of unusual or non-recurring nature should be reflected in the company's interim earnings statements.	Quarterly. Should be published within 45 days after end of the first, second, and third fiscal quarter. (No statement is required for the fourth quarter, since that period is covered by the annual report.) Five copies of release should be sent to the Exchange. Press release must be sent to one or more New York City newspapers regularly publishing financial news, and to one or more of the national newswires.	Prompt notification and press disclosure if earnings are unusual. File 10-Q and 10-K concurrently with SEC filings.	Immediate publicity; do not hold data until printed quarterly report is published and mailed. Release no later than 10-Q filing; annual results as soon as available. Information in news release must be consistent with 10-Q. Breakout of current quarter results together with year-to-date totals desirable in 2nd, 3rd, and 4th quarter releases.
Legal Proceedings	Form 10-Q at start or termination of proceedings and in any quarter when material development occurs (generally damage claims in excess of 10% of current assets); also any suit against company by an officer, director, or major stockholder. See Regulation S-K, Item 103. See also appendix entry entitled "environmental matters."	No notice to NYSE required unless proceeding bears on ownership, dividends, interest or principal of listed securities, or start of receivership bankruptcy, reorganization proceedings.	"Significant litigation." Public disclosure if material. Prompt notice to Exchange.	Prompt notification and public disclosure if material or if company must file report with SEC.	Public disclosure recommended if outcome of legal proceeding could have material effect on company and news of proceeding has not already become public. Court filings now commonly distributed to key business media with or without press release.
Merger: Acquisition or Disposition of Assets	Form 8-K if company acquires or disposes of a significant (10 percent of total assets or whole subsidiary) amount of assets or business other than in normal course of business. Proxy soliciting material or registration statement may also be required. Check	Form 8-K filed (where assets acquired). Immediate public disclosure. Prompt notice to Exchange where assets disposed of.	Form 8-K if filed, for acquisition or disposition of assets. Immediate public disclosure.	Prompt notification and public disclosure (8-K filed with SEC).	Exchange policy requires immediate announcement as soon as confidential disclosures relating to such important matters are made to "outsiders" (i.e., other than "top management" and their individual confidential "advisers"). Immediate public-

continued

Reporting Required for:	Securities and Exchange Commission	New York Stock Exchange	American Stock Exchange	National Association of Securities Dealers	Generally Recommended Publicity Practice, All Companies
	application of Rule 145 (b) of Securities Act of 1933, to any such transaction involving exchange of stock (see also Tender Offers).				ity, especially when assets consist of an entire product line, division, operating unit, or a "substantial" part of the business.
Merger: Commenting on Unusual Market Activity	After SEC ruling in *In re Carnation,* and appeals court decision in *Levinson, et al., v. Basic Industries,* company can state "no comment" about merger discussions, when stock shows unusual market activity. However, if company comments in response to Exchange or regulatory inquiry, it must do so truthfully, and acknowledge that merger discussions are taking place.	Prepare to make immediate public announcement concerning unusual market activity from merger negotiations. Immediate candid public statement concerning state of negotiations or development of corporate plans, if rumors are correct or there are developments. Make statement as soon as disclosure made to outsiders (from business appraisals, financing arrangements, market surveys, etc.). Public statements should be definite, regarding price, ratio, timing, any other pertinent information necessary to evaluation. Should include disclosures made to outsiders (NYSE Company Manual, Sections 202.01 and .03).	Promptly publicly disseminate previously undisclosed information contained in any "leak" that resulted in market action. If company unable to determine cause of market action, Exchange may suggest that company issue "no news" release, that there have been no undisclosed recent developments affecting company that would account for unusual market activity. Company need not issue public announcement at each stage of merger negotiations, but may await agreement in principle on specific terms, or point at which negotiations stabilize. However, publicly release announcement setting forth facts to clarify rumor or report containing material information. (See Company Guide, p. 4-7 to 4-8.)	Prompt notification and public disclosure if material or if company must file report with SEC.	Either issue "no comment" statement, or truthfully explain reason for market activity known to company. Comment asserting that company is "unaware of any reason" to explain market activity is a comment. If company knows the reason for market activity but denies its awareness, it has made a false comment, and is probably liable.
Projection: Forecast or Estimate of Earnings	See Reg. S-K General Policy (b). SEC policy encourages use of projections of future economic performance that have "a reasonable basis" and are presented in an appropriate format. Obli-	Immediate public disclosure when news goes beyond insiders and their confidential advisers.	Exchange warns against "unwarranted promotional disclosure," including premature announcements of products, and interviews with analysts and financial writers which would unduly	Prompt notification and public disclosure if material (NASD Schedule D).	Projections should be either avoided altogether or widely circulated with all assumptions stated. Projections by others may require correction by company if wrong but widely be-

continued

Disclosure Requirements

Reporting Required for:	Securities and Exchange Commission	New York Stock Exchange	American Stock Exchange	National Association of Securities Dealers	Generally Recommended Publicity Practice, All Companies
	gation to correct promptly when facts change. Should not discontinue or resume projections without clear explanation of action.		influence market activity.		lieved. Once having made projection, issuer has obligation to "update" it promptly if assumptions prove wrong. Press releases and other communications should include all information necessary to an understanding of the projection. Legal counsel should be consulted.
Stock Split, Stock Dividend, or Other Change in Capitalization	10-Q required for increase or decrease if exceeds 5% of amount of securities of the class previously outstanding. Notice to NASD or exchange 10 days before record date under Securities Exchange Act anti-fraud provisions.	Exchange suggests preliminary discussion. Immediate public disclosure and Exchange notification. Issuance of new shares requires prior listing approval. Either "Telephone Alert" procedure should be followed, or preferably, wire by TWX. Separate confirmation letter to Exchange. Company's notice to Exchange should indicate brokers' and nominees' requirements and date by which they must notify disbursing agent of full and fractional share requirements. Exchange will publicize this in its Weekly Bulletin or special circulars. *Notice regarding stock dividend, split, or distribution should include:* ratio of stock dividend or split; record date for holders entitled to receive distribution;	Immediate public disclosure and Exchange notification. Issuance of new shares requires prior listing approval. Treatment of fractional shares must be announced.	Prompt notification and public disclosure 10 days before record date. File one copy of 10b-17 Report (included in "Reporting Requirements for NASDAQ Companies") with officer's signature. File 10-Q concurrently with SEC filing.	Immediate publicity as soon as proposal becomes known to "outsiders" whether formally voted or not. Discuss early whether to describe transaction as "split," "dividend," or both and use terminology consistently.

continued

Reporting Required for:	Securities and Exchange Commission	New York Stock Exchange	American Stock Exchange	National Association of Securities Dealers	Generally Recommended Publicity Practice, All Companies
		conditions upon which transaction hinges; date for mailing of certificates for additional shares.			
Tender offer	Conduct and published remarks of all parties governed by Sections 13(d), 13(e), 14(d), 14(e) of the 1934 Act and regulations thereunder. Schedule 14D-1 disclosure required of raider. Target required to file Schedule 14D-9 for any solicitation or recommendation to security holders. (See also *Hart-Scott-Rodino* requirements.)	Consult Exchange Stock List Department in advance. Immediate publicity and notice to Exchange. Deliver offering material to Exchange no later than distribution date to shareholders. Consult Exchange when terms of tender at variance with Exchange principles regarding tender offers.	Consult Exchange Securities Division in advance. Immediate publicity and notice to Exchange.	Prompt notification and public disclosure (NASD Schedule D).	Massive publicity effort required; should not be attempted without thorough familiarity with current rules and constant consultation with counsel. Neither raider nor target should comment publicly until necessary SEC filings have been made. "Stop, look, listen" letter permitted under Rule 14D-9(e).

Annual Meeting Checklist

By Frank Widder

The following annual shareholder's meeting checklist can be adapted to serve as a "preflight" for almost any major meeting.

I. Meeting announcement
   A. Shareholder's proxy statement and general notice
   B. Investment houses', major brokers', and institutional investors' notice and invitation
   C. Financial media invitations
   D. Employee notice of meeting
   E. Guests

   Follow-up (by phone or in person)
   A. Investor relations contacts with major shareholders to determine participation, major areas of interest, potential problems
   B. Major investment houses involved with company
   C. Local financial press
   D. Guest relations

II. Management announcement
   A. Notify all key management personnel to make sure they will be there and arrange alternates for those who cannot make it.
   B. Notify all members of the board to determine their ability to make the meeting.
   C. Arrange flight times and book hotel in advance; guarantee arrival if necessary.

III. Management coaching
   A. Draft basic list of shareholder problems and questions.
   B. Arrange meeting with CEO and chairman to prepare answers, with key staff and legal department to run down answers, and practice those answers.
   C. Review and practice management speeches.

IV. Presentation materials
   A. Review orders for graphs and slides, compare with financial review speech.
   B. Screen any films.
   C. Review displays.

V. Agenda: order of presentations with approximate running times (in minutes)
   A. Introduction—chairman calls meeting to order and introduces board and management (4:00)
   B. Opening comments by chairman and review of overall activities of company (6:00)

C. President's message (with visuals) (15:00)
D. Financial report by vice president, finance (with slide highlights) (5:00)
E. Film (20:00)
F. Present proposals in proxy (limit each shareholder to one statement per issue; hand out ballots to shareholders at beginning) (20:00)
G. Voting, collect ballots (3:00)
H. General discussion (limit shareholders to one question each) (30:00)
I. Announce voting results (3:00)
J. Present company awards of appreciation (2:00)
K. Adjournment (1:00)—Total: 1 hour, 49 minutes

Agenda allows 20 minutes additional for discussion or for more questions during presentation of proposals. Final agenda will be printed and passed out by ushers at meeting.

VI. Site preparation
   A. Staff
      1. Electrician, lighting, and sound equipment specialists on hand from 8 A.M. through 5 P.M.
      2. Supervisor of custodial, security, and equipment staff
      3. Walkie-talkie communications network with equipment staff
      4. Waiters for lounge
      5. Caterers for lounge
   B. Parking
      1. Traffic direction displays at parking lot entrances
      2. Parking attendants directing traffic to proper area
      3. Signs pointing to meeting entrance in parking lot
   C. Entrance/reception
      1. Reception tables with pencils and guest roster
      2. Receptionists to staff tables and answer questions about facilities (need to be briefed beforehand)
      3. Well-marked rest areas and signs indicating meeting area
      4. Unarmed security to control crowd and provide protection
      5. Armed security located in discrete areas of meeting room
      6. Name tags for all representatives of company
   D. Display area
      1. Displays set up along walls, not to impede foot traffic, and checked for operation 24 hours in advance
      2. Representatives to staff each booth and be prepared for questions about display
      3. Tables to display necessary financial information—annual report, 10-K, proxy statement, quarterlies
   E. Lounge area
      1. Adequate seating for participants, guests
      2. Breakfast/luncheon tables
   F. Meeting areas
      1. Sound, lighting, video checks
      2. Sound mikes for all stage participants
      3. Additional speakers for amplification
      4. Alternate hookup in case of failures—sound, lighting, and video; alternate film in case of breakage

5. Large screen for slide and film
6. Slide and film projectors for presentation
7. Audio and lighting mixers
8. Portable, remote mikes with long cords for audience questions
9. Tape recorder hookup to record proceedings

G. Construction
1. Podium constructed high enough for everyone to have direct view of all participants
2. Area blocked off for board and management to view film
3. Area blocked off for lighting and sound equipment
4. Exits properly marked
5. Access to podium and all chairs necessary for seating board and management
6. Logo prominently displayed and lighted above podium

H. Staff
1. Ushers with flashlights at all entrances for seating
2. Security at far corners of room
3. Backstage technicians for sound emergencies
4. Remote mike monitors on both aisles or front and back of room
5. Photographer to shoot proceedings, displays, and key presentations

I. Stage seating arrangements
1. Podium in middle, chairs to either side
2. Arrange board members in tenure order
3. Management in hierarchy order
4. Chairman sits on board side
5. President on management side
6. Nameplates for all participants on podium
7. Glasses, water, ashtrays

J. Shareholder seating
1. First-come basis
2. Areas roped off for invited shareholders and guests
3. Areas roped off for film viewing by participants
4. Special area for members not represented on stage—public accountants, special staff, guests

VII. Final run-through
A. Day prior complete mock session of annual report, with key principals and timing of presentation—including possible questions and responses.
B. Review slide show and cues four hours before meeting.
C. Check screening room communications to begin film. Make sure time is allowed to clear stage.
D. Make sure award is ready for presentation.
E. Hand out scripts to key participants and technical people.

VIII. Day of meeting
A. Review with supervisor that all technical checks are O.K.
B. See that all displays are up and working.
C. Contact board and management people to check for emergencies in transportation. Arrange backup accommodations if necessary.
D. Sit-down breakfast with key participants to go over agenda and cover any last-minute questions.

E. Go to convention center, check in with supervisor, security head, parking attendant. Ensure copies of scripts at podium.
F. Greet participants and guide to lounge.
G. Wait for shareholders and investors, media. Be available for questions and arrange interviews.
H. Sit down and wait.
I. Guide participants, guests to luncheon in lounge. Make sure bar is set up.
J. Have a drink—and good night.

On-line Databases

Particularly important for public relations research are on-line databases, which store vast quantities of information on current and historical subjects. Some of the major service information vendors available to public relations practitioners are described here.

BRS Information Technologies
1200 Route 7
Latham, NY 12110
800-289-4277

For over a decade, this service has supplied a large number of databases, with primary emphasis on medical, engineering, educational, and business-oriented information. Price structure varies, according to the type of service selected. The Open Access Plan has an annual password fee of $80, a per connect-hour charge of between $10 and $139, depending on the service, and a telecommunications charge of about $12.

DIALOG Information Services, Inc.
Lockheed Corporation
3460 Hillview Avenue
Palo Alto, CA 94304
800-334-2564

DIALOG was started as a commercial venture in 1972 by the Lockheed Corporation. It is one of the largest on-line services, offering nearly 400 databases that range from business and economics to science and technology. DIALOG charges a $45 initiation fee and has a wide variation in connect-hour cost. Each database has a set hourly cost, ranging from $30 to $300. DIALOG is available 24 hours a day, seven days a week.

Dow Jones News/Retrieval
P.O. Box 300
Princeton, NJ 08543
800-522-3567

This is part of Dow Jones and Company, publisher of *The Wall Street Journal*. More than 60 databases are offered, primarily relating to business and economics, financial and investment services, and general news and information. *The Wall Street Journal* is available in summary form, as well as in its entirety. The fee structure for companies is complex. For individuals, costs start with a $29.95 sign-up fee and an $18 annual service fee that kicks in after the first year. Then, fees range from $.50 to $2.85 per minute for prime time and from $.08 to $.60 per minute for nonprime time. The service is available 24 hours a day.

DIALCOM Services, Inc.
2560 N. First Street
P.O. Box 49019
San Jose, CA 95161-9019
800-872-7654

DIALCOM, begun in 1970, was puchased in 1986 by British Telecom. It offers gateways to databases such as UPI, the Official Airline Guide, and the Bureau of National Affairs. It also offers gateway services to other on-line vendors, which enable customers to access databases offered on Dow Jones News/Retrieval Service, BRS, and DIALOG. The fee structure is based on the number of hours used, not databases accessed. Costs for accessing the gateway services are based on the rates charged by other vendors. The service operates 24 hours a day, seven days a week.

Facts on File
460 Park Avenue South
New York, NY 10016
212-683-2244

Facts on File summarizes information daily from leading U.S. and foreign periodicals, the publications of Commerce Clearing House, *Congressional Quarterly, Congressional Record, State Department Bulletin,* presidential documents, and official press releases. Subject areas are as diverse as the news of the day. The annual subscription fee is $575.

NewsNet, Inc.
945 Haverford Road
Bryn Mawr, PA 19010
800-345-1301

NewsNet was started in 1982 by Independent Publications. It offers primarily newsletters and wire services. There are more than 400 specialized business newsletters and wire services, covering more than 35 industries, including telecommunications, publishing, broadcasting, electronics and computers, energy, investment, accounting, and taxation. Prices range from $24 to more than $100 an hour, depending on the newsletter being accessed. There is also a monthly minimum charge of $15. NewsNet is available 24 hours a day.

LEXIS and NEXIS
Mead Data Central
9443 Springboro Pike
P.O. Box 933
Dayton, OH 45401
800-227-4908

LEXIS and NEXIS are two of the information services provided by this division of Mead Corporation. LEXIS is a legal information database containing the full text of case law from state, federal, and international courts; state and federal regulations; and other legal records. NEXIS is a full-text database containing 750 major newspapers, magazines, and newsletters. In 1988, a group of media in the NEXIS databank was organized as the Advertising and Public Relations Library, including news wires and communications-oriented publications. The fee structure is complex, but the range of costs varies from $6 to $50 for the search and $35 per hour for connect charges. Both services are available 24 hours a day on weekdays and all weekend, except from 2 A.M. to 10 A.M. Sunday.

Index